MW01358394

Sk̲wx̲wú7mesh Sníchim – Xwelíten Sníchim Sk̲exwts

Squamish – English Dictionary

Sḵwx̱wú7mesh Sníchim – Xwelíten Sníchim Sḵexwts

Squamish – English Dictionary

Sḵwx̱wú7mesh Uxwumixw Ns7éyx̱nitm ta Snewéyalh
SQUAMISH NATION EDUCATION DEPARTMENT
North Vancouver, British Columbia

in association with

UNIVERSITY OF WASHINGTON PRESS
Seattle & London

© 2011 by the Squamish Nation Education Department
Printed in the United States of America
16 14 12 11 10 5 4 3 2 1

All rights reserved.

Sḵwx̱wú7mesh Úxwumixw Ns7éyx̱nitm ta Snew̓íyalh
Squamish Nation Education Department
P.O. Box 86131, North Vancouver, B.C. V7L 4J5
www.squamish.net/services

University of Washington Press
P.O. Box 50096, Seattle, WA 98145 U.S.A.
www.washington.edu/uwpress

Library of Congress Cataloging-in-Publication Data

Sḵwx̱wú7mesh sníchim xwelíten sníchim : Sḵexwts = Squamish - English dictionary / Sḵwx̱wú7mesh Úxwumixw Ns7éyx̱nitm ta Snew̓íyalh = Squamish Nation Education Department.
p. cm.
"Squamish Nation Education Department, North Vancouver, British Columbia in association with University of Washington, Seattle"—T.p. verso.
Includes bibliographical references and index.
ISBN 978-0-295-99022-4 (pbk. : alk. paper)
1. Suquamish language—Dictionaries—English. 2. English language—Dictionaries—Suquamish. I. Squamish Nation Education Department. II. University of Washington. III. Title: Squamish-English dictionary.
PM2381.S64S59 2010
497'.94—dc22
2010010123

The paper used in this publication is acid-free and 90 percent recycled from at least 50 percent post-consumer waste. It meets the minimum requirements of American National Standard for Information Sciences—Permanence of Paper for Printed Library Materials, ANSI Z39.48-1984. ∞

Sḵwx̱wú7meshulh Sḵexwts Sḵéxwḵexw

The Squamish Dictionary Project Personnel

Tiná7 Ta na wa Nexwniw̓n ta a Ímats
From Teachings for Your Grandchildren/
The Squamish Language Elders Group

Nekwsáliya (Margaret Locke)
Kwináḵatamat (Lucille Nicholson)
Ts'elts'elmát (Addie Kermeen)
Skwetsátenat (Valerie Moody)
X̱ats'alánexw Tanáynexw (Alex Williams)
Tiyáltalut (Audrey Rivers)
Chiyálhiya (Lila Johnston)
Neḵwníḵwelut (Barbara Charlie)
Xwelap'últ (Stella Newman)

Kwiyáw̓it na nam̓ huyá7 (Late Elders' Group members)

Skwetsátenat-t (Doris Williams)
P'eḵálten-t (Ernie Harry)
X̱áleḵ'-t (Lawrence Baker)
Telsentsút-t (Frank Miranda)
Nora Desmond
Sx̱ananált-t (Yvonne Joseph)
Skwétsiya-t (Eva Lewis)
Frank Guerrero
Kwelíx̱welut-t (Tina Cole)
Kwítelut-t (Lena Jacobs)

Tiná7 Ta Sḵwx̱wú7mesh Úxwumixw Ns7éyx̱nitm ta Snew̓íyalh
From the Squamish Nation Department of Education

Ta na wa x̱el̓ (editors)

Vanessa Campbell, Associate Editor
T'nax̱wtn (Peter Jacobs), PhD Candidate, Editor-in-Chief

Ta na wa ch'áwalhn (contributing researchers)

Ḵ'etx̱ímtn (Alroy Baker)
Sekyú Siy̓ám̓ (Chief Ian Campbell)
Tseytsáyax̱mat-amáts (Rebecca Campbell)
Xwáchtenat (Kathy LaRock)

Tiná7 ta Hiyí Skwul̓aw̓txw (from the university community)

Elizabeth Currie

Dr. Leora Bar-el, University of Montana

Dr. Carrie Gillon, Co-editor, Arizona State University

Linda Watt

Kwélhiw̓it na chénchen̓s (administrative support)

Snítelwet (Deborah Jacobs)

Siyámiya (Damara Jacobs-Morris)

Kirsten Baker-Williams

Chrystal Nahanee, the map

I7x̱w stam i ti sḵexwts

Contents

Chet kw'enmantúmi / Foreword ix

Chet txwtéta7 tkwétsiw̓it nilh ta sts'its'áp'swit / Background xi

Ta Sḵwx̱wú7mesh sníchim / The Squamish Language xiv

Nilh welh axw xwekws ti sḵexwts / How to Use This Dictionary xvi

Nilh welh axw x̱el' ta Sḵwx̱wú7mesh sníchim / The Writing System xvi

Nilh welh axw yay̓lh ta "letters" / The Order of the Alphabet xvii

Na7xw chet wa txwtéta7 ta sḵexwts / Other Notes xvii

Guide to Pronunciation of the Sḵwx̱wú7mesh Alphabet 3

Grammatical Sketch of Sḵwx̱wú7mesh 7

Ta Sḵexwts / The Dictionary

Squamish – English 39

The Dictionary / Ta Sḵexwts

English – Squamish 223

Chet kw'enmantúmi

Foreword

Stl'i7-chet kwis chet kw'enmantumiwit, i7x̱w ta newyap na xwekws ti Sḵwx̱wú7meshulh sḵexwts. I7x̱w ta Siiy̓úxwa-chet na ch'áwatumulh kwis chet ḵéxwen i7x̱w ta sníchim-chet, chet kw'enmantúmiyap. I7x̱w ta stá7uxwlh na wa xwekws ti sḵexwts, chet kw'enmantúmiyap.

We would like to thank the Squamish People for entrusting us to undertake this work. We are grateful to the Elders and leaders who protected the language and saw it through until today and had the foresight many years ago to begin this sḵexwts – this great collection of words. We acknowledge the support of the Squamish Nation Trust and the Squamish Nation Chiefs and Council, both past and present. We acknowledge the members of the Sḵwx̱wú7meshulh Sḵexwts Sḵéxwḵexw (the Squamish Language Dictionary Project Personnel). And to all the teachers and the students who have gone over this dictionary and helped to make it a better dictionary, with your many funny, insightful and helpful comments, we thank you.

This Dictionary is targeted primarily for the people of the Squamish Nation. It strengthens ours hearts, though, to know that it will also offer other peoples, both First Nations and non-First Nations, insight into the thoughts and feelings of the Sḵwx̱wú7mesh Úxwumixw (the Squamish People). We would like to thank all of you who use this dictionary, since using our language is what makes it a living language. A dictionary is never really complete since a living language is always adding new words. We present this dictionary as a picture of where the Sḵwx̱wú7mesh Snichim was in the past up to where it is today. Our hope is for many more versions of the Sḵwx̱wú7mesh dictionary in the future to represent our living language.

Chen kw'enman-túmiyap (thanking you for your kind attention)

Snítelwet iy Siyámiya
Deborah Jacobs
Squamish Nation Education Department Head

Sḵwx̱wú7meshulh Temíxw

(Squamish Terrritory)

This is not an exhaustive list of Squamish Nation place names. It represents the permanent villages and/or landmarks. Some are occupied and others remain resource sites.

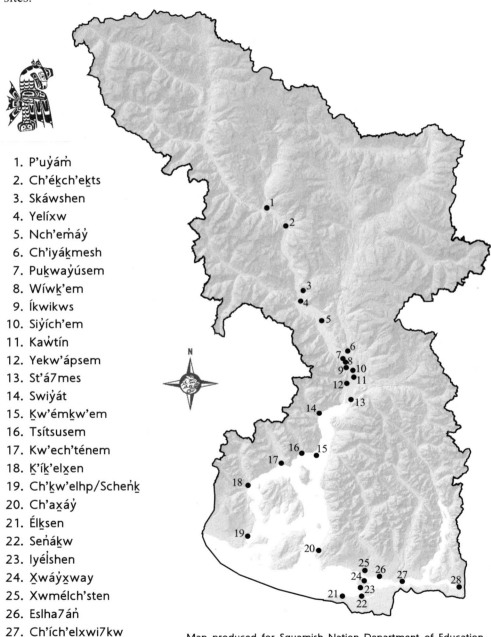

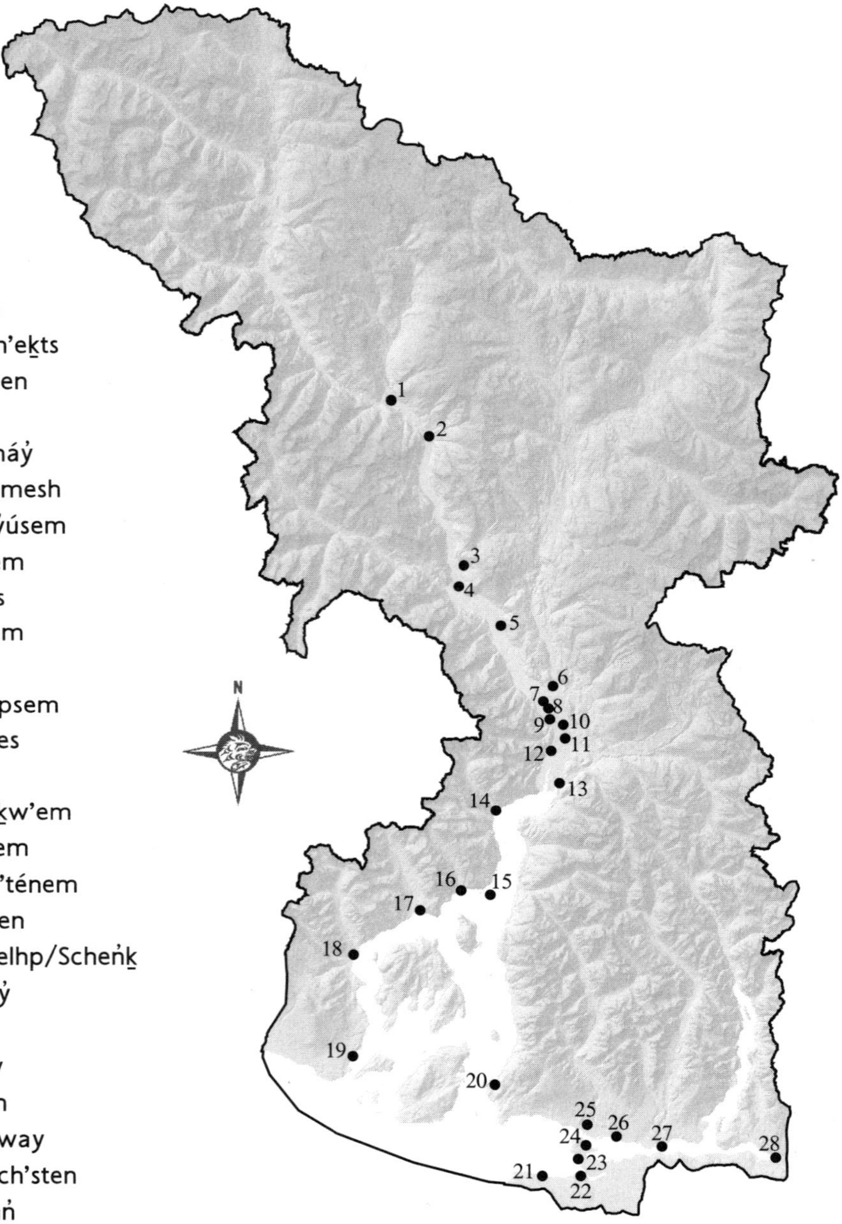

1. P’uy̓ám̓
2. Ch’éḵch’eḵts
3. Skáwshen
4. Yelíxw
5. Nch’em̓áy̓
6. Ch’iyáḵmesh
7. Puḵway̓úsem
8. Wíwḵ’em
9. Íkwikws
10. Siy̓ích’em
11. Kaw̓tín
12. Yekw’ápsem
13. St’á7mes
14. Swiy̓át
15. Ḵw’émḵw’em
16. Tsítsusem
17. Kw’ech’ténem
18. Ḵ’íḵ’elx̱en
19. Ch’ḵw’elhp/Schen̓ḵ
20. Ch’ax̱áy̓
21. Élḵsen
22. Sen̓áḵw
23. Iyél̓shen
24. X̱wáy̓x̱way
25. Xwmélch’sten
26. Eslha7án̓
27. Ch’ích’elxwi7ḵw
28. Títem̓tsen

Map produced for Squamish Nation Department of Education
GIS Cartographer: Chrystal Nahanee

Chet txwtéta7 tkwétsiw̓it nilh ta sts'its'áp'swit

Background

This dictionary is based on the work of many different people over many, many years. In this brief introduction we will attempt a sketch of all the work and insight that informs this present effort. A dictionary is always a work in progress. This brief history is not comprehensive, and more work will still be written.

The 1800s

The first written collection of S<u>k</u>w<u>x</u>wú7mesh words was compiled by a German anthropologist named Franz Boas, in the 1880s. He did not record who the people were that he worked with. In the 1890s, another anthropologist, Charles Hill-Tout, also collected some S<u>k</u>w<u>x</u>wú7mesh words, sentences, and legends. He worked primarily with an old S<u>k</u>w<u>x</u>wú7mesh man named Melkw's, and an interpreter, Annie Carasco, whose mother was S<u>k</u>w<u>x</u>wú7mesh. He also worked with Annie Rivers and Chief Thomas.

Anthropologists and Linguists

In the 1930s another anthropologist, Homer Barnett, worked with Jimmy Frank. He collected information about traditional S<u>k</u>w<u>x</u>wú7mesh culture, as well as collecting some S<u>k</u>w<u>x</u>wú7mesh words. Then in 1956, a Dutch linguist, Aert H. Kuipers, wrote the first comprehensive grammar of our language: "The Squamish language: grammar, texts, dictionary." He worked with Isaac Jacob and his wife, Lizzie, and Alec Peters and his wife, Mary, and later he also worked with Chief Louis Miranda. In Kuipers' second volume he worked exclusively with Uncle Louis. The first volume was published in 1967 and the second volume in 1969. Kuipers' texts are a collection of S<u>k</u>w<u>x</u>wú7mesh legends, stories, speeches, and prayers. These texts were told in S<u>k</u>w<u>x</u>wú7mesh and translated into English.

The BC Native Language Project

In 1968 the BC Native Language Project undertook comprehensive documentation of the Sḵwx̱wú7mesh language and culture. Randy Bouchard and Dorothy Kennedy were the main collaborators on this project. They developed the writing system that we use today for the Sḵwx̱wú7mesh sníchim. This writing system was later officially adopted by Chief and Council circa 1980. Bouchard and Kennedy collected many word lists, stories, and cultural information about plants, animals, place names, etc. Many of our Sḵwx̱wu7mesh elders of that time contributed to this research. Uncle Louis was also part of this research. He, in fact, wrote hundreds of pages of legends, stories, language lessons, and other materials in the Sḵwx̱wú7mesh sníchim. Much of this was also recorded on reel-to-reel tape. A large part of our written collections on the Sḵwx̱wú7mesh sníchim are due to his work.

Wa X̱el̓ Ta Sḵwx̱wu7mesh – Sḵwx̱wú7mesh People Write

One of the earliest Sḵwx̱wú7mesh people to write Sḵwx̱wú7mesh in a consistent manner was the late Tim Moody, Sr., who used a form of shorthand for writing Sḵwx̱wú7mesh. He served as Secretary to Chief and Council for a number of years. He kept meticulous notes, recording ancestral names, place names, cultural terminology, and genealogies.

Teaching of the Sḵwx̱wú7mesh sníchim began in the late 1960s, first in St'á7mes with Dominic Charlie. Later, Uncle Louis began teaching the language in North Vancouver in the early 1970s. The first classes offered were adult night classes. Next, classes began at St. Thomas Aquinas (STA), with Moses Antone and Laura Band working alongside Uncle Louis. Eventually the Sḵwx̱wú7mesh sníchim program was offered in many of the elementary and high schools in North Vancouver. The teachers who joined Uncle Louis include: Val Moody, Vanessa Campbell, Yvonne Joseph, Kathy Joseph, Sandra Joseph, Chief Lawrence Baker, and Roy Baker. The next generation of teachers to follow include: Alice Guss, Elva Lewis, Becky Campbell, Ian Campbell, Vera Douglas, Ray Natrall, Ellen Mathias, Marie Natrall, and Peter Natrall. Classes also began in Squamish with Chief Alvie Andrews and Ernie Harry. Other teachers that followed them include Vera Douglas, Alice Guss, Elva Lewis, Carla George, Dale Harry, and Shirley Lewis. All these teachers have tested out different draft versions of the dictionary and have contributed many useful comments and corrections.

Ta Nexwníw̓n ta a Ímats / Teachings for Your Grandchildren

In 1993 the Ta Nexwníw̓n ta a Ímats (Teachings for Your Grandchildren) group was formed. This group of elders is our Language Elders Advisory Group for the Sk̲wx̲wú7mesh sníchim. The original group was comprised of Chief Lawrence Baker, Barbara Charlie, Tina Cole, Auntie Nora Desmond, Lena Jacobs, Yvonne Joseph, Eva Lewis, and Auntie Doris Williams. Over the years we have grown to include Hilda Duerden, Lila Johnston, Margaret Locke, Frank Miranda, Lucille Nicholson, Audrey Rivers, Addie Kermeen, and Alec Williams. Other elders that we have worked with in the past include Ernie Harry and Frank Guerrero. As mentioned, Ernie Harry was himself a language teacher who also developed a large collection of Sk̲wx̲wú7mesh language lessons and word lists.

The Elders group work together with the staff of the Sk̲wx̲wú7mesh Sníchim program: Alroy Baker, Kirsten Baker Williams, Vanessa Campbell, Peter Jacobs, Kathy Joseph-LaRock, and Val Moody. All these elders and language staff, as well as our many Sk̲wx̲wú7mesh sníchim students, past and present, have contributed to the creation of this dictionary. The continuing widespread use of our language by our community is the inspiration for this work.

Ta Sk̲wx̲wú7mesh Sníchim

The Squamish Language

Ta Sk̲wx̲wú7mesh sníchim (the Squamish language) is spoken in ta s7ulh temíxw (our territory). The traditional Sk̲wx̲wú7mesh territory extends from Stelk̲áya (Roberts Creek, which is between the towns of Gibsons and Sechelt), down to Elksen (Point Grey, around present-day UBC), throughout the whole of Burrard Inlet, up through Atl'k̲á7tsem (Howe Sound), and up along the Sk̲wx̲wú7mesh Stak̲w (the Squamish River) and Ch'iyák̲mesh Stak̲w (the Cheakamus River).

Ta Sk̲wx̲wú7mesh sníchim is an independent language that belongs to the Salish language family. Historically there were 23 Salish languages. These languages were spoken in Southern British Columbia, throughout Washington State, on the Oregon Coast, and into Idaho and Montana. The whole Salish language family consists of five branches, as shown in the following table (a branch of languages means that these languages share many things in common compared to another branch in the language family). Sk̲wx̲wú7mesh belongs to the Coast Salish branch of the Salish language family (some linguists prefer the term Central Salish instead of Coast Salish). There are 10 languages in the Coast Salish branch. Two of the branches (Bella Coola and Tillamook) have only one language in them. When there is a traditional Sk̲wx̲wú7mesh name for another Salish language, it is included in brackets (note that these different tribes also have their own name for their language, which may be different from either the English name or the Sk̲wx̲wú7mesh name for their language).

SALISH LANGUAGES

A. Bella Coola (British Columbia)

1. Bella Coola [Pélxwela]

B. Coast Salish (the coast of southern British Columbia and Washington)

2. Comox-Sliammon [Stsa7lhúlhtxw]
3. Pentlach – Comox and south
4. Sechelt [Shishá7lh]
5. Squamish [Skwxwú7mesh]
6. Halkomelem [Sk’emín̓em] – Island, Downriver, and Upriver
7. Nooksack [Xwsa7k]
8. Straits – Saanich, Samish, Lummi, etc.
9. Clallam – Port Angeles area
10. Lushootseed – Puget Salish
11. Twana – Hood Canal

C. Tsamosan (on the coast of southern Washington)

12. Quinalt
13. Lower Chehalis
14. Upper Chehalis
15. Cowlitz

D. Tillamook (on the coast of Oregon)

16. Tillamook

E. Interior Salish (the interior of BC, Washington, Idaho, Montana)

17. Lillooet [Lúxwels – Mt. Currie, Stl’al’mexw – Lillooet proper]
18. Thompson [Lhkápmexw]
19. Shuswap
20. Columbian
21. Okanagan
22. Kalispel-Spokane-Flathead
23. Coeur d’Alene

Nilh welh axw xwekws ti sk̲exwts

How to Use This Dictionary

Nilh welh axw x̲el' ta Sk̲wx̲wú7mesh sníchim

The Writing System

The writing system used in this dictionary is the official writing system that was adopted by Squamish Nation Chief and Council in 1980 for the Sk̲wx̲wú7mesh sníchim. A complete explanation is available in the BC Language Project lesson called "How to Write the Squamish Language," which is also on audio CD.

Note that sometimes you will find that the words in this dictionary are written slightly differently in other places, such as in old language lessons, signs, etc. Often this alternate spelling doesn't actually represent a different pronunciation. Take, for example, the word for Squamish. You will see it written two different ways using our writing system, but they both represent the same pronunciation:

Sk̲wx̲wúm'ish
Sk̲wx̲wú7mesh

On the other hand, sometimes a different spelling respresents a different pronunciation. In that case, in this dictionary, we have tried to write all the different pronunciations that we are aware of. For example, the following Sk̲wx̲wú7mesh word has two different pronunciations, but these different pronunciations do not change the meaning of the word:

ch'xwit ~ ch'xwut [ch' xwit] add on to (something). *verb(t)*.

What does ~ mean? The symbol ~ is used in this dictionary to indicate when there is more than one pronunciation of a Sk̲wx̲wú7mesh word.

Nilh welh axw yaẏlh ta "letters"
The Order of the Alphabet

The order of our alphabet follows English, with many additions:

a aa ch ch' e h i ii k k' kw kw' ḵ ḵ' ḵw ḵw'
l l' lh m ṁ n ṅ p p' s sh t t' tl' ts ts' u uu
w ẇ xw x̱ x̱w y ẏ 7

Note that when there is more than one letter in the Sḵwx̱wú7mesh alphabet that starts with the same English letter, each Sḵwx̱wú7mesh letter is treated as a separate letter in the dictionary. For example, there are five Sḵwx̱wú7mesh letters that start with the English letter *t*. They are **t**, **t'**, **tl'**, **ts**, and **ts'**. Each of these letters is treated as a separate letter in this dictionary. So, for example, you will find all the words that begin with **t** in one section, and in the next section all the words that begin with **t'**, and then all the words that begin with **tl'**, and so forth.

Note that the five hooked letters that have the hook on top (l', ṁ, ṅ, ẇ, ẏ) and the letters x, xw, and 7 do not have their own section in the dictionary. This is because these letters do not occur at the beginning of any words.

The long vowels (aa, ii, uu) do not have their own sections in the dictionary either, since there are not very many words that begin with long vowels.

Na7xw chet wa txwtéta7 ta sḵexwts
Other Notes

Hyphen after an entry: When an entry in the dictionary has a hyphen after it, this means that this Sḵwx̱wú7mesh word is always attached before a word (it is a prefix).

For example, the second word in the dictionary is a-, and the hyphen means that the word is a prefix. It is always attached before another Sḵwx̱wú7mesh word.

example: a- your
as in: a-sna your name
a-laṁ your house

Hyphen before an entry: When an entry has a hyphen before it, this means that the Sḵwx̱wú7mesh word is always attached following another Sḵwx̱wú7mesh word (it is a suffix). In the examples, the suffix is in boldface.

example: -ḵs nose
as in: x̱ewtl'**ḵs** have a broken nose

example: -shn foot
as in: xíḵ'**shn**am̓ scratch your foot

What type of word is it? At the end of the definition of every word there is a word in *italics*. This word tells what type of word the Sḵwx̱wú7mesh word is. Here is a list of all the types of words that we have in the dictionary. This information is designed for advanced learners.

adjective	*noun*	*quantifier*
adverb	*numeral*	*sentence*
clitic	*passive*	*suffix*
conjunction	*phrase*	*verb(i) = intransitive verb*
demonstrative	*place name*	*verb(p) = passive verb*
determiner	*prefix*	*verb(t) = transitive verb*
interjection	*preposition*	*vocative*
interrogative	*pronoun*	

For a couple of examples, let us look at the following two words in the dictionary:

temlh red ochre; red paint. *noun.*
temlhúsem paint one's face. *verb(i).*

Following the definition of the first word we have the word *noun.* This word in italics tells us that the Sḵwx̱wú7mesh word is a noun. Compare the next word from the Sḵwx̱wú7mesh dictionary, which is followed by *verb(i)*. This word in italics tells us that this Sḵwx̱wú7mesh word is an intransitive verb.

Where does the word come from? You will notice that some words also have additional information about where the word comes from. A number of new words in the last 150 years were borrowed from other languages. These languages were mainly Chenékwk̲en (Chinook Jargon), English, and Sk̲'emín'em, also known as Halkomelem, the language spoken along the lower Fraser Valley and southern Vancouver Island. A few words have also been borrowed from other First Nations languages here in B.C., and these words will also be noted.

Chenékwk̲en was a trade language that was used throughout the Pacific Northwest of British Columbia, Washington, Oregon, and Alaska. This language was based on First Nations languages that were spoken around Vancouver, WA, and it also had words from Nuchaanulh, from the west coast of Vancouver Island. Many words in Chenékwk̲en also came from French and English. The pronunciation of these words was changed to fit Chenékwk̲en. So, even though we have words in Sk̲wx̲wú7mesh that sound like French words, these words came to Sk̲wx̲wú7mesh from French through Chenékwk̲en.

Sk̲'emín'em is the Sk̲wx̲wú7mesh name for the language spoken along the Fraser Valley (from Yale to Musqueam) and on Vancouver Island (from Nanoose Bay down to Mill Bay). In English, a common name given to this language is Halkomelem. Some terms for new things or concepts have been borrowed into Sk̲wx̲wú7mesh from this neighbouring language.

Sḵwx̱wú7mesh Sníchim – Xwelíten Sníchim Sḵexwts

Squamish – English Dictionary

Guide to Pronunciation
of the Sḵwx̱wú7mesh Alphabet

The following is a brief guide to pronouncing the Sḵwx̱wú7mesh alphabet.

- You will notice that some Sḵwx̱wú7mesh letters are pronounced the same as in English.
- But many Sḵwx̱wú7mesh sounds do not have an equivalent sound in English. For these letters we have provided an approximate sound in English.
- Most Sḵwx̱wú7mesh vowels have more than one pronunciation. The difference in pronuncation depends on where the vowel occurs in the word. We have given examples of each of these different pronunciations.
- At the end of the chart, we have also given the pronunciation of vowel combinations; these sounds occur when a vowel is followed by **w** or **y**.

Sḵwx̱wú7mesh letter	Sounds like the *English* sound	Sḵwx̱wú7mesh example	English meaning
a	a as in *father*	chánat	three
aa	a as in *father*, but a longer version	x̱aam	to cry
ch	ch as in *church*	éncha	where?
ch'	ch as in *church*, but sharper	nch'u7	one
	u as in *cut*	men̓	child
e	i as in *ship*	mechen	lice
	oo as in *shook*	chexw	you
h	h as in *hat*		
i	ay as in *way*	ílhen	to eat
	i as in *machine*	siyáy̓	friend
ii	ay as in *way*, but a longer version	sliim	sandhill crane

Sḵwx̱wú7mesh letter	Sounds like the *English* sound	Sḵwx̱wú7mesh example	English meaning
k	cu as in *cue*	kat	to climb
k’	cu as in *cut*, but sharper	k’éxwa7	to play lacrosse
kw	qu as in *queen*	kweshú	pig
kw’	qu as in *queen*, but sharper	kw’as	warm, hot
ḵ	c as in *call*, but farther back in the throat	tḵach	eight
ḵ’	c as in *call*, but farther back in the throat, and sharper	meḵ’	to get full (from eating)
ḵw	qu as in *queen*, but farther back in the throat	ḵwenís	grey whale
ḵw’	qu as in *queen*, but farther back in the throat, and sharper	t’áḵw’entem	Saturday
l	l as in *laugh*	lúlum	to sing
l̓	l as in *laugh*, but with an abrupt stop	kwi chel̓áḵlh	yesterday
lh	similar to thl in *athlete*	ílhen	to eat
m	m as in *moon*	man	father
m̓	m as in *moon*, but with an abrupt stop	spahím̓	the wind
n	n as in *nine*	sna	a name
n̓	n as in *nine*, but with an abrupt stop	men̓	child
p	p as in *pen*	push	cat
p’	p as in *pen*, but sharper	p’áyaḵ	to get better, to get fixed
s	s as in *sign*	sáta7	aunt
sh	sh as in *shoe*	chésha7	mother

Sḵwx̱wú7mesh letter	Sounds like the *English* sound	Sḵwx̱wú7mesh example	English meaning
t	t as in *time*	tá7a	older lady, mom
t'	t as in *time*, but sharper	t'alh	to be shallow (about water)
tl'	similar to thl in *athlete*, but much sharper	tl'estl'ís	green
ts	ts as in *cats*	tsútsin	mouth
ts'	ts as in *cats*, but sharper	ts'es	nine
u	oa as in *boat*	úpen	ten
	oo as in *too*	shusháw̓	bones
uu	oa as in *boat*, but longer	yuu	to be careful
w	w as in *water*	swat	who?
w̓	w as in *water*, but with an abrupt stop	tew̓íń	raw
xw	similar to a whispered version of wh in *what*	xwey	to be born
x̱	a friction sound in the back of the throat	ex̱	Canada goose
x̱w	similar to x̱ but with rounded lips	sx̱wúsum	soapberries, Indian ice cream
y	y as in *yes*	yem	to be cranky
y̓	y as in *yes*, but with an abrupt stop	hay̓áń	to pacify a child
7	a glottal stop, similar to the stop in the middle of the word *oh-oh!*	chá7ixw	to get used to

Sk̲wx̲wú7mesh letter	Sounds like the *English* sound	Sk̲wx̲wú7mesh example	English meaning
Vowel combinations			
aw	ow as in *how*	haw	no, not
aw̓	ow as in *how*, but with an abrupt stop	lhaw̓	to escape
ay	y as in *why*	tay	to canoe-race
ay̓	y as in *why*, but with an abrupt stop	ay̓x̲	crab
ey	ey as in *hey*	k̲ey	bad
ey̓	ey as in *hey*, but with an abrupt stop	k̲ey̓tsám̓	to curse
ew	o as in *no*	k̲'ewm	to howl, shriek
ew̓	o as in *no*, but with an abrupt stop	hew̓áy̓m	want to go along
iw	ey you as in *hey, you!*	lhchiws	to get tired
iw̓	ey you as in *hey, you!*, but with an abrupt stop	miw̓	to come along with
uy	oy as in *toy*	huy	to be finished
uy̓	oy as in *toy*, but with an abrupt stop	puy̓ch	to dip head in water to get a drink

Grammatical Sketch of Sk̲wx̲wu7mesh

The following is a sketch of the grammar of Sk̲wx̲wú7mesh. This sketch is meant to give you a brief overview of how the Sk̲wx̲wú7mesh sníchim works. It will tell you some basic things you need to know in order to understand Sk̲wx̲wú7mesh or create your own Sk̲wx̲wú7mesh sentences.

A. Chen, Chexw . . . (I, you . . .)
The Subject in Sk̲wx̲wú7mesh

There are four ch- words that indicate the subject of a sentence:

chen *clitic*	I	or	chan *clitic*	I
chexw *clitic*	you	or	chaxw *clitic*	you
chet *clitic*	we	or	chat *clitic*	we
chap *clitic*	you all	or	cháyap [chá yap] *clitic*	you all

(Note that there is no difference in meaning between the variations in the plural forms).

Examples:

1. chen men wa ha7lh.	I'm doing OK.
2. nam̓ chen tuy.	I'm going across (to downtown Vancouver from North Vancouver, for example).
3. chexw men wa ha7lh.	Hello (literally, "You are well?")
4. nu chexw huy?	Are you done?
5. chet huy.	We're done.
6. chet es-hílkw.	We're ready to go.
7. ayás chap.	Be at peace (said to a group of people).
8. chap wa chánem?	What are you all doing?

B. Tíwa, álhi, kwétsiw̓it

(he, she, they)

Understood "he, she, they." In S<u>k</u>w<u>x</u>wú7mesh there is often no word for "he, she, they" when it is understood who we are talking about. Imagine a context where we are talking about your (female) teacher and someone asks:

9. **na éncha lha usáy̓elh?** Where is the teacher?

To answer this question, we could say any of the following:

10. **na wa em̓út.**	She's at home.
11. **na wa hem̓í.**	She's on her way here.
12. **na wa es<u>k</u>w'úy.**	She's sick.

Notice that in none of these answer sentences is there a word that refers to "she" since it is already understood who we are talking about. The same is true if we are referrring to "he" or "they" and it is understood who we are talking about. If we want to be specific, there are a number of different ways to say "he, she, they."

The most common words for "he, she, they." There are a number of words that are translated as "he," "she," and "they" in the Skwxwú7mesh sníchim. While English has only one word "he," Squamish has at least three different words for "he," three different words for "she," and three different words for "they." These Skwxwú7mesh words tell you whether the person is close enough for you to touch, not within reach, or not in sight!

tíwa [ti wa]	he, this [right here]; this one here [male] *demonstrative*
tsíwa [tsi wa]	she [right here]; this one here [female] *demonstrative*
iyáw̓it [i yá w̓it]	they [right here]; these people right here *demonstrative*
tay̓	he, that [over there; visible to speaker, but not within reach; male] *demonstrative*
álhi [á lhi]	she [over there; visible to speaker, but not within reach] *demonstrative*

íytsiw̓it ~ ítsiw̓it [íy tsi w̓it]	they [over there]; those people there [visible to speaker, but not within reach] *demonstrative*
kwétsi [kwé tsi]	he [not in sight]; that one [not in sight] *demonstrative*
kwélhi [kwé lhi]	she [not in sight; female] *demonstrative*
kwétsiw̓it [kwé tsi w̓it]	they [not in sight] *demonstrative*

These Squamish words usually follow the action word or descriptive word as shown in the following examples:

Examples:

13. na mi lhchiws tay̓. He [over there] got tired.
14. na wa chánem tay̓? What is he [over there] doing?
15. an wa kw'ákw'ay̓ álhi. She [over there] is really hungry.
16. na wa chánem álhi. What is she [over there] doing?
17. na nam̓ ts'kw'átsut kwétsiw̓it. They [not in sight] went for a run.
18. na wa chánem ítsiw̓it? What are they [over there] doing?

"He, she, they" using the ending -as. With a smaller group of words the ending -as is added to the verb when the subject is he, she, or they.

Examples:

19. na wa míkw'int-as ta tétxwem. S/he is, they are washing the car.
20. na kw'ách-nemsh-as. S/he, they saw me.
21. tl'íḵst-as eḵ' ta tála. S/he, they will bring the money.

You could also add álhi or tay̓ in these sentences, though it is not normally done:

22. na wa míkw'int-as tay̓/álhi ta tétxwem. S/he is washing the car.

Another way to say "they," using -wit. Another way to say "they" is to simply add the suffix -wit to the verb. Compare the following three examples with examples 19–21. Note that the only change is the addition of -wit.

23. **na wa míkw’int-as-wit ta tétxwem.** They are washing the car.
24. **na kw’ách-nemsh-as-wit.** They saw me.
25. **tl’íḵst-as-wit ta tála.** They will bring the money.

C. Past and Future Tense

Past tense. To make a sentence in the past tense the letter **t** is added to the end of the first word in the sentence. If there is a **ch-** word, the **t** goes at the end of this word.

Examples:

26. **chent naṁ ímesh.** I went for a walk.
27. **nu chexwt wa ts’its’áp’?** Were you working? Have you been working?

Quite often the past tense is not even indicated with the use of the **t** because it is understood from the context:

28. **chen naṁ ímesh.** I went for a walk.
29. **nu chexw wa ts’its’áp’?** Were you working? Have you been working? Are you working?

When there isn’t a **ch-** word, then the **t** attaches to the word **na7**, such as:

30. **na7t wa ts’its’áp’.** He was working. He used to work.
31. **na7t wa ísun-wit.** They were pulling (paddling). They used to pull (paddle).

Future tense. To make a sentence in the future tense the **ch-** word follows the first word of the sentence and the word **eḵ’** follows the **ch-** word:

Examples:

32. **naṁ chet eḵ’.** We will go.
33. **kw’áchnexw chexw eḵ’.** You will see it.
34. **huy chet eḵ’ kwą́yles.** We will finish tomorrow.
35. **huy chap eḵ’ kwáyles.** You all will finish tomorrow.

Sometimes, though, the future tense is not even indicated by **eḵ’** when it is understood simply by having the **ch-** word follow the first word of the sentence:

Example:

36. naṁ chen t'ukw'. I'm going to go home.
37. ts'its'áp' chet. We are going to work.

If there is no ch- word, then ek̲' simply follows whatever is the first word in the sentence, such as:

38. ts'its'áp' ek̲' ta úxwumixw. The village will work.
39. huy ek̲' kwayl es. S/he will work tomorrow.

D. nu, u
Asking Questions

When you are asking a question where you are trying to find out if something is true or not, you use one of two words: nu or u. Not every type of question uses one of these two words, only those looking for an answer of "yes" or "no"!

Questions about the past and present. The word nu is used for questions about things that have already happened (past tense), or about things that are still happening (present tense).

[The word nu is actually made up of the words na and u contracted into nu.]

Examples:

40. nu chexw ílhen? Did you eat?
41. nu chet huy? Are we done?
42. nu chap kw'ákw'aẏ? Are you all hungry?
43. nu chen tl'xwenk̲? Did I win?

Questions about the future. The word u is used for questions about the future. It is placed after the first word in the sentence.

Examples:

44. ílhen u chexw? Are you going to eat?
45. huy u chet ti stsi7s? Are we going to finish today?

E. Object Endings

What are object endings? Objects in Sḵwx̱wú7mesh are indicated by using endings. There are two different sets of object endings. One set begins with **t** and the other set begins with **n**. Let's call them **t**-objects and **n**-objects.

	t-objects	n-objects
me	-ts	-nemsh
us	-tumulh	-numulh
you (one person)	-tumi	-numi
you (more than one person)	-tumiyap	-numiyap
her/him/it	-t	-nexw
them	-twit	-nexw-wit

First of all, note that these endings are simply attached to the end of the action word, unlike in English where they are separate words:

Examples:

46. nu chexw kw'ách-*nemsh*?	Did you see *me*?
47. chexw wa kw'awch-*ts.*	You're staring at *me*!
48. ch'awa-*túmulh* chexw.	Help *us*!
49. ḵiḵ'-*túmi* chen.	I'll repay *you.*
50. ḵw'u7-*túmiyap* chet.	We will join *you all.*
51. chen kw'enman-*túmi.*	I thank *you.*
52. chet wa kw'enmaylh-chew̓an̓-*túmiyap.*	We are praying for *you all.*
53. chen lixw-*t.*	I put *it* down.
54. chen ḵiḵ'-*t.*	I repaid *him.*
55. chet uu-*twit.*	We invited *them.*
56. chet kw'ach-*nexw-wit.*	We saw *them.*
57. nu chexw cháy-*nexw-wit*.	Did you catch up to *them*?

Which Sḵwx̱wú7mesh words can take these object endings? (or a helpful hint in the English translation listings). Any word that has "him," "it," "them," or "someone" in the English translation in our dictionary is a word that can take an object ending. For example, look at the following words in our dictionary; any of these can take object endings.

These verbs take a **t**-object:

kw'acht [kw'ácht] look at (something); take a look at (something). *verb(t).*
ch'áwat [ch'á wat] help (someone). *verb(t).*
ḵwáyexwn [ḵwáy ye xwn] hire (someone). *verb(t).*
tkwáya7nmin [t kwá ya 7n min] hear (someone); listen to (someone). *verb(t).*
lúlumcheẇaṅ [lú lum chew ẇaṅ] sing for (someone); sing about (someone). *verb(t).*
lhḵ'i7s [lh ḵ'i7s] know (someone/something); acquainted with (someone/something), be; know how to do (something). *verb(t).*
ch'íwi7ni [ch'í wi ni] fed up with (someone), be; bothered by (someone), get. *verb(t).*
míshi [mí shi] bring it to (someone). *verb(t).*

These verbs take an **n**-object:

cháynexw [cháy nexw] catch up with (somebody). *verb(t).*
kw'áchnexw [kw'ách nexw] catch sight of (someone/something); see (someone/something). *verb(t).*

Which Sḵwx̱wú7mesh words can take these object endings? (or a helpful hint from the Sḵwx̱wú7mesh listings). Besides using the English definition, you can usually tell which words can take an object ending by the way the Sḵwx̱wú7mesh verb ends. The type of ending the verb has will also tell you whether to use a **t**-object or an **n**-object. Let's look at the **n**-objects first.

1. Sḵwx̱wú7mesh words that take an **n**-*object*. Sḵwx̱wú7mesh words that take an **n**-object end in **-nexw** in the dictionary. This **-nexw** is actually the object ending for him/her/it. Here are some examples from the dictionary of verbs that can take an **n**-object:

cháynexw [cháy nexw] catch up with (somebody). *verb(t).*
ch'em̓nexw [ch'ém̓ nexw] have bitten (something or someone); bite (something or someone) accidentally. *verb(t).*
kw'áchnexw [kw'ách nexw] catch sight of (someone/something); see (someone/something). *verb(t).*
súxwtnexw [súxwt nexw] recognize (someone). *verb(t).*

When you want to use one of the **n**-object endings, you just take the **-nexw** ending off, and add the ending you want to use. For example:

in example 58 below, we have replaced **-nexw** with **-numulh**;
in example 59, we have replaced **-nexw** with **-nemsh**;
in example 60, we have replaced **-nexw** with **-numi**;
in example 61, we have replaced **-nexw** with **-nemsh.**

58. **na cháy-numulh-aswit.** They caught up with us.
59. **na ch'ém̓-nemsh-as lha push.** The (female) cat bit me (by accident).
60. **chen kw'ách-numi.** I saw you.
61. **nu chexw súxwt-nemsh.** Do you recognize me?

2. S<u>k</u>w<u>x</u>wú7mesh words that take a ***t****-object.* We have five types of verbs in the dictionary that can take a **t**-object. They are: 2a) verbs that end in **t**, 2b) verbs that end in **n**, 2c) special words that end in **n**, 2d) verbs that end in **s**, and 2e) verbs with special endings.

2a) Words that end in ***t.*** A number of verbs as listed in the S<u>k</u>w<u>x</u>wú7mesh end with the letter **t**. This **t** is actually the **t**-object which means "him/her/it." For example:

kw'acht [kw'acht] look at (something); take a look at (something). *verb(t).*
ch'áwat [ch'á wat] help (someone). *verb(t).*
<u>k</u>waat [<u>k</u>wat] save (someone); rescue (someone). *verb(t).*
tsú<u>k</u>wut [tsú <u>k</u>wut] inform on (someone); report on (someone); squeal on (someone); betray (someone); tell on (someone). *verb(t).*

(Note that some of these verbs have a further vowel before the **t**. This vowel is the same as the vowel of the verb itself.)

If you want to have an object other than "him/her/it," just replace the **t** with another one of the **t**-objects, such as:

62. **chexw kw'ách-tumulh.** You looked at us.
63. **chen ch'áwa-tumi.** I helped you.
64. **chap <u>k</u>waa-ts.** You all saved me.
64. **chexw tsú<u>k</u>wu-tumulh.** You told on us.

Not every S<u>k</u>w<u>x</u>wú7mesh word, though, that ends in a **t** can take the object endings. You can go to the English translation to get help. If the word has *verb(i)* in the definition, then it is not a word that can take an object ending. For example:

k̲'ayt shout; holler. *verb(i).*

Note that, although this Sk̲wx̲wú7mesh word does end with t, there is no English translation such as "him" or "someone" added to the Sk̲wx̲wú7mesh listing. Also, it has *verb(i)* in its definition. If you want to say that you are "shouting at (someone)" in Sk̲wx̲wú7mesh, you have to first add the suffix listed in the dictionary as:

-en [-en] {added onto some words so that you can use the object endings, see section on "object endings"}. *suffix.*

k̲'áyten [k̲'áy ten] call (someone). *verb(t).*

Now you can add an object suffix, such as:

66. nu chexw k̲'áyten-ts? Did you holler at me? or, Did you call me?

Compare this to the verb without -en. It doesn't have an object ending.

67. na wa k̲'ayt. He is hollering.

2b) Words that end with an n. Another group of verbs, as listed in the Sk̲wx̲wú7mesh, end in the letter n. These verbs can also take the t-objects.

Examples:

k̲wáyexwn [k̲wá ye xwn] hire (someone). *verb(t).*
tselk̲w'án [tsel k̲w'án] kick (someone). *verb(t).*

Here are some sentence examples with these verbs:

68. k̲wáyexwn-tumi chet. We'll hire you.
69. na tselk̲w'án-ts-as. S/he kicked me.

2c) Special words that end in n. Another group of verbs, as listed in the Sk̲wx̲wú7mesh dictionary section, end in either of the following two endings. Notice that these endings themselve also end in an n.

Examples:

-miṅ [-miṅ] {complex transitivizer} to, with. *suffix.*
-cheẇaṅ [-cheẇ ẇaṅ] about, for, on behalf of. *suffix.*

Here are some examples from the dictionary:

na<u>x</u>chachmíń [na<u>x</u> chach miń] make motions with hands to (someone); signal to (someone) with the hand or hands. *verb(t).*

lúlumchew̓ań [lú lum chew w̓an] sing for (someone); sing about (someone). *verb(t).*

Here are some sentence examples with these verbs:

70. **chen wa na<u>x</u>chach-míń-tumi.** I'm making motions with my hands to you.
71. **lúlum-chew̓ań-tumiyap chet.** We will sing for you all.

2d) Words that end with an **s.** Another group of verbs, as listed in the S<u>k</u>w<u>x</u>wú7mesh dictionary section, end in the letter **s**:

kw'awchs look after (someone); see (someone), be able to.*verb(t).*

chénchenś [chén chenś] stand (something) up; steady (something). *verb(t).*

Here are some sentence examples with these verbs:

72. **kw'awchs-tumiyap chen e<u>k</u>'.** I will be looking after you all.
73. **chet wa chénchenś-tumi.** We are supporting you.

Not every word that ends in an **s** can take the object endings, just the ones that have "him," "someone," "it," or "them" in the English translation.

2e) Special endings. Another group of verbs, as listed in the S<u>k</u>w<u>x</u>wú7mesh dictionary section, have either of these two endings:

-ni {added onto some words so that you can use the object endings, see section on "object endings"} to; toward; with. *suffix.*

-shi {added onto some words so that you can use the object endings, see section on "object endings"} for; on behalf of; to. *suffix.*

Here are two examples from the dictionary with these endings:

cha7ixwní ~ cháy̓exwni [cha 7ixw ní] accustomed to (someone), be; used to (someone), be. *verb(t).*

lhémshi [lhém shi] pick berries for (someone) [berries which are picked individually, such as salmonberries]. *verb(t).*

Here are some sentence examples with these endings:

74. **na cha7ixwní-tumulh-as ta push.** The cat is used to us.
75. **na lhemshi-túmulh-as ta stá7uxwlh.** The children picked berries for us.

3. Some more notes about object endings

3a) Her or him? You may have noticed the two endings for him/her/it: **-t**, **-nexw**. We've looked at which verbs use **-t** and which use **-nexw**. But, how do you know when it means "her" instead of "him," or the other way around?

The answer is: You have to tell by the context. For example, imagine a conversation where we are talking about your teacher, Ms. Baker. Then I ask you the following question:

76. **nu chexw kw'ach-nexw kwi chel̓áḵlh?** Did you see her yesterday?

This question is not ambiguous between him or her because we already know we are talking about Ms. Baker. The context usually lets us know when we are referring to him, her, or it.

3b) The disappearing **t.** The **t** which means him/her/it disappears (gets deleted) sometimes. Whenever it follows a verb which ends in **n** or **s**, and the **t** is the last sound in the word, then the **t** gets deleted. Let's take, for example, two verbs that end in **n**: **yutsuṅ**, to shove (someone), and **lháts'i7n**, to bother (someone).

77. **chen yútsuṅ.** I shoved him/her.
78. **chexw wa lháts'i7n.** You're bothering him/her.

Notice that the **t**, which means him/her, is deleted in both sentences. If the **t** didn't get deleted then we would have the following (the * before the sentence means that the sentence is not correct):

79. ***chen yútsuṅ-t.** I shoved him/her.
80. ***chexw wa lháts'i7n-t.** You're bothering him/her.

The **t**, which means him/her, is also deleted in the same way with verbs that end in **s**, such as:

81. **chen lhḵ'i7s.** I know him/her.
82. **chet wa chénchens̓.** We are supporting her/him.

3c) What about "you"? You've probably noticed that there are many ways to say "you" in Sḵwx̱wú7mesh.

Let's review the words and object endings that are translated as "you" so far:

chexw you. *clitic.*
chap you all. *clitic.*
cháyap you all. *clitic.*
-umi you. (object) *suffix.*
-umiyap you all. (object) *suffix.*

The words for "you" in Sḵwx̱wú7mesh change according to whether we are referring to singular or plural, or subject or objects.

This is not the end of the story on "you." There is a further fact about Sḵwx̱wú7mesh when translating "you." There is no way to literally say "he helped you" or "she helped you" or "they helped you"! Instead, what you have to say in Sḵwx̱wú7mesh, translated literally, is "you were helped (by him, her, them)." For example:

83. **chexw ch'áwatem.** You were helped (by him, her, them), she/he/they helped you.

Note that normally these sentences are translated into English as "he helped you," or "she helped you," or "they helped you," based on the context of the conversation.

F. A Summary with Charts

We have looked at a lot of different possible ways of saying I, you, we, you all, he, she, and they. The following charts are a summary of everything we have looked at so far: the **ch-** words, the object endings, and the ways to say s/he, they.

Note that the parts of the charts left blank indicate things that can't be said in Sḵwx̱wú7mesh (nor in English). As an example, you don't say "I helped me." You would or may say "I helped myself" in English.

How do the charts work? The charts give all the possible combinations for sentences in the past or present tense. For example, if you want to say, "I helped you," look first at the left column for "I" and then at the top row for the column that says "you."

Using the dictionary, you will be guided to the construct:

84. **chen ch'áwa-tumi.** I helped you.

To try another example, constuct "You all helped him." First look at the left hand column for "you all." Then look at the top row for "him/her/it." You will find:

85. **chap ch'áwa-t.** You all helped him.

A number of the following charts show how the object endings combine with the different types of verbs that we've talked about. We have verbs that end with:

-t, such as: **kw'acht** to look at (someone/something)
-at, such as: **ch'áwat** to help (someone)
-n, such as, **k̲wáyexwn** to hire (someone)
-min, such as, **nax̲chachmíṅ** to make hand motions to (someone)
-cheẇaṅ, such as, **lúlum-cheẇaṅ** to sing for/about (someone)
-s, such as, **lhk̲'i7s** to know (someone/something)
-ni, such as, **k̲'ál̓ni** to be used to (someone)
shi, such as, **lhemshí** to pick berries for (someone)

Verb with Final –t

kw'ácht [kw'acht] look at (someone/something)

	me -ts	us -tumulh	you singular -tumi you plural -tumiyap	him/her/it -t them -twit
I chen			chen kw'ách-tumi-(yap)	chen kw'ách-t-(wit)
we chet			chet kw'ách-tumi-(yap)	chet kw'ách-t-(wit)
you chexw	chexw kw'ách-ts	chexw kw'ách-tumulh		chexw kw'ách-t-(wit)
you all chap	chap kw'ách-ts	chap kw'ách-tumulh		chap kw'ách-t-(wit)
s/he -as	na kw'ách-ts-as	na kw'ách-tumulh-as		na kw'ách-t-as-(wit)
they -aswit	na kw'ách-ts-aswit	na kw'ách-tumulh-aswit		na kw'ách-t-as-(wit)
by him by her by them	chen kw'ách-tem	chet kw'ách-tem	chexw/chap kw'ách-tem	na kw'ách-tem

Other verbs that end in **-t**: **ám̓ekt** to return (something), **wilkw't** to ask (someone), **kwélasht** to shoot (someone/something).

Verb with Final -at

ch'áwat [ch'á wat] help (someone)

	me **-ts**	us **-tumulh**	you singular **-tumi** you plural **-tumiyap**	him/her/it **-t** them **-twit**
I **chen**			**chen ch'áwa-tumi-(yap)**	**chen ch'áwa-t-(wit)**
we **chet**			**chet ch'áwa-tumi-(yap)**	**chet ch'áwa-t-(wit)**
you **chexw**	**chexw ch'áwa-ts**	**chexw ch'áwa-tumulh**		**chexw ch'áwa-t-(wit)**
you all **chap**	**chap ch'áwa-ts**	**chap ch'áwa-tumulh**		**chap ch'áwa-t-(wit)**
s/he **-as**	**na ch'áwa-ts-as**	**na ch'áwa-tumulh-as**		**na ch'awa-t-as-(wit)**
they **-aswit**	**na ch'áwa-ts-aswit**	**na ch'áwa-tumulh-aswit**		**na ch'awa-t-as-(wit)**
by him by her by them	**chen ch'áwa-tem**	**chet ch'áwa-tem**	**chexw/chap ch'áwa-tem**	**na ch'awa-tem**

Other verbs that end in **-at** (or **-et**, or **-it**, or **-ut**): **tsx̱et** to shove (someone/something), **lhích'it** to cut (someone/something), **shúkw'ut** to bathe (someone).

Verb with Final -n

k̲wáyexwn [k̲wáy ye xwen] hire (someone)

	me -ts	us -tumulh	you singular -tumi you plural -tumiyap	him/her/it-(t) them-(t)wit
I chen			chen k̲wáyexwn-tumi-(yap)	chen k̲wáyexwn-(wit)
we chet			chet k̲wáyexwn-tumi-(yap)	chet k̲wáyexwn-(wit)
you chexw	chexw k̲wáyexwn-ts	chexw k̲wáyexwn-tumulh		chexw k̲wáyexwn-(wit)
you all chap	chap k̲wáyexwn-ts	chap k̲wáyexwn-tumulh		chap k̲wáyexwn-(wit)
s/he -as	na k̲wáyexwn-ts-as	na k̲wáyexwn-tumulh-as		na k̲wáyexwn-t-as-(wit)
they -aswit	na k̲wáyexwn-ts-aswit	na k̲wáyexwn-tumulh-aswit		na k̲wáyexwn-t-as-(wit)
by him by her by them	chen k̲wáyexwn-tem	chet k̲wáyexwn-tem	chexw/chap k̲wáyexwn-tem	na k̲wáyexwn-tem

Other verbs that end in -miṅ: ip'áak̲w'ulhmiṅ to be afraid of (someone), x̲áamiṅ to cry for (someone), tkwáya7nmiṅ to listen to (someone).

Verb with –miṅ

naxchach-míṅ make hand motions to (someone); motion to (someone) with your hands

	me -ts	us -tumulh	you singular -tumi you plural -tumiyap	him/her/it-(t) them-(t)wit
I chen			chen naxchach-miṅ-tumi-(yap)	chen naxchach-miṅ-(wit)
we chet			chet naxchach-miṅ-tumi-(yap)	chet naxchach-miṅ-(wit)
you chexw	chexw naxchach-miṅ-ts	chexw naxchach-miṅ-tumulh		chexw naxchach-miṅ-(wit)
you all chap	chap naxchach-miṅ-ts	chap naxchach-miṅ-tumulh		chap naxchach-miṅ-(wit)
s/he -as	na naxchach-miṅ-ts-as	na naxchach-miṅ-tumulh-as		na naxchach-miṅ-t-as-(wit)
they -aswit	na naxchach-miṅ-ts-aswit	na naxchach-miṅ-tumulh-aswit		na naxchach-miṅ-t-as-(wit)
by him by her by them	chen naxchach-miṅ-tem	chet naxchach-miṅ-tem	chexw/chap naxchach-miṅ-tem	na naxchach-miṅ-tem-(wit)

Other verbs that end in -miṅ: ip'áakw'ulhmiṅ to be afraid of (someone), xáamiṅ to cry for (someone), tkwáya7nmiṅ to listen to (someone).

Verb with -cheẁan

lulum-cheẁan sing for/about (someone)

	me -ts	us -tumulh	you singular -tumi you plural -tumiyap	him/her/it-(t) them-(t)wit
I chen			chen lulum-cheẁaṅ-tumi-(yap)	chen lulum-cheẁaṅ-(wit)
we chet			chet lulum-cheẁaṅ-tumi-(yap)	chet lulum-cheẁaṅ-(wit)
you chexw	chexw lulum-cheẁaṅ-ts	chexw lulum-cheẁaṅ-tumulh		chexw lulum-cheẁaṅ-(wit)
you all chap	chap lulum-cheẁaṅ-ts	chap lulum-cheẁaṅ-tumulh		chap lulum-cheẁaṅ-(wit)
s/he -as	na lulum-cheẁaṅ-ts-as	na lulum-cheẁaṅ-tumulh-as		na lulum-cheẁaṅ-t-as-(wit)
they -aswit	na lulum-cheẁaṅ-ts-aswit	na lulum-cheẁaṅ-tumulh-aswit		na lulum-cheẁaṅ-t-as-(wit)
by him by her by them	chen lulum-cheẁaṅ-tem	chet lulum-cheẁaṅ-tem	chexw/chap lulum-cheẁaṅ-tem	na lulum-cheẁaṅ-tem-(wit)

Other verbs that end in **-cheẁaṅ:** **kw'enmáylh-cheẁaṅ** to pray for (someone), **kwíltencheẁaṅ** to fight for (someone), to fight about (something).

Verb with -s

lhk̲'i7s [lh k̲'i7s] know (someone)

	me -ts	us -tumulh	you singular -tumi you plural -tumiyap	him/her/it -t them -twit
I chen			chen lh'i7s-tumi-(yap)	chen lhk̲'i7s-(wit)
we chet			chet lhk̲'i7s-tumi-(yap)	chet lhk̲'i7s-(wit)
you chexw	chexw lhk̲'i7s-ts	chexw lhk̲'i7s-tumulh		chexw lhk̲'i7s-(wit)
you all chap	chap lhk̲'i7s-ts	chap lhk̲'i7s-tumulh		chap lhk̲'i7s-(wit)
s/he -as	na lhk̲'i7s-ts-as	na lhk̲'i7s-tumulh-as		na lhk̲'i7s-t-as-(wit)
they -aswit	na lhk̲'i7s-ts-aswit	na lhk̲'i7s-tumulh-aswit		na lhk̲'i7s-t-as-(wit)
by him by her by them	chen lhk̲'i7s-tem	chet lhk̲'i7s-tem	chexw/chap lhk̲'i7s-tem	na lhk̲'i7s-tem

Other verbs that end in in -s: siy̓ám̓s to treat (someone) with respect, to treat (someone) as a chief; chénchen̓s to support (someone), to steady (something); chicháy̓s to follow behind (someone), to be chasing (someone).

Verb with -ni

k̲’ál̓-ni believe in (someone)

	me -ts	us -tumulh	you singular -tumi you plural -tumiyap	him/her/it -t them -twit
I chen			chen k̲’ál̓-ni-tumi-(yap)	chen k̲’ál̓-ni-t-(wit)
we chet			chet k̲’ál̓-ni-tumi-(yap)	chet k̲’ál̓-ni-t-(wit)
you chexw	chexw k̲’ál̓-ni-ts	chexw k̲’ál̓-ni-tumulh		chexw k̲’ál̓-ni-t-(wit)
you all chap	chap k̲’ál̓-ni-ts	chap k̲’ál̓-ni-tumulh		chap k̲’ál̓-ni-t-(wit)
s/he -as	na k̲’ál̓-ni-ts-as	na k̲’ál̓-ni-tumulh-as		na k̲’ál̓-ni-t-as-(wit)
they -aswit	na k̲’ál̓-ni-ts-aswit	na k̲’ál̓-ni-tumulh-aswit		na k̲’ál̓-ni-t-as-(wit)
by him by her by them	chen k̲’ál̓-ni-tem	chet k̲’ál̓-ni-tem	chexw/chap k̲’ál̓-ni-tem	na k̲’ál̓-ni-tem

Other verbs that end in -ni: **tkwáya7nni** to listen to (someone), **álhey̓ni** to hurt (someone), **kwúlheni** to borrow it from (someone).

Verb with -shi

lhem-shi pick berries for (someone)

	me -ts	us -tumulh	you singular -tumi you plural -tumiyap	him/her/it -t them -twit
I chen			chen lhem-shi-tumi-(yap)	chen lhem-shi-t-(wit)
we chet			chet lhem-shi-tumi-(yap)	chet lhem-shi-t-(wit)
you chexw	chexw lhem-shi-ts	chexw lhem-shi-tumulh		chexw lhem-shi-t-(wit)
you all chap	chap lhem-shi-ts	chap lhem-shi-tumulh		chap lhem-shi-t-(wit)
s/he -as	na lhem-shi-ts-as	na lhem-shi-tumulh-as		na lhem-shi-t-as-(wit)
they -aswit	na lhem-shi-ts-aswit	na lhem-shi-tumulh-aswit		na lhem-shi-t-as-(wit)
by him by her by them	chen lhem-shi-tem	chet lhem-shi-tem	chexw/chap lhem-shi-tem	na lhem-shi-tem

Other verbs that end in **-shi**: **sát-shi** to hand to (someone), **ch'eẏ-shi** to take from (someone), **húyshi** to make for (someone).

G. Possessives

To indicate who something belongs to, you can use one of six possessives. Some of these possessives come before the word (prefixes), some come after the word (suffixes), and one comes in parts before and after the word.

The six possessives are:

singular		*plural*	
n-/en- . . .	my	**. . . -chet**	our
a- . . .	your (about 1 person)	**a- . . . -yap**	your (speaking to more than 1 person)
. . . -s	his, her, its	**. . . -swit**	their

So how do these possessives work? Let's first look at the possessives as they are attached to the Sḵwx̱wú7mesh word **snexwílh** canoe:

n-snexwílh	my canoe	**snexwílh-chet**	our canoe
a-snexwílh	your canoe (about 1 person)	**a-snexwílh-yap**	your canoe (about more than 1 person)
snexwílh-s	his /her /its canoe	**snexwílh-swit**	their canoe

My and your. In actuality these possessives do not usually appear by themselves. They usually appear with a *determiner* word (**ta/a** for "the"; **lha** when the "a" or "the" is a female; **kwa** when the "a" or "the" is male). The possessives **n-** and **a-** change sometimes when one of these determiners is present. For example, let's see what happens when the determiner **ta** is in use:

ten snexwílh	my canoe
ta a snexwílh	
or **ta7snexwílh**	your canoe (about 1 person)

Notice that **n-** attaches to the determiner word, **ta**, that preceeds it. It is usually pronounced as **ten,** although **tan** is a form some people use as well.

Notice that **a-** is pronounced as a separate sound, or it can be expressed as **ta**7.

These combinations are also true for the determiners **lha**, **kwa**, **kwi**, etc.

lhen sḵa7k	my younger sister	**lha a sḵa7k**	your younger sister
kwen sḵa7k	my younger brother	**kwa a sḵa7k**	your younger brother

Our. The ending for "our" is pronounced the same as the word for "we" in Sk̲wx̲wú7mesh: -chet.

The difference, though, is that the word for "our" is always attached after the word it is associated with. (Whereas the word with the sense of "we" is used interchangeably, before and sometimes after the action word it is tied to!)

Examples:

86. Nilh lam̓-chet ti. This is our house.

As compared to:

87. nam chet ílhen na7 ta lam̓-s. *We*'ll go and eat at her house.
88. chet nam̓ ílhen na7 ta lam̓-s. *We* went to eat at her house.

H. Endings with Specific Meanings

Sk̲wx̲wú7mesh has a rich collection of endings (suffixes) that have specific meanings. These are different from suffixes in the English language because of the specific nature of the meaning. In addition, there is often a separate full Sk̲wx̲wú7mesh word that has the same meaning as the shorter suffix.

There are two groups of endings, one for body parts and the other for other things.

For example, look at the word for "nose" in Sk̲wx̲wú7mesh sníchim:

mék̲sen [mek̲ sen] nose. *noun.*

The Sk̲wx̲wú7mesh sníchim suffix that means "nose" is:

-k̲s nose {full word: mék̲sen }; point; promontory; small oblong object. *suffix.*

Here is an example of this suffix on the word x̲ewtl', to break, as seen in the dictionary listing:

x̲ewtl'k̲s [x̲ewtl' k̲s] break one's nose. *verb(i).*

Note that the "specific ending" for nose, -k̲s, is similar to the basic Sk̲wx̲wú7mesh word mék̲sen. This is not always the case with all of these "specific endings," as shown in the following example:

yíy̓ulh [yi y̓ulh] fire; firewood. *noun.*
burn; have a fire burning. *verb(i).*

The Sḵwx̱wú7mesh sníchim suffix that refers to fire is:

-ayikwup ~ -ikwup [-a yi kwup] fire {full word: yíy̓ulh}. *suffix.*

Here are a couple of dictionary listings with this suffix:

lhich'ní7kwup [lhich' ni7 kwup] cut wood. *verb(i).*
hiyíkwup [hi yí kwup] big fire. *adjective.*

Body parts. Endings for body parts are shown in the following table. Note that for this category, the specific endings sometimes have other additional meanings, which are also given in the listing.

Specific ending/*suffix*	Refers to	Additional meanings	{ full word }
-a7n ~ -a7án	side	cheek	{ nexwmiyíwa7n }
-ach	arm; hand	edge of something	{ táxnten } { naxch }
-alap	thigh		{ smekw'álap }
-alxwtsalh	tongue		{ mekálxwtsalh }
-alhx̱a	neck; throat	windpipe; gullet	{ kénaxw } {x̱wumlhnalh}
-ans	tooth; teeth		{ yenís }
-apsám ~ -apsem ~ -psem	back of the neck		{ skapsm ~ stskapsm ~ stsekápsem }
-ax̱an	side		{ nexwmiyíwa7xan }
-ayan ~ -ay̓a7n	ear		{ kw'éla7n }
-ay̓ ~ -ay̓aḵin	guts; insides		{ ḵ'iyáx̱ }
-ay̓amixw	breast		{ st'elkwím̓ ~ st'elkwím }
-ay̓am̓it	shoulder		{ kweḵ'tán }
-ay̓ax̱a7n ~ -iy̓ax̱a7n ~ -iy̓ax̱an	arm		{ táxnten }
-ay̓eḵw ~ - iy̓eḵw	top; crown of head; top of head		{ nk'áy̓tsiy̓ekw }

Specific ending/*suffix*	Refers to	Additional meanings	{ full word }
-aẏk̲wshen	knee		{ kwéni7kwshen }
-ayus ~ -aẏus	eye	colour	{ k̲elúṁ }
-ch	back	half	{ staẏch }
-chis	hand		{ syelemchís /ring / for fingers}
-chk̲	side; hip		{ sk̲'ak̲'aẇchk̲, smiyiwchk̲, sk̲'ák̲'awchk̲, sk̲'íx̲uts'ch }
-chus	forehead		{ st'úkw'chus }
-inas	chest		{ s7ílinas }
-ek̲w ~ -k̲w	top; head	top of something	{ sme7ús }
-iws ~ -iẇs	inside; body		{ s7étswilh } { slálaẇ }
-k̲	bottom, behind, trunk	bottom of something	{ s7atsk }
-k̲n ~ -k̲in	throat, hair, language	head [in borrowed word]; top [in borrowed words]	{ x̲wúmlhnalh } { skw'úmaẏ } { sníchim }
-k̲s	nose	point; promontory; small oblong object	{ méksen }
-k̲saẏ	elbow		{ s7áẏksaẏ}
-k̲wáẏneẇas	stomach		{ kw'el̓}
-k̲wuẏach	finger		{ nixkwúẏach }
-k̲wuẏshen	toe		{ nixkwúẏshen }
-lhnay	throat,	inside of	{ x̲wúmlhnalh }
-shen	leg; foot	bottom of something	{ sxeṅ }
-ts	mouth	lip; edge; opening	{ tsútsin}
-tsk̲	chin		{ slestsk }
-us	face	front of something	{ s7átsus and sm7us }
-wilh	stomach; belly; bowels	container	{ s7étswilh } {snexwílh}

Other specific suffixes. The following is a list of some of the specific endings and some of their corresponding basic words. Where no basic word is given, that ending does not match the basic form. A sample word for that specific ending is given instead.

Specific ending/*suffix*	Refers to	Full word, or, example
-achxw	limb of tree; branch	{full word: st'exáchxw}
-alh	times; instances	k̲ex̲álh *many times* tsíyachisálh *five times*
-alhk̲wu	water [used in cooking]	{full word: stakw};
-a7lh	bed bedcover	{full word: yáy̓wes}
-alkwlh	dance, spirit	{full word: k̲w'iyílsh; strict sense: mílha7}
-amats'	rope, yarn, etc.; strands	hiyámats' *large-sized [about rope or other thread-like things]*
-amyexw	roots	{full word: t'kw'ámyexw}
-awań	roll of 50-60 blankets	chanatáẃan *150 blankets*
-awanexw	year; years	tsiyichisáwanexw *five years*
-awek̲w ~ -aẃak̲w	hat {full word: yási7k̲w}	
-aẃtxw ~ -txw	house; building; room	sk̲'ey̓áẃtxw *shed where salmon is dried*
-axwilh ~ -wilh ~ -ulh	canoe; container; stomach; belly; bowels	{full word: snexwílh}; {full word: s7étswilh}.
-ay̓	tree; bush	x̲ápay̓ay red *cedar tree; young cedar*
-ay̓ak̲ap	smell; taste	halháy̓ak̲ap *good-smelling; good-tasting*
-ayikwup ~ -ikwup	fire {full word: yíy̓ulh}	
-aylh ~ -ay̓lh ~ -íyalh	child; person; people	swenimáylh *child of dead brother, sister, or cousin; nephew, niece*
-ayuḿ	small object	ańusáyuḿ *two pieces e.g., two berries*
-ay̓ch ~ -i7ch	area; surface	x̲ch'ítay̓ch shortcut
-ay̓em	want to; wish to	{full word: stl'i7}

Specific ending/*suffix*	Refers to	Full word, or, example
-elwet ~ -elut ~ elwit ~ -lwit ~ -lwet	clothes; blanket	{full word: hém̓ten}
-i7k̲in	wool; animal hair	{full word: lemetu7íy̓k̲in};
-i7k̲w	obstruction; rapids	{full word: sch'i7í7k̲w}
-its'a ~ -ayts'a ~ -ayts'a7 ~ -ts'a	clothes	{full word: yek̲wáy̓ ~ yek̲w}
-iwa7 ~ -iwa	tree {full word: stsek̲ }	
-iwan	spirit; mind	{full word: sk̲wálwen}
-i7ups	tail	{full word: skw'ukw'ts}
-k̲ay̓s	weapon	{full word: wak̲áy̓stn}
-k̲	o'clock	tsíyachisk̲ *five o'clock*
-lhal	food	{full word: s7ílhen}
-lhsha7 ~ -alhsha7	multiple of ten	tk̲echalhshá7 *eighty*
-iw̓ilh	be at [a relative position in space or time]	chílhiw̓ilh *over, be; above, be; high up, be*
-min̓ ~ -min	piece; half; side	sek̲'mín *chopped wood; cuttings; waste wood after splitting*
-mesh	people	{full word: stélmexw} Ch'iyák̲-mesh *Salmon-weir-People*
-mut	piece; individual specimen	nch'ú7mut *one piece; one, be at; unity, be in; one unit, be*
-nep ~ -np ~ -nup	floor; ground	{full word: lhxénpten}; {full word: temíxw}
-tán ~ -tn ~ ten	instrument; implement	hálitn *chisel*
-ulh	belonging to; coming from [human or animal]	Sk̲wx̲wu7mesh-úlh *Squamish's own; belonging to the Squamish*
-ullh	young specimen (animal)	mix̲alh-úl-lh *bear cub*
-unexw	wave, waves in the ocean	k̲eyúnexw *rough, be [about water]; bad waves, be*
-uy̓s	large object; large piece; large chunk	hiyúy̓s *consisting of large pieces [referring to rocks, boulders, etc]*

I. Relative Clauses

A relative clause is a part of a sentence that is used to describe something. The subject of a relative clause is different than the **ch-** words. The subject looks like a **ch-** word without the **ch-** and it takes the form of a suffix to the action or verb. Here is a list of subject suffixes for relative clauses:

-an [-an] I *suffix*	**-at** [-at] we *suffix*
-axw [-axw] you *suffix*	**-ap ~ -ayap** [-ap] you all *suffix*
-as [-as] he; she *suffix*	**-aswit** [-as] they *suffix*

These endings are only used with words that can also take Sk̲wx̲wú7mesh object endings.

Relative clauses in English often begin with "that" or "which." Note that there is no word in Sk̲wx̲wú7mesh, though, that translates as simply "that" or "which."

In the following examples, the sentences start with **nilh ta lam̓** – "that's the house" – and the relative clauses are in italics:

89. **nilh ta lam̓** ***na kw'áchnexw-an.***	That's the house *that I saw*.
90. **nilh ta lam̓** ***na kw'áchnexw-axw.***	That's the house *that you saw.*
91. **nilh ta lam̓** ***na kw'áchnexw-as.***	That's the house *that s/he saw.*
92. **nilh ta lam̓** ***na kw'áchnexw-at.***	That's the house *that we saw.*
93. **nilh ta lam̓** ***na kw'áchnexw-ap.***	That's the house *that you all saw.*
94. **nilh ta lam̓** ***na kw'áchnexw-aswit***	That's the house *that they saw.*

Another common place to find relative clauses in Sk̲wx̲wú7mesh is in questions about:

stam what? *question word*	and	**swat** who? *question word*

95. **Stam kwi** ***nam̓st-an?***	What should I bring?
96. **Stam kwi** ***nam̓st-axw?***	What will you bring?
97. **Stam kwi** ***nam̓st-as?***	What will s/he bring?
98. **Stam kwi** ***nam̓st-at?***	What should we bring?

99. Stam kwi *naḿst-ap?* What will you all bring?
100. Stam kwi *naḿst-aswit?* What will they bring?
101. Swat kwi *naḿst-an?* Who should I bring
102. Swat kwi *na naḿst-axw?* Who did you bring?
103. Swat kwi *na naḿst-as?* Who did s/he bring?
104. Swat kwi *naḿst-at?* Who should we bring?
105. Swat kwi *na naḿst-ap?* Who did you all bring?
106. Swat kwi *na naḿst-aswit?* Who did they bring?

If the question word is the subject of the sentence, then there is no subject ending:

107. Swat kwi *na húynexw?* Who finished it?
108. Stam kwi *na wa húy̓s ta sáx̱wi7?* What is eating the grass?

J. Determiners and Demonstratives

In this section we will look at determiners and demonstratives. Determiners are similar to the English articles *the, a, an*. Demonstratives are similar to the English demonstratives *this, these, that, those*. There is much to be said about determiners and demonstratives, but we will only give a brief overview of some of the main things to learn about them in Sḵwx̱wú7mesh.

Determiners. Similar to articles in English, determiners in Sḵwx̱wú7mesh cannot stand alone. That is, they always have to have a word following them that they modify.

Determiners in Sḵwx̱wú7mesh

	Close	In sight, but not close (over there)	Not in sight	Cannot be seen
feminine	tsi	lha	kwlha	kwes
non-feminine	ti	ta	kwa	kwi
plural	iya	iytsi	kwetsi	

Determiners in Sḵwx̱wú7mesh, you will notice, have a lot more information than do articles in English. These determiners can be quite complex in their meaning. Here is the information that they provide:

- *How close something is:* close enough for you to touch, still in sight but not close enough to touch, fairly distant, or out of sight.
- *Feminine or non-feminine:* The feminine determiners are used with female people, female animals, or sometimes things that belong to a female person. The non-feminine determiners are used for males and for all inanimate things.
- *Singular or plural:* the feminine determiners are usually only used for singular, while the non-feminine are used for both singular and plural. There is also a set of plural determiners, but these don't distinguish between feminine or non-feminine.
- There are also determiners for things that haven't been seen yet or can never be seen, such as names, thoughts, feelings, desires, etc.

The following two examples show the difference between the feminine and the non-feminine determiners.

109. na wa ts'its'áp' *lha* slhánay̓.	The woman is working.
110. na wa ts'its'áp' *ta* swí7k̲a.	The man is working.

The next two examples show the difference between "close" and "in sight, but not close":

111. na wa í7tut *tsi* sk̲wemáy̓-chet.	Our (female) dog (right here) is sleeping.
112. na wa í7tut *lha* sk̲wemáy̓-chet.	Our (female) dog (over there) is sleeping.

The next two examples show the difference between "in sight, but not close" and "not in sight":

113. na wa ts'its'áp' *ta*-n man.	My dad (over there) is working.
114. na wa ts'its'áp' *kwa*-n man.	My dad (not in sight) is working.

The next two examples show the difference between "over there" and "cannot be seen":

115. ha7lh *ta* s7ílhen.	The food is good [the food is over there].
116. John *kwi* en-sna.	My name is John [my name cannot be seen].

The following two examples show the difference between "over there" (singular) and "over there" (plural):

117. na wa wuun *ta* sk̲wemáy̓. The dog is barking.
118. na wa wuun *iytsi* sk̲wemáy̓. Those dogs are barking.

Demonstratives. Demonstratives are similar to determiners. They, too, tell you if something is close by, in sight but not close, feminine or non-feminine, etc. One difference, though, is that the demonstratives can stand alone in a sentence. They can have a following word, but they don't need one, unlike the determiners. Demonstratives that refer to things (i.e., not people) that are "close by" are translated as "this" or "these." Demonstratives that refer to things at all the other distances are translated as "that" or "those."

Demonstratives in Sk̲wx̲wú7mesh

	Close by	Over there	Not in sight	Cannot be seen
feminine	tsíwa	álhi	kwélhi	kwesáwa
non-feminine	tí, tíwa	tay̓	kwétsi	kwiyáwa
plural	iyáw̓it	íytsiw̓it	kwétsiw̓it	kwiyáw̓it

The following three examples show the difference between feminine, non-feminine, and plural "over there" demonstratives:

119. na wa chánem *álhi*? What is she (over there) doing?
120. na wa chánem *tay̓*? What is he (over there) doing?
121. na wa chánem *íytsiw̓it*? What are they (over there) doing?

The following two examples show the difference between "over there" and "close by" demonstratives:

122. na wa chánem *tay̓*? What is he (over there) doing?
123. na wa chánem *tíwa*? What is he (close by) doing?

The following two examples show the difference between "over there" and "not in sight" demonstratives:

124. na wa chánem *tay̓*? What is he (over there) doing?
125. na wa chánem *kwétsi*? What is he (not in sight) doing?

The following two examples show the difference between "not in sight" and "cannot be seen" demonstratives. Notice that "cannot be seen" means that you haven't seen the person yet so you don't know who it is.

126. na wa chánem *kwétsi*? — What is he doing? (he's not in sight, but we know him)

127. na wa chánem *kwiyáwa*? — What is he doing? (he's not in sight, we can hear him, but we don't know who he is yet)

Ta Sk̲exwts / The Dictionary

Squamish – English

A a

a[a] [added to the end of a sentence, somewhat similar to "eh" in English; emphasizes sentence]. **Huy chexw a.** Thank you. **Nam̓ chen paym a.** I'm going to rest now. *clitic.*

a-[a-] you; your. **nilh a-si7l tsiwa.** This is your grandmother. **tsi7 u kwi a-tála?** Do you have any money? *prefix.*

aa[aa] ache; sore; hurt. **aa en-sk̲w**

aa ensk̲wálwen [aa n sk̲wál wen] I'm sorry.; I'm sad. *sentence.*

áak̲'alh [áa k̲'alh] bone stuck in throat, have. *verb(i).*

aak̲w [aak̲w] headache, have a. **chen aak̲w.** I have a headache. *adjective.*

aalstén̓emut [aal stén̓ ne mut] offended, be; feel sorry for oneself; sorry for oneself, feel. *verb(i).*

áan̓us [áan̓ nus] two animals. **an̓us ten push.** I have two cats. *numeral.*

aas [aas] hurt (something). **na áastas ta sx̲en̓s.** He hurt his foot. *verb(t).*

-ach [-ach] arm {full word: **táx̲nten**}; hand {full word: **nax̲ch**}. **ch'aháchi7m** lift up your arms. **x̲ewtl'ách** break your hand. *suffix.*

achcháwam ~ echcháwm ~ ns7achcháwam [ach chá wam] spawn. **na wa achcháwan ta tsáw̓in.** The coho are spawning. *verb(i).*

achcháwten [ach cháw ten] spawning place. *noun.*

-achxw [-achxw] limb of tree; branch {full word: **st'ex̲áchxw**}. **p'a7áchxwim̓** leaves start to take [spring]. **ts'xwáchxwim̓** leaves start to rot [autumn]. *suffix.*

ahánum [a há num] hunger [see also **skw'ákw'ay'**]. *noun.*

aháw̓amut [a háw̓ wa mut] odds and ends. *noun.*

aháy̓new̓as [a háy̓ new̓ was] fed up, be; sick and tired, be. *verb(i).*

ahíws [a híws] suffer. **chen ahíws.** I'm suffering. *verb(i).*

ahíwsentsut [a híw sen tsut] injure oneself. **haw k̲w'axw ahíwsentsut.** Don't injure yourself! *verb(i).*

ahúy̓numut [a húy̓ nu mut] act in vain; waste time in a vain effort. *verb(i).*

ak̲áy [a k̲áy] mischievious; rude. *adjective.*

ák̲'alh [á k̲'alh] choke. *verb(i).*

ak̲'ík̲'exw [a k̲'í k̲'exw] beat the drum slowly. *verb(i).*

ak̲wáy̓new̓as [a k̲wáy̓ new̓ was] indigestion, have. *verb(i).*

-alap [-a lap] thigh {full word **smekw'álap**}. **tsík̲alap** get stabbed in the thigh. *suffix.*

al̓íl̓a7 [a̓l lí7 la7] raspberry; raspberries. **ha7lhshen ta al'íl'a.** I like raspberries. *noun.*

al̓íl̓a7ay̓ [a̓l lí7 la 7ay̓] raspberry bush; raspberry bushes. **k̲ex̲ ta al'íl'a7ay̓ na7 ta npen̓em̓áy-chet.** There are a lot of raspberry bushes in our garden.*noun.*

-alkwlh [-al kwlh] dance {full word: **k̲w'iyílsh**). *suffix.*

al̓s [a̓ls] feel sorry for (someone); pity (someone). *verb(t).*

-alxwtsalh [-alxw tsalh] tongue {full word: **mek̲álxwtsalh**}. **tsik̲alxwtsálhen** stab at (someone's) tongue. *suffix.*

-alh [-alh] times; instances. **k̲ex̲álh** many times. **tsiyachisálh** five times. *suffix.*

álhey̓ [á lhey̓] hurt, get; injured, be. **nu chexw álhey̓.** Did you get hurt? *verb(i).*

álhey̓nexw [á lhey̓ nexw] hurt (something) [e.g., one's hands]. **chen álhey̓nexw tin nax̲ch.** I hurt my hand. *verb(t).*

álhey̓ni [á lhey̓ ni] hurt (someone). *verb(t).*

álhey̓shen [á lhey̓ shen] downpour of rain, be a. **na álhey̓shen ti stsi7s.** There was a downpour today. *verb(i).*

álhi [á lhi] she [over there]. **swat melh alhi.** Who is she [over there]? *demonstrative.*

-alhk̲wu [-alh k̲wu] water [used in cooking] {full word: **stak̲w**}; fluid. **ch'xwálhk̲wu7en** add water to (something) [**ch'exw** = increase]. *suffix.*

-alhsha7 ~ -lhsha7 [-alh sha7] multiple of ten. *suffix.*

-alhx̱a [-alh x̱a] neck; throat {full word: **ḵénaxw**}. **ch'eyxwálhx̱a** dry throat [**ch'eyxw** = dry]. *suffix.*

alhx̱án [alh x̱án] downstream area. *noun.*

alhx̱ánax̱an [alh x̱á na x̱an] long downstream side of house built with its long side perpendicular to river. *noun.*

alhx̱ániẇilh [alh x̱á ni ẇilh] downstream of it, be. *verb(i).*

alhx̱ánḵs [alh x̱ánḵs] short downstream side of house built with its long sides parallel to river. *noun.*

-amats' [-a mats'] rope, yarn, etc.; strands. **hiyámats'** large-sized [about rope or other thread-like things]. **aṅusámats'** two strands [of rope, wool, etc.]. *suffix.*

áṁeḵshi [áṁ meḵ shey] deliver it for (someone); deliver it to (someone); return it to (someone); return it for (someone). *verb(t).*

áṁeḵt [áṁ meḵt] deliver (something); return (someone/something); return (someone/something) home; see (someone) off; take (someone/something) home. *verb(t).*

-amyexw [-am yexw] roots {full word: **t'kw'ámyexw**}. *suffix.*

an [an] I. *clitic.*

an [an] really; very; too; excessively; act to a high degree; be to a high degree. **an kw'as ti skwáyel ti stsi7s.** It's very hot today. *adverb.*

-an [-an] I; my. *suffix.*

an ha7lh [an ha7 lh] very. *adverb.*

-an ~ -aṅ [-an] {added onto some words so that you can use the object endings, see section on "object endings," p. 12}. **sátaṅ** hand (something over). *suffix.*

-aṅ ~ -an [aṅ] {added onto some words so that you can use the object endings; see section on "object endings," p. 12}. *suffix.*

-anam ~ -anm [a nam] measure; time. *suffix.*

áṅaṁit [áṅ na meyt] let (someone) have his/her way. *verb(t).*

-anm ~ -anam [a nem] measure; time. *suffix.*

-ans [ans] tooth; teeth {full word: **yenís**}. **seḵ'sáḵ'ans** tooth ache. *suffix.*

ánulh [á nulh] agree; obey; consent. **chen ánulh.** I agree. *verb(i).*

ánuṅ [á nuṅ] allow (someone); give (someone) permission. **chen ánuṅtumi.** I allow you. *verb(t).*

áṅus [áṅ nus] two. **áṅus ta laṁs.** She has two houses. *numeral.*

áṅusalh [áṅ nu salh] twice. **na áṅusálh kwins na lúlum.** I sang twice. *verb(i).*

aṅusámats' [aṅ nu sá mats'] two strands [of wool, rope, etc.]. **men aṅusámats' ta na wa xwékwstan.** I'm only using two strands of wool. *numeral.*

aṅusawánexw [aṅ nu sa wá nexw] two years. **nekw aṅusawánexw lhen sḵa7ḵ.** My little sister is two years old. *verb(i).*

aṅusáyuṁ [aṅ nu sá yuṁ] two berries. **na lhemch'ántas ta aṅusáyuṁ yetwán.** She picked two salmonberries. *numeral.*

áṅusiwa ~ áṅuswa [áṅ nu sey wa] two trees. **na x̱itsḵántem ta áṅusiwa.** He cut down two trees. *numeral.*

áṅusḵ [áṅ nusḵ] two o'clock. **chet naṁ huyá7 na7 ta áṅusḵ.** We left at two o'clock. *noun.*

aṅusmíṅ [aṅ nus míṅ] after (someone), be; pursue (someone); double up on (someone); gang up on (someone) [about two people]. *verb(t).*

áṅusmut [áṅ nus mut] two pieces; put on two of the same thing. **p'i7t chexw ta áṅusmut.** Grab two pieces! *numeral.*

áṅuswa ~ áṅusiwa [áṅ nus wa] two trees. *numeral.*

aṅus7áyum mit [aṅ nus 7áy yum meyt] twenty cents. *noun.*

ap [ap] you all. *clitic.*

-ap ~ -ayap [-ap] you all; yours [plural]. *suffix.*

ápels [á pels] apple; apples. *noun.*

apelsáy [a pel sáy] apple tree; apple trees. *noun.*

ápeṅ [á peṅ] maggot; maggots [see also **íx̱wits'**]. *noun.*

ápeṅántm [á peṅ 'an tem] maggot-infested, get. *verb(p).*

-apsám ~ -apsem ~ -psem [ap sam] back of the neck {full word: **sḵapsm ~ stsḵapsm ~ stseḵápsem**}. *suffix.*

-apsem ~ apsám ~ -psem [ap sem] back of the neck {full word: **sk̲apsm ~ stsk̲apsm ~ stsek̲ápsem**}. *suffix.*

ap'á7en [a p'á 7en] small all-cedar bark basket. *noun.*

as [as] he, she, it, they. *clitic.*

-as [-as] he; she; it; they; his; her; its; their. *suffix.*

asch'eẇá [as ch'eẇ wá] careful to show respect, be. *verb(i).*

asxw [asxw] seal. *noun.*

ashn [á shn] pain in the leg, have a. *adjective.*

at [7at] we. *clitic.*

-at [-at] {added onto some words so you can use the object endings, see section on "object endings," p. 12}. *suffix.*

-at [-at] we, our. *suffix.*

átl'k̲a7tsem [átl' k̲a7 tsem] go into inlet; sail out of [harbour, bay, etc.]. *verb(i).* Howe Sound [see also **nexwnéwu7ts** and **txwnéwu7ts**]. *place name.*

átsak̲wan [á tsa k̲wan] roast (something). *verb(t).*

átsik̲en [á tseh k̲en] front side, be. *verb(i).*

atsk̲ [atsk̲] outside, be. *verb(i).* outdoors; outside [see also **átsk̲iw'ilh**]. *noun.*

átsk̲am [áts k̲am] go outside and sit down. *verb(i).*

átsk̲iẇilh [áts k̲i ẇilh] outside measurement, be; outside of the outside, be on the; be outside something. *verb(i).* outside [see also **atsk̲**]. *noun.*

átsnach ~ étsnach [áts nach] Burrard Reserve. *place name.* bay [see also **s7átsnach**]. *noun.*

átsus [á tsus] front of the house; front side [see also **s7átsus**]. *noun.*

-ats' ~ -ats'a [-ats'] genitals. *suffix.*

-ats'a ~ -ats' [-a ts'a] genitals. *suffix.*

-aẇak̲w ~ -awek̲w [-aẇ wak̲w] hat {full word: **yási7k̲w**}. *suffix.*

-awaṅ [-a waṅ] roll of 50–60 blankets. *suffix.*

-awanexw [-a wa nexw] year; years {full word: **syelánem**}. *suffix.*

-awek̲w ~ -aẇak̲w [-a wek̲w] hat {full word: **yási7k̲w**}. *suffix.*

aẇíts [aẇ wíts] fast; quick; quickly. *adjective.*

aẇítsanum [aẇ wí tsa num] quickness; swiftness. *noun.*

aẇt [aẇ t] behind, be; coming after, be; future, be; last, be. *verb(i).*

aẇt stélmexw [aẇ t stél mexw] people of times to come; future generations. *noun.*

áẇtiwilh [áẇ ti wilh] come from behind; put behind; behind it, be. *verb(i).*

-aẇtxw ~ -txw [-aẇ txw] house {full word: **laṁ**}; building; room. *suffix.*

axw [7axw] you. *clitic.*

-axw [-axw] you; your. *suffix.*

-axwilh ~ -wilh ~ -ulh [-a xwilh] canoe {full word: **snexwílh**}; container; stomach; belly; bowels {full word: **s7étswilh**}. *suffix.*

ax̲áchu7 [a x̲á chu7] little lake [see **x̲áchu7**]. *noun.* Beaver Lake [in Stanley Park]. *place name.*

-ax̲an [-a x̲an] side {full word: **nexwmiyíẇax̲an**}. *suffix.*

áx̲waẏ [á x̲waẏ] housefly; houseflies; blackfly; blackflies. *noun.*

-aẏ [-aẏ] tree; bush {full word: **stsek̲**}. *suffix.*

-aẏ ~ -aẏak̲in [-aẏ] guts {full word: **k'iyáx̲**}; insides. *suffix.*

-ay ~ -way [-ay] one another; each other. *suffix.*

-aẏak̲ap [-aẏ ya k̲ap] smell; taste. *suffix.*

-aẏak̲in ~ -aẏ [-aẏ ya k̲in] guts {full word: **k̲'iyáx̲**}; insides. *suffix.*

áyalhk̲w [áy yalh k̲w] beach. *noun.* down below, be; be on the beach. *verb(i).*

áyalhk̲wáx̲an [áy yalh k̲wá x̲an] long shoreward side of house built with its long sides parallel to the river. *noun.*

áyalhk̲wiẇilh [áy yalh k̲wi ẇilh] beach side of, be on the; towards the beach, be; below, be [i.e., closer to the beach]; shoreward side, be on the. *verb(i).*

áyalhk̲wk̲s [á yalh k̲wk̲s] short shoreward side of house built with its long sides perpendicular to the river. *noun.*

áyalhk̲wmiṅ [áy yalhk̲w miṅ] beach side of; place below someone; area below someone. *noun.*

-aẏaṁit [-aẏ yaṁ meyt] shoulder {full word: **kwek̲'tán**}. *suffix.*

-aẏamixw [-aẏ ya meyxw] breast {full word: **st'elk̲wíṁ** and **st'élk̲wim**). *suffix.*

ayan ~ -aẏa7n [-a yan] ear {full word: **k̲w'éla7n**}. *suffix.*
ayap [ay yap] you all. *clitic.*
-ayap ~ -ap [-ay yap] you all; yours [pl]. *suffix.*
ayás [ay yás] peace, be at; good time, have a. *verb(i).*
áyat [áy yat] cod; black codfish. *noun.*
ayát ~ áyet [a yát] do (something) gently; do (something) with care; do (something) with kindness; put (something) down gently; treat (someone) kindly. *verb(t).*
áyaxwat [á ya xwat] make use of (something); not allow (something) to go to waste. *verb(t).*
áyaxwnúmut [á yaxw nú mut] be a pity; pity, be a. *verb(i).* **áyaxwnúmut ek̲'** [á yaxw nú mut ek̲'] It's going to spoil, too bad! *phrase.*
áyaxws [áy yaxws] have scruples about (something); consider (something) a pity; spare (something). *verb(t).*
áyaxwtas [áy yaxw tas] it's a pity. *verb(t).*
-aẏax̲a7n ~ -iẏax̲a7n ~ -iẏax̲an [-aẏ ya x̲a 7n] arm {full word: **táx̲nten**}. *suffix.*
-aẏa7n ~ -ayan [-aẏ ya 7n] ear {full word: **k̲w'éla7n**}. *suffix.*
-aẏch ~ -i7ch [-aẏch] area; surface. *suffix.*
-aẏek̲w ~ - iẏek̲w [-aẏ yek̲w] top; crown of head; top of head {full word: **nk̲'áytsiẏek̲w**}. *suffix.*
-aẏem [-aẏ yem] want to {full word: **stl'i7**}; wish to. *suffix.*
áẏemustn [áẏ ye mus tn] mask. *noun.*
áyet ~ ayát [áy yet] do (something) gently; do (something) with care; do (something) with kindness; put (something) down gently; treat (someone) kindly. *verb(t).*
áyetsut [áy ye tsut] gently. *verb(i).*
áyexw [áy yexw] wasted food; wasted [anything]. *noun.*
-aẏi ~ -aẏin ~ i7aṅ [-aẏ yi] net. *suffix.*
-ayikwup ~ -ikwup [-a yi kwup] fire {full word: **yíẏulh**}. *suffix.*
aẏílem [aẏ yéh lem] sunny, be. *verb(i).*
-aẏin ~ -aẏi ~ -i7aṅ [-aẏ yin] net. *suffix.*
-ayips [-ay yips] clothespin {full word: **sáyips**}; button. *suffix.*
áyish [áy yish] relative of the same generation; sibling of opposite sex; cousin of opposite sex. *noun.*
aẏíx̲elh [aẏ yéh x̲elh] little crab [see **aẏx̲**]. *noun.*
aykw'álh ~ ikw'álh [ay kw'álh] babysit. *verb(i).*
aykw'álhs [ay kw'álhs] babysit (someone). *verb(t).*
-aẏk̲ [-aẏk̲] bottom; behind {full word: **a7k̲**]. *suffix.*
-aẏk̲wshen [-aẏk̲w shen] knee {full word: **k̲wéni7k̲wshen**}. *suffix.*
-aylh ~ -aẏlh ~ -íyalh [-aylh] child {full word: **meṅ**}; person; people. *suffix.*
-aẏlh ~ -aylh ~ -íyalh [-aẏlh] child {full word: **meṅ**}; person; people. *suffix.*
áẏnexw [áẏ nexw] alive, be. *verb(i).*
áynexw ~ s7áynexw ~ s7áynixw [áy nexw] eulachon from the Squamish River; small eulachon. *noun.*
áynexwan ~ áẏnexwan [áy ne xwan] bring (someone) back to life; endow (something) with life. *verb(t).*
áẏnexwan ~ áynexwan [áẏ ne xwan] bring (someone) back to life; endow (something) with life. *verb(t).*
aẏnexwének̲ [aẏ ne xwén nek̲] have power to cure. *verb(i).*
aẏnexwí7 [aẏ ne xwí7] come back to life. *verb(i).*
áynexwi7 [áy ne xwi7] come to life; revive. *verb(i).*
áẏnexwnexw [áẏ nexw nexw] save (someone). *verb(t).*
ays [ays] inside, be. *verb(i).*
ays [ays] put (something) inside. *verb(t).*
áysaẏch [áy saẏch] territory. *noun.*
áysiẇilh [áy si ẇilh] inside, be; inside of it, be. *verb(i).*
aẏtxw [aẏ txw] home, be; be at home; babysitting, be; home alone, be; sit with someone. *verb(i).*
áytxwmíṅen [áy txw míṅ nen] bequest to (someone); leave to (descendants). *verb(t).*
-ayts'a ~ -ayts'a7 ~ -its'a ~ -ts'a [-ay ts'a] clothes. *suffix.*
-ayts'a7 ~ -ayts'a ~ -its'a ~ -ts'a [-ay ts'a7] clothes. *suffix.*

-ayuṁ [-ay yuṁ] small object. *suffix.*
-aỷus [-aỷ yus] skin {full word: **kw'eḷáẇ**}; colour; animal hair; feathers; bark of tree. *suffix.*
-ayus ~ -aỷus [-ay yus] eye {full word: **k̲elúṁ**}. *suffix.*
-aỷus ~ -ayus [-aỷ yus] eye {full word: **k̲elúṁ**}. *suffix.*
aỷx̲ [aỷ x̲] crab. *noun.*
áỷx̲entem [áỷ x̲en tem] crab-infested, be. *verb(p).*
-a7án ~ -a7n [-a 7an] cheek {full word: **nexwmiyíwa7n**}. *suffix.*
á7aẇt [á 7aẇ t] coming after, be; following after, be; future, be. *verb(i).* after-birth. *noun.*
a7áyas [a 7áy yas] peace, be at [i.e., not at war]. *verb(i).*
á7aynexw ~ á7aỷnexw [á 7ay nexw] alive, be; lively, be. *verb(i).*
á7aỷnexw ~ á7aynexw [á 7aỷ nexw] alive, be; lively, be. *verb(i).*
a7a7ní7 [a 7a7 ní7] oldsquaw [type of duck]. *noun.*
a7k̲ [a7 k̲] defecate. *verb(i).*
-a7lh [-a7 lh] bed {full word: **yáỷwes**}; bedcover. *suffix.*
á7lhk̲en [á7 lh k̲en] sleet; wet snow, be. *verb(i).*
-a7n ~ -a7án [-a 7n] cheek {full word: **nexwmiyíwa7n**}. *suffix.*
a7tk̲ách [a7 t k̲ách] eight animals. *numeral.*
a7ú7 swí7k̲a [a 7ú7 swí7 k̲a] first man. *noun.*
a7ú7 ~ u7ú7 [a 7ú7] first, be. *verb(i).*
á7xwa [á7 xwa] light in weight; swift. *adjective.*
a7x̲mámin [a7 x̲ má min] defecate in pants. *verb(i).*
a- . . . -yap [7a- -yap] your all; your [pl]. *prefix.*

Ch ch

-ch [-ch] back {full word: **staỷch**}.*suffix.*
chácha7nem ~ chá7chanem [chá cha7 nem] doing what, be?; going where, be? *question word.*
ráchenat [chá cheń nat] three animals. *numeral.*
cháchshaỷ [chách shaỷ] give; give away presents; make presents. *verb(i).*
cháchu7 [chá chu7] hunt by canoe. *verb(i).*
chalh [chalh] soon; almost. *adverb.*
chan I do; I [emphatic]. *clitic.*
chánat [chá nat] three. *numeral.*
chanatálh [cha na tálh] three times. *verb(i).*
chanatámats' [cha na tá mats'] three strands [of wool, rope, etc.]. *numeral.*
chanatáwań [cha na tá wań] three rolls of 50 blankets. *numeral.*
chanatawánexw [cha na ta wá nexw] three years. *verb(i).*
chanatáyuḿ [cha na táy yuḿ] three berries. *numeral.*
chanatíwa [cha na tí wa] three trees. *numeral.*
chánatk̲ [chá na tk̲] three o'clock. *noun.*
chánatuys [chá na tuys] three rocks. *numeral.*
chanáxw [cha náxw] third; three times; thrice. *verb(i).*
chánaxwilh [chá na xwilh] three containers [pots, pans, canoes]. *numeral.*
chanáxwntsut [cha ná xwen tsut] make a third attempt; attempt for the third time; try for the third time. *verb(i).*
chánem [chá nem] do what?; go where? *question word; verb(i).*
chánxwyes [chán xw yes] three days. *verb(i).*
chap you all. *clitic.*
chas do what with (something)? *question word; verb(t).*
cháshi [chá shey] do what with (something)? *question word; verb(t).*
chat we. *clitic.*
chaxw you. *clitic.*
chawn [chaw wen] hum. *verb(i).*
chaỷ not be raining so hard; raining so hard, not be. *verb(i).*
cháyak̲em [cháy ya k̲em] follow behind someone; follow someone; pursue someone. *verb(i).*
cháyap [chá yap] you all. *clitic.*
cháỷexw ~ chá7ixw [chá7 yexw] used to, get; accustomed to, get. *verb(i).*
cháỷexwni ~ chá7ixwni [chá7 yexw ni] used to (someone), be; accustomed to (someone), be. *verb(t).*
chaylh ~ chiyálh [chaylh] soon. *adverb.*
cháymin [cháy min] Chinese person. *noun.*
chayn [chay yen] chase (someone); pursue (someone); follow (something). *verb(t).*
cháynexw [cháy nexw] catch up with (somebody). *verb(t).*
chá7chanem ~ chácha7nem [chá7 cha nem] going where, be?; doing what, be? *question word; verb(i).*
chá7chen [chá7 chen] delouse (someone). *verb(t).*
chá7i ~ chiyáy [chá 7i] nearly; almost; act to a small degree; a little; do something a little bit; barely. *adverb.*
chá7ixw ~ cháỷexw [chá 7ixw] accustomed to, get; used to, get. *verb(i).*
cháỷexwni [cha 7ixw ní] accustomed to (someone), be; used to (someone), be. *verb(t).*
cha7lh ~ chá7lha [cha7 lh] for a little while; little while. *adverb.*
chá7lha ~ cha7lh [chá7 lha] for a little while; little while. *adverb.*
cha7t [cha7 t] make (something). *verb(t).*
chá7twilh [chá7 twilh] build a canoe. *verb(i).*
checheḿúsn [che cheḿ ḿú sn] meeting (someone), be. *verb(t).*
chéchepx̲wem [ché chep x̲wem] brittle, be. *verb(i).*
checheẃát ~ escheche ẃát ~ escheẃát ~ scheẃát [che cheẃ ẃát] clever, be; smart, be; able, be; know how to do something; able to do something, be; can work well. *verb(i).*

chechshíw̓at [chech shí w̓at] urge (someone); pursuade (someone); coax (someone). *verb(t).*

chel̓áḵlh [chel7 lá ḵlh] yesterday [only in the phrase **kwi chel'áḵlh**]. *adverb.*

cheláw̓nexw [che láw̓ nexw] defeat (someone/something). *verb(t).*

chelína [che lí na] Chilean person. *noun.*

chelm [chél lem] eelgrass. *noun.*

chelhchílhshen [chelh chílh shen] high heel shoes. *noun.*

chelhḵw [chelh ḵw] fall through an opening [e.g., a hole in the floor]; pass through a hole or opening. *verb(i).*

chelhḵwáń [chelh ḵwáń] put (something) through a hole; shove (something) through a hole; throw (something) through a hole. *verb(t).*

chelhḵwéy ~ chelhḵwí ~ chélhḵwi [chelh ḵwéy] go through a hole; pass through opening. *verb(i).*

chelhḵwí ~ chélhḵwi ~ chelhḵwéy [chelh ḵwéy] go through a hole or opening; pass through opening. *verb(i).*

chélhḵwi ~ chelhḵwí ~ chelhḵwéy [chélh ḵwey] go through a hole or opening; pass through opening. *verb(i).*

chelhḵwnúmut [chelh ḵw nú mut] fall through a hole after trying to get through. *verb(i).*

chélhḵwshen [chélh ḵw shen] fall through a hole [about feet]. *verb(i).*

chemáy̓kwup [che máy̓ kwup] fetch wood. *verb(i).*

cheṁá7 [cheṁ ṁá7] piggyback; pack things on one's back; carry a load. *verb(i).*

chemá7n [che má 7n] carry (something) on one's back; pack (something) on one's back. *verb(t).*

chemá7ntway [che má 7n tway] piggyback each other. *verb(i).*

chemcheṁáy̓eḵw [chem cheṁ ṁáy̓ y̓eḵw] strap of basket over head. *noun.*

cheṁcheṁáylh [cheṁ cheṁ 7áylh] pack a child on one's back. *verb(i).*

chemcheṁá7s [chem cheṁ ṁá7 s] carrying (something) on the back, be. *verb(t).*

chéṁcheṁts [chéṁ cheṁ ts] lock one's mouth closed; clamp one's mouth shut [like a child who's pouting]. *verb(i).*

chéṁetn [chéṁ ṁe tn] pallial muscle of clam; packstrap; tumpline; shoulder strap of basket. *noun.*

cheṁtsám [cheṁ tsám] close one's mouth. *verb(i).*

chéṁus ~ ncheṁús ~ nchéṁus [chéṁ ṁus] meet; double, be; come together; together, come. *verb(i).*

chéṁusn ~ nchéṁusn [chéṁ ṁu sn] meet (someone); fold (something). *verb(t).*

chéṁusnew̓as [chéṁ ṁus new̓ w̓as] meet each other. *verb(i).*

chemx̱ [chem x̱, ur, ché mex̱] pitch; resin. *noun.*

chemx̱án [chem x̱án] pitch (something); apply pitch to (something); make (something) watertight with pitch. *verb(t).*

chemx̱áyus [chem x̱áy yus] put pitch in someone's eyes; have one's eyes closed up with pitch. *verb(i).*

chemx̱áyusan [chem x̱áy yu san] pitch (someone's) eyes; close (someone's) eyes up with pitch. *verb(t).*

chemx̱éwilh [chem x̱éw wilh] make canoe watertight with pitch. *verb(i).*

chen I. *clitic.*

cheńáw̓as ~ eschenáw̓as [cheń ńáw̓ w̓as] recline; lie down. *verb(i).*

chenchánat [chen chá nat] three people. *numeral.*

chenchánatay̓lh [chen chá na tay̓ lh] have three children. *verb(i).*

chéńchens [chéń chens] stand (something) up; steady (something). *verb(t).*

chéńchenstway [chéń chens tway] uphold one another; support one another. *verb(i).*

chenékwḵen [che nékw ḵen] speak Chinook [see also **chinúḵwḵin**]. *verb(i).*

cheńt [cheń t] hold (something) steady; support (something); steady (something). *verb(t).*

chéńtsut [chéń tsut] lean against it for support. *verb(i).*

chenxw [chen xw] I still [from **chen** + **xw**]. *clitic.*

-chep ~ -chp fire {full word: **yíy̓ulh**}. *suffix.*
chépani [**ché pa ni**] Japanese person. *noun.*
chépsan [**chép san**] take a wee bit off of (something) at a time. *verb(t).*
chepshán [**chep shán**] chip (something); take a small piece off of (something) [e.g., of wood]. *verb(t).*
chépxwem [**chép xwem**] brittle, be; weak, be; crunchy, be. *verb(i).*
chésha7 [**ché sha7**] mother. *noun.*
cheshá7min [**che shá7 min**] mother (someone); motherly towards (someone), be. *verb(t).* step-mother. *noun.*
cheshchésha7 [**chesh ché sha7**] mother to many [see **chésha7**]. *noun.*
cheshchésha7min [**chesh ché sha7 min**] mother to many, be. *verb(t).*
cheshchésha7ni [**chesh ché sha7 ni**] mother to (them) all. *verb(t).*
cheshn [**ché shen**] send (someone). *verb(t).*
cheshnám [**chesh nám**] send someone to do something. *verb(i).*
chet we. *clitic.*
-chet our. *suffix.*
-chew̓an [**-chew̓ w̓an**] {added onto some words so that you can use the object endings, see section on "object endings," p. 12}; on behalf of, for. *suffix.*
chewásh [**chew wásh**] wife. *noun.*
chewáshem [**che wá shem**] get a wife; propose marriage; act as go-between in a marriage proposal. *verb(i).*
chewashem̓áy̓m [**chew wa shem̓ máy̓ yem**] want to propose. *verb(i).*
chewchewásh [**chew chew wásh**] wives [sg: **chewásh**]. *noun.*
chexw you. *clitic.*
chexw huyá7 [**chexw hu yá7**] Goodbye. *sentence.*
chexw tl'ik̲ [**chexw tl'ehk̲**] Good day. [said to person arriving]; You have arrived. *sentence.*
chexw wa chánem [**chexw wa chá nem**] what are you doing? *sentence.*
chexw wa texwnch7ám̓ [**chexw wa txwen ch 7ám̓**] How are you? *sentence.*
chexwétem [**che xwé tem**] swelling on body, have. *verb(i).*
chex̲wentsút [**che x̲wen tsút**] splash [about fish]. *verb(i).*
cheyk̲sám [**cheyk̲ sám**] lose balance; fall off. *verb(i).*
chey̓k̲w [**chey̓ k̲w**] upside down, be; hang down [about head]; have one's head hanging down; go head-first. *verb(i).*
chey̓k̲wám [**chey̓ k̲wám**] dive head-first; nose-dive [e.g., bird]. *verb(i).*
chey̓k̲wán̓ [**chey̓ k̲wán̓**] turn (something) upside down. *verb(t).*
chéy̓k̲wentsut [**chey̓ k̲wen tsút**] turn oneself upside down. *verb(i).*
chéy̓k̲wsan [**chey̓ k̲w sán**] turn (someone) upside down. *verb(t).*
cheyn [**chéy yen**] cause (something) to lean over. *verb(t).*
cheyntm [**chéy yen tm**] lean over. *verb(p).*
chicháy̓ak̲em [**chey cháy̓ y̓a k̲em**] following behind someone, be; following, be. *verb(i).*
chicháy̓s [**chey cháy̓s**] following (something), be; chasing (something), be. *verb(t).*
chicháy̓stway [**chey cháy̓s tway**] following each other in single file, be. *verb(i).*
chichík̲'en [**chi chéh k̲'en**] mink. *noun.*
chíchip [**chí chip**] tickling, be. *verb(i).*
chíchipach [**chí chi pach**] ticklish hands, have. *verb(i).*
chichipáchen [**chi chi pá chen**] tickle (someone's) hands. *verb(t).*
chichipán [**chi chi pán**] tickle (someone). *verb(t).*
chíchipem [**chí chi pem**] ticklish feeling in throat, have a. *verb(i).*
chichipshnán̓ [**chi chip sh nán̓**] tickle (someone's) feet. *verb(t).*
chichipús [**chi chi pús**] ticklish face, have a. *adjective.*
chíchishkwstm [**chí chish kwes tm**] get left behind [in a race]; left behind [in a canoe race], be. *verb(p).*
chichm [**chí chem**] inner, be [in the sense of closer to shore]. *verb(i).*
chichm k̲w'émk̲w'm [**chí chem k̲w'ém k̲w'em**] inner Defence Island. *place name.*
chíchshem [**chích shem**] upper part of some place, be in the. *verb(i).*

chíkmen [chík men] Chinook money; Chinook. *noun.*
chíkmen tála [chík men tá la] silver dollar. *noun.*
chík̲wiṅ [chéh k̲wiṅ] smash (something); grind (something). *verb(t).*
chík̲wnexw [chéhk̲w nexw] smash (something) up. *verb(t).*
chílis [chéh lis] cherry; cherries. *noun.*
chilh [chilh] above; high. *adjective.* upper part; top. *noun.*
chilh temíxw [chilh te míxw] heaven. *noun.*
chílhiṅup [chí lhi ṅup] high ground. *noun.*
chílhiẇilh [chí lhi ẇilh] over, be; above, be; high up, be. *verb(i).*
chílhix̱en [chí lheh x̱en] top part of it. *noun.*
chilhná7nch' [chilh ná 7ench'] chief's daughter; girl of upper class. *noun.*
chilhs [chilhs] put (something) up high; have (something) up high; raise (something). *verb(t).*
chílhshi [chílh shey] put it up high for (someone); raise it for (someone). *verb(t).*
chinúkw [chi núkw] Chinook [see also **chikmen**]. *noun.*
chinúkwk̲in [chi núkw k̲in] speak Chinook jargon [see also **chenék̲wk̲en**]. *verb(i).* Chinook language. *noun.*
-chis [-chis] hand. *suffix.*
chíshem [chí shem] up away from the beach, be; area above, be. *verb(i).* place above; area higher up than when one is oneself. *noun.*
chishemáyak̲'in [chi she máy ya k̲'in] kitchen [see also **ílhenáw'txw**]. *noun.*
chíshemiẇilh [chí shem mi ẇilh] above, be [away from the beach]; landward side, be on the. *verb(i).*
chishkw [chish kw] distance, be in the; recede; ebb. *verb(i).*
chíshkwaẏus [chísh kwaẏ ẏus] bright-coloured. *adjective.*
chishkwts [chísh kwets] low tide, be [way out]; very low tide, be. *verb(i).*
chíshus [chí shus] face-to-face with dead person's spirit, be. *verb(i).*
chíwi7min [chí wi7 min] satisfy (someone). *verb(t).*
chiws ~ lhchiws [chiws] tired, get [short form]. *verb(i).*
chíx̱em [chéh x̱em] strong smell, have a. *verb(i).*
chíx̱emi7 [chéh x̱e mi7] stinky, be getting [about salmon that is being smoked]. *verb(i).*
chíx̱eṁk̲w [chéh x̱eṁ k̲w] "stinkhead" [type of smoked fish head]. *noun.*
chíx̱iṅ [chéh x̱iṅ] singe (something) over a fire. *verb(t).*
chiyálh ~ chaylh [chi yálh] soon. *adverb.*
chiẏáxw [chi ẏáxw] 1. quiver for arrows; 2. protocol. *noun.*
chiyáy ~ chá7i [chi yáy] act to a small degree; be to a small degree; a little; do something a little bit; nearly; barely; almost. *adverb.*
chiyáystexw [chi yáy stexw] just so much. *adverb.*
chíyetmixw [chí yet mixw] great horned owl. *noun.*
chi7cht [chi7 ch t] parent; parent or sibling of parent; father. *noun.*
chí7i7aẏ [chí 7i 7aẏ] strawberry plant; strawberry plants. *noun.*
-chk̲ hip {full word: **sk̲'aẇchk̲, smiyíwchk̲, sk̲'ák̲'aẇchk̲, sk̲íx̱uts'ch**}; side. *suffix.*
-chp ~ -chep fire {full word: **yíẏulh**}. *suffix.*
-chus [-chus] forehead {full word: **st'úkw'chus**}. *suffix.*
chx̱etm [che x̱é tem] swell. *verb(i).*

Ch' ch'

-ch' apparently. *clitic.*
ch'aa [ch'aa] surprised, be. *verb(i).*
ch'áatl'am [ch'aá tl'am] hunt; hunt deer. *verb(i).*
ch'ách'am [ch'á ch'am] rise; mount; go upward. *verb(i).*
ch'ách'em [ch'á ch'em] stinging feeling, have a. *verb(i).*
ch'ách'ewam [ch'á ch'eẁ ẁam] recount one's family tree or descent. *verb(i).*
ch'ách'lem [ch'á ch'el lem] give birth [old word for esmen']. *verb(i).*
ch'aháchi7m [ch'a há chi 7m] lift up one's arm. *verb(i).*
ch'aháy̓lhm [ch'a háy̓ lhem] lift up one's child to offer for marriage; raise one's child. *verb(i).*
ch'ahím̓ [ch'a hím̓] lift. *verb(i).*
ch'ahúsem [ch'a hú sem] lift up one's head. *verb(i).*
ch'am̓am [cha m̓am] cedar leaves. *noun.*
ch'áman [ch'á man] needle; needles. *noun.*
ch'ámem [ch'á mem] dead needle; dead needles. *noun.*
ch'áptstn [ch'áp ts ten] strap used with Indian baby basket. *noun.*
ch'ást'a [ch'ás t'a] splint. *noun.*
ch'ást'a7en [ch'ás t'a 7en] apply a splint to (someone); put splints on (someone). *verb(t).*
ch'átyay̓ ~ ch'ích'aya [ch'át yay̓] devil's club [type of plant; see also pá7pawtn]. *noun.*
ch'áwalhen [ch'á wa lhen] help. *verb(i).*
ch'áwat [ch'á wat] help (someone). *verb(t).*
ch'áwatway [ch'á wa tway] help each other. *verb(i).*
ch'áwatsut [ch'á wa tsut] help oneself. *verb(i).*
ch'áẁax̱an [ch'áẁ ẁa x̱an] widgeon [type of duck]. *noun.*
ch'aẁáy̓ [ch'aẁ ẁáy̓] spoon [modern]; wooden spoon. *noun.*
ch'awch'áẁstway [ch'aw ch'áẁ stway] help one another. *verb(i).*
ch'awnálhen [ch'aw ná lhen] help someone, manage to. *verb(i).*
ch'áẁneẁas [ch'áẁ ne ẁas] help one another/each other. *verb(i).*
ch'áwnexw [ch'áw nexw] helped (someone), have; have been of assistance to (someone); turn out to be of assistance to (someone). *verb(t).*
ch'awnúmut [ch'aw nú mut] help oneself. *verb(i).*
ch'awténm ~ tich'awténm [ch'aw té nem] come to ask someone for assistance; ask for assistance [in the form of supplies]. *verb(i).*
ch'awtn [ch'aw tn] helper; spiritual helper. *noun.*
ch'áxwch'axwḵsm [ch'áxw ch'axw ḵs m] limp, be. *verb(i).*
ch'áxwi7 [ch'á xwi7] stop talking; silent, be or become; fall silent. *verb(i).*
ch'áxwḵsen [ch'áxw ḵ sen] hit the ground with (something). *verb(t).*
ch'áyay̓ [ch'áy yay̓] what one's ch'emash is called after the death of one's spouse; deceased spouse's sibling or cousin. *noun.*
ch'áyay̓m ~ tich'áyay̓m [ch'áy yay̓ y̓m] marry deceased spouse's sibling or cousin. *verb(i).*
ch'áy̓i [ch'áy̓ y̓i] dry out [about living things]; die [about a tree]. *verb(i).*
ch'áytsut [ch'áy tsut] fast; diet, be on a; diet. *verb(i).*
ch'ay̓ús [ch'ay̓ y̓ús] fish spreader [see also ch'ay'ústn]. *noun.*
ch'ay̓ústn [ch'ay̓ yús tn] fish spreader used in barbecuing [see also ch'ay'ús]. *noun.*
ch'á7cham̓ [ch'á7 cham̓] go up (a hill, moutain); hike up; mount; rise (up a hill, mountain). *verb(i).*
ch'a7lhx̱w [ch'a7 lhxw] short cedar planks for roofing. *noun.*
ch'ch'ulh ~ ch'ich'úlh [ch' ch'ulh] collarbone. *noun.*

ch'ch'us ~ ch'ech'ús [ch' ch'us] sandfly; sandflies; no-see-um; no-see-ums. *noun.*
ch'ech'awátaỷ [ch'e ch'a wá taỷ] helping one another/each other, be. *verb(i).*
ch'ech'a7chám̓ [ch'e ch'a7 chám̓] ascending, be; going up, be [a hill, mountain, etc.]. *verb(i).*
ch'éch'epxwm [ch'é ch'ep xwem] shattering, be. *verb(i).*
ch'ech'etx̲álhs [ch'e ch'et x̲álhs] laughing, be. *verb(t).*
ch'éch'ewtl'em [ch'é ch'ew tl'em] many of them, be; teeming, be. *verb(i).*
ch'ech'eyxwí7 ~ ch'eych'eyxwí7 [ch'e ch'ey xwí7] dry, be getting. *verb(i).*
ch'ech'e7úsem [ch'e ch'e 7ú sem] go uphill. *verb(i).*
ch'ech'ich'ántm ~ ch'ich'ichántem [ch'e ch'i ch'án tm] convulsions, have; thrown into convulsions, be. *verb(p).*
ch'ech'ús ~ ch'ch'us [ch'e ch'ús] sandfly; sandflies; no-see-um; no-see-ums. *noun.*
ch'ech'xw [ch'ech' xw] increasing, be. *verb(i).*
ch'ekwx̲án [ch'ekw x̲án] fry (something). *verb(t).*
ch'ekwx̲ím̓ [ch'ekw x̲ím̓] frying, be. *verb(i).*
ch'ékwx̲tn [ch'ékw x̲ ten] frying pan. *noun.*
ch'ek̲' ~ ch'eyk̲' surprised, be. *verb(i).*
ch'ék̲'ni [ch'ék̲' ni] surprised by (something), be. *verb(t).*
ch'ek̲'númut [ch'ek̲' nú mut] surprise oneself. *verb(i).*
ch'elík̲'aỷus [ch'e léh k̲'aỷ yus] yellow slime mould. *noun.*
ch'elk̲ drop [about dry salmon from being overheated]. *verb(i).*
ch'elk̲áń [ch'el k̲áń] throw on a big dab of (something). *verb(t).*
ch'elk̲m [ch'el k̲m] drop [about fish]. *verb(i).*
ch'em̓ bite. *verb(i).*
ch'emásh [ch'e másh] in-laws of the same generation; sibling-in-law; cousin-in-law. *noun.*
ch'em̓chán [ch'em̓ chán] bite (someone's) back. *verb(t).*
ch'emch'emím̓ [ch'em ch'e mím̓] have something on one's breath [e.g., alcohol or food]. *verb(i).*
ch'émch'ems [ch'ém ch'ems] hold (something) between one's teeth. *verb(t).*
ch'ém̓ch'em̓ts [ch'ém̓ ch'em̓ts] mouth closed tightly, have the; tight-lipped, be; clamped shut, have one's mouth; have one's mouth clamped shut. *verb(i).*
ch'ém̓esh [ch'ém̓ mesh] herring spawn. *noun.*
ch'em̓k̲án [ch'em̓ k̲án] bite (something's) rear. *verb(t).*
ch'em̓nexw [ch'em̓ nexw] bitten (something or someone), have; bite (something or someone) accidentally. *verb(t).*
ch'em̓t bite (something or someone). *verb(t).*
ch'em̓tm [chem̓ tm] bitten, be; have a bite [as when fishing]. *verb(p).*
ch'ésk̲en [ch'és k̲en] golden eagle; snow eagle. *noun.*
ch'ésp'i [ch'és p'i] ugly, be. *verb(i).*
ch'esp'i7ús [ch'es p'i 7ús] ugly face, have an; ugly-faced. *adjective.*
ch'éshnech [ch'ésh nech] weasel. *noun.*
ch'etk̲w'án [ch'et k̲w'án] crumble (something) up; smash (something) up. *verb(t).*
ch'etxw [ch'et xw] carve; decorated with carving, be. *verb(i).*
ch'etxwán [ch'et xwán] carve (something). *verb(t).*
ch'etxwím̓ [ch'et xwím̓] carving, be. *verb(i).*
-ch'ew̓ań [ch'ew̓ w̓ań] [a suffix meaning for someone].
ch'ewch'áwni [ch'ew ch'áw ni] help (someone). *verb(t).*
ch'ewch'áwstway [ch'ew ch'áws tway] help one another. *verb(i).*
ch'éwilh ~ snch'éwilh [ch'éw wilh] half-brother; half-sister. *noun.*
ch'exw ~ ch'ixw [ch'exw] increase. *verb(i).*
ch'eỷ light eater, be a; fast; not eat much. *verb(i).*
ch'eych' [ch'ey ch'] virgin. *noun.* pure. *adjective.*
ch'eyk̲' ~ ch'ek̲' surprised, be. *verb(i).*
ch'éỷshi [ch'éỷ shi] take it from (someone); take it over (someone); take it away from (someone). *verb(t).*
ch'eyxw ~ ch'eỷxw dry. *adjective.*
ch'eỷxw ~ ch'eyxw dry. *adjective.*

ch'eyxwálhx̱a [ch'ey xwálh x̱a] dry throat, have a. *adjective.*
ch'eyxwán̓ ~ ch'ey̓xwán [ch'ey xwán̓] dry (something). *verb(t).*
ch'ey̓xwán ~ ch'eyxwán̓ [ch'ey̓ xwán] dry (something). *verb(t).*
ch'eyxwán̓tm [ch'ey xwán̓ tm] dry, get; thirsty, be. *verb(p).*
ch'eyxwán̓tsut [ch'ey xwán̓ tsut] dry oneself off. *verb(i).*
ch'eyxwáy̓ḵin [ch'ey xwáy̓ ḵin] dry throat, have a. *adjective.*
ch'eyxwáy̓ḵin ~ ch'eyxwíḵin [ch'ey xwáy̓ ḵin] thirsty; have a dry throat; dry throat, have a; want to drink. *adjective.*
ch'eyxwáy̓usn [ch'ey xwáy̓ yu sen] dry (someone's) tears. *verb(t).*
ch'eyxwáy̓usntsut [ch'ey xwáy̓ yu sen tsut] dry one's own tears. *verb(i).*
ch'eyxwíḵin ~ ch'eyxwáy̓ḵin [ch'ey xwéh ḵin] thirsty; have a dry throat; dry throat, have a; want to drink. *adjective.*
ch'ey̓xwím̓ [ch'ey̓ xwím̓] drying things, be. *verb(i).*
ch'eyxwimáw̓txw [ch'ey xwi máw̓ txw] shed where things are dried [see also ch'ixwi7áw'txw]. *noun.*
ch'eyxwí7 [ch'ey xwí7] dry, be; get dry. *verb(i).*
ch'éy̓xwnexw [ch'éy̓xw nexw] dry (something), manage to; dried (something), have. *verb(t).*
ch'eyxwnúmut [ch'eyxw nú mut] dry, get. *verb(i).*
ch'eyx̱ántsut [ch'ey x̱án tsut] make noise like a group of children; sound like a group of children; chattering, be. *verb(i).*
ch'e7chám̓ [ch'e7 chám̓] climb up a hill or mountain. *verb(i).*
ch'ich' [ch'ey ch'] turn around; twisted, be; twist. *verb(i).*
ch'ich'alíw̓en ~ nch'ích'elíw̓en [ch'i ch'a lí w̓en] grab all one can; greedy, be. *verb(i).*
ch'ich'án [ch'i ch'án] twist (something). *verb(t).*
ch'ich'ántsut [ch'i ch'án tsut] turn oneself around. *verb(i).*
ch'ích'aya ~ ch'átyay̓ [ch'í ch'ay ya] devil's club [type of plant; see also pá7pawtn]. *noun.*
ch'ích'ich' [ch'í ch'ich'] tangled; twisted. *adjective.*
ch'ich'ich'ántem ~ ch'ech'ich'ántm [ch'i ch'i ch'án tem] convulsions, have; thrown into convulsions, be. *verb(p).*
ch'ich'íin [ch'i ch'íin] lift (something); keep lifting (something). *verb(t).*
ch'ích'ikwem [ch'í ch'i kwem] furious, be; angry, be. *verb(i).*
ch'ích'imi7 [ch'í ch'i mi7] closer, be getting. *verb(i).*
ch'ích'is [ch'í ch'is] support (something). *verb(t).*
ch'ích'it [ch'í ch'it] next to someone, be; close second in a race, be a. *verb(i).*
ch'ích'its [ch'í ch'its] stay close to (someone) [literally, cause someone to be near]. *verb(t).*
ch'ich'itsántem [ch'i ch'i tsán tem] take food out of one's mouth [about sha7yu]. *verb(p).*
ch'ich'ixwí7 ~ ch'ech'ixwí7 [ch'i ch'i xwí7] dry, be getting. *verb(i).*
ch'ich'iyúy ~ ch'iyúy ~ sch'iyúy ~ sch'eych'eyúy [ch'i ch'i yúy] twins. *noun.*
ch'ich'ḵwán [ch'ich' ḵwán] strangle (someone). *verb(t).*
ch'ich'úlh ~ ch'ch'ulh [ch'i ch'úlh] collarbone. *noun.*
ch'ich'úsn [ch'i ch'ú sen] strangle (someone). *verb(t).*
ch'iiḵ [ch'eeh ḵ] come up; rise [about sun/moon]. *verb(i).*
ch'iim [ch'iim] raised, be; lift; raise. *verb(i).*
ch'iin [ch'iin] lift (something) up; raise (something). *verb(t).*
ch'íintsut [ch'íin tsut] take off [about a bird]; rise to the surface [in water]. *verb(i).*
ch'iinúmut [ch'ii nú mut] lift oneself up, manage to. *verb(i).*
ch'íkwi7tem [ch'í kwi7 tem] closing on, be. *verb(p).*
ch'ikwm [ch'i kwm] lose temper. *verb(i).*
ch'iḵ [ch'iḵ] rise [about sun/moon]. *verb(i).*
ch'iḵ ta lhḵaych' [ch'iḵ ta lh ḵaych'] The moon rises. *sentence.*
ch'íḵam̓ [ch'éh ḵam̓] envious, be; raise oneself slightly from a sitting position; rise from one's seat. *verb(i).*

ch'ik̲sán [ch'eh k̲ sán] lift up one end of (something). *verb(t).*

ch'ík̲'aluts [ch'éh k̲'a luts] thrush, have [a fungal infection of the mouth, usually found in children]. *verb(i).*

ch'ímiṅtsut [ch'í miṅ tsut] close, be getting [intentionally]; approach. *verb(i).*

ch'ími7 [ch'í mi7] near, get; approach; close to giving birth, be. *verb(i).*

ch'iṅáyusem [ch'iṅ náy yu sem] look up. *verb(i).*

ch'íshi [ch'í shi] lift it up for (someone). *verb(t).*

ch'ishnáṁ [ch'ish náṁ] lift up one's leg. *verb(i).*

ch'it [ch'it] close; near. *adjective.*

ch'ítaỷch ~ x̲ch'ítaỷch [ch'í taỷ ch] shortcut; nearest at opposite side [as across water]; area close to where one is going; area close to one's destination; area close to one's own territory. *noun.*

ch'íten [ch'í ten] move (something) closer; put (something) close; bring (something) close. *verb(t).*

ch'ítentsut [ch'í ten tsut] bring oneself closer; approach. *verb(i).*

ch'íti [ch'í ti] closer, get. *verb(i).*

ch'ítiṅ [ch'í tiṅ] gnaw on (something) [e.g., about a rat gnawing a hole in the wall]. *verb(t).*

ch'ítitem [ch'í ti tem] gnawed, be. *verb(p).*

ch'ítneẃas [ch'ít neẃ was] never parted, be; close together, be. *verb(i).*

ch'ítnexw [ch'ít nexw] brought (something) close, have. *verb(t).*

ch'its [ch'its] keep (something) close by. *verb(t).*

ch'íwi [ch'í wi] bothered, feel; annoyed, be; fed up, get. *verb(i).*

ch'íwi7min [ch'í wi7 min] bother (someone); bothersome to (someone), be. *verb(t).*

ch'íwi7ni [ch'í wi7 ni] fed up with (someone), be; bothered by (someone), get. *verb(t).*

ch'ixw ~ ch'exw [ch'ixw] fall through; increase. *verb(i).*

ch'ixwáyts'a7ten [ch'i xwáy ts'a7 ten] clothesline [see also **lhp'ayts'a7ten**]. *noun.*

ch'ixwi7áṅten [ch'i xwi 7áṅ ten] rack for drying nets. *noun.*

ch'ixwi7áẃtxw [ch'i xwi 7áẃ txw] drying shed [see also **ch'ixwimáw'txw**]. *noun.*

ch'íyakwem [ch'í ya kwem] furious, be. *verb(i).*

ch'iyák̲ [ch'i yák̲] fish trap; salmon weir. *noun.*

Ch'iyák̲mesh [ch'i yák̲ mesh] Salmon-weir place; People of the Salmon-weir; Cheakamus. *place name.*

ch'iyíkw'in [ch'i yí kw'in] pinch (someone). *verb(t).*

ch'iyíkw'in ~ ch'iyíkw'ní7n [ch'i yí kw'in] gnash one's teeth; clench one's teeth. *verb(i).*

ch'iyíkw'ní7n ~ ch'iyíkw'in [ch'i yí kw'e ní 7n] gnash one's teeth; clench one's teeth. *verb(i).*

ch'iyíp [ch'i yíp] close to edge, be; at the edge or end, be. *verb(i).*

ch'iyípach ~ sch'iyípach [ch'i yí pach] hand; lower arm. *noun.*

ch'íỷit [ch'í ỷit] take away from (someone). *verb(t).*

ch'iyúy ~ sch'iyúy ~ ch'ich'iyúy ~ sch'eych'eyúy [ch'i yúy] twins. *noun.*

ch'í7ch'ikwem [ch'í7 ch'i kwem] angry, be really. *verb(i).*

ch'i7í7k̲wm [ch'i 7éh7 k̲wem] go up rapids. *verb(i).*

ch'í7ten ~ nch'í7ten [ch'í7 ten] rattle; ritualist's rattle; rattle used by a person with magic power. *noun.*

ch'i7xw [ch'i7 xw] dry, be. *verb(i).*

ch'i7x̲ [ch'i7 x̲] tender; sensitive; sore. *adjective.*

ch'k̲'en [ch' k̲'en] file. *noun.*

ch'k̲wéla7 [ch' k̲wél la7] ball; Indian hockey game. *noun.*

ch'k̲w'ap [ch' k̲w'ap] tie up hair with one feather in it [in the Indian fashion]. *verb(i).*

ch'lhá7lew [ch' lhá7 lew] insect similar to a maggot [gets into dried salmon after it has been stored]; mite. *noun.*

ch'nch'u7 ~ nch'nch'u7 ~ ench'ench'u7 [ch'n ch'ú7] alone, be [about a person]. *verb(i).* one person. *numeral.*

ch'shaỷ [ch' shaỷ] Douglas fir [see also **ch'sháya**]; fir stick. *noun.*

ch'sháya [ch' shá ya] Douglas Fir [see also **ch'shaỷ**]. *noun.*

ch't'us [ch' t'us] jealous, be. *verb(i).*

ch'úch'usum ~ ch'úsum [ch'ú ch'u sum] act superior to someone; dislike. *verb(i).*

ch'um̓ [ch'um̓] split shakes. *verb(i).*

ch'um̓ún̓ [ch'um̓ mún̓] split (red cedar) into shakes. *verb(t).*

ch'usténamut [ch'us tén nam̓ mut] feel insulted; insulted, feel. *verb(i).*

ch'úsum ~ ch'úch'usum [ch'ú sum] act superior to somone; dislike. *verb(i).*

ch'úsumin̓ [ch'ú su min̓] not like (something). *verb(t).*

ch'út'a [ch'ú t'a] fall and get poked with a stick; pierced with sharp object, get; skewered, be. *verb(i).*

ch'út'a7n [ch'ú t'a 7en] pierce (something) with a stick, or sharp object. *verb(t).*

ch'útl'i7n [ch'ú tl'i 7n] cold, have chest stuck with. *verb(i).*

ch'úukw'a [ch'úu kw'a] skunk cabbage. *noun.*

ch'u7 ~ nch'u7 ~ snch'u7 [ch'u7] one. *numeral.*

ch'ú7wilh [ch'ú7 wilh] step-brother; step-sister. *noun.*

ch'xwálhk̲wu7en [ch' xwálh k̲wu 7en] add water to (something); add water to (food in a cooking pot). *verb(t).*

ch'xwit ~ ch'xwut [ch' xwit] add on to (something). *verb(t).*

ch'xwut [ch' xwut] add on to (something); increase (something); put more on to (something). *verb(t).*

E e

échaẏ [é chaẏ] give along; hand to someone to deliver. *verb(i).*
echcháwm ~ achcháwam ~ ns7achcháwam [7ech cháw wem] spawn. *verb(i).*
ehánum [e há num] hungry, be painfully; painfully hungry, be. *verb(i).*
ekwiyí [e kwi yí] play the shuttlecock and battledore game. *verb(i).*
ekw's [7ekw's] black katy chiton. *noun.*
ek̲a [7e k̲a] they say. *clitic.*
ek̲' [7ek̲'] will [future tense; see also **it'**]. *clitic.*
ek̲w [7ek̲w] fall out [about hair]. *verb(i).*
-ek̲w ~ -k̲w [-ek̲w] top; head {full word: **sme7ús**}. *suffix.*
ék̲wen [é k̲wen] remove hair from (a hide). *verb(t).*
ék̲wentsut [é k̲wen tsut] moult. *verb(i).*
ek̲wís [e k̲wís] narrow; thin [e.g., rope]; slim. *adjective.*
ek̲wísamats' [e k̲wí sa mats'] thin [about rope]. *adjective.*
ek̲wísaẏk̲in [e k̲wí saẏ k̲in] high-pitched voice, have a. *adjective.*
ek̲wísiẇa [e k̲wí si ẇa] thin [about tree]. *adjective.*
ek̲wísk̲s [e k̲wís k̲s] narrow nose, have a. *adjective.*
ek̲wísn [e k̲wí sn] make (something) narrow. *verb(t).*
ek̲wísus [e k̲wí sus] narrow-faced; narrow face, have a. *adjective.*
ek̲wtús [ek̲w tús] air-dried salmon; salmon, air-dried; dried whole salmon. *noun.*
ek̲w'í7tel [e k̲w'í7 tel] related, be; pair of brothers or sisters, be. *verb(i).* sibling; cousin; siblings and cousins [see also **sek̲w'í7tel ~ s7ek̲w'í7tel**]. *noun.*
eḷás ~ eḷés [eḷ lás] sea cucumber. *noun.*
eḷáshtel [eḷ lásh tel] group of two composed of siblings and/or cousins, be a; pair consisting of brother and sister, be a. *verb(i).*
eḷéli [eḷ 7él li] dream. *verb(i).*
eḷélini [eḷ 7él li ni] dreaming about (something/someone), be; vision about (something/someone), be having a. *verb(t).*
eḷés ~ eḷás [eḷ lés] sea cucumber. *noun.*
élini [é li ni] dream about (something/someone); vision about (something/someone), have a. *verb(t).*
elk̲áẏ [el k̲áẏ] supernatural creature. *noun.*
élk̲en [él k̲en] top, be at the. *verb(i).*
-elut ~ -elwit ~ -elwet ~ -lwit ~ -lwet [-e lut] clothes; blanket {full word: **hémten**}. *suffix.*
-elwet ~ -elut ~ elwit ~ -lwit ~ -lwet [-el wet] clothes; blanket {full word: **hémten**}. *suffix.*
-elwit ~ -elut ~ -elwet ~ -lwit ~ -lwet [-el it] clothes; blanket {full word: **hémten**}. *suffix.*
elháp [e lháp] gone short of one's intended spot, have; fall short. *verb(i).*
élhk̲aẏ [élh k̲aẏ] snake. *noun.*
elhtách [elh tách] parent; parents. *noun.*
elhtáchntsut [elh tá chen tsut] parent, become a. *verb(i).*
elhx̲án [elh x̲án] downstream area, be. *verb(i).*
elhx̲ániẇilh [elh x̲á ni ẇilh] lower side of village or river, be. *verb(i).*
elh7ílhen [elh 7í lhen] eat [about a group]. *verb(i).*
eṁemút [eṁ 7em mút] sit [about a group]. *verb(i).*
eṁí [eṁ mí] come. *verb(i).*
émilhán [é mi lhán] give (one's daughter) as a wife. *verb(t).*
émilhaẏlh [é mi lháẏ lh] give one's daughter in marriage. *verb(i).*
eṁíṁash [eṁ 7íṁ mash] walking around, be; walk [about a group]. *verb(i).*
eṁímats [eṁ 7í mats] grandchildren [sg: ímats]. *noun.*
eṁís [e ṁís] bring (something) here. *verb(t).*
emtl'áy [em tl'áy] knocked out, be. *verb(i).*

emút [e mút] sit down [said to someone standing up]; get up [said to someone lying in bed]. *verb(i).*

eṁút [eṁ mút] home, be at; living somewhere, be; sitting on something, be; sitting down, be. *verb(i).*

emúts [e múts] sit (someone) down. *verb(t).*

em7úmsem [em 7úm sem] awake, be [about a group]. *verb(i).*

en [7en] I. *clitic.*

-en [-en] {added onto some words so that you can use the object endings, see section on "object endings," p. 12}. *suffix.*

en sh7eylh [7ensh 7eylh] loved uncle or elder. *noun.*

en- ~ n- [7en-] my. *prefix.*

eńáńusmiń [eń 7áń nus miń] co-owned, be; own the same thing [about two people]. *verb(i).*

éncha [én cha] where, be?; which?; at which place?; at which time? *question word.*

énchas [én chas] put (something) where? *question word; verb(t).*

ench'ench'ú7 ~ nch'nch'u7 ~ ch'nch'u7 [en ch'en ch'ú7] one person. *numeral.* alone, be [about a person]. *verb(i).*

eńench'áyuṁ [eń 7en ch'áy yuṁ] one berry at a time, be. *verb(i).*

énmitsut [én mi tsut] commit suicide. *verb(i).*

ents [7ents] I. *pronoun.*

énuńtach [é nuń tach] middle child, be the. *verb(i).*

énwilh [én wilh] centre, be in the; man the centre of the boat; middle, be the. *verb(i).*

en7áńus [eń 7áń nus] two people. *numeral.*

eń7áńusaẏlh [eń 7áń nu saẏ lh] have two children. *verb(i).*

ep7úpen [ep 7ú pen] ten people. *numeral.*

ep7úpnaẏlh [ep 7ú pen naẏ lh] have ten children. *verb(i).*

ép'enshen [é p'en shen] redback salamander. *noun.*

es- [es-] [stative prefix]. *prefix.*

esáṁ [e sáṁ] covered, be. *verb(i).*

esáṁk̲w ~ es-háṁk̲w [e sáṁ k̲w] keep one's head covered; have a covered head. *verb(i).*

esáṁk̲ws [e sáṁ k̲ws] cover (someone) all up with a blanket or towel. *verb(t).*

esámtm [e sám tm] look worried; worried, look. *verb(p).*

esáp' [e sáp'] come to an end [of a trail]; finish a course; graduate. *verb(i).*

esáp'nexw [e sáp' nexw] finish (something) [e.g., reading a book]. *verb(t).*

esáp'shi [e sáp' shi] finish for (someone). *verb(t).*

esásxw [e sás xw] greased, be. *verb(i).*

esáẇtuỉa ~ saẇtúỉa [e sáẇ tuỉ ỉa] little finger [see also **etsím'ul'a** and **saw't̲k̲wúy'ach ~ saw't̲k̲wúl'a**]. *noun.*

eschánem [es chá nem] how? [literally, be doing what?]. *question word; verb(i).*

eschecheẇát ~ checheẇát ~ escheẇát ~ scheẇát [es che cheẇ wát] clever, be; smart, be; able, be; know how to do something; able to do something, be; can work well. *verb(i).*

eschécheẏnup [es ché cheẏ nup] sloping ground. *noun.*

eschechík̲' [es che chéhk̲'] look surprised; surprised, look. *verb(i).*

eschechíxw [es che chíxw] swelling, be. *verb(i).*

eschéchi7 [es ché chi7] tilted, be; leaning over, be; slanted, be; not horizontal, be. *verb(i).*

eschéchlhk̲wus [es chéch lh k̲wus] leaning with one's head through a window or door, be. *verb(i).*

eschék̲chek̲ [es chék̲ chek̲] spotted. *adjective.*

escheỉáẇ [es cheỉ láẇ] defeated, be; forfeit; lose. *verb(i).*

escheỉáẇs [es cheỉ láẇs] defeat (someone). *verb(t).*

eschelhk̲wús [es chelh k̲wús] lean head through window or door [either to look inside or outside of the house]. *verb(i).*

eschenáẇas ~ cheńáẇas [es chen náẇ was] recline; lie down. *verb(i).*

eschenáẇes [es chen náẇ wes] lie on one's back. *verb(i).*

eschewásh [es chew wásh] married, be [about a man]; wife, have a. *verb(i).*

escheẇát ~ scheẇát ~ eschecheẇát ~ checheẇát [es cheẇ wát] smart, be;

clever, be; able; able to do something, be; know how to do something; can work well. *verb(i).*

eschéych [es chéych] bed with someone, be in. *verb(i).*

eschíchen̓ [es chí chen̓] impure footprint, have an; footprint, have an impure. *verb(i).*

eschí7ch [es chí7 ch] lying down, be [about a group]; sleeping together, be. *verb(i).*

esch'áwatm [es ch'á wa tem] gift [e.g., of seeing the future in dreams]. *noun.* have that kind of gift. *verb(p).*

esch'áxw [es ch'áxw] quiet, be; silent, be. *verb(i).*

esch'ch'ín̓ [es ch' ch'ín̓] leaning on something, be. *verb(i).*

esch'ch'íxw [es ch' ch'íxw] little more than the other, be; excess, be in. *verb(i).*

esch'éch'ich' [es ch'é ch'ich'] twisted, be. *verb(i).*

esch'éch'ich' sp'útl'am [es ch'é ch'ich' sp'ú tl'am] plug tobacco. *noun.*

esch'ech'íxw [es ch'e ch'íxw] excess, be in. *verb(i).*

esch'ék̲ch'ek̲ ~ sch'ék̲ch'ek̲ [es ch'ék̲ ch'ek̲] dirty. *adjective.*

esch'ek̲ch'ék̲shn [es ch'ek̲ ch'ék̲ shn] dirty feet, have [about a group of people]. *verb(i).*

esch'em̓álxwtsalh [es ch'em̓ málxw tsalh] lisp [literally, have the tongue between the teeth]. *verb(i).*

esch'éxwk̲ [es ch'éxwk̲] fried bread; anything fried. *noun.*

esch'éy̓ch' [es ch'éy̓ch'] purified. *adjective.*

esch'ich'ík̲' [es ch'i ch'éhk̲'] surprised, be. *verb(i).*

esch'ích'm [es ch'í ch'em] reaching up to, be; being as high as, be; high as, be being as. *verb(i).*

esch'k̲wús [es ch' k̲wús] dirty face, have a. *adjective.*

esch'k̲w'áp [es ch' k̲w'áp] hair tied up in the Indian fashion, have [with a single feather]. *verb(i).*

esch'úsum [es ch'ú sum] shunned, be. *verb(i).*

esch'úsumni [es ch'ú sum ni] shun (someone). *verb(t).*

esch'xwúy̓s [es ch' xwúy̓s] larger amount, be a. *verb(i).*

esék̲' ~ lhsek̲' [e sék̲'] half [split off], be [see also **nt'ék̲w'ch**]. *verb(i).*

esém̓k̲wu [e sém̓ k̲wu] wrapped in a blanket, be. *verb(i).*

esem̓úm̓at [e sem̓ 7úm̓ mat] lazy. *adjective.*

esesaw̓án [e se sa w̓án] provided with food on trip, be; bring food for lunch. *verb(i).*

esesel̓ús [e se sel̓ lús] spun, be [about wool]. *verb(i).*

esesím̓ [e se sím̓] unconscious, be. *verb(i).*

esésixw [e sé sixw] fleeting glance. *verb(i).*

esések̲' [e sések̲'] cracked, be; half, be; torn, be; split, be. *verb(i).*

es-hám̓k̲w ~ esám̓k̲w [es hám̓ k̲w] keep one's head covered; have a covered head. *verb(i).*

es-hámk̲w ~ hamk̲w ~ ham̓k̲w [es hám k̲w] covered, be [by blanket, by snow, etc.]. *verb(i).*

es-hámk̲ws [es hám k̲ws] cover (someone) with a blanket. *verb(t).*

es-héch [es héch] more than, be. *verb(i).*

es-héchhich [es héch hich] braggart, be a; boastful, be. *verb(i).*

es-hílkw [es hílkw] ready to leave, be; be ready; be ready to go. *verb(i).*

es-húy [es húy] ready, be already; ready, be. *verb(i).*

es-húyiws ~ es-huy̓us [es húy yiws] dressed up, be; all dressed up, be. *verb(i).*

es-húys [es húys] made (something), have; keep (something). *verb(t).*

es-húy̓us ~ es-húyiws [es húy̓ yus] dressed up, be; all dressed up, be. *verb(i).*

esíik̲ [e séhk̲] under house, be. *verb(i).*

esí7ch [e sí7 ch] receive more. *verb(i).*

esí7chmin [e sí7 ch min] extra with regards to, be. *verb(i).*

eskáket [es ká ket] climbed up already, have. *verb(i).*

eskapú [es ka pú] jacket on, have a [see **kapú**]. *verb(i).*

eskwákwaẏ ~ eskwákwi [es kwá kwaẏ] hidden, be; hiding, be in; hiding, be. *verb(i).*

eskwákways [es kwá kways] hiding (something), be. *verb(t).*

eskwákwi ~ eskwákwaẏ [es kwá kwi] hidden, be; hiding, be in; hiding, be. *verb(i).*

eskwáyel [es kwá yel] during the day; in the daytime. *adverb.*

eskwékwep [es kwé kwep] mound. *noun.*

eskwekwín [es kwe kwín] state of rapture, be in a; rapture, be in a state of. *verb(i).*

eskwímkwim [es kwím kwim] red. *adjective.*

eskwkwá7tel [es kw kwá7 tel] living apart, be. *verb(i).*

eskwkwá7telneẇas [es kw kwá7 tel neẇ was] separated, be. *verb(i).*

eskwkwíṅ [es kw kwíṅ] long time, be a; old, be [about things]. *verb(i).*

eskwtáms [es kw táms] married, be [about a woman]; husband, have a. *verb(i).*

eskwúkwem [es kwú kwem] shore. *noun.* shore, be at the. *verb(i).*

eskwúkwsen [es kwúkw sen] light of the stars [sg: **eskwúsen**]. *noun.*

eskwúmshen [es kwúm shen] beach, have feet up on; feet up on beach, have. *verb(i).*

eskwúsen [es kwú sen] light of a star. *noun.*

eskwúẏts [es kwúẏts] funny, be; talk funny; joke. *verb(i).*

eskw'áy ~ skw'áy ~ kw'ay [es kw'áy] can't; impossible, be; unable, be; pregnant, be; cannot; wrong, be; amiss, be; powerless, be; very ill, be; defective, be; out of order, be. *verb(i).*

eskw'áychk̲ [es kw'áy ch k̲] crippled leg, have. *verb(i).*

eskw'áyiws [es kw'áy yiws] ignoble descent, be of [e.g., sons of skasnekem]. *verb(i).*

eskw'ékw'sh [es kw'ékw' sh] counted already, be. *verb(i).*

eskw'élkw'el [es kw'él kw'el] stomach ache, have a. *verb(i).* diarrhoea. *noun.*

eskw'élkw'elstm [es kw'él kw'els tem] diarrhoea, have. *verb(p).*

eskw'émkw'emts' [es kw'ém kw'em ts'] bony, be; skinny, be. *verb(i).*

eskw'úkw'sh [es kw'úkw'sh] counted, be. *verb(i).*

eskw'úkw'uts' [es kw'ú kw'uts'] crooked. *adjective.*

esk̲ák̲alhi7 [es k̲á k̲a lhi7] dark, be getting. *verb(i).*

esk̲ák̲tl' [es k̲ák̲ tl'] cloudy, be. *verb(i).*

esk̲ápk̲wep [es k̲áp k̲wep] bumpy, uneven surface, be. *verb(i).*

esk̲áxwk̲exw [es k̲áxw k̲exw] groups, be in. *verb(i).*

esk̲ék̲ [es k̲ék̲] make an even beat on a drum; even beat on a drum, make an. *verb(i).*

esk̲ek̲ích [es k̲e k̲ích] full, be [about the moon]. *verb(i).*

esk̲ék̲ms [es k̲é k̲ems] put away, be [about a dead body]. *verb(i).*

esk̲ék̲tl' [es k̲ék̲ tl'] obstructed, be. *verb(i).*

esk̲ék̲xw [es k̲ék̲ xw] gathered already, be; gathered together, be; group of fish, be a; school of fish, be a. *verb(i).*

esk̲ék̲xws [es k̲ék̲ xws] gather (them) up. *verb(t).*

esk̲énaxw [es k̲én naxw] greedy, be; overeaten, have. *verb(i).*

esk̲exwíwa7 [es k̲e xwí wa7] bunched together, be [about trees]. *verb(i).*

esk̲éxwneẇásen [es k̲éxw neẇ wa sen] group (them) together. *verb(t).*

esk̲éxwts [es k̲éxw ts] gathered together, be [about languages]. *verb(i).*

esk̲éxwts'a [es k̲éxw ts'a] gathered together, be [about a body of water]. *verb(i).*

esk̲éẏ [es k̲éẏ] bad, be [about terrain]. *verb(i).*

esk̲ík̲t [es k̲ík̲ t] bandaged, be. *verb(i).*

esk̲ík̲tl'teḷ [es k̲ík̲ tl' tel'] even, be [in a match]. *verb(i).*

esk̲ílhpay [es k̲ílh pay] flint gun. *noun.*

esk̲íyalh [es k̲í yalh] sickly, be. *verb(i).*

esk̲íyekw [es k̲í yekw] make a slow-paced beat; slow-paced beat, make a. *verb(i).*

esk̲í7k̲el ~ sk̲í7k̲el [es k̲í7 k̲el] not good at doing something, be; unskilled, be; unschooled, be; ignorant, be; not know how to do something. *verb(i).*

esk̲í7k̲elach [es k̲í7 k̲e lach] fumble with a package; clumsy, be. *verb(i).*

esk̲í7k̲elxw ~ sk̲í7k̲elxw [es k̲éh7 k̲elxw] not yet know how to do something; unskilled, be still; unschooled, be still. *verb(i).*

esk̲'ák̲'ey [es k̲'á k̲'ey] top of it, be on; on, be. *verb(i).*

esk̲'ák̲'eyshn [es k̲'á k̲'ey shn] stand with one's foot on it. *verb(i).*

esk̲'ants'x̲ánm ~ sk̲'ants'x̲ánm [es k̲ants' x̲á nm] back eddy; eddy. *noun.*

esk̲'áw [es k̲'áw] absolved, be; paid, be; paid for services rendered, be; have paid for services [e.g., the **sxw7umten** for a cure]. *verb(i).*

esk̲'áy [es k̲'áy] pass over top of something, just. *verb(i).*

esk̲'ek̲'éw̓ ~ esk̲'ék̲w'u7 ~ esk̲'ek̲w'ú7 ~ esk̲'ék̲'ew̓ [es k̲'e k̲'éw̓] with, be [more than one person]; together with, be. *verb(i).*

esk̲'ék̲'ew̓ ~ esk̲'ek̲w'ú7 ~ esk̲'ék̲w'u7 ~ esk̲'ek̲'éw̓ [es k̲'é k̲'ew̓] with, be [more than one person]; together with, be. *verb(i).*

esk̲'ek̲'ey̓ím̓ [es k̲'e k̲'ey̓ yím̓] camping, be; verb(i).

esk̲'ék̲'its [es k̲'é k̲'its] insufficient, be; not enough, be. *verb(i).*

esk̲'ek̲w'ú7 ~ esk̲'ék̲w'u7 ~ esk̲'ék̲'ew̓ ~ esk̲'ek̲'éw̓ [es k̲'e k̲w'ú7] with, be [more than one person]; together with, be. *verb(i).*

esk̲'ék̲w'u7 ~ esk̲'ek̲w'ú7 ~ esk̲'ék̲'ew̓ ~ esk̲'ek̲'éw̓ [es k̲'é k̲w'u7] with, be [more than one person]; together with, be. *verb(i).*

esk̲'ek̲w'ú7new̓as [es k̲'e k̲w'ú7 new̓ was] together, be. *verb(i).*

esk̲'elk̲'el̓p'í7k̲in [es k̲'el k̲'el' p'éh7 k̲in] curly hair, have. *verb(i).*

esk̲'ets'íchen [es k̲'e ts'í chen] place hands behind neck. *verb(i).*

esk̲'éw̓ ~ sk̲'ew̓ ~ sk̲w'u7 ~ esk̲w'ú7 [es k̲'éw̓] companion. *noun.*

esk̲'ewk̲'áw [es k̲'ew k̲'áw] bewitched, be. *verb(i).*

esk̲'eyk̲'eyx̲nít [es k̲'ey k̲'eyx̲ nít] recognize (someone). *verb(t).*

esk̲'ík̲'itl'us [es k̲'éh k̲'i tl'us] scar-faced; scarred face, have a; have scars on one's face. *adjective.*

esk̲'ík̲'iy̓im̓ [es k̲'éh k̲'ey̓ y̓im̓] camping, be [about a group]. *verb(i).*

esk̲'ík̲'s [es k̲'éh k̲'s] tied up, be. *verb(i).*

esk̲'ík̲'tel [es k̲'éhk̲' tel] evenly matched, be. *verb(i).*

esk̲'ík̲'xw [es k̲'éh k̲'xw] produce an interrupted beat [every second or fourth beat silent]. *verb(i).*

esk̲'iy̓ím̓ [es k̲'ey̓ y̓ím̓] camp overnight; camping, be. *verb(i).*

esk̲'tsám̓ ~ sk̲'tsam̓ [es k̲' tsám̓] run short [e.g., when sewing something]; short, be too; not quite reaching, be. *verb(i).*

esk̲'tsám̓ach [es k̲' tsám̓ m̓ach] out of reach, be; can't reach it. *verb(i).*

esk̲'tsám̓k̲s [es k̲' tsám̓ k̲s] short, be [when ends don't meet]. *verb(i).*

esk̲wáak̲wa [es k̲wáa k̲wa] worn out, be. *verb(i).*

esk̲wék̲wa7 [es k̲wé k̲wa7] hole in it, have a [e.g., pail, canoe, ground, clothes]; pierced, be. *verb(i).* hole. *noun.*

esk̲wék̲wa7k̲s ~ esnek̲wék̲wa7k̲s ~ sk̲wék̲wek̲s [es k̲wé k̲wa7 k̲s] perforation in nose, have a; pierced nose, have a. *verb(i).*

esk̲wek̲weháya7n [es k̲we k̲wa háy ya 7n] pierced ears, have. *verb(i).*

esk̲wék̲wey̓k̲w' [es k̲wé k̲wey̓k̲w'] crooked. *adjective.*

esk̲wék̲wey̓k̲w'ts [es k̲wé k̲wey̓ k̲w'ts] crooked jaw, have a. *adjective.*

esk̲wék̲wik̲w' [es k̲wé k̲wik̲w'] crooked, be. *verb(i).*

esk̲wek̲wúk̲wuwilh [es k̲we k̲wú k̲wu wilh] wrapped around a body, be. *verb(i).*

esk̲wélx̲w [es k̲wél x̲w] "white eye," have a; cataracts, have; half-blind, be. *verb(i).*

esk̲wém̓ts [es k̲wém̓ts] lumpy mouth, have a; crooked lip, have a. *adjective.*

esk̲wúk̲wel̓ [es k̲wú k̲wel'] thirsty, be; collected, be [about a small quantity of water]. *verb(i).*

esk̲wúk̲welayus [es k̲wú k̲wel lay yus] high tide, be. *verb(i).*

esk̲wuk̲wláy̓ak̲alh [es k̲wu k̲wel láy̓ ya k̲alh] pool. *verb(i); noun.*

esk̲wúk̲wus ~ sk̲wúk̲wus [es k̲wú k̲wus] head down, have ones; sneak; have

one's head lowered between shoulders. *verb(i).*
esk̲w'ek̲w'íl [es k̲w'e k̲w'éhl] done, be; ready for, be; ripe, be. *verb(i).*
esk̲w'él [es k̲w'él] cooked, be [already]. *verb(i).*
esk̲w'élt [es k̲w'élt] cooked (something), have. *verb(t).*
esk̲w'ík̲w't [es k̲w'éh k̲w't] very edge of a cliff. *verb(i).*
esk̲w'íwk̲ts [es k̲w'íw k̲ts] edge of anything; edge of a cliff. *verb(i).*
esk̲w'úk̲ws [es k̲w'ú k̲ws] hit (someone) many times; beat (someone) up. *verb(t).*
esk̲w'úk̲w'ulh [es k̲w'ú k̲w'ulh] aware of the perimeter, be; prepared to start, be; ready to start, be; sneaking, be[about an animal]; be ready [to race]; be prepared [to race]. *verb(i).*
esk̲w'úk̲w'utl' [es k̲w'ú k̲w'utl'] tucked in already, be. *verb(i).*
esk̲w'úy [es k̲w'úy] sick, be; dead, be. *verb(i).*
esk̲w'ú7 [es k̲w'ú7] with, be [one person]. *verb(i).*
esk̲w'ú7 ~ sk̲'ew̓ ~ sk̲w'u7 ~ esk̲'éw̓ [es k̲w'ú7] companion. *noun.*
esk̲w'ú7new̓as [es k̲w'ú7 new̓ was] together, be. *verb(i).* togetherness. *noun.*
eslép'lep' [es lép' lep'] wrinkled, be; warped, be all. *verb(i).*
eslil̓xwí7nup [es leh7 el̓ xwí7 nup] lie [sleep] on the floor. *verb(i).*
eslí7lxw [es léh 7elxw] lying, be; prostrate, be; lying down, be. *verb(i).*
eslí7s [es lí7s] kept (something) away, have. *verb(t).*
eslúl̓elh [es lúl̓ elh] move from one village to another. *verb(i).*
eslhák̲ [es lhák̲] whisper. *verb(i).*
eslhálhk̲en [es lhálh k̲en] quiet, be. *verb(i).*
eslhánch' ~ slhanch' [es lhánch'] careless [with things], be; rude, be; mean, be; bully, be a; rough, be. *verb(i).*
eslhánch'stem [es lhán ch's tem] sexually harrass (someone); teased sexually, be. *verb(p).*
eslhánch'tway [es lhánch' tway] mean to one another, be. *verb(i).*
eslhék̲' [es lhék̲'] basic family tree; close family. *verb(i).*
eslhék̲'new̓as [es lhék̲' new̓ was] close relatives, be; immediate family, be. *verb(i).*
eslhélha7 ~ slhélha7 [es lhé lha7] close to something, be very. *verb(i).*
eslhélhch [es lhélh ch] spit. *verb(i).*
eslhelhích [es lhe lhích] strongly singing war dance, be; singing war dance, be strongly [about a man]. *verb(i).*
eslhélhp' [es lhélhp'] hang over. *verb(i).*
eslhén̓ [es lhén̓] braided, be. *verb(i).*
eslhéts'lhets' [es lhéts' lhets'] riling people, be always. *verb(i).*
eslhéw̓lhew [es lhéw̓ lhew] get well; recover. *verb(i).*
eslhíkw'k̲w [es lhíkw' k̲w] hanging [on], be [about something hanging on a nail, the wall, etc.]. *verb(i).*
eslhílhkw' [es lhílh kw'] hand up. *verb(i).*
eslhílhkw'iws [es lhílh kw'íws] connected to it, be; related to someone, be. *verb(i).*
eslhílhn [es lhí lhen] caught in a net, be. *verb(i).*
eslhíshus [es lhí shus] slimy face, have a. *adjective.*
eslhk̲áych' [es lh k̲áy ch'] light of the moon; moonlight. *noun.*
eslhk̲én̓ [es lh k̲én̓] anchored, be. *verb(i).*
eslhk̲'í7s ~ lhk̲'i7s ~ slhk̲'i7s ~ sk̲'i7s ~ lhsk̲'i7s [es lh k̲'í7s] know (someone/something); acquainted with (someone/something), be; know how to do (something). *verb(t).*
eslhúk̲'ach [es lhú k̲'ach] skinned up, be all [about hands]. *verb(i).*
eslhx̲ílsh [es lh x̲ílsh] standing up, be [already]. *verb(i).*
esmám̓akw'as [es má7 ma kw'as] spend time with (someone); share in (someone's) sorrow or discomfort; sympathize with (someone). *verb(t).*
esmelmélch' [es mel mélch'] squished up, be [about berries, such as thimbleberries]. *verb(i).*
esmémen̓ [es mé men̓] have a child; child, have a. *verb(i).*
esmemey̓máy [es me mey̓ máy] forgetful, very; absent-minded. *adjective.*
esmém̓kw [es mém̓kw] covered one's head, have. *verb(i).* lumpy. *adjective.* lump [on skin, tree, etc.]. *noun.*

esmémś [es mémś] attached, be. *verb(i).*
esmémś [es mémś] attach to (something). *verb(t).*
esméń [es méń] give birth [LM: old word is **ch'ach'lem**]. *verb(i).*
esmíkw' [es míkw'] washed, be already. *verb(i).*
esḿík̲' [e seḿ méhk̲'] full already, be. *verb(i).*
esmímkw' [es mím kw'] washed, be; baptized, be. *verb(i).*
esmímk̲' [es mím k̲'] pressed down already, be. *verb(i).*
esmí7mitl' [es méh7 mitl'] crouch. *verb(i).*
esmúmey̓shen [es mú mey̓ shen] feet in the water, have one's; water, have one's feet in the water. *verb(i).*
esmúmi7 [es mú mi7] sunken, be. *verb(i).*
esnát [es nát] night time, be; night, be at; nocturnal, be. *verb(i).*
esnek̲wék̲wa7k̲s ~ esk̲wék̲wa7k̲s ~ sk̲wék̲wek̲s [es ne k̲wé k̲wa7 k̲s] perforation in nose, have a; pierced nose, have a. *verb(i).*
esnéńk̲wm [es néń k̲wem] sunny, be. *verb(i).*
esnéńp [es néń p] point, be to the. *verb(i).*
esnéńsh [es néńsh] lying on its side, be. *verb(i).*
esńíẃ [e seń níẃ] inside, be; within, be. *verb(i).*
esńíẃs [e seń níẃs] leave (something) inside [of a container]. *verb(t).*
esntl'úḿk̲ay̓us [e sen tl'úḿ k̲ay̓ yus] ball of the eye. *noun.*
esnuwákw'a [es nu wá kw'a] ring around the moon. *noun.*
espápey̓m [es pá pey̓ yem] resting, be. *verb(i).*
espeńúy̓txw [es peń núy̓ txw] underground house. *noun.*
espépeń [es pé peń] under ground, be. *verb(i).*
espépuḿ [es pé puḿ] swollen up, be. *verb(i).*
espétspets [es péts pets] doubled up, be. *verb(i).*
espx̲átm [es p x̲á tem] tight, be very; not quite reaching around something, be. *verb(i).*
esp'áp'ey̓ek̲s [es p'á p'i y̓ek̲s] make (something) right. *verb(t).*
esp'áp'iy̓ek̲ [es p'á p'i y̓ek̲] proper, be; in order, be; nothing wrong, have; just right, be; right, be just. *verb(i).*
esp'áp'iyik̲neẃas [es p'á p'i yehk̲ neẃ was] engaged, be; engaged to each other, be. *verb(i).*
esp'ék̲w [es p'ék̲w] slab. *noun.*
esp'ep'ílh [es p'e p'ílh] sober, be. *verb(i).*
estátel̓ [es tá tel̓] sound right; even, be. *verb(i).*
estek̲ís ~ stek̲ís [es te k̲ís] take it easy; slow, be; go slowly. *verb(i).*
estélanumut [es té la nu mut] offended, be. *verb(i).*
estela7áyus [es te la 7áy yus] wear glasses. *verb(i).*
estesás [es te sás] poor, be; impoverished, be; wretched, be [about person]. *verb(i).*
estestesás [es tes te sás] poor, be. *verb(i).*
estetel̓áyus [es te tel̓ 7áy yus] wearing glasses, be; glasses on, have one's. *verb(i).*
estétey̓ [es té tey̓] field; open area. *noun.*
estétey̓sh [es té tey̓sh] doing the same thing, just be; doing something, still be; extent, be the; be still; be yet. *verb(i).*
estétey̓wilh [es té tey̓ wilh] protected; safe. *adjective.*
estetích [es te tích] plain view, be in; visible, be; clear, be. *verb(i).*
estétx̲w [es tét x̲w] correct, be; right, be; definite, be. *verb(i).*
estétx̲ws [es tét x̲ws] make sure of (something). *verb(t).*
estéwak̲in ~ téwak̲in [es téw wa k̲in] mourning, be in. *verb(i).*
estéy̓sh [es téy̓sh] length, be the; same length, be exactly the. *verb(i).*
estítiḿ [es tí tiḿ] raining hard, be; trying hard, be. *verb(i).*
estítkw ~ títkw [es tít kw] sheltered; safe. *adjective.*
estk̲wú7ts [es t k̲wú7ts] blocking, be. *verb(i).*
estútuy [es tú tuy] leaning, be. *verb(i).*
estútx̲w [es tút x̲w] sticking in the ground, be. *verb(i).*
estx̲wáy̓a7n [es t x̲wáy̓ ya 7en] sharp of hearing, be. *verb(i).*

estx̲wáy̓us [es t x̲wáy̓ yus] see clearly/ plainly. *verb(i).*

estx̲wáy̓usem [es t x̲wáy̓ yu sem] look at carefully; examine. *verb(i).*

est'ák̲' [es t'ák̲'] across, be already. *verb(i).*

est'áneṁ [es t'á neṁ] shunned, be; marked, be; part, be. *verb(i).*

est'át'ek̲' [es t'á t'ek̲'] across, be; lying aross, be. *verb(i).*

est'át'elh [es t'á t'lh] way out, be [about the tide]. *verb(i).*

est'át'em [es t'á t'em] get out of someone's way. *verb(i).*

est'át'k̲'ayus [es t'át' k̲'ay yus] cross-eyed, be. *verb(i).*

est'át'k̲'neẃas [es t'át' k̲' neẃ was] crossing each other, be. *verb(i).*

est'át'xw [es t'á t'xw] sticking out [of a container, etc.], be. *verb(i).*

est'ek̲t'ík̲l ~ **st'ek̲t'ík̲l** [es t'ek̲ t'éh k̲l] muddy. *adjective.*

est'ék̲w' [es t'ék̲w'] half [broken off], be. *verb(i).* broken-off half. *noun.*

est'ék̲w'ch [es t'é k̲w'ch] half, be [e.g., a fish, a meal, etc.]. *verb(i).*

est'ék̲w't'ek̲w'k̲s ~ **t'ék̲w't'ek̲w'k̲s** [es t'ék̲w' t'ekw̲' k̲s] square. *adjective.*

est'et'aṅíw̓s [es t'e t'aṅ níw̓s] covering (something), be. *verb(t).*

est'ét'ch' [es t'ét' ch'] ravine [see also **estl'etl'esh**]. *noun.*

est'ét'elk̲w ~ **st'ét'elk̲w** [es t'é t'elk̲w] spot on something, be a; on, be [about a spot]. *verb(i).*

est'ét'kw' [es t'ét' kw'] dug already, be. *verb(i).* hole in the ground; pit [hole dug in the ground]; well [with drinking water]. *noun.*

est'ét'kw' stak̲w [es t'ét' kw' stak̲w] well water. *noun.*

est'ex̲t'x̲áchxw [es t'ex̲ t' x̲á chxw] many-limbed; branchy; have many limbs. *adjective.*

estl'átl'em [es tl'á tl'em] enough, be; fitting, be; sufficient, be; fit [about clothes]. *verb(i).*

estl'ék̲ [es tl'ék̲] spot. *noun.*

estl'éptl'epx̲ ~ **stl'éptl'epx̲** [es tl'ép tl'ep x̲] spotted; spots, have. *adjective.*

estl'étl'esh [es tl'é tl'esh] ravine [see also **est't'ch'**]. *noun.*

estl'éxw ~ **stl'exw** [es tl'éxw] defeated, be; loser [in a game or fight]. *noun.*

estl'éxws [es tl'éxws] defeat (someone). *verb(t).*

estl'ík̲numut [es tl'éhk̲ nu mut] arrived, have. *verb(i).*

estl'útl'k̲w [es tl'útl' k̲w] filed away, be; put away in a small space, be; corner, be in a. *verb(i).*

estl'útl'k̲ws [es tl'útl' k̲ws] hide (something). *verb(t).*

estséṁtseṁk̲w ~ **stséṁtseṁk̲w** [es tséṁ tseṁ k̲w] wrinkles [see also **lhelp'ús**]; creases. *noun.*

estsetsík̲w [es tse tséhk̲w] strong dancer, be a. *verb(i).*

estsetsíxw [es tse tsíxw] stay there for a while; disappeared, be; vanished, be; missing, be. *verb(i).*

estse7át [es tse 7át] no moon, be. *verb(i).*

estsík̲s [es tséhk̲s] stab (something/ someone) many times; stab (something/ someone) all over. *verb(t).*

estsítsixw [es tsí tsixw] camp over for a while; delayed, be; gone for a while, be. *verb(i).*

estsútsp [es tsúts p] resting on, be. *verb(i).*

ests'áts'i [es ts'á ts'i] shade. *noun.* purple. *adjective.* being in the shade, be. *verb(i).*

ests'elhts'úlh [es ts'elh ts'úlh] cold, be feeling; feeling cold, be. *verb(i).*

ests'éw̓k̲s [es ts'éw̓ k̲s] pointed, be. *verb(i).*

ests'exwts'íxw [es ts'exw ts'íxw] pitiful [about person]; helpful; ready to help. *adjective.* take pity on others. *verb(i).*

ests'iy̓úṁ [es ts'ey̓ yúṁ] stuck, be. *verb(i).*

ests'únts' [es ts'únts'] woman's private parts. *noun.*

ests'úts'p' [es ts'úts' p'] leaning, be. *verb(i).*

esúts [e súts] have feet on it; feet on it, have [e.g., carving]. *verb(i).*

eswéts'wets' ~ **swéts'wets'** [es wéts' wets'] touchy; fidgety; irritable. *adjective.*

esxwách'it [es xwá ch'it] light of a torch; torchlight. *noun.*

esxwáxwkw' [es xwáxw kw'] drunk, be. *verb(i).*

esxwékw'xwekw' [es xwékw' xwekw'] drunkard. *noun.*

esxwetxwút [es xwet xwút] rough [about surface]; bumpy [about surface]. *adjective.*
esxwexwá ~ esxwéxwa7 [es xwe xwá] diligent, be. *verb(i).*
esxwéxwa7 [es xwé xwa7] diligent, be. *verb(i).*
esxwexwíts [es xwe xwíts] cut right off, be. *verb(i).*
esxwéxwkw [es xwéxw kw] important, be; useful, be; use, be in; used, be. *verb(i).*
esxwéxwkws [es xwéxw kws] using (something), be. *verb(t).*
esxwéyxwey̓ ~ xwéyxwey ~ esxwíxwi7 [es xwéy xwey̓] visible, be; sticking out, be; appearing, be. *verb(i).*
esxwéyxweyḵ [es xwéy xweyḵ] showing, have one's rear end; rear end showing, have one's. *verb(i).*
esxwéyxwiy̓ach [es xwéy xwi y̓ach] visible as far as one's hands are concerned, be. *verb(i).*
esxwéyxwiy̓us [es xwéy xwi y̓us] visible as far as one's face is concerned, be. *verb(i).*
esxwíxwiḵ [es xwéh xwehḵ] jolly, be; good time, have a; euphoric, be; happy, be. *verb(i).*
esxwíxwi7 ~ esxwéyxwey̓ ~ xwéyxwey [es xwéy xwey̓] stick out; visible, be. *verb(i).*
esxw7umtnántsut [e sxw 7um ten nán tsut] become a **sxw7umten**. *verb(i).*
esx̱áx̱as [es x̱á x̱as] ready to go, be; anxious to do something, be. *verb(i).*
esx̱áx̱ay̓ [es x̱á x̱ay̓] crying all the time, be. *verb(i).*
esx̱él̓x̱el [es x̱él' x̱el] different colours, be of; variegated, be. *verb(i).*
esx̱ét' [es x̱ét'] suffer under a sxw7umten. *verb(i).*
esx̱ét'x̱et' [es x̱ét' x̱et'] bewitched; spell put on, have a. *adjective.*
esx̱éts [es x̱éts] talk rough. *verb(i).*
esx̱éts'ḵs [es x̱éts' ḵs] loud voice, have a. *adjective.*
esx̱ets'x̱íts' [es x̱ets' x̱íts'] shy, be [see also **es7í7x̱i** and **es7éx̱7ex̱i**]. *verb(i).*
esx̱éwtl'chḵ [es x̱éw tl' ch ḵ] broken hip, have a; lame. *adjective.*
esx̱éx̱el̓s [es x̱é x̱el's] etched it onto (something), have; drawn it onto (something), have; written it onto (something), have. *verb(t).*
esx̱éx̱ewtl' [es x̱é x̱ewtl'] broken. *adjective.*
esx̱ex̱éwtl'shen [es x̱e x̱éwtl' shen] broken leg, have a. *adjective.*
esx̱ex̱íḵ' [es x̱e x̱éhḵ'] cut one's hair really short. *verb(i).*
esx̱ex̱ílh [es x̱e x̱ílh] drunk, be really. *verb(i).*
esx̱ey̓x̱áy [es x̱ey̓ x̱áy] laughing, be. *verb(i).*
esx̱éy̓x̱i [es x̱éy̓ x̱ey] laughing all the time, be. *verb(i).*
esx̱íts ~ ex̱íts [es x̱íts] recline; lie; lie down. *verb(i).*
esx̱íts ~ ex̱íts [es x̱íts] lay (something) down. *verb(t).*
esx̱ítsḵ [es x̱íts ḵ] fallen, be. *verb(i).*
esx̱ix̱p'iy̓ách [es x̱ehx̱ p'i y̓ách] grab by the handfuls; handful, be a. *verb(i).*
esx̱wetx̱wút [es x̱wet x̱wút] lumpy, be; rough, be. *verb(i).*
esx̱wíḵw' [es x̱wéhḵw'] captive, be. *verb(i).*
esx̱wíx̱wel̓ay̓ḵ [es x̱wéh x̱wel̓ 7ay̓ ḵ] barefoot, be. *verb(i).*
esx̱wix̱wiḵw'úwilh [es x̱weh x̱weh ḵw'ú wilh] wrapped around someone's waist, be. *verb(i).*
esx̱wíx̱wḵw' [es x̱wíx̱w ḵw'] jail, be in; arrest, be under. *verb(i).*
esx̱wíx̱wḵw'i7ch [es x̱wíx̱w ḵw'i7 ch] tied up in a bundle, be; bundled up, be. *verb(i).*
esyáḵ [es yáḵ] picked, be already [about berries]. *verb(i).*
esyáḵwchew [es yáḵw chew] burn without fire. *verb(i).*
esyáyḵ' [es yáy ḵ'] lying, be [about a fallen tree]. *verb(i).*
esyáy̓x̱w [es yáy̓ x̱w] fluid condition, be in. *verb(i).*
esyéḵ [es yéḵ] berries that have already been picked; picked berries. *noun.*
esyéxwyexw [es yéxw yexw] bashful. *adjective.*
esyéy̓etl'ḵ' [es yéy̓ yetl'ḵ'] painted, be. *verb(i).*
esyéy̓x̱w [es yéy̓ x̱w] free, be; loose, be. *verb(i).*

esyíy̓ch' ~ syíy̓ch' [es yéy̓ ch'] filled, be; full, be. *verb(i).*
esyúlh [es yúlh] burnt, get. *verb(i).*
esyú7 [es yú7] forecaster; seer; fortune-teller. *noun.*
esyú7kw [es yú7 kw] stingy. *adjective.*
es7álh [es 7álh] quiet, be. *verb(i).*
es7álhk̲en [es 7álh k̲en] whispering, be. *verb(i).*
es7átetem [es 7á te tem] baggage; stuff; belongings. *noun.*
es7áy̓as ~ s7áy̓as [es 7áy̓ yas] engaged to (someone), be. *verb(t).*
es7áy̓astway [es 7áy̓ yas tway] engaged to one another, be. *verb(i).*
es7ay̓ílem [es 7ay̓ yéh lem] nice weather, be. *verb(i).*
es7á7aw̓ts [es 7á 7aw̓ ts] able, be; can; could; hurry, be in a. *verb(i).*
es7á7kwlesh [es 7á7 kwel lesh] wounded, be. *verb(i).*
es7á7tsiw̓en [es 7á7 tsi w̓en] pregnant, be. *verb(i).*
es7éch7ech [es 7éch 7ech] stutter; stuttering, be. *verb(i).*
es7éx̲7ex̲i ~ es7í7x̲i [es 7éx̲ 7e x̲i] shy, be [see also **esx̲ets'x̲íts'**]. *verb(i).*
es7íxwiwat ~ s7íxwiwat [es 7í xwi wat] jump [about fish]. *verb(i).*
es7í7x̲i ~ es7éx̲7ex̲i [es 7éh7 x̲i] shy, be [see also **esx̲ets'x̲íts'**]. *verb(i).*
es7úmsems [es 7úm sems] keep (someone) awake; awake, keep (someone). *verb(t).*
es7úmsm ~ s7úm̓sem [es 7úm sm] awake, be [see also **úmsem**]. *verb(i).*
es7úyumi7 [es 7úy yu mi7] slow working, be. *verb(i).*
eshan̓ melh [7e shan̓ melh] why then. *question word.*
eshán̓ ~ shan̓ [e shán̓] what's the matter with . . . ?; why?; what happened? *question word; verb(i).*
eshashemáy̓ch [e sha she máy̓ ch] rockbar; sandbar [see also **eshashem̓ín̓was**]. *noun.*
eshashem̓ín̓was [e sha shem̓ mín̓ was] bar in river; reef in river [see also **eshashemáy̓ch**]. *noun.*
esháshm [e shá shem] dry land, be on. *verb(i).*
eshéshiy̓us ~ shéshiy̓us [e shé shi y̓us] stubborn. *adjective.*
éshew̓en [é shew̓ wen] sneeze. *verb(i).*
eshíshch' [e shísh ch'] bushy terrain, be; bushes, be in the; surrounded by, be [bushes]; amidst vegetation, be; brush, be in the; amidst the trees, be. *verb(i).*
eshíshch'shen [e shísh ch' shen] bushes, have feet in; feet in bushes, have. *verb(i).*
eshúkw' [e shúkw'] bath, have had a; received a bath, have; bathed, be. *verb(i).*
esh7íl ~ sh7il [esh 7éhl] elder sibling [a term of address; respectful form]. *vocative.*
-et [-et] {added onto some words so that you can use the object endings, see section on "object endings"}. *suffix.*
etl'ím [e tl'ím] short [in length]. *adjective.*
etl'ím skwáyel [e tl'ím skwáy yel] short day, be a. *verb(i).*
etl'ímay̓k̲wem [e tl'í may̓ k̲wem] short [about person]. *adjective.*
etl'ím̓en [e tl'ím̓ men] shorten (something). *verb(t).*
etsím [e tsím] little; small [about object]. *adjective.* a little. *verb(i).*
etsími7 [e tsí mi7] smaller. *adjective.*
etsím̓ts [e tsím̓ts] small mouth, have a. *adjective.*
etsím̓ul̓a [e tsím̓ mul̓ 7a] little finger [see also **saw't̓k̲wúy'ach ~ saw't̓k̲wúl'a** and **esáw'tul'a ~ saw'túl'a**]. *noun.*
etsím̓us [e tsím̓ mus] little face, have a. *adjective.*
etsímxw [e tsím xw] little ones. *noun.*
étsnach ~ átsnach [éts nach] Burrard Reserve. *place name.* bay [see also **s7átsnach**]. *noun.*
etstsím [ets tsím] little; small [about animals]. *adjective.*
ets7útsis [ets 7ú tsis] wear (something); keep (something) on. *verb(t).*
ets'ánax̲an [e ts'á na x̲an] inside back of house. *noun.*
ets'k̲'án̓tsut [ets' k̲án̓ tsut] throb. *verb(i).*
ets'wás [ets' wás] beg. *verb(i).*
ets'7íts'am [ets' 7í ts'am] wear a blanket; wearing, be. *verb(i).*

ets'7íts'aṁs [ets' 7í ts'aṁs] wear (clothes). *verb(t).*

ewáyani7m [ew wáy ya ni 7em] yawn. *verb(i).*

ewáya7m [ew wáy ya 7em] yawn. *verb(i).*

eẇús ~ u7ús [eẇ wús] egg; eggs. *noun.*

éxwa7t [é xwa7 t] give it to (someone); hand it to (someone). *verb(t).*

exw7úxwumixw [exw 7ú xwu mixw] visitor; guest; villagers. *noun.*

ex̱ [7ex̱] Brandt Canadian goose; wild goose. *noun.*

ex̱ch'ch [7ex̱ ch'ch] vertabra [see also **ex̱ts'ch ~ nexw7éx̱ts'ch ~ nx̱ats'ch**]. *noun.*

ex̱íts ~ esx̱íts [e x̱íts] recline; lie; lie down. *verb(i).*

ex̱íts ~ esx̱íts [e x̱íts] lay (something) down. *verb(t).*

ex̱ts'ch ~ nexw7éx̱ts'ch ~ nx̱ats'ch [éx̱ ts' ch] backbone [see also **ex̱ch'ch**]. *noun.*

ex̱7í7x̱iṅ [ex̱ 7éh7 x̱iṅ] call (someone) down; call (someone) names. *verb(t).*

éx̱wu7n [é x̱wu 7en] cough. *verb(i).*

ex̱w7éx̱wu7n [ex̱w 7é x̱wu 7en] cough all the time. *verb(i).*

ey ~ i ~ iy [7ey] and; or. *conjunction.*

eẏáẏach [eẏ 7áẏ yach] hanging on [with one's hands], be. *verb(i).*

eykw'álhen [ey kw'á lhen] babysit (someone). *verb(t).*

eykw'álhs [ey kw'álhs] babysit (someone). *verb(t).*

eyḵ [7eyḵ] or. *conjunction.*

eylh ~ ilh [7eylh] dear; cousin [term of address] [see also **sh7eylh ~ sh7ilh**]. *vocative.*

éẏuts ~ s7éẏuts [éẏ yuts] mouth of a river. *noun.*

éyu7ts [éy yu7 ts] sharp-edged; sharp edge, have a. *adjective.*

é7enwilh [é 7en wilh] halfway, be. *verb(i).*

H h

háhalhi7 ~ hahelhí7 ~ hehelhí7 [há ha lhi7] better, be; better, be getting. *verb(i).*
hahááwk̲ [ha háwk̲] passing away, be. *verb(i).*
hahá7lh ~ há7ha7lh [ha há7 lh] good [about a group of people]. *adjective.*
hahelhí7 ~ háhalhi7 ~ hehelhí7 [ha he lhí7] better, be getting; better, be. *verb(i).*
hák̲wnexw [hák̲w nexw] smell (something). *verb(t).*
hal-hílitsut [hal héh li tsut] rolling around, be. *verb(i).*
hálitn [há li tn] chisel. *noun.*
halh therefore; then. *conjunction.*
halháy̓ak̲ap [ha lháy̓ ya k̲ap] good-smelling; good-tasting. *adjective.*
halháy̓um̓ [ha lháy̓ yum̓] good [about berries]. *adjective.*
halháyus ~ halháy̓us [ha lháy yus] good colour, have a. *adjective.*
halháy̓us ~ halháyus [ha lháy̓ yus] good colour, have a. *adjective.*
halhí7 ~ helhí7 [ha lhí7] better, be; better, get; feel good; good, become. *verb(i).*
ham ~ ham̓ come; covered, be; come home. *verb(i).*
ham̓ ~ ham covered, be; come home; come. *verb(i).*
háma [há ma] hammer. *noun.*
hám̓en [hám̓ men] cover (someone) with a blanket. *verb(t).*
hám̓entsut [hám̓ men tsut] cover oneself with a blanket. *verb(i).*
hámi7n [há mi 7en] make a grab [about a group]. *verb(i).*
hamk̲w ~ es-hámk̲w ~ hám̓k̲w [ham k̲w] covered, be [by blanket, by snow, etc.]. *verb(i).*
ham̓k̲w ~ hamk̲w ~ es-hámk̲w [ham̓ k̲w] covered, be [by blanket, by snow, etc.]. *verb(i).*
hám̓k̲wam [hám̓ k̲wam] cover one's head. *verb(i).*
ham̓k̲wáń [ham̓ k̲wáń] cover (something/someone) with a blanket. *verb(t).*
hans tell (someone); inform (someone). *verb(t).*
hatá7a [ha tá 7a] aunty (a term of address). *vocative.*
háts'ek̲ [há ts'ek̲] venereal disease. *noun.* venereal disease, have a. *verb(i).*
haw no; not be; be not the case; do not. *verb(i).*
haw k̲'axw an x̲étsx̲etsetsut [haw k̲'axw an x̲éts x̲e tse tsut] Don't overdo it. *verb(i).*
hawk̲ be none; there is no; there is not; none; die. *verb(i).*
hawk̲ k̲ stam na shánas [hawk̲ stam na shán nas] Nothing happened. *sentence.*
hawk̲ stam nothing. *verb(i).*
hawk̲ swat no one; none of them. *verb(i).*
háwk̲an [háw k̲an] erase (something). *verb(t).*
háwk̲i7 [háw k̲i7] no longer be; give out; be no more. *verb(i).*
haws disagree with (someone); refuse (someone); decline (one's daughter's suitor). *verb(t).*
háwshi [háw shi] deny (someone). *verb(t).*
háxwatsut [há xwa tsut] closer, be getting. *verb(i).*
hay̓áń [hay̓ yáń] pacify (someone's) child. *verb(t).*
há7ha7lh ~ hahá7lh [há7 ha7 lh] good [about people]. *adjective.*
ha7lh good. *adjective.*
ha7lhánan [ha7 lhá nan] peace, be at; good mood, be in a. *verb(i).* kindness; peaceful atmosphere; goodness. *noun.*
ha7lhínup [ha7 lhí nup] fixed and leveled off, be; prepared, be [about ground, e.g., in preparation for a house]. *verb(i).*
ha7lhmíń [ha7 lh míń] better than someone/something, be. *verb(i).*
há7lhnew̓as [há7 lh new̓ was] good wishes, have. *verb(i).*
ha7lhnítem [ha7 lh ní tem] go well for (someone who has died); do good for (someone). *verb(p).*
ha7lhs [ha7 lhs] like (something). *verb(t).*
há7lhstway [há7 lhs tway] like one another. *verb(i).*

ha7mákwlh [ha7 má kwelh] accident, have an; injured, be. *verb(i).*
ha7mákwlhmiń [ha7 má kwlh miń] hurt (someone). *verb(t).* hurt, reason for someone getting. *noun.*
ha7mákwlhnexw [ha7 má kwlh nexw] hurt (someone) unintentionally, have. *verb(t).*
héchaw̓ni [hé chaw̓ ni] accuse (someone). *verb(t).*
héchew̓ [hé chew̓] accuse someone of taking something belonging to one; missing something, be. *verb(i).*
hehá7lh [he há7 lh] bad. *adjective.*
hehelhí7 ~ háhalhi7 ~ hahelhí7 [he he lhí7] better, be; better, be getting. *verb(i).*
hehiyí [he hi yí] big, be getting. *verb(i).*
hékwiy̓ik̲w [hé kwi y̓ik̲w] great-great-great-grandparent/aunt/uncle; great-great-great-grandchild. *noun.*
hel̓kw pocket knife. *noun.*
helháyak̲in [he lháy ya k̲in] good-sounding [about drum]. *adjective.*
helhí7 skwáyel [he lhí7 skwáy yel] It's getting to be a fine day. *sentence.*
helhí7 ~ halhí7 [he lhí7] get better; good, become; feel good. *verb(i).*
hem̓í [hem̓ mí] come. *verb(i).*
hemík̲w [he méhk̲w] lie with head towards one. *verb(i).*
hem̓íni [hem̓ mí ni] come to (someone). *verb(t).*
hemlch [he mlch] contagious disease, have an [one symptom of which is that one spits blood ("a kind of TB," IJ)]. *verb(i).* contagious disease, name of particular [see also **ts'xwínas, ts'kw'i7ns**, and **sts'ekw'í7ens**]. *noun.*
hem̓sh tomboy. *noun.*
hém̓ten [hém̓ ten] blanket. *noun.*
heńús [heń nús] looking [in the direction of the speaker], be. *verb(i).*
heńúsm ~ txwheńúsm [heń nú sm] look [in the direction of the speaker]. *verb(i).*
héńxwilhem [héń xwi lhem] gas boat. *noun.*
hep fall down [e.g., an old tree on house]. *verb(i).*
hepét [he pét] knock (something) down. *verb(t).*
hew̓álus ~ hewa7áy̓m ~ hew̓áy̓m [hew̓ wá lus] wish to accompany someone ["old people's language for **hew̓áy̓m**," LM]; want to go with someone; want to go along. *verb(i).*
héwan [héw wan] dog; hound [normal word is sqwemay']. *noun.*
hew̓áy̓m ~ hewa7áy̓m ~ hew̓álus [hew̓ wáy̓ yem] wish to accompany someone; want to go someone with; want to go along. *verb(i).*
hewá7 [hew wá7] accompany someone; go with someone. *verb(i).*
hewa7áy̓m ~ hew̓áy̓m ~ hew̓álus [hew wa 7áy̓ yem] wish to accompany someone; want to go with someone; want to go along. *verb(i).*
hewa7ní [hew wa7 ní] accompany (someone). *verb(t).*
hew̓él̓ch [hew̓ wel' ch] play string game [e.g., cat's cradle]. *verb(i).*
hew̓él̓em [hew̓ wel' lem] play. *verb(i).*
hew̓ít [hew̓ wít] rat. *noun.*
hew̓itúllh [hew̓ wi túl lh] baby rat [see **hew̓ít**]. *noun.*
hew̓úl̓em [hew̓ wul' lem] play. *verb(i).*
hey̓ek̲wíń ~ hey̓k̲wíń [hey̓ ye k̲wíń] lamp; torch; candle; light [such as an electrical light]. *noun.*
hey̓k̲wíń ~ hey̓ek̲wíń [hey̓ k̲wíń] lamp; torch; candle; light [such as an electrical light]. *noun.*
hey̓k̲wínayus [hey̓ k̲wí nay yus] go deer pit lamping; pit lamp for deer [on land]. *verb(i).*
heyk̲wt tkwi tl'etl'xwítay [heyk̲wt t kwi tl'etl' xwí tay] challenge (someone) to a race. *verb(t).*
heyk̲wt ~ hey̓k̲wt invite (someone) on a hunting trip; propose to (someone) to do something together; suggest to (someone) to do something together. *verb(t).*
hey̓k̲wt ~ heyk̲wt propose to (someone) to do something together; suggest to (someone) to something together; invite (someone) on a hunting trip. *verb(t).*
hich [hich] extra. *adjective.*
híchit [hí chit] increase (something); add to (something). *verb(t).*

híchi7tsut [hí chi7 tsut] brag about oneself; boast. *verb(i).*
híhiḵi [héh heh ḵi] crawling under, be; going under, be. *verb(i).*
híhil̓it [héh heh̓l lit] rolling (something), be. *verb(t).*
híhil̓itsut [héh heh̓l li tsut] rolling, be. *verb(i).*
hihiy̓ám̓ [hi hi y̓ám̓] get home. *verb(i).*
hiḵ [hiḵ] knocked out, be; never come to; unconscious, be. *verb(i).*
híḵi [héh ḵi] crawl under; go under. *verb(i).*
híḵit [héh ḵit] put (something) underneath. *verb(t).*
hílit [héh lit] roll (something) [e.g., under a tree]. *verb(t).*
hílitsut [héh li tsut] roll. *verb(i).*
hilkw [hilkw] get ready [to go]. *verb(i).*
hilkwántsut [hehl kwán tsut] get oneself ready to go. *verb(i).*
hiṅ [hiṅ] long time, be a; later on, be; take a long time. *verb(i).*
hiṅ eḵ' [hiṅ 7eḵ'] last a long time. *adverb.*
hiṅítsut [hiṅ ní tsut] brag of a murder; brag about a killing. *verb(i).*
híntu [hín tu] person from India, Pakistan, etc.; Indian (from India); Pakistani. *noun.*
hiw ~ hiẇ [hiw] upstream, be. *verb(i).* upstream region. *noun.*
hiẇ ~ hiw [hiẇ] upstream, be. *verb(i).* upstream area. *noun.*
hiwhiẇám [hiw hiẇ wám] have success [used only in the phrase: **haw kwelh na hiwhiw'ám**, "they had no success"]. *verb(i).*
hiẇíḵn [hi ẇéh ḵen] those sitting in front [closest to the fire]. *verb(i).*
híẇiṅtsut [hí ẇiṅ tsut] go upstream [only about salmon]; put oneself forward. *verb(i).*
híẇi7 [hí ẇi7] closer to the front or fire, get. *verb(i).*
híẇḵan [híẇ ḵan] move (someone) up; shove (something); push (something). *verb(t).*
hiẇḵm [hiẇ ḵm] have sexual intercourse; sexual intercourse, have. *verb(i).*
hiẇḵw [hiẇḵw] up around head, be; up front, be; front, be in. *verb(i).*
híẇḵwam̓ [híẇ ḵwam̓] move ahead. *verb(i).*
híẇḵwḵantsut [híẇḵw ḵan tsut] move oneself up. *verb(i).*
hiẇḵwts' [hiẇ ḵwts'] headwaters, be up at. *verb(i).*
hiẇtsáṅ [híẇ tsaṅ] hang up (a net). *verb(t).*
híẇtsim̓ [híẇ tsim̓] hang up nets; hanging up a net, be. *verb(i).*
hiẇtstn [hiẇts tn] net floater line. *noun.*
hiy̓ám̓ [hi y̓ám̓] come home; return home; get home. *verb(i).*
hiyámats' [hi yá mats'] thick; large-sized [about rope, or other thread-like things]. *adjective.*
hiy̓ám̓nexw [hi y̓ám̓ nexw] get (something) home; brought (something) home, have; bring (something) home. *verb(t).*
hiy̓am̓númut [hi yam̓ nú mut] get home; get home, manage to; get home finally; got home finally, have. *verb(i).*
hiyáts'a [hi yá ts'a] big genitals, have. *adjective.*
hiyáy [hi yáy] miss something. *verb(i).*
hiyí [hi yí] big; large. *adjective.*
hiyí syátshen [hi yí see yát shen] big country. *noun.*
hiyíkwup [hi yí kwup] big fire. *adjective.*
hiyíḵw [hi yéhḵw] head cover used by a **sxw7umten**. *noun.*
hiyímiṅ [hi yí miṅ] bigger than someone or something, be. *verb(i).*
hiyíẇa [hi yí7 wa] thick [about tree]. *adjective.*
hiyíwilh [hi yí wilh] up, be. *verb(i).*
hiyíws [hi yíws] big-bodied person, be; big body, have [about person]. *verb(i).*
hiyí7ts [hi yí7ts] big mouth, have a; large mouth, have a. *adjective.*
hiyí7umesh [hi yí 7u mesh] kind of big. *adjective.*
hiyúnexw [hi yú nexw] big waves. *noun.*
hiyúy̓s [hi yúy̓s] consisting of large pieces [referring to rocks, boulders, etc.]. *adjective.*
hiyú7yem [hi yú7 yem] alright, be; good order, be in. *verb(i).*
hí7chistn [hí7 chis tn] poker (for a fire). *noun.*
huhuystwáy̓ [hu huys twáy̓] quarrel. *verb(i).*

huhú7chem [hu hú7 chem] spring tide, be. *verb(i).*
húmi7n [hú mi 7n] descend on it [as a swarm of flies]. *verb(i).*
huy [huy] stop; finish; but; ultimate; only; finished, be. *verb(i).*
huỷ [huỷ] go. *verb(i).*
huy aẁt [huy aẁt] last, be very; last one, be the. *verb(i).*
huy chexw a [huy chexw 7a] Thank you. *sentence.*
huỷ melh halh [huỷ melh halh] Goodbye. *sentence.*
huy melhálh [huy me lhálh] goodbye. *sentence.*
huyálhtsut [huy yálh tsut] final, be. *verb(i).*
huyá7 [hu yá7] depart; go away; leave. *verb(i).*
huyá7aỷm [hu yá 7aỷ yem] want to go. *verb(i).*
huyá7nexw [hu yá7 nexw] take (something) away finally. *verb(t).*
huyá7numut [hu yá7 nu mut] leave, finally get to. *verb(i).*
huyá7s [hu yá7s] take (someone) away; send (someone) away. *verb(t).*
huyiwsán [huy yiw sán] dress (someone) up. *verb(t).*
húyiwsem [hú yiw sem] dressed up, get all; dress up. *verb(i).*
húyiyanexw [húy yi ya nexw] finished, be [about season]. *verb(i).*
húỷk̲áỷsm [húỷ k̲áỷ sem] get one's weapons in readiness; ready one's weapons. *verb(i).*
húynexw [húy nexw] finish (something); complete (something). *verb(t).*
húỷnexw [húỷ nexw] finish eating (something); consume (something); taste (something). *verb(t).*
huynúmut [huy nú mut] done, be. *verb(i).*
huys [huys] fire (someone). *verb(t).*
huỷs [huỷs] finish eating (something); eating (something), finish; eat (something). *verb(t).*
húỷska [húỷs kya] let us do it. *clitic.*
húyshi [húy shey] make it for (someone). *verb(t).*
huỷts [huỷts] finish eating; eating, finish. *verb(i).*
huyú [hu yú] act suddenly. *verb(i).*
húyut [húy yut] give shape to (something); make (something); mould (something); prepare (something). *verb(t).*

I i

i [7i] here, be. *verb(i).*
i [7i] [event occurs close to the present; may be occurring right now]. *clitic.* here, be. *verb(i).*
i- [i–] switch; move back and forth. *prefix.*
i chen men wa ha7lh [7i chen men wa ha7 lh] I am doing okay. *sentence.*
i chen tl'iḵ [7i chen tl'iḵ] Hello.; Good day. [greeting used by person arriving]; I have arrived. *sentence.*
i chexw huyá7 [7i chexw hu yá7] Are you leaving? *sentence.*
i ti ~ i tti [7i ti] here, be. *verb(i).*
i tti ~ i ti [7i t ti] here, be. *verb(i).*
i ẇach' nilh [7i ẇach' nilh] it apparently turned out to be. *adverb.*
i ~ ey ~ iy [7i] and; or. *conjunction.*
-i ~ -i7 ~ -y [–i] [inchoative suffix]; become; get. *suffix.*
íchnexw [ích nexw] receive (a message); hear (a message); informed about (something), be. *verb(t).*
ich'ahàchi7m [i ch'a há chi 7em] lift up one's arms alternatingly. *verb(i).*
ích'ishnam [í ch'ish nam] lift up one's legs alternatingly. *verb(i).*
iiḵ [eehḵ] downtown; uptown. *noun.*
ikw [7ikw] then; until; when. *conjunction.*
íkwi [í kwi] and. *conjunction.*
-ikwup ~ -ayikwup [–i kwup] fire {full word: yíẏulh}. *suffix.*
íkwusem [í kwu sem] comb one's hair. *verb(i).*
íkwusiṁ [í kwu siṁ] card [wool]. *verb(i).*
íkwusn [í kwu sn] comb (someone). *verb(t).*
íkwustn [í kwus tn] comb; carding implement [for wool]. *noun.*
ikw'álh ~ aykw'álh [i kw'álh] babysit. *verb(i).*
íkw'imin [í kw'i min] sea urchin shells. *noun.*
ikw'íyentn [i kw'í yen tn] urchin net. *noun.*
íḵ'alhtn [éh ḵ'alh ten] gorge hook. *noun.*
íḵ'in [éh ḵ'in] scrape (hides). *verb(t).*
iḵw' [7iḵw'] rubbed, be. *verb(i).*
íḵw'in [éh ḵw'in] wipe (something); rub (something) off. *verb(t).*
íḵw'intsut [éh ḵw'in tsut] rub oneself off. *verb(i).*
íl̓ilay [í7 li lay] young fir tree; young fir trees. *noun.*
ilh ~ eylh [7ilh] dear; cousin [term of address] [see also sh7eylh~ sh7ilh]. *vocative.*
ílhchi [ílh chi] bow. *noun.* man the bow of a boat/canoe. *verb(i).*
ílheḵa [í lhe ḵa] other side, be on the. *verb(i).* other side. *noun.*
ílheḵa7min [í lhe ḵa7 min] other side [of a body of water]. *noun.*
ílhen [í lhen] eat. *verb(i).*
ilheṅám [i lheṅ nám] go pick berries; pick berries, go; go berry picking. *verb(i).*
ílhenáẇtxw [í lhen náẇ txw] kitchen [see also chishemáyak'in]; restaurant. *noun.*
ilheṅáẏem [i lheṅ náẏ yem] want to eat. *verb(i).*
ílhenaylh ~ ílhenaẏlh [í lhen naylh] feed the dead; give extra food away; have a feast with extra food; feast with extra food, have a. *verb(i).*
ílhenaẏlh ~ ílhenaylh [í lhen naẏ lh] feed the dead; give extra food away; have a feast with extra food; feast with extra food, have a. *verb(i).*
ílhenaylhs [í lhen naylhs] feed (the dead). *verb(t).*
ilheṅíwlh [i lheṅ níwlh] go out to eat; eat, go out to. *verb(i).*
ilhennúmut [i lhen nú mut] eat, manage to. *verb(i).*
ílhens [í lhens] feed (someone). *verb(t).*
ilhnexw [7ilh nexw] eat (something), manage to. *verb(t).*
ilhteṅáẏ [ilh teṅ náẏ] swamp gooseberry [older growth stage bush with more distinctive and numerous spines; see also ḵel'íplhḵay']. *noun.*
ilhténten [ilh tén ten] medicine to restore appetite [e.g., tl'asip, the licorice fern root]. *noun.*

iṁ [iṁ] baby boy at birth; newborn baby boy. *noun.*
-iṁ [-iṁ ~ -iṁ] {active intransitive suffix}. *suffix.*
-im ~ -iṁ [-im ~ -im] {intransitive suffix}. *suffix.*
-iṁ ~ -im [-iṁ ~ iṁ] {intransitive suffix}. *suffix.*
ímats [í mats] grandchild. *noun.*
ímen [í men] also; too. *adverb.*
ímesh [í mesh] walk. *verb(i).*
ímeshnumut [í mesh nu mut] be able to walk; manage to walk; walk, be able to; walk, manage to. *verb(i).*
iṁímesh [im 7í mesh] walk, be just starting to. *verb(i).*
iṁshálkwlh [iṁ shál kwlh] take a trek into the woods on spirit song search [about novice dancer]. *verb(i).*
imshálkwu ~imshálkwu7ts [im shál kwu] search for **syewen** in the ocean. *verb(i).*
imshálkwu7ts ~ imshálkwu [im shál kwu7ts] search for **syewen** in the ocean. *verb(i).*
íṁshen [íṁ shen] baby girl at birth; newborn baby girl. *noun.*
imshlhálem [imsh lhá lem] begging for food, be [about young dancer]. *verb(i).*
-in ~ -iṅ [-in ~ -in] {added onto some words so that you can use the object endings, see section on "object endings," p. 12}. *suffix.*
-iṅ ~ -in [-iṅ ~ -in] {added onto some words so that you can use the object endings, see section on "object endings," p. 12}. *suffix.*
ína [í na] one, the; other, the. *noun.*
ínak̲a [í na k̲a] across from, be. *verb(i).*
ínak̲skwu [í nak̲s kwu] other side of river. *noun.*
-inas [-i nas] chest {full word: **s7ílinas**}. *suffix.*
inayíwilh ~ ináẏwilh [i nay yí wilh] other side; each side; either side. *noun.* beyond, be. *verb(i).*
ináẏwilh ~ inayíwilh [i náẏ wilh] each side; other side; either side. *noun.* beyond, be. *verb(i).*
ínet [í net] say what?; what did . . . say? *question word; verb(i).*
ínexw [í nexw] view. *verb(i).*
ínexwan [í ne xwan] view (something). *verb(t).*
iṅinyáx̲a7n [iṅ 7in yá x̲a 7en] thunder; Thunderbird. *noun.*
íniẇilh [í ni ẇilh] other side of something. *verb(i).*
ip'áak̲w'ulh ~ p'áak̲w'alh ~ p'á7k̲w'alh [i p'áa k̲w'ulh] afraid; scared; get scared. *adjective.*
ip'áak̲w'ulhimin [i p'áa k̲w'u lhi min] frightening, be. *verb(i).*
ip'áak̲w'ulhmin [i p'áa k̲w'ulh min] scare (someone). *verb(t).*
ip'áak̲w'ulhni [i p'áa k̲w'ulh ni] scared of (someone/something), be; frightened of (someone/something), get. *verb(t).*
ip'áak̲w'ulhs [i p'áa k̲w'ulhs] scare (someone); frighten (someone). *verb(t).*
ip'áchn [i p'á chen] grab (someone's) hands. *verb(t).*
ip'áchs [i p'áchs] hold (someone's) hand. *verb(t).*
íp'alh [í p'alh] look after children. *verb(i).*
ip'áẏlh [i p'áẏ lh] hold a baby in one's arms. *verb(i).*
ip'a7ámats'em [i p'a 7á ma ts'em] place hands on hip. *verb(i).*
ip'a7áysus ~ xwp'a7áysus [i p'a 7áy sus] cave; hollow in rock. *noun.*
ip'a7íṁ ~ ip'i7íṁ ~ p'a7íṁ [i p'a 7íṁ] hold it in one's hands. *verb(i).*
ip'a7úẏwilh [i p'a 7úẏ wilh] hold on to a canoe, dragging it along in the water. *verb(i).*
íp'in [í p'in] wipe (something). *verb(t).*
íp'ip'is [í p'i p'is] holding on to (something), be. *verb(t).*
íp'is [í p'is] carry (something/someone) in one's arms; grab (something/someone); hold (something/someone). *verb(t).*
ip'i7íṁ ~ ip'a7íṁ ~ p'a7íṁ [i p'i 7íṁ] hold it in one's hands. *verb(i).*
is [7is] keep (something) here; have (something) here. *verb(t).*
is [7is] fine; nice; good time, have a; make merry; agreeable. *adjective.*
íṡaẇen [í saẇ wen] chew (something) [about human]. *verb(t).*
íṡaẇi [í saẇ wi] chew [about human]. *verb(i).*

iséyk̲'k̲s [i séy k̲' k̲s] go back and forth from one end to the other. *verb(i).*

iséyk̲'shn ~ isík̲'shn [i séyk̲' shn] transfer weight repeatedly from one foot to the other. *verb(i).*

isík̲'shn ~ iséyk̲'shn [i séhk̲' shen] transfer weight repeatedly from one foot to the other. *verb(i).*

ísun [í sun] canoe pulling, be; paddle; make strokes; strokes, make. *verb(i).*

isuṅáẏm [i suṅ náẏ yem] want to paddle. *verb(i).*

ísunt [í sunt] paddle (someone/something). *verb(t).*

it [7it] finish; finished, be; done, be. *verb(i).*

-it [–it ~ –it] {added onto some words so that you can use the object endings, see section on "object endings," p. 12}. *suffix.*

ítech [í tech] in plain sight, be. *verb(i).*

itiṁúsem [i tiṁ mú sem] look around; look in all directions. *verb(i).*

íttut [ít tut] fall asleep; slept, have finally. *verb(i).*

ítut [í tut] sleep. *verb(i).*

itutálhx̲a [i tu tálh x̲a] appetite, have no; full [literally, have a sleepy throat]. *adjective.*

itutnúmut [i tut nú mut] sleep, manage to get to. *verb(i).*

ítuts [í tuts] put (someone) to sleep. *verb(t).*

it' [7it'] {future tense; this word is no longer in common use; see **ek̲'**}. *clitic.*

ítl'eṁk̲ [í tl'eṁ k̲] short ass, have a. *adjective.*

ítl'i [í tl'i] not moving, be; still, be; keep still; refrain from action; yet, be; all the time; still. *verb(i).*

ítl'is [í tl'is] leave (something) alone. *verb(t).*

ítl'itl'i [í tl'i tl'i] keep still. *verb(i).*

itl'iyáy [i tl'i yáy] hover [about a bird]. *verb(i).*

ítl'i7atk̲wum [í tl'i 7at k̲wum] no tide, be; still, be [about water]; standing water, be. *verb(i).*

ítsi ~ íytsi [í tsi] those. *demonstrative.*

ítsiẇit ~ íytsiẇit [í tsi ẇit] those [people]. *demonstrative.*

-its'a ~ -ayts'a ~ -ayts'a7 ~ -ts'a [–i ts'a] clothes. *suffix.*

íts'am [í ts'am] get dressed. *verb(i).*

íts'ams [í ts'ams] dress (someone). *verb(t).*

-iwa ~ -iwa7 [–i wa] tree {full word: **stsek̲**}. *suffix.*

-iwan [–i wan] spirit; mind. *suffix.*

iẇánilh [i ẇá nilh] it turned out to be something other than expected. *adverb.*

íẇas ~ yeẇás [í ẇas] fish with hook and line; fish by means of a hook; fish with line ["mooching"]; fish with rod; fish with line in a river; angle [for fish]. *verb(i).*

iẇáyti lhkwun [i ẇáy tilh kwun] maybe. *clitic.*

iẇáyti ~ wáyti [i ẇáy ti] maybe; I think; may. *adverb.*

-iwa7 ~ -iwa [–i wa7] tree {full word: **stsek̲**}. *suffix.*

-iẇilh [–i ẇilh] be at [a relative position in space or time]. *suffix.*

-iws ~ -iẇs [–iws] inside {full word: **s7étswilh**}; body {full word: **slálaẇ**}. *suffix.*

-iẇs ~ -iws [–iẇs] inside {full word: **s7étswilh**}; body {full word: **slálaẇ**}. *suffix.*

íxwitsut [í xwi tsut] cry unstoppably; bawl. *verb(i).*

ixwn [7i xwn] give (something); make a present of (something). *verb(t).*

ixwn [7i xwn] small [about person]; "too young." *adjective.*

ix̲ [7ix̲] scraped, be; scratch. *verb(i).*

íx̲i ~ í7x̲i [éh x̲i] ashamed, be; shame, have. *verb(i).*

íx̲itsut [éh x̲i tsut] scratch oneself. *verb(i).*

íx̲iyen [éh x̲ey yen] insult (someone). *verb(t).*

ix̲m [7i x̲m] borrow. *verb(i).*

íx̲maẏm [éhx̲ maẏ yem] want to borrow. *verb(i).*

ix̲míṅ [ehx̲ míṅ] borrow something from (someone). *verb(t).*

ix̲mnúmut [eh x̲em nú mut] borrow it, manage to. *verb(i).*

íx̲wiṅ [éh x̲wiṅ] sweep (something). *verb(t).*

íx̲wits' [éh x̲wits'] housefly eggs; mites; maggots [see also **ápen'**]. *noun.*

ix̲wits'ántm ~ ix̲wits'éntm [eh x̲wi ts'án tem] infested with maggots, be. *verb(p).*

ix̱wits'éntm ~ ix̱wits'ántm [eh x̱wi ts'én tem] infested with maggots, be. *verb(p).*

íx̱wits'n [éh x̱wi ts'en] infest (something) with housefly eggs, maggots or mites. *verb(t).*

ix̱wtn [7ix̱w tn] broom. *noun.*

iy ~ i ~ ey [7iy] and; or. *conjunction.*

iyá [i yá] these. *demonstrative.*

iyáleẇen [i yá la7 wen] echo. *verb(i).*

iẏálḵep [i ẏál ḵep] Alaska blueberry; Alaska blueberries. *noun.*

iẏálḵpaẏ [i ẏál ḵ paẏ] Alaska blueberry bush; Alaska blueberry bushes. *noun.*

-íyalh ~ -aylh ~ -aẏlh [-í yalh] child {full word: meṅ}; person; people. *suffix.*

iyás [i yás] make merry; have a good time. *verb(i).*

iyáwa [i yá wa] they [right here]; them [right here]. *determiner.*

iyáẇit [i yá ẇit] these [people right here]. *demonstrative.*

-iẏax̱an ~ -iẏax̱a7n ~ -aẏax̱a7n [-i ẏa x̱an] arm {full word: táx̱nten}. *suffix.*

-iẏax̱a7n ~ -aẏax̱a7n ~ -iẏax̱an [-i ẏa x̱a 7n] arm {full word: táx̱nten}. *suffix.*

iẏáẏs [eẏ 7áẏs] wait for (someone/something). *verb(t).*

iẏáẏshim [eẏ 7áẏ shim] wait. *verb(i).*

iẏáẏulh [eẏ yá7 yulh] aboard, be. *verb(i).*

-iẏeḵw ~ -aẏeḵw [-i ẏeḵw] top; crown of head; top of head {full word: nḵ'áytsiẏeḵw}. *suffix.*

íyeṅtsut [í yeṅ tsut] groan. *verb(i).*

iẏím [i ẏím] strong; brave [about a person]. *adjective.*

iẏím ta sḵwalwens [i ẏím ta sḵwál wens] His heart is strong. *sentence.*

iẏímen [i ẏí men] strengthen (something). *verb(t).*

iẏími7 [i ẏí mi7] strong, get. *verb(i).*

iẏíms [i ẏíms] strengthen (something). *verb(t).*

íytsi ~ ítsi [íy tsi] those. *demonstrative.*

íytsiẇit ~ ítsiẇit [íy tsi ẇit] those [people]. *demonstrative.*

íẏuts [í7 yuts] mouth of river; river's mouth. *noun.*

íyu7ts [í yu7 ts] sharp. *adjective.*

iyu7tsán [i yu7 tsán] sharpen (something). *verb(t).*

íyu7tsḵs [í yu7 ts ḵs] sharp-pointed; sharp point, have a; sharp [about small oblong objects; e.g., knives]. *adjective.*

íyu7tstn [í yu7 ts ten] sharpener; whetstone. *noun.*

i7 [eh7] yes. *interjection.*

-i7 ~ -i ~ -y [-i7] [inchoative suffix]; become; get. *suffix.*

-i7aṅ ~ -aẏin ~ -aẏi [-i 7aṅ] net. *suffix.*

i7áyish [i 7áy yish] siblings of opposite sex; cousins of opposite sex [sg: áyish]. *noun.*

-i7ch ~ -aẏch [-eẏ ch] area; surface. *suffix.*

i7ílhen ~ í7ilhen [i 7í lhen] eating, be. *verb(i).*

í7ilhen ~ i7ílhen [í 7i lhen] eating, be. *verb(i).*

í7imesh ~ í7iṁesh ~ í7mash [í 7i mesh] walking, be. *verb(i).*

í7iṁesh ~ í7imesh ~ í7mash [í 7iṁ mesh] walking, be. *verb(i).*

i7ip'áaḵw'ulhni [i 7i p'áa ḵw'ulh ni] afraid of (someone), be. *verb(t).*

i7íyu7ts [i 7í yu7 ts] sharp. *adjective.*

i7íyu7ts lheḵ'lhḵ'átachxw [i 7í yu7 ts lheḵ' lh ḵ'á ta chxw] Scotch thistle. *noun.*

-i7ḵin [-i7 ḵin] wool {full word: lemetu7í7ḵin}; animal hair. *suffix.*

-i7ḵw [-i7ḵw] obstruction; rapids {full word: sch'i7í7ḵw}. *suffix.*

i7líwen [i7 lí wen] lucky. *adjective.*

í7mash ~ í7iṁesh ~ í7imesh [í7 mash] walking, be. *verb(i).*

í7mḵiya [í 7em ḵi ya] young mountain goat. *noun.*

-i7n [-i 7n] {added onto some words so you can use the object endings, see section on "object endings," p. 12}. *suffix.*

í7sun [í7 sun] paddling, be; making strokes, be; strokes, be making; pulling canoe, be. *verb(i).*

í7sunḵan [í7 sun ḵan] paddle for (someone). *verb(t).*

í7tut [í7 tut] asleep, be; sleeping, be. *verb(i).*

í7tutem [í7 tu tem] sleepy, be. *verb(i).*

-i7ups [-i 7ups] tail {full word: skw'ukw'ts}. *suffix.*

í7x̱i ~ íx̱i [éh7 x̱i] ashamed, be; shame, have. *verb(i).*

i7x̱w [7i7 x̱w] all; every. *adverb.* all gone, be; used up, be. *verb(i).*

i7x̱w éncha [eh7 x̱w én cha] everywhere. *adverb.*

i7x̱w stam [7i7 x̱w stam] everything. *noun.*

i7x̱w swat [7i7 x̱w swat] everyone. *noun.*

í7x̱wax̱w [éh7 x̱wax̱w] everybody; all of them. *noun.*

í7x̱wex̱wit [éh7 x̱we x̱wit] all of them. *noun.*

i7x̱ws [7i7 x̱ws] eat all of (something); finish (something); use (something) up. *verb(t).*

K k

ka [kya] {imperative; makes a stronger command; ex. **tl'iya ka**. "Stop it."}. *suffix.*

kákat [kyá kyat] climbing up, be. *verb(i).*

kákaw [kyá kyaw] descending, be [from a tree or hill]. *verb(i).*

kapú [kya pú] coat. *noun.*

kapú7m [kya pú 7m] put one's jacket on. *verb(i).*

kapú7n [kya pú 7en] put (someone's) coat on for him/her. *verb(t).*

kat ~ ket [kyat] climb up a tree or mountain; go up; ascend; climb. *verb(i).*

katnúmut [kyat nú mut] get up [a hill, a tree], finally. *verb(i).*

kats [kyats] move (something) up higher. *verb(t).*

kaw ~ kew [kyaw] descend [from a hill or tree]. *verb(i).*

káwat [kyá wat] bring (something) down. *verb(t).*

kaws [kyaws] bring (something) down to the beach; take (something) down; bring down (something) [e.g., a deceased person's name]. *verb(t).*

káw̓shenam [kyáw̓ she nam] change course [straight down; about river]. *verb(i).*

ket ~ kat [kyet] ascend; climb; climb up a tree or mountain; go up. *verb(i).*

kew ~ kaw [kyew] descend [from a hill or tree]. *verb(i).*

kewkáwim̓ [kyew kyáw wim̓] sing song of a dead person [literally, bring down]. *verb(i).*

kéwkew [kyéw kyew] make a number of trips [to carry something] down. *verb(i).*

kewkéwim̓ [kyew kyéw im̓] sing the song of a dead person. *verb(i).*

kílila [kyí li la] butterfly. *noun.*

kim̓ [kyim̓] nurse; take the breast; breastfeed [slang, children's language]. *verb(i).*

kítu7 [kyí tu7] swing. *noun.*

kítu7 tl'a stéwak̲in [kyí tu7 tl'a stéw wa k̲in] Orange honeysuckle. *noun.*

kíy̓a [kéy̓ ya] granny; mother. *noun.* mamma. *vocalic.*

klexw play 'pulling fingers' game. *verb(i).*

kli7tsán ~ lekli7tsán [kli7 tsán] lock (something). *verb(t).*

kshaws ~ kwsháwes blue jay. *noun.*

K' k'

k'ák'eltx̱ [k'á k'el tx̱] play **slhahál**; gamble. *verb(i).*

k'élk'ech [k'él k'ech] wolverine. *noun.*

k'éxwa7 [k'é xwa7] play lacrosse [modern]. *verb(i).*

k'éxwa7ten [k'é xwa7 ten] lacrosse stick. *noun.*

k'xwum [k'xwum] make a basket. *verb(i).*

Kw kw

kw [added to the end of a word, for example: **nekw** = **na** + **kw**, **chenkw** = **chen** + **kw**]; now; then; already. *clitic.*

kwa the, a (masculine, not present). *determiner.*

kwa wenlh tinená7t [kwa wenlh ti ne ná7t] my late father [literally, the late one who I came from]. *noun.*

kwaan [kwaan] relieve (someone). *verb(t).*

kwáchem [kwá chem] holler; scream; yell. *verb(i).*

kwákway̓el [kwá kway̓ 7el] dawn, be; dawning, be. *verb(i).*

kwalh opaque; fogged up. *adjective.*

kwálhi7 [kwá lhi7] opaque, become; foggy, become. *verb(i).*

kwan get better; recover. *verb(i).*

kwánatsut [kwá na tsut] take it easy. *verb(i).*

kwániws [kwá niws] recover; get well. *verb(i).*

kwank̲w relieved, be [about headache]. *verb(i).*

kwáshan [kwá shan] cut (wound); lance (boil). *verb(t).*

kwáshan̓tsut [kwá shan̓ tsut] lance oneself; cut oneself. *verb(i).*

kwáshat [kwá shat] cut (wound); lance (boil). *verb(t).*

kwáshatsut [kwá sha tsut] cut oneself to let out bad blood; lance oneself. *verb(i).*

kwashtn [kwash tn] **sxw7umten**'s knife. *noun.*

kwáwa [kwá wa] he [absent]; husband [term used by wife]. *demonstrative.*

kwaw̓it [kwa w̓it] they [not present]. *demonstrative.*

kway hide. *verb(i).*

kwáyan [kwáy yan] hide (something). *verb(t).*

kwáyantsut [kwáy yan tsut] hide oneself. *verb(i).*

kwáyel [kwáy yel] next day, be the. *verb(i).* tomorrow; day; sky. *noun.*

kwáy̓kway̓ [kwáy̓ kway̓] hide from one another; play hide and seek. *verb(i).*

kwáylayl ítut [kwáyl layl 7í tut] sleep during the day. *verb(i).*

kwáylayus [kwáyl lay yus] blue eyes, have. *adjective.*

kwáyles [kwáyl les] tomorrow, be. *verb(i).*

kwáyles txwná7nat [kwáy̓l 7es txw ná7 nat] tomorrow night. *adverbial phrase.*

kwayutsmin [kwa yuts min] murder (someone). *verb(t).*

kwáyutsmixw [kwáy yuts mixw] kill someone; murder someone. *verb(i).*

kwáyutsmixwn [kwáy yuts mi xwen] murder (someone) [see also **kwayutsmin**]; kill (someone). *verb(t).* act of murder, the. *noun.*

kwá7kwelh [kwá7 kwelh] jellyfish. *noun.*

kwá7sek̲w [kwá7 sek̲w] scalp. *noun.*

kwchétem [kwché tem] crowd. *verb(i).*

kwécha k̲ens [kwé cha k̲ens] Indian dancer's leggings. *noun.*

kwekwáchem [kwe kwá chem] cry out really loud. *verb(i).*

kwekwchám̓ [kwekw chám̓] hollering, be. *verb(i).*

kwékwem̓em ~ k̲wék̲wem̓em [kwé kwem̓ mem] thumping, be always; making a thumping sound, be; heavy feet, have [about person walking]; walking heavily, be; stomping, be; thump continuously. *verb(i).*

kwékwetxwm [kwé kwet xwem] roar [as a waterfall does]; make a rumbling noise. *verb(i).*

kwekwín̓ ~ kwukwín̓ [kwe kwín̓] long time ago; long since. *noun.*

kwekwiy̓ín̓tsut [kwe kwi y̓ín̓ tsut] doing, be; acting, be; behave; behave strangely; behave irregularly; "do everything." *verb(i).*

kwekwntál̓ [kwe kwen tál'] wrestle. *verb(i).*

kwek̲eléylstn [kwe k̲el léyls ten] music. *noun.*

kwék̲i7n [kwé k̲i 7en] flash. *verb(i).*

kwek̲' ~ k̲wek̲' ~ k̲w'ek̲' surprised, be; look with surprise. *verb(i).*

kwélash [kwél lash] fire a gun; shoot; shoot string; sting [about a bee]. *verb(i).*
kwelashnálhn [kwel lash ná lhn] shoot, manage to. *verb(i).*
kwélashnexw [kwél lash nexw] shoot (something), manage to; shoot (something) accidentally. *verb(t).*
kwelashnúmut [kwel lash nú mut] shoot oneself accidentally; take a shot, manage to; get a shot off, able to; get a chance to shoot. *verb(i).*
kwélasht [kwél lasht] fire at (something); shoot at (something); shoot (something). *verb(t).*
kwelashtsút [kwel lash tsút] shoot oneself intentionally. *verb(i).*
kwelkwélash [kwel kwél lash] shooting, be. *verb(i).*
kwelkwélasht [kwel kwél lasht] shoot (something) continuously. *verb(t).*
kwélmexwus [kwél me xwus] fine-work basket; red cedar root basket [with watertight weave]. *noun.*
kwelúl̓ay [kwel lú7 'lay] red alder tree. *noun.*
kwelh split, be [e.g., a log]. *verb(i).*
kwelhch split in half, be; split open, be. *verb(i).*
kwelhchán̓ [kwelh chán̓] split (something) in half [about something large, like a log]. *verb(t).*
kwélhi [kwé lhi] she [not present]. *demonstrative.*
kwélhk̲i7n [kwélh k̲i 7en] make a noise. *verb(i).*
kwelhn [kwe lhn] split (something). *verb(t).*
kwelh7áy̓nexw [kwelh 7áy̓ nexw] spirit of the water. *noun.*
kwemi7 [kwe mi7] blush; red, get. *verb(i).*
kwémi7 [kwém mi7] sound. *verb(i).*
kwémi7n [kwém mi 7en] thump [i.e., the sound of something dropping]; make a thumping sound. *verb(i).*
kwemkwemshenám̓ [kwem kwem shen nám̓] stamping, be; go fast while bouncing. *verb(i).*
kwémkwemts ~ skwém̓kwem̓ts [kwém kwemts] skinny. *adjective.* female salmon after spawning. *noun.*
kwém̓kwets' ~ skwúm̓kwum̓ts' ~ skwém̓kwemts' [kwém̓ kwets'] lump. *noun.*
kwemkwím [kwem kwím] red; gold [money]. *adjective.*
kwemkwím tála [kwem kwím tá la] gold. *noun.*
kwemkwúm [kwem kwúm] get ashore [about group]. *verb(i).*
kwémts'i7 [kwém ts'i7] thin, get very; emaciated, become. *verb(i).*
kwen begin singing one's power song; singing one's power song, begin; start; get into a state of rapture; rapture, get into a state of; begin doing something; start being possessed (while dancing). *verb(i).*
kwenám̓in [kwe ná7 min] scallop shell; scallop shells. *noun.*
kwénatsut [kwén na tsut] come through. *verb(i).*
kweniws [kwe niws] hold new dancer during first dance. *verb(i).*
kwenkwéns [kwen kwéns] get (someone) started. *verb(t).*
kwenkwenshenám̓ [kwen kwen shen nám̓] making a lot of thumping noises, be. *verb(i).*
kwens really do (something); do (something), really. *verb(t).*
kwépentsut [kwé pen tsut] swelling on body, have. *verb(i).*
kwepkwúpits [kwep kwú pits] children of parent's older sibling; older siblings; elder cousins; elder siblings [sg: **kwúpits**]. *noun.*
kwes a, any, some [feminine]. *determiner.*
kwes wenlh tinená7t [kwes wenlh ti ne ná7t] my late mother. *noun.*
kwésem [kwé sem] short and stubby, be; heavy-set, be [about person]. *verb(i).*
kwéshnach [kwésh nach] price. *noun.*
kwéshnacht [kwésh nacht] price (something). *verb(t).*
kweshú [kwe shú] pig. *noun.*
kwétxwem [kwét xwem] make a roaring noise in a stove [e.g., fire]. *verb(i).*
kwétxwet [kwét xwet] scramble for (the **swals**); grab up (the **swals**). *verb(t).*
kwétxwi7n [kwét xwi 7en] make a rumbling noise. *verb(i).*
kwetxwmts [kwet xwmts] have a "heavy," deep voice; "heavy," deep voice, have a. *verb(i).*

kwet'k̲í7n [kwet' k̲í 7en] crack finger joints. *verb(i).*

kwetl'i7 [kwe tl'i7] rusty, get. *verb(i).*

kwétsi [kwé tsi] he, that [not present]. *demonstrative.*

kwétsi siy̓ám̓ smex̲wíws [kwé tsi si y̓ám̓ sme x̲wíws] Chief Smallpox [term of fearful respect, used when smallpox was especially virulent]. *phrase.*

kwétsit [kwé tsit] he [deceased male]. *demonstrative.*

kwétsiw̓it [kwé tsi w̓it] they [not here]. *demonstrative.*

kwétsi7n [kwé tsi 7en] flash [about a light]. *verb(i).*

kwétsmin [kwéts min] dancer's rattle. *noun.*

kwéts'i7n [kwé ts'i 7en] sharp point of spear or hunting knife. *noun.*

kwew̓í7 [kwew̓ wí7] leave something with someone [for safekeeping]. *verb(i).*

kwéxwemay̓ [kwé xwem may̓] white fir [silver]. *noun.*

kwexwkwúxwmin ~ k̲wexwk̲wexwmín [kwexw kwúxw min] deer hooves. *noun.*

kwey̓ús [kwey̓ yús] starve. *verb(i).*

kwi [kwi ~ kwi] a, any, some. *determiner.*

kwi aw̓t stelmexw [kwi 7aw̓t stel mexw] people of times to come; future generations. *noun.*

kwi chel̓ák̲lh [kwi chel̓ 7á k̲lh] yesterday. *phrase.*

kwi hem̓í lhk̲aych' [kwi hem̓ mí lh k̲aych'] next month. *adverbial phrase.*

kwi hem̓í syel̓ánem [kwi hem̓ mí syel̓ 7á nem] next year. *adverbial phrase.*

kwi nch'u7 lhk̲aych' [kwi n ch'u7 lh k̲aych'] next month. *adverbial phrase.*

kwi nch'u7 syel̓ánem [kwi n ch'u7 syel̓ 7á nem] next year. *adverbial phrase.*

kwi ses [kwi ses] that s/he; when s/he. *clitic.*

kwi tpánu [kwi t pánu] last year. *adverbial phrase.*

kwi txwná7nat [kwi txw ná7 nat] last night. *adverbial phrase.*

kwi tx̲íx̲ta txwná7nat [kwi t x̲éhx̲ ta txw ná7 nat] on the evening of the day before yesterday. *adverbial phrase.*

kwi xwey lhk̲aych' [kwi xwey lh k̲aych'] next month. *phrase.*

kwi x̲aw̓s lhk̲aych' [kwi x̲aw̓s lh k̲aych'] next month. *phrase.*

kwikwáy [kwi kwáy] hide [about a group]. *verb(i).*

kwikwitsám [kwi kwi tsám] joke. *verb(i).*

kwik̲máman [kwehk̲ má man] cure (hides). *verb(t).*

kwílten [kwíl ten] fight; war. *verb(i).*

kwíltenchew̓án̓ [kwíl ten chew̓ wán̓] fight for (someone); fight over (something). *verb(t).*

kwíltenstway [kwíl tens tway] fight one another. *verb(i).*

kwíltn ~ kwíntel [kwíl tn] fight. *verb(i).*

kwílhimin̓ [kwí lhi min̓] bothersome, be. *verb(t).*

kwins [kwins ~ kwins] that I [future]; when I [future]. *clitic.*

kwins na [kwins na ~ kwins na] that I; when I. *clitic.*

kwíntel ~ kwíltn [kwín tel] fight. *verb(i).*

kwis [kwis ~ kwis] that you [future]; when you [future]. *clitic.*

kwis na [kwis na ~ kwis na] that you; when you. *clitic.*

kwis tex̲wl̓ám̓ es-húy [kwis tex̲w 'lám̓ es húy] be your very best. *phrase.*

kwiyá [kwi yá] him over there [just out of sight]. *demonstrative.*

kwiyáwa [kwi yá wa] that guy over there [can't see him and don't know who he is]. *demonstrative.*

kwiyáw̓it [kwi yá7 wit] these people [not sure of who they are]. *demonstrative.*

kwíyentem [kwí yen tem] pursued by angry person, be; called down, get; get after (someone); bawl (someone) out. *verb(p).*

kwíyin [kwí yin] do to (someone); give (someone) a tough time [in a fight, game, etc.]; make (money). *verb(t).*

kwíyin̓tsut [kwí yin̓ tsut] get into action; do something; accomplish something. *verb(i).*

kwíyukw [kwí yukw] milt of fish. *noun.*

kwí7kwelh [kwí7 kwelh] small canoe. *noun.*

kwlha the, a [feminine, not present]. *determiner.*

kwlhawa [kwlha wa] her [not present]. *demonstrative.*
kwlhaẃit [kwla ẃit] those ladies [not here yet]. *demonstrative.*
kwsáwa [kw sá wa] she [can't be seen and unknown to speaker]. *demonstrative.*
kwshámin [kw shá min] ancestral name. *noun.*
kwsháwes ~ kshaws [kw shá wes] blue jay. *noun.*
kwtams husband. *noun.*
kwtl'étsut [kw tl'é tsut] jump from fright. *verb(i).*
kwtsi7ts [kw tsi7ts] ritualist; person with magic power. *noun.*
kwtsí7tsi7 [kw tsí7 tsi7] become a ritualist; ritualist, become a. *verb(i).*
kwukw [kwukw] cook. *verb(i).*
kwukwíń ~ kwekwíń [kwu kwíń] long time ago; long since. *adverb.*
kwúkwtsem [kwúkw tsem] walking strongly and smartly, be; strutting, be. *verb(i).*
kwúkwuḿ [kwú kwuḿ] coming up [a hill], be; ascending, be; going uphill, be; going up, be [up the shore, from water]. *verb(i).*
kwúlhen [kwú lhen] borrow it. *verb(i).*
kwúlheni [kwú lhe ni] borrow it from (someone). *verb(t).*
kwúlhens [kwú lhens] borrow (something); lend (something); lend it to (someone). *verb(t).*
kwum [kwum] go ashore; go upward; ascend. *verb(i).*
kwumch ~ kwuḿch [kwumch] go over a hill or mountain [rather than around it]; go over a top or ridge. *verb(i).*
kwuḿch ~ kwumch [kwuḿ ch] go over a hill or mountain [rather than around it]; go over a top or ridge. *verb(i).*
kwúḿkwum [kwúḿ kwum] go into the bush [about a group]. *verb(i).*
kwums ~ kwuḿs [kwums] take (someone/something) ashore; take (something) up [from the ground]; take (something) upward. *verb(t).*
kwuḿs ~ kwums [kwuḿs] take (something) up [from the ground]; take (something) upward; take (someone/something) ashore. *verb(t).*
kwúmshi [kwúm shey] bring it up the hill for (someone); take it ashore for (someone); take it up the hill for (someone). *verb(t).*
kwúpits [kwú pits] older sibling; elder sibling; elder cousin; child of parent's older sibling. *noun.*
kwúsen [kwú sen] star. *noun.*
kwút-tseḿ [kwút tseḿ] pucker one's lips. *verb(i).*
kwútusem [kwú tu sem] pull a long face in anger. *verb(i).*
kwúxwmin ~ k̲wúxwmin [kwúxw min] deer hoof. *noun.*
kwu7 [kwu7] pulled apart, be; pulled off, be [about bark]. *verb(i).*
kwú7kwuwel̓s [kwú7 kwu wel̓s] highbush cranberry; highbush cranberries. *noun.*
kwu7kwuwél̓saẏ [kwu7 kwu wél̓ saẏ] highbush cranberry bush; highbush cranberry bushes. *noun.*
kwu7n [kwu 7n] peel off a layer from (something) [especially thick bark]; pull (something) off. *verb(t).*
kwu7s [kwu7s] spring salmon. *noun.*

Kw' kw'

kw'a together with [only with lh]. *clitic.*
kw'aa [kw'aa] I don't know. *interjection.*
kw'aach' [kw'aach'] dogfish; shark. *noun.*
kw'ach look at. *verb(i).*
kw'acháy̓s [kw'a cháy̓s] look over something. *verb(i).*
kw'achémeṅ ~ kw'échmeṅ [kw'a ché meṅ] mirror. *noun.*
kw'achmámin [kw'ach má min] look inside. *verb(i).*
kw'áchmin [kw'ách min] vision. *noun.*
kw'achmixwaylh [kw'ach mi xwaylh] show pictures in the longhouse; exhibit. *verb(i).*
kw'áchmixws [kw'ách mixws] show it to (someone). *verb(t).*
kw'áchnalhn [kw'ách na lhen] see, be able to; see, finally. *verb(i).*
kw'áchnamen [kw'ách na men] see for oneself. *verb(i).*
kw'áchnexw [kw'ách nexw] catch sight of (someone/something); see (someone/something). *verb(t).*
kw'acht look at (something); take a look at (something). *verb(t).*
kw'áchusnexw [kw'á chus nexw] see (someone's) face. *verb(t).*
kw'ach'áḵalh [kw'a ch'á ḵalh] shark, type of. *noun.*
kw'ach'áy̓inkwu [kw'a ch'áy̓ yin kwu] shark, type of. *noun.*
kw'ách'sen [kw'ách' sen] set (something) near the fire to heat. *verb(t).*
kw'ákw'asi7 [kw'á kw'a si7] become warm; warm, become; become hot; hot, become; become summer; summer, become. *verb(i).*
kw'ákw'ay̓ [kw'á kw'ay̓] very hungry, be; hungry, be very. *verb(i).*
kw'ákw'ayakw'ni [kw'á kw'ay yakw' ni] suspect (someone). *verb(t).*
kw'akw'ch [kw'akw' ch] looking, be. *verb(i).*
kw'akw'chsténaṁut [kw'akw' ch sté na ṁut] look at oneself; careful, be; watch oneself. *verb(i).*
kw'akw'cht [kw'akw' cht] looking at (someone/something), be; watching (someone/something), be. *verb(t).*
kw'ákw'chust [kw'ákw' chust] stare at (someone). *verb(t).*
kw'ákw'em [kw'á kw'em] circle when flying. *verb(i).*
kw'ákw'stsam [kw'á kw's tsam] toasting the **xwastn**, be [literally, warming it for the mouth]. *verb(i).*
kw'ákw'xwa7 ~ kw'íkw'ixwa7 [kw'ákw' xwa7] little box [see **kw'áxwa7**]. *noun.*
kw'ala̱kwusnálhen [kw'a7 la ḵwus ná lhen] finally beat someone. *verb(i).*
kw'ála̱kwust [kw'á7 la ḵwust] hitting (someone), keep; club (someone); beat (someone) up. *verb(t).*
kw'ála7ḵwus [kw'á la7 ḵwus] club. *noun.*
kw'aṅí [kw'a ṅí] move from one canoe to another. *verb(i).*
kw'aṅíṁ [kw'aṅ níṁ] transfer from one container to another. *verb(i).*
kw'áṅnexw [kw'áṅ nexw] spilt (something), have already. *verb(t).*
kw'as hot; warm; scald; singe; burn. *adjective.*
kw'as skwáyel [kw'as skwáy yel] warm weather. *verb(i).*
kw'ásach [kw'á sach] burnt hands, have. *adjective.* burn one's hands. *verb(i).*
kw'ásalḵen [kw'á sal ḵen] sunstroke, have. *verb(i).*
kw'ásalxwtsalh [kw'á salxw tsalh] burn one's tongue. *verb(i).*
kw'asamút [kw'a sa mút] dress up warmly. *verb(i).*
kw'ásan [kw'á san] heat (something) up. *verb(t).*
kw'ásay̓us [kw'á say̓ yus] warm food near fire. *verb(i).*
kw'asayúsen [kw'a say yú sen] singe hair on (a seal); singe the outer skin of (a red cod). *verb(t).*
kw'ásem [kw'á sem] heat up ["toast"] fish. *verb(i).*

kw'ási7 [kw'á si7] get hot; hot, get; become warm or hot; warm, become. *verb(i).*
kw'askw'ás [kw'as kw'ás] hot; warm; scald; singe; burn. *verb(i).*
kw'askw'ásts [kw'as kw'ásts] burning one's mouth, be. *verb(i).*
kw'ásmut [kw'ás mut] hot, be [about clothes]; dress warmly. *verb(i).*
kw'ásshen [kw'ás shen] burnt foot, have a. *adjective.*
kw'asts burn one's mouth. *verb(i).*
kw'át'an [kw'á t'an] mouse. *noun.*
kw'át'em [kw'á t'em] listless, be; lazy, be. *verb(i).*
kw'atl' sex, have. *verb(i).*
kw'átl'an [kw'á tl'an] sex with (someone), have. *verb(t).*
kw'áwaschk̲ [kw'á was chk̲] jaw. *noun.*
kw'awch watching, be. *verb(i).*
kw'awchs look after (someone); see (someone), be able to. *verb(t).*
kw'awcht [kw'aw cht] watching (someone), be. *verb(t).*
kw'áwchus [kw'áw chus] staring, be. *verb(i).*
kw'áwchust [kw'áw chust] staring at (someone), be. *verb(t).*
kw'áwenek̲ [kw'á wen nek̲] curse someone. *verb(i).*
kw'áwi7 [kw'á wi7] talk too much; ailing, be; sighing, be. *verb(i).*
kw'awkw'chústway [kw'aw kw' chús tway] facing each other, be [about people]. *verb(i).*
kw'áxwa7 [kw'á xwa7] box. *noun.*
kw'ay wrong, be; cannot. *verb(i).*
kw'ay̓ hungry, be; worse, be getting [about sick person]. *verb(i).*
kw'ay ~ skw'ay ~ eskw'áy [kw'ay] can't; impossible, be; unable, be; pregnant, be; cannot; wrong, be; amiss, be; powerless, be; very ill, be; defective, be; out of order, be. *verb(i).*
kw'áyat [kw'áy yat] train (someone) to be a sxw7umten; purify (someone). *verb(t).*
kw'áyatsut [kw'áy ya tsut] train to become a sxw7umten; purify onself. *verb(i).*
kw'ayáylhm [kw'ay yáy lhem] purify ritually. *verb(i).*
kw'áynexw [kw'áy nexw] made (someone) pregnant, have. *verb(t).*
kw'áy̓nexw [kw'áy̓ nexw] make (someone) hungry; hungry, make (someone). *verb(t).*
kw'ay̓númut [kw'ay̓ nú mut] hungry, finally get. *verb(i).*
kw'ay̓s make (someone) hungry; hungry, make (someone). *verb(t).*
kw'ayshít [kw'ay shít] refuse (someone) permission. *verb(t).*
kw'a7ém̓ch [kw'a 7ém̓ch] burst [e.g., a boil]. *verb(i).*
kw'chustn ~ nkw'ekw'chústn ~ nkw'chustn ~ kw'ek̲wchústn [kw' chús ten] window; mirror. *noun.*
kw'echkw'áchnexw [kw'ech kw'ách nexw] see (someone) [about a group]. *verb(t).*
kw'echkw'áchn̓was [kw'ech kw'á chen̓ was] see one another. *verb(i).*
kw'échkw'ech [kw'éch kw'ech] expecting someone, be. *verb(i).*
kw'echkw'echnít [kw'ech kw'ech nít] expect (someone); look forward to (something). *verb(t).*
kw'échmen ~ kw'achémen̓ [kw'éch men] mirror. *noun.*
kw'échmen̓ ~ kw'achémen̓ [kw'éch men̓] mirror. *noun.*
kw'ech' strong smell, have; strong-smelling, be; rancid odour, have a; smell rancid. *verb(i).*
kw'éch'tnshen [kw'éch' ten shen] ice skates. *noun.*
kw'ékw'chi7n [kw'ékw' chi 7en] have a look at the content of one's net; look at the content of one's net, have a. *verb(i).*
kw'ekw'chustnáw̓txw [kw'ekw' chus ten náw̓ txw] window of house. *noun.*
kw'ekw'iyúkw [kw'e kw'i yúkw] small fishhook. *noun.*
kw'ekw'k̲wáystn [kw'ekw' k̲w'áys ten] implements for beating wool [sg: k̲w'k̲waystn ~ k̲w'k̲waystn]. *noun.*
kw'ekw'sáyus [kw'ekw' sáy yus] singe feathers on a bird. *verb(i).*
kw'ekw'shát [kw'ekw' shát] counting (them), be. *verb(t).*
kw'ekw'tsáyus ~ kw'ikw'tsáyus [kw'ekw' tsáy yus] pluck feathers; pluck a fowl. *verb(i).*

kw'é<u>k</u>em̓ts [kw'é <u>k</u>em̓ts] wide open. *adjective.*
kw'é<u>k</u>'en [kw'é <u>k</u>'en] cut open (game or fish). *verb(t).*
kw'e<u>k</u>wchústn ~ nkw'ekw'chústn ~ kw'chustn ~ nkw'chustn [kw'e<u>k</u>w chús ten] window; mirror. *noun.*
kw'el̓ stomach. *noun.*
kw'el̓áw̓ [kw'el̓ láw̓] human skin; fish skin; animal skin; skin, fish, animal or human. *noun.*
kw'el̓áw̓ach [kw'el̓ láw̓ wach] skin on hands. *noun.*
kw'el̓áw̓iws [kw'el̓ láw̓ wiws] skin. *noun.*
kw'el̓áw̓shen [kw'el̓ láw̓ shen] skin on foot. *noun.*
kw'elch' dried herring. *noun.*
kw'el<u>k</u>tsáṅ [kw'el <u>k</u> tsáṅ] knock on (something). *verb(t).*
kw'el<u>k</u>tsím̓ [kw'el <u>k</u> tsím̓] knock on door. *verb(i).*
kw'elh fellow; co-. *adjective.*
kw'elh spill accidentally. *verb(i).*
kw'elh wa chet <u>x</u>aam [kw'alh wa chet <u>x</u>aam] group consisting of parents of surviving spouse and parents of deceased spouse. *noun.*
kw'elhch<u>k</u>áṅ [kw'elh ch <u>k</u>áṅ] water (plants) around the roots. *verb(t).*
kw'élhey̓e<u>k</u>wem [kw'é lhey̓ ye·<u>k</u>wem] spill water on middle of one's head. *verb(i).*
kw'élhey̓<u>k</u>wem [kw'é lhey̓ <u>k</u>wem] spill water on one's head. *verb(i).*
kw'élhkw'elh [kw'élh kw'elh] spill repeatedly; spilling, be. *verb(i).*
kw'élhkw'elhnexw [kw'élh kw'elh nexw] spill (something) accidentally; have spilled (something). *verb(t).*
kw'elhkw'lhát [kw'elh kw' lhát] pouring (something), be [about a group]. *verb(t).*
kw'elhnálhen [kw'elh ná lhen] spill it, finally; spill it, manage to. *verb(i).*
kw'élhnexw [kw'élh nexw] spill (something) already; spilt (something) accidentally, have; have spilt (something) accidentally; have spilt (something); spilt (something), have; spill a lot of (something); keep spilling (something); spill (something) accidentally. *verb(t).*
kw'elhs spill (something). *verb(t).*
kw'elhsyú7yuxwa [kw'elh syú7 yu xwa] co-elder. *noun.*
kw'elhtl'í7new̓ás [kw'elh tl'í7 new̓ was] partners; friends to each other. *noun.*
kw'elh7áynexw [kw'elh 7áy nexw] soul; spirit [see also **wa lh7áy̓nexw**]. *noun.*
kw'emaylháw̓txw ~ kw'enmaylháw̓txw [kw'em may lháw̓ txw] church. *noun.*
kw'emkw'úm̓ [kw'em kw'úm̓] codfish spawn. *noun.*
kw'éna [kw'én na] look at that! *interjection.*
kw'eṅáṅ [kw'e ṅáṅ] use (a ladle); ladle (something). *verb(t).*
kw'enáyachtn [kw'en náy yach ten] ladle [deep serving spoon]. *noun.*
kw'eṅím̓ [kw'eṅ ním̓] ladle some out. *verb(i).*
kw'éṅ<u>k</u>en [kw'éṅ <u>k</u>en] choked drinking water, get [cf. t'ekwínas]. *verb(i).*
kw'enlh wa <u>x</u>aam [kw'enlh wa <u>x</u>aam] group of three consisting of parent(s) of surviving spouse and parent(s) of deceased spouse. *noun.*
kw'enmán [kw'en mán] thank (someone); greet (someone); offer one's condolence to (someone). *verb(t).*
kw'enmáylh [kw'en máylh] pray. *verb(i).*
kw'enmaylháw̓txw ~ kw'emaylháw̓txw [kw'an may lháw̓ txw] church. *noun.*
kw'enmaylhchew̓án [kw'en maylh chew̓ wán] pray for (someone). *verb(t).*
kw'éṅnexw [kw'éṅ nexw] spilt (something), have already; move (something) from one container to another. *verb(t).*
kw'enus [kw'e nus] aim. *verb(i).*
kw'eṅúsn [kw'eṅ nú sen] aim at (someone/something). *verb(t).*
kw'éṅwilhn [kw'éṅ wi lhen] step over (something). *verb(t).*
kw'eskw'ás [kw'es kw'ás] warmer, be getting [about weather]. *verb(i).*
kw'éshnexw [kw'ésh nexw] count (them) already. *verb(t).*
kw'étxwem [kw'ét xwem] come loose. *verb(i).*
kw'étl'kw'etl' [kw'étl' kw'etl'] sex, be someone who is always having. *verb(i).*
kw'étsen [kw'é tsen] pluck (something); pull out (feathers). *verb(t).*
kw'ets'alá<u>k</u>s [kw'e ts'al lá<u>k</u>s] adze. *verb(i).*

kw'ets'alá<u>k</u>sen [kw'e ts'al lá<u>k</u> sen] adze (something). *verb(t).*

kw'ets'kw'úts'untsut [kẃ'ets' kw'ú ts'un tsut] zigzag [e.g., in a canoe]. *verb(i).*

kw'ewxwayúsem [kw'ew xway yú sem] not look for fear. *verb(i).*

kw'exweláwet [kw'e xwe lá wet] rainproof coat. *noun.*

kw'exwkw'áxwa7 [kw'exw kw'á xwa7] boxes [sg: **kw'áxwa7**]. *noun.*

kw'exwús [kw'e xwús] hail [meteorological]. *verb(i).*

kw'eykw'áy [kw'ey kw'áy] disabled, be. *verb(i).*

kw'ich' [kw'ich'] skin any animal; butcher fish; clean fish, fowl or game; cut up fish. *verb(i).*

kw'ích'in [kw'í ch'in] skin (something); clean (fish, fowl or game); cut up (something); operate on (someone). *verb(t).*

kw'ich'tn [kw'ich' tn] fish knife; salmon knife; knife used to clean animals. *noun.*

kw'ikw'áy [kw'i kw'áy] go wrong. *verb(i).*

kw'ikw'áynew̓as [kw'i kw'áy new̓ was] have a disagreement resulting in a quarrel; disagreement resulting in a quarrel, have a; have a falling out; falling out, have a. *verb(i).*

kw'íkw'en ~ kw'íkw'in [kw'í kw'en] few animals. *verb(i).* how many animals? *question word; verb(i).*

kw'íkw'ilhiw̓ [kw'í kw'i lhiw̓] live with wife's people. *verb(i).*

kw'íkw'in ~ kw'íkw'en [kw'í kw'in] few animals. *verb(i).* how many animals? *question word; verb(i).*

kw'íkw'ixwa7 ~ kw'ákw'xwa7 [kw'í kw'i xwa7] little box [see **kw'áxwa7**]. *noun.*

kw'íkw'iyas [kw'í kw'i yas] stall (someone); keep (someone) from going. *verb(t).*

kw'íkw'<u>k</u>wémn [kw'íkw' <u>k</u>wé men] hatchet; little axe [see **<u>k</u>w'a<u>k</u>wemén ~ <u>k</u>w'<u>k</u>wémn**]. *noun.*

kw'íkw'lets' [kw'íkw' lets'] pin feather; feathers. *noun.*

kw'íkw'sáyus [kw'íkw' sáy yus] burn off the hairs of a [seal] skin. *verb(i).*

kw'ikw'tsáyus~ kw'ekw'tsáyus [kw'ikw' tsáy yus] pluck feathers; pluck a fowl. *verb(i).*

kw'ílhiw̓ [kw'í lhiw̓] move to live at wife's village; go and stay with one's wife's people. *verb(i).*

kw'ílhkw'ilh [kw'ílh kw'ilh] tippy, be. *verb(i).*

kw'ilhkw'ilhátsut [kw'ilh kw'i lhá tsut] rock a canoe. *verb(i).*

kw'in [kw'in] few; a few; little; some. *verb(i).* how many?; how much? *question word; verb(i).*

kw'inálh [kw'i nálh] how many times? *question word; verb(i).*

kw'ínamats' [kw'í na mats'] few strands of wool. *verb(i).*

kw'ínawanexw [kw'í na wa nexw] what age?; how old?; how many years old? *question word; verb(i).*

kw'ínaxwilh [kw'í na xwilh] few canoes. *verb(i).* how many canoes? *question word; verb(i).*

kw'íni7 [kw'í ni7] few, become. *verb(i).*

kw'ínkw'en ~ kw'ínkw'in [kw'ín kw'en] few people. *verb(i).* how many people? *question word; verb(i).*

kw'ínkw'in ~ kw'ínkw'en [kw'ín kw'in] few people. *verb(i).* how many people? *question word; verb(i).*

kw'ínlhyes [kw'ín lhyes] what day? *question word; verb(i).*

kw'inmút [kw'in mút] how many pieces? *question word; verb(i).*

kw'its'kw'its'lé<u>k</u>em [kw'its' kw'its' lé <u>k</u>em] fall head over heels. *verb(i).*

kw'í<u>x</u>ta [kw'í<u>x</u> ta] animal hide. *noun.*

kw'iyamlhnáym [kw'i yamlh náy yem] stingy with food, be. *verb(i).*

kw'iyáshi [kw'i yá shey] refuse (someone). *verb(t).*

kw'iyáshi [kw'i yá shey] refuse (someone). *verb(t).*

kw'iyát ~ kw'íyat [kw'i yát] refuse (someone); refuse to give to (someone); insist that (someone) refrain from doing something. *verb(t).*

kw'íyat ~ kw'iyát [kw'í yat] refuse to give to (someone); refuse (someone); insist that (someone) refrain from doing something. *verb(t).*

kw'iyátsut [kw'i yá tsut] refuse. *verb(i).*

kw'í7<u>k</u>tn [kw'í7 <u>k</u> ten] animal skin; fur; skin [animal]. *noun.*

kw'i7k̲'áń [kw'i7 k̲'áń] rock (a boat). *verb(t).*
kw'i7tn ~ nekw'í7tn [kw'í7 ten] ladder. *noun.*
kw'í7xwem [kw'í7 xwem] screech; make a noise [about screech owl]. *verb(i).* screech owl. *noun.*
kw'k̲ach [kw' k̲ach] hang broken on a tree [about branch]; have a branch hanging off. *verb(i).*
kw'k̲waystn ~ k̲w'k̲waystn [kw' k̲wáys ten] implement for beating wool; implement for beating mountain goat wool. *noun.*
kw'k̲winstn [kw' k̲wíns ten] spring-tied tree [type of weapon]. *noun.*
kw'lhálhk̲wu7n [kw' lhálh k̲wu 7en] pour (something); strain off water from (something) [while cooking]. *verb(t).*
kw'lham [kw' lhám] empty berries into a different container. *verb(i).*
kw'lháḿen [kw' lháḿ men] fill (something) with liquid. *verb(t).*
kw'lhat [kw' lhát] spill (something); pour (something) out. *verb(t).*
kw'lhátsut [kw' lhá tsut] capsize [about a canoe]. *verb(i).*
kw'lhaých overflow. *verb(i).*
kw'lháyusem [kw' lháy yu sem] splash one's eyes. *verb(i).*
kw'lhá7lhen [kw' lhá7 lhen] pour water over (someone) who is lying in bed. *verb(t).*
kw'lhiḿ [kw'lhiḿ] spilling, be. *verb(i).*
kw'lhíyak̲waḿ [kw' lhí ya k̲waḿ] smear over one's face. *verb(i).*
kw'lhúsem [kw' lhú sem] smear one's face. *verb(i).*
kw'lhúsen [kw' lhú sen] pour water on (someone/something); water (plant). *verb(t).*
kw'sham confess. *verb(i).*
kw'shat count (them). *verb(t).*
kw'shiḿ [kw'shiḿ] count them; number them. *verb(i).*
kw'úlhnexw [kw'úlh nexw] seem to know (something) is around; know (something) is around, seem to. *verb(t).*
kw'ulhnúmut [kw'ulh nú mut] feel some unseen thing. *verb(i).*
kw'úmutsut [kw'ú mu tsut] weak but willing to try, be. *verb(i).*
kw'únut' [kw'ú nut'] porpoise. *noun.*
kw'úpuntsut ~ kw'úp'untsut [kw'ú pun tsut] wrinkled, become. *verb(i).*
kw'up'chk̲ [kw'up' chk̲] rotten tree [dead]; deadfall tree. *noun.*
kw'úp'chk̲ań [kw'úp' ch k̲ań] pull out (plants). *verb(t).*
kw'up'k̲ [kw'up'k̲] uprooted, be [about tree]. *verb(i).*
kw'úp'untsut ~ kw'úpuntsut [kw'ú p'un tsut] wrinkled, become. *verb(i).*
kw'utl'kw [kw'utl'kw] salt water. *noun.*
kw'útswilhen [kw'úts wi lhen] bang on (a canoe). *verb(t).*
kw'úts'un [kw'ú ts'un] bend (something) [in several directions]; make (something) crooked. *verb(t).*
kw'úts'untsut [kw'ú ts'un tsut] crooked, have gone. *verb(i).*
kw'úwen [kw'ú wen] raise (something) up a little bit in order to get a look at it. *verb(t).*
kw'uykw [kw'uykw] fishhook [general term]; large fishhook. *noun.*
kw'uykwél̓shen [kw'uy kwel' shen] fishing line; trolling line. *noun.*
kw'úykwem [kw'úy kwem] troll. *verb(i).*

Ḵ ḵ

ḵ not real [used in negative sentences and sentences where the outcome is not certain]. *clitic.*

-ḵ bottom, behind {full word: s7atsḵ}; trunk. *suffix.*

-ḵ o'clock. *suffix.*

-ḵa side. *suffix.*

ḵáḵalhi7 [ḵá ḵa lhi7] dark, be just getting. *verb(i).*

ḵáḵatl' [ḵá ḵatl'] cloudy, be getting. *verb(i).*

ḵaḵel̓ántsut [ḵa ḵel̓ 7án tsut] babyish, be [e.g., when an older kid wants to get noticed]. *verb(i).*

ḵaḵn [ḵa ḵn] housepost. *noun.*

ḵaḵ'n [ḵa ḵ'n] brake (something); slow (something) down. *verb(t).*

ḵáḵ'ntsut [ḵá ḵ'en tsut] slow down. *verb(i).*

ḵálax̱wus [ḵá la x̱wus] two-year old deer [with one-pronged antlers]. *noun.*

ḵalílḵem [ḵa léhl ḵem] spoil a child. *verb(i).*

ḵal̓ḵ wild rosebud. *noun.*

ḵál̓ḵalilh [ḵál' ḵa lilh] Giant Cannibal Woman. *noun.*

ḵál̓ḵay [ḵál' ḵay] wild rosebush. *noun.*

ḵal̓s chexw [said to someone when they trip or drop something]. *phrase.*

ḵálx̱aẏ [ḵál x̱aẏ] ironwood tree; hardhack. *noun.*

ḵalh ~ ḵ'alh ever; never [only used in certain sentences with "haw" and "txwhaw"]. *clitic.*

ḵálhayu [ḵá lha yu] gaff hook; fishing hook. *noun.*

ḵaṅ cheat; rob; steal. *verb(i).*

ḵan ~ ḵen ~ ḵ'an ~ ḵ'en I. *clitic.*

ḵáṅan [ḵáṅ nan] put a little bit of pressure on (something). *verb(t).*

ḵáṅen [ḵáṅ nen] rob (someone). *verb(t).*

ḵanlhálem [ḵan lhá lem] steal food; eat secretly. *verb(i).*

ḵáṅshi [ḵáṅ shey] steal from (someone). *verb(t).*

ḵáp'ḵap'tsaylh ~ sḵáp'ḵap'tsaylh [ḵáp' ḵap' tsaylh] bat [type of animal]. *noun.*

ḵap'ḵwáṅ [ḵap' ḵwáṅ] cover (someone's) head. *verb(t).*

ḵatán [ḵa tán] give (someone) a steam bath; cause (someone) to take a steam bath. *verb(t).*

ḵatántsut [ḵa tán tsut] take a sweatbath; take a steam bath. *verb(i).*

ḵatúseṅ [ḵa tú seṅ] hug (someone). *verb(t).*

ḵatl' cloudy, be. *verb(i).*

ḵátl'en [ḵá tl'en] block (something); stop (something). *verb(t).*

ḵátl'shnaṁ ~ ḵetl'shnáṁ [ḵátl' shnaṁ] stop walking; stop suddenly; brace one's footing [e.g., when slipping down a hill]. *verb(i).*

ḵáts'en [ḵá ts'en] stop (something) from leaking. *verb(t).*

ḵax̱ make a lot of noise [about crows]; caw. *verb(i).*

ḵáx̱chewaṅtem [ḵáx̱ cheẇ waṅ tem] make a lot of noise [about crows]; caw. *verb(p).*

ḵax̱ḵex̱ás [ḵax̱ ḵe x̱ás] wasteful, be. *verb(i).*

ḵáyalhkwup [ḵáy yalh kwup] ashes [see also ḵwáyalhkwup and p'ich't]. *noun.*

ḵáẏiws [ḵáẏ yiws] left hand. *noun.* left-handed. *adjective.*

ḵáẏḵsém [ḵáẏḵ sém] sneeze through the left nostril [a sign of bad luck]. *verb(i).*

-ḵaẏs weapon. *suffix.*

ḵaẏt tips of fish. fin [for propulsion] *noun.*

ḵáẏus [ḵáẏ yus] left eye. *noun.*

ḵa7ís ~ ḵá7is [ḵa 7ís] little while; soon. *adverb.*

ḵá7is ~ ḵa7ís [ḵá 7is] little while; soon. *adverb.*

ḵcháyuṁ [ḵ cháy yuṁ] full-grown [about berries, etc.]. *adjective.*

ḵchuẏs [ḵchuẏs] full-grown [about larger fruit]. *adjective.*

ḵech full, be [about the moon]; full grown, be; full-blown, be; well-developed, be. *verb(i).*

ḵéchḵech [ḵéch ḵech] increase [about the moon]. *verb(i).*

k̲ek̲ch ~ k̲ék̲ech [k̲ek̲ ch] increasing, be [about the moon]. *verb(i).*

k̲ék̲ech ~ k̲ek̲ch [k̲é k̲ech] increasing, be [about the moon]. *verb(i).*

k̲ek̲eẏí7 [k̲e k̲eẏ yí7] bad, be getting; mouldy, be getting; become bad; spoil. *verb(i).*

k̲ék̲eẏx̲em [k̲é k̲eẏ x̲em] movie; theatre. *noun.*

k̲ek̲lími7 [k̲e k̲el lí mi7] be becoming weak; weak, be becoming. *verb(i).*

k̲ék̲xwen [k̲ék̲ xwen] gathering (something), be; putting (things) away, be. *verb(t).*

k̲ek̲x̲í7 [k̲e k̲x̲í7] increase; multiply; numerous, be. *verb(i).*

k̲ék̲'em [k̲é k̲'em] hard to paddle [slow]; hard pulling, be [about canoe]. *verb(i).*

k̲ek̲'k̲'ítsut [k̲ek̲' k̲'í tsut] stubborn and wanting to be begged, be. *verb(i).*

k̲ék̲wilh [k̲é k̲wilh] brand-new canoe. *noun.*

k̲eleṁí7 [k̲e le ṁí7] muddy, be [saltwater condition that occurs every April]. *verb(i).*

k̲el̓íplhk̲aẏ [k̲el̓ lí plh k̲aẏ] swamp gooseberry [younger growth-stage bush; see also **ilhten'áy'**]. *noun.*

k̲elk̲el̓ [k̲el k̲el'] spoil; waste, go to; go to waste. *verb(i).*

k̲elk̲él̓ [k̲el k̲él] spoiled; wrecked. *adjective.*

k̲elk̲el̓ílt [k̲el k̲el̓ lílt] spoil (something) [intentionally]. *verb(t).*

k̲el̓k̲el̓ílt [k̲el' k̲el̓ lílt] waste (something). *verb(t).*

k̲elk̲él̓nexw [k̲el k̲él̓ nexw] spoil (something); have spoiled (something). *verb(t).*

k̲él̓k̲eluṁ [k̲él̓ k̲e luṁ] eyes [sg: k̲lum']. *noun.*

k̲elk̲ímut [k̲el k̲í mut] clumsy. *adjective.*

k̲elh reinjure a wound. *verb(i).*

k̲elheẇálstn ~ k̲elhẇálstn [ke lheẇ wáls ten] mat-creaser [implement used in making mats]. *noun.*

k̲elhẇálstn ~ k̲elheẇálstn [k̲elh ẇál sten] mat-creaser [implement used in making mats]. *noun.*

k̲emáni [k̲e má ni] black turban [type of sea snail]. *noun.*

k̲ems packed together, be. *verb(i).*

k̲eṁsám [k̲eṁ sám] funeral. *noun.*

k̲emsán [k̲em sán] gather (things) together; pack (things) together. *verb(t).*

k̲emsántsut [k̲em sán tsut] pack one's belongings. *verb(i).*

k̲emsíṁ [k̲em síṁ] get one's stuff ready; tidy up. *verb(i).*

k̲éṁsnexw [k̲éṁs nexw] buried (something), have just; put away a corpse, just; finished packing (something), be; tidied (something) up, have. *verb(t).*

k̲en ~ k̲an ~ k̲'en ~ k̲'an I. *clitic.*

k̲énaxw [k̲é naxw] neck [front part of]; throat. *noun.*

k̲éṅk̲en ~ k̲éṅk̲eṅ [k̲éṅ k̲en] steal. *verb(i).* thief. *noun.*

k̲éṅk̲eṅ ~ k̲éṅk̲en [k̲éṅ k̲eṅ] steal. *verb(i).* thief. *noun.*

k̲eṅlhálem [k̲eṅ lhá lem] steal something to eat. *verb(i).*

k̲enp go down; set [about sun or moon]. *verb(i).*

k̲ensheẇáẏem [k̲en shew wáẏ yem] retrace one's family tree; retraced, be. *verb(i).*

k̲ep' ~ nk̲ep' ~ nek̲ép' close [on its own]; shut [on its own]. *verb(i).*

k̲ép'k̲p'us [k̲ép' k̲ p'us] looking down, be; lie facing down. *verb(i).*

k̲ep'tán [k̲ep' tán] door. *noun.*

k̲ep'tnáy [k̲ep' t náy] closet. *noun.*

k̲ep'úsem [k̲e p'ú sem] put one's head down; look down[ward]; direct one's glance downward. *verb(i).*

k̲es ~ k̲'es if s/he; when s/he. *clitic.*

k̲esnáṅ [k̲es náṅ] miss a shot at something. *verb(i).*

k̲esnáṅen [k̲es náṅ nen] miss (something) [opposite of hit]. *verb(t).*

k̲etlháytns [k̲et lháy tens] bow tie. *noun.*

k̲étx̲eṁ [k̲ét x̲eṁ] slip down; slip; slide. *verb(i).*

k̲étx̲eṁshen [k̲ét x̲eṁ shen] slip; slip [about foot]; lose one's footing. *verb(i).*

k̲etl' stopped, be. *verb(i).*

k̲etl'shnáṁ ~ k̲átl'shnaṁ [k̲etl' shnáṁ] stop walking; stop suddenly; brace one's footing [e.g., when slipping down a hill]. *verb(i).*

k̲exw gather; get together; gathered together, be. *verb(i).*

k̲éxwen [k̲é xwen] collect (something); gather (them) together; invite (people); pick (berries). *verb(t).*
k̲exwím̓ [k̲e xwím̓] collect them. *verb(i).*
k̲exwk̲exwntsút [k̲exw k̲e xwen tsút] gather together. *verb(i).*
k̲exwnew̓ásn [k̲exw new̓ wá sen] get (them) together; gather (them) together. *verb(t).*
k̲éxwnexw [k̲éxw nexw] gather (something). *verb(t).*
k̲exwní7kwup [k̲exw ní7 kwup] gather firewood. *verb(i).*
k̲exwntsút [k̲e xwen tsút] crowd together. *verb(i).*
k̲ex̲ many, be; much, be; plenty, be. *verb(i).*
k̲ex̲álh [k̲e x̲álh] many times; often. *verb(i).*
k̲ex̲álh tála [k̲e x̲álh tá la] lots of money. *adverb.*
k̲ex̲álhen [k̲e x̲á lhen] do something many times to (someone). *verb(t).*
k̲ex̲áxwilh [k̲e x̲á xwilh] many canoes. *verb(i).*
k̲éx̲em ~ k̲éx̲en [k̲é x̲em] snort [about deer]. *verb(i).*
k̲éx̲en ~ k̲éx̲em [k̲é x̲en] snort [about deer]. *verb(i).*
k̲éx̲k̲ex̲ [k̲éx̲ k̲ex̲] many people. *adverb.*
k̲ex̲mín̓tem [k̲ex̲ mín̓ tem] after (someone), be; pick on (someone) [about a group]. *verb(p).*
k̲ex̲s give (someone) lots. *verb(t).*
k̲ey bad. *adjective.*
k̲éyas [k̲éy yas] [term of derision]. *interjection.*
k̲ey̓át [k̲e y̓át] bad to (someone), be. *verb(t).*
k̲eyáy̓ak̲ap [k̲ey yáy̓ ya k̲ap] stink; taste bad. *verb(i).*
k̲ey̓ím̓ut [k̲ey̓ yí7 mut] ugly; ugly looking. *adjective.*
k̲éyi7 [k̲éy yi7] spoiled, be; become bad; bad, become; spoil. *verb(i).*
k̲eyí7inas [k̲ey yí 7i nas] disheartened, be. *verb(i).*
k̲éyk̲ey [k̲éy k̲ey] bad, be [about people]. *verb(i).*
k̲eyk̲eyáy̓ itut [k̲ey k̲ey yáy̓ 7i tut] bad dream; nightmare. *noun.*
k̲éy̓k̲eyts [k̲éy̓ k̲eyts] swearing, be. *verb(i).*
k̲eyk̲iyí7 [k̲ey k̲i yí7] unsettled, be very. *verb(i).*
k̲ey̓múts [k̲ey̓ múts] keep (someone) company. *verb(t).*
k̲éy̓nexw [k̲éy̓ nexw] scold (someone). *verb(t).*
k̲éyni [k̲éy ni] allergic to (something), be. *verb(t).*
k̲eys dislike (something/someone); hate (something/someone). *verb(t).*
k̲éystway [k̲éys tway] hate one another; dislike one another. *verb(i).*
k̲ey̓tsám̓ [k̲ey̓ tsám̓] curse. *verb(i).*
k̲eyúnexw [k̲ey yú nexw] rough, be [about water]; bad waves, be. *verb(i).*
k̲eyús [k̲ey yús] ugly. *adjective.*
k̲ey̓ús [k̲ey̓ yús] shady side of mountain. *noun.*
k̲éyuts ~ k̲éyutsk̲s [k̲éy yuts] blunt-edged; have a blunt edge; blunt. *adjective.*
k̲éy̓utsin [k̲éy̓ yu tsin] curse (someone). *verb(t).*
k̲éy̓utsin sníchim [k̲éy yu tsin sní chim] cursing words. *noun.*
k̲éy̓utsinem [k̲éy̓ yu tsi nem] put a spell on someone [about ritualist]; cursed, be. *verb(p).*
k̲éyutsk̲s ~ k̲éyuts [k̲éy yuts k̲s] blunt-edged; have a blunt edge; blunt. *adjective.*
k̲éywilh [k̲éy wilh] cranky. *adjective.*
k̲ikw [k̲ikw] cave in. *verb(i).*
k̲ik̲ix̲ítsut [k̲eh k̲eh x̲í tsut] sliding, be; skating along, be. *verb(i).*
k̲ík̲p'iy̓ek̲w [k̲éhk̲ p'i y̓ek̲w] small shelter [made, e.g., of branches]. *noun.*
k̲ík̲p'usem [k̲éhk̲ p'u sem] look down on/into the water [for fish to spear] while shading the eyes. *verb(i).*
k̲ik̲x̲ [k̲i k̲x̲] many animals. *adverb.*
k̲ik̲'t [k̲ik̲'t] repay (someone). *verb(t).*
k̲ík̲wes [k̲éh k̲wes] type of plant. *noun.*
k̲íl̓sew ka [k̲íl' sew kya] [person startled from an accident would use this phrase]. *interjection.*
k̲ílus [k̲éh lus] beautiful [as in scenery]. *adjective.*
k̲ilxwtn [k̲il xw tn] way of tying a dog. *noun.*
k̲ilh [k̲ilh] almost; very near; come close to. *adverb.*

ki̱ḿki̱ms [ki̱ḿ ki̱ms] keep (them) together for safekeeping. *verb(t).*
ki̱ḿki̱ḿxwáyeḵwshen [ki̱ḿ ki̱ḿ xwáy yeḵw shen] kneecap. *noun.*
-ki̱n ~ -ḵn [-ki̱n] throat {full word: x̱wúmlhnalh}; hair {full word: sḵw'úmaý}; language {full word: sníchim}; head [in borrowings]; top [in borrowings]. *suffix.*
ki̱ńki̱ńx̱ni [ki̱ń ki̱ń x̱ ni] shadow. *noun.*
kí̱p'intsut [kí̱ p'in tsut] tighten up, as in a cramp [about muscle]. *verb(i).*
ki̱tachí7n [ki̱ ta chí 7en] bandage (someone's) hand. *verb(t).*
kí̱teń [kí̱ teń] bring (something) up. *verb(t).*
kí̱tiń [kí̱ tiń] bandage (something). *verb(t).*
ki̱tḵw [ki̱tḵw] new dancer's headband [made of cedar bark]. *noun.*
ki̱tn [ki̱ tn] belt [woman's]. *noun.*
kí̱t-shen [kí̱t shen] rags around legs. *noun.*
ki̱t-shnáń [ki̱t shnáń] bandage (someone's) foot. *verb(t).*
kí̱t-shtn [kí̱tsh ten] band [of cloth]. *noun.*
kí̱tl'em [kí̱ tl'em] make a noise from big wind [about house]. *verb(i).*
kí̱tsem [kí̱ tsem] creak [e.g., door]; squeak [e.g., buggy, door, mouse]. *verb(i).*
ki̱wki̱ẃx̱ántsut [ki̱w ki̱ẃ x̱án tsut] turning itself into a steelhead at the head of the Squamish River, be [about salmon]. *verb(i).*
kí̱x̱iń [ḵéh x̱iń] make (something) smaller or even by chopping. *verb(t).*
kí̱x̱item [ḵéh x̱i tem] slip and fall; slip; slide. *verb(p).*
kí̱x̱itsut [ḵéh x̱i tsut] slide; slither; slip. *verb(i).*
ki̱x̱ḵántem [ki̱x̱ ḵán tem] slide on one's behind. *verb(p).*
ki̱x̱ḵántsut [ḵehx̱ ḵán tsut] slip [on purpose]. *verb(i).*
kí̱x̱shenaḿ [ḵéhx̱ she naḿ] slide one's feet; ice-skate. *verb(i).*
ki̱x̱shnáńtem [ḵehx̱ shnáń tem] slip; have one's foot slip. *verb(p).*
kí̱x̱wilh [ḵéh x̱wilh] chisel with an adze. *verb(i).*
kí̱x̱wus [ḵéh x̱wus] blind. *adjective.*
ki̱x̱wúsn [ḵeh x̱wú sen] wave (stick, weapon, etc.) at someone. *verb(t).*
ki̱ýát [ki̱ ýát] again; do again; another. *adverb.*
ki̱ýutsinem syewen [ki̱ ýu tsi nem sye wen] ritualist's spell on someone. *noun.*
ki̱7ḵaýús [ḵeý ḵaý yús] dark side of the mountain. *noun.*
ki̱7ḵétx̱em [ḵeh7 ḵét x̱em] slipping, be. *verb(i).*
kí̱7ḵi [ḵéh7 ḵey] soft [e.g., butter]. *adjective.*
ki̱7ḵi7í7 [ḵeh7 ḵeý 7í7] get soft; soft, get; become soft. *verb(i).*
ḵlim [ḵlim] weak [about a person]. *adjective.*
ḵlímeńtsut [ḵ lí meń tsut] make oneself weak. *verb(i).*
ḵlími7 [ḵ lí mi7] weak, get; become weak. *verb(i).*
ḵluḿ [ḵluḿ] eye. *noun.*
ḵlumstm [ḵlum stm] have one's eyes on it. *verb(p).*
-ḵn ~ -ki̱n [-ḵn] throat {full word: x̱wúmlhnalh}; hair {full word: sḵw'úmaý}; language {full word: sníchim}; head [in borrowings]; top [in borrowings]. *suffix.*
ḵneskw when he/she/they. *clitic.*
ḵp'alstn ~ ḵp'áýeḵwshen ~ ḵp'áýeḵwstn [ḵ p'ál sten] kneecap. *noun.*
ḵp'áýeḵwstn ~ ḵp'áýeḵwshen ~ ḵp'alstn [ḵ p'áý yeḵw sten] kneecap. *noun.*
ḵp'áýeḵwshen ~ ḵp'alstn ~ ḵp'áýeḵwstn [ḵ p'áý yeḵw shen] kneecap. *noun.*
ḵp'á7elch [ḵ p'á 7elch] cover; lid. *noun.*
ḵp'a7elchán [ḵ p'a 7el chán] put lid on (box). *verb(t).*
ḵp'et ~ nḵp'et ~ neḵp'ét [ḵ p'ét] close (something); shut (something). *verb(t).*
ḵp'i7ḵwm [ḵ p'i7 ḵwm] upset canoe/can/box; turn canoe/can/box over. *verb(i).*
-ḵs nose {full word: méḵsen}; point; promontory; small oblong object. *suffix.*
-ḵsaý elbow {full word: s7áýḵsaý}. *suffix.*
ḵtiḿ [ḵ tiḿ] fishing spot for a dip net. *noun.*
ḵtiń [ḵ tiń] pool in river [where the fish swim around]. *noun.*
ḵts'aḿ [ḵ ts'aḿ] stuck, get; won't flow [about water]. *verb(i).*
ḵxwus [ḵxwus] assembled, be; together, be [about people]. *verb(i).*

k̲xwúsem [k̲ xwú sem] gather people together; get together; assemble. *verb(i).*
k̲xwúsmin [k̲ xwús min] gang up on (someone). *verb(t).*

k̲x̲i7 [k̲ x̲i7] be getting more; more, be getting; become much; much, become; become many; many, become. *verb(i).*

K̲' k̲'

k̲'aa7 [k̲'aa7] caught, get; remain stuck [about something thrown, etc.]. *verb(i).*

k̲'ák̲'aw [k̲'á k̲'aw] skate [type of fish]. *noun.*

k̲'ák̲'axwi7 [k̲'á k̲'a xwi7] callous, gradually become. *verb(i).*

k̲'ák̲'ey̓k̲ [k̲'á k̲'ey̓k̲] sitting on something, be. *verb(i).*

k̲'ak̲'ts [k̲'a k̲'ts] hanging up, be. *verb(i).*

k̲'ák̲'tsan̓ [k̲'ák̲' tsan̓] hang (something) up [e.g., meat]. *verb(t).*

k̲'ák̲w'es [k̲'á k̲w'es] sudden, be; suddenly; going right behind, be. *verb(i).*

k̲'al̓ believe; obey; consent; agree. *verb(i).*

k̲'ál̓en [k̲'ál̓ 7en] believe (someone); believe in what (someone) says; obey (someone). *verb(t).*

k̲'ál̓ni [k̲'ál̓ ni] believe in (someone). *verb(t).*

k̲'áltxwiyu [k̲'ál txwi yu] hang on to. *verb(i).*

k̲'alh ~ k̲alh ever; never [only used in certain sentences with "haw," and "txwhaw"]. *clitic.*

k̲'an ~ k̲'en ~ k̲an ~ k̲en I. *clitic.*

k̲'ánatsut [k̲'á na tsut] return; return to it; come back. *verb(i).*

k̲'án̓atsutíwes [k̲'án̓ na tsu tí wes] oars used to row a boat. *noun.*

k̲'ánatsutnexw [k̲'á na tsut nexw] have got (something) back again; got (something) back again, have; be again in possession of (something); possession of (something), be again in. *verb(t).*

k̲'an̓átsutúsm [k̲'an̓ ná tsu tú sem] look behind. *verb(i).*

k̲'ánatsutshi [k̲'á na tsut sheyt] return it to (someone). *verb(t).*

k̲'ániwan [k̲'á ni wan] bring back a lost spirit; look for a sick person's spirit [as done by sxw7umten while performing a cure]; perform a spirit quest. *verb(i).*

k̲'ániwanen [k̲'á ni wa nen] look for (a sick person's lost spirit); perform a spirit quest for (a sick person's lost spirit). *verb(t).*

k̲'ank̲'án̓atsut [k̲'an k̲'án̓ na tsut] going backwards, be; backwards, be going; walk back and forth. *verb(i).*

k̲'ap' ~ k̲'ep' catch a disease; infected, get; seized, be; included, be. *verb(i).*

k̲'áp'achi7n [k̲'á p'a chi 7en] grab (someone's) hand; seize (someone's) hand [especially with mouth or beak]. *verb(t).*

k̲'ap'achí7ntm [k̲'a p'a chí 7en tem] caught by the hand, be. *verb(p).*

k̲'áp'an [k̲'á p'an] give (someone) a disease; infect (someone). *verb(t).*

k̲'áp'nem [k̲'áp' nem] have been included; included, have been. *verb(t).*

k̲'áp'new̓ásn [k̲'áp' new̓ wa sen] tie (them) together [e.g., the ends of two ropes]. *verb(t).*

k̲'áp'nexw [k̲'áp' nexw] catch (a disease). *verb(t).*

k̲'áp'tsam̓ [k̲áp' tsam̓] put hand over mouth. *verb(i).*

k̲'ásat [k̲'á sat] ask for (something). *verb(t).*

k̲'át'am [k̲'á t'am] sweet. *adjective.*

k̲'atl'n [k̲'a tl'n] wash away (ground) [as done by a swollen river]. *verb(t).*

k̲'atl'n [k̲'a tl'n] stop (someone who is moving). *verb(t).*

k̲'áts'chan̓ [k̲'áts' chan̓] put arms around (someone); hold one's arms around (someone's) body. *verb(t).*

k̲'ats'íchn ~ nk̲'ats'íchn [k̲'a ts'í chen] hold one's arms on the back. *verb(i).*

k̲'áts'usen [k̲'á ts'u sen] hug (someone); hold one's arms around (someone's) head or neck; put arms around (someone's) head or neck. *verb(t).*

k̲'aw get paid; paid, get; pay. *verb(i).*

k̲'áwalhen [k̲'á wa lhen] paid, be; punished, be; atone; expiate; do penance; penance, do. *verb(i).*

k̲'áwalhens [k̲'á wa lhens] punish (someone). *verb(t).*

k̲'áwat [k̲'á wat] pay (someone); pay (someone) for a cure. *verb(t).*

k̲'aw̓íchshen ~ sk̲'aw̓íchshen [k̲'aw̓ wích shen] dorsal fin. *noun.*

k̲'aẇítshen [k̲'aẇ wít shen] fish fin. *noun.*
k̲'awnálhen [k̲'aw ná lhen] get paid; paid, get. *verb(i).*
k̲'awnúmut [k̲'aw nú mut] finally get paid; paid, finally get. *verb(i).*
k̲'axw hard; hardened; callous. *adjective.*
k̲'axw if you; when you; you. *clitic.*
k̲'áxwi7 [k̲'á xwi7] hard, become [about bread or food]; callous, become. *verb(i).*
k̲'áx̲aṅtsut [k̲'á x̲aṅ tsut] sway back and forth; go backwards; backwards, go; bend over backwards. *verb(i).*
k̲'ay high up, be; top, be on. *verb(i).*
k̲'aẏáṁin [k̲'aẏ yá7 min] clam shell; clam shells. *noun.*
k̲'áyaṅ [k̲'áy yaṅ] put (something) on top. *verb(t).*
k̲'áyaṅtsut [k̲'áy yan tsut] mount an animal; ride (a horse, etc.). *verb(i).*
k̲'áẏem [k̲'áẏ yem] make a lot of noise. *verb(i).*
k̲'ayéṅten [k̲'ay yéṅ ten] stick used to raise fish up to the drying racks. *noun.*
k̲'aẏk̲ chair. *noun.*
k̲'aẏk̲áṁ [k̲'aẏ k̲áṁ] sit [on a chair]; sit down [on any raised surface]. *verb(i).*
k̲'áẏmin [k̲'áẏ min] campsite. *noun.*
k̲'aynewásen [k̲'ay neẇ wá sen] pile (something) up. *verb(t).*
k̲'ayt shout; holler. *verb(i).*
k̲'áyten [k̲'áy ten] call (someone). *verb(t).*
k̲'áyx̲ak̲' [k̲'áy x̲ak̲'] little shelter. *noun.*
k̲'á7a [k̲'á 7a] get hung up; hung up, get. *verb(i).*
k̲'á7maẏ [k̲'á7 maẏ] maiden; young woman; lady. *noun.*
k̲'á7maẏaẏlh [k̲'á7 maẏ 7aẏ lh] maiden daughter. *noun.*
k̲'chétem [k̲' ché tem] suck blood; fill up [about mosquitoes]. *verb(p).*
k̲'ech' fill out [as in body]. *verb(i).*
k̲'ek̲'iẏás [k̲'e k̲'i ẏás] barrel. *noun.*
k̲'ék̲'p'nach [k̲'ék̲' p' nach] tow. *verb(i).*
k̲'ek̲'síṅ [k̲'ek̲' síṅ] entire, be. *verb(i).*
k̲'ek̲'síṅ ti siyát-shen [k̲'ek̲' síṅ ti si yát shen] world. *noun.*
k̲'ek̲'tús [k̲'ek̲' tús] pass in front of it; pass by. *verb(i).*
k̲'ek̲'túsn [k̲'ek̲' tú sen] go around the front side of (something). *verb(t).*
k̲'ek̲'x̲átaẏ [k̲'ek̲' x̲á taẏ] argue; debate. *verb(i).*
k̲'ek̲'x̲átaẏní [k̲'ek̲' x̲á taẏ ní] argue about (something). *verb(t).*
k̲'ék̲'x̲el [k̲'ék̲' x̲el] tin can. *noun.*
k̲'eláak̲'a ~ k̲'elák̲'ela [k̲'e láa k̲'a] crow. *noun.*
k̲'elák̲'ela ~ k̲'eláak̲'a [k̲'e lá k̲'e la] crow. *noun.*
k̲'elch'án [k̲'el ch'án] put (someone) in seclusion. *verb(t).*
k̲'élch'tn [k̲'él ch' ten] baby's tent [a new dancer's tent]. *noun.*
k̲'elk̲' wound around, be. *verb(i).*
k̲'elk̲'án [k̲'el k̲'án] coil (something); wind (something) around. *verb(t).*
k̲'élk̲'elk̲' [k̲'él k̲'elk̲'] get tangled up around it; tangled up around it, get. *verb(i).*
k̲'élk̲'elp' [k̲'él k̲'elp'] tangled [about string, hair, etc.]. *adjective.*
k̲'elk̲'elp'í7k̲in [k̲'el k̲'el p'í7 k̲in] curly hair, have. *verb(i).*
k̲'elk̲w'úẏsen [k̲'el k̲w'úẏ sen] coil (something) up; wind (string) into a ball. *verb(t).*
k̲'elp'án [k̲'el p'án] curl (something). *verb(t).*
k̲'elp'ántsut [k̲'el p'án tsut]
1. curling up, be.
2. curling one's own hair, be. *verb(i).*
k̲'elp'íṁ [k̲'el p'íṁ] curl. *verb(i).*
k̲'elx̲áyus [k̲'el x̲áy yus] pupil of the eye. *noun.*
k̲'élya [k̲'él ya] sweathouse; steambath. *noun.* take a steambath. *verb(i).*
k̲'elhmáẏ [k̲'elh máẏ] yellow cedar tree. *noun.*
k̲'émasaynup [k̲'é ma say nup] leave space. *verb(i).*
k̲'eṁásaẏnúpem [k̲'eṁ má saẏ nú pem] make room. *verb(i).*
k̲'emásaynúpen [k̲'e má say nú pen] make room for (something). *verb(t).*
k̲'emel̇áẏ [k̲'e mel̓ láẏ] maple tree. *noun.*
k̲'émen [k̲'é men] swallow (something). *verb(t).*
k̲'emíṅem [k̲'e mí7 nem] Halkomeylem language [see also **Sk̲'emín'em**]. *noun.* speak the Halkomeylem language. *verb(i).*
k̲'emk̲'ámay [k̲'em k̲'á may] threaten [someone who is present]. *verb(i).*

k̲'emk̲'ámt [k̲'em k̲'ámt] threaten (someone who is present). *verb(t).*

k̲'émk̲'emay [k̲'ém k̲'e may] maidens; young women; young ladies [sg: **q'á7may'**]. *noun.*

k̲'émnexw [k̲'ém nexw] swallow (something). *verb(t).*

k̲'emts'áṅ [k̲'em ts'áṅ] catch (something) with purse-seine or drag-seine. *verb(t).*

k̲'emts'íṁ [k̲'em ts'íṁ] catch with purse-seine or drag-seine. *verb(i).*

k̲'en ~ k̲'an ~ k̲an ~ k̲en I. *clitic.*

k̲'énexw ~ k̲'énnexw [k̲'é nexw] return (something); get (something) back; be again in possession of (something); possession of (something), be again in. *verb(t).*

k̲'énnexw ~ k̲'énexw [k̲'én nexw] return (something); get (something) back; be again in possession of (something); possession of (something), be again in. *verb(t).*

k̲'enp'án [k̲'en p'án] coil (something) up. *verb(t).*

k̲'ensheWáẏem [k̲'en she wáẏ yem] retrace one's steps. *verb(i).*

k̲'epkwtsáṁ [k̲'ep kw tsáṁ] have one's teeth chattering; chattering, be [about teeth]. *verb(i).*

k̲'ep' ~ k̲'ap' seized, be; catch a disease; infected, get; included, be. *verb(i).*

k̲'es ~ k̲es if s/he; when s/he. *clitic.*

k̲'esápsem [k̲'e sáp sem] tired neck, get a; tired neck, have a. *adjective.*

k̲'esíws [k̲'e síws] tired of waiting, be; get tired waiting; impatient, get. *verb(i).*

k̲'ésshen [k̲'és shen] tired feet, have; get tired feet. *verb(i).*

k̲'etcháṅ [k̲'et cháṅ] go behind (something); behind (something), go; go around back of (something); around back of (something), go. *verb(t).*

k̲'etiẏek̲wáṅ [k̲'e teẏ ye k̲wáṅ] go around the head of (something); around the head of (something), go. *verb(t).*

k̲'etk̲sán [k̲'et k̲ sán] go around the point of (something); around the point of (something), go. *verb(t).*

k̲'et-shnáṅ [k̲'et shnáṅ] go around the feet of (someone lying down); around the feet of (someone lying down), go. *verb(t).*

k̲'etx̲án [k̲'et x̲án] make a rattling noise; rap; make a clattering noise. *verb(i).*

k̲'etx̲ántsut [k̲'et x̲án tsut] rattling, be; fast noise, be a. *verb(i).*

k̲'etx̲iẏúlhn [k̲'et x̲eẏ yú lhen] rap (a dish). *verb(t).*

k̲'etl'kw [k̲'e tl'kw] misfire. *verb(i).*

k̲'ets blocked. *adjective.*

k̲'ets' get more than one in one shot from gun. *verb(i).*

k̲'ets'iwá7sentem [k̲'e ts'i wá7 sen tem] prevent one from using (something). *verb(p).*

k̲'ets'k̲'áts'chesténaṁut [k̲'ets' k̲'áts' ches tén naṁ mut] cross one's arms over one's chest; hug oneself. *verb(i).*

k̲'ets'k̲'áts'chs [k̲'ets' k̲'áts' chs] holding (someone) around the waist, be. *verb(t).*

k̲'éts'shen [k̲'éts' shen] have two legs together; two legs together, have. *verb(i).*

k̲'eẇáchi7m [k̲'eẇ wá chi 7em] pull in one's hand. *verb(i).*

k̲'ewát [k̲'e wát] stick for keeping time; drumstick. *noun.*

k̲'ewátem [k̲'ew wá tem] keep time with sticks; drum on boards with stick. *verb(i).*

k̲'eẇát-shen [k̲'eẇ wát shen] stick for hanging meat on to smoke. *noun.*

k̲'ewm shriek; howl; whistle [about animal, steamboat, etc.]. *verb(i).*

k̲'ewms honk (a horn). *verb(t).*

k̲'eẇneẇás ~ k̲w'u7neẇás ~ k̲w'ú7neẇas [k̲'eẇ neẇ wás] together, be; meet accidentally. *verb(i).*

k̲'éẇneẇasn ~ k̲w'ú7neẇasn [k̲'éẇ neẇ wa sen] put (them) together; gather (them) together; assemble (them); join (them). *verb(t).*

k̲'eẇshnám [k̲'eẇ shnám] pull in one's leg. *verb(i).*

k̲'eẇúsem [k̲'eẇ wú sem] pull face back; pull in one's head. *verb(i).*

k̲'exwk̲'áxwi7 [k̲'exw k̲'á xwi7] hard and stale, get; callous, become very. *verb(i).*

k̲'exwú7lh [k̲'e xwú7 lh] West Coast-style canoe; Chinook canoe. *noun.*

ḵ'ex̱ḵ'áx̱entsut [ḵ'ex̱ ḵ'á x̱en tsut] rock back and forth. *verb(i).*

ḵ'ex̱ḵ'íx̱ [ḵ'ex̱ ḵ'íx̱] black. *adjective.*

ḵ'ex̱ḵ'íx̱ines sts'eḵw'í7ḵes [ḵ'ex̱ ḵ'í x̱i nes sts'e ḵw'í7 ḵes] black-chested woodpecker. *noun.*

ḵ'éx̱min [ḵ'éx̱ min] Indian consumption plant [seed used in fire to purify air]. *noun.*

ḵ'ey̓áw̓txw [ḵ'ey̓ 7áw̓ txw] smokehouse. *noun.*

ḵ'eym camp; stay overnight. *verb(i).*

ḵ'ey̓shn [ḵ'ey̓ shn] small bullrush mat. *noun.*

ḵ'eyt daylight, be. *verb(i).*

ḵ'eytl' heal; healed up, be. *verb(i).*

ḵ'eytl'án̓ [ḵ'ey tl'án̓] heal (a wound) [about medicine]. *verb(t).*

ḵ'eytl'ánay̓ ~ ḵ'éytl'tanay̓ [ḵ'ey tl'á nay̓] medicinal plant [general term]. *noun.*

ḵ'éytl'tanay̓ ~ ḵ'eytl'tánay̓ [ḵ'éytl' ta nay̓] medicinal plant [general term]. *noun.*

ḵ'e7ílmi7 [ḵ'e 7éhl mi7] old, get; aged, be; old, be very. *verb(i).*

ḵ'íḵ'ix̱i7 [ḵ'éh ḵ'eh x̱ey̓] black, be getting. *verb(i).*

ḵ'íḵ'p'ikw [ḵ'éhḵ' p'ikw] temporary shelter. *noun.*

ḵ'is [ḵ'is] tied, be; knotted, be. *verb(i).*

ḵ'ísayípstn [ḵ'í sa yíps ten] button. *noun.*

ḵ'isayípstn hem̓tn [ḵ'i say yíp sten hém̓ ten] button blanket. *noun.*

ḵ'ísin̓ ~ nk'ísin [ḵ'í sin̓] tie (something) up; know (something) together. *verb(t).*

ḵ'ísin̓tsut [ḵ'í sin̓ tsut] tie up. *verb(i).*

ḵ'ísnumut [ḵ'ís nu mut] all in, be finally [e.g., after a hunting expedition]. *verb(i).*

ḵ'iswílhn [ḵ'is wí lhen] tie (something) around the middle. *verb(t).*

ḵ'íswilhtn [ḵ'ís wilh ten] mooring line. *noun.*

ḵ'it [ḵ'it] morning, be; early daylight, be [later than **natlh**]. *verb(i).*

ḵ'itl' [ḵ'itl'] speak about some very strong person. *verb(i).*

ḵ'itl'án̓ [ḵ'i tl'án̓] chew [especially grass; about animal]. *verb(t).*

ḵ'ítl'usen [ḵ'í tl'u sen] oppose (someone). *verb(t).*

ḵ'íts'iy̓eḵw [ḵ'í ts'ey̓ yeḵw] gabled roof. *noun.*

ḵ'íw̓it [ḵ'í7 wit] put (something) over the top; put (something) around something. *verb(t).*

ḵ'íw̓itsut [ḵ'í7 wi tsut] turn around a bend. *verb(i).*

ḵ'íw̓its'a [ḵ'í7 wi ts'a] string up wool on the loom. *verb(i).* sticks on which the wool is strung up. *noun.*

ḵ'iwḵs [ḵ'iwḵs] get to the end of a trip; end of a trip, get to the; go around the bend; around the bend, go. *verb(i).* length in a canoe race. *noun.*

ḵ'íw̓nem [ḵ'íw̓ nem] enveloped in (something), get; caught in (something), get [e.g., bad weather]. *verb(p).*

ḵ'ixwúsm [ḵ'i xwú sem] go against [wind or current]. *verb(i).*

ḵ'ix̱ [ḵ'ix̱] black. *adjective.*

ḵ'íx̱i7 [ḵ'éh x̱ey̓] black, get. *verb(i).*

ḵ'iyát [ḵ'i yát] consider (someone) to not be worthy; consider (someone) too small or weak. *verb(t).*

ḵ'iyátl'an [ḵ'i yá tl'an] snail. *noun.*

ḵ'iyáx̱ [ḵ'ey yáx̱] guts; intestines. *noun.*

ḵ'iyáx̱an [ḵ'ey yá x̱an] stockade; fortification; fort; fence. *noun.*

ḵ'iyáx̱atkwu7m [ḵ'ey yá x̱at kwu 7m] eddy; whirl [about water in a whirlpool]. *verb(i).*

ḵ'iyáx̱en [ḵ'ey yá x̱en] fence. *noun.*

ḵ'iyáx̱enen [ḵ'ey yá x̱e nen] fence (something) in. *verb(t).*

ḵ'iyí7ch [ḵ'ey yí7 ch] elk; moose. *noun.*

ḵ'í7chintem [ḵ'í7 chin tem] hang up [e.g., hooves on "stick" for protection]. *verb(p).*

ḵ'i7chtn [ḵ'í7 ch ten] wool braided for protection at wrist, below knees, and at ankles. *noun.*

ḵ'i7t [ḵ'i7t] late morning, be. *verb(i).*

ḵ'í7x̱em [ḵ'í7 x̱em] leave food behind; preserve it; leave some for a future occasion. *verb(i).*

ḵ'í7x̱iya [ḵ'éh7 x̱ey ya] black person. *noun.*

ḵ'lháy̓aḵap [ḵ' lháy̓ ya ḵap] strong odour, be a. *verb(i).*

ḵ'p'ax̱w ~ ts'ichn [ḵ' p'axw] hazelnut; nut [general term]. *noun.*

ḵ'tusn [ḵ' tu sn] go around the front side of (something). *verb(t).*

k̲'tsam̓ [k̲' tsám̓] faint; fall short [about stone thrown]. *verb(i).*

k̲'tsám̓achi7n [k̲' tsám̓ ma chi 7en] put (something) out of reach. *verb(t).*

k̲'ts'ap [k̲' ts'ap] tie up hair in back. *verb(i).*

k̲'ts'íchen [k̲' ts'í chen] walk with hands behind back. *verb(i).*

Ḵw ḵw

-ḵw ~ -eḵw top; head {full word: **sme7ús**}. *suffix.*

ḵwaa [**ḵwaa**] perforated, be; have a hole through it; hole through it, have a. *verb(i).*

ḵwaach [**ḵwaach**] shot through the back, be. *verb(i).*

ḵwaaḵ [**ḵwaaḵ**] have hole in the bottom of a canoe or pot; hole in the bottom of a canoe or pot, have a; holed, be. *verb(i).*

ḵwaan ~ ḵwan [**ḵwaan**] make a hole in (something); pierce (something); perforate (something). *verb(t).*

ḵwaat [**ḵwaat**] save (someone). *verb(t).*

ḵwachán̓ [**ḵwa chán̓**] make a hole in back of (something). *verb(t).*

ḵwach't burp; belch. *verb(i).*

ḵwach'ts make (someone) burp. *verb(t).*

ḵwaháya7ni7n [**ḵwa háy ya7 ni 7en**] pierce (someone's) ear. *verb(t).*

ḵwaḵán [**ḵwa ḵán**] put a hole in the bottom of (something). *verb(t).*

ḵwáḵsán [**ḵwáḵ sán**] pierce (someone's) nose; perforate (someone's) nose. *verb(t).*

ḵwaḵ'p cod lure. *noun.*

ḵwálhshen [**ḵwálh shen**] clear up [about the weather]; stop raining. *verb(i).*

ḵwan ~ ḵwaan perforate (something); make a hole in (something); pierce (something). *verb(t).*

ḵwánexw [**ḵwá nexw**] have made a hole in (something); made a hole in (something), have; make a hole in (something) accidentally; perforated (something), have; perforate (something) accidentally. *verb(t).*

ḵwanúmut [**ḵwa nú mut**] have saved onself; save oneself; have escaped; escape. *verb(i).*

ḵwat save (someone); rescue (someone). *verb(t).*

ḵwáts'ayúsem [**ḵwá ts'a yú sem**] try to recognize. *verb(i).*

ḵwáx̱nis [**ḵwáx̱ nis**] chum salmon; dog salmon. *noun.*

ḵwáyalhkwup [**ḵwáy yalh kwup**] embers [see also **ḵáyalhkwup** and **ḵweḵwúlh**]. *noun.*

ḵwayax̱wsténam̓ut [**ḵwa yax̱ws tén nam̓ mut**] ask for a job. *verb(i).*

ḵwáyexw [**ḵwáy yexw**] hire someone. *verb(i).*

ḵwáyexwn [**ḵwáy ye xwen**] hire (someone). *verb(t).*

ḵwayḵs seagull [when it is mature and has a large and yellowish-orange coloured beak]. *noun.*

-ḵwáy̓new̓as [**-ḵwáy̓ ne w̓as**] stomach {full word: **kw'el̓**}. *suffix.*

ḵwáy̓tsay [**ḵwáy̓ tsay**] hemlock tree. *noun.*

ḵwáy̓tsayachxw [**ḵwáy̓ tsa ya chxw**] hemlock bough; hemlock boughs. *noun.*

ḵwa7álhḵwu [**ḵwa 7álh ḵwu**] broth. *noun.*

ḵwchet vomit (something) up; spit (blood). *verb(t).*

ḵwchim̓ [**ḵw chim̓**] hemmorage; spit blood; vomit. *verb(i).*

ḵwéḵcheḵ [**ḵwéḵ cheḵ**] surprised, be. *verb(i).*

ḵweḵí7 [**ḵwe ḵéy̓**] blaze. *verb(i).*

ḵweḵ' ~ kweḵ' ~ ḵw'eḵ' surprised, be; look with surprise. *verb(i).*

ḵwéḵ'tan [**ḵwéḵ' tan**] shoulder. *noun.*

ḵweḵwel-háy̓ [**ḵwe ḵwel háy̓**] young second-growth Douglas fir tree. *noun.*

ḵwéḵwelhḵem [**ḵwé ḵwelh ḵem**] making a sharp noise continually, be; knocking repeatedly, be; rapping on something repeatedly, be; making a thumping noise, be. *verb(i).*

ḵwéḵwem̓em ~ kwékwem̓em [**ḵwé ḵwem̓ mem**] making a thumping noise, be; thumping, be always; heavy feet, have [about person walking]; stomping, be; walking heavily, be; thump continuously. *verb(i).*

ḵweḵwtḵ [**ḵweḵw tḵ**] passing by, be; going by, be [in space or time]. *verb(i).*

ḵweḵwtḵán̓ [**ḵweḵwt ḵán̓**] passing by (something/someone), be; going by (something/someone), be. *verb(t).*

k̲wek̲wtúniy̓ik̲w [k̲wek̲w tú ni y̓ehk̲w] soft spot on baby's head. *noun.*

k̲wek̲wúlh [k̲we k̲wúlh] embers [see also k̲wáyalhkwup]. *noun.*

k̲weláwa [k̲we lá wa] nodding onion. *noun.*

k̲welk̲wálwen [k̲wel k̲wál wen] think; decide; plan; make up one's mind. *verb(i).*

k̲wélk̲wel [k̲wél k̲wel] talkative, be; talk excessively; talk too much. *verb(i).*

k̲wélulusni [k̲wél lu lus ni] miss (someone). *verb(t).*

k̲welh drift ashore. *verb(i).*

k̲wélhi7n [k̲wé lhi 7en] western birch tree. *noun.*

k̲wélhk̲i7n [k̲wélh k̲i 7en] make a sharp noise; rap on something; knock. *verb(i).*

k̲welhk̲m [k̲welh k̲m] make a thumping noise; thumping noise, make a; sharp noise, make a; rap; knock. *verb(i).*

k̲welhk̲tsím̓ [k̲welh k̲ ts'ím̓] knock on the door. *verb(i).*

k̲welhk̲wlháy̓ [k̲welh k̲w lháy̓] lots of driftwood; mass of driftwood [sg: k̲wlháy̓]. *noun.*

k̲wem̓ch burst [as of a balloon]; pout. *verb(i).*

k̲wem̓chán [k̲wem̓ chán] crush (something); crack (something); burst (something) [by two-sided pressure; e.g., nits]. *verb(t).*

k̲wemchúl̓s [k̲wem chúl's] bog cranberry. *noun.*

k̲wemchúl̓say̓ [k̲wem chúl' say̓] bog cranberry bush. *noun.*

k̲wem̓xw knuckle. *noun.*

k̲wém̓x̲wshen [k̲wém̓x̲w shen] ankle. *noun.*

k̲wenálhp [k̲we nálhp] Indian hellebore [type of plant]. *noun.*

k̲wen̓ímach [k̲wen̓ ní mach] mosquito; mosquitoes. *noun.*

k̲wenís [k̲we nís] whale. *noun.*

k̲wenísen [k̲we ní sen] turn (someone) into a whale. *verb(t).*

k̲wéni7k̲wshen [k̲wé neh7 k̲w shen] knee. *noun.*

k̲wepk̲wúpus [k̲wep k̲wú pus] dog [type of long-haired dog with wool hanging over its eyes]. *noun.*

k̲wetk̲ pass by; go by [referring to either a place or time]. *verb(i).*

k̲wetk̲ tpanu [k̲wetk̲ t pa nu] last year. *adverb.*

k̲wetk̲án [k̲wet k̲án] pass by (something). *verb(t).*

k̲wetk̲pli [k̲wet k̲ pli] past; gone by. *verb(i).*

k̲wetk̲wétshem [k̲wet k̲wét shem] foggy, be. *verb(i).*

k̲wexwk̲wexwmín ~ kwexwkwúxwmin [k̲wexw k̲wexw mín] deer hooves. *noun.*

k̲wéx̲k̲en [k̲wéx̲ k̲en] have hoarse voice [about person]. *verb(i).*

k̲wéx̲k̲eni7 [k̲wéx̲ k̲e ney̓] hoarse from singing, be. *verb(i).*

k̲wex̲nís [k̲wex̲ nís] sea lion. *noun.*

k̲wex̲tsám̓ [k̲wex̲ tsám̓] throw one's voice. *verb(i).*

k̲wéx̲tsut [k̲wéx̲ tsut] struggle before dying. *verb(i).*

k̲wex̲wk̲wúx̲w [k̲wex̲w k̲wúx̲w] blond. *adjective.*

k̲wey low tide, be [furthest out]. *verb(i).*

k̲wey̓ way out, be [about sea]; be at lowest ebb; ebb, be at lowest [about tide]. *verb(i).*

k̲wey̓k̲w ~ k̲weyk̲w crooked. *adjective.*

k̲wéy̓k̲way ~ k̲wéy̓k̲wey [k̲wéy̓ k̲way] discuss; talk. *verb(i).*

k̲wéy̓k̲ways ~ k̲wéy̓k̲weys [k̲wéy̓ k̲ways] talk to (someone); discuss with (someone). *verb(t).*

k̲wéy̓k̲waystway [k̲wéy̓ k̲ways tway] talk to each other. *verb(i).*

k̲wéy̓k̲wey ~ k̲wéy̓k̲way [k̲wéy̓ k̲wey] discuss; talk. *verb(i).*

k̲wéy̓k̲weys ~ k̲wéy̓k̲ways [k̲wéy̓ k̲weys] discuss with (someone); talk to (someone). *verb(t).*

k̲wey̓k̲weysténam̓ut [k̲wey̓ k̲weys tén nam̓ mut] talk to oneself. *verb(i).*

k̲wéyk̲weytem [k̲wéy k̲wey tem] chop up the ground; till the ground. *verb(i).*

k̲weyk̲w' ~ k̲wey̓k̲w crooked. *adjective.*

k̲wey̓k̲w'tsám̓ [k̲wey̓ k̲w' tsám̓] twist one's mouth; pull one's jaw sideways. *verb(i).*

k̲wey̓s cook by boiling. *verb(i).*

k̲wey̓sán [k̲wey̓ sán] boil (something); boil (food). *verb(t).*

k̲we7úp ~ k̲wu7úp [k̲we 7úp] wild crabapple. *noun.*

k̲we7úpaỷ ~ k̲wu7úpaỷ [k̲we 7ú paỷ] wild crabapple tree. *noun.*
k̲wík̲x̲en [k̲wéhk̲ x̲en] cured hide. *noun.*
k̲wík̲wi [k̲wéh k̲wey] copper. *noun.*
k̲wík̲wi slemchís [k̲wéh k̲wey slem chís] copper ring. *noun.*
k̲wík̲witam [k̲wéh k̲wey tam] exactly full, be; filled to the brim, be. *verb(i).*
k̲wík̲witem [k̲wéh k̲wey tem] overflowing, be. *verb(i).*
k̲wík̲witsawilhtn [k̲wéh k̲wey tsa wilh ten] skids for launching a canoe. *noun.*
k̲wík̲wmes [k̲wéhk̲w mes] hair hat [used by Cowichan dancers; not originally used by Squamish]. *noun.*
k̲wílayus [k̲wéh lay yus] red flowering currant; rain flower. *noun.*
k̲wílayusaỷ [k̲wéh lay yu saỷ] red flowering currant bush; rain flower bush. *noun.*
k̲wílhus [k̲wí lhus] wedge; yew wooden wedge. *noun.*
k̲wíninas [k̲wí ni nas] hairy chest, have a. *adjective.*
k̲wíniyatsen [k̲wí ni ya tsen] Pacific tomcod [also called whitefish]. *noun.*
k̲wíṅi7 [k̲wíṅ ni7] hairy, become. *verb(i).*
k̲wiyám [k̲wi yám] fallen needles on ground, an old word for "moss"; leaves that have already fallen; dead leaves and needles [of evergreen trees]. *noun.*
k̲wí7nexw [k̲wí7 nexw] doubt (someone). *verb(t).*
k̲wlhaỷ [k̲w lhaỷ] driftwood; log. *noun.*
k̲wlhi7 [k̲w lheỷ] land ashore. *verb(i).*
k̲wlhi7shn [k̲w lhéỷ shen] shoe; shoes. *noun.*
k̲wlhi7shnáṁ [k̲w lheỷ shnáṁ] put one's shoes on. *verb(i).*
k̲wpíchen [k̲w pí chen] sand. *noun.*
k̲wtáytsn [k̲w táy tsen] sturgeon. *noun.*
k̲wts'i7n [k̲w ts'í 7en] flash. *verb(i).*
k̲wuch's [k̲wuch's] person who drinks a lot of water. *noun.*
k̲wúk̲wul̓tstn [k̲wú k̲wu̓lts ten] dipper for water. *noun.*
k̲wúk̲wusem [k̲wú k̲wu sem] porcupine. *noun.*
k̲wul [k̲wul] come in [about water]. *verb(i).*
k̲wulachí7m [k̲wul la chí 7em] scoop up water with one's hands. *verb(i).*
k̲wúlaỷus [k̲wúl laỷ yus] high tide, be. *verb(i).*
k̲wulíṁ [k̲wul líṁ] get some water; water, get some. *verb(i).*
k̲wúl̓iṁ [k̲wú̓l liṁ] dip water. *verb(i).*
k̲wul̓k̲ [k̲wul'k̲] come in stern of canoe [about water]. *verb(i).*
k̲wúlshi [k̲wúl sheyt] get water for (someone); water for (someone), get. *verb(t).*
k̲wult [k̲wult] dip (water) out. *verb(t).*
k̲wúlhuṅtsut [k̲wú lhuṅ tsut] be swimming closely together near the shore while going to the spawning grounds [about group of fish]. *verb(i).*
k̲wúmaỷt [k̲wú maỷt] relative. *noun.*
k̲wúmun [k̲wú mun] bend around (something); bend (something). *verb(t).*
k̲wúmutsut [k̲wú mu tsut] bent, get. *verb(i).*
k̲wúscheṁ [k̲wús cheṁ] hump one's back. *verb(i).*
k̲wúsi [k̲wú si] bend over; stoop over. *verb(i).*
k̲wúsuṅtem [k̲wú suṅ tem] stooped over from age, be [about person]. *verb(p).*
k̲wútusem [k̲wú tu sem] pull long face in anger; change expression in anger. *verb(i).*
k̲wuwí7ach [k̲wu wí 7ach] callous. *adjective.*
k̲wuxwk̲wuxwyá7k̲em ~ k̲wuxwk̲wuxwyé7k̲em [k̲wuxw k̲wuxw yá7 k̲em] slide down. *verb(i).*
k̲wuxwk̲wuxwyé7k̲em ~ k̲wuxwk̲wuxwyá7k̲em [k̲wuxw k̲wuxw yé7 k̲em] slide down. *verb(i).*
k̲wúxwmin ~ kwúxwmin [k̲wúxw min] deer hoof. *noun.*
k̲wúx̲wi [k̲wú x̲wey] blond, become. *verb(i).*
k̲wuy [k̲wuy] snagged, be; hooked up, get; catch upon a snag. *verb(i).*
-k̲wuỷach [-k̲wu ỷach] finger {full word: nix̲k̲wúỷach}. *suffix.*
-k̲wuỷshen [-k̲wuỷ shen] toe {full word: nix̲k̲wúỷshen}. *suffix.*
k̲wu7úp ~ k̲we7úp [k̲wu 7úp] crabapple. *noun.*
k̲wu7úpaỷ ~ k̲we7úpaỷ [k̲wu 7ú paỷ] crabapple tree. *noun.*
k̲wú7us ~ snk̲wú7us ~ nk̲wú7us [k̲wú 7us] tear; tears. *noun.*

Ḵw’ ḵw’

ḵw’áḵ’am [ḵw’á ḵ’am] bellow [about sea-lions, etc.]. *verb(i).*

ḵw’aḵwemén ~ ḵw’ḵwémn [ḵw’a ḵwe mén] axe [see also t’ḵwémen]. *noun.*

ḵw’áḵw’ats’ [ḵw’á ḵw’ats’] rising, be; coming in, be [about tide]. *verb(i).*

ḵw’áḵw’aẏ [ḵw’á ḵw’aẏ] tame, very; friendly. *adjective.*

ḵw’áḵw’aẏáx̲ [ḵw’á ḵw’aẏ yáx̲] excuse [me]. *verb(i).*

ḵw’aḵw’aẏáx̲ ka [ḵw’a ḵw’aẏ yáx̲ ka] Be cautious going past!; Excuse me. [said when trying to get past someone]. *sentence.*

ḵw’áḵw’i [ḵw’á ḵw’ey] tame [about animal]. *adjective.*

ḵw’áḵw’iyán [ḵw’á ḵw’ey yán] make (something) tame. *verb(t).*

ḵw’áḵw’iẏeḵ’ [ḵw’á ḵw’eẏ yeḵ’] turned opposite, be; opposite, be turned. *verb(i).*

ḵw’alh gunpowder [see also ts’úlayus]. *noun.*

ḵw’ámi [ḵw’á mi] lonely. *adjective.*

ḵw’ámini [ḵw’á mi ni] lonely for (someone), be. *verb(t).*

ḵw’an ~ ḵw’en if I [future tense]; I. *clitic.*

ḵw’ap if you all [future tense]; you all. *clitic.*

ḵw’as if s/he [future tense]; s/he. *clitic.*

ḵw’at if we [future tense]; we. *clitic.*

ḵw’ats’ high tide, be; come in; rise [about the tide]. *verb(i).*

ḵw’axw if you [future tense]; you. *clitic.*

ḵw’aẏ tame; reserved; distant [about person]. *adjective.*

ḵw’áyaḵ’ántsut ~ ḵw’áyḵ’antsut [ḵw’á ya ḵ’án tsut] turn oneself right over. *verb(i).*

ḵw’áyaḵ’n ~ ḵwáyḵ’an [ḵw’á ya ḵ’en] turn (something) over. *verb(t).*

ḵw’áyat [ḵw’áy yat] fire (a canoe). *verb(t).*

ḵw’áẏat [ḵw’áẏ yat] tame (something). *verb(t).*

ḵw’áẏatsut [ḵw’áẏ ya tsut] change to a friendly disposition [after being angry]. *verb(i).*

ḵw’áẏchep [ḵw’áẏ chep] soot. *noun.*

ḵw’áyeḵ’ [ḵw’á yeḵ’] turned inside out, be; inside out, be turned. *verb(i).*

ḵw’áyḵ’an ~ ḵw’áyaḵ’n [ḵw’áy ḵ’an] turn (something) over. *verb(t).*

ḵw’áyḵ’antsut ~ ḵw’áyaḵ’ántsut [ḵw’áy ḵ’an tsut] turn oneself right over. *verb(i).*

ḵw’áyḵw’aẏax̲ [ḵw’áy ḵw’aẏ yax̲] shy, be; nervous; wild, be [about animal]. *verb(i).*

ḵw’áyḵw’ayḵ’ [ḵw’áy ḵw’ayḵ’] turning, be [when sleeping]. *verb(i).*

ḵw’áẏnexw [ḵw’áẏ nexw] friendly with (someone), have become. *verb(t).*

ḵw’á7axwt [ḵw’á 7axwt] struggle before dying. *verb(i).*

ḵw’ech’e7láḵinem [ḵw’e ch’el̓ lá ḵi nem] cry out really loud. *verb(i).*

ḵw’eḵ split, be [about tree]; split apart with one trunk to top end, be [about tree]. *verb(i).*

ḵw’eḵ’ ~ ḵweḵ’ ~ kweḵ’ surprised, be; look with surprise. *verb(i).*

ḵw’eḵways [ḵw’e ḵways] beat wool into workable wool. *verb(i).*

ḵw’eḵw’enáʔm [ḵw’e ḵw’e ná 7em] puberty, reach; reach puberty [about male]; have one’s voice be changing [about a young man]. *verb(i).*

ḵw’eḵw’íḵw’ehatl’ ~ seḵw’íḵw’ehats [ḵw’e ḵw’éh ḵw’e hatl’] swallow [type of bird]. *noun.*

ḵw’el cooked, be; ripe, be; done, be. *verb(i).*

ḵw’elámaẏ [ḵw’el lá maẏ] berry bush; fruit tree. *noun.*

ḵw’éla7en [ḵw’él la 7en] ear. *noun.*

ḵw’élem [ḵw’él lem] barbecue meat or fish. *verb(i).*

ḵw’élemay [ḵw’él le may] berry basket. *noun.*

ḵw’élen [ḵw’él len] cook (something). *verb(t).*

ḵw’elíx̲iya [ḵw’e léh x̲ey ya] small green cod. *noun.*

k̲w'elk̲'chís [k̲w'el k̲' chís] mole [type of animal]. *noun.*

k̲w'elk̲wám̓ [k̲w'el k̲wám̓] start to ripen [about berries]. *verb(i).*

k̲w'elk̲wán̓ [k̲w'el' k̲wán̓] barbecue (fish heads). *verb(t).*

k̲w'elm̓xwáy̓ [k̲w'el lem̓ xwáy̓] wild blackberry bush [see **sk̲w'elm'xw**]. *noun.*

k̲w'elnálhen [k̲w'el ná lhen] get it cooked; cooked, get it; manage to get it cooked; cooked, manage to get it. *verb(i).*

k̲w'élshi [k̲w'él shey] cook for (someone). *verb(t).*

k̲w'elt cook (something). *verb(t).*

k̲w'élten [k̲w'él ten] forked barbecuing knife or stick. *noun.*

k̲w'elts'áchxwem [k̲w'el ts'ách xwem] bent, be; stunted, be [about a tree]. *verb(i).*

k̲w'elús [k̲w'el lús] over-smoked fish [from too much heat, causing the skin to separate from the flesh, so that the oil goes rancid]. *noun.*

k̲w'emk̲w'úm [k̲w'em k̲w'úm] kelp, lots of [sg: **k̲w'um̓**]. *noun.*

k̲w'en ~ k̲w'an if I (future); I. *clitic.*

k̲w'eník̲w'ay [k̲w'e néh k̲w'ay] cottonwood tree. *noun.*

k̲w'etl'íwen ~ k̲w'utl'íwen [k̲w'e tl'í wen] animal intestines [word only used in legends]. *noun.*

k̲w'ets' wet. *adjective.*

k̲w'éts'en [k̲w'é ts'en] wet (something); make (something) wet. *verb(t).*

k̲w'éts'entsut [k̲w'é ts'en tsut] soak himself. *verb(i).*

k̲w'ets'mámim̓ [k̲w'ets' má mim̓] pee one's pants. *verb(i).*

k̲w'ets'númut [k̲w'ets' nú mut] wet oneself accidentally. *verb(i).*

k̲w'éx̲wa7k̲s [k̲w'é x̲wa7 k̲s] looks up [about red-faced dancer; a song break where they cry]; perform a dance characterized by the shaking of the head. *verb(i).* dancer, type of. *noun.*

k̲w'ey̓ús [k̲w'ey̓ yús] springtime, be. *verb(i).*

k̲w'éywilh [k̲w'éy wilh] burn sliver off bottom of canoe. *verb(i).*

k̲w'ich'tn [k̲w'ich' tn] sinew from the back of the deer. *noun.*

k̲w'ík̲'in [k̲w'éh k̲'in] rip (fish or animal) open. *verb(t).*

k̲w'ík̲w'ik̲w' [k̲w'éh k̲w'ehk̲w'] small black-headed seagull; seagull, small black-headed; Bonaparte gull. *noun.*

k̲w'ík̲w'ishétsut [k̲w'éh k̲w'i shé tsut] play. *verb(i).*

k̲w'ík̲w'lus ~ nk̲w'ík̲w'lus ~ nk̲w'ík̲w'lwas [k̲w'éhk̲w' lus] stick for holding salmon above fire; dried salmon put away for winter use. *noun.*

k̲w'ík̲w'tl'us [k̲w'éhk̲w' tl'us] target-shooting arrow. *noun.*

k̲w'ín̓exw [k̲w'í7 nexw] animals. *noun.*

k̲w'ítin̓ [k̲w'í tin̓] put (something) close to the edge. *verb(t).*

k̲w'ítin̓tsut [k̲w'í tin̓ tsut] move closer to the edge. *verb(i).*

k̲w'ixwántsut [k̲w'i xwán tsut] growl [as in stomach]. *verb(i).*

k̲w'iyílsh [k̲w'i yílsh] dance. *verb(i).*

k̲w'iyílsh7ay̓em [k̲w'i yílsh 7ay̓ yem] want to dance. *verb(i).*

k̲w'iyítk̲ [k̲w'i yítk̲] gull. *noun.*

k̲w'iy̓úk̲w' [k̲w'ey̓ yúk̲w'] fish stomach. *noun.*

k̲w'k̲waystn ~ kw'k̲waystn [k̲w' k̲ways tn] implement for beating mountain goat wool; implement for beating wool. *noun.*

k̲w'k̲wémn ~ k̲w'ak̲wemén [k̲w' k̲wé men] axe [see also **t'k̲wémen**]. *noun.*

k̲w'pel [k̲w' pel] small fish, similar to a small cod [never known to be eaten]. *noun.*

k̲w'shet play with (something/someone). *verb(t).*

k̲w'shétsut [k̲w' shé tsut] play; play a game; play a drum. *verb(i).*

k̲w'shetsutáy̓m [k̲w' she tsu táy̓ yem] want to play. *verb(i).*

k̲w'ts'i7 [k̲w' ts'i7] wet, get; become wet. *verb(i).*

k̲w'uk̲w [k̲w'uk̲w] hit accidentally, get. *verb(i).*

k̲w'uk̲wéyelh [k̲w'u k̲wéy yelh] whip with boughs [while training]. *verb(i).*

k̲w'úk̲wik̲w [k̲w'ú k̲wehk̲w] sea wrack [type of seaweed]. *noun.*

k̲w'úk̲wi7ek̲wń ~ k̲w'uk̲wk̲wán [k̲w'ú k̲weẏ 7e k̲weń] hit (someone) on the head. *verb(t).*

k̲w'uk̲wk̲wán ~ k̲w'úk̲wi7ek̲wń [k̲w'uk̲w k̲wán] hit (someone) on the head. *verb(t).*

k̲w'uk̲wneẃásen [k̲w'uk̲w neẃ wá sen] hit (them) together. *verb(t).*

k̲w'úk̲wnexw [k̲w'úk̲w nexw] hit (someone) accidentally; strike (someone) accidentally. *verb(t).*

k̲w'uk̲wnúmut [k̲w'uk̲w' nú mut] hit oneself accidentally. *verb(i).*

k̲w'úk̲wustn [k̲w'ú k̲w'us ten] fish club [more common term is **sla7mats**]; war club. *noun.*

k̲w'úk̲wut [k̲w'ú k̲wut] hit (someone) with a stick; beat (someone); strike (someone). *verb(t).*

k̲w'úk̲wutsut [k̲w'ú k̲wu tsut] hit oneself deliberately. *verb(i).*

k̲w'uk̲w'úk̲ws [k̲w'u k̲w'úk̲ws] hitting (someone), be always. *verb(t).*

k̲w'úk̲w'uts'i7 [k̲w'ú k̲w'u ts'eẏ] be getting fat; fat, be getting. *verb(i).*

k̲w'úk̲w'uy [k̲w'ú k̲w'uy] dying, be. *verb(i).*

k̲w'úlhutsut [k̲w'ú lhu tsut] prepare to start. *verb(i).*

k̲w'um̓ [k̲w'um̓] bull kelp. *noun.*

k̲w'únek̲ [k̲w'ú nek̲] dear [term of endearment for younger relative]. *noun.*

k̲w'úp'un [k̲w'ú p'un] put (something) in pleats [as in a dress]; pleat (something) [as in a dress]. *verb(t).*

k̲w'utl'íwen ~ k̲w'etl'íwen [k̲w'u tl'í wen] intestinal worm. *noun.*

k̲w'útl'un [k̲w'ú tl'un] tuck (something) in. *verb(t).*

k̲w'uts [k̲w'uts] fat. *adjective.*

k̲w'útsem [k̲w'ú tsem] rinse laundry. *verb(i).*

k̲w'útsi7 [k̲w'ú tsi7] fat, get. *verb(i).*

k̲w'útsuń [k̲w'ú tsuń] fatten (someone); make (someone) fat. *verb(t).*

k̲w'útsuńtsut [k̲w'ú tsuń tsut] make oneself fat. *verb(i).*

k̲w'uts'lhnáyn [k̲w'uts' lh náy yen] choke (someone). *verb(t).*

k̲w'úts'uń [k̲w'ú ts'uń] wring (something). *verb(t).*

k̲w'uwínstn [k̲w'u wín stn] suspenders. *noun.*

k̲w'ux̲wáẏusem [k̲w'u x̲wáẏ yu sem] glance. *verb(i).*

k̲w'ux̲wáẏusin [k̲w'u x̲wáẏ yu sin] glance at (something). *verb(t).*

k̲w'úx̲wim̓ [k̲w'ú x̲wim̓] look sideways. *verb(i).*

k̲w'úx̲wuń [k̲w'ú x̲wuń] glance at (something); look sideways at (something). *verb(t).*

k̲w'uy [k̲w'uy] die [singular]; paralyzed, be. *verb(i).*

k̲w'úẏaẃtxw [k̲w'úẏ 7aẃ txw] hospital. *noun.*

k̲w'úyayítut [k̲w'úy yay yí tut] dead tired, be. *verb(i).*

k̲w'úyek̲' [k̲w'úy yek̲'] beat up. *verb(i).*

k̲w'uynálhen [k̲w'uy ná lhen] kill it. *verb(i).*

k̲w'úynexw [k̲w'úy nexw] kill (game or fish); have caught (something); caught (something), have. *verb(t).*

k̲w'uynúmut [k̲w'uy nú mut] kill oneself. *verb(i).*

k̲w'úyut [k̲w'úy yut] beat (someone) up; vanquish (someone); lick (someone) in a fight. *verb(t).*

k̲w'u7n [k̲w'u 7n] bring (something) close to one's body to heat it. *verb(t).*

k̲w'u7neẃás ~ k̲'eẃneẃás ~ k̲w'ú7neẃas [k̲w'u7 neẃ wás] together, be; meet accidentally. *verb(i).*

k̲w'ú7neẃas ~ k̲w'u7neẃás ~ k̲'eẃneẃás [k̲w'ú7 neẃ was] together, be; meet accidentally; get together. *verb(i).*

k̲w'u7neẃásm [k̲w'u7 neẃ wá sem] get together; together, get. *verb(i).*

k̲w'ú7neẃasn ~ k̲'éẃneẃasn [k̲w'ú7 neẃ wa sen] put (them) together; gather (them) together; assemble (them); join (them). *verb(t).*

k̲w'ú7nexw [k̲w'ú7 nexw] get (something) together; included (something/someone), have; include (something/someone) accidentally. *verb(t).*

k̲w'u7t [k̲w'u7t] join (someone); include (someone/something); put (something) into a collection. *verb(t).*

k̲w'ú7tsut [k̲w'ú7 tsut] included, be. *verb(i).*

k̲w'xwélwet [k̲w' xwél wet] waterproof garment. *noun.*

k̲w'x̲wúy̓k̲wuy̓ach [k̲w' x̲wúy̓ k̲wuy̓ yach] fingernail; fingernails. *noun.*

k̲w'x̲wúy̓k̲wuy̓shen [k̲w' x̲wúy̓ k̲wuy̓ shen] toenail; toenails. *noun.*

L l

lakalestí [la kya les tí] Eucharist. *noun.*
lakáltem [la kyál tem] play cards. *verb(i).*
laklás [la klás] grace. *noun.*
lam whiskey; alcoholic beverage; alcohol [general term]. *noun.*
laṁ house. *noun.*
laṁ tl'a míx̲alh [laṁ tl'a méh x̲alh] den of black bear; lair of black bear. *noun.*
laṁán [laṁ mán] house location; permanent encampment. *noun.*
lamáẇtxw [la máẇ txw] beer parlour [see lam]. *noun.*
lánexw [lá nexw] take advantage of (someone). *verb(t).*
laplepx̲wáṅtsut [lap lep x̲wáṅ tsut] making a noise, be [about a group]. *verb(i).*
laplít [la plít] priest; minister. *noun.*
laplitntsut [la pli tn tsut] make himself out to be a priest [see laplit]. *verb(i).*
laplít7an [la plít 7an] make (someone) out to be a priest [see laplit]. *verb(t).*
láp'entsut [lá p'en tsut] out of shape, be; wrinkled, become; warped, be; skewed, be. *verb(i).*
lashás [la shás] angel. *noun.*
latám [la tám] table. *noun.*
la7chs [la7 chs] basket [one-pound berry basket for measuring]. *noun.*
leklí [le klí} key. *noun.* lock something. *verb(i).*
lekli7tsán ~ kli7tsán [le kli7 tsán] lock (something). *verb(t).*
lekw bitter taste, have a. *adjective.*
lekwá ~ lekwín [le kwá] Cross, the; crucifix; cross. *noun.*
lekwák̲w [le kwák̲w] rooster. *noun.*
lekwín ~ lekwá [le kwín] cross; cruxifix; Cross, the. *noun.*
lekwi7n [le kwi 7n] make (the sign of the cross). *verb(t).*
lekw' give off odour [about gall, when vomiting]. *verb(i).*
lelch' yellow; bright yellow. *adjective.*
lél̇epx̲wm [lél̇ lep x̲wem] noisy, be. *verb(i).*
lemetú [le me tú] sheep. *noun.*
lemetu7íẏk̲in [le me tu 7éẏ k̲in] make sounds like a sheep [see lemetu]. *verb(i).*
lemetu7í7k̲in [le me tu 7éh7 k̲in] wool; sheep's wool [see lemetu]. *noun.*
lemláṁ [lem láṁ] houses [sg: laṁ]. *noun.*
lémxwi7n [lém xwi 7en] thumping noise, make a; make a thumping noise; bumping noise, make a [e.g., a pot that falls, without breaking]. *verb(i).*
lepáptism [le páp tism] baptism [word used in the Catechism]. *noun.*
lepát [le pát] cup. *noun.*
lépeskwi7 [lé pes kweẏ] pilot bread; biscuit. *noun.*
leplásh [le plásh] lumber. *noun.*
leplepát [lep le pát] cups [sg: lepat]. *noun.*
lepl̇eplit [lep lep lit] priests [sg: laplit]. *noun.*
léplepx̲wem [lép lep x̲wem] making lots of noise, be. *verb(i).*
lepx̲wáṅtsut [lep x̲wáṅ tsut] make noise. *verb(i).*
les deep; low. *adjective.* bottom; lower part. *noun.*
les yíẏulh [les yéh7 yulh] hell [literally, low fire]. *noun.*
lesák̲ [le sák̲] bag; sack. *noun.*
lésen [lé sen] lower (something); humble (something). *verb(t).*
lésiẇilh [lé si ẇilh] underneath, be; under, be. *verb(i).*
les7álhx̲a [les 7álh x̲a] deep throat. *verb(i).*
letx̲ [le tx̲] vibrate; shake [as at explosion or heavy fall]. *verb(i).*
létx̲i7n [lét x̲i 7en] crash and shake. *verb(i).*
lewx̲ rib; ribs. *noun.*
lexwlíxw [lexw líxw] fall down; fall down while walking. *verb(i).*
lexwlíxwalh [lexw lí xwalh] settled down, be. *verb(i).*
lik̲ [lik̲] receive it at a potlatch. *verb(i).*
lílaṁ ~ lí7laṁ [lí laṁ] small house; little house [see laṁ]. *noun.*
lílat [lí lat] railroad. *noun.*

lil̓s ~ **li7ls** [lil's] under, being; below, being. *verb(i).*
lítem̓ [lí tem̓] thumping noise, make a. *verb(i).*
lixw [lixw] fall down; be laid down; laid down, be; put it down; hand it down. *verb(i).*
líxwayíwa7ntem [lí xwa yí wa 7en tem] replace (a person's) lost spirit. *verb(p).*
lixwáy̓lhem ~ **líxway̓lhem** [li xwáy̓ lhem] give daughter in marriage; offer daughter in marriage. *verb(i).*
líxway̓lhem ~ **lixwáy̓lhem** [lí xway̓ lhem] give daughter in marriage; offer daughter in marriage. *verb(i).*
líxway̓shen [lí xway̓ shen] reach the flatlands or valley floor. *verb(i).*
líxwelh [lí xwelh] settle down. *verb(i).*
lixwik̲án [leh xweh k̲án] pass out (food) at a potlatch. *verb(t).*
lixwk̲wm [lixw k̲wm] fall on the tops [about snow on the mountains]. *verb(i).*
líxwshi [líxw sheyt] give (daughter) in marriage. *verb(t).*
lixwt [lixwt] put (an object) down; give (one's daughter) in marriage. *verb(t).*
líxwtsut [líxw tsut] lie down. *verb(i).*
líx̲witem [li x̲wi tem] fast beat made with wood beaters for Indian dance or Indian war dance; accompanied by a fast beat, to abe; drum a fast rhythm. *verb(p).*
líx̲witsut [léh x̲wey tsut] make a noise. *verb(i).*
liyám [li yám] devil. *noun.*
liyámulh [li yá mulh] devil's [see **liyam**]. *adjective.*
lí7lam̓ ~ **lílam̓** [lí7 lam̓] little house; small house [see **lam̓**]. *noun.*
lí7latam ~ **lí7litam** [lí7 la tam] little table [see **latam**]. *noun.*
li7lemlám̓ [li7 lem lám̓] little houses; small houses [see **lam̓**; sg: **lí7lam̓** ~ **lílam̓**]. *noun.*
lí7litam ~ **lí7latam** [lí7 li tam] little table [see **latam**]. *noun.*
lí7lk̲ [léh 7elk̲] cheap; easy. *adjective.*
li7lk̲s [li 7lk̲s] find (something) easy to do; make (something) easy. *verb(t).*
li7ls ~ **lil̓s** [li 7ls] under, being. *verb(i).*
lí7shi [lí7 sheyt] put it away for (someone). *verb(t).*
li7t [li7t] store (something) away; put (something) away [for safekeeping]. *verb(t).*
lúlum [lú lum] sing. *verb(i).*
lulum̓áy̓m [lu lum̓ 7áy̓ yem] wish to sing. *verb(i).*
lúlumchew̓an [lú lum chew̓ wan] sing for (someone); sing about (someone). *verb(t).*
lúlumin [lú lu min] sing to (someone). *verb(t).*
lúlums [lú lums] make (someone) sing. *verb(t).*
Lúx̲wels [lu xwels] Mount Currie people. *noun.*
-lwet ~ **-lwit** ~ **-elut** ~ **-elwit** ~ **-elwet** [-lwet] clothes; blanket {full word: **hém̓ten**}. *suffix.*
-lwit ~ **-lwet** ~ **-elut** ~ **-elwit** ~ **-elwet** [-lwit] clothes; blanket {full word: **hém̓ten**}. *suffix.*

LH lh

lh {predicative clitic with relative meaning}. *clitic.*
lha the, a [feminine]. *determiner.*
lhach dim; dark. *adjective.*
lháchi7 [**lhá chi7**] twilight, be; dusk, be. *verb(i).*
lhach'tn [**lhách' ten**] knife [see also **sk̲'ápitaxw ~ sk̲'ápitixw**]. *noun.*
lhakw'ámentm [**lha kw'á men tem**] receive one's **syewen**. *verb(p).*
lhák̲at [**lhá k̲at**] whisper to (someone). *verb(t).*
lhák̲em [**lhá k̲em**] whisper. *verb(i).*
lhák̲'lhek̲'elel̓men [**lhák̲' lhe k̲'el lel̓ men**] making inquiries, be. *verb(i).*
lhák̲wanstn [**lhá k̲wans ten**] brooch for the chest. *noun.*
lhák̲wemaya7n [**lhá k̲we may ya 7en**] earache, have an. *adjective.*
lhak̲w'achí7m [**lha k̲w'a chí 7em**] clap; clap hands. *verb(i).*
lhak̲w'achí7n [**lha k̲w'a chí 7en**] slap (someone's) hand. *verb(t).*
lhák̲w'an [**lhá k̲w'an**] slap (someone). *verb(t).*
lhák̲w'antsut [**lhá k̲w'an tsut**] snow really hard. *verb(i).*
lhak̲w'ey̓ek̲wán [**lha k̲w'ey̓ ye k̲wán**] slap (someone) on the head. *verb(t).*
lhák̲w'k̲an̓ [**lhák̲w' k̲an̓**] spank (someone). *verb(t).*
lhák̲w'lhak̲w'shenam [**lhák̲w' lhak̲w' she nam**] slapping with one's feet, be. *verb(i).*
lhák̲w'usn [**lhá k̲w'u sen**] slap (someone's) face. *verb(t).*
-lhal food {full word: **s7ílhen**}. *suffix.*
lhálhachi7 [**lhá lha chi7**] be getting dimmer; dimmer, be getting; be getting dark; dark, be getting. *verb(i).*
lhálhak̲m [**lhá lha k̲m**] whispering to oneself, be. *verb(i).*
lhálhaw̓ [**lhá lhaw̓**] running away, be; recovering, be. *verb(i).*
lhálhetx̲em [**lhá lhet x̲em**] shaking from rage, be. *verb(i).*
lhalhéy̓ [**lha lhéy̓**] approaching, be. *verb(i).*
lhám̓an [**lhám̓ man**] dampen (something). *verb(t).*
lham̓áy̓ [**lham̓ máy̓**] seagrass; surf-grass. *noun.*
lham̓í7 [**lham̓ mí7**] damp, get. *verb(i).*
lhan ~ lhen when I. *clitic.*
lhánew̓ásen [**lhá new̓ wá sen**] pile (things) up. *verb(t).*
lhap ~ lhep when you all. *clitic.*
lhaplhipayúsm [**lhap lhi pay yú sem**] fluttering, be [about eyes]. *verb(i).*
lháp'en [**lhá p'en**] hang (something) up to dry; hang (something). *verb(t).*
lhas ~ lhes when s/he, when they. *clitic.*
lhásem [**lhá sem**] Chocolate lily; Indian rice. *noun.*
lhashán [**lha shán**] place on (something) [as a blanket over a mat]. *verb(t).*
lhat ~ lhet when we. *clitic.*
lhats' restless. *adjective.*
lháts'i [**lhá ts'i**] fed up, be. *verb(i).*
lháts'ini [**lhá ts'i ni**] fed up with (someone), be. *verb(t).*
lháts'i7n [**lhá ts'i 7en**] bother (someone). *verb(t).*
lháts'new̓as [**lháts' new̓ was**] get two or more with one shot. *verb(i).*
lháts'new̓ásn [**lháts' new̓ wá sen**] combine (them); put (them) together [can also be used for killing two ducks with one shot]. *verb(t).*
lhaw̓ escape; run away [about a captive]; recover; get away. *verb(i).*
lháw̓at ~ lháw̓et [**lháw̓ wat**] cure (someone); heal (someone). *verb(t).*
lháw̓en [**lháw̓ wen**] run away from (someone). *verb(t).*
lhaw̓ének̲ [**lhaw̓ wén nek̲**] sing **sxw7umten**'s song; cure; perform a cure; heal. *verb(i).*
lháw̓et ~ lháw̓at [**lháw̓ wet**] cure (someone); heal (someone). *verb(t).*

lháwichen [lháw wi chen] humpback salmon; pink salmon; salmon, pink or humpback. *noun.*
lháw̓k̲amay̓ [lháw̓ k̲a may̓] Pacific dogwood tree. *noun.*
lháw̓k̲em [lháw̓ k̲em] mussel. *noun.*
lháwlik̲w ~ alháwlik̲w [lháw lik̲w] big raft [see also **t'álhi7k̲w**]. *noun.*
lháw̓nexw [lháw̓ nexw] healed (someone), have; cured (someone), have. *verb(t).*
lháw̓numut [lháw̓ nu mut] get away, manage to. *verb(i).*
lhaw̓s ~ lhew̓s elope with (someone); cause (someone) to elope. *verb(t).*
lháw̓stway [lháw̓ stway] elope. *verb(i).*
lhaxw ~ lhexw when you. *clitic.*
lháx̲walu [lhá x̲wa lu] stick tongue out. *verb(i).*
lhay̓án [lha y̓án] dim (light); decrease (fire). *verb(t).*
lhá7a [lhá 7a] touched, be. *verb(i).*
lhá7entsutiwes [lhá 7en tsu ti wes] approach someone. *verb(i).*
lha7í7 [lha 7í7] approach; get near/close; come/go towards; sexually forward, be. *verb(i).*
lha7lhahíws [lha7 lha híws] related, be. *verb(i).*
lha7lhch [lha 7lhch] surface of it, be on the; top, be on; high up, be. *verb(i).*
lha7lhchách ~ slhá7lhchach [lha7 lh chách] top of hand; back of the hand. *noun.*
lhá7lhchan [lhá7 lh chan] put (something) on the surface of it. *verb(t).*
lhá7lhchiw̓ilh [lhá7 lh chi7 wilh] top, be on. *verb(i).*
lha7n [lha 7n] touch (something) [with hands]; approach (something). *verb(t).*
lhchiws [lh chiws] tired, get. *verb(i).*
lhchiwsn [lh chiw sn] tire (someone) out. *verb(t).*
lhchíwsni [lh chíws ni] tired of (someone), be. *verb(t).*
lhch'ímen [lh ch'í men] comb. *noun.*
lhech smell from burning; give off a strong burning smell [e.g., burning rags or feathers]. *verb(i).*
lhech'lhách'tn [lhech' lhách' ten] knives [sg: **lhách'tn**]. *noun.*
lhech'lhích's [lhech' lhích's] cutting (something) up continuously, be. *verb(t).*
lhekwáyusen [lhe kwáy yu sen] peck (someone's) eye out. *verb(t).*
lhékwem [lhé kwem] peck. *verb(i).*
lhékwen [lhé kwen] peck at (something). *verb(t).*
lhekwlhúkwuń [lhekw lhú kwuń] push (something) away in all directions; scatter (something). *verb(t).*
lhek'éta [lhe ky'éh ta] Plains-style Indians. *verb(i).*
lhekw' grazed, be just. *verb(i).*
lhekw'lhíkw'shn [lhekw' lhíkw' shen] stumble along; trip when one's foot gets caught; stumbling, be. *verb(i).*
lhek̲ arrive on other shore; get to the other side [of a body of water]. *verb(i).*
lhek̲eńéwilhtn [lhe k̲eń 7éw wilh ten] anchor line. *noun.*
lhek̲s take (something) across the gulf. *verb(t).*
lhek̲'ch [lhek̲' ch] broad back, have a. *adjective.*
lhek̲'chalhshá7 [lhek̲' chalh shá7] fifty. *numeral.*
lhek̲'chalhshá7 i kwi nch'u7 [lhek̲' chalh shá7 7i kwi n ch'u7] fifty one. *numeral.*
lhek̲'cháń [lhek̲' cháń] halve (something). *verb(t).*
lhék̲'es [lhé k̲'es] red laver seaweed. *noun.*
lhek̲'k̲s [lhek̲' k̲s] flat nose, have a. *adjective.*
lhek̲'lhék̲w'ilh [lhek̲' lhé k̲w'ilh] lumbago, have. *verb(i).*
lhek̲'lhk̲'átachxw [lhek̲' lh k̲'á ta chxw] broad-leafed, be; broad leaves, have. *verb(i).*
lhek̲wlhak̲wemáya7en [lhek̲w lha k̲we máy ya 7en] earache, be having an. *verb(i).*
lhek̲w' shedding bark, be [about tree]; come off [about bark on tree].
lhek̲w'lhák̲w'an [lhek̲w' lhá k̲w'an] slap (someone) many times. *verb(t).*
lhelekwínes [lhe le kwí nes] "taking out from the chest" [name of a supernatural being that eats people's hearts]. *noun.*
lhel̓k̲ soaked, be. *verb(i).*
lhelk̲'ém [lhel k̲'ém] inhale [when smoking]. *verb(i).*

lhélnach [lhél nach] cheek of rear end; butt cheek. *noun.*
lhelp'ách [lhel p'ách] wrinkles on hand, have; wrinkly hands, have. *verb(i).*
lhelp'í7 [lhel p'í7] saggy arms, have; wrinkles, have. *verb(i).*
lhelp'shn [lhelp' shn] wrinkles on legs, have; flapping foot, have a. *adjective.*
lhelp'ús [lhel p'ús] wrinkles [see also **estsém'tsem'k̲w ~ stsém'tsem'k̲w**]. *noun.*
lhelp'úsi7 [lhel p'ú si7] loose skin, have; wrinkles, have. *verb(i).*
lhelwá7stay [lhel wá7 stay] sit side by side. *verb(i).*
lhelwá7stays [lhel wá7 stays] put (them) side by side; pack (them) close together. *verb(t).*
lhelh- eat; drink; ingest; smoke; take in; chew. *prefix.*
lhelha7í [lhe lha 7í] approaching, be. *verb(i).*
lhelhchéchmx̲ [lhelh ché chem x̲] chew gum; chew resin. *verb(i).*
lhelhchíws [lhelh chíws] tired, be. *verb(i).*
lhélhemxw [lhé lhemxw] raining, be; raining hard, be; raining continuously, be. *verb(i).*
lhélhenay [lhé lhe nay] miss someone. *verb(i).*
lhelhenáya ~ lhelhenáy̓a ~ lhelhená7ya [lhe lhe náy ya] dragonfly. *noun.*
lhelhenáy̓a ~ lhelhená7ya ~ lhelhenáya [lhe lhe náy̓ ya] dragonfly. *noun.*
lhelhená7ya ~ lhelhenáya ~ lhelhenáy̓a [lhe lhe ná7 ya] dragonfly. *noun.*
lhélheyts'em [lhé lhey ts'em] emitting sparks, be. *verb(i).*
lhelhmíx̲alhay̓m [lhelh méh x̲a lhay̓ yem] want to eat bear meat. *verb(i).*
lhelhnts'k̲wú7tstn [lhe lhen ts' k̲wú7ts ten] smoke a pipe. *verb(i).*
lhélhp'i7 [lhélh p'i7] flabby arms, have. *verb(i).*
lhelhseplín [lhelh se plín] eat bread. *verb(i).*
lhelhsk̲áwts [lhelh sk̲áwts] eat potatoes. *verb(i).*
lhelhsméyts [lhelh sméyts] eat meat. *verb(i).*
lhelhsp'útl'am [lhelh sp'ú tl'am] smoke cigarettes; smoke [tobacco]. *verb(i).*
lhelhsts'úk̲wi7 [lhelh sts'ú k̲wi7] eat fish. *verb(i).*
lhelhtí [lhelh tí] drink tea. *verb(i).*
lhelhyí7yulh [lhelh yéh7 yulh] eat fire. *verb(i).*
lhemch' [lhe mch'] knocked off, be [about top of something]; break off; chipped off, be; get chipped off. *verb(i).*
lhemch'án [lhem ch'án] pick (something) in handfuls [for berries, such as huckleberries]; rake (berries) off a berry bush [e.g., huckleberries]; chip (something) off. *verb(t).*
lhemch'ím̓ [lhem ch'ím̓] pick berries in handfuls [e.g., huckleberries]. *verb(i).*
lhémch'nexw [lhém ch' nexw] chipped (something) off, have; chip (something) off accidentally; picked (berries) in handfuls, have [e.g., huckleberries]. *verb(t).*
lhémen [lhé men] pick (berries) individually [e.g., salmonberries, raspberries]. *verb(t).*
lhem̓í [lha7 mí] soaked, be. *verb(i).*
lhemím̓ [lhe mím̓] pick berries individually. *verb(i).*
lhémk̲w'a [lhém k̲w'a] sole [type of fish]. *noun.*
lhemlhemt'íyay̓ [lhem lhem t'í yay̓] "getting their wings wet" [of birds, mosquitoes]. *verb(i).*
lhém̓lhem̓ts' [lhém̓ lhem̓ ts'] pimply, be; pock-marked, be. *verb(i).*
lhém̓lhem̓ts'us [lhém̓ lhem̓ ts'us] pockmarked face, have a; pockmarked face, with. *adjective.*
lhémshi [lhém sheyt] pick berries for (someone) [berries which are picked individually, such as salmonberries]. *verb(t).*
lhemts'án [lhem ts'án] nick (something), just. *verb(t).*
lhem̓xw rain. *verb(i).*
lhemxwnítem [lhemxw ní tem] caught out in the rain, be; rained out, be; out when it starts raining, be; become wet [about snow]. *verb(p).*
lhemx̲wí7 [lhem x̲wí7] slimy, get. *verb(i).*
lhen ~ lhan when I. *clitic.*

lhéṅem [lhéṅ nem] braid the edges of a cattail mat [literally, weave]. *verb(i).*

lheni7él̓wes [lhe ni 7él̓ wes] woman's paddle. *noun.*

lhenlhéṅt [lhen lhéṅt] weaving (something) all the time, be. *verb(t).*

lheṅt weave (blankets). *verb(t).*

lhep ~ **lhap** when you all. *clitic.*

lhep' get hung up; hung up, get; hang it. *verb(i).*

lhes bitter; sour. *adjective.*

lhes ~ **lhas** when s/he, when they. *clitic.*

lhesh play pulling "lazy stick" contest; play tug-of-war [using a stick]. *verb(i).*

lhésheṅ [lhé sheṅ] jerk (something); pull (something). *verb(t).*

lhet ~ **lhat** when we. *clitic.*

lhétx̲em [lhét x̲em] shiver; tremble [from fear or cold]. *verb(i).*

lhetx̲úsem [lhet x̲ú sem] shaking, have one's head. *verb(i).*

lhét'em [lhé t'em] catch herring with herring rake. *verb(i).*

lhét'emten [lhé t'em ten] herring rake. *noun.*

lhet'kw'áyusm [lhet' kw'áy yu sem] splash one's eyes with water. *verb(i).*

lhét'kw'em [lhét' kw'em] sprinkled, get. *verb(i).*

lhet'kw'íṁ [lhet' kw'íṁ] sprinkle. *verb(i).*

lhet'kw'íwsntsut [lhet' kw'íw sen tsut] shower, have a. *verb(i).*

lhet'kw'úsn [lhet' kw'ú sen] sprinkle (something) with water. *verb(t).*

lhet'k̲em [lhet' k̲em] shaking, be [about a person]. *verb(i).*

lhét'k̲emiws [lhét' k̲em miws] shaking, have whole body. *verb(i).*

lhétsnech [lhéts nech] cormorant. *noun.*

lhets'lhúts' [lhets' lhúts'] scabby, become; itchy, become. *verb(i).*

lhewíl̓ew [lhew wí7 lew] shell clams. *verb(i).*

lheẇíṁ [lheẇ wíṁ] elope. *verb(i).*

lhewíts'a7m [lhew wí ts'a 7em] take off blanket; undress oneself. *verb(i).*

lheẇíts'n [lheẇ wí ts'en] strip (something); undress (someone). *verb(t).*

lhewk̲íṁ [lhew k̲'íṁ] Canada blueberry. *noun.*

lhewk̲íṁay [lhew k̲íṁ may] Canada blueberry bush. *noun.*

lheẇs ~ **lhaẇs** cause (someone) to elope; elope with (someone); steal (someone). *verb(t).*

lhexw ~ **lhaxw** when you. *clitic.*

lhexwlháxwala [lhew lhá xwa la] stick tongue out. *verb(i).*

lhéxwlhsha7 i kwi áṅus [lhéxwlh sha7 7i kwi áṅ nus] thirty two. *numeral.*

lhéxwlhsha7 i kwi nch'u7 [lhéxwlh sha7 7i kwi n ch'u7] thirty one. *numeral.*

lhexwlhshá7 ~ **lhéxwlhsha7** [lhexw lh shá7] thirty. *numeral.*

lhéxwlhsha7 ~ **lhexwlhshá7** [lhéxw lh sha7] thirty. *numeral.*

lhex̲wáchi7m [lhe x̲wá chi 7em] spit on one's hands. *verb(i).*

lhex̲wáṁen [lhe x̲wáṁ men] spit into (something). *verb(t).*

lhéx̲wen [lhé x̲wen] spit on (something/someone); spit at (something/someone). *verb(t).*

lhex̲wút [lhe x̲wút] spit (something) out. *verb(t).*

lhich' [lhich'] cut; be cut. *verb(i).*

lhích'ach [lhí ch'ach] cut one's hand. *verb(i).*

lhích'chk̲iṁ [lhí ch' ch k̲iṁ] bail hay. *verb(i).*

lhích'elk̲ín [lhí ch'el k̲ín] cut, have one's hair; shorn, have one's hair; have one's hair cut off; have one's hair shorn off. *verb(i).*

lhích'elk̲ínem [lhí ch'el k̲í nem] cut off one's hair. *verb(t).*

lhích'elhx̲a7m [lhí ch'elh x̲a 7em] cut one's neck deliberately. *verb(i).*

lhich'ilhx̲á7n [lhi ch'ilh x̲á 7en] cut (someone's) neck. *verb(t).*

lhích'it [lhí ch'it] cut (something); shear (something). *verb(t).*

lhích'nexw [lhích' nexw] cut (something) accidentally; cut (something), have. *verb(t).*

lhich'ní7kwup [lhich' ní7 kwup] cut wood. *verb(i).*

lhích'tn [lhích' tn] saw. *noun.*

lhích'us [lhích' us] wind-dried salmon from the Fraser River. *noun.*

lhiils [lhiils] sinew [see also **lhits'**]. *noun.*

lhikw' [lhikw'] hooked, be; hooked [up], get; get hooked. *verb(i).*
lhíkw'ach [lhí kw'ach] hooked in one's hand, get. *verb(i).*
lhíkw'in [lhí kw'in] hang (something) up; hang (something); hook (something) up; butt (something) [about horned animals]. *verb(t).*
lhikw'íwan [lhi kw'í wan] be sorry. *verb(i).*
lhikw'ḵw [lhikw' ḵw] get caught on a hook [about fish]. *verb(i).*
lhíkw'lhikw'iws [lhíkw' lhi kw'iws] related, be; hooked all over the body, be. *verb(i).*
lhíkw'nexw [lhíkw' nexw] hooked (something), have; have hooked (something) up; hung (something), have; have hung (something) up. *verb(t).*
lhíkw'shen [lhíkw' shen] stumble. *verb(i).*
lhíkw'shnan [lhíkw' shnan] trip (someone). *verb(t).*
lhiḵ' [lhiḵ'] always; often. *adverb.*
lhíḵwachn [lhéh ḵwa chen] skinless part of salmon cut in half. *noun.*
lhíḵw'in [lhéh ḵw'in] pull (something) apart. *verb(t).*
lhilháts' [lhi lháts'] make fun of. *verb(i).*
lhilháts'n [lhi lhá ts'en] make fun of (someone). *verb(t).*
lhilháts't [lhi lháts't] ridicule (soeone); rile (someone); belittle (someone). *verb(t).*
lhílhay [lhí lhay] miss. *verb(i).*
lhilháy̓l [lhi lháy̓ 7el] offended, be; take offence. *verb(i).*
lhilhemáyum̓ [lhi lhe máy yum̓] picked clean, be [about berries]. *verb(i).*
lhílhew̓its' [lhí lhew̓ wits'] naked, be. *verb(i).*
lhílhipm [lhí lhi pm] blink; blinking, be. *verb(i).*
lhílhipmayus [lhí lhip may yus] blink one's eyes. *verb(i).*
lhílhix̱tem [lhéh lhehx̱ tem] slobbering, be; drooling. be. *verb(i).*
lhílhḵw'us [lhílh ḵw'us] slanted roof, have a [as opposed to gabled]. *adjective.*
lhílhx̱i7lsh [lhílh x̱i 7elsh] standing, be; standing up, be. *verb(i).*
lhim̓ [lhim̓] accepted, be; approved, be [e.g., as a fiancé]. *verb(i).*
lhím̓mit [lhím̓ mit] accept (someone); approve (someone) [e.g., as a fiancé for one's daughter]; pull (something) towards oneself. *verb(t).*
lhim̓íxwstem [lhim̓ míxws tem] accuse (someone). *verb(p).*
lhím̓nexw [lhím̓ nexw] accept (someone); acquired (something/someone), have; possession of (something/someone), be. *verb(t).*
lhin [lhin] caught [in a net], get; strapped up, be. *verb(i).*
lhín̓chán̓ [lhín̓ chán̓] strap (something) on one's back. *verb(t).*
lhín̓elstn [lhín̓ nels ten] bridle. *noun.*
lhinḵstn ~ nlhinḵstn [lhinḵ stn] nose ornament. *noun.*
lhín̓nexw [lhín̓ nexw] caught (something) in a net, have. *verb(t).*
lhipay̓úsm [lhi pay̓ yú sem] blink one's eyes. *verb(i).*
lhiplh [lhi plh] blink. *verb(i).*
lhiplhtn [lhi plh tn] eyelash; eyelashes. *noun.*
lhitán̓ [lhi tán̓] sprinkle (liquid); splash (liquid). *verb(t).*
lhitúsn [lhi tú sen] sprinkle (something/someone) with water; splash water on (something/someone); besprinkle (something/someone). *verb(t).*
lhit' [lhit'] give something away at a feast; distribute gifts at a potlatch. *verb(i).*
lhít'in [lhí t'in] scatter (something). *verb(t).*
lhít'it [lhí t'it] scatter (something); give (something) around [especially gifts at a potlatch]; distribute (something). *verb(t).*
lhít'itsut [lhí t'i tsut] depart from one another. *verb(i).*
lhits' [lhits'] sinew [see also **lhiils**]. *noun.*
lhits' melḵw [lhit's melḵw] Adam's apple. *noun.*
lhits'em [lhi ts'em] emit sparks. *verb(i).*
lhíwix̱wusentem [lhí weh x̱wu sen tem] dab [dancer's paint] on quickly. *verb(p).*
lhíxwel̓ech [lhí xwel̓ lech] three hundred. *numeral.*
lhíxwshenantem [lhíxw she nan tem] trip. *verb(p).*
lhix̱t [lhix̱t] saliva. *noun.*

lhíx̱tem [lhéhx̱ tem] spit run from mouth, have; slobber. *verb(i).*

lhíx̱wem [lhí x̱wem] slug. *noun.*

lhiy̓áts' [lhi y̓áts'] tight squeeze, be a. *verb(i).*

lhí7lhach'tn [lhí7 lhach' ten] small knife [see lhách'tn]. *noun.*

lhí7neḵ [lhí7 neḵ] breechcloth; loincloth. *noun.*

lhí7ni [lhí7 ni] draw closer to (one). *verb(t).*

lhkwám̓en [lh kwám̓ men] hollow (something) out. *verb(t).*

lhkwun [lh kwun] don't know; might; must be; maybe; probably; possibly. *clitic.*

lhḵápten [lh ḵáp ten] line connecting the harpoon heads to the pole or connecting gaffhook head to pole. *noun.*

lhḵaych' [lh ḵaych'] moon. *noun.*

lhḵén̓at [lh ḵén̓ nat] anchor (something). *verb(t).*

lhḵén̓ten [lh ḵén̓ ten] anchor. *noun.*

lhḵ'at [lh ḵ'at] broad; wide; flat [river, clothes, etc.]. *adjective.*

lhḵ'átchus [lh ḵ'át chus] wide forehead, have a; broad forehead, have a. *adjective.*

lhḵ'átus [lh ḵ'á tus] broad face, have a. *adjective.*

lhḵ'áy̓nup [lh ḵ'áy̓ nup] broad, be [about beach]. *verb(i).*

lhḵ'i7s ~ sḵ'i7s ~ eslhḵ'í7s ~ slhḵ'i7s ~ lhsḵ'i7s [lh ḵ'í7s] know (someone/something); acquainted with (someone/something), be; know how to do (something). *verb(t).*

lhḵ'í7stway [lh ḵ'í7s tway] know one another. *verb(i).*

lhḵwíw̓ilh [lh ḵwí7 wilh] suck blood [about mosquitoes]. *verb(i).*

lhmáḵ'a [lh má ḵ'a] patella; limpet. *noun.*

-lhnay [-lh nay] throat, inside of {full word: x̱wúmlhnalh}. *suffix.*

lhna7 [lh na7] place. *noun.*

lhp'áyts'a7ten [lh p'áy ts'a7 ten] clothesline [see also ch'ixwáyts'a7ten]. *noun.*

lhseḵ' ~ eséḵ' [lh séḵ'] half [split off], be. *verb(i).*

lhsíḵ'mit [lh séhḵ' mit] nickle [literally, half a dime]. *noun.*

lhsḵ'i7s ~ eslhḵ'í7s ~ lhḵ'i7s ~ slhḵ'i7s ~ sḵ'i7s [lh sḵ'í7s] know (someone/something); acquainted with (someone/something), be; know how to do (something). *verb(t).*

-lhsha7 ~ -alhsha7 [-lh sha7] multiple of ten. *suffix.*

lhukw [lhukw] out of the way, be. *verb(i).*

lhúkwun̓ [lhú kwun̓] scatter (something) around; push (something) out of the way. *verb(t).*

lhúḵwḵam̓ [lhúḵw ḵam̓] splash water [about skipper of canoe]. *verb(i).*

lhúḵwun [lhú ḵwun] dig into (something). *verb(t).*

lhuḵw' [lhuḵw'] peeled off, be [as heavy bark of tree]. come off [about skin] *verb(i).*

lhúḵw'un [lhú ḵw'un] peel (thin bark). *verb(t).*

lhúlhuḵw'ay̓ [lhú lhu ḵw'ay̓] Arbutus tree. *noun.*

lhúlhusi7 [lhú lhu si7] drifting back in the river, be continually. *verb(i).*

lhum̓ [lhum̓] eat soup. *verb(i).*

lhup [lhup] late, be; out of reach, be; way off, be; away from the edge [e.g., an object on a table]. *verb(i).*

lhúpun [lhú pun] put (something) out of reach; put (something) away. *verb(t).*

lhúpuntsut [lhú pun tsut] put oneself way back; move away. *verb(i).*

lhus [lhus] drift back [as in a canoe]. *verb(i).*

lhus [lhus] drop [as of barbecued fish]; slide down. *verb(i).*

lhúsi [lhú si] move down; go down [about health]. *verb(i).*

lhúsum̓ [lhú sum̓] lower [as sail in a canoe]; slide down. *verb(i).*

lhúsun̓ [lhú sun̓] lower (something) down. *verb(t).*

lhút'un [lhú t'un] sip (tea or water); slurp (something). *verb(t).*

lhuts [lhuts] touched, be just. *verb(i).*

lhuts' [lhuts'] scabby, be; itch. *verb(i).*

lhx̱áy̓tstn [lh x̱áy̓ts ten] plate; platter [white]. *noun.*

lhx̱áy̓tstnay̓ [lh x̱áy̓ts ten nay̓] dish shelf; cupboard. *noun.*

lhx̲énpten [lh x̲én p ten] floor. *noun.*
lhx̲ilsh [lh x̲ilsh] stand; stand up. *verb(i).*
lhx̲ilshnúmut [lh x̲ilsh nú mut] stand up finally; stand up, manage to. *verb(i).*
lhx̲wélhch [lh x̲wélh ch] spit. *verb(i).*
lh7i [lh 7i] place [near to where one is; cf. **lhna7**]. *noun.*

M m

-m [suffix used on certain intransitive verbs]. *suffix.*
maalh [maalh] come on. *adverb.*
máchen [má chen] testicle. *noun.*
mákwlhnexw ~ má7kwlhnexw [má kwlh nexw] hurt (something) unintentionally; hurt (someone) accidentally; get (someone) hurt. *verb(t).*
mákwutsinem [má kwu tsi nem] start budding; budding, start. *verb(i).*
mákw'alhnayem [má kw'alh nay yem] won't eat because one's friend won't; join someone in fasting. *verb(i).*
mákw'atsut [má kw'a tsut] punish oneself for the sake of another; share someone's fate voluntarily. *verb(i).*
mák̲a7 [má k̲a7] snow. *noun.*
mak̲' coarse; thick [about rope, yarn, wool, etc.]. *adjective.*
mák̲'amats' [má k̲'a mats'] heavy, be [about cord or yarn]; thick, be [about rope]. *verb(i).*
mák̲wam [má k̲wam] Indian tea; moss; dry swamp; swamp. *noun.*
malk̲w scattered around, be; mixed, be. *verb(i).*
málk̲wnew̓as [málk̲w new̓ was] mixed together, be. *verb(i).*
málk̲wnew̓ásn [málk̲w new̓ wa sen] mix (them) up; confuse (them) [e.g., shoes or clothes]. *verb(t).*
malk̲wt mix (something). *verb(t).*
mam father; daddy. *vocative.*
máma [má ma] dad [see also **man**]. *noun.*
mamakw'útsin [ma ma kw'ú tsin] sticky burrs of bedstraw. *noun.*
mamakw'útsinay̓ [ma ma kw'ú tsi nay̓] bedstraw. *noun.*
mámi7 [má mi7] bait. *noun.*
mámi7n [má mi 7en] bait (something). *verb(t).*
mamts'á7n [mam ts'á 7en] showing off, be. *verb(i).*
mamts'á7nem [mam ts'á7 nem] flirting, be. *verb(i).*
man father [see also **máma**]. *noun.*
man̓alhánan [man̓ na lhá nan] respected feeling. *noun.*
manan̓ílh [ma nan̓ nílh] themselves. *noun.*
manáts'a ~ manáts'i [ma ná ts'a] drum [specifically a skin drum]. *noun.*
manáts'i ~ manáts'a [ma ná ts'i] drum [specifically, a skin drum]. *noun.*
manáts'i7m [ma ná ts'i 7em] beat a drum [see **manáts'a**]. *verb(i).*
mat mat. *noun.*
mátl'en [má tl'en] smear (someone); smear (someone) with dirt; make (someone) dirty; dirty, make (someone). *verb(t).*
mátl'et [má tl'et] take revenge on (someone). *verb(t).*
matl'mín̓ [matl' mín̓] dirty (someone). *verb(t).* dirty. *verb(i).* reason for someone getting dirty. *noun.*
mátl'nexw [mátl' nexw] revenge on (someone), get; repay (someone); take revenge for (someone). *verb(t).*
mátl'nexw [mátl' nexw] dirty (someone). *verb(t).*
mátl'ntsut [má tl'en tsut] dirty himself. *verb(i).*
matl'númut [matl' nú mut] revenge, get. *verb(i).*
mátl'tsut [mátl' tsut] avenge oneself; get even. *verb(i).*
máts'ulh [má ts'ulh] pus. *noun.*
máwan̓ [má wan̓] side with (someone) in an argument; support (someone) in an argument; defend (someone); take (someone's) part. *verb(t).*
may forget. *verb(i).*
máyk̲wsmut [máy k̲ws mut] go into a trance; trance, go into a; pass out. *verb(i).*
máy̓muyun [máy̓ muy yun] put (something) in the water; dip (something) repeatedly in the water. *verb(t).*
máy̓muyuntsut [máy̓ muy yun tsut] dip oneself in water. *verb(i).*
máynexw [máy nexw] forget (something); have forgotten (something). *verb(t).*

ma7át [ma 7át] spawned out, be [about salmon]. *verb(i).* salmon after spawning. *noun.*
ma7áti7 [ma 7á ti7] deteriorate [about salmon after spawning]. *verb(i).*
ma7ayachí7m [ma 7a ya chí 7em] release one's grip. *verb(i).*
ma7áyk̲' [ma 7áyk̲'] set net. *verb(i).*
má7chen [má7 chen] bone. *noun.*
má7kwelh [má7 kwelh] fart [see also **tek̲'** and **pu7k̲**]; get hurt; hurt, get. *verb(i).*
má7kwlhnexw ~ mákwlhnexw [má7 kwlh nexw] hurt (someone) accidentally; get (someone) hurt; hurt (something) unintentionally; have hurt (someone). *verb(t).*
má7k̲wel [má7 k̲wel] padlock. *noun.*
mechemí7 [me che mí7] slow down [about water]. *verb(i).*
méchen [mé chen] louse; lice. *noun.*
mechen̓ántem [me chen̓ 7án tem] infected with lice, be; lousy, be. *verb(p).*
méchenten [mé chen ten] fine-toothed comb; comb, fine-toothed. *noun.*
méchmechem [méch me chem] no wind, be; slack tide, be; move slowly [about water]. *verb(i).*
mekwshn [mekw shn] socks. *noun.*
mekwshnám̓ [mekw shnám̓] wrap one's own leg up in something. *verb(i).*
mekwtn [mekw tn] blanket; burial blanket. *noun.*
mékwu7 [mé kwu7] wrapped, be. *verb(i).*
mékwu7n [mé kwu 7en] wrap (something); cover (something). *verb(t).*
mékw'em [mé kw'em] find it; pick it up. *verb(i).*
mek̲álxwtselh [me k̲álxw tselh] tongue. *noun.*
mék̲sen [mék̲ sen] nose. *noun.*
mek̲' full, be [from eating]. *verb(i).*
mek̲'étsut [me k̲'é tsut] fill up; overeat. *verb(i).*
mek̲'mík̲' [mek̲' méhk̲'] press down. *verb(i).*
mek̲'númut [mek̲' nú mut] full, be finally; manage to get full. *verb(i).*
mék̲wem [mé k̲wem] loose, be. *verb(i).*
mek̲weméy̓ [me k̲we méy̓] come loose; loose, come. *verb(i).*
mék̲wen [mé k̲wen] loosen (something). *verb(t).*
mék̲wmek̲w [mék̲w mek̲w] loose, be. *verb(i).*
mek̲wú7shtn [me k̲wú7sh ten] moccasins [see also **stl'ék̲'shen**]. *noun.*
mélalus [mé la lus] raccoon. *noun.*
meláshis [me lá shis] molasses. *noun.*
mélch'tsut [mélch' tsut] struggle [before dying]. *verb(i).*
melelus7úl-lh [me le lus 7úl-lh] baby raccoon [see **mélalus**]. *noun.*
melk̲w larynx. *noun.*
mélmelx̲wíts'a ~ smélmelx̲wits'a ~ smalmelx̲wíts'a [mél mel x̲wi ts'a] dipper [type of bird]. *noun.*
melmílch' [mel mílch'] confused, be; mixed up, be; get mixed up [about things or mentally]. *verb(i).*
melmílkw [mel mílkw] mouldy, be getting. *verb(i).*
melyá7 [mel yá7] marry; get married. *verb(i).*
melh so; then. *clitic.*
melhalh [me lhalh] [used only in the phrase **huy' melhalh**]. *clitic.*
melhmílha7 [melh mí lha7] dancing a bunch, be. *verb(i).*
memelshenám [me mel she nám] walk at edge of water. *verb(i).*
mém̓etk̲wm [mém̓ met k̲wem] bubbling, be. *verb(i).*
memets'ín̓tm ~ smemets'ín̓entem [me me ts'ín̓ tem] squirted by a skunk, get [literally, get skunked]. *verb(p).*
mémey̓ [mé mey̓] sinking, be; going down, be [in the water]. *verb(i).*
mémkw'em [mém kw'em] picking things up, be. *verb(i).*
memkw'útsin [mem kw'ú tsin] burr [small]. *noun.*
memtl'ítsut [mem tl'í tsut] try to best one another. *verb(i).*
memtl'ús [mem tl'ús] dirty face, have a. *adjective.*
men̓ son; daughter; child; offspring. *noun.*
men ch'ích'its [men ch'í ch'its] right behind (someone). *verb(t).*
men em̓út [men 7e m̓út] remain sitting; sitting, remain. *verb(i).*
men eslhélha7 ~ men slhélha7 [men es lhé lha7] right behind something. *verb(i).*

men eshán̓ melh [men e shán̓ melh] why? *question phrase; adverb.*
men huy [meh huy] only; always. *adverb.*
men huys [men huys] let (someone) be; never mind (someone); ignore (someone). *verb(t).*
men i [men 7i] stay; stay here. *verb(i).*
men iy̓áy̓ulh [men 7ey̓ y̓á7 yulh] left aboard, be; aboard, be. *verb(i).*
men í7im̓esh [men í 7im̓ mesh] travel on foot. *verb(i).*
men k̲á7is [men k̲á 7is] go on a short trip; short trip, go on a. *verb(i).*
men na7s leave (something) there. *verb(t).*
men nch'ench'ú7 [men ch'en ch'ú7] alone, be. *verb(i).* one of them.
men nímalh [men ní malh] we ourselves. *pronoun.*
men slhélha7 ~ men eslhélha7 [men slhé lha7] right behind something. *verb(i).*
men swátes [men swá tes] anybody; just whoever. *pronoun.*
men shan why? *question word; adverb.*
men shan̓ melh why, then? *question word; adverb.*
men txwhuy [men txw huy] all one does. *verb(i).*
men t'ut [men t'ut] as always; former; old; previously. *adverb; adjective.*
men tl'ay still; yet; as previously. *adverb.*
men tl'ik̲' [men tl'ik̲'] always. *adverb.*
men tl'ítsus [men tl'í tsus] try to out do one another. *verb(i).*
men wa í7im̓esh [men wa 7í 7im̓ mesh] wander around. *verb(i).*
men yalh just [recently]; recently; for the first time. *adverb.*
men ~ mn just; only; then. *clitic.*
menílh [me nílh] same; similar; he himself; himself; she herself; herself. *noun.*
mén̓men [mén̓ men] children; offspring [sg: **men̓**]. *noun.*
ménya [mén ya] battleship. *noun.*
mes stuck to something, get; adhere; stick to something. *verb(i).*
mésen [mé sen] gall bladder; gall. *noun.*
mésen̓ [mé sen̓] stick (something) on it; put (them) together; connect (them). *verb(t).*
mesíwsem [me síw sem] hitch up [horses]. *verb(i).*
mesnew̓ás [mes new̓ wás] stuck together, get; put together, get. *verb(i).*
mesnew̓ásen [mes new̓ wá sen] join (them) together. *verb(t).*
-mesh people {full word: **stélmexw**}. *suffix.*
métk̲wem [mét k̲wem] bubble; bubble up; froth. *verb(i).*
metmútaw̓i [met mú taw̓ wi] sit on someone's lap. *verb(i).*
metmútk̲wem [met mút k̲wem] lying with hands raised behind head, be. *verb(i).* lying with hands raised behind head. *place name.*
metmútk̲ws [met mút k̲ws] have (someone's) head resting on one's arm; support (someone's) head. *verb(t).*
metmúts [met múts] hold (someone) on one's lap. *verb(t).*
met' limber; supple; pliable. *adjective.*
met'étsut [me t'é tsut] bend; give way [e.g., about a plank under a weight]. *verb(i).*
metl' dirty, get; stained, get. *verb(i).*
metl'ách [me tl'ách] dirty, get one's hands. *verb(i).*
metl'áyam̓it [me tl'áy yam̓ mit] dirty, get one's shoulder. *verb(i).*
métl'iy̓ek̲w [mé tl'i y̓ek̲w] great-grandchild. *noun.*
métl'metl' [métl' metl'] dirty, be; splashed with mud or dirt, be. *verb(i).*
métsk̲w'i7n [méts k̲w'i 7en] doubled up knee, have a. *verb(i).*
mets'entín [me ts'en tín] honourable pride. *noun.*
mex̲míx̲alh [mex̲ méh x̲alh] bears [black]; black bears [sg: **míx̲alh**]. *noun.*
méx̲weya [mé x̲we ya] bellybutton; navel. *noun.*
mey sink. *verb(i).*
meymáy̓ ~ smeymáy̓ ~ smemey̓máy̓ [mey máy̓] forgetful [see also **esmemey'máy**]; get lost [old meaning]; lose one's way [old meaning]. *adjective.*
méymey [méy mey] drown. *verb(i).*
méymey̓em [méy mey̓ yem] ripple. *verb(i).*
meymúy [mey múy] flood over. *verb(i).*
mi chelhk̲wi [mi chelh k̲wi] pass through a hole hither or this way. *verb(i).*

mi ch'ik̲ [mi ch'ik̲] dawn, be. *verb(i).*
mi k̲atl' [mi k̲atl'] become cloudy; cloudy, become. *verb(i).*
mi nách'i [mi ná ch'i] change expression. *verb(i).*
mi sham [mi sham] come to the surface. *verb(i).*
mi wuk̲w' [mi wuk̲w'] come downstream. *verb(i).*
mi yeẇáṅ [mi yeẇ wáṅ] come first. *verb(i).*
mi ~ ṁi [mi] come; become; start. *verb(i).*
ṁi ~ mi [ṁi] come; become; start. *verb(i).*
míchem [mí chem] spread out, be. *verb(i).*
mikw' [mikw'] washed; clean. *adjective.*
míkw'achi7m [mí kw'a chi 7em] clean one's hands; wash one's hands. *verb(i).*
mikw'achí7n [mi kw'a chí 7en] wash (someone's) hands. *verb(t).*
míkw'aẏák̲inan [mí kw'aẏ yá k̲i nan] wash the insides of (an animal). *verb(t).*
míkw'i [mí kw'i] clean, become [can be used for ritual cleansing as well]. *verb(i).*
míkw'in [mí kw'in] clean (something); wash (something). *verb(t).*
míkw'intsut [mí kw'in tsut] wash oneself. *verb(i).*
mikw'mámin [mikw' má min] wash the dishes. *verb(i).*
míkw'mikw' [míkw' mikw'] clean. *verb(i).*
mikw'míkw'shn [mikw' míkw' shen] clean feet, have [about a group of people]. *verb(i).*
míkw'shnaṁ [míkw' shnaṁ] clean one's feet; wash one's feet. *verb(i).*
míkw'shnan [míkw' shnan] wash (someone's) feet. *verb(t).*
mikw'tn [mikw' tn] dance [performed before a wedding]. *noun.*
mikw'tsm [mikw' tsm] wash one's own mouth. *verb(i).*
míkw'us [mí kw'us] clean face, have a. *adjective.*
míkw'usm [mí kw'u sem] wash one's face. *verb(i).*
míkw'usn [mí kw'u sen] wash (someone's) face. *verb(t).*
mík̲sem [méhk̲ sem] have canoe pointing this way; point canoe in this direction. *verb(i).*
mik̲' [mik̲'] fish with net [in river]. *verb(i).*
mík̲'in [méh k̲'in] press (something) down. *verb(t).*
mík̲'intsut [méh k̲'in tsut] dunk oneself in the water when bathing. *verb(i).*
mik̲'neẇásen [mehk̲' neẇ wá sen] press (them) together. *verb(t).*
mík̲wi7n [méh k̲wi 7en] eased up from pain, be. *verb(i).*
mík̲w'usem [méh k̲w'u sem] duck someone's head under water. *verb(i).*
milch't [milch't] confuse (someone). *verb(t).*
mílha7 [mí lha7] dance an Indian winter dance. *verb(i).* Indian winter dance. *noun.*
milha7áẇtxw [mi lha 7áẇ txw] dance house [see also **tl'ashnáw'txw**]. *noun.*
mílha7s [mí lha7s] make (someone) dance; dance, make (someone). *verb(t).*
mílha7uyts [mí lha 7uyts] dancing gear. *noun.*
mímikw'uẏs [mí mi kw'uẏs] round ["washed"] stone; large pebble. *verb(i).*
míṁiṅ [mí7 miṅ] doll. *noun.*
míṁna [míṁ na] child. *noun.*
míṁna lhk̲aych' [míṁ nalh k̲aych'] January. *noun.*
mimts' [mimts'] old man's beard [type of lichen]. *noun.*
mimúy [mey múy] flooded, be; flooded out, be. *verb(i).*
-miṅ [-miṅ] {complex transitivizer}. *suffix.*
-min ~ -miṅ [-min] piece; half; side. *suffix.*
-miṅ ~ -min [-miṅ] piece; half; side. *suffix.*
míni [mí ni] bring (someone) here. *verb(t).*
miṅmiṅúllh ~ smíṅminullh ~ smíṁna7ullh [miṅ miṅ 7úllh] young of any animal; animal cub. *noun.*
mis ~ ṁis [mis] bring (something). *verb(t).*
ṁis ~ mis [ṁis] bring (something). *verb(t).*
míshi [mí sheyt] bring it to (someone). *verb(t).*
mit [mit] dime. *noun.*
míten [mí ten] wood duck. *noun.*
mítl'ela [mí tl'e la] play "hit the bones" game. *verb(i).*
mítl'intsut [mí tl'in tsut] duck; stoop. *verb(i).*
mítsaṁ [mí tsaṁ] send word this way. *verb(i).*

mítsiǹtsut [mí ts'iǹ tsut] squat. *verb(i).*
miẁ [miẁ] come along; come here. *verb(i).*
míẁnexw [míẁ nexw] bring (someone) along. *verb(t).*
míxwintsut [mí xwin tsut] bob up and down on a board or branch. *verb(i).*
míxwi7 [mí xwi7] melted, be. *verb(i).*
míx̱alh [méh x̱alh] black bear; bear [black]. *noun.*
mix̱alhálkwlh [meh x̱a lhál kwlh] perform a bear dance; dance a bear dance. *verb(i).*
mix̱alhúl-lh [meh x̱a lhúl-lh] bear cub. *noun.*
míx̱alhulh [méh x̱a lhulh] black bear's; belonging to a black bear. *adjective.*
míx̱wmex̱w [méhx̱w mex̱w] soft, be [about grease or butter]. *verb(i).*
miyách [mi yách] barbed spear point; salmon harpoon; spear for catching salmon; spearhead; harpoon with string. *noun.*
míyatsut [mí ya tsut] submerge oneself; go down [in the water]. *verb(i).*
miyíw [mi yíw] side; edge. *noun.*
miyíẁax̱an ~ smiyíẁax̱an [mi yí7 ẁa x̱an] side; edge [of anything]. *noun.*
miyíẁts [mi yíẁts] riverbank; water's edge. *noun.*
miyú7ts [mi yú7 ts] make cheaper. *verb(i).*
mí7meḵsen [mí7 meḵ sen] little nose [see **méḵsen**]. *noun.*
mn ~ men just; only; then. *clitic.*
-msh me [used only with **-nexw** verbs]. *suffix.*
mukwtst ~ nexwmúkwutsin [múkw tst] kiss (someone). *verb(t).*
múkwuts [mú kwuts] kiss. *verb(i).*
múkwutsin [mú kwu tsin] kiss (someone). *verb(t).*
mul [mul] sledgehammer. *noun.*
múla [mú la] lumber mill. *noun.*
múl̓ḵstn [múl' ḵs ten] shoulder blade. *noun.*
múl̓sem [múl' sem] bog blueberry; large swamp blueberry. *noun.*
múl̓seṁaẏ [múl' seṁ maẏ] bog blueberry bush. *noun.*
múlutsinem [mú lu tsi nem] not willing to discuss a dead person, be. *verb(i).*
múṁten [múṁ ten] blue grouse; grouse [blue]. *noun.*
mumú7nexw [mu mú7 nexw] drop (them) continuously. *verb(t).*
músmes [mús mes] cow. *noun.*
-mut [-mut] piece; individual specimen. *suffix.*
mútaẁi [mú taẁ wi] sit down on someone's lap. *verb(i).*
mútḵem [mút ḵem] sit on the ground. *verb(i).*
mut' [mut'] drown. *verb(i).*
mutl'ts [mutl' ts] smothered, get. *verb(i).*
mútl'un [mú tl'un] put hand over (someone); suffocate (someone); crush (someone) [by one-sided pressure]. *verb(t).*
múx̱wutsut [mú x̱wu tsut] get revenge. *verb(i).*
muy [muy] touched by rising water, be; submerge; soaked, be. *verb(i).*
muẏaẏi [mu ẏa ẏi] set out one's net. *verb(i).*
múynexw [múy nexw] get (something) into the water. *verb(t).*
múyuṅ [mú yuṅ] put (something) in the water; soak (something). *verb(t).*
múyuntsut [mú yun tsut] go into the water deliberately; submerge. *verb(i).*
múyuẏsen [múy yuẏ sen] boil (something) by means of hot stones. *verb(t).*
mu7n [mu 7n] drop (something) intentionally; release (something); let go of (something). *verb(t).*
mú7nexw [mú7 nexw] drop (something) accidentally; have dropped (something). *verb(t).*

N n

n- my; me; I. *prefix.*
n- ~ en- my. *prefix.*
-n ~ -ṅ {added onto some words so that you can use the object endings, see section on "object endings," p. 12}. *suffix.*
-ṅ ~ -n {added onto some words so that you can use the object endings, see section on "object endings," p. 12}. *suffix.*
n- ~ nexw- ~ xw- {location}. *prefix.*
na here; there [said when handing something to someone]. *interjection.*
na [indicates that something has happened or is happening at the moment]. *clitic.*
na k̲eṅp ta lhk̲aych' [na k̲eṅp ta lh k̲aych'] The moon set. *sentence.*
na k̲eṅp ta snék̲wem [na k̲eṅp ta sné k̲wem] The sun set. *sentence.*
na téxwlam [na téxw lam] There is no wind. *sentence.*
na wí7xwem ta kwúsen [na wí7 xwem ta kwú sen] There was a falling star. *sentence.*
na yulh ta stsék̲tsek̲ [na yulh ta stsék̲ tsek̲] There was a forest fire. *sentence.*
naa ~ na7 [naa] name. *verb(i).*
náatsut [náa tsut] identify oneself; introduce oneself. *verb(i).*
naaẃ [naaẃ] dear [expression used by man and wife speaking to one another]. *clitic.*
nach' different; wrong; several; some. *adjective.*
nách'ani7m [ná ch'a ni 7em] make a difference; change one's diet. *verb(i).*
nách'aẃalh [ná ch'aẃ walh] separate bed. *noun.*
nách'aẃich [ná ch'aẃ wich] one hundred. *numeral.*
nách'aẃtxw [ná ch'aẃ txw] separate house, be in; another room, be in; next room, be in. *verb(i).* one house. *numeral.*
nach'áxw [na ch'áxw] once; one time. *verb(i).*
nách'axwilh [ná ch'a xwilh] one container [pots, pans, canoes]. *numeral.*
nach'aẏúsn [na ch'aẏ yú sen] change (someone's) appearance; change the colour of (something). *verb(t).*
nách'en [ná ch'en] transform (something); change (something). *verb(t).*
nách'i [ná ch'i] different, become; change. *verb(i).*
nach'íṁ [na ch'íṁ] beautiful; handsome; pretty. *adjective.*
nach'í7mixw [na ch'í7 mixw] unsettled, be. *verb(i).*
nách'nach'entsut [nách' na ch'en tsut] changing one's appearance, be. *verb(i).*
nach's find (something/someone) strange. *verb(t).* let another go. *verb(t).*
naháṁ [na háṁ] get home; come home. *verb(i).*
naháylhem [na háy lhem] give out names to descendants; give a name to a person. *verb(i).*
nahím [na hím] call one's name. *verb(i).*
nák̲nak̲entsut [nák̲ na k̲en tsut] bob and weave. *verb(i).*
nak̲'álhnexw [na k̲'álh nexw] hit (target). *verb(t).*
nak̲w'ú7wilhan [na k̲w'ú7 wi lhan] go aboard a canoe with (someone). *verb(t).*
-nalhn [-na lhn] {suffix usually translated as manage to, finally,}. *suffix.*
naṁ go. *verb(i).*
naṁáẏm [naṁ 7áẏ yem] wish to go. *verb(i).*
náṁen [náṁ men] go and get (something or someone); pick (someone) up. *verb(t).*
naṁnúmut [naṁ nú mut] go, finally; get to go. *verb(i).*
naṁs take (someone) somewhere. *verb(t).*
náṁshi [náṁ sheyt] take to (someone). *verb(t).*
-naṁut [-na ṁut] {reflexive suffix used with causative stems}. *suffix.*
nan call out (someone's) name; call or give (someone) a name; name (someone); call (someone). *verb(t).*
nánach' [ná nach'] doing wrong, be; wrong, be doing; wrong, be. *verb(i).*

nánaṁ [ná naṁ] go to; going along, be; going, be; moving, be. *verb(i).*

nánaṁs [ná naṁs] take (someone) along. *verb(t).*

nántsut [nán tsut] introducing oneself, be; saying one's own name, be. *verb(i).*

nápus [ná pus] cedar-bark cape. *noun.*

náp'tsaṅ [náp' tsaṅ] put food in (someone's) mouth. *verb(t).*

násteṁay [nás teṁ may] Saskatoon berry plant [see **snastem**]. *noun.*

nat night, be. *verb(i).*

natlh early morning, be [earlier than **ḵ'it**]. *verb(i).*

nax̱ch hand. *noun.*

nax̱cháchi7m [nax̱ chá chi 7em] signal with the hand or hands. *verb(i).*

nax̱chachmín [nax̱ chach mín] make motions with hands to (someone); signal to (someone) with the hand or hands. *verb(t).*

nax̱wáxwaẏ [na x̱wá xwaẏ] red-hot, be. *verb(i).*

náyat [náy yat] scold (someone). *verb(t).*

náyatsut [náy ya tsut] regret. *verb(i).*

na7 at [location or time]; on; in. *preposition.* there is; there, be; absent, be. *verb(i).*

na7 ta les down below, be. *phrase.*

na7 ~ naa name. *verb(i).*

na7áẏin [na 7áẏ yin] leave one's net; set out one's net. *verb(i).*

na7lhkwun [na 7lh kwun] maybe. *clitic.*

ná7nat [ná7 nat] evening, be. *verb(i).*

na7s make (something) one's business; leave (something) there; care about (something). *verb(t).*

na7xw still [from **na7** + **xw**]. *clitic.*

nchecheṁúsen [n che cheṁ mú sen] meet (someone). *verb(t).*

ncheṁús ~ nchéṁus ~ chéṁus [n cheṁ mús] meet; double, be; come together; together, come. *verb(i).*

nchéṁus ~ ncheṁús ~ chéṁus [n chéṁ mus] meet; double, be; come together; together, come. *verb(i).*

nchéṁusn ~ chéṁusn [n chéṁ mu sen] meet (someone); fold (something). *verb(t).*

nchíshus [n chí shus] come face-to-face with a dead spirit; meet [a spirit]. *verb(i).*

nch'aṁ ~ txwnch7aṁ ~ txwncha7áṁ [n ch'áṁ] how?; what kind?; how much? *question word; verb(i).* any kind. *verb(i).*

nch'áẇan [n ch'áẇ wan] one roll of 50 blankets. *numeral.*

nch'áyuṁ [n ch'áy yuṁ] one berry. *numeral.*

nch'áẏuẇam [n ch'áẏ yu7 ẇam] family [the descendants of one head]. *noun.*

nch'élmexw [n ch'él mexw] stranger. *noun.*

nch'élnech [n ch'él nech] lyrics; words to a song. *noun.*

nch'élnechiṁ [n ch'él ne chiṁ] sing out lyrics; sing the words to a song. *verb(i).*

nch'ích'elíẇen ~ ch'ich'alíẇen [n ch'í ch'e lí7 wen] grab all one can; greedy, be. *verb(i).*

nch'íwa [n ch'í wa] one tree. *numeral.*

nch'í7ten ~ ch'í7ten [n ch'í7 ten] ritualist's rattle; rattle; rattle used by a person with magic power. *noun.*

nch'nch'áẏlh [n ch'en ch'áẏ lh] have one child. *verb(i).*

nch'nch'u7 ~ ench'ench'ú7 ~ ch'nch'u7 [n ch'en ch'ú7] one human. *numeral.* alone, be [about a person]. *verb(i).*

nch'nch'u7ni [n ch'n ch'u7 ni] one (thing) for each, be. *verb(t).*

nch'u7 ~ ch'u7 ~ snch'u7 [n ch'u7] one. *numeral.*

nch'u7ḵ [n ch'u7ḵ] one o'clock. *noun.*

nch'u7ḵs [n ch'u7 ḵs] one small oblong object. *adjective.*

nch'ú7mut [n ch'ú7 mut] one piece. *numeral.* one, be at; unity, be in; one unit, be. *verb(i).*

nch'ú7muts [n ch'ú7 muts] give (someone) one. *verb(t).*

nch'ú7uẏs [n ch'ú 7uẏs] one large rock; one large piece; one chunk. *numeral.*

nechníchim [nech ní chim] bawl out; make a speech; talk [about group]; talk a lot. *verb(i).*

nechníchimiṅ [nech ní chi miṅ] bawl (someone) out; tell (someone). *verb(t).*

nech'nách' [nech' nách'] anyone [from a group of people]. *adjective.*

nech'nách'neẇas [nech' nách' neẇ was] differ from each other. *verb(i).*

nech'nech'íṁ [nech' ne ch'íṁ] beautiful [about group of women]; handsome [about group of men]. *adjective.*
nekw already. *clitic.*
nekw k̲wetk̲ tex̲w skwáyel [nekw k̲wetk̲ tex̲w skwáy yel] afternoon. *phrase.*
nekw tl'íyi7 stélmexw [nekw tl'í yi7 stél mexw] adult. *noun.*
nekwálhk̲wu7n [ne kwálh k̲wu 7en] stir (a liquid) [e.g., soup]. *verb(t).*
nékweṁ ~ nekwm [né kweṁ] move; start an engine; shake; stir. *verb(i).*
nékwen [né kwen] drive (a car); shake (something). *verb(t).*
nékwentsut [né kwen tsut] move around; move one's residence; make movements. *verb(i).*
nekwíyalh [ne kwéy yalh] rock one's baby. *verb(i).*
nekwm ~ nékweṁ [né kwm] move; stir; shake; start an engine. *verb(i).*
nekwnekwúsem [nekw ne kwú sem] shake one's head. *verb(i).*
nékwnexw [nékw nexw] move (something), manage to; move (something) accidentally; manage to move (something). *verb(t).*
nekwúsem [ne kwú sem] shake one's head. *verb(i).*
nekwúẏik̲w [ne kwúẏ yehk̲w] juice. *noun.*
nekw'í7tn ~ kw'i7tn [ne kw'í7 ten] ladder. *noun.*
nek̲ép' ~ nk̲ep' ~ k̲ep' [ne k̲ép'] close [on its own]; shut [on its own]. *verb(i).*
nek̲p'ét ~ nk̲p'et ~ k̲p'et [nek̲ p'ét] close (a door or box); shut (a door or box). *verb(t).*
nek̲'ák̲'eẏk̲ [ne k̲'á k̲'eẏk̲] sit on something. *verb(i).*
nek̲'álh [ne k̲'álh] in the way, be; in front of it, be; bar passage; hit, be; run into, be. *verb(i).*
nek̲'álhentsut [ne k̲'á lhen tsut] butt it. *verb(i).*
nek̲'álhn [ne k̲'á lhen] put (something) in the way. *verb(t).*
nek̲'álhnexw [ne k̲'álh nexw] hit (something) accidentally; run into (something) by chance; strike (an obstacle) accidentally. *verb(t).*
nek̲'álhs [ne k̲'álhs] hit (something). *verb(t).*
nek̲'ánatsut [ne k̲'á na tsut] return to where one was. *verb(i).*
nek̲'áyiwstn [ne k̲'áy yiws ten] drying pole for fish; roasting rack. *noun.*
nek̲'á7k̲'aẏk̲ [ne k̲'á7 k̲'aẏk̲] sitting on a chair, be. *verb(i).*
nek̲'ík̲'els [ne k̲'éh k̲'els] deceive (someone); fool (someone). *verb(t).*
nek̲'ík̲'eẇch [ne k̲'éh k̲'eẇch] balance oneself lying with the back across something; balanced, be; equilibrium, be in. *verb(i).*
nek̲'ílus [ne k̲'éh lus] intelligent; sensible; clever; smart; wise. *adjective.*
nek̲'íts'iẏik̲w [ne k̲'éh ts'i ẏehk̲w] crown of the head; top of the head; comb of a bird. *noun.*
nek̲wáchi7m [ne k̲wá chi 7em] warm one's hands. *verb(i).*
nek̲wálhk̲wu7n [ne k̲wálh k̲wu 7en] stir (something). *verb(t).*
nek̲wcháṁ [nek̲w cháṁ] heat oneself. *verb(i).*
nek̲wéltn [ne k̲wél tn] voice. *noun.*
nék̲wen [né k̲wen] warm (something) near the fire. *verb(t).*
nék̲wentsut [né k̲wen tsut] heat oneself; warm oneself. *verb(i).*
nek̲wshnáṁ [nek̲w shnáṁ] warm one's feet. *verb(i).*
nek̲wúyuẏ [ne k̲wúy yuẏ] floor on canoe to protect bottom. *noun.*
nek̲w'núk̲w' [nek̲w' núk̲w'] get all poked up; poked up, get all. *verb(i).*
nek̲w'úyachxw [ne k̲w'úy ya chxw] withering leaves, have [in the fall]. *adjective.*
nek̲w'úyiwan [ne k̲w'ú yi wan] not dare; afraid to, be. *verb(i).*
nelhm [ne lhm] rumble. *verb(i).*
nelhnílht [nelh nílht] go through the same (thing). *verb(t).*
nelhnílhtsut [nelh nílh tsut] connect oneself to something. *verb(i).*
nemá [ne má] forbidden; taboo. *adjective.*
nemán [ne mán] mourning for (someone), be in; forbid (someone). *verb(t).*
nemántsut [ne mán tsut] deny oneself. *verb(i).*

némi7n [ném mi 7en] make a soft plunking sound [e.g., cat jumping from table or distant cannon]. *verb(i).*

nemnáam [nem náam] overdo it. *verb(i).*

nénew̓ets [né new̓ wets] sail into [harbour, bay, etc.]. *verb(i).*

nén̓kwem [nén̓ kwem] moving, be. *verb(i).*

nen̓k̲wíchen [nen̓ k̲wí chen] warm oneself by the sun. *verb(i).*

nep follow. *verb(i).*

-nep ~ -np ~ -nup [-nep] floor {full word: **lhx̲énpten**}; ground {full word: **temíxw**}. *suffix.*

nepí [ne pí] get on to the road or trail. *verb(i).*

nesk̲ínem [nes k̲í nem] oil one's hair. *verb(i).*

nesk̲í7n [nes k̲í 7en] make a whispering sound. *verb(i).*

néshen [né shen] put (something) on its side. *verb(t).*

neshús [ne shús] fire log. *noun.*

new you. *pronoun.*

néwa [néw wa] husband or wife [term of address used by spouse]. *vocative.*

néwakw'a [néw wa kw'a] coffin. *noun.*

new̓ámim̓ ~ nexwnew̓ámim̓ [new̓ wá mim̓] load a gun; fill a can. *verb(i).*

-new̓as ~ -nw̓as [-ne w̓as] {suffix meaning: one another, both, each other}. *suffix.*

new̓áy̓usm [new̓ wáy̓ yu sem] grow into a tree [about bark]. *verb(i).*

néw̓en [néw̓ wen] put (something) inside; put (something) into it. *verb(t).*

new̓í [new̓ wí] enter. *verb(i).*

néwi ~ new [néw wi] you. *pronoun.*

new̓k̲sán [new̓ k̲ sán] put (a bullet) in a gun; put (a plug) in a socket. *verb(t).*

new̓k̲w hit on the head. *verb(i).*

new̓mámin [new̓ má min] put (a plug) in a socket. *verb(t).*

néw̓nacht [néw̓ nacht] pay (someone). *verb(t).*

new̓néw̓nech [new̓ néw̓ nech] repaying, be. *verb(i).*

news let it be you. *verb(t).*

new̓tsám̓ [new̓ tsám̓] phone call, make a. *verb(i).*

new̓tstn ~ nexwnéw̓tstn [néw̓ts ten] telephone. *noun.*

néwyap [néw yap] you guys. *pronoun.*

-nexw {an ending usually translated as: managed to, finally, accidentally, have. limited-control transitivizier}. *suffix.*

nexw- ~ n- {location}. *prefix.*

nexwá7s [ne xwá7s] leave behind for (someone). *verb(t).*

nexwchílhiwilh [nexw chí lhi wilh] over the side, be. *verb(i).*

nexwch'ít [nexw ch'ít] closer, be; close by, be; right by, be. *verb(i).*

nexwhiw̓k̲sán ~ nexwhíwk̲sán ~ nexwíwk̲sán [nexw hiw̓ k̲ sán] stick it into (someone's) nose. *verb(t).*

nexwhíwk̲sán ~ nexwhiw̓k̲sán ~ nexwíwk̲sán [nexw híwk̲ sán] stick it into (someone's) nose. *verb(t).*

nexwhiyáyus ~ xwiyáyus [nexw hi yá yus] big eyes, have; big-eyed [see also **x̲wechx̲wáchayus**]. *adjective.*

nexwhiyík̲s ~ nexwiyík̲s [nexw hi yéhk̲s] big nose, have a; big-nosed. *adjective.*

nexwik̲w'úsn ~ nexwyek̲w'úsn [ne xweh k̲w'ú sen] sharpen (a knife). *verb(t).*

nexwíwk̲sán ~ nexwhíwk̲sán ~ nexwhiw̓k̲sán [ne xwíw k̲ sán] stick it into (someone's) nose. *verb(t).*

nexwiyáy̓us ~ nexw7ey̓áy̓us [ne xwi yáy̓ yus] far-sighted; clear-sighted. *adjective.*

nexwiyík̲s ~ nexwhiyík̲s [ne xwi yéhk̲s] big nose, have a; big-nosed. *adjective.*

nexwiyíwilh [ne xwi yí wilh] stout. *adjective.*

nexwlámay [nexw lá may] bottle. *noun.*

nexwleklíts [nexw lek líts] lock door. *verb(i).*

nexwlek̲we7áy [nexw le k̲wa 7áy] pocket. *noun.*

nexwlí7lim̓ay ~ xwlí7lim̓ay [nexw lí7 li7 may] little bottle [see **nexwlámay**]. *noun.*

nexwlí7lk̲ [nexw léh 7elk̲] cheap. *adjective.*

nexwlí7ls [nexw léh 7els] eventful, be; special, be very. *verb(i).*

nexwmets'en̓álpk̲em [nexw me ts'en̓ 7ál p k̲em] tell a lie. *verb(i).*

nexwmets'ńálk̲p ~ nexwmets'tńálk̲p ~ xwméts'tńálk̲p ~ xwmets'ńálk̲p [nexw me ts'en̓ 7ál k̲p] lie; falsehood. *noun.* tell a lie. *verb(i).*

nexwmets'tńálk̲p ~ xwméts'tńálk̲p ~ xwmets'ńálk̲p ~ nexwmets'ńálk̲p [nexw me ts'eń 7ál k̲p] lie; falsehood. *noun.* tell a lie. *verb(i).*
nexwmíkw'shn [nexw míkw' shen] clean feet, be always having. *verb(i).*
nexwmiyíw̓ax̲an ~ xwmiyíw̓ax̲an [nexw mi yí7 wa x̲an] side. *noun.*
nexwmiyíwa7n ~ xwmiyíwa7n [nexw mi yí wa 7en] cheek. *noun.*
nexwmúkwutsin ~ mukwtst [nexw mú kwu tsin] kiss (someone). *verb(t).*
nexwmú7ts ~ xwmu7ts [nexw mú7ts] drop something from one's mouth. *verb(i).*
nexwnákwnakwk̲am [nexw nákw nakw k̲am] walking, shaking one's rear end, be. *verb(i).*
nexwnew̓ám̓en [nexw new̓ wám̓ men] fill (something) with a solid; load (a gun). *verb(t).*
nexwnew̓ámim̓ ~ new̓ámim̓ [nexw new̓ wá mim̓] load a rifle; fill a can. *verb(i).*
nexwnew̓éyelh ~ nexwniw̓éyalh [nexw new̓ wéy yelh] give advice; teach; advise; instruct; instruct a child. *verb(i).*
nexwnew̓ít ~ nexwníw̓it [nexw new̓ wít] teach (someone); instruct (someone); advise (someone). *verb(t).*
nexwnew̓íwstn [nexw new̓ wíws ten] place to keep clothes; container; box; trunk. *noun.*
nexwnéw̓tstn ~ new̓tstn [nexw néw̓ts ten] telephone. *noun.*
nexwnéwu7ts [nexw né wu7ts] go into inlet. *verb(i).* Howe Sound [see also **atl'k̲a7tsem** and **txwnéwu7ts**]. *place name.*
nexwníchimtn [nexw ní chim ten] "where one's voice comes from". *noun.*
nexwnílhus [nexw ní lhus] resemble. *verb(i).*
nexwnílhusnew̓as [nexw ní lhus new̓ was] resemble one another. *verb(i).*
nexwnínew̓ [nexw ní new̓] upbringing, have the; well brought up, be. *verb(i).*
nexwnínlhewá7nem [nexw nín lhew wa7 nem] put oneself in someone's place; commiserate. *verb(i).*
nexwníw̓ [nexw níw̓] advice; teaching; upbringing; instructions; ways; fashion; manners. *noun.*
nexwníw̓en [nexw ní7 wen] instruct (someone); pay attention to (someone's) instruction. *verb(t).*
nexwníw̓eni [nexw ní7 wen ni] pay attention to (someone). *verb(t).*
nexwniw̓éyalh ~ nexwnew̓éyelh [nexw ni w̓éy yalh] teach; advise; instruct; instruct a child; give advice. *verb(i).*
nexwníw̓it [nexw ní7 wit] advise (someone); instruct (someone). *verb(t).*
nexwníw̓iwsentem [nexw ní7 wiw sen tem] sex with (someone), have. *verb(p).*
nexwníw̓mamin [nexw níw̓ ma min] loaded, be [about gun]. *verb(i).*
nexwnútk̲s [nexw nút k̲s] talking through one's nose, be; talk nasally; produce nasal sounds; make a nasal twang. *verb(i).*
nexws- {prefix creating agent nouns}. *prefix.*
nexwschecháchshay̓ [nexws che chách shay̓] generous person. *adjective.*
nexwschíchip [nexws chí chip] ticklish. *adjective.*
nexwskwéy [nexw skwéy] diligent; energetic. *adjective.*
nexwskw'enmáylh [nexws kw'en máylh] praying all the time, be; someone who prays all the time, be; have the habit of praying all the time; habit of praying all the time, have the. *verb(i).*
nexwsk̲'ek̲'elk̲'ál̓ [nexws k̲'e k̲'el k̲'ál̓] credulous; gullible. *adjective.* sucker [someone who is easily fooled]. *noun.*
nexwsk̲'elk̲'ál̓ [nexws k̲'el k̲'ál̓] obedient. *adjective.*
nexwsk̲wéy̓k̲wi [nexws k̲wéy̓ k̲wi] talkative. *adjective.*
nexwslhich'álhx̲a [nexws lhi ch'álh x̲a] spirit who cuts people's throats. *noun.*
nexwsmemey̓máy̓ [nexws me mey̓ máy̓] person who is always absent-minded; absent-minded person; forgetful person. *noun.*
nexwsmey̓máy̓ [nexws mey̓ máy̓] person who is always forgetting; person who is always getting lost. *noun.*
nexwsnéńp [nexws néń p] go along

the road; walk right on a trail [of an animal]. *verb(i).*

nexwsníchim [nexws ní chim] great talker; someone who talks a lot. *noun.*

nexwspepiy̓átulh [nexws pe pi y̓á tulh] hunter. *noun.*

nexwspipisténʼak̲ [nexws pi pis ténʼ nak̲] jealous, always be. *verb(i).*

nexwstek̲tk̲ának̲ [nexws tek̲ t k̲á nak̲] asking suspiciously whether one has said bad things about him/her, be always; suspicious, be; paranoid, be. *verb(i).*

nexwsteptpúlhim̓ [nexws tep t pú lhim̓] stretch skins all the time. *verb(i).*

nexwsts'eyts'áyx̲aylh [nexws ts'i ts'áy x̲aylh] habit of rushing people, be in the. *verb(i).*

nexwswéts'wets'áy̓lh ~ nexwswewts'áy̓lh [nexws wéts' we ts'áy̓ lh] given to teasing people, be. *verb(i).*

nexwswewts'áy̓lh ~ nexwswéts'wets'áy̓lh [nexws wew ts'áy̓ lh] given to teasing people, be. *verb(i).*

nexwsx̲éyx̲ ~ nexwsx̲éy̓x̲ [nexws x̲éyx̲] warrior. *noun.*

nexwsx̲éy̓x̲ ~ nexwsx̲éyx̲ [nexws x̲éy̓x̲] warrior. *noun.*

nexwsx̲wex̲wiy̓ám̓ [nexws x̲we x̲wey̓ yám̓] storyteller. *noun.*

nexwsx̲wik̲w'em [nexw sx̲wi k̲w'em] police officer. *noun.*

nexwsyétsyets [nexws yéts yets] tattletale. *noun.*

nexwsyúlhim̓ [nexws yú lhim̓] burning. *noun.*

nexws7ílhen [nexws 7í lhen] eater. *adjective.*

nexws7ilhením [nexws 7i lhe ním] good appetite, have a. *verb(i).*

nexws7usáyelh [nexws 7u sáy yelh] teacher. *noun.*

nexws7ú7x̲wim̓ [nexws 7ú7 x̲wim̓] carver. *noun.*

nexwshétshtam [nexw shét shtam] diver. *noun.*

nexwtá7 [nexw tá7] around there, be; go by way of some place. *verb(i).*

nexwtí7 [nexw tí7] around here, be; come by way of some place. *verb(i).*

nexwt'át'em [nexw t'á t'em] miss a shot. *verb(i).*

nexwts'its'usnítus [nexw ts'i ts'us ní tus] sad face, have a. *adjective.*

nexwúk̲w'uts ~ nxwúkw'us [ne xwú k̲w'uts] whole dried salmon. *noun.*

nexwwániw̓an [nexw wá ni7 wan] impatient waiting, get. *verb(i).*

nexwwáw̓sh [nexw wáw̓sh] those sitting in the last row; those sitting farthest away from the fire; those sitting in the back row. *noun.*

nexwwéchwechk̲s ~ wéchwechk̲s [nexw wéch wech k̲s] broad-nosed; flat-nosed; wide nostril nose, have a. *adjective.*

nexwyál̓yelx̲ay [nexw yál̓ yel x̲ay] look around searching. *verb(i).*

nexwyaw̓ánʼshn [nexw yaw̓ wánʼ shen] legs in front, be with; legs in front, have one's; do something feet first. *verb(i).*

nexwyawapáy [nexw ya wa páy] mast. *noun.*

nexwyek̲w'úsn [nexw ye k̲w'ú sen] sharpen (a knife). *verb(t).*

nexwyelx̲áy̓ [nexw yel x̲áy̓] look around searching. *verb(i).*

nexwyém̓tenan ~ nexwyem̓tnán [nexw yém̓ te nan] put a belt on (someone). *verb(t).*

nexwyém̓tn [nexw yém̓ tn] belt. *noun.*

nexwyem̓tnán ~ nexwyém̓tenan [nexw yem̓ ten nán] put a belt on (someone). *verb(t).*

nexwyiy̓ulháy [nexw yi7 yu lháy] stove. *noun.*

nexwyíy̓ulhtn [nexw yí7 yulh ten] fire hearth; fireplace. *noun.*

nexwyukwá7min [nexw yu kwá7 min] "what belongs to a stingy person." *noun.*

nexwyútsim̓ [nexw yú tsim̓] someone that crowds or shoves. *noun.*

nexw7átsach [nexw 7á tsach] wrist; palm of hand. *noun.*

nexw7átshen ~ nexw7átsshn [nexw 7át shen] sole of foot; bottom of foot. *noun.*

nexw7átsiyax̲a7en [nexw 7á tsi ya x̲a 7en] armpits. *noun.*

nexw7átsshn ~ nexw7átshen [nexw

7áts shen] sole of foot; bottom of foot. *noun.*

nexw7áts'k̲ [nexw 7áts' k̲] outside, be. *verb(i).*

nexw7aw̓ítsay̓ [nexw 7aw̓ wí tsay̓] fast worker, be a; active, be; energetic person, be an. *verb(i).*

nexw7áwiwánm [nexw 7á wi wá nem] discouraged, be; surprised, be very; disagreeably surprised, be. *verb(i).*

nexw7áx̲wn [nexw 7á x̲wen] admire (something/someone). *verb(t).*

nexw7áy̓ [nexw 7áy̓] changed, be; exhange. *verb(i).*

nexw7áy̓amustn [nexw 7áy̓ ya mus ten] mask. *noun.*

nexw7áy̓entsut [nexw 7áy̓ yen tsut] transform oneself. *verb(i).*

nexw7áyits'á7n [nexw 7áy yi ts'a 7en] change the blanket of (the dead). *verb(t).*

nexw7áy̓its'm ~ snexw7ayits'á7m [nexw 7áy̓ yi ts'em] change of clothes. *noun.*

nexw7áy̓n [nexw 7áy̓ yen] change (something) around; train in or follow (a tradition); replace (something); represent (something); change (something). *verb(t).*

nexw7áy̓s [nexw 7áy̓s] trade (something); exchange (something); trade (something) in; change (something). *verb(t).*

nexw7áysay̓ch [nexw 7áy say̓ch] go by inside way; go by inside route [e.g., between Bowen Island and the mainland]. *verb(i).*

nexw7áy̓stway̓ [nexw 7áy̓s tway̓] trade; exchange with each other. *verb(i).*

nexw7éncha [nexw 7én cha] go by which way?; go by which route?; go by what means? [by canoe, by foot, etc.]; go how? *question word; verb(i).*

nexw7étchus [nexw 7ét chus] jealous; envious; begrudging. *adjective.*

nexw7étchusem [nexw 7ét chu sem] envied, be. *verb(p).*

nexw7étchusni [nexw 7ét chus ni] jealous of (someone), be; envious of (someone), be; begrudging of (someone), be. *verb(t).*

nexw7éx̲ts'ch ~ ex̲ts'ch ~ nx̲ats'ch [nexw 7éx̲ ts'ch] backbone. *noun.*

nexw7ey̓áy̓us ~ nexwiyáy̓us [nexw 7ey̓ yáy̓ yus] clear-sighted; far-sighted. *adjective.*

nexw7éy̓wilh [nexw 7éy̓ wilh] kind; good-natured. *adjective.*

nexw7iy̓áy̓ulh [nexw 7ey̓ y̓á7 yulh] travel by canoe; travel by any conveyance (e.g., a car); aboard, be. *verb(i).*

nexw7íy̓em [nexw 7éy̓ yem] clear, be [about water]. *verb(i).*

nexw7í7ik̲s [nexw 7éy̓ 7ehk̲s] keen of scent, be; good sense of smell, have a. *verb(i).*

nexw7í7xwen̓us [nexw 7éy̓ xwen̓ nus] sad-looking; sad look, have a. *adjective.*

nexw7út'us [nexw 7ú t'us] pout; long face, have a. *verb(i).*

nex̲én̓etn [ne x̲én̓ ne ten] animal tracks; footprints. *noun.*

nex̲éwtl'ch [ne x̲éw tl'ch] broken spine, have a. *adjective.*

nex̲wék̲wal [ne x̲wé k̲wal] pocket. *noun.*

nex̲wésshn [ne x̲wés shen] marrow. *noun.*

nex̲wéts'k̲w'tn [ne x̲wets'k̲w tn] arrow notch. *noun.*

nex̲wík̲w' [ne x̲wik̲w'] arrested, be. *verb(i).*

nex̲wík̲w'in [ne x̲wi k̲w'in] put (someone) in jail; tie (someone) up; arrest (someone). *verb(t).*

nex̲wíl̓em [ne x̲wi l'em] empty, be. *verb(i).*

nex̲wíl̓min̓ [ne x̲wil' min̓] emptied bottle, be an. *verb(i).*

nex̲wíl̓shi [ne x̲wil' shi] open for (someone). *verb(t).*

nex̲wil̓tsán̓ ~ nex̲wil̓tsen̓ [ne x̲wil' tsan̓] open (a box). *verb(t).*

nex̲wíl̓tsen̓ ~ nex̲wil̓tsán̓ [ne x̲wil' tsen̓] open (a box). *verb(t).*

nex̲wíx̲welem [ne x̲wi x̲we lem] leave space. *verb(i).*

nex̲wíx̲wel̓ts [ne x̲wi x̲wel'ts] opened, be [about a door, window, etc.]. *verb(i).*

ney̓ch high seas. *noun.*

néyney̓ch [ney ney̓ch] front of house; front room. *noun.*

nhin̓ítsut ~ nin̓ítsut [n hi n̓i tsut] brag about one's success with a person of the opposite sex. *verb(i).*

-ni [-ni] {added onto some words so that you can use the object endings, see section on "object endings"}. *suffix.*

nicháyak̲'in [ni cha ya k̲'in] front of house. *noun.*
níchim [ni chim] speak; talk. *verb(i).*
níchimin [ni chi min] tell (someone). *verb(t).*
nichimnúmut [ni chim nu mut] talk, manage to. *verb(i).*
níchimstway [ni chims tway] talk to one another. *verb(i).*
níkwit [ni kwit] swing (someone). *verb(t).*
níkwitsut [ni kwi tsut] swing oneself; swinging, be. *verb(i).*
nikw'íyalh [ni kw'i yalh] rock one's baby. *verb(i).*
ník̲im̓ [ni k̲im̓] dodge; duck. *verb(i).*
ník̲'i [ni k̲'i] want to go and see someone; feel a wish to be with someone. *verb(i).*
ník̲'i [ni k̲'i] spoiled, get; soft, get [about meat or fish, e.g., when leaving fish in]. *verb(i).*
ník̲wusm [ni k̲wu sm] nod one's head. *verb(i).*
ník̲w'em [ni k̲w'em] soft [as cloth]; smooth; soft; fine [about materials]. *adjective.*
ník̲w'emen [ni k̲w'e men] make (something) smooth. *verb(t).*
nik̲w'em̓í7 [ni k̲w'e m̓i7] soft, getting [about down feathers]. *verb(i).*
ník̲w'mayits' [nik̲w' ma yits'] soft cloth, be a. *verb(i).*
ník̲w'umay̓ [ni k̲w'u may̓] soft hair, have. *verb(i).*
nilh [nilh] it is; that is; that's the one. *verb(i).*
nílhen [ni lhen] compare (someone). *verb(t).*
nílhnew̓as [nilh ne w̓as] look alike; be the same; same, be the. *verb(i).*
nímalh [ni malh] us; we. *pronoun.*
ninaháy̓lhm [ni na hay̓ lhm] give a name to a child. *verb(i).*
niná7min [ni na7 min] nickname. *noun.*
nin̓chím̓s [nin̓ chim̓s] question (someone). *verb(t).*
nínch'u7 [nin ch'u7] one animal. *numeral.*
ninicháyak̲'in [ni ni cha ya k̲'in] front room. *noun.*
nin̓ítsut ~ nhin̓ítsut [ni n̓i tsut] brag about one's success with a person of the opposite sex. *verb(i).*
níni7ch [ni ni7 ch] outer, be [in the sense of "farther offshore"]. *verb(i).*
nín̓kwemshen [nin̓ kwem shen] moving one's feet, be. *verb(i).*
nínkwk̲wuy̓shnem [ninkw k̲wuy̓sh nem] move one's toes; move one's feet [e.g., to the music]; tap one's feet. *verb(i).*
nix̲k̲wúy̓ach [nix̲ k̲wu y̓ach] finger. *noun.*
nix̲k̲wúy̓shen [nix̲ k̲wuy̓ shen] toe. *noun.*
ni7ch [ni7 ch] out in deep water, be; deep water, be out in. *verb(i).* deep sea. *noun.*
nk'ísin ~ k̲'ísin̓ [n k'i sin] tie (something) up; know (something) together. *verb(t).*
nkw'amtn [n kw'am tn] when the eagle comes to take a dead person away. *noun.*
nkw'chustn ~ nkw'ekw'chústn ~ kw'chustn ~ kw'ek̲wchústn [nkw' chus tn] window; mirror. *noun.*
nkw'ekw'chústn ~ kw'chustn ~ kw'ek̲wchústn ~ nkw'chustn [n kw'ekw' chus tn] mirror; window. *noun.*
nkw'el̓áw̓us [n kw'e l'a w̓us] skin on face. *noun.*
nk̲áp'tsan [n k̲ap' tsan] cover (someone's) mouth. *verb(t).*
nk̲élten [n k̲el ten] allergic, be. *verb(i).*
nk̲ep' ~ nek̲ép' ~ k̲ep' [n k̲ep'] close [on its own]; shut [on its own]. *verb(i).*
nk̲ep'tán ~ nk̲ep'tn [n k̲ep' tan] door [the more common word is shewalh]; cover. *noun.*
nk̲ep'tn ~ nk̲ep'tán [n k̲ep' tn] door [the more common word is **shewalh**); cover. *noun.*
nk̲p'et ~ k̲p'et ~ nek̲p'ét [nk̲ p'et] close (something); shut (something). *verb(t).*
nk̲x̲am̓ [nk̲ x̲am̓] hold much; contain a lot; eat much. *verb(i).*
nk̲'ats'íchn ~ k̲'ats'íchn [n k̲'a ts'i chn] hold one's arms on the back. *verb(i).*
nk̲'ísin [n k̲'i sin] tie (something) up; knot (something) together. *verb(t).* knot. *noun.*
nk̲wík̲wix̲ [n k̲wi k̲wix̲] sitting with legs open, be. *verb(i).*
nk̲wí7k̲wistn [n k̲wi7 k̲wis tn] little cooking pot [see **nk̲wi7stn**]. *noun.*
nk̲wi7stn [n k̲wi7 stn] cooking pot. *noun.*
nk̲wúyum̓ [n k̲wu yum̓] child after twins. *noun.*
nk̲wú7us ~ snk̲wú7us ~ k̲wú7us [n k̲wu 7us] tear; tears. *noun.*

nk̲w'áyak̲' [n k̲w'a yak̲'] turn inside out. *verb(i).*

nk̲w'áyk̲'an [n k̲w'ay k̲'an] turn (something) inside out. *verb(t).*

nk̲w'elk̲s [n k̲w'elk̲s] cholic, be; bile, be full of. *verb(i).*

nk̲w'ík̲w'lus ~ k̲w'ík̲w'lus ~ nk̲w'ík̲w'lwas [n k̲w'ik̲w' lus] stick for holding salmon above fire; dried salmon put away for winter use. *noun.*

nk̲w'ík̲w'lwas ~ nk̲w'ík̲w'lus ~ k̲w'ík̲w'lus [n k̲w'i k̲w'l was] stick for holding salmon above fire; dried salmon put away for winter use. *noun.*

nk̲w'úk̲wey̓ek̲w [n k̲w'u k̲we y̓ek̲w] hit on the head, get. *verb(i).*

nk̲w'úk̲wey̓ek̲wán [n k̲w'u k̲w'e y̓e k̲wan] hit (someone) on the top of the head. *verb(t).*

nk̲w'ú7nexw [n k̲w'u7 nexw] partner. *noun.*

nk̲w'ú7wilh [n k̲w'u7 wilh] partner in a canoe. *noun.*

nlhakw'máy [n lhakw' may] windpipe; vein [literally, breath-container]. *noun.*

nlhák̲w'us [n lha k̲w'us] slap on the face. *verb(i).*

nlhex̲wk̲ [n lhex̲wk̲] coward, be a. *verb(i).*

nlhink̲stn ~ lhink̲stn [n lhink̲ stn] nose ornament. *noun.*

nmí7antsut [n mi 7an tsut] commit suicide. *verb(i).*

nmi7antsutáy̓m [n mi 7an tsu ta y̓m] suicidal, be. *verb(i).*

-np ~ -nup ~ -nep [-np] floor {full word: **lhx̲énpten**}; ground {full word: **temíxw**}. *suffix.*

npen̓em̓áy ~ pen̓em̓áy [n pe n̓e m̓ay] garden. *noun.*

np'ahách [n p'a hach] palm of hand. *noun.*

np'ats' [n p'ats'] frozen [about river]. *adjective.*

np'a7ám̓in ~ p'a7ám̓in [n pa 7a m̓in] handle [e.g., for a bucket]; haft. *noun.*

np'a7shn [n p'a7 shn] sole of foot. *noun.*

nsa7álh [n sa 7alh] low, be [about sound]. *verb(i).*

nsa7ústn [n sa 7us tn] towel. *noun.*

nsélus ~ sélus [n se lus] spin wool; spin thread. *verb(i).* spinning wool. *noun.*

nsesa7álhi [n se sa 7a lhi] fainter and fainter, be getting [about a sound off in the distance]. *verb(i).*

nset'k̲'íws ~ set'k̲íws [n set' k̲'iws] side of body. *noun.*

nsex̲á7x̲em ~ sex̲á7x̲em [n se x̲a7 x̲em] pigeon [wild]. *noun.*

ns-húhupit ~ súhupit ~ nsúhupit [ns hu hu pit] rabbit. *noun.*

nsists'k̲ [n sis ts'k̲] sitting on the ground, be. *verb(i).*

nsk̲ínem [n sk̲i nem] put on hair oil; rub oil in one's hair; oil one's hair. *verb(i).*

nsk̲i7 [n sk̲i7] underbrush; brushy terrain. *noun.* brushy place, be; brushy, be very. *verb(i).*

nsk̲'ák̲'i tkwi stek̲íw [n sk̲'a k̲'i t kwi ste k̲iw] travel by horse; horseback ride. *verb(i).*

nsmék̲w'á7 ~ smek̲w'á7 [n sme k̲w'a7] great blue heron. *noun.*

nsnen̓p [n snen̓p] follow [road, path]; on, be [a road]. *verb(i).*

nsúhupit ~ súhupit ~ ns-húhupit [n su hu pit] rabbit. *noun.*

nswa7 [n swa7] mine. *adjective.*

nswú7wu ~ swú7wu [n swu7 wu] cougar. *noun.*

nsx̲íp'im [n sx̲i p'im] hawk. *noun.*

ns7achcháwam ~ achcháwam ~ echcháwm ~ s7achcháwam [ns 7ach cha wam] spawn. *verb(i).* crescent gunnel; penpoint gunnel; conger eel. *noun.*

ns7alh [ns 7alh] low; soft [about voice]. *adjective.*

ns7ey ~ s7ey [ns 7ey] loud. *adjective.*

ns7eyk̲w [ns 7eyk̲w] loud speaker, be a. *verb(i).*

ns7eyx̲ [ns 7eyx̲] look after someone. *verb(i).*

ns7éyx̲ni [ns 7eyx̲ ni] babysit (someone); look after (someone); witness to (a statement), be a; keep (a name) in good repute. *verb(t).*

ns7eyx̲sténam̓ut [ns 7eyx̲ ste na m̓ut] take care of oneself; behave oneself; behave carefully. *verb(i).*

ns7it ~ s7it [ns 7it] act completely; really. *verb(i).*

ns7í7x̱ni [ns 7i 7x̱ ni] watch (statement); take care of (statement); witness to (statement), be; keep (name) in good repute. *verb(t).*
nsháwiẏups [n sha wi ẏups] tailbone; tail end. *noun.*
nshaẇk̲s [n shaẇk̲s] bridge of nose; nose, bridge of. *noun.*
nsháẇus ~ sháẇus [n sha ẇus] cheekbone. *noun.* skinny. *adjective.*
nshech'k̲ [n shech'k̲] splinter in the rear end, have a. *adjective.*
ntahíṅet [n ta hi ṅet] depend on someone. *verb(i).*
ntahíṅetni [n ta hi ṅet ni] depend on (someone). *verb(t).*
ntak̲wtn ~ tak̲wtn ~ sntak̲wtn [n tak̲w tn] bucket. *noun.*
ntala7áy ~ tála7ay [n ta la 7ay] purse; money bag [see **tála**]. *noun.*
ntala7áyus [n ta la 7a yus] glasses [see **tála**]. *noun.*
ntáx̱wustn [n ta x̱wus tn] curtain. *noun.*
nta7áẇeni [n ta 7a ẇe ni] think about (something/someone). *verb(t).*
nta7áẇn ~ ta7áẇn [n ta 7a ẇn] expect; think; consider. *verb(i).*
ntelk̲t [n telk̲t] answer (someone). *verb(t).*
ntelk̲tn [n telk̲ tn] answer. *noun.*
ntélhchis [n telh chis] stone hammer. *noun.*
ntemxw [n te mxw] short-tailed animal. *noun.*
ntik̲w' ~ tik̲w' [n tik̲w'] bump; run aground [about boat]. *verb(i).*
ntík̲w'iẏek̲w [n tik̲w'i ẏek̲w] bump the top of one's head. *verb(i).*
ntík̲w'us ~ tík̲w'us [n ti k̲w'us] bump one's head. *verb(i).*
nt'ek̲w'ch [n te k̲w'ch] half, be [see also **esék̲' ~ lhsek̲'**]; half full, be [about bottle]. *verb(i).*
nt'ek̲w'cháṅ [n tek̲w' chaṅ] cut (something) in half. *verb(t).*
nt'ik̲wm [n ti k̲wm] cold, has the quality of being [e.g., a house]; drafty. *adjective.*
ntl'iwk̲s [n tl'iwk̲s] clams in one's nose; boogers. *noun.*
ntl'i7 [n tl'i7] stingy. *adjective.*
ntl'í7tán ~ ntl'i7tn [n tl'i7 tan] hideout. *noun.*
ntl'i7tn ~ ntl'i7tán [n tl'i7 tn] hideout. *noun.*
ntl'up [n tl'up] numb bum, have a. *adjective.*
ntsekwtn [n tsekw tn] bow string. *noun.*
ntséwiyekw [n tse wi yekw] gabled ends, have. *verb(i).*
nts'ahémin [n ts'a he min] temples [anatomical]. *noun.*
nts'ák̲iyik̲w [n ts'a k̲i yik̲w] bald head, have a; bald. *adjective.*
nts'ák̲'iẏek̲w ~ ts'ák̲'iẏek̲w [n ts'a k̲'i ẏek̲w] bald. *adjective.*
nts'ak̲'k̲ [n ts'ak̲' k̲] hit on the bottom, get. *verb(i).*
nts'á7lhten [n ts'a 7lh ten] seed [of salmonberry, apple, orange, etc.]. *noun.*
nts'ex̱shn [n ts'ex̱ shn] have one's shoes wear out; wear out, have one's shoes; have worn-out shoes; shoes, have worn-out. *verb(i).*
nts'íts'xwus [n ts'its' xwus] pitiful looking; sad-faced; have a sad face. *adjective.*
nts'k̲wu7tstn ~ ts'k̲wu7tstn ~ snts'k̲wu7tstn [nts' k̲wu 7ts tn] smoking pipe; pipe [for smoking]. *noun.*
nts'úysus ~ ts'úysus [n ts'uy sus] crazy face, have a; crazy-faced. *adjective.*
nu question particle. *clitic.*
nu chexw men wa ha7lh [nu chexw men wa ha 7lh] Are you well? *sentence.*
nu chexw na7 taẏ [nu chexw na7 taẏ] Are you there? *sentence.*
nuk̲w [nuk̲w] midday, be; noon, be. *verb(i).*
nuk̲ws [nuk̲ws] game using two pieces of rubber tied on a stick. *noun.* play that game. *verb(i).*
nuk̲w' [nuk̲w'] poked, get. *verb(i).*
nuk̲w'nálhen [nuk̲w' na lhen] poke it finally; poke it accidentally; poke it, manage to. *verb(i).*
núk̲w'shen [nuk̲w' shen] get sliver in foot; sliver in foot, get a. *verb(i).*
nuk̲w'tsk̲wú7n [nuk̲w'ts k̲wu 7n] peg (a canoe). *verb(t).*
núk̲w'un [nu k̲w'un] poke (something). *verb(t).*
-numut [-nu mut] {reflexive suffix}. *suffix.*
núnstem [nun stem] call out to (someone). *verb(p).*

núṅutam [nu ṅu tam] humming sound, make a [e.g., of people in another room]; make an indistinct hum [about people talking]. *verb(i).*

-nup ~ -np ~ -nep [-nup] floor {full word: **lhx̱énpten**}; ground {full word: **temíxw**}. *suffix.*

nuun [nuun] hailing (the house), be. *verb(t).*

nuuw [nuuw] hello. *interjection.*

nú7nacht [nu7 nacht] repay (someone). *verb(t).*

nxwúkw'us ~ nexwúḵw'uts [n xwu kw'us] whole dried salmon. *noun.*

nx̱ats'ch ~ nexw7éx̱ts'ch ~ ex̱ts'ch [n x̱a ts'ch] backbone. *noun.*

nx̱etx̱ít7ayus ~ x̱etx̱ít7ayus [n x̱et x̱it 7a yus] far-sighted; able to see at great distance. *adjective.*

nx̱éx̱el̓ch [n x̱e x̱el'ch] marks on the back, be having. *verb(i).*

nx̱eya7mán [n x̱e ya7 man] make (someone) laugh. *verb(t).*

nx̱eya7mnúmut [n x̱e ya 7m nu mut] smile, manage to. *verb(i).*

nx̱iya7mán [n x̱i ya7 man] make (someone) laugh. *verb(t).*

nx̱iyá7ms [n x̱i ya 7ms] smile. *verb(i).*

nx̱weḵw'ál [n x̱we ḵw'al] pocket [any type]. *noun.*

nx̱wesshn [n x̱wes shn] marrow. *noun.*

nx̱wil̓ts ~ x̱wil̓ts [n x̱wil'ts] open, be; open it. *verb(i).*

nx̱wil̓tsáṅ ~ x̱wil̓tsáṅ ~ x̱wil̓tsn ~ nx̱wil̓tsn ~ x̱wíl̓tseṅ [n x̱wil' tsaṅ] open (something). *verb(t).*

nx̱wil̓tsn ~ nx̱wil̓tsáṅ ~ x̱wil̓tsáṅ ~ x̱wil̓tsn ~ x̱wíl̓tseṅ [n x̱wil' tsn] open (something). *verb(t).*

nx̱wíl̓tsnexw ~ x̱wíl̓tsnexw [n x̱wil'ts nexw] have opened (something); opened (something), have; open (something); manage to open (something); get (something) open. *verb(t).*

nx̱wítl'ulh [n x̱wi tl'ulh] 1/4 cup; 1/2 cup; partial measure [less than a cup]. *verb(i).*

nx̱wuts'ch [n x̱wuts' ch] bruised back, have a; have a bruised back. *adjective.*

n7áy̓ach [n 7a y̓ach] holding on with one's hands, be. *verb(i).*

P p

páak̲wen [páa k̲wen] put (kettle) on stove. *verb(t).*

paalt [paalt] skim (something) off. *verb(t).*

paaltm [páal tem] skimmed off, be. *verb(p).*

páchan [pa chan] spread (something); spread out (something). *verb(t).*

páchan̓tsut [pa chan̓ tsut] spread out, be; spread [e.g., people from an ancestor or shoots from a weed]. *verb(i).*

paháyikwup [pa ha yi kwup] blow into fire. *verb(i).*

paháyumen [pa ha yu men] clear leaves and twigs from (blueberries or huckleberries). *verb(t).*

pahím̓ [pa him̓] blow [about the wind]. *verb(i).*

pahím̓ni [pa him̓ ni] blow at (something/someone). *verb(t).*

pahím̓nitem [pa him̓ ni tem] caught by the wind, be; come to one [about wind]. *verb(p).*

pákwan̓ [pa kwan̓] cut (meat). *verb(t).*

pákw'en [pa kw'en] put (something) over smoke of fire. *verb(t).*

pakw'k̲án̓ [pakw' k̲an̓] put (pot) over heat. *verb(t).*

pák̲'em [pa k̲'em] bloom. *verb(i).*

pák̲w'an [pa k̲w'an] scatter (feathers, seeds, etc.); dust (something) up. *verb(t).*

pák̲w'usem [pa k̲w'u sem] powder one's face. *verb(i).*

pák̲w'ustn [pa k̲w'us tn] face powder. *noun.*

pálapála [pa la pa la] deer fern; sword fern. *noun.*

pápey̓m [pa pe y̓m] want to rest; resting now, be. *verb(i).*

Pápiyek̲ [pa pi yak̲] Brockton Point; Vancouver Lighthouse. *place name.*

pápk̲'am [pap k̲'am] flower; bloom, be in. *verb(i).*

pápu7ten [pa pu7 ten] goatsbeard [type of plant]. *noun.*

pasm [pa sm] budding, be; sprouting, be; coming out, be [about plants]. *verb(i).*

paw tired muscles from overexertion, get. *verb(i).*

pawshn [paw shn] sore feet from exertion, get. *verb(i).*

páyem [pa yem] rest. *verb(i).*

páy̓iya [pa y̓i ya] grandfather. *noun.*

paym̓áy̓m [pay m̓a y̓m] want to rest. *verb(i).*

paymnúmut [paym nu mut] rest finally; rest, get to. *verb(i).*

payms [payms] make (someone) rest. *verb(t).*

pa7áchxw [pa 7a chxw] budding a lot, be; sprouting a lot, be. *verb(i).*

pa7áchxwim̓ [pa 7ach xwim̓] taking, be [about leaves on a tree]; spring-raining, be. *verb(i).*

pá7chalem [pa7 cha lem] two-headed snake. *noun.*

pá7pa [pa7 pa] fuzzy; wooly. *adjective.*

pá7pawtn [pa7 paw tn] devil's club [type of plant; see also **ch'átyay'** and **ch'ích'aya**]; plant that relieves muscle soreness. *noun.*

pa7pa7í7k̲in [pa7 pa 7i7 k̲in] dog ["fluffy hide" type]. *noun.*

pekcha7ám̓ [pek cha 7am̓] take a picture. *verb(i).*

pekcha7ántsut [pek cha 7an tsut] take a picture of oneself. *verb(i).*

pékw'em [pe kw'em] flying dust, be. *verb(i).*

pékw'en [pe kw'en] scatter (something) in clouds. *verb(t).*

pékw'entsút [pe kw'en tsut] make dust. *verb(i).*

pékw'i7n [pe kw'i 7n] splashed, be; splash. *verb(i).*

pekw'n [pe kw'n] scatter (something). *verb(t).*

pek̲pák̲ [pek̲ pak̲] scattered all over, be [as of ducks or dead birds]. *verb(i).*

pek̲wpúk̲w [pek̲w puk̲w] mouldy. *adjective.*

pek̲w'pák̲w' [pek̲w' pak̲w'] scattered all over, be. *verb(i).*

pelk̲wám [pel k̲wam] kneel. *verb(i).*
Pelpála [pel pa la] Bella Bella people. *noun.*
pélpelk̲w [pel pelk̲w] kneeling, be. *verb(i).*
Pélxwla [pelxw la] Bella Coola people. *noun.*
pelh flat taste, have; no taste, have. *adjective.*
pelhts [pelh ts] thicked-lipped, be; thick lips, have. *adjective.*
peṁí7ach [pe ṁi 7ach] blister. *noun.*
pen buried, get; buried, be. *verb(i).*
penáṁen [pe na ṁen] fill up hole in ground. *verb(t).*
penáyus [pe na yus] something in one's eye. *noun.*
pená7k̲ [pe na7 k̲] match [for camping]. *noun.*
péṅem [pe ṅem] plant things. *verb(i).*
peṅeṁáy ~ **npeṅeṁáy** [pe ṅe ṁay] garden. *noun.*
peṅk̲wáṅ [peṅ k̲waṅ] bury (something); cover (something) with ground. *verb(t).*
pent bury (something). *verb(t).*
pepahíṁ [pe pa hiṁ] windy, be; blowing, be [about the wind]. *verb(i).*
pépa7achxw [pe pa 7a chxw] green, becoming [about trees]; sprouting, be; budding, be. *verb(i).*
pepeẏátulh [pe pe ẏa tulh] hunt small animals; hunting trip on a canoe, be on a; hunting in a canoe, be. *verb(i).*
pépeych'm [pe pey ch'm] emitting sparks, be; causing sparks, be; sparking, be. *verb(i).*
pépeẏtsm [pe peẏ tsm] bubbling, be. *verb(i).*
pépkw'am [pep kw'am] making dust or smoke, be; form clouds or puffs of dust; smoke; dusty, be very. *verb(i).*
peplhúlhi7 [pep lhu lhi7] thicker, be getting. *verb(i).*
pepseṅá7 [pep se ṅa7] wild lily of the valley [plant leaves used for eyewash]. *noun.*
pepseṅá7ay [pep se ṅa 7ay] wild lily of the valley plant. *noun.*
peptítsut [pep ti tsut] competing, be; competion, have a; match, have a. *verb(i).*
peptúsm [pep tu sm] along the waterfront, go; waterfront, go along the. *verb(i).*
pepuk̲áṁ [pe pu k̲aṁ] wind, go with the; go with the wind. *verb(i).*
pépuṁ ~ **púpuṁ** [pe puṁ] swelling, be [e.g., bread]. *verb(i).*
pépxweyek̲w ~ **péxweyek̲w** [pep xwe yek̲w] light-coloured hair, have. *verb(i).*
pepxwí7 [pep xwi7] faded, be getting; fading, be; pale, be getting. *verb(i).*
peshpúshullh [pesh pu shullh] kittens [sg: **pushúllh**; see **push**]. *noun.*
pets bent, be; folded, be. *verb(i).*
pétsem [pe tsem] bent, get. *verb(i).*
pétsen [pe tsen] fold (something); tuck (something) in; bend (something) [in one direction]. *verb(t).*
pétsentsut [pe tsen tsut] fold itself over. *verb(i).*
petsiẏúsn [pe tsi ẏu sn] make a dent in (something); make a fold in (something). *verb(t).*
pétspetsen [pets pe tsen] fold (something). *verb(t).*
péẇem [pe ẇem] make waves by dragging something in water. *verb(i).*
pewpáw [pew paw] tightened up and tired, get [about body]; sore muscles, get. *verb(i).*
péxweyek̲w ~ **pépxweyek̲w** [pe xwe yek̲w] light-coloured hair, have. *noun.*
pex̲ erect, be. *verb(i).*
péx̲wen [pe x̲wen] spit medicine on (someone); blow (something) out; spit at (someone). *verb(t).*
péx̲wilh [pe x̲wilh] short wide canoe. *noun.*
péyatulh [pe ya tulh] hunt in a canoe; hunting trip in a canoe, go on a [literally, launch canoe]. *verb(i).*
peych'áṅ [pey ch'aṅ] hit (someone) with burning cedar wood [was done to troublesome children]. *verb(t).*
péych'em [pey ch'em] spark; cause sparks; flash; burst [about flour]; explode [about dust or flowers]; burst out. *verb(i).*
peylh smudged, be; erased, be. *verb(i).*
peylhán [pey lhan] scatter (something); erase (something); scatter (ordered things). *verb(t).*
peym fall overboard; fall into the water; throw overboard. *verb(i).*
peymán [pey man] throw (something) overboard. *verb(t).*
peymántsut [pey man tsut] throw oneself overboard. *verb(i).*

péy̓tsem [pey̓ tsem] bubble; froth. *verb(i).*
pích'i7n [pi ch'i 7n] flash [about a light]. *verb(i).*
pikw'álxwim [pi kw'al xwim] smoke fish a lot; smoke salmon. *verb(i).*
pikw'áń [pi kw'ań] smoke (fish/meat) a little bit; smoke (something). *verb(t).*
píkw'pikw'pikw' [pikw' pikw' pikw'] all in after a long run, be. *verb(i).*
pik̲w' [pik̲w'] make spread motion in **slhahál** game [pick the two outside]. *verb(i).*
pípa [pi pa] paper. *noun.*
pípa tála [pi pa ta la] paper money [bills]. *noun.*
pipixwáyus [pi pi xwa yus] blueback [type of fish]. *noun.*
pisténak̲ [pis te ńak̲] jealous. *adjective.*
pítsintsut [pi tsin tsut] force one's way into a small spot. *verb(i).*
píts'ayusn [pi ts'a yu sn] squeeze (someone's) eyes. *verb(t).*
píts'in [pi ts'in] jam (something). *verb(t).*
pixw [pixw] falling, be [about leaves]; removed, be [about berries from a bush, dust from clothing, etc.]. *verb(i).*
píxwachxw [pi xwa chxw] fall from being shaken; drop from being shaken [about leaves]. *verb(i).*
píxwayk̲ińtn [pi xway k̲iń tn] brush for cleaning clothing. *noun.*
pixwayts'á7tn [pi xway ts'a7 tn] brush. *noun.*
píxwa7lhm [pi xwa7 lhm] clean one's bed. *verb(i).*
píxwin [pi xwin] brush (something) using a brush; brush off (clothes). *verb(t).*
pix̲súun [pix̲ súun] person [only used in the Catechism]. *noun.*
piyís [pi yis] murrelet [type of bird]. *noun.*
pí7pek̲'láchxwm [pi7 pek̲' lach xwm] yellow leaves, get [about trees in autumn]. *verb(i).*
pkw'et [p kw'et] make (a lot of smoke) from pipe or cigarette. *verb(t).*
pkw'úyin [p kw'u yin] crosspiece in a boat; crossbar in a canoe. *noun.*
pláw̓a7 [pla wa7] air bladder of fish [used as a container for oil]. *noun.*
plhétem [plhe tem] force (someone) out of his/her spot. *verb(p).*
plhits ~ plhúlhayts'a [plhits] thick cloth. *adjective.*
plhulh [plhulh] thick. *adjective.*
plhúlhayts'a ~ plhits [plhu lhay ts'a] thick cloth. *adjective.*
Pná7lx̲ets' [p na 7l x̲ets'] Kuper Island. *place name.*
-psem ~ -apsám ~ -apsem neck {full word: **sk̲apsm ~ stsk̲apsm ~ stsek̲ápsem**}. *suffix.*
ptakwem [p ta kwem] fern, type of. *noun.*
ptsiḿ [p tsiḿ] fold. *verb(i).*
púk̲wi7 [pu k̲wi7] mouldy, get. *verb(i).*
púk̲w'emi7 [pu k̲w'e mi7] foamy, be. *verb(i).*
puk̲w'k̲sm [puk̲w' k̲sm] snort; make a snorting sound. *verb(i).*
púk̲w'tsaḿ [puk̲w' tsaḿ] toot a horn. *verb(i).*
puḿ [puḿ] swell. *verb(i).*
puḿch [puḿch] swell up [as of bread]; swollen back, have a; swelling on the back, have a. *verb(i).*
puḿíḿ [pu ḿiḿ] make yeast bread. *verb(i).*
púpuḿ ~ pépuḿ [pu puḿ] swelling, be [e.g., bread]. *verb(i).*
push [push] cat. *noun.*
púsham [pu sham] flying dry snow, be. *verb(i).*
pushúllh [pu shullh] kitten [see **push**]. *noun.*
putíẃas [pu ti ẃas] oar. *noun.*
putputíẃas [put pu ti ẃas] oars [sg: **putíẃas**]. *noun.*
pútsuń [pu tsuń] twist (a cedar bough) to make a rope. *verb(t).*
puuk̲áḿ [puu k̲áḿ] go with the wind [while canoeing]. *verb(i).*
puuk̲w [puuk̲w] strong wind making the snow fly on mountain peaks, be. *verb(i).*
puum [puum] make waves [about the bow of a fast moving boat]. *verb(i).*
puuḿ [puuḿ] swell up [about bread]. *verb(i).*
puut [puut] blow on (something) with mouth; blow (something). *verb(t).*
puutm [puu tem] blown off, be [by the wind]. *verb(p).*
púxwem [pu xwem] steam. *verb(i).*
puxwmíń [puxw miń] the stomach part left after a hunter finishes cleaning a deer. *noun.*

púxwun [**pu xwun**] blow (something) with mouth. *verb(t).*

puých [**puých**] dip head in water to get drink; drink directly from river [without scooping up water]. *verb(i).*

pu7k̲ [**pu7k̲**] fart [see also **tek̲'** and **má7kwelh**]. *verb(i).*

pú7k̲aým [**pu7 k̲a ým**] want to fart. *verb(i).*

pú7k̲w'em [**pu7 k̲w'em**] blowing sound, make a [e.g., whale letting out water or air from its blow hole]. *verb(i).*

pxwaýs [**p xwaýs**] snort [about sea-lions, etc.]. *verb(i).*

pxwaystn [**p xways tn**] blow-hole [of a whale or dolphin]. *noun.*

pxwáýus [**p xwa ýus**] faded; have a faded colour. *adjective.*

pxwi7 [**p xwi7**] pale, get/become; fade. *verb(i).*

px̲wiḿ [**p xwiḿ**] blow [e.g., **sxw7umten**]. *verb(i).*

P'eẁyáḿ [**p'eẁ yaḿ**] name of a place in Squamish. *place name.*

P' p'

p'áak̲w'alh ~ ip'áak̲w'ulh ~ p'á7k̲w'alh [p'áa k̲w'alh] scared; get scared; afraid. *adjective.*
p'áats'ay [p'áa ts'aẏ] stink currant bush [sp'aats']. *noun.*
p'áchi7n [p'a chi 7n] shake hands with (someone). *verb(t).*
p'áchntway [p'a chn tway] hold hands. *verb(i).*
p'ach' hot; glowing hot; red hot [about fire or person in fever, not water or weather]. *adjective.*
p'ách'eṅtsut [p'a ch'eṅ tsut] heat up. *verb(i).*
p'ách'i7 [p'a ch'i7] hot, get. *verb(i).*
p'ákwam [p'a kwaṁ] come to surface of water; come to shore [about a canoe]; land [about a canoe]. *verb(i).*
p'ákwan [p'a kwaṅ] launch (canoe or boat); put (something) in the water. *verb(t).*
p'ákwaṅtsut [p'a kwaṅ tsut] rise to surface; come to surface of water. *verb(i).*
p'ákwilh [p'a kwilh] launch canoe. *verb(i).*
p'ákwilhen [p'a kwi lhen] float (a canoe). *verb(t).*
p'akwm [p'a kwṁ] rise to the surface of the water. *verb(i).*
p'ákw'an [p'a kw'an] make use of (something) almost useless; use (something) almost useless; use (something) as a last resort; make do with (something); use (something) for the lack of anything better. *verb(t).*
p'ak̲wtn [p'ak̲w tn] jackscrew. *noun.*
p'ák̲w'uen [p'a k̲w'u sen] powder (someone). *verb(t).*
p'alk̲' sprained, be. *verb(i).*
p'álk̲'nexw [p'alk̲' nexw] sprain (something). *verb(t).*
p'álk̲w'ach [p'al k̲w'ach] sprained ankle, have a. *adjective.*
p'álk̲w'achnexw [p'al k̲w'ach nexw] sprain (someone's) hand. *verb(t).*
p'álk̲w'shen [p'alk̲w' shen] sprain one's ankle. *verb(i).*
p'aṁáṅ ~ p'áṁan [p'a ṁaṅ] blacken (something) over a fire; colour (something) with smoke from fire. *verb(t).*
p'áṁan ~ p'aṁán [p'a ṁan] blacken (something) over a fire; colour (something) with smoke from fire; blacken (something) by holding it in smoke. *verb(t).*
p'áp'ach' [p'a p'ach'] fever, have a; really hot; feverish; hot. *adjective.*
p'áp'akwilh ~ p'íp'ikwilh [p'a p'a kwilh] play with toy canoe. *verb(i).*
p'áp'aẏak̲en [p'a p'a ẏa k̲en] fixing (something) up, be; correcting (something), be; curing (someone), be. *verb(t).*
p'áp'ekw [p'a p'ekw] float. *verb(i).*
p'áts'an [p'a ts'an] sew (something). *verb(t).*
p'áts'im [p'a ts'iṁ] sew. *verb(i).*
p'áts'iyen [p'a ts'i yen] repair net. *verb(i).*
p'áts'iyeṅten [p'a ts'i yeṅ ten] net-making twine. *noun.*
p'ats'neẇásn [pa'ts' ne ẇa sn] stitch (things) together. *verb(t).*
p'áts'nexw [p'ats' nexw] sewn (something), have. *verb(t).*
p'ats'tenáy [p'ats' te naẏ] sewing box. *noun.*
p'ats'tn [p'ats' tn] needle. *noun.*
p'áxwem [p'a xwem] quiet, be [about person]. *verb(i).*
p'áyak̲ [p'a yak̲] fixed, be; get well; recover. *verb(i).*
p'áyak̲alhen [p'a ya k̲a lhen] prepare someone to do something. *verb(i).*
p'ayak̲á7lhm [p'a ya k̲a7 lhm] make one's bed. *verb(i).*
p'áyak̲en [p'a ya k̲en] fix (something); repair (something); fix up (something); correct (something); cure (someone). *verb(t).*
p'ayak̲éntsut [p'a ya k̲en tsut] get oneself ready; train oneself for sports. *verb(i).*
p'áyak̲im [p'a ya k̲iṁ] make bread. *verb(i).*
p'ayak̲nálhen [p'a yak̲ na lhen] fixed, get; fix it finally. *verb(i).*

p'áyaḵnexw [p'a yaḵ nexw] fix (something), manage to. *verb(t).*
p'ayḵáy̓s [p'ay ḵay̓s] stop an argument; get a weapon. *verb(i).*
p'a7áchiyelh [p'a 7a chi yelh] shake hands; take a child by the hand. *verb(i).*
p'a7áchi7n [p'a 7a chi 7n] shake (someone's) hand; grab (someone) by the hand. *verb(t).*
p'a7áchnexw [p'a 7ach nexw] hold (someone's) hand accidentally; catch (someone's) hand; grab (someone's) hand, manage to; have hold of (someone's) hand. *verb(t).*
p'a7áchxwim [p'a 7ach xwim] start to take on trees [about leaves in the spring]. *verb(i).*
p'a7ám̓in ~ np'a7ám̓in [p'a 7a m̓in] handle [e.g., for a bucket]; haft. *noun.*
p'a7áya7ní7n [p'a 7a ya7 ni 7n] grab (someone) by the ear. *verb(t).*
p'a7ím̓ ~ ip'a7ím̓ ~ ip'i7ím [pa 7im̓] hold it in one's hands. *verb(i).*
p'á7ḵw'alh ~ ip'áaḵw'ulh ~ p'áaḵw'alh [p'a7 ḵw'alh] scared; afraid; get scared. *adjective.*
p'a7úts'us ~ p'úuts'us ~ p'e7úts'us [p'a 7u ts'us] cradle. *noun.*
p'ékwa7en [p'e kwa 7en] split (shakes). *verb(t).*
p'ékwilh [p'e kwilh] bring down to the shore unfinished canoe-hull from the place where it was made [canoes are hollowed out wherever the tree is felled]. *verb(i).*
p'ékwp'ekw [p'ekw p'ekw] floating high, be; light in the water, be; floating easily, be. *verb(i).*
p'ekwtín [p'ekw tin] net float; "cork." *noun.*
p'éḵen [pe' ḵen] make one's way through (bushy spot). *verb(t).*
p'eḵ' white. *adjective.*
p'eḵ'élwet [p'e ḵ'el wet] whiteman's blanket; white blanket. *noun.*
p'eḵ'í7 [p'e ḵ'i7] white, become; bleached, get. *verb(i).*
p'eḵw split, be. *verb(i).*
p'eḵwtn [p'eḵw tn] froe [type of tool]. *noun.*
p'éḵwu7n [p'e ḵwu 7n] split (something) [e.g., cedar shakes]. *verb(t).*
p'eḵw'p'íḵw' [p'eḵw' p'iḵw'] brown; yellow. *adjective.* yellow paint [kind that is found in the mountains]. *noun.*
p'eḵw'ús [p'e ḵw'us] pale face, have a. *adjective.*
p'elách'm [p'e la ch'm] small type of canoe made of cedar in such a way that the heart of the tree is at the bottom of the boat; canoe, small type. *noun.*
p'elách'm snexwílh [p'e la ch'm sne xwilh] small type of canoe made of cedar in such a way that the heart of the tree is at the bottom of the boat; canoe, small type. *noun.*
p'éli7 [p'e li7] skin and bones, be; thin bark, have. *verb(i).*
p'elḵ'án [p'el ḵ'an̓] glance at (something); take a quick look at (something) and then look away. *verb(t).*
p'élḵ'nexw [p'elḵ' nexw] catch a glimpse of (something). *verb(t).*
p'elḵw'ách [p'el ḵw'ach] sprain a wrist. *verb(i).*
p'elp'al̓aḵwúsi7 [p'el p'a l'a ḵwu si7] face-peeling skin condition, have a. *verb(i).*
p'eltl'án [p'el tl'an̓] knead (dough); squeeze (something) in one's hands; crush (something); squash (something). *verb(t).*
p'eltl'í7 [p'el tl'i7] crushed, be. *verb(i).*
p'elh sober up; sober, be. *verb(i).*
p'elhch explode. *verb(i).*
p'elhḵw'ách [p'elh ḵw'ach] sprained wrist or any part of arm, have a. *adjective.*
p'élhḵw'shen [p'elhḵw' shen] sprained ankle or any part of leg, have a. *adjective.*
p'elhnúmut [p'elh nu mut] sober up finally. *verb(i).*
p'em̓án [p'e m̓an̓] put (something) over smoke to colour. *verb(t).*
p'en̓tskwú7 [p'en̓ts kwu7] edge of water. *noun.*
p'ép'elḵ'em [p'e p'el ḵ'em] shimmering, be. *verb(i).*
p'ep'elḵ'emáchxw [p'e p'el ḵ'e ma chxw] trembling aspen. *noun.*

p'ép'eykw'm [p'e p'ey kw'm] churning, be; agitated, be [about water, or object in it]. *verb(i).*

p'ép'ikw'm [p'e p'i kw'm] churning, be; agitated, be. *verb(i).*

p'ep'í7 [p'e p'i7] captive, be taken; prisoner, be taken; brought in as a prisoner, be. *verb(i).*

p'ep'í7nexw [p'e p'i7 nexw] getting (something), have been. *verb(t).*

p'ep'sí [p'ep' si] coming to shore, be; landing, be. *verb(i).*

p'es get to shore; shore, get to; land; go to shore. *verb(i).*

p'ésen [p'e sen] bring (something) to shore. *verb(t).*

p'esentsút [p'e sen tsut] steer one's boat to shore. *verb(i).*

p'eskw'án [p'es kw'an] squeeze (something) with tongs. *verb(t).*

p'eskw'elhnáyen [p'es kw'elh na yen] choke (someone); squeeze (someone's) neck. *verb(t).*

p'eskw'úy̓ ~ sp'eskw'úy [p'es kw'uy̓] mountain goat wool. *noun.*

p'ésp'es [p'es p'es] landing ashore, be. *verb(i).*

p'ésxwem [p'es xwem] crusty. *adjective.*

p'es7álhx̲a [p'es 7alh x̲a] choking, be. *verb(i).*

p'eshnáń ~ p'i7shnán [p'esh nań] grab (someone's) foot or leg. *verb(t).*

p'étx̲numut [p'e tx̲ nu mut] avoid something, manage to. *verb(i).*

p'ewáy [p'e way̓] flounder [black-dotted]. *noun.*

p'eyákw'as [p'e ya kw'as] alder bark basket. *noun.*

p'eykw'm [p'ey kw'm] churn; agitated, be [about water or object in it]. *verb(i).*

p'eyk̲w' rotten wood. *noun.*

p'eyts'em [pey ts'em] emit sparks. *verb(i).*

p'e7úts'us ~ p'úuts'us ~ p'a7úts'us [p'e 7u ts'us] cradle basket; cradle. *noun.*

p'e7úts'usn [p'e 7u ts'u sn] put (a baby) in its cradle. *verb(t).*

p'ich't [p'ich' t] ashes [see also **k̲áyalhkwup**]; charcoal; cinders; black paint; coal. *noun.*

p'ích'tusem [p'ich' tu sem] paint one's face black; put charcoal on one's face [as done by dancers]. *verb(i).*

p'ík̲san ~ p'i7k̲sán [p'ik̲ san] get a hold of (someone's) nose; grab (someone's) nose. *verb(t).*

p'ik̲w' [p'ik̲w'] nighthawk. *noun.*

p'ík̲w'i7 [p'ik̲w'i7] yellow, become. *verb(i).*

p'ik̲w's [p'ik̲w's] point (them) both ways [spreading both thumb and index-finger in **slhahál**]. *verb(t).*

p'ílhk̲'antsut [p'ilh k̲'an tsut] come alongside. *verb(i).*

p'ílhk̲'i [p'ilh k̲'i] go alongside in a canoe; alongside in a canoe, go. *verb(i).*

p'ílhk̲'neẁásn [p'ilhk̲' ne ẁa sn] put (them) side by side. *verb(t).*

p'íneẁas [p'i ne ẁas] marry each other; get married. *verb(i).*

p'íp'a7em [p'i p'a 7em] log jam. *noun.*

p'íp'ikwilh ~ p'áp'akwilh [p'i p'i kwilh] play with toy canoe; shove a little canoe in the water. *verb(i).*

p'ip'íy̓em [p'i p'i y̓em] overflow. *verb(i).*

p'ip'k̲' [p'ip' k̲'] white [about animals]. *adjective.*

p'its' [p'its'] bruised, be; jammed, be; trapped, get; squeezed, get. *verb(i).*

p'íts'ach [p'i ts'ach] jammed hands, have; get one's hand caught [in something squeezing]. *verb(i).*

p'íts'in [p'i ts'in] squeeze (something) together; squeeze (something). *verb(t).*

p'its'k̲w [p'its'k̲w] squeezed between two things, get [about head]. *verb(i).*

p'its'lhnáy̓n [p'i ts'lh na y̓n] strangle (someone). *verb(t).*

p'íts'nexw [p'its' nexw] squeeze (something), manage to; squeeze (something) accidentally. *verb(t).*

p'its'shn [p'its' shn] get one's foot caught [in something squeezing]. *verb(i).*

p'i7áx̲aní7n [p'i 7a x̲a ni 7n] grab (someone) by the arm. *verb(t).*

p'i7áya7n [p'i 7a ya 7n] grab (someone's) ear. *verb(t).*

p'i7k̲sáń ~ p'ík̲san [p'i7k̲ sań] grab (someone's) nose; get a hold of (someone's) nose. *verb(t).*

p'í7k̲sim [p'i7k̲ sim̓] begin; grab by the nose. *verb(i).*

p'í7k̲wań [p'i7 k̲wań] grab (someone's) head. *verb(t).*

p'í7nalhen [p'i7 na lhen] get (something), manage to [e.g., a deer]; taken, have. *verb(t).*

p'í7nexw [p'i7 nexw] catch (something); get (something); have (something); hold (something); take (someone) prisoner; have a hold of (something); have caught (something); found (something), have; received (something), have; have got (something). *verb(t).*

p'í7shi [p'i7 shi] take it from (someone). *verb(t).*

p'i7shnáń ~ p'eshnán [p'i7 shnań] grab (someone's) leg or foot. *verb(t).*

p'í7shnexw [p'i7 shnexw] have hold of (someone's) leg. *verb(t).*

p'i7t [p'i7t] take (something); grab (something); seize (something). *verb(t).*

p'í7tway [p'i7 tway] mate. *verb(i).*

p'í7tsan [p'i7 tsan] feed (someone) [about new dancers]; grab (someone's) mouth; squeeze (someone's) mouth. *verb(t).*

p'lhet [p' lhet] sober (someone) up. *verb(t).*

p'lhétsut [p' lhe tsut] straighten oneself up. *verb(i).*

p'lhiws [p' lhiws] revive; sober up; come to [after fainting]. *verb(i).*

p'lhi7 [p' lhi7] sober up. *verb(i).*

p'lhúsem [p' lhu sem] wash face with water. *verb(i).*

p'si ~ p'si7 [p' si] come ashore; land; go to shore. *verb(i).*

p'si7 ~ p'si [p' si7] come ashore; land; go to shore. *verb(i).*

p'tusm [p' tu sm] cross oneself; make the sign of the cross. *verb(i).*

p'úk̲w'am [p'u k̲w'am] foam. *verb(i).*

p'úp'utl'am [p'u p'u tl'am] smoking, be [cigarettes]. *verb(i).*

p'útl'am [p'u tl'am] smoke [about a fire]; smoky, be; hazy, be [like fog]. *verb(i).*

p'úuts'us ~ p'a7úts'us ~ p'e7úts'us [p'úu ts'us] cradle. *noun.*

S s

s- {turns verbs into nouns}. *prefix.*
-s {added onto some words so that you can use the object endings; see section on "object endings," p. 12}. *suffix.*
-s his, hers, its. *suffix.*
sa [similar in meaning to the Skwxwu7mesh word **ti** "this"]. *determiner.*
saam [saam] covered, be. *verb(i).*
saats [saats] leftover food. *noun.* left over, be. *verb(i).*
sáklament [sak la ment] Sacrament [word used in the Catechism]. *noun.*
śákwi7 [sa kwi7] hoarse, become. *verb(i).*
sakw'súkw' [sakw' sukw'] staggering, be. *verb(i).*
sak̲' tear; rip. *verb(i).*
sák̲'an ~ sák̲'en [sa k̲'an] rip (something); tear (something); split (something). *verb(t).*
sák̲'en ~ sák̲'an [sa k̲'en] rip (something); tear (something); split (something). *verb(t).*
sák̲'nexw [sak̲' nexw] torn (something), have. *verb(t).*
sák̲wula [sa k̲wu la] unit of measurement from shoulder to top of finger of right hand. *noun.*
sák̲w'ilhen [sa k̲w'i lhen] split (a canoe) in half. *verb(t).*
sálu [sa lu] girl who picks berries. *noun.*
san my [close by]. *clitic.*
sásatim̓ [sa sa tim̓] passing something over, be. *verb(i).*
satachí7m [sa ta chi 7m] give one's hand. *verb(i).*
sátan̓ [sa tan̓] pass (something); hand (something) over; give (something). *verb(t).*
sátan̓tsut [sa tan̓ tsut] hand oneself over. *verb(i).*
sátat [sa tat] deceased aunt; deceased female cousin of parents. *noun.*
sáta7 ~ s-háta7 [sa ta7] aunt; female cousin of parents. *noun.*
sátim̓ [sa tim̓] offer it; give it. *verb(i).*
sátk̲wuy̓achí7m [sat k̲wu y̓a chi 7m] offer one's finger; give one's finger [in order to play **klexw**]. *verb(i).*
sátshi [sat shi] give (someone) something. *verb(t).*
saw̓án [sa w̓an] food for a trip; packed lunch; food taken on trip; boxed lunch. *noun.*
saw̓an̓áy [sa w̓a n̓ay] lunch bucket. *noun.*
saw̓án̓en [sa w̓a n̓en] provide lunch for (someone); give (someone) food for lunch. *verb(t).*
saw̓án̓s [sa w̓an̓s] make lunch for (someone); give (someone) food for lunch; provide lunch for (someone). *verb(t).*
saw̓t youngest child; junior-line children or cousins. *noun.*
saw̓tk̲wúl̓a ~ saw̓tk̲wúy̓ach [saw̓t k̲wu l'a] little finger [see also **etsím̓ul'a** and **esáw̓tul'a ~ saw̓túl'a**]. *noun.*
saw̓tk̲wúy̓ach ~ saw̓tk̲wúl̓a [saw̓t k̲wu y̓ach] little finger [see also **etsím̓ul'a** and **esáw̓tul'a ~ saw̓túl'a**]. *noun.*
sáw̓tk̲wuy̓shen [saw̓t k̲wuy̓ shen] little toe. *noun.*
saw̓túl̓a ~ esáw̓tul̓a [saw̓ tu l'a] little finger [see also **etsím̓ul'a** and **saw̓tk̲wúy'ach ~ saw̓tk̲wúl'a**]. *noun.*
saxw ~ sax̲w greased, be. *verb(i).*
sáxwan̓ ~ sáx̲wan̓ [sa xwan̓] rub (someone) with oil. *verb(t).*
sáx̲an̓ [sa x̲an̓] scrape (something). *verb(t).*
sáx̲tsam̓ [sax̲ tsam̓] shave. *verb(i).*
sax̲w ~ saxw greased, be. *verb(i).*
sáx̲wan̓ ~ sáxwan̓ [sa x̲wan̓] rub (someone) with oil. *verb(t).*
sax̲way̓úsem [sa x̲wa y̓u sem] walk in a dazed condition. *verb(i).*
sáx̲wi7 [sa x̲wi7] grass; hay; straw. *noun.*
sáx̲wk̲wam̓ [sax̲w k̲wam̓] oil one's own hair; put hair oil on; rub oil in one's hair. *verb(i).*
sax̲wmámin [sax̲w ma min] oil something on the inside. *verb(i).*
sáyam [sa yam] bitter; sour; harsh [about wind]. *adjective.*

sayamáyum̓ [sa ya ma yum̓] unripe [about a berry]. *adjective.*
sayamlíwen [sa yam li wen] brave. *adjective.*
sáy̓em̓s [sa y̓em̓s] drafty. *adjective.*
sáyips [sa yips] pin; clothespin. *noun.*
sáyi7n ~ sáy̓i7n [sa yi 7n] audible, be; heard, be. *verb(i).*
sáy̓i7n ~ sáyi7n [sa y̓i 7n] audible, be; heard, be. *verb(i).*
sá7say̓em [sa7 sa y̓em] hearing a song from nature, be. *verb(i).*
sa7sx̱w [sa7 sx̱w] damp. *adjective.*
sá7sx̱wi7 [sa7s x̱wi7] damp, become. *verb(i).*
scháchshay̓ [schach shay̓] thing [to be] given away. *noun.*
scháyilhen [scha yi lhen] fish on their run to spawn up river; fish [collective, all kinds; a "high" word]. *noun.*
scháyminulh [schay mi nulh] belonging to a Chinese person; Chinese. *adjective.*
schá7ḵwem [scha7 ḵwem] smelt. *noun.*
schá7twilh [scha7 twilh] boat. *noun.*
scha7tx̱ [scha7 tx̱] halibut. *noun.*
schéchen̓ [sche chen̓] lean against it. *verb(i).*
schelíl̓s [sche lil's] happen. *verb(i).*
schelhḵwí [schelh ḵwi] narrow passage. *noun.*
schelhna7ench' [schelh na 7ench'] girl raised strictly. *noun.*
schem̓á7 [sche m̓a7] burden. *noun.*
schenáwes [sche na wes] lying down on back, be. *verb(i).*
schéshen [sche shen] messenger. *noun.*
schew̓át ~ eschew̓át ~ eschechew̓át ~ chechew̓át [sche w̓at] clever, be; smart, be; know how to do something; able to do something, be. *verb(i).*
schíchlawem [schich la wem] huge thing that could be sasquatch. *noun.*
schíchlhach [schich lhach] drumstick. *noun.*
schilh [schilh] woman's firstborn. *noun.*
schilhts [schilh ts] upper lip. *noun.*
schílhus [schi lhus] hill. *noun.*
schíshmax̱an [schish ma x̱an] long landward side side of house built with its long sides parallel to the river [also known as yekw'ayaḵ'in]. *noun.*
schishmḵs [schish mḵs] short landward side of house built with its long sides perpendicular to the river; upper end of a village. *noun.*
schí7i [schi 7i] strawberry. *noun.*
schi7i7áy̓ [schi 7i 7ay̓] strawberry plant. *noun.*
schí7ulh [schi 7ulh] fish right up to the spawning grounds; spring salmon [very first run during high water; literally, way up above]. *noun.*
schlhútsin [sch lhu tsin] roof. *noun.*
sch'ach splinter; sliver [in finger]. *noun.*
sch'áḵw'els [sch'a ḵw'els] fork. *noun.*
sch'ámts'a7ten [sch'am ts'a7 ten] mat-making needle for bullrush mat; weaving needle; needle [weaving]. *noun.*
sch'áwatn [sch'a wa tn] helper [usually spiritual]. *noun.*
sch'ay̓ dead tree; snag. *noun.*
sch'á7miḵw [sch'a7 miḵw] great-grandparent/aunt/uncle; great-grandchild. *noun.*
sch'ech'íxw [sch'e ch'ixw] extra. *adjective.*
sch'éḵch'eḵ ~ esch'éḵch'eḵ [sch'eḵ ch'eḵ] dirty. *adjective.*
sch'eḵ' dirt. *noun.*
sch'élḵ'es [sch'el ḵ'es] slingshot. *noun.*
sch'elxwiḵw [sch'el xwiḵw] Chilliwack. *place name.*
sch'elxwi7ḵw [sch'el xwi7ḵw] Chilliwack people. *noun.*
sch'épxwel̓ [sch'ep xwel'] wart. *noun.*
sch'etxw [sch'e txw] anything carved; totem pole. *noun.*
sch'etxwim̓ [sch'et xwim̓] carving. *noun.*
sch'etxwínes [sche't xwi nes] brooch; decoration carried on chest. *noun.*
sch'ex̱wḵ' fried bread; bannock. *noun.*
sch'eych'eyúy ~ ch'ich'iyúy ~ ch'iyúy ~ sch'iyúy [sch'ey ch'e yuy] twins. *noun.*
sch'eyḵ ~ sch'iḵ [sch'eyḵ] sunrise. *noun.*
sch'e7úsem [sch'e 7u sem] hillside; sidehill; slope. *noun.*
sch'ich'íḵ [sch'i ch'iḵ] surprised, be. *verb(i).*
sch'ích'inu [sch'i ch'i nu] cone of evergreen tree. *noun.*
sch'ikw [sch'ikw] narrow passage; strait; mountain pass. *noun.*

sch’ik̲ ~ sch’eyk̲ [sch’ik̲] sunrise. *noun.*

sch’íwi7min [sch’i wi7 meyn] bothersome, be; nuisance, be a. *verb(i).*

sch’iyámut [sch’i ya mut] take away. *verb(i).*

sch’iyípach ~ ch’iyípach [sch’i yi pach] lower arm; hand. *noun.*

sch’iyípk̲wuy̓shen [sch’i yip k̲wuy̓ shen] toes. *noun.*

sch’iyípshen [sch’i yip shen] lower leg; shin bone; foot. *noun.*

sch’iyúy ~ ch’iyúy ~ ch’ich’iyúy ~ sch’eych’eyúy [sch’i yuy] twins. *noun.*

sch’i7í7k̲w [sch’i 7i7k̲w] rapids. *noun.*

sch’k̲wéla7 [sch’ k̲we la7] “puck” in the hockey-like game of ch’k̲wela7. *noun.*

sch’k̲w’ap [sch’ k̲w’ap] feather [as part of Indian hairdo]; feather put in hair. *noun.*

sch’tish [sch’ tish] rope made of twisted cedar bark. *noun.*

sch’tíshm [sch’ ti shm] harpoon line of cedar bark. *noun.*

sch’úlha7 [sch’u lha7] leaf [of any tree]. *noun.*

sécheẃ [se cheẃ] accused of taking something, be. *verb(i).*

sekéṁkem [se keṁ kem] bumblebee [see also sesemáy’]. *noun.*

sekw go astray; astray, go. *verb(i).*

sekwelásh ~ skwel̓ásh ~ s7ekwel̓ásh [se kwe lash] gun; rifle. *noun.*

sekwí7kwlus ~ s7ekwí7kwlus [se kwi7 kwlus] large butterfly [whose appearance is followed by the run of the kwu7s]. *noun.*

sek̲sík̲ [sek̲ sik̲] fly away [about bunch of birds]. *verb(i).*

sek̲’ split, be; ripped, be; cracked, be; middle, be the; half, be. *verb(i).*

sek̲’ lhk̲aych’ [sek̲’ lh k̲aych’] half moon, be. *verb(i).*

sek̲’ skwáyel [sek̲’ skwa yel] half a day, be. *verb(i).*

sek̲’ snat midnight. *phrase.*

sek̲’cháṅ [sek̲’ chaṅ] split (something); split (something) in half. *verb(t).*

sek̲’eṅí7kwup ~ sek̲’ní7kwup ~ sek̲níkwup [se k̲’e ṅi7 kwup] chop firewood; split firewood. *verb(i).*

sek̲’íṁ [se k̲’iṁ] split it; split wood. *verb(i).*

sek̲’k̲wáṅ [sek̲’ k̲waṅ] split (a head) in two [can refer particularly to skewering a fish head for barbecuing]. *verb(t).*

sek̲’máy̓us [sek̲’ ma y̓us] well-grained for splitting, be [about a log]. *verb(i).*

sek̲’mín [sek̲’ min] chopped wood; cuttings; waste wood after splitting. *noun.*

sek̲’míntway [sek̲’ min tway] divide and share; split and share. *verb(i).*

sek̲’níkwup ~ sek̲’ní7kwup ~ sek̲’eṅí7kwup [sek̲’ ni kwup] split firewood; chop firewood. *verb(i).*

sek̲’ní7kwup ~ sek̲’ení7kwup ~ sek̲’níkwup [sek̲’ ni7 kwup] split firewood; chop firewood. *verb(i).*

sek̲’sák̲’an [sek̲’ sa k̲’an] tear (something) continuously. *verb(t).*

sek̲’sák̲’ans [sek̲’ sa k̲’ans] toothache, have a. *adjective.*

sék̲’wilh [sek̲’ wilh] torn body, have a; ripped up [about body]. *adjective.*

sek̲’wílhn [sek̲’ wi lhn] separate (something). *verb(t).*

sek̲w’ek̲w’í7nexw ~ s7ek̲w’7ek̲w’í7nexw ~ s7uk̲w’uk̲w’íṅexw [se k̲w’e k̲w’i7 nexw] bird [general term]. *noun.*

sék̲w’ek̲w’i7tel ~ s7ék̲w’7ek̲w’i7tel ~ s7ék̲w’ek̲w’itel ~ sék̲w’7ek̲w’itel [se k̲w’e k̲w’i7 tel] siblings; cousins [sg: ek̲w’í7tel and sek̲w’í7tel ~ s7ek̲w’itel]. *noun.*

sek̲w’ík̲w’ehats ~ k̲w’ek̲w’ík̲w’ehatl’ [se k̲w’i k̲w’e hats] swallow [type of bird]. *noun.*

sek̲w’í7tel ~ s7ek̲w’í7tel [se k̲w’i7 tel] sibling; cousin; relative; siblings and cousins [see also ek̲w’í7tel]. *noun.*

sék̲w’7ek̲w’itel ~ sék̲wek̲w’itel ~ s7ék̲w’7ek̲w’itel ~ s7ék̲w’ek̲w’itel [sek̲w’7e k̲w’i tel] siblings; cousins [sg: ek̲w’í7tel and sek̲w’í7tel ~ s7ek̲w’itel]. *noun.*

seláwa7 [se la wa7] pitiful, be; pitiful person, be a sort of. *verb(i).*

séliy̓ay̓ [se li y̓ay̓] Oregon grape bush. *noun.*

sel̓í7shi [se l’i7 shi] keep it for (someone). *verb(t).*

selk̲’m [sel k̲’m] hang down. *verb(i).*

selk̲w sad, become. *verb(i).*

selk̲wmíṅ [selk̲w miṅ] cause of sorrow; sorrow, cause of. *noun.*

sélk̲wtsut [selk̲w tsut] lonely, get; feel sad; sad, feel. *verb(i).*

sel̓selíws ~ silsilíws ~ sisilíws [sel' se liws] frightened, get; nervous, be; get the creeps. *verb(i).*

sél̓seltn [sel' sel tn] spindle whorl. *noun.*

selsí7l [sel si 7l] grandparents [sg: **si7l ~ si7la**]. *noun.*

seltém [sel tem] spin (something) [e.g., wool]. *verb(t).*

sélus ~ nsélus [se lus] spinning wool. *noun.* spin wool; spin thread. *verb(i).*

selúsen [se lu sen] spin (something). *verb(t).*

seṁ faint; knocked out, be; pass right out. *verb(i).*

seṁá7mak̲a [se ṁa7 ma k̲a] snowbird. *noun.*

seṁúṁat [se ṁu ṁat] lazy. *adjective.*

seṁúṁati7 [se ṁu ṁa ti7] lazy, be getting. *verb(i).*

semyú7 [sem yu7] less than. *verb(i).*

sen then I; and I; when I [from **s** + **7an**]. *conjunction.*

sen my [from **sa** + **n**]. *determiner.*

sensíntl' [sen sintl'] senior-line children or cousins; cousins from a senior line; children from a senior line; elder children [sg: **sintl'**]. *noun.*

sep stiff. *adjective.*

sepík̲ [se pik̲] yellow salmonberry. *noun.*

sepíts' [se pits'] stiff cloth. *adjective.*

sepíwa [se pi wa] hard wood. *adjective.*

sepíws [se piws] stiff body. *adjective.*

sepíwsi7 [se piw si7] stiff body, get a. *verb(i).*

sepiyáx̲a7en [se pi ya x̲a 7en] stiff arm, have a. *adjective.*

sepí7 [se pi7] stiff, get. *verb(i).*

seplín [se plin] bread. *noun.*

sepspíwsntm [sep spiw sn tm] chill creep up one's back [from cold or fright], have a. *verb(p).*

ses then s/he. *conjunction.*

sesaẇán [se sa ẇan] take food along on a trip. *verb(i).*

sesaẇáṅen [se sa ẇa ṅen] make lunch for (someone). *verb(t).*

sesaẇaṅí7m [se sa ẇa ṅi 7m] make lunch for oneself. *verb(i).*

sesáẇt [se saẇt] younger children; junior-line children; junior-line cousins [sg: **saw't**]. *noun.*

séselk̲'em [se sel k̲'em] swaying, be; hanging, be; hang. *verb(i).*

seselk̲'eṁús [se sel k̲'e ṁus] hanging face, have a. *verb(i).*

séselk̲'mk̲ [se sel k̲'mk̲] hanging from one's rear end, be having something. *verb(i).*

séselk̲'mk̲s [se sel k̲'mk̲s] hanging from one's nose, be having something. *verb(i).*

séselk̲'mshn [se sel k̲'m shn] dangling, have one's legs. *verb(i).*

séselk̲w [se selk̲w] sad; lonely; lonesome; sorry; unhappy. *adjective.*

séselk̲wi7 [se sel k̲wi7] lonely, become. *verb(i).*

séselk̲wni [se selk̲w ni] lonesome for (someone), be; long for (someone); miss (someone); sad about (someone), be; sorry about (someone/something), be. *verb(t).*

séselk̲wtsut [se selk̲w tsut] feeling sorry for oneself, be. *verb(i).*

seselk̲w7ús [se selk̲w 7us] sad-faced; sad face, have a. *adjective.*

séselts'em [se sel ts'em] whistling noise, make a; make a whistling noise [as of a kettle]. *verb(i).*

séselts'emk̲s [se sel ts'emk̲s] wheezing, be. *verb(i).*

sesemáẏ [se se maẏ] bee; bumblebee [see also **sekém'kem**]; blackjacket; yellow-jacket. *noun.*

sésetk̲wem [se set k̲wem] lukewarm, be. *verb(i).*

séseẇaẏ ~ séseẇyay [se se ẇaẏ] go right by; go right through [e.g., arrow through object, person running in the front and out the back door]. *verb(i).*

seseẇít [se se ẇit] try to get (someone's) attention [by signs, sounds]. *verb(t).*

séseẇyay ~ séseẇaẏ [se seẇ yay] go right by; go right through [e.g., arrow through object, person running in the front and out the back door]. *verb(i).*

seseyk̲'áẏch [se sey k̲'aẏch] pass over a ridge; climb over a mountain. *verb(i).*

séseyk̲'ts [se seyk̲' ts] crossing over a river, bridge, lake, etc., be. *verb(i).*

seseẏx̲ [se seẏx̲] drifting. *verb(i).*
sésiwi7 [se si wi7] catch a glimpse of something. *verb(i).*
sésiẇyay [se siẇ yay] instantly. *verb(i).*
sesk̲'míntway [sesk̲' min tway] dividing and sharing, be. *verb(i).*
sespí7 [ses pi7] become stiff; stiff, become. *verb(i).*
sésx̲wa7 [ses x̲wa7] urinating, be. *verb(i).*
setk̲wán [set k̲wan] heat (something) in an oven. *verb(t).*
set'k̲'íws ~ nset'k̲'íws [set' k̲'iws] side of body. *noun.*
setsk̲'etsántsut [sets k̲'e tsan tsut] grind one's teeth. *verb(i).*
sets'imts'imáymixw [se ts'im ts'i may mixw] caterpillar. *noun.*
séts'ishen [se ts'i shen] berry seeds. *noun.*
sets'íts'itx̲em [se ts'i ts'it x̲em] grasshopper. *noun.*
sets'úts'umam ~ ts'úts'uṁam [se ts'u ts'u mam] chickadee. *noun.*
seẇíẇ [se ẇiẇ] awkward, be; unable, be. *verb(i).*
seẇíẇlus ~ swáẇlus [se ẇiẇ lus] young men [sg: **swíẇlus**]. *noun.*
seẇúl̓em ~ s-heẇúl̓em [se ẇu l'em] toy. *noun.*
sexwsáxwi7 [sexw sa xwi7] northern lights. *noun.*
sex̲ bitter; sour; strong [about taste]. *adjective.*
sex̲á7x̲em ~ nsex̲á7x̲em [se x̲a7 x̲em] pigeon [wild]. *noun.*
séx̲wa7 [se x̲wa7] urinate. *verb(i).* urine. *noun.*
séx̲wa7n [se x̲wa 7n] urinate on (something). *verb(t).*
sex̲wn [se x̲wn] cut strips of (skin). *verb(t).*
sex̲wsáx̲wi7 [sex̲w sa x̲wi7] grasslands; prairie. *noun.*
seẏíx̲yix̲es [se ẏix̲ yi x̲es] giant salamander. *noun.*
seyk̲' clay; "hardpan." *noun.*
séyk̲'ach ~ sík̲'ach [sey k̲'ach] switch hands [e.g., when paddling with the one-bladed paddle or in **slhahál**]. *verb(i).*
seyk̲'áẏch [sey k̲'aẏch] take a short cut; go around something when travelling; pass over a mountain ridge. *verb(i).*
seyk̲'k̲s [seyk̲' k̲s] pass over a flat surface; pass over water. *verb(i).*
seyk̲'k̲sán [seyk̲' k̲san] turn (something) around lengthwise. *verb(t).*
seyk̲'ts [seyk̲' ts] cross over a road or bridge. *verb(i).* bridge. *noun.*
seyx̲ drift; drift downstream. *verb(i).*
seyx̲á7m [sey x̲a 7m] use a driftnet. *verb(i).*
seyx̲á7mten [sey x̲a 7m ten] driftnet. *noun.*
se7áchi7m [se 7a chi 7m] wipe one's hands. *verb(i).*
se7á7ems [se 7a 7ems] shawl. *noun.*
se7líl [se7 lil] dowry; ransom. *noun.* sell "Indian blanket." *verb(i).*
se7pík̲wem [se7 pi k̲wem] walk in one's sleep. *verb(i).*
se7sk̲' [se7 sk̲'] chips of wood [for starting fire]. *noun.*
se7úsm [se 7u sm] wipe one's face. *verb(i).*
se7x̲ [se 7x̲] parent- or child-in-law. *noun.*
síiẏaṁ [síi ẏaṁ] chiefs; honoured ones [sg: **siy'ám'**]. *noun.*
síiyaẏ [síi yaẏ] friends [sg: **siyaẏ**]. *noun.*
siiyúxwa ~ síiẏuxwa [sii yú xwa] elders; old people [sg: **syú7yuxwa**]. *noun.*
síiẏuxwa ~ siiyúxwa [síi ẏu xwa] elders; old people [sg: **syú7yuxwa**]. *noun.*
sikw' [sikw'] ripped, get. *verb(i).*
síkw'in [si kw'in] tear (something). *verb(t).*
síkw'it [si kw'it] tear (something). *verb(t).*
sikw'íwen [si kw'i wen] underarms. *noun.*
síkw'nexw [sikw' nexw] rip (something). *verb(t).*
sik̲ [sik̲] fly. *verb(i).*
sik̲ch [sik̲ch] shingles [roof]. *noun.*
sik̲stm [sik̲ stm] blown away by the wind, get. *verb(p).*
sík̲'ach ~ séyk̲'ach [si k̲'ach] switch hands [e.g., when paddling with a one-bladed paddle or in **slhahál**]. *verb(i).*
sik̲'k̲sán [sik̲' k̲san] turn (something) around lengthwise. *verb(t).*
sík̲'shen [sik̲' shen] switch feet. *verb(i).*
sík̲wintem [si k̲win tem] rip (something) up. *verb(p).*
sil [sil] cloth. *noun.*
sílawilh [si la wilh] lining for a cradle. *noun.*
sil̓áẇtxw [si l'aẇ txw] tent. *noun.*
silsilíws ~ sel̓selíws ~ sisilíws [sil si liws] get the creeps; nervous, be; frightened, get. *verb(i).*

sílha7 [si lha7] buy it; purchase it. *verb(i).*
silha7án ~ sílh7an ~ sílha7n [si lha 7an] buy (something). *verb(t).*
silha7áys [si lha 7ays] shopping, be. *verb(i).*
sílha7chaṁ [si lha7 chaṁ] buy clothing. *verb(i).*
sílha7n ~ silha7án ~ sílh7an [si lha 7n] buy (something). *verb(t).*
sílha7shi [si lha7 shi] buy it for (someone). *verb(t).*
sílh7an ~ silha7án ~ sílha7n [silh 7an] buy (something). *verb(t).*
siṁáṅ [si ṁaṅ] leftover [of food]; surplus of anything. *noun.*
sin [sin] move over. *verb(i).*
sína7kw [si na7kw] old mountain goat. *noun.*
sínin ~ sínit [si nin] move (something) over; move (something) from one place to another. *verb(t).*
sínit ~ sínin [si nit] move (something) over; move (something) from one place to another. *verb(t).*
sínitsut [si ni tsut] move over. *verb(i).*
sínnexw [sin nexw] move (something) over accidentally; moved (something) accidentally, have. *verb(t).*
sínshnam [sin shnam] move one's foot [over]. *verb(i).*
sintl' [sintl'] oldest child; senior-line child or cousin; elder child; child from a senior line; cousin from a senior line. *noun.*
sintl'ak̲wúỷach [sin tl'a k̲wu ỷach] thumb. *noun.*
sintl'ak̲wúỷshen [sin tl'ak̲wuỷ shen] big toe. *noun.*
síntl'aywilh [sin tl'ay wilh] oldest of . . . . *noun.*
sísik̲ smemel̓útsin [séh sehk̲ sme mel̓ lú tsin] [séy seyk̲ sme mel̓ lú tsin] flying squirrel. *noun.*
sisík̲ ~ sísik̲ [si sik̲] flying, be. *verb(i).*
sísik̲ ~ sisík̲ [si sik̲] flying, be. *verb(i).*
sisilíws ~ silsilíws ~ sel̓selíws [si si liws] get the creeps; frightened, get; nervous, be; scared, get; afraid, become. *verb(i).*
sisilíwsmen [si si liws men] something that is frightening; creepy thing. *noun.*
sisilíwsshn [si si liws shn] have one's feet get frightened; frightened, have one's feet get. *verb(i).*
sisiwiyínek̲ [si si wi yi nek̲] on guard, be [aware]. *verb(i).*
sísix̲wim [si si x̲wim] wading, be; wade. *verb(i).*
sísi7 [si si7] uncle; male cousins of parents. *noun.*
sísi7t [si si7t] deceased uncle; deceased male cousin of parents. *noun.*
síst'k̲'els [sist' k̲'els] single-bladed; single blade, have a. *adjective.*
síst'k̲'els k̲w'k̲wémen [sist' k̲'els k̲w' k̲we men] single-bladed axe. *noun.*
síshulhni7en [si shulh ni 7en] pay attention to (someone). *verb(t).*
sítk̲wachi7m [sit k̲wa chi 7m] warming hands, be. *verb(i).*
sitn [si tn] basket [generic]. *noun.*
sít'it [si t'it] start (a song). *verb(t).*
síts'k̲aṁ [sits' k̲aṁ] sit on ground. *verb(i).*
siẇ ~ s-hiẇ [siẇ] head of river; upstream region. *noun.*
síẇach ~ s-híẇach [si ẇach] front leg. *noun.*
siwáỷ ~ siẇay ~ s-hiẇay [si waỷ] right away; soon; sooner; quick; quicker; quickly. *adverb.*
siẇay ~ siwáỷ ~ s-hiẇay [si ẇay] sooner; soon; quick; quicker; right away; quickly. *adverb.*
síwayk̲ [si wayk̲] pants. *noun.*
síwi [si wi] aware of something that one can't see, be; attentive, become; prick one's ears. *verb(i).*
siẇíṅ [si ẇiṅ] witchcraft; spiritual power [of **kwtsi7ts**, exercised through words]. *noun.*
siẇí7k̲a [si ẇi7 k̲a] men [sg: **swí7k̲a**]. *noun.*
síẇsiẇxwk̲aỷmixw [siẇ siẇxw k̲aỷ mixw] centipede. *noun.*
six̲ás ~ syex̲ás [si x̲as] large rock; rock [large]; boulder. *noun.*
síx̲wim [si x̲wim] wade; walk into the water. *verb(i).*
siỷáṁ [si ỷaṁ] chief; highly honoured person; rich person. *noun.*
siỷáṁn [si ỷa ṁn] make (someone) a chief. *verb(t).*
siỷáṁs [si ỷaṁs] treat (someone) like a chief; respect (someone) like a chief. *verb(t).*

siy̓ám̓ulh [si y̓a m̓ulh] chief's; belonging to a chief. *adjective.*
siy̓ám̓ulh sk̲wálwen [si y̓a m̓ulh sk̲wal wen] big man's words [literally, a chief's thoughts]. *noun.*
siyáy̓ [si yay̓] friend. *noun.*
siyáy̓ay̓ [si ya y̓ay̓] related to someone, be; friendly terms with someone, be on. *verb(i).*
siy̓áy̓us [si y̓a y̓us] dizzy from spiritual power, be; dizzy, be getting; high, be getting [while drinking]. *verb(i).*
siy̓á7 [si y̓a7] sweetheart. *noun.*
siy̓á7ten [si y̓a7 ten] widows; widowers [sg: **syá7ten**]. *noun.*
siy̓ích' [si y̓ich'] full [e.g., a container]. *adjective.*
siy̓íx̲ix̲as [si y̓i x̲i x̲as] *noun.* large lizard.
si7áchtn [si 7ach tn] napkin. *noun.*
si7inúptn [si 7i nup tn] mop. *noun.*
sí7k̲am̓ [si7 k̲am̓] wipe one's rear end. *verb(i).*
sí7k̲sam̓ [si7k̲ sam̓] wipe one's nose. *verb(i).*
si7k̲stn [si7k̲ stn] tissue. *noun.*
si7k̲tn [si7k̲ tn] toilet paper. *noun.*
si7l ~ sí7la [si 7l] grandparent; grandaunt; granduncle. *noun.*
sí7la ~ si7l [si7 la] grandparent; grandaunt; granny [term of address]; granduncle. *noun.*
si7n [si 7n] wipe (something). *verb(t).*
sí7sek̲' [si7 sek̲'] kindling. *noun.*
si7semáchxw [si7 se ma chxw] yarrow [type of plant]. *noun.*
sí7sintl' [si7 sintl'] grizzly [term of respect]; taboo name for grizzly bear. *noun.*
sí7tsam̓ [si7 tsam̓] wipe one's mouth. *verb(i).*
si7úsm [si 7u sm] wipe one's face. *verb(i).*
si7úsn [si 7u sn] wipe (someone's) face. *verb(t).*
skásnekem [skas ne kem] illegitimate child. *noun.*
skáti [ska ti] crazy. *adjective.*
skati7ús [ska ti 7us] crazy-faced; crazy face, have a. *adjective.*
skem̓ts littleneck clam; clam [littleneck]. *noun.*
skepalú7 [ske pa lu7] mongrel. *noun.*
skeskásnekem [skes kas ne kem] illegitimate children [sg: **skásnekem**]. *noun.*
sketk carrot [originally referred to a type of wild carrot]. *noun.*
skikimelú7 [ski ki me lu7] minnow. *noun.*
skim̓ [skim̓] breast [children's term]. *noun.*
skwákwel ~ swákwel [skwa kwel] loon. *noun.*
skwáyel [skwa yel] blue. *adjective.* sky; day; daylight. *noun.*
skwayutsmin [skwa yuts min] murdered (someone), have. *verb(t).*
skwá7wach [skwa7 wach] sturgeon. *noun.*
skwekwá7tl [skwe kwa7 tl] living apart, be; divorced, be; separated, be. *verb(i).*
skwekwích [skwe kwich] not much room, be; tight squeeze, be. *verb(i).*
skwekwiy̓ín̓tsut [skwe kwi y̓in̓ tsut] do what one does. *verb(i).* what what one is doing. *noun.*
skwekwi7ín̓tem [ske kwi 7in̓ tem] what happens to one; what befalls one. *noun.*
skwel̓ásh ~ s7ekwel̓ásh ~ sekwel̓ásh [skwe l'ash] rifle; gun. *noun.*
skwelkwélts [skwel kwelts] Western Grebe [type of bird]. *noun.*
skwém̓kwem̓ts ~ kwémkwemts [skwem̓ kwem̓ts] skinny. *adjective.* female salmon after spawning. *noun.*
skwém̓kwemts' ~ skwúm̓kwum̓ts' ~ kwém̓kwets' [skwem̓ kwemts'] lump. *noun.*
skwemúm [skwe mum] escaped into the bush, be all; flee into the bush [upward from village on the shore]. *verb(i).*
skwen former state. *noun.*
skweníwsem [skwe niw sem] heart [used for heart of new dancer]; heartbeat. *noun.*
skweshnách [skwesh nach] price. *noun.*
skwetl' rust. *noun.*
skwéxwnach [skwexw nach] patch of wood without underbrush. *noun.*
skwikwekwiy̓ín̓tsut [skwi kwe kwi y̓in̓ tsut] small actions. *noun.*
skwíkwi7 [skwi kwi7] stump of tree. *noun.*
skwíts'ay̓ [skwi ts'ay̓] burr. *noun.*
skwi7s [skwi7s] butt of tree. *noun.*
skwtsa7ts [skw tsa7ts] island. *noun.*

skwtsi7ts [skw tsi7ts] relative. *noun.*
skwul [skwul] school. *noun.* go to school. *verb(i).*
skwúlsem [skwul sem] mink pelts used by **sxw7umten**. *noun.*
skwum [skwum] cedar kettle or tub. *noun.*
skwúma [skwu ma] ratfish. *noun.*
skwúṁechn [skwu ṁe chn] humpback; humpback salmon [alternate name for **lhaw'ichen**]. *noun.*
skwúṁkwuṁts' ~ skwéṁkwemts' ~ kwéṁkwemts' [skwuṁ kwuṁts'] lump. *noun.*
sk'ák'eltx̲ [sk'a k'el tx̲] bone used in **slhahál**. *noun.*
sk'éxwa7 [sk'e xwa7] lacrosse match. *noun.*
sk'ínu7 [sk'i nu7] hunting dog. *noun.*
skw'áchmixwaẏlh [skw'ach mi xwa ẏlh] showing of pictures; something to be exhibited; exhibit. *noun.*
skw'ákw'aẏ [skw'a kw'aẏ] hunger [see also **ahánum**]. *noun.*
skw'ay ~ eskw'áy ~ kw'ay can't; impossible, be; unable, be; pregnant, be; cannot; wrong, be; amiss, be; powerless, be; very ill, be; defective, be; out of order, be. *verb(i).*
skw'áyatsut [skw'a ya tsut] training. *noun.*
skw'ek̲ák̲ [skw'e k̲ak̲] robin. *noun.*
skw'ek̲w'íl̓ [skw'e k̲w'il'] fully ripe, be [about berries]. *verb(i).*
skw'enmáylh [skw'en maylh] prayer. *noun.*
skw'eykw'ayach [skw'ey kw'a yach] out of order, be [i.e., not work]. *verb(i).*
skw'eykw'iyúts ~ skw'ikw'iyúts [skw'ey kw'i yuts] slaves [sg: **skw'iyúts**]. *noun.*
skw'ikw'íwes [skw'i kw'i wes] parents of child-in-law [sg: **skw'íwes**]. *noun.*
skw'íkw'iyuts [skw'i kw'i yuts] little slave [see **skw'iyúts**]; domestic animal; pet. *noun.*
skw'ikw'iyúts ~ skw'eykw'iyúts [skw'i kw'i yuts] slaves [sg: **skw'iyuts**]. *noun.*
skw'íts'ay [skw'i ts'ay] sea eggs; small green sea urchin. *noun.*
skw'íwes [skw'i wes] sibling's parent-in-law; co-parent-in-law; any close in-law; in-law, any close; child-in-law's sibling. *noun.*
skw'íẏechen ~ skw'í7achn [skw'i ẏe chen] grizzly bear [term used only in **syewen**]. *noun.*
skw'iyúts [skw'i yuts] slave. *noun.*
skw'í7achn ~ skw'íẏechen [skw'i 7a chn] grizzly bear. *noun.*
skw'lháẏak̲alh [skw'lha ẏa k̲alh] place where water runs over anything [falls, rapids, stones in mountain stream, etc.]. *noun.*
skw'ukw'ts [skw'ukw' ts] tail. *noun.*
sk̲aalx̲ [sk̲aal x̲] root digger; digging stick; stick for digging clams. *noun.*
sk̲ák̲el [sk̲a k̲el] baby; infant. *noun.*
sk̲amún [sk̲a mun] underground house. *noun.*
sk̲aṅ something stolen; stolen goods. *noun.*
sk̲apsm ~ stsk̲apsm ~ tsek̲ápsem [sk̲ap sm] back of the neck. *noun.*
sk̲áp'k̲ap'tsaylh ~ k̲'áp'k̲ap'tsaylh [sk̲ap' k̲ap' tsaylh] bat [type of animal]. *noun.*
sk̲atl' cloud; clouds. *noun.*
sk̲awts potato. *noun.*
sk̲áxwk̲axw [sk̲axw k̲axw] grouped together, be. *verb(i).*
sk̲áẏach [sk̲a ẏach] left hand. *noun.*
sk̲áyiws ~ sk̲áẏiws [sk̲a yiws] left side. *noun.*
sk̲áẏiws ~ sk̲áyiws [sk̲a ẏiws] left side. *noun.*
sk̲áẏk̲a ~ sk̲áẏshen [sk̲aẏ k̲a] left foot. *noun.*
sk̲áẏshen ~ sk̲áẏk̲a [sk̲aẏ shen] left foot. *noun.*
sk̲a7k̲ younger sibling; child of parent's younger sibling. *noun.*
sk̲ek̲ích [sk̲e k̲ich] full moon. *noun.*
sk̲ek̲xw [sk̲e k̲xw] gathering. *noun.*
sk̲el̓áẃ [sk̲e l'aẃ] beaver. *noun.*
sk̲életsun [sk̲e le tsun] dance hand movement with both hands at side at shoulder. *noun.*
sk̲elúlax̲en [sk̲e lu la x̲en] deer hooves [term used only in legends]. *noun.*
sk̲elh sore. *noun.*
sk̲em cedar kettle or tub. *noun.*
sk̲emsíṁ [sk̲em siṁ] funeral. *noun.*
sk̲ewk̲' raven. *noun.*
sk̲éyep ~ sk̲eyp [sk̲e yep] hit chest so that blood comes shooting out of mouth [a

type of **syewen**]; perform a dance characterized by the use of a rattle. *verb(i).*

sk̲eyp ~ sk̲éyep hit chest so that blood comes shooting out of mouth [a type of **syewen**]; perform a dance characterized by the use of a rattle. *verb(i).*

sk̲eẏtsáṁ [sk̲eẏ tsaṁ] swear words. *noun.* swearing. *verb(i).*

sk̲eẏúnek̲ [sk̲e ẏu nek̲] mean. *adjective.*

sk̲eyúẏwilh [sk̲e yuẏ wilh] old canoe; canoe, old. *noun.*

sk̲ik̲p'ach [sk̲ik̲ p'ach] fist. *noun.*

sk̲iẇx̲ [sk̲iẇx̲] steelhead. *noun.*

sk̲íx̲wuts'ch [sk̲i x̲wu ts'ch] hip [see also **sk̲'ák̲'aw'chk̲, sk̲'aw'chk̲, smiyíwchk̲**]. *noun.*

sk̲íyalh [sk̲i yalh] crybaby; diapers. *noun.*

sk̲í7eṁk̲w [sk̲i 7eṁk̲w] devilfish; octopus [the more common word is **st'elx̲wts'**]. *noun.*

sk̲í7k̲el ~ esk̲í7k̲el [sk̲i7 k̲el] ignorant, be; unschooled, be; not know how to do something; not good at doing something, be; unskilled, be. *verb(i).*

sk̲í7k̲elxw ~ esk̲í7k̲elxw [sk̲i7 k̲elxw] not yet know how to do something; unskilled, be still; unschooled, be still. *verb(i).*

sk̲'aatl' [sk̲'aatl'] otter; river. *noun.*

sk̲'ák̲'aẇchk̲ ~ sk̲'aẇchk̲ [sk̲'a k̲'aẇchk̲] hip [see also **sk̲íx̲wuts'ch, smiyíwchk̲**]; side of body. *noun.*

sk̲'ants'x̲ánm ~ esk̲'ants'x̲ánm [sk̲'ants' x̲a nm] eddy; back eddy. *noun.*

sk̲'ápitaxw ~ sk̲'ápitixw [sk̲'a pi taxw] knife [see also **lhách'tn**]. *noun.*

sk̲'ápitixw ~ sk̲'ápitaxw [sk̲'a pi tixw] knife [see also **lhách'tn**]. *noun.*

sk̲'aw payment. *noun.*

sk̲'áwalhen [sk̲'a wa lhen] punishment. *noun.*

sk̲'aẇchk̲ ~ sk̲'ák̲'aẇchk̲ hip [see also **sk̲íx̲uts'ch, smiyíwchk̲**]; side of body. *noun.*

sk̲'aẇíchshen ~ k̲'aẇíchshen [sk̲'a ẇich shen] dorsal fin. *noun.*

sk̲'ék̲'eẇ ~ sk̲'ek̲'éẇ ~ sk̲'ék̲w'u7 ~ sk̲'ek̲w'ú7 [sk̲'e k̲'eẇ] companions [sg: **sk̲'ew' ~ sk̲w'u7 ~ esk̲'ew' ~ esk̲w'u7**]. *noun.*

sk̲'ek̲'éẇ ~ sk̲'ék̲w'u7 ~ sk̲'ek̲w'ú7 ~ sk̲'ék̲'eẇ [sk̲'e k̲'eẇ] companions [sg: **sk̲'ew' ~ sk̲w'u7 ~ esk̲'ew' ~ esk̲w'u7**]. *noun.*

sk̲'ek̲w'ú7 ~ sk̲'ék̲'eẇ ~ sk̲'ek̲'éẇ ~ sk̲'ék̲w'u7 [sk̲'e k̲w'u7] companions [sg: **sk̲'ew' ~ sk̲w'u7 ~ esk̲'ew' ~ esk̲w'u7**]. *noun.*

sk̲'ék̲w'u7 ~ sk̲'ek̲w'ú7 ~ sk̲'ék̲'eẇ ~ sk̲'ek̲'éẇ [sk̲'e k̲w'u7] companions [sg: **sk̲'ew' ~ sk̲w'u7 ~ esk̲'ew' ~ esk̲w'u7**]. *noun.*

sk̲'ek̲w'ú7chk̲ [sk̲'e k̲w'u7 chk̲] cross. *noun.*

sk̲'ek̲w'ú7ṅwas [sk̲'e k̲w'u 7ṅ was] together, be. *verb(i).*

sk̲'émel [sk̲'e mel] paddle. *noun.*

sk̲'énk̲'enp' [sk̲'en k̲'enp'] full of bends, be; bends, be full of; doubled up, be all [about person]. *verb(i).*

sk̲'enp' bend; elbow of pipe. *noun.*

sk̲'énts'x̲anem [sk̲'ents' x̲a nem] back eddy. *noun.*

sk̲'étl'k̲'etl' [sk̲'etl' k̲'etl'] bracket fungus. *noun.*

sk̲'eẇ ~ sk̲w'u7 ~ esk̲'eẇ ~ esk̲w'u7 [sk̲'eẇ] companion. *noun.*

sk̲'ewátem [sk̲'e wa tem] beat [of a song]. *noun.*

sk̲'ewk̲'áw [sk̲'ew k̲'aw] person who has been cursed by **sxw7umten**. *noun.*

sk̲'ewm cry; howl. *noun.*

sk̲'éx̲k̲'ex̲ [sk̲'ex̲ k̲'ex̲] muskrat. *noun.*

sk̲'eẏ smoked salmon; dried smoked salmon cut up thin. *noun.*

sk̲'eẏáẇtxw [sk̲'e ẏaẇ txw] shed where salmon is dried. *noun.*

sk̲'ík̲'imel [sk̲'i k̲'i mel] little paddle; paddle [little] [see **sk̲'émel**]. *noun.*

sk̲'ík̲'itl' [sk̲'i k̲'itl'] scars [sg: **sk̲'itl'**]. *noun.*

sk̲'ík̲w'u7 [sk̲'i k̲w'u7] mate. *noun.*

sk̲'itl' [sk̲'itl'] scar. *noun.*

sk̲'iyáx̲atk̲wu7em [sk̲'i ya x̲at k̲wu 7em] whirlpool. *noun.*

sk̲'i7s ~ eslhk̲'í7s ~ lhk̲'i7s ~ slhk̲'i7s ~ lhsk̲'i7s [sk̲'i7s] know (something/someone); acquainted with (someone/something), be; know how to do (something). *verb(t).*

sk̲'í7x̲iya7ulh [sk̲'i7 x̲i ya 7ulh] belonging to a black person. *adjective.*

sk̲'tsaṁ ~ esk̲'tsáṁ [sk̲' tsaṁ] short, be too; run short [e.g., when sewing something]; not quite reaching, be. *verb(i).*
sk̲wacháẏs [sk̲wa chaẏs] underground tunnel. *noun.*
sk̲waháya7n [sk̲wa ha ya 7n] hole in ear; holes in ears [as in pierced ears]. *noun.*
sk̲wak̲s hole in nose. *noun.*
sk̲wálwen [sk̲wal wen] heart [as seat of affections or spiritual]; mind; opinion. *noun.*
sk̲wék̲wek̲s ~ esk̲wék̲wa7k̲s ~ esnek̲wék̲wa7k̲s [sk̲we k̲wek̲s] pierced nose, have a. *adjective.*
sk̲wék̲weṁch ~ sk̲wu7mchen [sk̲we k̲weṁch] hunched back, have a; hunchbacked. *adjective.*
sk̲welx̲w cataract; "white eye". *noun.*
sk̲wemáẏ [sk̲we maẏ] dog. *noun.*
sk̲wemáẏak̲in [sk̲we ma ẏa k̲in] wool blanket [made of mixed dog and mountain goat hair]. *noun.*
sk̲wemaẏáẃtxw [sk̲we ma ẏaẃ txw] doghouse. *noun.*
sk̲wemaẏúllh [sk̲we ma ẏullh] puppy. *noun.*
sk̲wemaẏúmesh [sk̲we ma ẏu mesh] doglike. *adjective.*
sk̲wemaẏús [sk̲we ma ẏus] face like a dog, have a; dog-faced. *adjective.*
sk̲wemk̲wemáẏ [sk̲wem k̲we maẏ] dogs [sg: **sk̲wemay'**]. *noun.*
sk̲wetk̲álhyes [sk̲wet k̲alh yes] Monday. *noun.*
sk̲wétshem ~ sk̲wétshen [sk̲wet shem] fog. *noun.*
sk̲wétshen ~ sk̲wétshem [sk̲wet shen] fog. *noun.*
sk̲wets' ruffed grouse; grouse [ruffed]. *noun.*
sk̲wexwnách [sk̲wexw nach] valley. *noun.*
sk̲wéẏk̲wey [sk̲weẏ k̲wey] talk; conversation; discussion. *noun.*
sk̲weyk̲wtáẏmesh [sk̲weyk̲w taẏ mesh] dwarf [if you see one don't tell anyone]. *noun.*
sk̲we7íls [sk̲we 7ils] copper. *noun.*
sk̲wik̲w [sk̲wik̲w] marmot. *noun.*
sk̲wík̲wems [sk̲wi k̲wems] hair hat. *noun.*
sk̲win- . . . . [sk̲win-] hair on . . . . *prefix.*
sk̲wínach [sk̲wi nach] arm hair [including hair on the hands]. *noun.*
sk̲wínats' [sk̲wi nats'] pubic hair. *noun.*
sk̲wiṅch [sk̲wiṅch] back hair. *noun.*
sk̲wíninas [sk̲wi ni nas] chest hair. *noun.*
sk̲wíniws [sk̲wi niws] body hair. *noun.*
sk̲winiyáx̲a7n [sk̲wi ni ya x̲a 7n] underarm hair; armpit hair. *noun.*
sk̲wink̲s [sk̲wink̲s] nose hair. *noun.*
sk̲wínk̲wen [sk̲win k̲wen] rosary; beads [small]. *noun.*
sk̲wínshen [sk̲win shen] leg hair. *noun.*
sk̲wints [sk̲wints] beard. *noun.*
sk̲wiẏápsem [sk̲wi ẏap sem] back of the head. *noun.*
sk̲wlha7lk̲ [sk̲w lha 7lk̲] wave hitting beach. *noun.*
sk̲wúk̲wel̓ [sk̲wu k̲wel'] tide pool; pond; bucket of water; small quantity of collected water. *noun.*
sk̲wúk̲wus ~ esk̲wúk̲wus [sk̲wu k̲wus] head down, have; sneak; have the head lowered between shoulders. *verb(i).*
sk̲wúk̲wuts'ayus [sk̲wu k̲wu ts'a yus] cross-eyed. *adjective.*
sk̲wu7mchen ~ sk̲wék̲weṁch [sk̲wu 7m chen] hunched back, have a; hunchbacked. *adjective.*
sk̲w'ax̲ slough; marshy water. *noun.*
sk̲w'chem [sk̲w' chem] boil; abscess. *noun.*
sk̲w'ek̲wchs [sk̲w'ek̲w chs] red huckleberry; huckleberry [red]. *noun.*
sk̲w'ek̲wchsáẏ [sk̲w'e k̲wch saẏ] huckleberry plant [red]. *noun.*
sk̲w'ék̲w'ipa [sk̲w'e k̲w'i pa] fawn [yearling]. *noun.*
sk̲w'elám [sk̲w'e lam] berry [general term]. *noun.*
sk̲w'elámaẏ [sk̲w'e la maẏ] berry bush [general term]. *noun.*
sk̲w'élem [sk̲w'e lem] barbecued salmon. *noun.*
sk̲w'elemáy [sk̲w'e le may] berry basket. *noun.*
sk̲w'elk̲w'eláṁ [sk̲w'el k̲w'e laṁ] berries [sg: **sk̲w'elám**]. *noun.*
sk̲w'elṁxw [sk̲w'el ṁxw] blackberry [wild]; wild blackberry [see **k̲w'elm'xwáy'**]. *noun.*
sk̲w'elhk̲ínes [sk̲w'elh k̲i nes] brooch. *noun.*

sk̲w'ík̲w'ishetsut ~ sk̲w'ík̲w'ishétsut [sk̲w'i k̲w'i she tsut] little toy [see **sk̲w'shétsut**]. *noun.*

sk̲w'ík̲w'ishétsut ~ sk̲w'ík̲w'ishetsut [sk̲w'i k̲w'i she tsut] little toy [see **sk̲w'shétsut**]. *noun.*

sk̲w'ílk̲w'elem tl'a élhk̲ay̓ [sk̲w'il k̲w'e lem tl'a 7elh k̲ay̓] little berry of the snake [another term for the black twinberry; see **titin'ústnay̓**]. *noun.*

sk̲w'k̲wem [sk̲w' k̲wem] new dancer's staff [with deerhooves on top]. *noun.*

sk̲w'k̲w'il̓ [sk̲w' k̲w'il'] berry, fully ripe [general term]. *noun.*

sk̲w'shétsut [sk̲w' she tsut] toy. *noun.* fun. *adjective.*

sk̲w'shétsut snexwílh [sk̲w' she tsut sne xwilh] toy canoe. *noun.*

sk̲w'úmay̓ [sk̲w'u may̓] head hair; hair. *noun.*

sk̲w'úmay̓ tl'a k̲w'um̓ [sk̲w'u may̓ tl'a k̲w'um̓] kelp leaves [literally, hair of the kelp]. *noun.*

sk̲w'úmk̲w'emay̓ [sk̲w'um k̲w'e may̓] fishing line [modern]. *noun.*

sk̲w'únek̲ [sk̲w'u nek̲] youngest, dearest child; [term of pity used for the youngest child of a family; "poor, wretched fellow"]. *noun.*

sk̲w'ut'shen [sk̲w'ut' shen] crooked leg, have a; crooked-legged. *adjective.*

sk̲w'uy [sk̲w'uy] sickness; disease. *noun.*

sk̲w'úynexw [sk̲w'uy nexw] catch (something); kill (something). *verb(t).* bag of game or fish; haul of game or fish; catch of game or fish. *noun.*

sk̲w'uy̓úmish [sk̲w'u y̓u mish] kind of sick, be [not sure what the illness is]; sickly, be. *verb(i).*

sk̲w'u7 ~ sk̲'ew̓ ~ esk̲'ew̓ ~ esk̲w'ú7 [sk̲w'u7] spouse; companion; partner. *noun.* with, be. *verb(i).*

sk̲w'ú7new̓as [sk̲w'u7 ne w̓as] company. *noun.*

slaay̓ [slaay̓] Douglas fir bark; thick bark; bark [thick]. *noun.*

slakáltem [sla kal tem] deck of cards. *noun.*

slálaw̓ [sla law̓] body. *noun.*

slálaw̓s ta swí7k̲a [sla law̓s ta swi7 k̲a] man's private parts [literally, body of the man]. *noun.*

slá7mats [sla7 mats] fish club; club for killing large fish. *noun.*

slemchis [slem chis] ring. *noun.*

slem̓k̲s ~ slhem̓k̲ eleven o'clock. *noun.*

slép'lep'áw̓ak̲w [slep' le p'a w̓ak̲w] old warpy hat [used jokingly]. *noun.*

sles bottom. *noun.*

slesk̲ river bottom. *noun.*

slests lower lip. *noun.*

slestsk̲ [sles tsk̲] chin. *noun.*

sléway̓ ~ sléwi7 [sle way̓] cedar bark; inner red cedar bark. *noun.*

sléway̓uyt [sle wa y̓uyt] blanket made of cedar bark. *noun.*

sléwi7 ~ sléway̓ [sle wi7] inner red cedar bark; cedar bark. *noun.*

sliim [sliim] sandhill crane. *noun.*

slil [slil] bunch of native blankets. *noun.*

slil̓sáy̓ek̲s [slil' sa y̓ek̲s] petticoat. *noun.*

slil̓xwí7nup [slil' xwi7 nup] lowland. *noun.*

slim [slim] white long-legged crane-like bird [makes a krrr-sound]; sandhill crane. *noun.*

slish [slish] fish slime. *noun.*

slishm [sli shm] rope made of twisted cedar withes. *noun.*

slix̲wáy̓shn ~ slíx̲way̓shn [sli x̲way̓ shn] foot of mountain; valley; area where the ground levels off. *noun.*

slíx̲way̓shn ~ slix̲wáy̓shn [sli x̲way̓ shn] foot of mountain; valley; area where the ground levels off. *noun.*

sluk̲' [sluk̲'] half dollar. *noun.*

slúlum [slu lum] song. *noun.*

sluxw [sluxw] arrowhead [one which detaches]. *noun.*

slhahál [slha hal] bone game; gambling. *noun.*

slhákw'amay [slha kw'a may] windpipe. *noun.*

slhákw'em [slha kw'em] one's breath; breath. *noun.*

slhákw'emachs [slha kw'e machs] pulse beat. *noun.*

slhálhen̓ay [slha lhe n̓ay] female [animal]. *adjective.*

slhálhen̓ay míx̲alh [slha lhe n̓ay mi x̲alh] female bear. *noun.*

slhálhen̓ay sx̲wí7shen [slha lhe n̓ay sx̲wi7 shen] doe; female deer. *noun.*

slhálhk̲'an [slhalh k̲'an] modest person; well-behaved person; nice person; respectable person. *noun.*
slhánaẏ [slha naẏ] woman. *noun.*
slhánaẏi7 [slha na ẏi7] woman, become a. *verb(i).*
slhanch' ~ eslhánch' careless [with things], be; rude, be; mean, be; bully, be a; rough, be. *verb(i).*
slhaẇének̲ [slha ẇe nek̲] "power song"; song sung by sxw7umten while healing. *noun.*
slhaẇíṅ [slha ẇiṅ] mattress [originally referred to a large cattail mat]. *noun.*
slhawt' herring. *noun.*
slhá7elkw' [slha 7elkw'] in-laws [general term]. *noun.*
slha7lhch [slha7 lhch] outside [of an object]; surface. *noun.*
slhá7lhchach ~ lha7lhchách [slha 7lh chach] top of the hand; back of the hand. *noun.*
slha7lhchshn [slha7 lhch shn] top of foot. *noun.*
slha7lhútxw [slha7 lhutxw] roof. *noun.*
slhek̲tál̓ [slhek̲ tal'] double blanket. *noun.*
slhék̲'wilh [slhek̲' wilh] torso; trunk of tree. *noun.*
slhélha7 ~ eslhélha7 [slhe lha7] close to something, be very. *verb(i).*
slhelhchéchmx̲ [slhelh chech mx̲] resin for chewing; chewing gum. *noun.*
slheṁ choke on water; swallow the wrong way. *verb(i).*
slhemch' chip; chipped-off piece. *noun.*
slheṁk̲ ~ sleṁk̲s ~ slheṁk̲s eleven o'clock. *noun.*
slheṁk̲s ~ slheṁk̲ ~ sleṁk̲s eleven o'clock. *noun.*
slhéṁlhem [slheṁ lhem] dew. *noun.*
slhéṁlheṁkw' [slheṁ lheṁkw] acne; skin disorder [general term]. *noun.*
slhems extra. *adjective.*
slheṁxw [slhe ṁxw] rain. *noun.*
slheṁxwmáchexw [slhe ṁxw ma chexw] dew on branches. *noun.*
slheṁxwmáchxw [slhe ṁxw ma chxw] moisture dripping from trees. *noun.*
slheṅ woven mat; woven material [general term]; mat. *noun.*
slhenlhánaẏ [slhen lha naẏ] women [sg: slhánaẏ]. *noun.*
slheṅyúllh [slheṅ yullh] young girl [see slhánaẏ]. *noun.*
slhe7án [slhe 7an] head of bay. *noun.*
slhích'apsm [slhi ch'ap sm] modern haircut [to shoulder-level]. *noun.*
slhich'lk̲n [slhi ch'l k̲n] dog [old word for sk̲wemáẏ; this kind of dog had its hair used for making cloth]. *noun.*
slhich'm [slhi ch'm] strips. *noun.*
slhik̲w [slhik̲w] flesh. *noun.*
slhik̲wáylh [slhi k̲waylh] parent- or child-in-law after death of own child. *noun.*
slhík̲wus [slhi k̲wus] fish cheek. *noun.*
slhílhkw'iws [slhilh kw'iws] connected, be; hooked, be. *verb(i).*
slhímel [slhi mel] yellow shiner perch; minnow; "shiner." *noun.*
slhíplhipiyax̲a7ens [slhip lhi pi ya x̲a 7ens] fin. *noun.*
slhíts'em [slhi ts'em] spark. *noun.*
slhí7lhaẇiṅ tl'a wex̲és [slhi7 lha ẇiṅ tl'a we x̲es] frog leaves [literally, little bed of the frog]. *noun.*
slhk̲'i7s ~ eslhk̲'í7s ~ sk̲'i7s ~ lhk̲'i7s ~ lhsk̲'i7s [slh k̲'i7s] know (something/someone); acquainted with (someone/something), be; know how to do (something). *verb(t).*
slhuṁ [slhuṁ] soup. *noun.*
slhuts' [slhuts'] scabies. *noun.*
slhuxw [slhuxw] arrowhead [type that breaks off the shaft when it hits something]. *noun.*
smalmelx̲wíts'a ~ mélmelx̲wíts'a ~ smélmelx̲wits'a [smal mel x̲wi ts'a] dipper [type of bird]. *noun.*
smaṅánlh [sma ṅa nlh] high-class person; person of high class [also used to address a woman, as a counterpart to siẏáṁ]. *noun.*
smánit [sma nit] mountain; high mountain. *noun.*
smánitm [sma ni tm] turn into stone. *verb(i).*
smant rock; stone. *noun.*
smántn [sman tn] turn (something) into stone. *verb(t).*
smáts'en [sma ts'en] proud. *adjective.*

smáyk̲wsmut [smayk̲w smut] trance. *noun.*
smáyl̓ilh [smay l'ilh] giant wild person; "wild people." *noun.*
smekw burl; lump on a tree; lump; protuberance. *noun.*
smékwmekw [smekw mekw] bumpy [surface]. *adjective.*
smekw'álap [sme kw'a lap] thigh; upper leg. *noun.*
smekw'a7ál [sme kw'a 7al] graveyard [see also **stéwak̲in**]; grave; dead man's cache. *noun.*
smékw'em [sme kw'em] find. *noun.*
smek̲sáń [smek̲ sań] visor. *noun.*
smék̲'nech [smek̲' nech] arrow notch; arrow used for practise; small game arrow. *noun.*
smek̲w'á7 ~ **nsmék̲w'á7** [sme k̲w'a7] great blue heron. *noun.*
smek̲w'ú7ts [sme k̲w'u7 ts] food sent home for women and children; leftovers from a feast; food donation [after a feast]. *noun.*
smélmelx̲wits'a ~ **mélmelx̲wíts'a** ~ **smalmelx̲wíts'a** [smel mel x̲wi ts'a] dipper [type of bird]. *noun.*
smélhx̲wel [smelh x̲wel] Indian plum. *noun.*
smelhx̲weláy̓ [smelh x̲we lay̓] Indian plum bush. *noun.*
smemel̓útsin [sme me l'u tsin] squirrel. *noun.*
smemets'íń [sme me ts'iń] skunks [sg: **smets'íń**]. *noun.*
smemets'íńentem ~ **memets'íńtm** [sme me ts'i ńen tem] squirted by a skunk, get. *verb(p).*
smemey̓máy̓ ~ **meymáy̓** ~ **smeymáy̓** [sme mey̓ may̓] forgetful [see also **esmemey'máy**]. *adjective.*
smém̓kw clot. *noun.*
smemn [sme mn] give birth; bear child; in labour, be. *verb(i).*
smeńálhen [sme ńa lhen] make (someone) respectable. *verb(t).*
smeńálhs [sme ńalhs] treat (someone) like a high-class person; respect (someone). *verb(t).*
sméńhem [smeń hem] descendants; generations below; posterity; children. *noun.*
smenmańálh [smen ma ńalh] high-class people [sg: **smańálh**]. *noun.*
smenmánit [smen ma nit] mountains [sg: **smánit**]. *noun.*
smenmántm [smen man tm] rocky shore, be a. *verb(i).*
sméschem [smes chem] brown bear. *noun.*
smesch'íń [smes ch'iń] birthmark. *noun.*
smetk̲sn [smetk̲ sn] snot. *noun.*
smet'áni [sme t'a ni] dice game. *noun.*
smét'k̲sen [smet'k̲ sen] mucus. *noun.*
smets'álk̲en [sme ts'al k̲en] brain. *noun.*
smets'íń [sme ts'iń] skunk. *noun.*
sméts'mets'em [smets' me ts'em] proud of oneself, be; stuck-up, be; kind of showing off, be; flirting, be. *verb(i).*
smex̲wíws [sme x̲wiws] smallpox. *noun.*
smeymáy̓ ~ **meymáy̓** ~ **smemey̓máy̓** [smey may̓] forgetful [see also **esmemey'máy**]. *adjective.*
smeyts meat. *noun.*
smeytsáns [smey tsans] gums. *noun.*
smeytsk̲w meat head. *noun.*
sme7ík̲' [sme 7ik̲'] full for a while, have been; full, be [from eating]. *verb(i).*
sme7ús [sme 7us] head [of human, animal, fish]. *noun.*
sme7úsk̲w [sme 7usk̲w] fish head; salmon head. *noun.*
smíkw'ayts'a7m [smi kw'ay ts'a 7m] washing; laundry. *noun.*
smílha7 [smi lha7] Indian winter dance. *noun.*
smimkw' [smimkw'] washed. *adjective.*
smím̓na7ullh ~ **smíńminullh** ~ **mińmińúllh** [smim̓ na 7ullh] animal cub; young of any animal. *noun.*
smíńminullh ~ **mińmińúllh** ~ **smím̓na7ullh** [smiń mi nullh] animal cub; young of any animal. *noun.*
smiyíw̓ax̲an ~ **miyíw̓ax̲an** [smi yi w̓a x̲an] side of body; edge [of anything]. *noun.*
smiyíwchk̲ [smi yiwchk̲] hip [see also **sk̲íx̲wuts'ch, sk̲'ák̲'aw'chk̲, sk̲'aw'chk̲**]. *noun.*
smí7mant [smi7 mant] pebbles; little stone [see **smant**]. *noun.*
sm̓us [sm̓us] face. *noun.*
sna ~ **sna7** name; title. *noun.*
snách'ulh [sna ch'ulh] another's; the other's; other's, the. *adjective.*
snahím̓ [sna him̓] naming. *noun.*

snástem [snas tem] Saskatoon berry [see **nástem'ay**]. *noun.*
snat night. *noun.*
sna7 ~ **sna** name; title. *noun.*
sna7m [sna 7m] spiritual power of a **sxw7umten** [exercised through dancing and singing]. *noun.*
snch'éwilh [sn ch'e wilh] half-brother; half-sister; half-sibling. *noun.*
snch'ínak̲ [sn ch'i nak̲] spouse of spouse's sibling. *noun.*
snch'ínek̲ [sn ch'i nek̲] spouse's in-laws of the same generation. *noun.*
snch'u7 ~ **nch'u7** ~ **ch'u7** [sn ch'u7] one. *numeral.*
snéch'elhp [sne ch'elhp] small river canoe; canoe, small river. *noun.*
snékwem [sne kwem] beat [e.g., as of a heart]. *noun.*
snékwen [sne kwen] movements [to something, e.g., the beats of a song]. *noun.*
snek̲'álhs [sne k̲'alhs] wound. *noun.*
snék̲wem [sne k̲wem] sun. *noun.*
snélhem [sne lhem] make a racket; be noisy. *verb(i).*
snemá [sne ma] penance; forbidden thing; taboo thing. *noun.*
snésk̲en [snes k̲en] hair oil. *noun.*
snewákw'a [sne wa kw'a] ring around the moon. *noun.*
snew̓ínas [sne w̓i nas] half a fathom, measured from breast bone to finger. *noun.*
snew̓íyelh [sne w̓i yelh] advice. *noun.*
snexwílh [sne xwilh] canoe; Squamish canoe. *noun.* raid some place; go on a raid. *verb(i).*
snexwnexwílh [snexw ne xwilh] canoes [sg: **snexwilh**]. *noun.*
snexw7ayits'á7m ~ **nexw7áy̓its'm** [snexw 7a yi ts'a 7m] change of clothes. *noun.*
sníchim [sni chim] language; speech; word. *noun.*
sní7nixwilh [sni7 ni xwilh] toy canoe; model canoe [see **snexwílh**]. *noun.*
snk̲wú7us ~ **k̲wú7us** ~ **nk̲wú7us** [sn k̲wu 7us] tear; tears. *noun.*
snk̲w'úyiwan [sn k̲w'u yi wan] not dare to; afraid to. *verb(i).*
sntak̲wtn ~ **ntak̲wtn** ~ **tak̲wtn** [sn tak̲w tn] bucket. *noun.*
snts'k̲wú7tstn ~ **nts'k̲wu7tstn** ~ **ts'k̲wu7tstn** [snts' k̲wu7ts tn] smoking pipe; pipe [for smoking]. *noun.*
spahím̓ [spa him̓] wind. *noun.*
spák̲'em [spa k̲'em] flower. *noun.*
spák̲'em s7íxwalh [spa k̲'em s7i xwalh] flower child; hippie. *noun.*
spak̲'em̓áw̓txw [spa k̲'e m̓aw̓ txw] flower shop. *noun.*
spálhx̲en [spalh x̲en] meadow; flats; flatland; prairie. *noun.*
spánanexw [spa na nexw] blue camas. *noun.*
spáxwpxwéi̓k̲sen [spaxwp xwel'k̲ sen] puffball [literally, dust on nose]. *noun.*
spekw'm [spe kw'm] dust. *noun.*
spelk̲wach [spel k̲wach] small span [unit of measurement from thumb and knuckle of bent index-finger]. *noun.*
spéńem [spe ńem] plant; seed; shoot for planting. *noun.*
speńem̓áy [spe ńe m̓ay] vegetables. *noun.*
spenúy'txw [spe nuy̓ txw] "keekwilee house" [house sunk in ground]. *noun.*
spexw stomach where tripe comes from; tripe; animal stomach. *noun.*
spexw pale. *adjective.*
spipisténak̲ [spi pis te nak̲] jealous. *adjective.*
sptach [sp tach] unit of measurement from elbow of right arm to tip of finger. *noun.*
spúmim̓ [spu mim̓] yeast bread. *noun.*
spúshem [spu shem] spray. *noun.*
spúxwam [spu xwam] steam; smoke; dust. *noun.*
sp'aats' [sp'aats'] stink currant [see **p'áats'ay'**]; Indian currant. *noun.*
sp'ach' sparks; heat [intense heat, as from a fire]. *noun.*
sp'ák̲w'us [sp'a k̲w'us] bald eagle. *noun.*
sp'áyak̲ [sp'a yak̲] bread, homemade. *noun.*
sp'áyak̲im̓ [sp'a ya k̲im̓] bread, baked; bread, home-made; bread [which one has baked; literally, preparation]. *noun.*
sp'á7wik̲w [sp'a7 wik̲w] Derby hat. *noun.*
sp'ek̲wa7ím̓ [sp'e k̲wa 7im̓] split-off material. *noun.* split something. *verb(i).*
sp'elách'em [sp'e la ch'em] bobcat. *noun.*
sp'éi̓xwem [sp'el' xwem] lung; lungs; milt. *noun.*

sp'ep'elách' [sp'e p'e lach'] snipe [type of bird]. *noun.*

sp'eskw'úy nexwyém̓tn [sp'es kw'uy nexw yem̓ tn] new Indian dancer's belt. *noun.*

sp'eskw'úy̓ ~ p'eskwúy̓ [sp'es kw'uy̓] moutain goat wool. *noun.*

sp'etl'tn [sp'etl' tn] clay used in making Indian blankets, kind of; white paint [used in making blankets]. *noun.*

sp'éxwi7k̲s [sp'e xwi7k̲s] tender part of nose of fish. *noun.*

sp'íp'lhk̲'new̓as [sp'i p'lhk̲' ne w̓as] side by side, be; side by side, come. *verb(i).*

sp'iyákw'us [sp'i ya kw'us] alderbark basket. *noun.*

sp'úk̲w'em [sp'u k̲w'em] foam. *noun.*

sp'útl'am [sp'u tl'am] smoke; tobacco. *noun.*

stak̲íw̓aw̓txw [sta k̲i w̓aw̓ txw] barn [see **stek̲íw**]. *noun.*

stak̲iwúllh ~ stek̲iw̓úllh [sta k̲i wullh] foal; colt; young horse [see **stek̲íw**]. *noun.*

stak̲w river; water. *noun.*

stam what? *question word; noun.*

stamáw̓txw ~ tamáw̓txw [sta maw̓ txw] what kind of house is it? *question word; verb(i).*

stamáy̓ ~ tamáy̓ [sta may̓] what kind of tree is it? *question word; verb(i).*

stam̓áy̓ak̲ap [sta m̓a y̓a k̲ap] what kind of smell is it? *question word; verb(i).*

staméwilh ~ taméwilh [sta me wilh] what kind of canoe is it? *question word; verb(i).*

stam̓í7k̲in [sta m̓i7 k̲in] what kind of wool is it? *question word; verb(i).*

stamsh warrior; great fighter. *noun.*

státax̲ay̓s [sta ta x̲ay̓s] rough land; sheer bluff; cliff; sheer cliff. *noun.*

statkw even, be. *verb(i).*

stáx̲ay̓s [sta x̲ay̓s] bluff; cliff. *noun.*

stáyak̲shnam̓ [sta yak̲ shnam̓] steps. *noun.*

stáyalh [sta yalh] child of living sibling; child of living cousin; nephew; niece; sibling's child. *noun.*

stay̓ápsem [sta y̓ap sem] back of head. *noun.*

stay̓ch back [of body or house]; back side; space behind something. *noun.*

stá7uxwlh [sta 7uxwlh] children; child. *noun.*

stek'ín [ste k'in] Haida people. *noun.*

stek̲íw [ste k̲iw] horse. *noun.*

stek̲iw̓úllh ~ stak̲iwúllh [ste k̲i w̓ullh] foal; colt; young horse. *noun.*

stek̲shn [stek̲ shn] cliff. *noun.*

stek̲tak̲íw [stek̲ ta k̲iw] horses [sg: **stek̲iw**]. *noun.*

stek̲' fart. *noun.*

stek̲wták̲w [stek̲w tak̲w] rivers [sg: **stak̲w**]. *noun.*

stélk̲wim ~ st'elk̲wím̓ [stel k̲wim] breast. *noun.*

stélmexw [stel mexw] Indian; person; human being. *noun.*

stélmexwulh [stel me xwulh] Indian's; belonging to an Indian. *adjective.*

stélmexwulh sts'its'áp' [stel me xwulh sts'i ts'ap'] Indian work. *noun.*

steltélmexw [stel tel mexw] persons; people [sg: **stélmexw**]. *noun.*

stém̓k̲wek̲s [stem̓ k̲wek̲s] blunt pointed. *adjective.*

stém̓xwalh [stem̓ xwalh] cloth made of dog's hair with plumes of fireweed. *noun.*

stémx̲wulh [stem x̲wulh] blanket of fiber of cottonwood. *noun.*

steta7átal̓ [ste ta 7a tal'] even, be; equal, be [in strength, size, etc.]; tied, be [in a canoe race]. *verb(i).*

stéwak̲in [ste wa k̲in] corpse; dead; grave; graveyard [see also **smekw'a7ál**]. *noun.*

stewtáw̓ [stew taw̓] glare; brightness. *noun.*

stewtá7uxwlh [stew ta 7uxwlh] children [sg: **stá7uxwlh**]. *noun.*

stey̓sh same size, be the; extent, be the; enough, be; be all; measure something; size something. *verb(i).*

stíta7 [sti ta7] covering, be; being on, be. *verb(i).*

stítim̓ [sti tim̓] working hard, be. *verb(i).*

stíy̓iws ~ stíyiyews [sti y̓iws] ornament. *noun.*

stíyiyews ~ stíy̓iws [sti yi yews] ornament. *noun.*

stí7tas [sti7 tas] have one of (something); one of (something), have. *verb(t).*

stkwáya7n [st kwa ya 7n] hearing. *noun.*

stk̲áya ~ tk̲áya7 [st k̲a ya] wolf [term used in longhouse]. *noun.*
stup [stup] stove. *noun.*
st'akw'usachálh [st'a kw'u sa chalh] seventh time. *noun.*
st'ák̲'its' [st'a k̲'its'] crosswise, be. *verb(i).*
st'ák̲'its'áw̓txw [st'a k̲'i ts'aw̓ txw] log house. *noun.*
st'ák̲w'em [st'a k̲w'em] thimbleberry [see **t'ák̲w'emay'** and **t'ek̲w't'ak̲w'emáy'**]. *noun.*
st'al fillet. *noun.*
st'amáy̓s [st'a may̓s] pointer [in **slhahál**]. *noun.*
st'ashem [st'a shem] child of a slave; low-class person; disrespected people [e.g., illegitimate children]. *noun.*
st'ashemántsut [st'a she man tsut] make oneself out to be a low-class person. *verb(i).*
st'áshemni [st'a shem ni] treat (someone) like a low-class person. *verb(t).*
st'át'k̲'new̓as [st'at'k̲' ne w̓as] cross. *noun.*
st'ech'shn [st'ech' shn] toe jam. *noun.*
st'ek̲ís ~ estek̲ís [st'e k̲is] take it easy; slow, be; go slowly. *verb(i).*
st'ek̲t'ík̲l ~ est'ek̲t'ík̲l [st'ek̲ t'i k̲l] muddy. *adjective.*
st'ek̲w' break in a song, type of. *noun.*
st'ek̲w'áy̓ch [st'e k̲w'ay̓ch] shortcut. *noun.*
st'ék̲w't'ek̲w's [st'ek̲w' t'ek̲w's] Cut-up-in-chunks. *place name.*
st'elkáyus [st'el ka yus] wart on face near eye, have a. *adjective.*
st'elkw' spot [on an animal]. *noun.*
st'elkw'áyus [st'el kw'a yus] spot-eyed. *adjective.*
st'elk̲wím̓ ~ stélk̲wim [st'el k̲wim̓] bosom; breast. *noun.*
st'elmú7t ~ stl'elmú7t [st'el mu7t] old person. *noun.*
st'élt'elkw' [st'el t'elkw'] spotted like a dog. *adjective.*
st'el̓úllh [st'e l'ullh] fawn [newborn]. *noun.*
st'élx̲wets' ~ st'elx̲wts' [st'el x̲wets'] devilfish; octopus. *noun.*
st'elx̲wts' ~ st'élx̲wets' [st'el x̲wts'] octopus; devilfish. *noun.*
st'em̓ flip; snap up. *verb(i).*
st'em̓k̲w scalped, be. *verb(i).*
st'emsh braid. *noun.*
st'emt'ám [st'em t'am] errors; something wrong. *noun.*
st'ét'elk̲w ~ est'ét'elk̲w [st'e t'elk̲w] spot on something, be a; on, be [about a spot]. *verb(i).*
st'éwak̲w' [st'e wak̲w'] mud, a kind of. *noun.*
st'ex̲ branch; prong of antler. *noun.*
st'ex̲t'x̲áchxw [st'ex̲t x̲a chxw] branches [sg: **st'x̲achxw**]. *noun.*
st'éy̓k̲ay [st'ey̓ k̲ay] soaked fish; dried salmon soaked in water. *noun.*
st'ík̲el [st'i k̲el] mud. *noun.*
st'ik̲w [st'ik̲w] cold. *noun.* cold weather, be. *verb(i).*
st'í7k̲wem [st'i7 k̲wem] spark from a fire; large spark. *noun.*
st'kw'im̓ [st' kw'im̓] pit; dugout. *noun.*
st'k̲w'élhnalh snexwílh [st' k̲w'elh nalh sne xwilh] "cut-off" canoe; canoe, "cut-off." *noun.*
st'úkw'chus ~ st'úk̲wchus [st'ukw' chus] forehead. *noun.*
st'úk̲wchus ~ st'úkw'chus [st'uk̲w chus] forehead. *noun.*
st'x̲achxw [st' x̲a chxw] knot [in a tree]; branch; limb [of a tree]. *noun.*
st'x̲áyus ~ st'x̲áyusem [st' x̲a yus] lightning. *noun.*
st'x̲áyusem ~ st'x̲áyus [st' x̲a yu sem] lightning. *noun.*
st'x̲i [st' x̲i] fork in a stream, river or road. *noun.*
stl'álk̲em [stl'al k̲em] rare; special; supernatural. *adjective.* monster. *noun.*
stl'ál̓x̲en ~ tl'ál̓x̲en [stl'al' x̲en] snowshoe; snowshoes. *noun.*
stl'alhálem [stl'a lha lem] grizzly bear. *noun.*
stl'amkw' tainted salmon eggs; salmon eggs preserved for winter use. *noun.*
stl'átl'am [stl'a tl'am] right size, be the. *verb(i).*
stl'áx̲wtl'x̲way̓lh [stl'ax̲w tl'x̲wa y̓lh] dog whelp; litter of pups; young of any animal. *noun.*
stl'a7áshen [stl'a 7a shen] invited guest. *noun.*
stl'ék̲'shen [stl'ek̲' shen] moccasin; moccasins [see also **mek̲wú7shtn**]. *noun.*

stl'elmú7t ~ st'elmú7t [stl'el mu7t] old person. *noun.*
stl'eltl'elmút [stl'el tl'el mut] old people [sg: **stl'elmút ~ st'elmut**]. *noun.*
stl'elú7em [stl'e lu 7em] cockle. *noun.*
stl'eplk̲n [stl'e pl k̲n] feathers; down [as in the small feathers from a bird; cf. **stl'palk̲n**]. *noun.*
stl'epnách [stl'ep nach] saucer. *noun.*
stl'éptl'epx̲ ~ estl'éptl'epx̲ [stl'ep tl'e px̲] spotted like a chicken. *adjective.*
stl'epx̲w [stl'e px̲w] beat a drum very rapidly; make a fast drumbeat [almost a ruffle, with one drumstick]. *verb(i).*
stl'etl'elmú7tentsut [stl'e tl'el mu7 ten tsut] get old; old, get; age. *verb(i).*
stl'ets beat a drum rapidly; beat a slow rhythm [on drum or otherwise]. *verb(i).*
stl'exw ~ estl'éxw loser [in a game, fight]. *noun.*
stl'exwtl'éxw [stl'exw tl'exw] logger. *noun.*
stl'ík̲w'am [stl'i k̲w'am] smoke from house fire; smoke. *noun.*
stl'ik̲w'em̓áw̓txw [stl'i k̲w'e m̓aw̓ txw] smokehouse. *noun.*
stl'itl'á7alk̲em [stl'i tl'a 7al k̲em] bugs [literally, a bunch of little supernatural things; sg: **stl'itl'í7lk̲m**]. *noun.*
stl'itl'í7lk̲m [stl'i tl'i 7l k̲m] bug [general term; literally, little monster]. *noun.*
stl'i7 [stl'i7] want; like; desire. *verb(i).* dear; thing desired or wanted; desire. *noun.*
stl'k̲ilh [stl' k̲ilh] relative [general term]. *noun.*
stl'pál̓k̲en [stl' pal' k̲en] feather; feathers. *noun.*
stl'píw̓en [stl' pi w̓en] shirt. *noun.*
stsátsam̓áxwilh [stsa tsa m̓a xwilh] two canoes travelling together. *noun.*
stsátsi7n [stsa tsi 7n] blood. *noun.*
stsá7tsk̲ay [stsa7 tsk̲ay] salmonberry shoots; thimbleberry shoots; "saskies." *noun.*
stsa7tsk̲ay̓íwa [stsa7 tsk̲a y̓i wa] large shoot [general term; usually in its second year]; one-year-old shoots. *noun.*
stsa7x̲áy̓ [stsa7 x̲ay̓] crybaby, be a. *verb(i).*
stsá7yem [stsa7 yem] guest, be a. *verb(i).*
stsek̲ tree; branch; wood; log; stick. *noun.*
stsek̲ápsem ~ sk̲apsm ~ stsk̲apsm [stse k̲ap sem] back of the neck. *noun.*
stsék̲i7 [stse k̲i7] sockeye salmon. *noun.*
stsék̲tsek̲ [stsek̲ tsek̲] forest; trees; woodland; bunch of trees [sg: **stsek̲**]. *noun.*
stsem̓á [stse m̓a] second [thing]. *noun.*
stsemántsut [stse man tsut] second attempt. *noun.*
stsém̓tsem̓k̲w ~ estsém̓tsem̓k̲w [stsem̓ tsem̓k̲w] wrinkles [see also **lhelp'ús**]; creases. *noun.*
stsewásem [stse wa sem] bet. *noun.*
stséxwem [stse xwem] waterfall; falls. *noun.*
stsey̓ end. *noun.*
stséy̓k̲s last; end [of something extended in length]; endpoint. *noun.*
stsítsiyiw̓an [stsi tsi yi w̓an] satisfy (someone). *verb(t).*
stsíyus [stsi yus] clothes; costume. *noun.*
stsi7s [stsi7s] today [only in the phrase **ti stsi7s**]. *noun.*
stsk̲apsm ~ sk̲apsm ~ stsek̲ápsem [stsk̲ap sm] back of the neck. *noun.*
stsúntem [stsun tem] what is told. *noun.*
stsúyay̓ [stsu yay̓] leather buckskin; leather. *noun.*
stsúyay̓wit [stsu yay̓ wit] buckskin shirt. *noun.*
sts'ák̲shelik̲w ~ ts'ák̲shelik̲w [sts'ak̲ she lik̲w] rock cod. *noun.*
sts'ak̲' bruise. *noun.*
sts'áts'ey [sts'a ts'ey] shade. *noun.*
sts'ayx̲tsutánan [sts'ayx̲ tsu ta nan] hastiness. *noun.*
sts'á7k̲in [sts'a7 k̲in] cattail; bullrush. *noun.*
sts'ekw' bug; bugs; worm; worms. *noun.*
sts'ekw'í7ens [sts'e kw'i 7ens] consumption; tuberculosis; TB [see also **hemlch, ts'xwínas,** and **ts'kw'i7ns**]. *noun.*
sts'ekw'nítem [sts'ekw' ni tem] wormy, get. *verb(p).*
sts'ékw'ts'ekw' [sts'ekw' ts'ekw'] wormy, be. *verb(i).*
sts'ek̲wts'úk̲wi7 [stsek̲w ts'u k̲wi7] catch any salmon by any method. *verb(i).* fish, a lot of; school of fish. *noun.*
sts'em fish with line [not with a rod]; stillfishing; angle [not with a rod]; "mooching." *verb(i).*

sts'émkwa [sts'em kwa] tommycod; kelp greenling. *noun.*
sts'enáy̓ ~ sts'nay̓ ~ ts'nay̓ [sts'e nay̓] bullhead. *noun.*
sts'ét'k̲'em [sts'et' k̲'em] drop of water. *noun.*
sts'ik̲' [sts'ik̲'] clay; mud. *noun.*
sts'im̓ [sts'im̓] oil for eating. *noun.*
sts'íts'ak̲in [sts'i ts'a k̲in] little bullrush. *noun.*
sts'its'áp' [sts'i ts'ap'] job; work. *noun.*
sts'its'úys [sts'i ts'uys] crazy; mad; crazy fellow, be a. *adjective.*
sts'iwk̲' [sts'iwk̲'] red elderberry [see **ts'íwk̲ay̓**]. *noun.*
sts'íwk̲'ay̓ ~ ts'íwk̲ay̓ [sts'iw k̲'ay̓] elderberry tree. *noun.*
sts'nay̓ ~ ts'nay̓ ~ sts'enáy̓ [sts' nay̓] bullhead. *noun.*
sts'úk̲wi7 [sts'u k̲wi7] salmon; fish [general term]. *noun.*
sts'uk̲w'i7án [sts'u k̲w'i 7an] turn (someone) into a salmon. *verb(t).*
sts'uunts' [sts'uunts'] vulva. *noun.*
sts'úysánan [sts'uy sa nan] foolish ways. *noun.*
súhupit ~ ns-húhupit ~ nsúhupit [su hu pit] rabbit. *noun.*
sukw' [sukw'] stagger. *verb(i).*
sukw'amáw̓txw [su kw'a maw̓ txw] lodging made of cedar bark. *noun.*
súkw'em [su kw'em] outer red cedar bark; cedar bark. *noun.*
suk̲sántem [suk̲ san tem] have its dampness removed [about firewood]. *verb(p).*
suk̲w [suk̲w] whole dried deer. *noun.*
suk̲w' [suk̲w'] side of dried deer. *noun.*
súlchis [sul chis] soldier. *noun.*
sulsúlchis [sul sul chis] soldiers [sg: **súlchis**]. *noun.*
sum̓ [sum̓] smell [give off an odour]; stink. *verb(i).* smell. *noun.*
sum̓ay̓ák̲in [su m̓a y̓a k̲in] have smelly insides or intestines [about game]. *verb(i).*
sum̓nálhen [sum̓ na lhen] smell it; start to smell it. *verb(i).*
súm̓nexw [sum̓ nexw] smell (something). *verb(t).*
sum̓ún̓ [su m̓un̓] smell (something); sniff at (something). *verb(t).*
sunimáylh ~ swanimáylh [su ni maylh] deceased sibling's child. *noun.*
súsukw' [su sukw'] stagger along. *verb(i).*
súsum̓ [su sum̓] smell the stink; smell; stink. *verb(i).*
súsum̓nexw [su sum̓ nexw] smelling (something), be. *verb(t).*
-sut [-sut] {reflexive suffix}. *suffix.*
sútich [su tich] north; north wind; "Squamish wind"; cold north wind. *noun.*
sút'un [su t'un] inhale (something) [as in smoking]. *verb(t).*
suts [suts] brushed by. *verb(i).*
suuk̲sántem [suuk̲ sán tem] draw water from (wood). *verb(p).*
suun [suun] blow a sore; control weather. *verb(i).*
súxwten [suxw ten] identify (someone/something). *verb(t).*
súxwtim̓ [suxw tim̓] try to recognize someone. *verb(i).*
suxwtnálhen [suxwt na lhen] recognize, manage to; manage to recognize. *verb(i).*
súxwtnexw [suxwt nexw] recognize (someone). *verb(t).*
sux̲wsux̲wmíw̓as [sux̲w sux̲w mi w̓as] paddle quietly. *verb(i).*
súyay̓ch [su yay̓ch] wall mats [sg: **súyi7ch**]. *noun.*
súyiws ~ s-húyiws [su yiws] costume. *noun.*
súyi7ch [su yi7ch] wallmat [see also **tax̲ch**]. *noun.*
súyumay̓lh [su yu ma y̓lh] ceremony [involving donations] of "bringing out" a girl. *verb(i).*
súyum̓en [su yu m̓en] make expenditures in honour of (something/someone); spend goods or money in honour of (something/someone). *verb(t).*
súyum̓entem [su yu m̓en tem] honoured with donations, be. *verb(p).*
súyuy̓ [su yuy̓] cured hide. *noun.*
swaam [swaam] geoduck; horse clam. *noun.*
swacháy̓ [swa chay̓] perch [pile or striped]. *noun.*
swách'it [swa ch'it] torch; lamp. *noun.*
swákwel ~ skwákwel [swa kwel] loon [common]. *noun.*

swálam [swa lam] echo. *noun.*
swals scramble gift. *noun.*
swanimáylh ~ sunimáylh [swa ni maylh] deceased sibling's child. *noun.*
swat who? *question word; noun.*
swáw̓lus ~ sew̓íw̓lus [swaw̓ lus] young men [sg: swíw'lus]. *noun.*
swáwts'apsem [swaw ts'ap sem] neck pain. *noun.*
swáwts'aych [swaw ts'aych] back pain. *noun.*
swáwts'inas [swaw ts'i nas] chest pain. *noun.*
swa7 belonging; object possessed by someone. *noun.*
swa7 sk̲wálwen [swa7 sk̲wal wen] one's business. *noun.*
swa7ám̓ [swa 7am̓] relatives; close relative; ancestors. *noun.*
swá7elt [swa 7elt] creek. *noun.*
swa7s his; his own; hers; her own. *adjective.*
swá7swit [swa7 swit] their own; theirs. *adjective.*
swa7tk̲ [swa7 tk̲] stern man; stern of a boat. *noun.*
swa7tshn [swa7 tshn] tail-part of fish [see also sx̲ép'shen]. *noun.*
swék̲w'elh ~ swéwk̲w'elh ~ swek̲w'elhúyt [swe k̲w'elh] mountain goat blanket. *noun.*
swek̲w'elhúyt ~ swék̲w'elh ~ swéwk̲w'elh [swe k̲w'e lhuyt] mountain goat blanket. *noun.*
swelwá7lt [swel wa7 lt] creeks [sg: swá7elt]. *noun.*
swenimáylh [swe ni maylh] child of dead brother, sister, or cousin; nephew, niece. *noun.*
swetáwlh [swe tawlh] bridge. *noun.*
swéts'wets' ~ eswéts'wets' [swets' wets'] irritable; touchy; fidgety. *adjective.*
swewa7ám̓ [swe wa 7am̓] relatives [sg: swa7ám̓]. *noun.*
swéwk̲w'elh ~ swék̲w'elh ~ swek̲w'elhúyt [swew k̲w'elh] mountain goat blanket. *noun.*
swéy̓wey̓k̲a [swey̓ wey̓ k̲a] male [animal]. *adjective.*
swéy̓wey̓k̲a sx̲wí7shen [swey̓ wey̓ k̲a sx̲wi7 shen] buck. *noun.*
swé7u [swe 7u] called, be; named, be. *verb(i).*
swé7ustem [swe 7us tem] called that, be; named that, be. *verb(p).*
switn [swi tn] fishing net; spider web. *noun.*
swíw̓lus [swiw̓ lus] *noun.* young man.
swiw̓lus7áńtsut [swiw̓ lus 7ań tsut] teenage boy, become a. *verb(i).*
swí7k̲a [swi7 k̲a] man. *noun.*
swí7k̲as [swi7 k̲as] make (someone/something) out to be a man. *verb(t).*
swi7k̲a7áńtsut [swi7 k̲a 7ań tsut] manhood, going into. *verb(i).*
swi7k̲a7áws [swi7 k̲a 7aws] old man. *noun.*
swi7k̲a7í7 [swi7 ka 7i7] man, become a. *verb(i).*
swí7k̲a7ullh [swi7 k̲a 7ullh] young boy. *noun.*
swí7u [swi 7u] eulachon from the Fraser River. *noun.*
swi7xwí7k̲wm [swi7 xwi7 k̲wm] rapids. *noun.*
swú7wu ~ nswú7wu [swu7 wu] cougar. *noun.*
sxw- acting for; in the place of; step-(relative). *prefix.*
sxwaháy̓us ~ sxwháy̓us [sxwa ha y̓us] dropoff. *noun.*
sxwákw'ichn [sxwa kw'i chn] dogfish skin; sandpaper. *noun.*
sxwák̲amentsut [sxwa k̲a men tsut] roar [i.e., roar of the north wind]. *verb(i).*
sxwalítnulh [sxwa lit nulh] belonging to a white person. *adjective.*
sxwalítnulh sníchim [sxwa lit nulh sni chim] white man's language. *noun.*
sxwaxw pigmy owl; saw-whet owl. *noun.*
sxwáxwkw'us [sxwaxw kw'us] drunkard, be a. *verb(i).*
sxwa7ns [sxwa7 ns] half-dried salmon. *noun.*
sxwchésha7 [sxw che sha7] stepmother; wife of uncle. *noun.*
sxwch'á7mik̲w [sxw ch'a7 mik̲w] great-grandparent of spouse. *noun.*
sxwékwiy̓ik̲w [sxwe kwi y̓ik̲w] great-great-great-grandparent, and all the same generation of relatives, of one's spouse. *noun.*
sxwelawú7 [sxwe la wu7] turnip. *noun.*

sxwelhch saliva. *noun.*
sxwétkwem [sxwet kwem] flame. *noun.*
sxwéwk̲en ~ xwéwk̲en [sxwew k̲en] swan. *noun.*
sxwéxwa7 [sxwe xwa7] ambitious; diligent; good worker. *adjective.*
sxwexwkw important; useful. *adjective.*
sxweym dung [euphemism for **s7a7k̲**; see also **sx̱wits'**]. *noun.*
sxwéyxweyk̲ [sxwey xweyk̲] lively; happy. *adjective.*
sxwéyxweys [sxwey xweys] showing (something), be. *verb(t).*
sxweyxweỷúỷs [sxwey xwe ỷuỷs] rock that sticks out. *noun.*
sxwháỷus ~ sxwaháỷus [sxw ha ỷus] dropoff. *noun.*
sxwiim̓ [sxwiim̓] discarded thing; something gotten rid of or thrown away; something discarded. *noun.*
sxwimála [sxwi ma la] shop; store. *noun.*
sxwkwúpits [sxw kwu pits] older step-brother. *noun.*
sxwk̲w'áyek̲w [sxw k̲w'a yek̲w] pole [e.g., for a clothesline]. *noun.*
sxwman [sxw man] stepfather; husband of aunt. *noun.*
sxwmats'tn [sxw mats' tn] warrior's spear. *noun.*
sxwmeṅ [sxw meṅ] stepchild. *noun.*
sxwm̓úmten [sxw m̓um ten] Indian doctors [sg: **sxw7umten**]. *noun.*
sxwse7x̱ [sxw se 7x̱] husband's or wife's step-parent; step-child's husband or wife. *noun.*
sxwsi7l [sxw si 7l] grandparent/aunt/uncle of spouse; step-grandparent/aunt/uncle. *noun.*
sxwsts'its'áp' [sxw sts'i ts'ap'] one who works in place of someone else. *noun.*
sxwsx̱ex̱l̓ [sxw sx̱e x̱l'] secretary. *noun.*
sxwts'ép'iỷik̲w [sxw ts'e p'i ỷik̲w] great-great-grandparent/aunt/uncle of spouse. *noun.*
sxwúxwlem [sxwuxw lem] whistle. *noun.*
sxwuxwupíws [sxwu xwu piws] hives. *noun.*
sxw7ímats [sxw 7i mats] grandchild of spouse's siblings or cousins; step-grandchild. *noun.*
sxw7úmten [sxw 7um ten] Indian doctor. *noun.*
sxw7úmteni7 [sxw 7um te ni7] become a **sxw7úmten**; Indian doctor, become an. *verb(i).*
sxw7umtnáwek̲w [sxw 7umt na wek̲w] **sxw7úmten**'s hat. *noun.*
sx̱aam [sx̱aam] cry. *noun.*
sx̱amíṅtsut [sx̱a miṅ tsut] lament; cry for oneself. *noun.* also a verb.
sx̱áx̱elk̲w [sx̱a x̱elk̲w] have cut hair; have trimmed hair; cut hair, have; trimmed hair, have. *verb(i).*
sx̱ayts' murre [type of bird]. *noun.*
sx̱a7mts [sx̱a 7mts] sap; juice. *noun.*
sx̱el̓ colours. *noun.*
sx̱él̓x̱el [sx̱el' x̱el] coloured material. *noun.* coloured [about material]. *adjective.*
sx̱élx̱elch' [sx̱el x̱elch'] black brant [type of bird]. *noun.*
sx̱ém̓x̱em [sx̱em̓ x̱em] horsetail [type of plant]. *noun.*
sx̱ém̓x̱em [sx̱em̓ x̱em] kidney. *noun.*
sx̱eṅ leg; foot. *noun.*
sx̱éṅx̱en [sx̱eṅ x̱en] legs; feet [sg: **sx̱eṅ**]. *noun.*
sx̱ép'shen [sx̱ep' shen] fish tail [see also **swa7tshn**]. *noun.*
sx̱esháyup'em [sx̱e sha yu p'em] breathing. *noun.*
sx̱éta7k̲s [sx̱e ta7 k̲s] far end [of a lake]. *noun.*
sx̱et' hit by sxw7umten's curse, be. *verb(i).*
sx̱étsni7kwup [sx̱ets ni7 kwup] fire log "aiming" direction of fire; log around which fire is built, big. *noun.*
sx̱eẇ salmon backbone; dried salmon backbone. *noun.*
sx̱ex̱lh [sx̱e x̱ilh] drunk, be really. *verb(i).*
sx̱ex̱p'íchen [sx̱ex̱ p'i chen] chipmunk. *noun.*
sx̱ip'im [sx̱i p'im] chickenhawk. *noun.*
sx̱ítl'us [sx̱i tl'us] cut face. *noun.*
sx̱itsk̲ [sx̱itsk̲] fallen timber. *noun.*
sx̱í7kwen ~ x̱í7kwen [sx̱i7 kwen] kidney. *noun.*
sx̱i7tsáỷlh [sx̱i7 tsa ỷlh] lullaby. *noun.*
sx̱í7x̱a7us [sx̱i7 x̱a 7us] originating from, be [with reference to the locality where one's ancestors were created]. *verb(i).*

sx̱p'ekw' [sx̱ p'ekw'] cartilage. *noun.*
sx̱wáwinas [sx̱wa wi nas] bone in center of chest. *noun.*
sx̱wáyx̱wey [sx̱way x̱wey] ceremonial mask. *noun.*
sx̱weḵwíchen ~ x̱weḵwíchen [sx̱we ḵwi chen] spider's web; net; spider. *noun.*
sx̱wéḵw'lhnalh ~ sx̱wéḵw'lhnilh [sx̱we ḵw'lh nalh] handkerchief; kerchief. *noun.*
sx̱wéḵw'lhnilh ~ sx̱wéḵw'lhnalh [sx̱e ḵw'lh nilh] kerchief; handkerchief. *noun.*
sx̱wel̓áx̱ḵin [sx̱we l'ax̱ ḵin] big deer with many "spikes" and a grey forehead. *noun.*
sx̱weláyshn [sx̱we lay shn] rill. *noun.*
sx̱wem current; tide; swift tide; rapids; rushing current. *noun.*
sx̱wem̓ presents; things given away [e.g., at a potlatch]. *noun.*
sx̱wes grease [liquid]; oil; fat. *noun.*
sx̱wétl'ḵin [sx̱wetl' ḵin] cushion. *noun.*
sx̱wets'ḵw' joint of body; cut; place of division. *noun.*
sx̱wets'ḵw'ách [sx̱wets' ḵw'ach] wrist. *noun.*
sx̱wets'ḵw'íws [sx̱wets' ḵw'iws] joints of body [sg: **sx̱wets'ḵw'**]. *noun.*
sx̱wéts'ḵw'shen [sx̱wets'ḵw' shen] ankle. *noun.*
sx̱wex̱weḵwíchen [sx̱we x̱we ḵwi chen] spider. *noun.*
sx̱wéx̱wel [sx̱we x̱wel] valley. *noun.*
sx̱wex̱wiy̓ám̓ [sx̱we x̱wi y̓am̓] legend; mythical story; myth. *noun.*
sx̱wíḵw'iws [sx̱wi ḵw'iws] leggings used in dancing. *noun.*
sx̱wíl̓nach [sx̱wil' nach] wild onion; onion [wild]. *noun.*
sx̱wish [sx̱wish] varied thrush [type of bird]. *noun.*
sx̱wits' [sx̱wits'] poop [see also **sxweym**]. *noun.*
sx̱wíw̓ach [sx̱wi w̓ach] plainfin midshipman [type of fish]; eulachon; candlefish. *noun.*
sx̱wix̱w [sx̱wix̱w] sparrow. *noun.*
sx̱wí7shen [sx̱wi7 shen] deer. *noun.*
sx̱wi7shenálkwlh [sx̱wi7 she nal kwlh] perform a deer dance; dance a deer dance. *verb(i).*
sx̱wí7shnus [sx̱wi7 shnus] dummy [literally, deer-face]. *noun.*
sx̱wúḵw'en [sx̱wu ḵw'en] snore. *noun.*
sx̱wuḵw'tn [sx̱wuḵw' tn] canoe pole. *noun.*
sx̱wumḵs [sx̱wumḵs] fish nose. *noun.*
sx̱wúp'a7en [sx̱wu p'a 7en] bead necklace; necklace. *noun.*
sx̱wúsum [sx̱wu sum] soapberry; soapberries. *noun.*
sx̱wúsumay̓ ~ x̱wúsumay̓ [sx̱wu su may̓] soapberry plant. *noun.*
sx̱wútl'ekw [sx̱wu tl'ekw] bracken fern. *noun.*
sx̱wúyum [sx̱wu yum] grey hair, have. *verb(i).*
sx̱wúyumḵw [sx̱wu yumḵw] grey hair. *noun.*
syahách [sya hach] right hand. *noun.*
syahíws ~ yahíws [sya hiws] right arm; right side. *noun.*
syahús [sya hus] right eye [see also **yahus**]. *noun.*
syáḵa ~ syáshen [sya ḵa] right foot. *noun.*
syáshen ~ syáḵa [sya shen] right foot. *noun.*
syátshen [syat shen] lowlands; land; mainland; country. *noun.*
syaw̓án̓ [sya w̓an̓] 1. place of origin; 2. ancestry. *noun.*
syá7ten [sya7 ten] widow; widower. *noun.*
syekw'ḵs [syekw' ḵs] short upriver side of house built with its long sides parallel to the river. *noun.*
syeḵ berry already picked [general term]; root already picked [general term]; "harvest"; gathered berries or roots. *noun.*
syel̓ánem ~ yel̓ánem [sye l'a nem] year. *noun.*
syelemchís [sye lem chis] ring [for the finger]. *noun.*
syetl'ḵ' paint [see also **yétl'ḵ'ten**]. *noun.*
syets true story; story [realistic]. *noun.*
syétsem [sye tsem] report; news; information. *noun.*
syew̓ predictor. *noun.*

syéwen [sye wen] guardian spirit and song; song. *noun.*
syew̓ín̓ [sye w̓in̓] ritualist's incantation; special [magical] words; words of a kwtsi7ts; magic power. *noun.*
syex̱ás ~ six̱ás [sye x̱as] large rock; rock [large]; boulder. *noun.*
syex̱éyx̱as ~ syex̱yex̱ás [sye x̱ey x̱as] large rocks; rocks [large]; boulders [sg: syex̱ás]. *noun.*
syex̱yex̱ás ~ syex̱éyx̱as [syex̱ ye x̱as] boulders; rocks [large]; large rocks [sg: syex̱ás]. *noun.*
syik̲ [syik̲] snow. *noun.*
syilík̲' [syi lik̲'] top [spinning toy]. *noun.*
syíy̓ch' ~ esyíy̓ch' [syiy̓ch'] filled, be; full, be. *verb(i).*
syúlhim̓ [syu lhim̓] food or clothing burnt at funeral. *noun.*
syúyk̲w'ula ~ syuyk̲w'úlu7 [syuy k̲w'u la] trout; any type of trout-like fish; rainbow trout. *noun.*
syuyk̲w'úlu7 ~ syúyk̲w'ula [syuy k̲w'u lu7] rainbow trout; any trout-like fish; trout. *noun.*
syú7yuxwa [syu7 yu xwa] old person; elder. *noun.*
syu7yuxwa7áws [syu7 yu xwa 7aws] older person. *noun.*
syu7yuxwa7í7 [syu7 yu xwa 7i7] old, getting [about people or things]. *verb(i).*
s7áay̓u [s7aa y̓u] pinto abalone. *noun.*
s7achcháwam ~ ns7achcháwam [s7ach cha wam] crescent gunnel; penpoint gunnel; conger eel. *noun.*
s7ahíws [s7a hiws] pains in body. *noun.*
s7án̓usmut [s7a n̓us mut] second piece. *noun.*
s7ásxwulh [s7ax xwulh] seal's; belonging to a seal. *adjective.*
s7ásxwulh sxwes [s7as xwulh sxwes] seal fat. *noun.*
s7áti7nes [s7a ti7 nes] strap of basket over chest. *noun.*
s7átsak̲w [s7a tsak̲w] roast potatoes. *noun.*
s7átsik̲en [s7a tsi k̲en] front of the neck. *noun.*
s7átsiy̓ek̲w [s7a tsi y̓ek̲w] man's private parts. *noun.*
s7atsk̲ rear end; bottom. *noun.*
s7átsnach [s7ats nach] bay [see also átsnach ~ étsnach]. *noun.*
s7átsus [s7a tsus] front side [see also átsus]; face. *noun.*
s7ats'ám̓es [s7a ts'a m̓es] shawl. *noun.*
s7aw̓t afterbirth. *noun.*
s7aw̓tk̲ hind leg. *noun.*
s7axw rockslide; landslide; snowslide. *noun.*
s7áx̱wa ~ s7áx̱wa7 [s7a x̱wa] butter clam. *noun.*
s7áx̱wa7 ~ s7áx̱wa [s7a x̱wa7] butter clam. *noun.*
s7áy̓ak̲w'a [s7a y̓a k̲w'a] younger siblings; group of younger siblings; younger children of parents' younger siblings [sg: sk̲a7k̲]. *noun.*
s7ay̓án̓ ~ s7ey̓án̓ [s7a y̓an̓] side of house [see also say'n'; s7i7 n']; wall. *noun.*
s7áy̓as ~ es7áy̓as [s7a y̓as] engaged to (someone), be. *verb(t).*
s7ay̓áx̱ [s7a y̓ax̱] leaking canoe; leak; crack. *noun.* cracked, be; have a leak. *verb(i).*
s7áy̓ek̲shen ~ s7áy̓k̲shen [s7a y̓ek̲ shen] heel. *noun.*
s7ayk̲s ~ s7ay̓k̲s point of any sharp object; point of land; teat; short end of [rectangular] house; promontory. *noun.*
s7ay̓k̲s ~ s7ayk̲s point of any sharp object; point of land; teat; short end of [rectangular] house; promontory. *noun.*
s7áyk̲say elbow. *noun.*
s7áy̓k̲shen ~ s7áy̓ek̲shen [s7ay̓k̲ shen] heel. *noun.*
s7áynexw [s7ay nexw] life; spirit [see also kw'elh7áynexw]. *noun.*
s7áynexw ~ áynexw ~ s7áynixw [s7ay nexw] eulachon from the Squamish River; small eulachon. *noun.*
s7áynixw ~ áynexw ~ s7áynexw [s7ay nixw] eulachon from the Squamish River; small eulachon. *noun.*
s7á7ik̲ [s7a 7ik̲] not genuine. *adjective.*
s7á7kwlash [s7a7 kwlash] wounded, be. *verb(i).*
s7á7kwlashs [s7a7 kwlashs] wound (someone). *verb(t).*
s7a7k̲ feces; dung. *noun.*
s7á7tam̓ [s7a7 tam̓] baggage; things; stuff; thing. *noun.*

s7á7teṁay [s7a7 te ṁay] bag for belongings. *noun.*

s7a7ú7 [s7a 7u7] first. *noun.*

s7a7x̲íts [s7a7 x̲its] lying down, be. *verb(i).*

s7ekwel̓ásh ~ skwel̓ásh ~ sekwel̓ásh [s7e kwe l'ash] rifle; gun. *noun.*

s7ekwiyí [s7e kwi yi] shuttlecock and battledore game. *noun.*

s7ekwí7kwlus ~ sekwí7kwlus [s7e kwi7 kwlus] large butterfly [whose appearance is followed by the run of the kwu7s]. *noun.*

s7ekw'á7kwelash [s7e kw'a7 kwe lash] wound it; wounded, be. *verb(i).*

s7ekw'á7kwlash [s7e kw'a7 kwlash] rifles; guns [sg: s7ekwel'ásh ~ skwel'ásh ~ sekwel'ásh]. *noun.*

s7ék̲ek̲ [s7e k̲ek̲] younger sibling; youngest of family [term of pity not as strong as sk̲w'unek̲]. *noun.*

s7ék̲w'ek̲w'itel ~ sék̲w'7ek̲w'itel ~ sék̲wek̲w'itel ~ s7ék̲w'7ek̲w'itel [s7e k̲w'e k̲w'i tel] siblings; cousins [sg: ek̲w'í7tel and sek̲w'í7tel ~ s7ek̲w'itel]. *noun.*

s7ek̲w'í7tel ~ sek̲w'í7tel [s7e k̲w'i7 tel] sibling; cousin; relative; siblings and cousins [see also ek̲w'í7tel]. *noun.*

s7ek̲w'7ek̲w'í7nexw ~ s7uk̲w'uk̲w'íṅexw ~ sek̲w'ek̲w'í7nexw [s7ek̲w' 7e k̲w'i7 nexw] bird [general term]. *noun.*

s7ék̲w'7ek̲w'i7tel ~ s7ék̲w'ek̲w'itel ~ sék̲w'7ek̲w'itel ~ sék̲wek̲w'itel [s7ek̲w' 7e k̲w'i7 tel] siblings; cousins [sg: ek̲w'í7tel and sek̲w'í7tel ~ s7ek̲w'itel]. *noun.*

s7el̓éli [s7e l'e li] dreams [sg: s7eli]. *noun.*

s7éli [s7e li] dream; vision; guardian spirit. *noun.*

s7élis [s7e lis] see (something) in a dream. *verb(t).*

s7elk̲n [s7el k̲n] top. *noun.*

s7elk̲'ét [s7el k̲'et] grab and sling (something). *verb(t).*

s7émilh [s7e milh] one who was given in marriage. *noun.*

s7émnexw [s7em nexw] gift. *noun.*

s7enám [s7e nam] pole of gaffhook; pole of harpoon; spear; spearshaft. *noun.*

s7enwilhk̲wúẏach ~ s7enwilhúl̓a [s7en wilh k̲wu ẏach] middle finger. *noun.*

s7enwilhúl̓a ~ s7enwilhk̲wúẏach [s7en wi lhu l'a] middle finger. *noun.*

s7etsím [s7e tsim] little; small. *adjective.*

s7étswilh [s7ets wilh] guts; stomach; bowels; inside, the. *noun.*

s7ets7útsiyim [s7ets 7u tsi yim] earrings, a pair of. *noun.*

s7ey ~ ns7ey loud. *adjective.*

s7eẏáṅ ~ s7aẏáṅ [s7e ẏan] wall. *noun.*

s7éẏuts ~ éẏuts [s7e ẏuts] mouth of the river. *noun.*

s7ik̲ch [s7ik̲ ch] roof. *noun.*

s7ílinas [s7i li nas] chest. *noun.*

s7iltxw [s7il txw] roof of cedar shakes; long cedar planks [used for walls or roofing]; Indian house. *noun.*

s7ílhchi [s7ilh chi] bow of boat/canoe. *noun.*

s7ílhen [s7i lhen] food. *noun.*

s7ímesh [s7i mesh] walk. *noun.*

s7íṅach [s7i ṅach] other hand. *noun.*

s7ínak̲a [s7i na k̲a] one of a pair. *noun.*

s7ínak̲wa [s7i na k̲wa] other head. *noun.*

s7ip'a7íṁ [s7i p'a 7iṁ] burden; load. *noun.*

s7ip'ip'áak̲w'ulh [s 7i p'i p'áa k̲w'ulh] cowardly, be; scaredy cat, be a. *verb(i).*

s7it ~ ns7it [s7it] act completely; really. *verb(i).*

s7ítut [s7i tut] sleep. *noun.*

s7íts'am ~ s7íts'aṁ [s7i ts'am] attire; anything one wears. *noun.*

s7íts'aṁ ~ s7íts'am [s7i ts'aṁ] attire; anything one wears. *noun.*

s7íxwalh [s7i xwalh] toddler; child; baby. *noun.*

s7íxwalhiwa [s7i xwa lhi wa] sapling; shoots of any tree. *noun.*

s7íxwa7 [s7i xwa7] generous, be. *verb(i).*

s7íxwiwat ~ es7íxwiwat [s7i xwi wat] jump [about fish]. *verb(i).*

s7íx̲i [s7i x̲i] shame. *noun.*

s7iẏimtán [s7i ẏim tan] strongest of . . . . *noun.*

s7iyíxw [s7i yixw] legend of how the Squamish eulachons appeared. *noun.*

s7íyu7tsáx̲an [s7i yu7 tsa x̲an] sharp edge [of something]. *noun.*

s7i7áẏk̲s [s7i 7aẏ k̲s] points, of any sharp object; points of land; teats; short ends of [rectangular] house [sg: **s7ay'k̲s ~ s7ayk̲s**]. *noun.*

s7uk̲w'uk̲w'íṅexw ~ sek̲w'ek̲w'í7nexw ~ s7ek̲w'7ek̲w'í7nexw [s7u k̲w'u k̲w'i ṅexw] bird [general term]. *noun.*

s7ulh [s7ulh] ours. *adjective.*

s7úṁsem ~ es7úmsm [s7uṁ sen] awake, be [see also **úmsem**]. *verb(i).*

s7útsiyiṁ [s7u tsi yiṁ] earring; earrings; handcuffs. *noun.*

s7úxwen [s7u xwen] ice. *noun.*

s7úxwumixw [s7u xwu mixw] neighbour. *noun.*

s7uys [s7uys] entrance. *noun.*

Sh sh

s-háta7 ~ sáta7 [s ha ta7] aunt; female cousin of parents. *noun.*
s-hew̓iwsem [s he w̓iw sem] accompany when travelling. *verb(i).*
s-hew̓úl̓em ~ sew̓úl̓em [s he w̓u l'em] toy. *noun.*
s-hiw̓ ~ siw̓ [s-hiw̓] upstream region; head of river. *noun.*
s-híw̓ach ~ síw̓ach [s hi w̓ach] front leg. *noun.*
s-hiw̓ay ~ siw̓ay ~ siwáy̓ [s-hi w̓ay] soon; sooner; quick; quicker; quickly; right away. *adverb.*
s-hiyí [s-hi yi] big part of . . . . *noun.*
s-huyáy̓lh [s hu ya y̓lh] woman's last child. *noun.*
s-húyiws ~ súyiws [s-hu yiws] costume. *noun.*
shách'els [sha ch'els] reed; sharp grass. *noun.*
sham going out, be [about water]; low tide, be; in shallow water, be; stick out of the water. *verb(i).*
shámaṅ [sha maṅ] bring (something) out of the water; bring (something) to the surface of the water; stick (something) out of the water. *verb(t).*
shámaṅtsut [sha maṅ tsut] rise to the surface; come to the surface of the water. *verb(i).*
shamshám̓cham̓ [sham sham̓ cham̓] finning, be [about porpoises or orcas/ killer whales]; swim so that the backfin repeatedly emerges from the water. *verb(i).*
shaṅ ~ esháṅ what's the matter with . . . ?; why?; what happened? *question word; verb(i).*
shapl̓ts [sha pl'ts] shoveller [type of bird]; spoonbill duck. *noun.*
shásham̓ [sha sham̓] going out, be; ebbing, be [about tide]. *verb(i).*
sháshamk̲w [sha shamk̲w] emerge with head above the water. *verb(i).*
sháshem [sha shem] gone out, have [about tide]. *verb(i).*
shásheṅtsut [sha sheṅ tsut] go out quietly. *verb(i).*
shat shot; lead; ammunition. *noun.*
shátax̲en [sha ta x̲en] net line sinker; sinker-line on net. *noun.*
shát-shtam [shatsh tam] goldeneye duck. *noun.*
shat' surface after being under water for some time. *verb(i).*
shát'an [sha t'an] bring (something) up to the surface; ladle (something). *verb(t).*
shát'antsut [sha t'an tsut] surface, help oneself come up to the; surface, make oneself come up to; help oneself come up to the surface; make oneself come up to the surface. *verb(i).*
shat'tn [shat' tn] ladle [type of serving spoon]. *noun.*
shaw̓ bone. *noun.*
sháwik̲ [sha wik̲] carrot. *noun.*
shaw̓k̲w skull. *noun.* loud person. *adjective.*
sháw̓min [shaw̓ min] pieces of bone. *noun.*
shaw̓tsk̲ bony-faced; bony face, have a. *adjective.*
sháw̓us ~ nsháw̓us [sha w̓us] cheekbone. *noun.* skinny. *adjective.*
sháxwlhus [shaxw lhus] deadpan face, have a; absent-minded, be; unaware of surroundings, be; stare, just. *verb(i).*
sháy̓ay [sha y̓ay] gills of a fish. *noun.*
shá7yu [sha7 yu] corpse; dead; screech owl; co-wife. *noun.* lie dead. *verb(i).*
shech'ách [she ch'ach] splinter in one's hand, have a. *verb(i).*
shech'shích'i [shech' shi ch'i] go into the bushes [about a group]. *verb(i).*
shech'shn [shech' shn] sliver in one's foot, have a. *verb(i).*
shekw'shúkw'em [shekw' shu kw'em] bathe together [about a group]. *verb(i).*
shek̲ finished giving a potlatch, get; finished, be; completed, be; over, be. *verb(i).*
shék̲i7n [she k̲i 7n] give a big sigh [about a dancer]; sigh. *verb(i).*
shek̲lhálem [shek̲ lha lem] make a big sigh;

make a big sigh [about a dancer]; catch breath when finishing crying; out of breath, be. *verb(i).*

shek̲w sunk in the mud, be. *verb(i).*

shék̲wu [she k̲wu] sob. *verb(i).*

shék̲w'i7n [she k̲w'i 7n] sob. *verb(i).*

shék̲w'u7m [she k̲w'u 7m] sob. *verb(i).*

shel̓ penis. *noun.*

shelshal̓u7éntem ~ shelshá7lutem [shel sha l'u 7en tem] haunted, be getting. *verb(p).*

shelshá7lutem ~ shelshal̓u7éntem [shel sha7 lu tem] haunted, be getting. *verb(p).*

shelshelk̲áẏus [shel shel k̲a ẏus] stye. *noun.*

shemán [she man] enemy. *noun.*

shemánentway [she ma nen tway] enemies to one another, be. *verb(i).*

shemáneẇas [she ma ne ẇas] fall out; quarrel. *verb(i).*

shéma7n [she ma 7n] fish with a dip net; dip-net. *verb(i).*

shéma7nten [she ma 7n ten] dip net. *noun.*

shemshám [shem sham] run aground [in a boat]; get stuck on the bottom [of the water]. *verb(i).*

-shen leg; foot {full word: sx̲eṅ}. *suffix.*

sheṅch slay someone. *verb(i).*

shepshípmk̲w [shep shi pmk̲w] spiked hair, have ["how they wear their hair today"]. *verb(i).*

sheshemáṅemneẇas [she sheṁ ma ṅem ne ẇas] enemies with one another, be. *verb(i).*

shésheẇay [she she ẇay] growing, be; grow all over. *verb(i).*

shéshewch'm [she shew ch'm] make a rustling noise while walking through the bush [about leaves]; make a noise while moving in the bushes. *verb(i).*

shésheych'm [she shey ch'm] good, be feeling; feeling good, be. *verb(i).*

shésheẏik̲ [she she ẏik̲] digging around, be. *verb(i).*

shéshiẏus ~ eshéshiẏus [she shi ẏus] stubborn. *adjective.*

sheshtáṁ [shesh taṁ] swim under water; dive continuously. *verb(i).*

sheshúlhni [she shulh ni] pay attention to (someone). *verb(t).*

shewálh [she walh] door; road; path; trail. *noun.*

shéẇalhms [she ẇa lhms] take out (a dead body) through the door. *verb(t).*

shewálhshi [she walh shi] break trail for (someone). *verb(t).*

sheẇám [she ẇam] advertise work beforehand. *verb(i).*

shéway [she way] grow. *verb(i).*

shewaẏálhx̲a [she wa ẏalh x̲a] growing in one's throat, have something. *verb(i).*

shewaẏántsut [she wa ẏan tsut] growing up, be. *verb(i).*

shewayáẏlhem [she wa yaẏ lhem] bring up a child; raise a child. *verb(i).*

shéwayiṁ [she wa yiṁ] adopted child; child, adopted; ward. *noun.*

shewaẏnúp ~ shéwaẏnup ~ shewáẏnup [she waẏ nup] weed. *noun.*

shewáẏnup ~ shewaẏnúp ~ shéwaẏnup [she waẏ nup] weed. *noun.*

shéwaẏnup ~ shewaẏnúp ~ shewáẏnup [she waẏ nup] weed. *noun.*

sheẇsh burnt to nothing, be; singed, be. *verb(i).*

shewsháṅ [shew shaṅ] scorch (something); singe (something). *verb(t).*

shewshewálhshi [shew she walh shi] break trail for (someone). *verb(t).*

sheẇshík̲in [sheẇ shi k̲in] get its wool singed; singed, get its wool. *verb(i).*

shéychep [shey chep] fire drill. *noun.*

sheych' all around, be. *verb(i).*

sheych'án [shey ch'an] circle (something) [inside of longhouse]; turn (something) around. *verb(t).*

sheych'ántsut [shey ch'an tsut] move around something; turn oneself around; circle around. *verb(i).*

shéych'em [shey ch'em] dizzy from drinking, be; dizzy, be getting. *verb(i).*

sheykw clam. *noun.* dig clams. *verb(i).*

sheylh darling. *interjection.*

-shi [-shi] {added onto some words so that you can use the object endings, see section on "object endings," p. 12}; for; on behalf of. *suffix.*

shich'átsut [shi ch'a tsut] move around something; turn oneself around. *verb(i).*

shích'i [shi ch'i] go into the bush. *verb(i).*

shích'us [shi ch'us] harpoon [for hunting seals, sea-lions, porpoises, etc.]. *noun.*
shiim [shiim] parted, be. *verb(i).*
shíimneẁas [shíim neẁ was] parted from one another, be. *verb(i).*
shímshalkwlh [shim shal kwlh] receive **syewen** [about new dancer]. *verb(i).*
shípemk̲w [shi pemk̲w] bushy head, have a. *adjective.*
shípintsut [shi pin tsut] put up its hair [about animals]. *verb(i).*
shishá7yu7ntem [shi sha7 yu 7n tem] ghosted, be; encounter with a ghost, have an [see also **tewak̲inántem**]. *verb(p).*
shisheẁánsem [shi she ẁan sem] pick one's teeth. *verb(i).*
shíshich ~ **shishích'** [shi shich] confused, be; mixed up, be. *verb(i).*
shíshichnexw [shi shich nexw] confuse (someone). *verb(t).*
shishích' ~ **shíshich** [shi shich'] confused, be; mixed up, be. *verb(i).*
shishich'áṅtsut [shi shi ch'aṅ tsut] spinning around, be. *verb(i).*
shíshik̲ [shi shik̲] nosy. *adjective.*
shishík̲' [shi shik̲'] interested. *adjective.*
shíshipem [shi shi pem] restless, be getting [about spirits]. *verb(i).*
shishiyétel [shi shi ye tel] co-wives. *noun.*
shishiẏúkw'aẏuṁ [shi shi ẏu kw'a ẏuṁ] solid round objects. *adjective.*
shíshi7ch [shi shi 7ch] round; spherical. *adjective.*
shishuyaní7ntm [shi shu ya ni 7n tm] show dimples in one's cheeks [e.g., when experiencing a sour taste]. *verb(p).*
-shi [-shi] {added onto some words so you can use the object endings, see section on "object endings," p. 12}. *suffix.*
shítim [shi tim] wishing for someone else's food, be. *verb(i).*
shítimmiṅ [shi tim miṅ] covet (something). *verb(t).*
shít'im [shi t'im] stretch one's neck. *verb(i).*
shitl' [shitl'] [disgusted remark]. *interjection.*
shíẁelhx̲a7n [shi ẁelh x̲a 7n] stick (a fish) through the gills. *verb(t).*
shíẁets [shi ẁets] thread fish onto a single stick through the mouth and the gills. *verb(i).*
shiẁetsán [shi ẁe tsan] put (fish) on stick [through gills]. *verb(t).*
shíẁetstn ~ **shiẏútstn** [shi ẁets tn] single stick onto which fish are threaded; spit for drying fish [e.g., herring]. *noun.*
shiẏúkw'ayuṁ [shi ẏu kw'a yuṁ] one whole [small] piece. *adjective.*
shíyukw'k̲w [shi yukw' k̲w] barbecued fish head. *noun.*
shiẏúkw'uẏs [shi ẏu kw'uẏs] one whole [large] piece. *adjective.*
shiẏúkw'uẏs smant [shi ẏu kw'uẏs smant] one whole rock. *noun.*
shiyútsin [shi yu tsin] dropoff at bottom of beach. *noun.*
shiẏútstn ~ **shíẁetstn** [shi ẏuts tn] spit for drying fish [e.g., herring]; single stick onto which fish are threaded. *noun.*
shí7mu7t [shi7 mu7t] whole piece of . . . . *noun.*
shí7sheway [shi7 she way] twig. *noun.*
shk̲étsut [shk̲e tsut] finish it; get ready. *verb(i).*
shk̲weṅ cross over a gulf or ocean; go far out into the sea; cross a wide stretch of water. *verb(i).* ocean. *noun.*
shtam dive. *verb(i).*
shtams put (something) under water. *verb(t).*
shúkwa [shu kwa] sugar. *noun.*
shúkwa7án [shu kwa 7an] add sugar to (something). *verb(t).*
shukwa7áy [shu kwa 7ay] sugar container. *noun.*
shukw' [shukw'] bathe. *verb(i).*
shukw'éyalh [shu kw'e yalh] bathe one's child. *verb(i).*
shúkw'um [shu kw'um] bathe. *verb(i).*
shukw'umáẁtxw [shu kw'u maẁ t̲xw] bathroom; bath house. *noun.*
shúkw'ut [shu kw'ut] bathe (someone). *verb(t).*
shupálitn [shu pa li tn] iron. *noun.*
shúpen [shu pen] *verb(i).* whistle. *noun.*
shupeṅáẏm [shu pe ṅa ẏm] want to whistle. *verb(i).*
shupns [shu pns] whistle at (someone). *verb(t).*
shúshantsut [shu shan tsut] get oneself out quickly. *verb(i).*
shusháẁ [shu shaẁ] bones [sg: **shaẁ**]. *noun.*

shusháw̓em [shu sha w̓em] bony, be. *verb(i).*
shusháw̓us [shu sha w̓us] [literally: bone-faced], be. *verb(i).*
shúshpen [shush pen] whistling, be; whistling repeatedly, be; whistling prolongedly [e.g., a melody, or the whistling of a bird], be. *verb(i).*
shúshukw'ay̓m [shu shu kw'a y̓m] wish to swim; want to swim. *verb(i).*
shushúpns [shu shu pns] whistling at (someone), be. *verb(t).*
shuwayálhx̱a [shu wa yalh x̱a] sore throat, have a. *verb(i).*
shúyu [shu yu] greet; appear before someone dies [about spirits]. *verb(i).*
shúyut [shu yut] bore a hole in (something). *verb(t).*
shúyuy̓n [shu yu y̓n] make holes in (something) with an awl. *verb(t).*
shú7mayus ~ shú7nayus [shu7 ma yus] come into contact with dead spirit; come face-to-face with spirit. *verb(i).*
shú7nayus ~ shú7mayus [shu7 na yus] come face-to-face with spirit; come into contact with dead spirit. *verb(i).*
shú7shukw'um [shu7 shu kw'um] bathing, be. *verb(i).*
sh7eylh ~ sh7ilh [sh7eylh] friend; dear. *noun.*
sh7il ~ esh7íl [sh7il] elder sibling [term of address; respectful form]. *vocative.*
sh7ilh ~ sh7eylh [sh7ilh] friend; dear. *noun.*

T t

t {past tense}. *clitic.*
t- to; by. *prefix.*
-t {added onto some words so that you can use the object endings, see section on "object endings," p. 12}. *suffix.*
-t the late . . . . *suffix.*
ta a, the [usually refers either to a male or to something generic; rarely occurs with females]. *determiner.*
ta ína [ta 7i na] other side, the; one, the; the other. *phrase.*
ta new you! *interjection.* you. *noun.*
ta néwyap [ta new yap] you all! *interjection.* you all. *noun.*
taam [taam] leak [about roof or house]. *verb(i).*
tahíṁ ~ ta7híṁ [ta hiṁ] make; do; build; weave. *verb(i).*
tákw'en [ta kw'en] tighten (something); pull (something) tight. *verb(t).*
táka7lh [ta ka 7lh] brome grass; sweet cicely. *noun.*
táknexw [tak nexw] felt (something), have; feel (something); sense (something). *verb(t).*
takw drink. *verb(i).*
tákwaṅ [ta kwaṅ] drink (something). *verb(t).*
tákwaẏm [ta kwa ẏm] want to drink. *verb(i).*
tákwilh [ta kwilh] bail a canoe. *verb(i).*
tákwilhen [ta kwi lhen] bail (a canoe). *verb(t).*
tákwilhtn ~ tákwuẏen ~ tákwi7n [ta kwilh tn] bailer. *noun.*
tákwi7n ~ tákwilhtn ~ tákwuẏen [ta kwi 7n] bailer. *noun.*
takwtn ~ ntakwtn ~ sntakwtn [takw tn] bucket. *noun.*
tákwuẏen ~ tákwilhtn ~ tákwi7n [ta kwu ẏen] bailer. *noun.*
tákw7aylh [takw 7aylh] give the dead something to drink. *verb(i).*
tákw'en [ta kw'en] straighten (something); make (something) straight. *verb(t).*
tal do as the other did. *verb(i).*
tála [ta la] money. *noun.*
tála7ay ~ ntala7áy [ta la 7ay] money bag; purse [see **tala**]. *noun.*
talh fathom; length from arm to arm outstretched. *noun.*
tamáẇtxw ~ stamáẇtxw [ta maẇ txw] what kind of house is it? *question word; verb(i).*
tamáẏ ~ stamáẏ [ta maẏ] what kind of tree is it? *question word; verb(i).*
tamétwilh ~ staméwilh [ta me wilh] what kind of canoe is it? *question word; verb(i).*
tan my [**ta** + **n**]. *determiner.*
-tan {superlative}. *suffix.*
-tán ~ -tn ~ ten instrument; implement. *suffix.*
tátaknexw [ta tak nexw] feel (something); sense (something); suspect (someone). *verb(t).*
tátaẏs [ta taẏs] butt in. *verb(i).*
tátaywilhs [ta tay wilhs] go alongside (a canoe); alongside (a canoe), go. *verb(t).*
táteleltas [ta te lel tas] keep time. *verb(i).*
tátsaṅ [ta tsaṅ] pat (something); pet (something); stroke (something). *verb(t).*
taw bright. *adjective.*
taẇán [ta ẇan] brighten (something); illuminate (something). *verb(t).*
taẇí7 [ta ẇi7] bright, get/become; brighten; light, become. *verb(i).*
taẇí7nim [ta ẇi7 ni tm] caught by the light, get; bright on one, get. *verb(p).*
táwn town. *noun.*
taẇtewálakep [taẇ te wa la kep] bracket fungus [term only used for **syewen**; literally, echo]. *noun.*
táẇtsaṁ [taẇ tsaṁ] shop for food. *verb(i).*
táxaṅ [ta xaṅ] spread (something) out vertically. *verb(t).*
taxch wall mat [small mat made from cattail; hung in the back-part of the house; see also **súyi7ch**]. *noun.*
táxchaṅ [tax chaṅ] spread (something)

in the back; cover (someone's) back; spread (something) behind [vertically]. *verb(t).*

tax̱ntn [ta x̱n tn] arm; shoulder joint; upper arm. *noun.*

táx̱tsaṁ [tax̱ tsaṁ] cover one's mouth [with one's hand]. *verb(i).*

táx̱tsaṅ [tax̱ tsaṅ] cover (something) [vertically; as of a door]. *verb(t).*

táx̱wi7min [ta x̱wi7 min] bother (someone); nuisance to (someone), be a. *verb(t).*

táx̱wtex̱wayani7m [tax̱w te x̱wa ya ni 7m] making sure of the news, be. *verb(i).*

táx̱wusen [ta x̱wu sen] cover (something) [vertically; as of a window]. *verb(t).*

táx̱wustn [ta x̱wus tn] curtain. *noun.*

tay canoe-race; race [in canoes]. *verb(i).*

taẏ he there; that one there [visible to speaker, but not within touching distance]. *demonstrative.*

táẏach [ta ẏach] take part in. *verb(i).*

táyaḵen [ta ya ḵen] move (something); give (something). *verb(t).*

táyaḵi [ta ya ḵi] move [from one house to another]. *verb(i).*

táyaḵshneṁ [ta yaḵ shneṁ] take a step. *verb(i).*

taẏch behind, be. *verb(i).*

taẏch back [of house]; space behind something; back side [see also **stay'ch**]. *noun.*

taẏcháyaḵ'in [taẏ cha ya ḵ'in] back of the house. *noun.*

táychiwilh [tay chi wilh] back of the house; behind of . . . . *noun.* behind something, be. *verb(i).*

taẏémtn ~ tíminshen [ta ẏem tn] calf of leg. *noun.*

tayéwilh ~ táywilh [ta ye wilh] race canoe; war canoe; canoe, race or war. *noun.*

taytáẏaḵi [tay ta ẏa ḵi] move [residence] all the time. *verb(i).*

taẏts follow [a song or another speech]. *verb(i).*

taẏtsáṁ ~ ti7tsáṁ [taẏ tsaṁ] follow someone's speech with one's own speech. *verb(i).*

táywilh ~ tayéwilh [táy wilh] modern race canoe; race canoe; war canoe; canoe, race or war. *noun.*

ta7- undergo; located, be; have something happen to itself. *prefix.*

tá7a [ta 7a] it happened; undergo; located, be; have something happen to itself. *verb(i).*

tá7a [ta 7a] mom, mum; mother; mamma. *noun.*

ta7ám [ta 7am] happen to someone. *verb(i).*

ta7ánu [ta 7a nu] good at doing something, be. *verb(i).*

ta7áẇn ~ nta7áẇn [ta 7a ẇn] think; expect; consider. *verb(i).*

ta7híṁ ~ tahíṁ [ta7 hiṁ] make; do; build; weave. *verb(i).*

ta7ḵs head for; in the direction of, be; direction of, be in the. *verb(i).*

ta7ḵsám [ta7ḵ sam] head for; face; go straight towards. *verb(i).*

ta7ḵsáṅ [ta7ḵ saṅ] head (one's canoes) for. *verb(t).*

tá7lem [ta7 lem] parallel, be; lengthwise, be. *verb(i).*

tá7lems [ta7 lems] put (something) lengthwise; put (them) down parallel to each other. *verb(t).*

tá7lnexw [ta 7l nexw] found out (something), have; learnt (something), have; understood (something), have; know (something). *verb(t).*

ta7lt [ta 7lt] learn (something); study (something). *verb(t).*

tá7nexw [ta7 nexw] build (something); made (something), have; finish making (something). *verb(t).*

ta7s make (something); build (something); construct (something). *verb(t).*

tá7shen [ta7 shen] running that way, be [about river]. *verb(i).*

tá7shi [ta7 shi] do for (someone); make for (someone). *verb(t).*

ta7ts address. *verb(i).*

tá7tsaṁ [ta7 tsaṁ] address. *verb(i).*

tá7tsan [ta7 tsan] answer (someone) back. *verb(t).*

ta7úsem [ta 7u sem] look in a certain direction; look [away from speaker]; look up; take a look. *verb(i).*

tech in plain sight, be. *verb(i).*

techtechnís [tech tech nis] hummingbird. *noun.*

tekw dented, be. *verb(i).*
tekw' tight, be [e.g., about clothes]; cheap, be; tight wad, be a. *verb(i).*
tekw'em̓í7 [te kw'e m̓i7] tight, become. *verb(i).*
tek̲ wiped out by enemy, be. *verb(i).*
tek̲ pinned down, be. *verb(i).*
ték̲k̲ách [tek̲ k̲ach] eight days. *verb(i).*
tek̲mín [tek̲ min] diaphragm. *noun.*
ték̲tek̲ [tek̲ tek̲] involved in, be. *verb(i).*
tek̲tk̲ách [tek̲t k̲ach] eight people. *numeral.*
tek̲' fart [see also **pu7k̲** and **má7kwelh**]. *verb(i).*
tek̲'númut [tek̲' nu mut] fart accidentally. *verb(i).*
tek̲wtík̲w [tek̲w tik̲w] muddy [muddier than ts'iq'i7]. *adjective.*
tek̲wtúk̲w [tek̲w tuk̲w] red snapper. *noun.*
tek̲w' straight, be. *verb(i).*
ték̲w'em [te k̲w'em] straight, be; go straight; go straight ahead; keep straight; steer; captain, be. *verb(i).*
ték̲w'ems [te k̲w'ems] steer (something); keep (something) straight. *verb(t).*
ték̲w'emtn [te k̲w'em tn] rudder. *noun.*
tel̓étsnech [te l'ets nech] east; east wind. *noun.*
tel̓míxws [tel' mixws] make (something) known; reveal (something). *verb(t).*
tél̓new̓as [tel' ne w̓as] friends, become. *verb(i).*
tél̓nexw [tel' nexw] discover (something); find out about (something); realize (something). *verb(t).*
tel̓núm̓ut [tel' nu m̓ut] realize; come to [after fainting]. *verb(i).*
tel̓tel̓númut [tel' tel' nu mut] studying who one is, be. *verb(i).*
teltíwet [tel ti wet] west; west wind. *noun.*
tel̓wánim [tel' wa nim] think things over. *verb(i).*
telyésh [tel yesh] south wind; "American wind." *noun.*
telhchís [telh chis] rock mallet used for splitting or making a canoe. *noun.*
tem time; season. *adjective.*
tem achcháwem ~ tem eshcháwm [tem ach cha wem] spawning season [salmon; approximately mid-August to mid-October]. *noun.*
tem cháyilhen [tem cha yi lhen] September. *noun.*
tem ek̲wáyanexw [tem e k̲wa ya nexw] autumn; fall; November. *noun.*
tem eshcháwm ~ tem achcháwem [tem esh chawm] time for salmon to spawn [approximately mid-August to mid-November]. *noun.*
tem kwáx̲nis [tem kwax̲ nis] September [when the dog-salmon run; old word for **tem cháyilhen**]. *noun.*
tem kwu7s [tem kwu7s] time of spring salmon [approximately July]. *noun.*
tem kw'eskw'ás [tem kw'es kw'as] June; summer. *noun.*
tem k̲w'élemexw [tem k̲w'e le mexw] July [when the blackberries are ripe]. *noun.*
tem lhawt' March; herring time. *noun.*
tem mílha7 [tem mi lha7] dancing season. *noun.*
tem p'í7tway [tem p'i7 tway] October. *noun.*
tem p'í7tway ta sx̲wí7shen [tem p'i7 tway ta sx̲wi7 shen] rutting season of the deer [literally, when the deer mate; old word for **tem p'i7tway**]. *noun.*
tem s7áynixw [tem s7ay nixw] time of the eulachon [approximately April]. *noun.*
tem t'ák̲a7 [tem t'a k̲a7] August [when the salalberries are ripe]. *noun.*
tem t'ik̲w [tem t'ik̲w] winter. *noun.*
tem tsá7tsk̲ay [tem tsa7ts kay] April [when salmonberry shoots are collected]. *noun.*
tem welhx̲s [tem welh x̲s] February. *noun.*
tem yetwán [tem yet wan] May [when the salmonberries ripen]. *noun.*
tem yeys summer [old word for **tem kw'eskw'ás**]. *noun.*
tem̓áy̓t [te m̓ay̓t] wish for (a certain kind of food); get hungry for (something); hungry for (something), get. *verb(t).*
temchál̓ek̲w [tem cha l'ek̲w] south; south wind. *noun.*
temíxw [te mixw] land; earth; dirt. *noun.*
temíxwiy̓ik̲w [te mi xwi y̓ik̲w] great-great-great-great-grandparent/uncle/aunt; great-great-great-great-grandchild. *noun.*

temlh red ochre; red paint. *noun.*
temlhán [tem lhan] paint (someone) with red paint. *verb(t).*
témlhepsem [tem lhep sem] pileated woodpecker; woodpecker [pileated]. *noun.*
temlhíwsem [tem lhiw sem] paint one's body. *verb(i).*
témlhḵwáṁ [temlh ḵwaṁ] paint one's hair. *verb(i).*
temlhúsem [tem lhu sem] paint one's face. *verb(i).*
temsḵw'shétsut [tems ḵw'she tsut] make a plaything of it; treat it irreverently. *verb(i).*
temslhilháts'mixwaẏlh [tem slhi lhat's mi xwa ẏlh] let people mock one; let people mock one's name. *verb(i).*
temstl'í7 [tem stl'i7] close to someone, be; favourite, be the. *verb(i).*
temstl'í7s [tem stl'i7s] love (someone). *verb(t).*
temswá7 [tem swa7] owner. *noun.*
temtám [tem tam] when? *question word; verb(i).*
témus [te mus] sea otter; velvet. *noun.*
-ten ~ -tn ~ -tán instrument; implement. *suffix.*
tení7i7 [te ni 7i7] spirit touches one and one goes numb. *verb(i).*
ténḵsen [tenḵ sen] mallard duck. *noun.*
tesás [te sas] pitiful. *adjective.*
tesasténaṁut [te sas te na ṁut] feel sorry for oneself. *verb(i).*
tesí7 [te si7] cold, become; feel cold; have a cold [about human]. *verb(i).*
tesí7ach [te si 7ach] cold hands, have. *adjective.*
tesí7n [te si 7n] cool (something) off. *verb(t).*
tesí7ntsut [te si 7n tsut] cool oneself off. *verb(i).*
tesí7shn [te si7 shn] cold feet, have. *adjective.*
testesás [tes te sas] poor [about people]. *adjective.*
tesh granny. *noun.*
tetaṁ [te taṁ] leaking, be [about roof or house]. *verb(i).*
tetaẇí7 [te ta ẇi7] bright, become; light, become. *verb(i).*
teta7áṁ [te ta 7aṁ] happening to someone, be. *verb(i).*
teta7ús [te ta 7us] face a certain direction. *verb(i).*
tetelástelwit [te te las tel wit] married, be. *verb(i).*
tetél̓neẇas [te tel' ne ẇas] man and wife, be; married to each other, be. *verb(i).*
tethíṁ [tet hiṁ] building, be. *verb(i).*
tétiẏex̱w [te ti ẏex̱w] busy, be. *verb(i).*
tet-si7 [tet si7] feel cold; cold, feel. *verb(i).*
tétus [te tus] face this way. *verb(i).*
tetúsayusem [te tu sa yu sem] face [look] the other way. *verb(i).*
tetúsem [te tu sem] face this way. *verb(i).*
tétxwem [tet xwem] car; beat [e.g., as of a heart]. *noun.*
tetx̱wáya7ní7m ~ tx̱wáya7ní7m [tet x̱wa ya7 ni 7m] make sure. *verb(i).*
tetstíts [tet stits] lean; skinny [about person]. *adjective.*
tetstítsi7 [tet sti tsi7] skinny, become. *verb(i).*
tetstítsntsut [tet sti tsn tsut] skinny, make oneself; skinny, get. *verb(i).*
téwaḵin ~ estéwaḵin [te wa ḵin] mourning, be in. *verb(i).*
téwaḵin ~ tíwiḵen [te wa ḵin] mourn. *verb(i).*
tewaḵinántem [te wa ḵi nan tem] ghosted, be; encounter with a ghost, have an [see also **shishá7yu7ntem**]. *verb(p).*
teẇá7n [te ẇa 7n] tilt (something). *verb(t).*
teẇíṅ [te ẇiṅ] raw; unripe. *adjective.*
tewíṅxw [te wiṅxw] berry [general term; not yet ripe]. *noun.*
téxwilh [te xwilh] buy a canoe. *verb(i).*
tex̱w straightened out; settled; correct. *adjective.*
tex̱w eḵ' later. *adverb.*
tex̱w skwáyel [tex̱w skwa yel] noon. *noun.*
tex̱wáṁ ~ tex̱wl̓áṁ ~ tex̱wláṁ [te x̱waṁ] really; truly; exactly; completely. *adverb.*
téx̱wa7ch [te x̱wa 7ch] bow [type of weapon]. *noun.*
tex̱wl̓áṁ men i7 [tex̱w l'aṁ men 7i7] good fit, be a really. *adverb.*

te_xwlám̓ ~ te_xwl̓ám̓ ~ te_xwám̓ [te_xw lam̓] really; truly; exactly; completely. *adverb.*

te_xwl̓ám̓ ~ te_xwlám̓ ~ te_xwám̓ [te_xw l'am̓] really; truly; exactly; completely. *adverb.*

téy̓e_xw [ye y̓e_xw] bothered, be. *verb(i).*

téy̓e_xwt [te y̓e_xwt] bother (someone). *verb(t).*

téy̓e_xwtsut [te y̓e_xw tsut] bothering, be. *verb(i).*

teytayak_shnám̓ [tey ta yak_sh nam̓] making lots of steps, be. *verb(i).*

téytk_in [teyt k_in] speak the Stó:lo language. *verb(i).*

téy̓wilh [tey̓ wilh] protected. *adjective.*

téy̓wilhn ~ tíw̓ilhn [tey̓ wi lhn] protect (something); defend (someone/something). *verb(t).*

téy̓wilhtn [tey̓ wilh tn] shelter. *noun.*

ti [ti] this one; he here. *demonstrative.*

ti [ti] the, a [close to speaker]. *determiner.*

ti- [ti-] make; build; weave. *prefix.*

ti- [ti-] from. *prefix.*

ti stsi7s [ti stsi7s] today. *adverbial phrase.*

ti txwná7nat [ti txw na7 nat] tonight. *adverbial phrase.*

tichám [ti cham] do so; say so. *verb(i).*

tichém_x [ti chem_x] firm, become [about glue, putty, etc.]. *verb(i).*

tichíchishem [ti chi chi shem] inshore wind, be. *verb(i).*

ticht [ticht] doing (something), be. *verb(t).*

tich'awténm ~ ch'awténm [ti ch'aw te nm] come to ask someone for assistance; ask for assistance [in the form of supplies]. *verb(i).*

tich'áyay̓m ~ ch'áyay̓m [ti ch'a ya y̓m] marry deceased spouse's sibling or cousin. *verb(i).*

tiha7lhí7 [ti ha7 lhi7] good now, be. *verb(i).*

tihem̓í [ti he m̓i] come this way; approach. *verb(i).* approaching. *adjective.*

tihúy [ti huy] finished, be. *verb(i).*

tikw [tikw] get away from rough weather. *verb(i).*

tik_'esk_'isayípstn [ti k_'es k_'i sa yip stn] make buttons. *verb(i).*

tik_w [tik_w] dirty [about water]; muddy. *adjective.*

tik_wáyatk_wu [ti k_wa yat k_wu] muddy [about water]. *adjective.*

tik_wúk_wel̓ [ti k_wu k_wel'] drink, be getting a; getting a drink, be. *verb(i).*

tik_w' ~ ntik_w' [tik_w'] bump; run aground [about boat]. *verb(i).*

tík_w'nem [tik_w' nem] bumped, get. *verb(p).*

tík_w'new̓as [tik_w' ne w̓as] bump together. *verb(i).*

tík_w'us ~ ntík_w'us [ti k_w'us] bump one's head. *verb(i).*

tilám̓ [ti lam̓] build a house. *verb(t).*

tilél̓s [ti lel's] from below, be; below, be from. *verb(i).*

tilél̓s stak_w [ti lel's stak_w] spring water; well water. *noun.*

tim̓á [ti m̓a] as, be; like, be; seem; accordingly, be; so, be. *verb(i).*

tim̓ak_sáń [ti m̓ak_ sań] turn (something) around; make a U-turn with (a car). *verb(t).*

tim̓ák_sem [ti m̓ak_ sem] turn around a canoe, car, etc.; make a U-turn [with car]. *verb(i).*

tim̓ás [ti m̓as] do as one is told [literally, do as (someone) tells one]; obey (someone); act like (someone/something); make like (someone/something). *verb(t).*

tim̓áshi [ti m̓a shi] agree with (someone). *verb(t).*

timát [ti mat] make a mat. *verb(i).*

timéń [ti meń] produce offspring [used only in the phrase **timeń ta sesemay̓**]. *verb(i).*

timéń ta sesemáy̓ [ti meń ta se se may̓] honey [literally, child of the bee]. *phrase.*

tímin [ti min] muscle; strength. *noun.*

tíminshen ~ tay̓émtn [ti min shen] calf of leg [literally, leg muscle]. *noun.*

tímit [ti mit] perform (something) with all one's might. *verb(t).*

tímitsut [ti mi tsut] exert oneself; rain hard. *verb(i).*

tim̓úsem [ti m̓u sem] look behind; look the other way; look around; turn so that one faces the other way. *verb(i).*

tinán [ti nan] soothe. *verb(t).*

tiná7 [ti na7] from, be; originate from. *verb(i).*

tiná7 i7x̱w [ti na7 7i7 x̱w] from everywhere, be. *verb(i).*
tinéneyċh [ti ne neyċh] offshore wind, be an; south, be from the [literally, be from the high seas]. *verb(i).*
tíntin [tin tin] bell. *noun.* ring a bell. *verb(i).*
tiseplín [ti se plin] go get bread; get bread, go; bread, go get. *verb(i).*
tiseẁáẏ [ti se ẁaẏ] right now. *adverb.*
tisé7sḵ' [ti se7 sḵ'] make chips of wood [for starting fire]. *verb(i).*
tisḵwú7ḵwu [ti sḵwu7 ḵwu] thirsty, be. *verb(i).*
tisḵw'shétsut [tisḵw' she tsut] make toys. *verb(i).*
tismeḵ'méḵ'm [ti smeḵ' me ḵ'm] overeat; stuff oneself [full of food]. *verb(i).*
tistséḵ [tis tseḵ] go logging; logging, go. *verb(i).*
tístsut [tis tsut] dance with a very rapid stamping of the feet [for which the **stl'epxw** serves as an accompaniment; this was done by a group of people, going three times around the house, after which one dancer starts dancing a **milha7**]. *verb(i).*
tists'úḵwi7 [tis ts'u ḵwi7] fish for salmon. *verb(i).*
tisxwám [tis xwam] starve to death; die from hunger. *verb(i).*
tísxweẏúsm [tis xwe ẏu sm] starve. *verb(i).*
tisyétsem [tis ye tsem] tell news. *verb(i).*
tisyéwan [tis ye wan] sing one's **syewen**. *verb(i).*
tisyeẁíṅ [tis ye ẁiṅ] use ritual words; ritual words, use; use magic power. *verb(i).*
tis7ílhen [tis 7i lhen] look for food. *verb(i).*
tisháṁ [ti shaṁ] get like. *verb(i).*
tishéykw [ti sheykw] go to get clams; get clams, go; clams, go get. *verb(i).*
titála [ti ta la] go to get some money; make money; get some money, go. *verb(i).*
titátaẏch [ti ta taẏch] come from behind. *verb(i).*
tititcháṁ [ti ti chaṁ] doing something else, be. *verb(i).*
titiṅústnaẏ [ti ti ṅust naẏ] black twinberry bush; snakeberry bush. *noun.*
titiẁéṅeḵ [ti ti ẁe ṅeḵ] surveying, be; wandering around, be. *verb(i).*
titkw ~ estítkw [tit kw] safe; sheltered. *adjective.*
títḵin [tit ḵin] speak the Sto:lo language. *verb(i).*
titúyntsaṁ [ti tuyn tsaṁ] make a [verbal] will. *verb(i).*
titúyntsaṁnumut [ti tuyn tsaṁ nu mut] make a [verbal] will, manage to. *verb(i).*
tit'álaḵ [ti t'a laḵ] target shooting, be. *verb(i).*
tits'áts'eẏx̱ [ti ts'a ts'eẏx̱] right now. *adverb.*
tits'úp' [ti ts'up'] connected, become. *verb(i).*
tiw [tiw] jarred, be. *verb(i).*
tíwa [ti wa] this one here; he here. *demonstrative.*
tíwa ts'umlh [ti wa ts'umlh] now. *adverbial phrase.*
tiẁásiẁilh [ti ẁa si ẁilh] both sides of something, be. *verb(i).*
tíwash [ti wash] land a canoe. *verb(i).*
tíwiḵen ~ téwaḵin [ti wi ḵen] mourn. *verb(i).*
tíẁilhn ~ téẏwilhn [ti ẁi lhn] defend (someone/something); protect (someone/something). *verb(t).*
tixw [tixw] get down. *verb(i).*
tix̱ḵwuẏachí7m [tix̱ ḵwu ẏa chi 7m] spread one's fingers. *verb(i).*
tix̱w [tix̱w] stripped off, be [about branches]. *verb(i).*
tíx̱wachxw [ti x̱wa chxw] branch stripped from a tree. *noun.*
tíx̱wachxwn [ti x̱wach xwn] strip (limbs off tree). *verb(t).*
tíx̱wiṅ [ti x̱wiṅ] rip (something) off accidentally [as of branches on a tree]; strip (limbs off tree). *verb(t).*
tiyách [ti yach] fight back. *verb(i).*
tíyam [ti yam] clear a large area of land. *verb(i).*
tiyáyusen [ti ya yu sen] lean against (something). *verb(t).*
tíyen [ti yen] clear (a small area of land). *verb(t).*
tí7ax̱w [ti 7ax̱w] get excited; excited, get; busy, get; get busy. *verb(i).*
ti7áy [ti 7ay] teapot. *noun.*
ti7cháṁ [ti7 chaṁ] fight back. *verb(i).*
ti7cht [ti7 cht] do (something). *verb(t).*
ti7éncha [ti 7en cha] from where?; where? *question word; verb(i).*

ti7énchas [ti 7en chas] get (something) from where? *question word; verb(t).*
ti7es7ásxw [ti 7es 7asxw] go for seals; seal hunting, be. *verb(i).*
ti7í [ti 7i] from here, be. *verb(i).*
ti7shám̓ [ti7 sham̓] do it; sex, have. *verb(i).*
tí7shexw [ti7 shexw] say; do. *verb(i).*
tí7shnexw [ti7 shnexw] got (something) to a certain point, have; got (someone) in a certain condition, have. *verb(t).*
ti7tsám̓ [ti7 tsam̓] follow someone's speech with one's own speech. *verb(i).*
tkwáya7n [t kwa ya 7n] hear; listen. *verb(i).*
tkwaya7ní7m [t kwa ya7 ni 7m] listen. *verb(i).*
tkwayá7nmin [t kwa ya 7n min] hear (someone); listen to (someone). *verb(t).*
tkwáya7nmixws [t kwa ya 7n mixws] listen to (someone); listen to something or someone, have (someone). *verb(t).*
tkwáya7nni [t kwa ya 7n ni] listen to (someone). *verb(t).*
tkwaya7nnúmut [t kwa ya 7n nu mut] hear finally; hear, manage to. *verb(i).*
tkwétsi [t kwe tsi] of that, of him [see **kwetsi**]. *demonstrative.*
tkwi [t kwi] of the, a [see **kwi**].*determiner.*
tk̲ach [t k̲ach] eight. *numeral.*
tk̲achámats' [t k̲a cha mats'] eight strands [of wool, rope, etc.]. *numeral.*
tk̲áchawanexw [t k̲a cha wa nexw] eight years. *verb(i).*
tk̲achk̲ [t k̲achk̲] eight o'clock. *noun.*
tk̲ap [t k̲ap] fish dam. *noun.*
tk̲at [t k̲at] accuse (someone); confront (someone); call to account (someone) suspected of spreading rumours about one; ask (someone) if he/she really said something; ask (someone) what is going on; ask (someone) why he/she is saying something. *verb(t).*
tk̲ay̓ [t k̲ay̓] do something else; go out for the evening. *verb(i).*
tk̲áya [t k̲a ya] wolf. *noun.*
tk̲áya7 ~ stk̲áya [t k̲a ya7] wolf. *noun.*
tk̲aya7úmesh [t k̲a ya 7u mesh] wolf-like. *adjective.*
tk̲echálh [t k̲e chalh] eight times. *verb(i).*
tk̲echalhshá7 [t k̲e chalh sha7] eighty. *numeral.*
tk̲'ák̲'an̓átsut [t k̲'a k̲'a n̓a tsut] returning the way one has come, be. *verb(i).*
tk̲'ánatsut [t k̲'a na tsut] return [move back in the same direction]. *verb(i).*
tk̲'ax̲ [t k̲'ax̲] fall backward. *verb(i).*
tk̲'ay [t k̲'ay] top of something, be on. *verb(i).*
tk̲wám̓entsut [t k̲wa m̓en tsut] appear [about big hole, as on road]. *verb(i).*
tk̲wu7ts [t k̲wu7ts] blocked, be. *verb(i).*
tk̲wú7tsen [t k̲wu7 tsen] block (something). *verb(t).*
tlhu7lhúsi [tlhu7 lhu si] slipping, be. *verb(i).*
-tn ~ -ten ~ -tán instrument; implement. *suffix.*
tnulh [t nulh] numb. *adjective.*
tpánu [t pa nu] season; next year; last year. *noun.*
tpánu es ek̲' [t pa nu 7es 7ek̲'] next year. *phrase.*
tpúlhim̓ [t pu lhim̓] stretch animal skin on stretching board. *verb(i).*
tpulhn [t pu lhn] stretch out (a hide); stretch (a hide) on board frame. *verb(t).*
tpúlhtn [t pulh tn] frame for tanning hides; stretching-board; frame for weaving blankets. *noun.*
ttay̓ [t tay̓] of him, that [see **tay̓**]. *demonstrative.*
tti [t ti] of this [see ti]. *demonstrative; determiner.*
túk̲wut [tu k̲wut] go easy with (something); save (something). *verb(t).*
túmlk̲elh [tu ml k̲elh] starfish. *noun.*
tut [tut] a bit; barely; sort of; a little; a little distance. *adverb.*
tut ch'itentsut [tut ch'i ten tsut] seen walking around, be [about dead person]. *verb(i).*
tut ns7ey [tut ns 7ey] talk a little louder. *verb(i).*
tutáw̓ [tu taw̓] bright. *adjective.* light. *noun.*
tutáw̓ikwup [tu ta w̓i kwup] bright fire. *adjective.*
tutkwemkwím [tut kwem kwim] kind of red; pink. *adjective.*
tutnexwch'ít [tut nexw ch'it] little close, be a; close, be a little. *verb.*
tútuk̲wut [tu tu k̲wut] save (something) for later. *verb(t).*

túxwun [tu xwun] run (something) out [e.g., a rope]. *verb(t).*

túx̱wuntsut [tu x̱wun tsut] string out. *verb(i).*

tuy [tuy] cross over large body of water; go across a body of water. *verb(i).*

tuyn [tuyn] abandon (something/someone); leave (something/someone). *verb(t).*

tuyntwáy̓wit [tuyn twaẏ wit] separate [about spouses]. *verb(i).*

tuyts [tuyts] cross a river; go across a river. *verb(i).*

tuẏún ~ túẏun [tu ẏun] lean (something) over; put (something) at an incline. *verb(t).*

túẏun ~ tuẏún [tu ẏun] lean (something) over; put (something) at an incline. *verb(t).*

tuẏúntsut [tu ẏun tsut] lean over. *verb(i).*

txw- {out of control}. *prefix.*

-txw ~ -aẇtxw house {full word: **laṁ**}; building; room. *suffix.*

txwaw ~ txwhaw no longer the case, be; no more, be. *verb(i).*

txwawk̲ ~ txwhawk̲ exist no longer; no longer be there. *verb(i).*

txwáyak̲ep [txwa ya k̲ep] go another way; take alternate route. *verb(i).*

txwchacha7ném [txw cha cha7 nem] where is . . . going? *question word; verb(i).*

txwchánem [txw cha nem] go where? *question word; verb(i).*

txwchas [txw chas] what to do with (something)? *question word; verb(t).*

txwchelhk̲w [txw chelhk̲w] fall in hole; move through it; through it, be. *verb(i).*

txwchenchánat [txw chen cha nat] three people left, only; only three people left. *numeral.*

txwch'a7ch [txw ch'a7ch] go up a mountain; go upward. *verb(i).*

txwch'ech'a7úsm [txw ch'e ch'a 7u sm] go uphill; uphill, go. *verb(i).*

txwch'eṁt [txw ch'eṁt] bite (someone) accidentally. *verb(t).*

txwch'eẏxwíṁ [txw ch'eẏ xwiṁ] dry something, just. *verb(i).*

txweṁí ~ txwheṁí ~ txwṁi ~ txwmi [txwe ṁi] come this way; come towards this way; towards this way, be. *verb(i).*

txweṅús ~ txwheṅús ~ txwnu7s [txwe ṅus] looking [in the direction of the speaker], be. *verb(i).*

txwháṁk̲w [txw haṁk̲w] head covered, get. *verb(i).*

txwháṁk̲waṁ [txw haṁ k̲waṁ] covered up, be. *verb(i).*

txwhaw ~ txwaw [txw haw] no more, be; no longer the case, be. *verb(i).*

txwhawk̲ ~ txwawk̲ [txw hawk̲] exist no longer; no longer be there. *verb(i).*

txwheṁí ~ txweṁí ~ txwmi ~ txwṁi [txw he ṁi] come this way; come towards this way; towards this way, be. *verb(i).*

txwheṁíni [txw he ṁi ni] come at (someone). *verb(t).*

txwheṅús ~ txweṅús ~ txwnu7s [txw he ṅus] looking [in the direction of the speaker], be. *verb(i).*

txwheṅúsm ~ heṅúsm [txw he ṅu sm] look [in the direction of the speaker]. *verb(i).*

txwhik̲ ~ txwik̲ [txw hik̲] fall under something; move under something; under something, be; move to the space under something. *verb(i).*

txwhílitsut [txw hi li tsut] roll oneself. *verb(i).*

txwhiẇ ~ txwiẇ [txw hiẇ] go up a little further [stream]; resume; advance; move on; move forward; move upstream; on something, be; forward, be; upstream, be; move upstream. *verb(i).*

txwhiyú7 [txw hi yu7] suddenly. *adverb.*

txwhuy ~ txwuy [txw huy] remaining; to no purpose; all [that remains]; be all that is left; left, be all that is. *adverb.*

txwik̲ ~ txhik̲ [txwik̲] move under something; under something, be; fall under something; move to the space under something. *verb(i).*

txwiẇ ~ txwhiẇ [txwiẇ] go up a little further [stream]; resume; move on; move forward; move upstream; on something, be; forward, be; upstream, be; advance. *verb(i).*

txwiwnúmut [txwiw nu mut] resume, manage to. *verb(i).*

txwiws [txwiws] do (something) again. *verb(t).*
txwkákat [txw ka kat] go upward. *verb(i).*
txwkat [txw kat] climb up; rise up. *verb(i).*
txwkats [txw kats] hoist (something) up. *verb(t).*
txwkaw [txw kaw] go down towards the water; down towards the water, go. *verb(i).*
txwkawchs [txw kawchs] cross (a mountain or hill). *verb(t).*
txwkáẇshenam [txw kaẇ she nam] change course and come straight downward [about water]. *verb(i).*
txwkwtams [txw kwtams] married, get; get married [about a woman]. *verb(i).*
txwkwum [txw kwum] go up on the beach; up on the beach, go; beach, go up on the; go up. *verb(i).*
txwkw'in [txw kw'in] just a few, be; few, be just a. *verb(i).*
txwkw'ínkw'in [txw kw'in kw'in] just a few left, be; few left, be just a; few, become [about people]; left over in small numbers, be [about people]. *adverb.*
txwk̲álachen ~ txwtsek̲álachen ~ txwtsk̲álachen [txw k̲a la chen] fall back [suddenly]. *verb(i).*
txwk̲áẏiwsm [txw k̲a ẏiw sm] point to the left side. *verb(i).*
txwk̲'ak̲'aṅátsut [txw k̲'a k̲'a ṅa tsut] returning the way one has come, be. *verb(i).*
txwk̲'ay [txw k̲'ay] go on top of it; on top of it, be. *verb(i).*
txwk̲'eẇ [txw k̲'eẇ] don't go as far. *verb(i).*
txwk̲w'iyílsh [txw k̲w'i yilsh] dance suddenly. *verb(i).*
txwk̲w'uy [txw k̲w'uy] dead tired, be. *verb(i).*
txwlixw [txw lixw] laid down, have been [without permission, e.g., as of a marker]. *verb(i).*
txwlhchiws [txwlh chiws] tired, get/become. *verb(i).*
txwlhep' [txw lhep'] doubled up over, be [about land]. *verb(i).*
txwlhép' [txw lhep'] hung up, get. *verb(i).*
txwmi ~ txwṁi ~ txweṁí ~ txwheṁí [txw mi] come this way; come towards this way; towards [this way], be. *verb(i).*
txwṁi ~ txwmi ~ txweṁí ~ txwheṁí [txw ṁi] come towards this way; towards [this way], be; come this way. *verb(i).*
txwmik̲'s [txw mik̲'s] point (them) down [in **slhahál**]. *verb(t).*
txwmiyíẇax̲an [txw mi yi ẇa x̲an] move to the side of something; side of something, be to the. *verb(i).*
txwmuy [txw muy] fall in the water [and sink]. *verb(i).*
txwnách'awtx̣w [txw na ch'aw tx̣w] visit. *verb(i).*
txwnách'aẇtxwni [txw na ch'aẇ txw ni] visit (someone). *verb(t).*
txwnách'aẇtxwtn [txw na ch'aẇ txw tn] visitor. *noun.*
txwnaṁ [txw naṁ] for [something desired]; than; to; towards; against [something disliked]. *preposition.* hence, be; that-a-way, be; go along; move along; go to; with a view to, be; {also used as a comparison word}. *verb(i).*
txwnánaṁ [txw na naṁ] gone, be; toward, be; in the direction of something, be; that-a-way, be; go to. *verb(i).*
txwnanch'áẇtxw [txw nan ch'aẇ txw] make many visits; visiting, be always. *verb(i).*
txwna7 [txw na7] land onto. *verb(i).*
txwná7nat [txw na7 nat] night. *noun.*
txwncha7áṁ ~ txwnch7aṁ ~ nch'aṁ [txwn cha 7aṁ] how?; what kind?; how much? *question word; verb(i).* any kind. *verb(i).*
txwnch7aṁ ~ txwncha7áṁ ~ nch'aṁ [txw nch 7aṁ] how?; what kind?; how much? *question word; verb(i).* any kind. *verb(i).*
txwnch7áṁneẇas [txw nch 7aṁ ne ẇas] how are they related? *question word; verb(i).*
txwnch7aṁs [txw nch 7aṁs] ask what price for (something)? *question word; verb(t).*
txwnch'nch'u7 [txwn ch'n ch'u7] one left, just; left alone; remain as the only person; alone, left. *numeral.*
txwnéneẇets [txw ne ne ẇets] coming into the harbour, bay, etc., be. *verb(i).*

txwnep [txw nep] hit upon; happen upon; stumble upon. *verb(i).*
txwneẁ [txw neẁ] into, be; fall into; land into. *verb(i).*
txwnéwu7ts [txw ne wu7ts] go into an inlet; move inland. *verb(i).* inlet. *noun.* Howe Sound. *place name.*
txwnu7s ~ txwheńús ~ txweńús [txw nu7s] looking [in the direction of the speaker], be. *verb(i).*
txwpelk̲w [txw pelk̲w] go down on one's knees; kneel; fall on one's knees. *verb(i).*
txwpen [txw pen] land in the dirt; dirt, be in the. *verb(i).*
txwpeym [txw peym] fall into the water; fall overboard. *verb(i).*
txwp'ilhk̲' [txw p'ilhk̲'] alongside, come right; come right alongside. *verb(i).*
txwp'í7nalhn [txw p'i7 na lhn] catch, manage to. *verb(i).*
txwp'i7s [txw p'i7s] catch (something) [that has been thrown]. *verb(t).*
txwp'i7t [txw p'i7t] catch (something). *verb(t).*
txwstl'atl'm [txws tl'a tl'm] alright now, be. *verb(i).*
txwshaẁ [txw shaẁ] all bone, be; become all bone; all bone, become; become very thin; thin, become very; reduced to bone, be; skinny, become very. *verb(i).*
txwshich' [txw shich'] in the bush, be. *verb(i).*
txwtaỷch [txw taỷch] follow behind somebody; go behind; behind, be. *verb(i).*
txwta7 [txw ta7] reach there; speak about it; land on it; on it, be. *verb(i).*
txwtéta7 [txw te ta7] talk about something/someone; discuss something/someone. *verb(i).*
txwteta7nít [txw te ta7 ni] talk about (someone). *verb(t).*
txwtéta7us [txw te ta 7us] looking the other way, be. *verb(i).*
txwtim̓úsem [txw ti m̓u sem] look the other way; look around; turn so that one faces the other way. *verb(i).*
txwti7 [txw ti7] onto, be; up to, be; down to, be; move onto; move up to; move down to. *verb(i).*
txwtuy [txw tuy] go across a small body of water; go in the direction of the other side of a body of water; set out from shore [of river, strait, etc.]. *verb(i).*
txwt'am [txw t'am] miss; guess wrong [in **slhahál**]; stray from. *verb(i).*
txwt'át'em [txw t'a t'em] miss. *verb(i).*
txwt'axw [txw t'axw] fall out of a container; move out of a container; out of a container, be; come out. *verb(i).*
txwt'ekw [txw t'ekw] land in the mud; stuck in the mud, get. *verb(i).*
txwt'ixw [txw t'ixw] downward to the ground, be. *verb(i).*
txwt'ukw' [txw t'ukw'] go home; home, go. *verb(i).*
txwtl'iẁ [txw tl'iẁ] have to run away; run away, have to. *verb(i).*
txwtl'íya7 [txw tl'i ya7] have to stop; stop, have to. *verb(i).*
txwtl'uk̲w' [txw tl'uk̲w'] fall into an out-of-the-way-space. *verb(i).*
txwtsekw [txw tsekw] go aground in canoe; run aground. *verb(i).*
txwtsek̲álachen ~ txwk̲álachen ~ txwtsk̲álachen [txw tse k̲a la chen] fall backwards; fall back [suddenly]. *verb(i).*
txwtsk̲álachen ~ txwk̲álachen ~ txwtsek̲álachen [txwtx k̲a la chen] fall back [suddenly]; fall backwards; fall on one's back. *verb(i).*
txwtsut [txw tsut] say to someone. *verb(i).*
txwtsútsut [txw tsu tsut] saying, be. *verb(i).*
txwts'its'áp' [txw ts'i ts'ap'] work unexpectedly. *verb(i).*
txwuy ~ txwhuy [txwuy] remaining; to no purpose; all [that remains]; be all that is left; left, be all that is. *adverb.*
txwwash [txw wash] back of the room, be in the; move to the back of the room [the space farthest away from the fire]. *verb(i).*
txwwí7xwéy [txw wi7 xwey] go downwards. *verb(i).*
txwwúk̲w'i ~ wúk̲w'i ~ wuk̲w' ~ wúwk̲w'i [txw wu k̲w'i] go downstream. *verb(i).*
txwwúwuk̲w'i [txw wu wu k̲w'i] going downstream, be. *verb(i).*

txwxwech'shí7 [txw xwech' shi7] go to the space between; move to the space between; space between, be in the; come to the space between. *verb(i).*
txwyahíwsem [txw ya hiw sem] turn to the right; point to the right side. *verb(i).*
txwyulh [txw yulh] burned accidentally, be; land in the fire; fire, be in the. *verb(i).*
txwyulhim̓ [txw yu lhim̓] burning, do a kind of [e.g., of garbage]. *verb(i).*
txw7alhx̱án [txw 7alh x̱an] go to the area below. *verb(i).*
txw7átsiḵn [txw 7a tsi ḵn] front of something/someone, be; move in front of something/someone; go to the space in front of something/someone. *verb(i).*
txw7átsus [txw 7a tsus] go to the front side; front side, be at the. *verb(i).*
txw7ats'ḵ [txw 7ats'ḵ] go outside. *verb(i).*
txw7áy̓aḵam̓ [txw 7a y̓a ḵam̓] change the topic [on purpose]; do something else [on purpose]. *verb(i).*
txw7á7iḵ [txw 7a 7iḵ] change the subject. *verb(i).*
txw7énwilh [txw 7en wilh] move to the centre; centre, be in the. *verb(i).*
txw7ilhn [txw 7i lhn] eat suddenly. *verb(i).*
txw7ín̓et [txw 7i n̓et] saying what, be?; about what, be? [about speech]. *question word; verb(i).*
txw7úmich [txw 7u mich] go upstream; go up [the coast, the river]; upstream, be; move upstream. *verb(i).*
txw7umsm [txw 7um sm] wake up unexpectedly. *verb(i).*
txw7utsḵ [txw 7utsḵ] go outside; move to the outdoors; outdoors, be. *verb(i).*
txw7utsus [txw 7u tsus] face, be just a. *verb(i).*
txw7uys [txw 7uys] go inside suddenly or unexpectedly. *verb(i).*
tx̱íx̱ta [tx̱ix̱ ta] day before last; day after next; day before yesterday; day after tomorrow. *noun.*
tx̱íx̱ta txwná7nat [tx̱ix̱ ta txw na7 nat] on the evening of the day after tomorrow. *adverbial phrase.*
tx̱íx̱ta7áwanas [tx̱ix̱ ta 7a wa nas] [when it is] the year after next. *adverb.*
tx̱íx̱ta7áwanexw [tx̱ix̱ ta 7a wa nexw] year before last year; year after next year; last year. *noun.*
tx̱wáya7ní7m ~ tetx̱wáya7ní7m [tx̱wa ya7 ni 7m] make sure. *verb(i).*
tx̱wáy̓usem [tx̱a y̓u sem] look at carefully; direct one's glance at something. *verb(i).*
tx̱wáy̓usnexw [tx̱wa y̓us nexw] caught sight of (someone), have. *verb(t).*

T' t'

t'aaṁ [t'aaṁ] removed, be. *verb(i).*
t'ach'apáx̲tn [t'a ch'a pax̲ tn] net-hanging twine. *noun.*
t'ákw'en [t'a kw'en] dig (something). *verb(t).*
t'ákw'us [t'a kw'us] point; indicate. *verb(i).*
t'akw'usách [t'a kw'u sach] seven. *numeral.*
t'akw'usachálh [t'a kw'u sa chalh] seven times. *verb(i).*
t'akw'usachámats' [ta kw'u sa cha mats'] seven strands [of wool, rope, etc.]. *numeral.*
t'akw'usáchk̲ [t'a kw'u sachk̲] seven o'clock. *noun.*
t'ákw'usen [t'a kw'u sen] point at (something). *verb(t).*
t'akw'usíṁ [t'a kw'u siṁ] point. *verb(i).*
t'ákw'ustn [t'a kw'us tn] index finger. *noun.*
t'ák̲a7 [t'a k̲a7] salal berry. *noun.*
t'ák̲a7 [t'a k̲a7] bruised [so that the skin has the colour of a salal berry]. *adjective.*
t'ák̲a7aẏ [t'a k̲a 7aẏ] salal berry bush. *noun.*
t'ák̲a7ayus [t'a k̲a 7a yus] black eye, have a. *adjective.*
t'ak̲' crosswise, become. *verb(i).*
t'ák̲'ach [t'a k̲'ach] six. *numeral.*
t'ák̲'ách [t'a k̲'ach] six days. *verb(i).*
t'ak̲'achálh [t'a k̲'a chalh] six times. *verb(i).*
t'ak̲'achámats' [ta k̲'a cha mats'] six strands [of wool, rope, etc.]. *numeral.*
t'ak̲'acháxwilh [t'a k̲'a cha xwilh] six [containers]. *numeral.*
t'ák̲'achk̲ [t'a k̲'achk̲] six o'clock. *noun.*
t'ák̲'aṁ [t'a k̲'aṁ] alight; land [about bird; e.g., on tree]. *verb(i).*
t'ák̲'an [t'a k̲'an] put (something) across. *verb(t).*
t'ák̲'em [t'a k̲'em] land [about bird]. *verb(i).*
t'ak̲'its'áẇtxw [t'a k̲'i ts'aẇ txw] log cabin. *noun.*
t'ák̲'neẇasn [t'ak̲' ne ẇa sn] cross (two things). *verb(t).*
t'ák̲wel̓ [t'a k̲wel'] drought, be a; dry, be; evaporated, be; gone dry, have; go dry [e.g., a well]. *verb(i).*
t'ák̲w'emaẏ [t'a k̲w'e maẏ] thimbleberry bush [see **st'ák̲w'em** and **t'ek̲w't'ak̲w'emáy'**]. *noun.*
t'ák̲w'en [ta k̲w'en] break (a rope); cut (a rope) in two. *verb(t).*
t'ák̲w'entem [t'a k̲w'en tem] cut (a rope). *verb(p).* Saturday. *noun.*
t'álaw [t'a law] muscles [of body]. *noun.*
t'alh shallow. *adjective.*
t'álhi [t'a lhi] shallow, get. *verb(i).*
t'álhik̲wan [t'a lhi k̲wan] make a raft from (something). *verb(t).*
t'álhi7k̲w [t'a lhi7k̲w] raft [see also **lháwlik̲w ~ alháwlik̲w**]. *noun.*
t'am guess in **slhahál**; "throw the white bone in **slhahál**." *verb(i).*
t'aṁán [t'a ṁan] put (something) aside; remove (something); move (something) over. *verb(t).*
t'ámat [t'a mat] guess (something). *verb(t).*
t'ámatsut [t'a ma tsut] on the alert, be; alert, be on the; leery, be; on one's guard, be; afraid, be. *verb(i).*
t'amáẏs [t'a maẏs] pointer in **slhahál**, be the. *verb(i).*
t'aṁéy ~ t'aṁí [t'a ṁey] get away; leave; get out of the way; go away; get away; move over. *verb(i).*
t'aṁí ~ t'aṁéy [t'a ṁi] get away; leave; get out of the way; go away; get away; move over. *verb(i).*
t'ámin [t'a min] animal hair. *noun.*
t'amkw' salmon eggs. *noun.*
t'ámnem [t'am nem] (someone) got one; outguessed, be. *verb(p).*
t'ámnexw [t'am nexw] guessed (someone), have; eliminate (player of the opposite team) by guessing in which hand s/he is holding the **t'ámten**. *verb(t).*
t'áṁshi [t'aṁ shi] remove from (someone). *verb(t).*
t'áṁshnaṁ [t'aṁ shnaṁ] divert water. *verb(i).*
t'ámten [t'am ten] white bone in **slhahál**. *noun.*

t'anam̓áchtn [t'a na m̓ach tn] basketful [type of measurement]. *noun.*

t'ánam̓en [t'a na m̓en] measure (something); mark (something); weigh (something). *verb(t).*

t'ánamtn [t'a nam tn] measure; time. *noun.*

t'anemnách [t'a nem nach] pattern for making clothes. *noun.*

t'ánem̓tn [t'a nem̓ tn] measurement; net-marking buoy; mark; sign. *noun.*

t'an̓íw̓ [t'a n̓iw̓] disappear; out of sight, be/get; stand in the shade. *verb(i).*

t'an̓íw̓n [t'a n̓i w̓n] remove (something) out of sight; put (something) in the shade. *verb(t).*

t'an̓íw̓ntsut [t'a n̓i w̓n tsut] stand in the shade. *verb(i).*

t'an̓íws [t'a n̓iws] put (something) out of the way. *verb(t).*

t'ápi7 [t'a pi7] stop leaking; have stopped leaking; not leaking anymore, be. *verb(i).*

t'ápk̲am [t'ap k̲am] get out of the rain; out of the rain, get; take shelter from the rain; shelter from the rain, take. *verb(i).*

t'áplhni [t'a plh ni] snub (someone). *verb(t).*

t'áp'elh [t'a p'elh] shut one's eyes [in disgust]; snub. *verb(i).*

t'ashénem [t'a she nem] war dance, do a. *verb(i).*

t'át'ak̲ayus [t'a t'a k̲a yus] black-eyed. *adjective.*

t'át'alh [t'a t'alh] loom [for weaving blankets]; horizontal pole of a loom. *noun.*

t'át'alhi [t'a t'a lhi] shallow, get. *verb(i).*

t'át'am̓átsut [t'a t'a m̓a tsut] leery, be; on one's guard, be; afraid, be; watchful, be. *verb(i).*

t'át'ayak̲' [t'a t'a yak̲'] angry, be; mad, be. *verb(i).*

t'at'kw'usách [t'at' kw'u sach] seven animals. *numeral.*

t'át'k̲'ach [t'at' k̲'ach] six animals. *numeral.*

t'axw taken out of a container, be; come out of a container; come out. *verb(i).*

t'áxwan̓ [t'a xwan̓] take (something) out of a container. *verb(t).*

t'áxwi [t'a xwi] come out. *verb(i).*

t'áyak̲' [t'a yak̲'] angry, get. *verb(i).*

t'áyak̲'ni [t'a yak̲' ni] angry at (someone), be. *verb(t).*

t'ayak̲'númut [t'a yak̲' nu mut] finally get mad; mad, finally get; angry involuntarily, get [in spite of oneself]. *verb(i).*

t'áyak̲w'us [t'a ya k̲w'us] angry face, have an. *adjective.*

t'áyamay̓ [t'a ya may̓] first growth of young red cedar tree. *noun.*

t'á7nalhen [t'a7 na lhen] get a taste; manage to taste; taste, manage to. *verb(i).*

t'á7nexw [t'a7 nexw] tasted (something), have; tried (something), have. *verb(t).*

t'a7t taste (something); test (something); try (something); sample (something). *verb(t).*

t'á7tsut [t'a7 tsut] attempt; try. *verb(i).*

t'á7x̲wetem [t'a7 x̲we tem] out of control because of rage, be. *verb(i).*

t'chach [t' chach] cane; walking stick; walking staff. *noun.*

t'échu [t'e chu] open space in woods. *noun.*

t'ech' hand or foot cracking, have; cracking, have hand or foot. *verb(i).*

t'éch'i7n [t'e ch'i 7n] clear after a rain storm, become really; become really clear after a rain storm [about day or night]. *verb(i).*

t'ech'k̲ám̓ [t'ech' k̲am̓] use a pole to jump; jump, use a pole to. *verb(i).*

t'ech'shn [t'ech' shn] cracked foot from heat, have. *verb(i).*

t'ech't'ách'ach [t'ech' t'a ch'ach] split hands, have. *verb(i).*

t'éch't'ech' [t'ech' t'ech'] split. *adjective.*

t'ekw get stuck in the mud; stuck in the mud, get; soggy, be. *verb(i).*

t'ekwínas [te kwi nas] choked [by food], get [cf. **kw'én'k̲en**]. *verb(i).*

t'ekws explode; fired, be [about gun]. *verb(i).*

t'ekwsán [t'ekw san] explode (something). *verb(t).*

t'ekwshn [t'ekw shn] feet stuck in mud, get. *verb(i).*

t'ékwt'ekw [t'ekw t'ekw] muddy, very. *adjective.*

t'ekwt'kwí7 [t'ekwt' kwi7] muddy, get very; muddy, be very. *verb(i).*

t'ékw'enp [t'e kw'enp] dig; dig the ground. *verb(i).*

t'ékw'kw'usách [t'ekw' kw'u sach] seven days. *verb(i).*

t'ékw'nexw [t'ekw' nexw] dug (something) up, have. *verb(t).*

t'ekw'tákw'en [t'ekw' ta kw'en] dig (something) up. *verb(t).*

t'ekw't'ákw'usách [t'ekw' t'a kw'u sach] seven people. *numeral.*

t'ek̲t'á7k̲a7 [t'ek̲ t'a7 k̲a7] bruised, be; bruised all over, be. *verb(i).*

t'ek̲t'k̲áy̓ [t'ek̲t' k̲ay̓] vine maple tree. *noun.*

t'ek̲'t'ák̲'ach [t'ek̲' t'a k̲'ach] six people. *numeral.*

t'ek̲w' break [as of a rope]; bruised, be. *verb(i).*

t'ek̲w'k̲sán [t'ek̲w' k̲san] cut off the end of (something). *verb(t).*

t'ek̲w'míṅ [t'ek̲w' miṅ] broken-off half. *noun.*

t'ék̲w'tek̲w'k̲s ~ est'ék̲w'tek̲w'k̲s [t'ek̲w' tek̲w' k̲s] square. *adjective.*

t'ek̲w't'ak̲w'emáy̓ [t'ek̲w' t'a k̲w'e may̓] thimbleberry tree [see **st'ák̲w'em** and **t'ák̲w'emay'**]. *noun.*

t'élchepsem [t'el chep sem] surf scoter [type of duck with white spot on back of neck]; black duck. *noun.*

t'élem [t'e lem] wild cherry; cherry [wild]. *noun.*

t'eleṁáy̓ [t'e le ṁay̓] wild cherry tree; cherry tree [wild]. *noun.*

t'elkáyus [t'el ka yus] wart on one's face, have a. *adjective.*

t'elk̲áṅ [t'el k̲aṅ] used with making mud pies; dab (something) on; apply a big dab of (something). *verb(t).*

t'elk̲wáṅ [t'el k̲waṅ] nurse (a baby). *verb(t).*

t'elk̲wáṅ [t'el k̲waṅ] put (something) as a dot on. *verb(t).*

t'elk̲wíṁ [t'el k̲wiṁ] breastfeed; nurse [about a baby]. *verb(i).*

t'elk̲wímay̓lh [t'el k̲wi ma y̓lh] nurse one's child; have one's child nursing. *verb(i).*

t'elk̲wíṁay̓m [t'el k̲wi ṁa y̓m] want to be nursed; want to be breastfed. *verb(i).*

t'elk̲wíṁs [t'el k̲wiṁs] nurse (a baby). *verb(t).*

t'elts'áṅ [t'el ts'aṅ] squirt (something). *verb(t).*

t'elh fat person [slang]; any wild game in late winter. *noun.*

t'élhk̲eṁ [t'elh k̲eṁ] slippery [e.g., sports or ice]. *adjective.*

t'elhk̲'ántsut [t'elh k̲'an tsut] struggle. *verb(i).*

t'élhk̲'em [t'elh k̲'em] diligent, be; energetic, be. *verb(i).*

t'elhk̲w'án [t'elh k̲w'an] claw (someone). *verb(t).*

t'elhnáym ~ tl'elhnáym [t'elh naym] go on a prolonged hunting trip [camping in the mountains]. *verb(i).*

t'elht'ílhikw'entem [t'elh t'i lhi kw'en tem] pulled apart, be [e.g., by a grizzly]. *verb(p).*

t'eṁách [t'e ṁach] chop one's hand accidentally. *verb(i).*

t'eṁáchn [t'e ṁa chn] chop (someone's) hand. *verb(t).*

t'éṁen [t'e ṁen] chop (something). *verb(t).*

t'emk̲w ~ t'eṁk̲w bump one's head; hurt one's head. *verb(i).*

t'eṁk̲w ~ t'emk̲w hurt one's head; bump one's head. *verb(i).*

t'emk̲wáṅ [t'em k̲waṅ] chop (someone's) head off. *verb(t).*

t'emshán [t'em shan] braid (something). *verb(t).*

t'éṁshen [t'eṁ shen] chopped foot, have a. *verb(i).*

t'emshíṁ [t'em shiṁ] braid. *verb(i).*

t'emshk̲wáṁ [t'emsh k̲waṁ] braid one's own hair. *verb(i).*

t'éṁshn [t'eṁ shn] hurt one's foot; bump one's foot. *verb(i).*

t'emt'ám [t'em t'am] go astray. *verb(i).*

t'émt'em [t'em t'em] wren; snowbird. *noun.*

t'émt'em [t'em t'em] cagey, be. *verb(i).*

t'émt'eṁn [t'em t'e ṁn] chop (something) up. *verb(t).*

t'emt'emuyíṁ [t'em t'e mu yiṁ] patch up all the time. *verb(i).*

t'émt'emuy̓n [t'em t'e mu y̓n] repair (them) all the time. *verb(t).*

t'éṁus [t'e ṁus] hurt one's face. *verb(i).*

t'émuy̓en [t'e mu y̓en] patch (something) up; repair (something). *verb(t).*

t'émuy̓íṁ [t'e mu y̓iṁ] repair; patch up. *verb(i).*

t'émuy̓n [t'e mu y̓n] repair (something); patch (something) up. *verb(t).*

t'em̓xw gooseberry [wild]. *noun.*
t'em̓xwáy̓ [t'em̓ xway̓] wild gooseberry bush; gooseberry bush, wild. *noun.*
t'ep heavy paste. *noun.*
t'es go down [about swelling]. *verb(i).*
t'éskw'em [t'es kw'em] creak. *verb(i).*
t'éskw'i7n [t'es kw'i 7n] creak. *verb(i).*
t'et'em̓án [t'e t'e m̓an] getting (something) out of the way, be. *verb(t).*
t'ét'emen [t'e t'e men] chopping (something), be. *verb(t).*
t'et'eninwilh [t'e t'e nin wilh] line up canoes. *verb(i).*
t'ét'eskw'i7n [t'e t'es kw'i 7n] creaking, be. *verb(i).*
t'ét'ey̓k̲i [t'e t'ey̓ k̲i] soaking, be [about dried salmon in water]. *verb(i).*
t'ét'ey̓k̲wm [t'e t'ey̓ k̲wm] throw off sparks; cause many sparks. *verb(i).*
t'et'i7náy̓en̓ [t'e t'i7 na y̓en̓] side. *noun.*
t'et'mítel̓ [t'et' mi tel'] determine which team gets the extra stick and begins holding the bones in **slhahál**. *verb(i).*
t'ets' bitter. *adjective.*
t'éwelek̲w ~ t'éwlik̲w [t'e we lek̲w] barbecued salmon head; skin, with attached flesh, that is peeled off whole barbecued salmon heads. *noun.*
t'éwlik̲w ~ t'éwelek̲w [t'ew lik̲w] barbecued salmon head; skin, with attached flesh, that is peeled off whole barbecued salmon heads. *noun.*
t'exwt'áxw [t'exw t'axw] put away in a box and fall out, be. *verb(i).*
t'exwt'áxwan̓ [t'exw t'a xwan̓] take some of (something) out of a container; take (things) out one by one. *verb(t).*
t'exwt'áxwi7 [t'exw t'a xwi7] out of [a container], get. *verb(i).*
t'éx̲malhsha7 [t'ex̲ malh sha7] sixty. *numeral.*
t'éx̲t'ex̲ts [t'ex̲ t'ex̲ts] have one's mouth open; open mouth, be with an; with an open mouth, be [as from surprise]. *verb(i).*
t'ex̲t'x̲áchxwem [t'ex̲t' x̲ach xwem] branchy, be. *verb(i).*
t'ex̲t'x̲áy̓us [t'ex̲t' x̲a y̓us] eyes open, have one's. *verb(i).*
t'ex̲tsám̓ [t'ex̲ tsam̓] open one's mouth. *verb(i).*
t'éykw'tsut [t'eykw' tsut] grumble. *verb(i).*
t'ey̓k̲án ~ t'éy̓k̲ay̓en [t'ey̓ k̲an] soak (something). *verb(t).*
t'éy̓k̲ay̓en ~ t'ey̓k̲án [t'ey̓ k̲a y̓en] soak (something). *verb(t).*
t'éy̓k̲i [t'ey̓ k̲i] soaked, be [about dried salmon in water]. *verb(i).*
t'ey̓k̲wm [t'ey̓ k̲wm] throw off large sparks; throw off large chips of glowing [cedar] wood; flame; spark. *verb(i).*
t'eyt'éykw' [t'ey t'eykw'] mad at oneself, be getting; complaining, be; grumbling, be. *verb(i).*
t'éyt'ey̓k̲wm [t'ey t'ey̓ k̲wm] spark; throw off sparks. *verb(i).*
t'íchim [ti chim] swim. *verb(i).*
t'ík̲'i [t'i k̲'i] mushy, become. *verb(i).*
t'ik̲w [t'ik̲w] cold [about air or weather]. *adjective.*
t'ík̲wi7 [t'i k̲wi7] cold, get [about air or weather]; cold, be getting [about air or weather]. *verb(i).*
t'ík̲wi7nitm [t'i k̲wi7 ni tm] caught by cold weather, get. *verb(p).*
t'ik̲wmámin [t'ik̲w ma min] cold inside a house. *adjective.*
t'ík̲w'i [t'i k̲w'i] soft, become [about fish]. *verb(i).*
t'ín̓in̓ [t'i n̓in̓] line (them) up in a row. *verb(t).*
t'in̓ín̓tsut [t'i n̓in̓ tsut] walk alongside of it. *verb(i).*
t'ít'ichim [t'i t'i chim] swimming, be. *verb(i).*
t'ít'ik̲wi7 [t'i t'i k̲wi7] time between autumn and early winter, be the; cold, be getting. *verb(i).*
t'ít'ixwi7 [t'i t'i xwi7] coming down, be; descending, be [e.g., from a hill]. *verb(i).*
t'íts'em [t'i ts'em] ooze out. *verb(i).*
t'íw̓in [t'i w̓in] move (something) to less heat; remove (something) from the fire. *verb(t).*
t'íw̓tes [t'iw̓ tes] amazed at such speed, be. *verb(i).*
t'ixw [t'ixw] descend [e.g., from a hill]; reach level country. *verb(i).* flat land. *adjective.*
t'íxwi [t'i xwi] down, be; descend; go down. *verb(i).*

t'íxwiṅ [t'i xwiṅ] take (something) down. *verb(t).*
t'íx̱iyachi7m [t'i x̱i ya chi 7m] put up hand to protect oneself. *verb(i).*
t'i7n [t'i 7n] deer call, make a; make a deer call. *verb(i).*
t'í7nten [t'i 7n ten] deer-calling instrument. *noun.*
t'í7tk̲em [t'i7t k̲em] soaked, be. *verb(i).*
t'kwínas ~ t'kwínus [t' kwi nas] choke; stuck in throat, be; go down the wrong pipe. *verb(i).*
t'kwínus ~ t'kwínas [t' kwi nus] choke; stuck in throat, be; go down the wrong pipe. *verb(i).*
t'kw'ámyexw [t' kwam yexw] root [general term]. *noun.*
t'kw'íṁ [t' kw'iṁ] dig; dig a pit; cut oneself off from someone. *verb(i).*
t'kw'íṁek̲ [t' kw'i ṁek̲] deadfall; snag; driftwood. *noun.*
t'k̲et [t' k̲et] accuse (someone); belittle (someone); insult (someone). *verb(t).*
t'k̲'ax̱ [t' k̲ax̱] fall backwards. *verb(i).*
t'k̲wémen [t' k̲we men] axe [see also k̲w'ak̲wemén ~ k̲w'k̲wémn]. *noun.*
t'k̲w'aẏch [t k̲w'aẏch] take a short cut; cut across (water or mountains); go across a stretch of water where the opposite shore is closest. *verb(i).*
t'k̲w'eṅ [t' k̲w'eṅ] break loose. *verb(i).*
t'k̲w'iṁ [t' k̲w'iṁ] cut up; chop. *verb(i).*
t'pi [t' pi] soggy, become. *verb(i).*
t'sháyen [t' sha yen] ears full of wax, have; wax, have one's ears be full of wax. *verb(i).*
t'úkwiẏen [t'u kwi ẏen] bounce away; bound. *verb(i).*
t'ukw' [t'ukw'] go home. *verb(i).*
t'ukw'áẏm [t'u kw'a ẏm] wish to go home; want to go home. *verb(i).*
t'ukw's [t'ukw's] take (something) home; bring (something) home. *verb(t).*
t'ut [t'ut] former; previously. *adverb.*
t'út'lhem [t'ut' lhem] flea. *noun.*
t'út'lhemántm [t'ut' lhe man tm] flea-ridden, be. *verb(p).*
t'út'ukw' [t'u t'ukw'] going home, be. *verb(i).*
t'út'ukw's [t'u t'ukw's] bringing (something) home, be; taking (something) home, be. *verb(t).*
t'uẏt [t'uẏt] medicine. *noun.*
t'uẏtenam [t'uẏ te nam] taking medicine, be. *verb(i).*
t'uẏtenamen [t'uẏ te na men] give (someone) medicine. *verb(t).*
t'úẏtentsut [t'uẏ ten tsut] take medicine. *verb(i).*
t'uẏtn [t'uẏ tn] administer medicine to (someone); give medicine to (someone). *verb(t).*
t'u7 [t'u7] pull a muscle; strain; strained, be. *verb(i).*
t'ú7ach [t'u 7ach] sprained hand, have a. *adjective.*
t'ú7achen [t'u 7a chen] pull a muscle in (someone's) hand. *verb(t).*
t'u7k̲w [t'u7k̲w] pull a muscle in one's head. *verb(i).*
t'ú7xwaẏ [t'u7 xwaẏ] balsam fir; white fir. *noun.*
t'x̱atsn [t'x̱a tsn] three-year old deer [with two-pronged antlers]. *noun.*
t'x̱áẏus [t'x̱a ẏus] lightning. *noun.*
t'x̱áẏusm [t'x̱a ẏu sm] lightning; open one's eyes. *verb(i).*
t'x̱áẏusmnumut [t'x̱a ẏu sm nu mut] open one's eyes; able to open one's eyes, be. *verb(i).*

Tl' tl'

tl'a of the, a; to the, a; by the, a; {oblique case}. *determiner.*
tl'ákwan [tl'a kwan] stamp (something); mark (something). *verb(t).*
tl'ákw'x̲en [tl'akw' x̲en] goose. *noun.*
tl'ak̲t long [space or time]. *adjective.*
tl'ak̲t lhk̲aych' [tl'ak̲t lh k̲aych'] December; last month of the year. *noun.*
tl'ák̲tamats' [tl'ak̲ ta mats'] long torso, have a. *adjective.*
tl'ák̲taw̓txw [tl'ak̲ taw̓ txw] longhouse. *noun.*
tl'ák̲tax̲an [tl'ak̲ ta x̲an] long-sided house; longhouse. *verb(i).*
tl'ák̲tay̓ch [tl'ak̲ tay̓ch] long hair, have; long back, have a. *adjective.*
tl'ák̲tay̓k̲wem [tl'ak̲ tay̓ k̲wem] tall [about a person]. *adjective.*
tl'ák̲tiw̓a [tl'ak̲ ti w̓a] tall [about a tree]. *adjective.*
tl'ák̲tiyups [tl'ak̲ ti yups] ring-necked pheasant. *noun.*
tl'ák̲tus [tl'ak̲ tus] long face, have a; long-faced, be. *adjective.*
tl'ák̲wan̓ [tl'a k̲wan̓] stamp (something). *verb(t).*
tl'ák̲wentsut [tl'a k̲wen tsut] snow heavy flakes. *verb(i).*
tl'ak̲w' all accounted for, be; accounted for, be all. *verb(i).*
tl'alt keep (something). *verb(t).*
tl'ál̓x̲en [tl'al' x̲en] snowshoe; snowshoes. *noun.*
tl'álhem [tl'a lhem] salt; salt water. *noun.*
tl'am enough, be. *verb(i).*
tl'amt do (something) [about group]. *verb(t).*
tl'an when I. *clitic.*
tl'ap when you all. *clitic.*
tl'ápat [tl'a pat] diminish (something); lower (something); slow (something) down; let (something) down; check (something). *verb(t).*
tl'ápatsut [tl'a pa tsut] hold oneself in check. *verb(i).*
tl'as when s/he; when it; when they. *clitic.*
tl'asíp [tl'a sip] licorice root; licorice tea [type of fern found on maple tree]; maple syrup; maple sugar. *noun.*
tl'ashn ~ tl'a7áshn ~ tl'a7áshen [tl'a shn] feast; party; dance. *noun.* give a potlatch; invite to a feast. *verb(i).*
tl'ashnáw̓txw [tl'ash naw̓ txw] party house; dance house [see also **milha7áw'txw**]. *noun.*
tl'at when we. *clitic.*
tl'átl'i [tl'a tl'i] venture; try. *verb(i).*
tl'áts'en [tl'a ts'en] make (something) tight; stop (something) leaking. *verb(t).*
tl'axw when you. *clitic.*
tl'áx̲wetem [tl'a x̲we tem] laugh hard. *verb(p).*
tl'ay still; yet; as previously [always preceded by **men**]. *clitic.*
tl'áyayax̲its' [tl'a ya ya x̲its'] die in one's sleep. *verb(i).*
tl'a7áshen ~ tl'ashn ~ tl'a7áshn [tl'a 7a shen] feast; party; dance. *noun.* give a potlatch; invite to a feast. *verb(i).*
tl'a7áshn ~ tl'ashn ~ tl'a7áshen [tl'a 7a shn] feast; party; dance. *noun.* invite to a potlatch; give a potlatch. *verb(i).*
tl'a7í [tl'a 7i] expensive, become. *verb(i).*
tl'a7ímen ~ tl'a7ímin [tl'a 7i men] vein; sinew. *noun.*
tl'a7ímin ~ tl'a7ímen [tl'a 7i min] vein; sinew. *noun.*
tl'a7m [tl'a 7m] get a wife by blanket marriage; wife by blanket marriage, get a; Indian proposal, make an; make an Indian proposal; proposal, make an Indian. *verb(i).*
tl'ech close together, be [with small openings; e.g., about stakes of a fence or mesh of a net]. *verb(i).*
tl'échptn [tl'echp tn] awl; piercer. *noun.*
tl'ékwentsut [tl'e kwen tsut] ease off [about pain]. *verb(i).*
tl'ek̲ break out [about bunch of pimples or rashes]. *verb(i).*
tl'ek̲tín [tl'ek̲ tin] lungs. *noun.*

tl'ek̲ttl'ák̲ti7k̲in [tl'ek̲t tl'ak̲ ti7 k̲in] long-haired [about an animal]. *adjective.*
tl'ek̲ttl'ák̲tshn [tl'ek̲t tl'ak̲ tshn] long-legged; long legs, have. *adjective.*
tl'ek̲túẏt [tl'ek̲ tuẏt] long coat; overcoat. *noun.*
tl'ek̲' black. *adjective.*
tl'ek̲'tn [tl'ek̲' tn] liver; gall. *noun.*
tl'ék̲wentem [tl'e k̲wen tem] easing, be [about a poultice applied]. *verb(p).*
tl'ek̲w' dark. *adjective.*
tl'ek̲w'mámin [tl'ek̲w' ma min] dark inside a house. *adjective.*
tl'elákwan [tl'e la kwan] in great sorrow or trouble, be; sorrow, be in great; trouble, be in great. *verb(i).*
tl'elakwaṅánan [tl'e la kwa ṅa nan] blow [as in an unfortunate event]; misfortune. *noun.*
tl'elekwán [tl'e le kwan] have something bad happen; receive a blow [figuratively]. *verb(i).*
tl'eĺíṁ [tl'e l'iṁ] receive help; receive much help from someone. *verb(i).*
tl'eĺíṁntsut [tl'e l'i ṁn tsut] rely on someone. *verb(i).*
tl'eltl'élnup [tl'el tl'el nup] home settlement; place of origin; real home. *noun.*
tl'elhnáyem [tl'elh na yem] hunt mountain goat. *verb(i).*
tl'elhnáym ~ t'elhnáym [tl'elh naym] go on a prolonged hunting trip [camping in the mountains]. *verb(i).*
tl'emkw'án [tl'em kw'an] crack (something) with one's teeth [e.g., nits, gum, sunflower seeds]. *verb(t).*
tl'émk̲en [tl'em k̲en] all day, be; all night, be; whole day or night, be a; do for a whole day or whole night. *verb(i).*
tl'emk̲'áẏ [tl'em k̲'aẏ] Western yew tree. *noun.*
tl'emtl'íṁ [tl'em tl'iṁ] go short of. *verb(i).*
tl'ení [tl'e ni] deer [term used only in **syewen**]. *noun.* dance a deer dance. *verb(i).*
tl'enk̲ ~ tl'e7énk̲ give a potlatch. *verb(i).* potlatch. *noun.*
tl'enk̲áẇtxw ~ tl'e7enk̲áẇtxw [tl'en k̲aẇ txw] potlatch house. *noun.*
tl'eṅsh rip. *verb(i).*
tl'eptl'áp [tl'ep tl'ap] numb. *adjective.*
tl'epx̲wáṅ [tl'ep x̲waṅ] throw (things); drop (small objects) [producing a rattling sound]. *verb(t).*
tl'épx̲weṁ [tl'ep x̲weṁ] fall [about a bunch of stuff]; drop out of something. *verb(i).*
tl'estl'ís [tl'es tl'is] green; pale [colour of grass]. *adjective.*
tl'esh rip off; released because hooked-up part rips, be [e.g., fish]. *verb(i).*
tl'éshtl'ensh [tl'esh tl'ensh] ripped, be [e.g., fish]. *verb(i).*
tl'eshts rip off [about a fish on a hook]. *verb(i).*
tl'étx̲em [tl'et x̲em] slippery, be; shiny, be [e.g. wood]. *verb(i).*
tl'etl' grass used for basket-making, type of. *noun.*
tl'etl'atás [tl'e tl'a tas] curious. *adjective.*
tl'etl'ch'ál̓k̲m [tl'etl' ch'al' k̲m] stalk an animal. *verb(i).*
tl'etl'ewk̲'éṁ [tl'e tl'ew k̲'eṁ] shining, be; shiny, be. *verb(i).*
tl'etl'exwítaẏ [tl'e tl'e xwi taẏ] gamble. *verb(i).*
tl'étl'iyi7 [tl'e tl'i yi7] middle-aged, be [literally, stop one's development]. *verb(i).*
tl'étl'iyi7 stélmexw [tl'e tl'i yi7 stel mexw] middle-aged person. *noun.*
tl'etl'k̲w'í7 [tl'etl' k̲w'i7] getting dark, be; dark, be getting. *verb(i).*
tl'etl'shí7k̲w [tl'etl' shi7k̲w] defecate. *verb(i).*
tl'etl'shí7k̲ws [tl'etl' shi7 k̲ws] defecate (something). *verb(t).*
tl'etl'shí7k̲wstem [tl'etl' shi7k̲w stem] have something in one's feces. *verb(p).*
tl'ets' packed tight, be. *verb(i).*
tl'éts'em [tl'e ts'em] close together; knitted tight, be; watertight, be. *verb(i).*
tl'ets'úyen [tl'e ts'u yen] cram (something); stuff (something); force (something) full. *verb(t).*
tl'ets'wíyen [tl'ets' wi yen] pack them tightly together. *verb(i).*
tl'éxwen [tl'e xwen] pick (blueberries or huckleberries with leaves). *verb(t).*
tl'exwtl'exwénk̲ [tl'exw tl'e xwenk̲] winning all the time, be. *verb(i).*

tl'ex̲w hard; strong [about materials]. *adjective.*

tl'éx̲wtl'éx̲w [tl'ex̲w tl'ex̲w] oyster. *noun.*

tl'ex̲wtl'ex̲wíẇilh [tl'ex̲w tl'e x̲wi ẇilh] constipation, have; indigestion, have. *verb(i).*

tl'éẏek̲wayusm ~ tl'iyik̲wayúsm [tl'e ẏe k̲wa yu sm] close one's eyes tightly. *verb(i).*

tl'eyk̲' get caught; caught, get; trapped, get. *verb(i).*

tl'eyk̲'áls [tl'ey k̲'als] put fish on split barbecuing stick. *verb(i).*

tl'eyk̲'án [tl'ey k̲'an] squeeze (something) with tongs; grip (something); pinch (something). *verb(t).*

tl'eyk̲'áẏstn [tl'ey k̲'aẏ stn] tongs; stick for arranging things in a fire. *noun.*

tl'eyk̲'íts'tn [tl'ey k̲'its' tn] clothespin. *noun.*

tl'éyk̲'nexw [tl'eyk̲' nexw] catch (an animal) in a trap; have caught (an animal) in a trap. *verb(t).*

tl'éyk̲'shen [tl'eyk̲' shen] trap [leg-hold]; snare. *noun.* get one's foot caught. *verb(i).*

tl'e7énk̲ ~ tl'enk̲ [tl'e 7enk̲] give a potlatch. *verb(i).* potlatch. *noun.*

tl'e7enk̲áẇtxw ~ tl'enk̲áẇtxw [tl'e 7en k̲aẇ txw] potlatch house. *noun.*

tl'ich'ayúsm [tl'i ch'a yu sm] peek; spy. *verb(i).*

tl'ích'it [tl'i ch'it] sneak up to (something); stalk (something). *verb(t).*

tl'ích'itsut [tl'i ch'i tsut] go very quietly. *verb(i).*

tl'ích'k̲aẏusem [tl'ich' k̲a ẏu sem] look at sideways; peep; peer. *verb(i).*

tl'íkw'en [tl'i kw'en] kinnikinnick berry. *noun.*

tl'íkw'enaẏ [tl'i kw'e naẏ] kinnikinnick berry plant. *noun.*

tl'ik̲ [tl'ik̲] arrive here; arrive. *verb(i).*

tl'ik̲ chexw [tl'ik̲ chexw] Hello [said to person arriving]; You have arrived. *sentence.*

tl'ik̲n [tl'i k̲n] approach (someone) sexually. *verb(t).*

tl'ik̲nálhn [tl'ik̲ na lhn] bring oneself here, manage to. *verb(i).*

tl'ík̲nexw [tl'ik̲ nexw] brought (something) here, have. *verb(t).*

tl'ik̲númut [tl'ik̲ nu mut] get here, manage to [similar to **tl'ik̲sténaṁut**]. *verb(i).*

tl'ik̲s [tl'ik̲s] bring (something) here; bring (something). *verb(t).*

tl'ik̲sténaṁut [tl'ik̲ ste na ṁut] get here, manage to [similar to **tl'ik̲númut**]. *verb(i).*

tl'ík̲shi [tl'ik̲ shi] bring it to (someone). *verb(t).*

tl'ík̲'eni7tn [tl'i k̲'e ni7 tn] loom, vertical pole of a; pole of a loom, vertical. *noun.*

tl'ik̲w'm [tl'i k̲w'm] smoke [e.g., about a stove]. *verb(i).*

tl'ími7k̲in [tl'i mi7 k̲in] dog [short-haired type]. *noun.*

tl'íṅa [tl'i ṅa] eulachon grease; eulachon oil. *noun.*

tl'íni ~ tl'í7ni [tl'i ni] desire (someone); wish for (something). *verb(t).*

tl'ípentsut [tl'i pen tsut] curl up; disguise oneself; hide. *verb(i).*

tl'íp'intsut [tl'i p'in tsut] duck down. *verb(i).*

tl'is [tl'is] green. *adjective.*

tl'ísitsut [tl'i si tsut] inquire; try to find out. *verb(i).*

tl'ísi7 [tl'i si7] green, get; pale, get. *verb(i).*

tl'ísusi7 [tl'i su si7] green, get. *verb(i).*

tl'is7ántsut [tl'is 7an tsut] pale, become. *verb(i).*

tl'itl'ch'álk̲m [tl'itl' chal' k̲m] sneak up. *verb(i).*

tl'ítl'elx̲iws [tl'i tl'el x̲iws] Dolly Varden trout; speckled trout. *noun.*

tl'ítl'ep [tl'i tl'ep] reef. *noun.*

tl'ítl'eptn [tl'i tl'ep tn] dress. *noun.*

tl'itl'eptnáẏk̲ [tl'i tl'ept naẏk̲] underpants; undershirt [see also **tl'itl'eptnáẏts'a**]. *noun.*

tl'itl'eptnáẏts'a [tl'i tl'ept naẏ ts'a] undershirt [see also **tl'itl'eptnáẏk̲**]. *noun.*

tl'itl'ich'ítsut [tl'i tl'i ch'i tsut] sneak along. *verb(i).*

tl'ítl'ik̲ [tl'i tl'ik̲] arriving, be. *verb(i).*

tl'ítl'ik̲w'm [tl'i tl'i k̲w'm] smoking, be [e.g. about a stove]. *verb(i).*

tl'ítl'isi7 [tl'i tl'i si7] jaundiced. *adjective.* jaundice. *noun.*

tl'ítl'ish [tl'i tl'ish] go check up on someone; check up on someone, go. *verb(i).*

tl'ítl'ix̲waẏ [tl'i tl'i x̲waẏ] brook trout. *noun.*

tl'ítl'i7aẏlh [tl'i tl'i 7a ẏlh] love one's child. *verb(i).*

tl'iẇ [tl'iẇ] run away [about a captive]. *verb(i).*

tl'íẇnexw [tl'iẇ nexw] have liberated (someone); liberated (someone), have; free (someone). *verb(t).*

tl'íẇnumut [tl'iẇ nu mut] escape [from something]; manage to escape. *verb(i).*

tl'íxwans [tl'i xwans] lose a tooth. *verb(i).*

tl'ix̲áṅtsut [tl'i x̲aṅ tsut] throb [about a sore]. *verb(i).*

tl'íya7 ~ tl'í7i7 [tl'i ya7] stop; quit. *verb(i).*

tl'íyen [tl'i yen] stop (something); quit (something). *verb(t).*

tl'iyik̲wayúsm ~ tl'éẏek̲wayusm [tl'i yi k̲wa yu sm] close one's eyes tightly. *verb(i).*

tl'iyík̲wiṅ [tl'i yi k̲wiṅ] squeeze (something). *verb(t).*

tl'íyi7 ~ tl'íya7 [tl'i yi7] stop; quit. *verb(i).*

tl'i7 [tl'i7] difficult; dear; expensive; valuable; important; dangerous; excessive. *adjective.*

tl'i7áẇ [tl'i 7aẇ] help with feast; help, just; go to another village to look for wife. *verb(i).*

tl'í7neẇas [tl'i7 ne ẇas] love one another; like each other; have a liking for each other. *verb(i).*

tl'í7ni ~ tl'íni [tl'i7 ni] desire (someone); wish for (something). *verb(t).*

tl'i7s [tl'i7s] like (someone); love (someone); want (something). *verb(t).*

tl'i7sténaṁut [tl'i7 ste na ṁut] love oneself; in love with oneself, be. *verb(i).*

tl'í7stway [tl'i7 stway] love one another; like each other. *verb(i).*

tl'í7tsut [tl'i7 tsut] make oneself hard to see. *verb(i).*

tl'kwéni7 [tl' kwe ni7] deaf, be. *verb(i).*

tl'kwéni7i ~ tl'kwní7i [tl' kwe ni 7i] become deaf; deaf, become. *verb(i).*

tl'kwní7i ~ tl'kwéni7i [tl'kw ni 7i] become deaf; deaf, become. *verb(i).*

tl'k̲ílh [tl' k̲ilh] give birth. *verb(i).*

tl'k̲íws [tl' k̲iws] rash, have a. *verb(i).*

tl'k̲w'ánan [tl' k̲w'a nan] darkness. *noun.*

tl'k̲w'aẏ [tl' k̲w'aẏ] salmon milt; soft salmon roe. *noun.*

tl'k̲w'ík̲en [tl' k̲w'i k̲en] dark spot on the road. *noun.*

tl'k̲w'i7 [tl' k̲w'i7] dark, get. *verb(i).*

tl'k̲w'í7nitem [tl' k̲wi7 ni tem] caught by darkness, get. *verb(p).*

tl'pat [tl' pat] bag; inner cedar bark basket; cedar bark basket [inner]. *noun.*

tl'pi7 [tl' pi7] pale, get. *verb(i).*

tl'shátsut [tl' sha tsut] scatter in all directions. *verb(i).*

tl'sháx̲en [tl' sha x̲en] burst (something) open. *verb(t).*

tl'tl'áwik̲w [tl' tl'a wik̲w] hat made of straw; straw hat. *noun.*

tl'uk̲'mí7 [tl'uk̲' mi7] become shiny; shiny, become. *verb(i).*

tl'uk̲wí7 [tl'u k̲wi7] crawl into something; go hide [as of a fish or rat, etc.]. *verb(i).*

tl'úk̲wun [tl'u k̲wun] hide (something). *verb(t).*

tl'úk̲w'un [tl'u k̲w'un] stick (something) into; force (something) in; plug (something) in. *verb(t).*

tl'úk̲w'wilh [tl'uk̲w' wilh] cork a boat. *verb(i).*

tl'up [tl'up] numb [from sitting in one position]. *verb(i).*

tl'úpshen [tl'up shen] fall asleep [about leg]; numb feet, have. *adjective.*

tl'up' [tl'up'] retracted, be; driven back, be [e.g., a wick in a lamp or nail in the end of a stick]. *verb(i).*

tl'úp'un [tl'u p'un] turn down (a light). *verb(t).*

tl'utl'íẇ [tl'u tl'iẇ] flee [about group of people]. *verb(i).*

tl'uts' [tl'uts'] close together, be. *verb(i).*

tl'úts'achxw [tl'u ts'a chxw] limbs close together, have; close-limbed [about tree]. *adjective.*

tl'úts'uṅ [tl'u ts'uṅ] put (them) close together; pack (them) close together. *verb(t).*

tl'ú7u [tl'u 7u] resting after a pain, be. *verb(i).*

tl'xwenk̲ win a contest; win. *verb(i).*

tl'xwet beat (someone) in a contest; vanquish (someone); win (something); master (something) [e.g., a language]. *verb(t).*

tl'xwétem [tl'xwe tem] overdo something; lose [the game or the fight]; overpowered, be. *verb(p).*

tl'x̲wáy̓lhem [tl'x̲way̓ lhem] brood; sit on eggs. *verb(i).*

tl'x̲wi7 [tl'x̲wi7] hard, get; harden; congeal. *verb(i).*

Ts ts

-ts mouth {full word: **tsútsin**}; lip; edge; opening. *suffix.*
-ts me. *suffix.*
tsaaẏ [tsaaẏ] go to see [about group]; interested in someone coming, be; come out of the house to look at something unusual or interesting [see also **ts'ats'alh**]. *verb(i).*
tsach send things. *verb(i).*
tsahímelh [tsa hi melh] fish with a harpoon; gaff. *verb(i).*
tsákw'shenam [tsakw' she nam] stretch legs. *verb(i).*
tsak̲w bleed. *verb(i).*
tsak̲wáya7n [tsa k̲wa ya 7n] bleeding ear, have a. *verb(i).*
tsam̓á [tsa m̓a] second; two times; twice. *verb(i).*
tsam̓án̓tsut [tsa m̓an̓ tsut] make a second attempt; attempt a second time; try a second time. *verb(i).*
tsámaxwilh [tsa ma xwilh] two containers [pots, pans, canoes]. *numeral.*
tsám̓ich [tsa m̓ich] two hundred. *numeral.*
tsámyas [tsam yas] two days. *numeral.*
tsántem [tsan tem] breathe hard from being tired; pant. *verb(p).*
tsápnexw [tsap nexw] distract (someone). *verb(t).*
tsápshen [tsap shen] less, get; get less [about rain]; stop raining; clear up. *verb(i).*
tsásan̓ [tsa san̓] feel (something) with hands; perceive (something) by touch. *verb(t).*
tsásnexw [tsas nexw] feel (something). *verb(t).*
tsatsk̲s ~ tsa7tsk̲s [tsats k̲s] feel around for fish with butt end of harpoon. *verb(i).*
tsáẇin [tsa ẇin] coho. *noun.*
tsáxwtsexwsténam̓ut [tsaxw tsexw ste na m̓ut] tossing, be [when sleeping]; throwing oneself around, be. *verb(i).*
tsáx̲wam [tsa x̲wam] stretch out one's arms; reach out; stick out one's hand. *verb(i).*
tsayiyíts'entem [tsa yi yi ts'en tem] search (one's) clothing. *verb(p).*
tsá7tsaxw [tsa7 tsaxw] happy; joyful; content; glad. *adjective.*
tsá7tsaxwi7 [tsa7 tsa xwi7] happy, get. *verb(i).*
tsá7tsaxwni [tsa7 tsaxw ni] happy about (someone), be; happy for (someone), be; content about (something), be. *verb(t).*
tsa7tsk̲s ~ tsatsk̲s [tsa7ts k̲s] feel around for fish with butt end of the harpoon. *verb(i).*
tsehénem [tse he nem] do a war dance; war dance, do a; dance, do a war. *verb(i).*
tsekw finish [e.g., a story]. *verb(i).*
tsekw pulled, be. *verb(i).*
tsékwem̓ [tse kwem̓] want to leave but something holds one back. *verb(i).*
tsékwem̓ni [tse kwem̓ ni] interested in (something), be. *verb(t).*
tsékwen [tse kwen] pull (something); tug (something). *verb(t).*
tsékwilh ~ tsékwilhen [tse kwilh] pull a canoe ashore. *verb(i).*
tsékwilhen ~ tsékwilh [tse kwi lhen] pull (a canoe) ashore. *verb(t).*
tsekwk̲ám [tsekw k̲am] pull oneself back; withdraw; back away. *verb(i).*
tsékwtsekwen [tsekw tse kwen] pull (them) on. *verb(t).*
tsék̲en [tse k̲en] stand (something) up [e.g., pole or mast]. *verb(t).*
tsek̲tsek̲shenám̓ [tsek̲ tsek̲ she nam̓] on back with feet put up in the air, be. *verb(i).*
tsek̲tsek̲wús ~ tsék̲tsek̲wus [tsek̲ tse k̲wus] lying down on one's back, be; looking up, be; looking upwards, be. *verb(i).*
tsék̲tsek̲wus ~ tsek̲tsek̲wús [tsek̲ tse k̲wus] lying down on one's back, be;

looking up, be; looking upwards, be. *verb(i).*

tsek̲tsk̲áy̓ek̲wshn [tsek̲ts k̲a y̓ek̲w shn] lie on back with knees drawn up. *verb(i).*

tsek̲wíyu7 [tse k̲wi yu7] dig up the bones of the dead; exhume body. *verb(i).*

tsek̲wlh [tse k̲wlh] Indian paint fungus [a dark brown substance obtained from certain trees, which is boiled and used as a face lotion to prevent sunburn]. *noun.*

tsek̲wúsem [tse k̲wu sem] look up; look upwards. *verb(i).*

tsek̲wyulh [tsek̲w yulh] unidentified mortuary office ["when the body of the dead is moved, the **tsek̲wyulh** picks up the bones"]. *noun.*

tsek̲w' worked up, get really [about Indian dancer]. *verb(i).*

tsek̲w'new̓ásen [tsek̲w' ne w̓a sen] pile upon (one another). *verb(t).*

tsék̲w'ya [tsek̲w' ya] dog whelp. *noun.*

tselk̲w'án [tsel k̲w'an] kick (someone). *verb(t).*

tselk̲w'ím̓ [tsel k̲w'im̓] kick. *verb(i).*

tselk̲w'k̲án [tselk̲w' k̲an] kick (someone) in the rear. *verb(t).*

tsélk̲w'nexw [tselk̲w' nexw] kick (someone) accidentally; manage to kick (someone); have kicked (someone). *verb(t).*

tseltselk̲w'án [tsel tsel k̲w'an] kicking (something) repeatedly, be. *verb(t).*

tsépshan [tsep shan] cut (something) a little at a time. *verb(t).*

tsestsástem [tses tsas tem] feel (someone) up. *verb(p).*

tsétsantem [tse tsan tem] breathe rapidly. *verb(p).*

tsétsaw̓an [tse tsa w̓an] satisfy (someone). *verb(t).*

tsetséy̓k̲s [tse tsey̓k̲s] coming to an end, be. *verb(i).*

tsetsiw̓ántsut [tse tsi w̓an tsut] satisfied with self, be. *verb(i).*

tsetsíx̲w [tse txix̲w] puberty, reach; reach puberty [about a female]. *verb(i).*

tsetsiy̓ák̲wustay̓ [tse tsi y̓a k̲wus tay̓] share; divide. *verb(i).*

tsetskw'átsut [tsets kw'a tsut] running, be. *verb(i).*

tsetskw'ít [tsets kw'it] frighten (someone); startle (someone). *verb(t).*

tsétsxwes [tsets xwes] thrown, be. *verb(i).*

tsewás [tse was] flat; level; even; equal; smooth. *adjective.*

tsewásin̓up [tse wa si n̓up] flat land; level ground. *adjective.*

tsewásm [tse wa sm] bet. *verb(i).*

tsewasmín̓ [tse was min̓] bum from (someone); bet (someone). *verb(t).*

tsewasmín̓ [tse was min̓] something used for betting; betting, something used for. *noun.*

tsewásn [tse wa sn] level (something) off; make (something) even. *verb(t).*

tsewátsut chaxw [tse wa tsut chaxw] do your best.; be well prepared. *sentence.*

tsexw hit by something thrown, get; get hit. *verb(i).*

tsexw disappear. *verb(i).*

tsexwáyak̲ap [tse xwa ya k̲ap] die away [about sound]. *verb(i).*

tsexwím̓ [tse xwim] throw. *verb(i).*

tséxwiy̓ek̲w [tse xwi y̓ek̲w] get hit on top of the head; hit on top of the head, get. *verb(i).*

tsexwn [tse xwn] throw something at (someone/something); [aim to] hit (someone/something). *verb(t).*

tséxwnexw [tsexw nexw] hit (something), have; hit (something) accidentally. *verb(t).*

tsexws throw (something); throw (something) down; throw (something) away. *verb(t).*

tsexwstm [tsexw stm] fall over; stroke, have a [literally, get thrown]. *verb(p).*

tsexwshít [tsexw shi] throw to (someone). *verb(t).*

tsexwshítway [tsexw shi way] play catch. *verb(i).*

tsex̲nálhen [tsex̲ na lhen] push by oneself. *verb(i).*

tséx̲ném [tsex̲ nem] pushed, be. *verb(p).*

tséx̲nexw [tsex̲ nexw] pushed (someone), have; push (someone) accidentally. *verb(t).*

tséx̲wus [tse x̲wus] come to a dead end on account of high bluff. *verb(i).*

tsey finished, be; ready, be. *verb(i).*

tséyk̲new̓ásn [tseyk̲ ne w̓a sn] divide (something) up. *verb(t).*

tseyk̲s ~ tsey̓k̲s end; last, be; final, be; end of a story, be the. *verb(i).*

tsey̓k̲s ~ tseyk̲s end; last, be; final, be; end of a story, be the. *verb(i).*

tsey̓k̲sán [tsey̓k̲ san] end (a story); finish (something); make an end of (something). *verb(t).*

tsi [tsi] this, the, a [female, within reach]. *determiner.*

tsíkw'i7n [tsi kw'i 7n] startled, be/get; frightened, be. *verb(i).*

tsik̲ [tsik̲] poked, be/get; stabbed, be/get; speared, be/get. *verb(i).*

tsík̲alap [tsi k̲a lap] stabbed in the thigh, get. **nu chexw tsík̲alap.** Did you get stabbed in the thigh? *verb(i).*

tsik̲alxwtsálhen [tsi k̲alxw tsa lhen] stab at (someone's) tongue. **na wa tsik̲alxwtsálhentem ta sesemáy̓.** the bee was stabbing at his tongue. *verb(t).*

tsik̲alhx̲á7n [tsi k̲alh x̲a 7n] stab (someone) in the throat. *verb(t).*

tsík̲ansn [tsi k̲an sn] stab (someone) in the teeth. *verb(t).*

tsik̲apsámen [tsi k̲ap sa men] stab (someone) in the back of the head. *verb(t).*

tsík̲ay̓ám̓it [tsi k̲a y̓a m̓it] get poked/stabbed in the shoulder; poked in the shoulder, get; stabbed in the shoulder, get. *verb(i).*

tsík̲ay̓ám̓itn [tsi k̲a y̓a m̓i tn] stab (someone) in the shoulder. *verb(t).*

tsik̲áya7ní7n [tsi k̲a ya7 ni 7n] stab (someone) in the ear. *verb(t).*

tsík̲a7an [tsi k̲a 7an] get poked/stabbed in the cheek; stabbed in the cheek, get; poked in the cheek, get. *verb(i).*

tsík̲a7áni7n [tsi k̲a 7a ni 7n] stab (someone) in the cheek. *verb(t).*

tsík̲in̓ [tsi k̲in̓] spear (something); stab (something); poke (something); give (something) a single poke in the fire. *verb(t).*

tsik̲ínas [tsi k̲i nas] get poked/stabbed in the chest; poked in the chest, get; stabbed in the chest, get. *verb(i).*

tsik̲inásn [tsi k̲i na sn] stab (someone) in the chest. *verb(t).*

tsík̲iy̓ek̲w [tsi k̲i y̓ek̲w] get poked/stabbed on the top of the head; poked on the top of the head, get; stabbed on the top of the head, get. *verb(i).*

tsik̲iy̓ek̲wán [tsi k̲i y̓e k̲wan] stab (someone) on the top of the head. *verb(t).*

tsik̲k̲án [tsik̲ k̲an] stab (someone) in the behind. *verb(t).*

tsik̲tsán [tsik̲ tsan] stab (someone) in the mouth. *verb(t).*

tsik̲tsk̲ [tsik̲ tsk̲] get poked/stabbed in the chin; poked in the chin, get; stabbed in the chin, get. *verb(i).*

tsík̲'in [tsi k̲'in] push (something) around the fire; stab (something); stir up (fire); work (something) around in the fire. *verb(t).*

tsík̲'intsut [tsi k̲'in tsut] throb really bad. *verb(i).*

tsik̲wálch [tsi k̲walch] dig up potatoes. *verb(i).*

tsípin̓tsut [tsi pin̓ tsut] duck; stoop; flinch. *verb(i).*

tsipix̲áyx̲ [tsi pi x̲ayx̲] farthest north. *noun.*

tsiplháyus [tsip lha yus] eyelashes [see also **tsíplhten**]. *noun.*

tsíplhten [tsi plh ten] eyelashes [see also **tsiplháyus**]; eyebrows [see also **tsúman**]. *noun.*

tsíptspi7lhten [tsipts pi 7lh ten] bird's nest. *noun.*

tsit [tsit] paint (someone's) face. *verb(t).*

tsítin̓ [tsi tin̓] decoration. *noun.*

tsitín̓en [tsi ti n̓en] blend (something). *verb(t).*

tsitín̓en [tsi ti n̓en] decorate (something/someone). *verb(t).*

tsítsaw̓in [tsi tsa w̓in] coho [small type; see **tsáw'in** and **tsi7tsáw'in**]. *noun.*

tsitsey̓áchis [tsi tse y̓a chis] five animals. *numeral.*

tsítsixw [tsi tsixw] arriving there, be just. *verb(i).*

tsitsíyachis [tsi tis ya chis] five people. *numeral.*

tsítskw'i7n [tsits kw'i 7n] startled, be. *verb(i).*

tsitsk̲ ~ tsi7ts [tsitsk̲] steep; steep terrain. *adjective.*

tsítsut [tsi tsut] paint oneself. *verb(i).*

tsíwa [tsi wa] she here; this one here [female]. *demonstrative.*
tsixw [tsixw] arrive there; get somewhere; reach destination. *verb(i).*
tsixw kwáyl̓es [tsixw kway l'es] tomorrow. *adverb.*
tsíxwach [tsi xwach] reached, be just about. *verb(i).*
tsíxway̓m [tsi xwa y̓m] want to arrive there. *verb(i).*
tsíxwen [tsi xwen] reach (something); arrive at (something). *verb(t).*
tsíxwni [tsixw ni] arrive at (something). *verb(t).*
tsixwnúmut [txixw nu mut] get there; manage to get there. *verb(i).*
tsixws [tsixws] get (someone) there. *verb(t).*
tsix̱ [tsix̱] fast drum beat. *noun.*
tsíx̱iw̓as [tsi x̱i w̓as] paddle rapidly. *verb(i).*
tsix̱shn [tsix̱ shn] take fast steps; walk quickly. *verb(i).*
tsix̱ts [tsix̱ts] speak quickly; talk quickly. *verb(i).*
tsíx̱wem [tsi x̱wem] steady flow, be a. *verb(i).*
tsiyách [tsi yach] loincloth; menstrual pad. *noun.*
tsíyáchis [tsi ya chis] five days. *verb(i).*
tsíyachis ~ tsíyichis [tsi ya chis] five. *numeral.*
tsíyachisálh [tsi ya chi salh] five times. *verb(i).*
tsiyachisálhntsut [tsi ya chi sa lhn tsut] make a fifth attempt; attempt a fifth time; try for the fifth time. *verb(i).*
tsiyachisámats' [tsi ya chi sa mats'] five strands [of wool, rope, etc.]. *numeral.*
tsiyachisáyum̓ [tsi ya chi sa yum̓] five berries. *numeral.*
tsíyachisk̲ [tsi ya chisk̲] five o'clock. *noun.*
tsiyák̲en [tsi ya k̲en] divide (something); divide off (a part from a whole). *verb(t).*
tsíyay̓tstn [tsi yay̓ts tn] table cover. *noun.*
tsiyek̲new̓ásn [tsi yek̲ ne w̓a sn] separate (them). *verb(t).*
tsíyel̓sen [tsi yel' sen] sharpen (a point). *verb(t).*
tsíyel̓stn [tsi yel' stn] whetstone. *noun.*
tsíyel̓txwem [tsi yel't xwem] build a house. *verb(i).*
tsiyéwelhtn [tsi ye welh tn] canoe shed; canoe shelter. *noun.*
tsíyichis ~ tsíyachis [tsi yi chis] five. *numeral.*
tsiyichisálhk̲wu [tsi yi chi salh k̲wu] five rivers. *numeral.*
tsiyichisáns [tsi yi chi sans] five teeth. *numeral.*
tsiyichisáwanexw [tsi yi chi sa wa nexw] five years. *numeral.*
tsiyichisáw̓txw [tsi yi chi saw̓ txw] five houses. *numeral.*
tsiyichisáxwilh [tsi yi chi sa xwilh] five canoes. *numeral.*
tsiyichisáyum̓ [tsi yi chil sa yum̓] five berries. *numeral.*
tsiyichisíwa7 [tsi yi chi si wa7] five trees. *numeral.*
tsíyichisuy̓s [tsi yi chi suy̓s] five dollars; five rocks. *numeral.*
tsiyíchsten [tsi yich sten] tablecloth; table cover. *noun.*
tsi7 [tsi7] have; some, be; there is [available]; exist; born, be. *verb(i).*
tsi7tsáw̓in [tsi7 tsa w̓in] coho [small; see also **tsítsaw'in**]. *noun.*
tsi7tsk̲ [tsi7 tsk̲] steep; steep terrain. *adjective.*
-tsk̲ chin {full word: **slestsk̲**}. *suffix.*
tsk̲álachn [tsk̲a la chn] fall backwards; lie on one's back. *verb(i).*
tsk̲an̓tn [tsk̲an̓ tn] pot hanger. *noun.*
tsúk̲wut [tsu k̲wut] inform on (someone); report on (someone); squeal on (someone); betray (someone); tell on (someone). *verb(t).*
tsúman [tsu man] eyebrow; eyebrows [see also **tsíplhten**]. *noun.*
tsum̓k̲wúy̓shen [tsum̓ k̲wuy̓ shen] sprain one's toe. *verb(i).*
tsun [tsun] tell (someone); order (someone). *verb(t).*
tsuntm [tsun tm] told, be; said, be. *verb(p).*
tsúntsut [tsun tsut] tell oneself something. *verb(i).*
tsúpen [tsu pen] pad (something); wrap (something). *verb(t).*
tsúpiy̓en [tsu pi y̓en] land softly. *verb(i).*
tsut [tsut] say; think; be of the opinion; opinion, be of the; have the idea; idea, have the; make believe. *verb(i).*

tsut [tsut] try. *verb(i).*
tsútsin [tsu tsin] mouth. *noun.*
tsutsuy̓úsem [tsu tsu y̓u sem] erratically swimming back downstream after spawning, be [about salmon]. *verb(i).*
tsúyum̓en [tsu yu m̓en] spend money or blankets on (someone). *verb(t).*
tsúyun [tsu yun] peel (something) [e.g., bark]; remove (something) [e.g., bark]. *verb(t).*
tsu7p [tsu7p] paw for food [about animal]. *verb(i).*
tsxwus [tsxwus] hit in the face, get. *verb(i).*
tsx̱álem [tsx̱a lem] sword fern. *noun.*
tsx̱et shove (someone); push (someone). *verb(t).*
tsx̱im̓ [tsx̱im̓] shove. *verb(i).*
ts7it [ts7it] true. *adjective.*

Ts' ts'

-ts' bones; spine. *suffix.*
-ts'a ~ -its'a ~ -ayts'a ~ -ayts'a7 [-ts'a] clothes. *suffix.*
ts'a ~ ts'aa hit, get; hurt, get; bump. *verb(i).*
ts'aa ~ ts'a [ts'aa] hit, get; hurt, get; bump. *verb(i).*
ts'aak̲w [ts'aak̲w] bumped head, have a; punched in the head, get; bump one's head; hit in the head, get. *verb(i).*
ts'aan ~ ts'an punch (someone); hit (someone). *verb(t).*
ts'aaẏ [ts'aaẏ] shaded, get; sheltered, be [from wind, sun, rain, etc.]. *verb(i).*
ts'áchaṅ [ts'a chaṅ] punch (someone) on the back. *verb(t).*
ts'aháyexwtn [ts'a ha yexw tn] instrument for taking off cedar bark; instrument for beating inner red cedar bark. *noun.*
ts'aháyusn [ts'a ha yu sn] punch (someone) in the eye. *verb(t).*
ts'ahíṁ [ts'a hiṁ] punch; throw punches. *verb(i).*
ts'ahús [ts'a hus] bump one's face; get hit in the face; hit in the face, get. *verb(i).*
ts'ak̲ bald, become; lose one's hair or fur. *verb(i).*
ts'ák̲chus [ts'ak̲ chus] bald forehead, have a. *adjective.*
ts'ak̲s bump one's nose; get hit on one's nose; hit on one's nose, get. *verb(i).*
ts'ak̲sán ~ ts'ák̲san [ts'ak̲ san] punch (someone) in the nose. *verb(t).*
ts'ák̲san ~ ts'ak̲sán [ts'ak̲ san] punch (someone) in the nose. *verb(t).*
ts'ák̲shelik̲w ~ sts'ák̲shelik̲w [ts'ak̲ she lik̲w] rock cod. *noun.*
ts'ak̲' hit, get. *verb(i).*
ts'ák̲'ach [ts'a k̲'ach] hit on the hands, get. *verb(i).*
ts'ák̲'alxwtsalh [ts'a k̲'alxw tsalh] hit on the tongue, get. *verb(i).*
ts'ák̲'an [ts'a k̲'an] hit and crush (something); hit (something) [especially when one takes two things and bumps them together]. *verb(t).*
ts'ák̲'ans [ts'a k̲'ans] hit on the tooth, get. *verb(i).*
ts'ák̲'apsm [ts'a k̲'ap sm] hit on the back of the head or neck, get. *verb(i).*
ts'ák̲'ax̲n [ts'a k̲'ax̲n] hit on the side, get. *verb(i).*
ts'ak̲'ayámit [ts'a k̲'a ya mit] hit on the shoulder, get. *verb(i).*
ts'ák̲'aẏan [ts'a k̲'a ẏan] hit on the ear, get. *verb(i).*
ts'ak̲'ayí7k̲wshen [ts'a k̲'a yi7k̲w shen] hit on the knee, get. *verb(i).*
ts'ák̲'aẏus [ts'a k̲'a ẏus] hit on the eye, get. *verb(i).*
ts'ák̲'a7en [ts'a k̲'a 7en] hit on the cheek, get. *verb(i).*
ts'ak̲'ch [ts'a k̲'ch] hit on the back, get. *verb(i).*
ts'ak̲'chk̲ [ts'ak̲' chk̲] hit on the hip, get. *verb(i).*
ts'ák̲'chus [ts'ak̲' chus] hit on the forehead, get. *verb(i).*
ts'ák̲'inas [ts'a k̲'i nas] hit on the chest, get. *verb(i).*
ts'ák̲'iwilh [ts'a k̲'i wilh] hit on the stomach, get. *verb(i).*
ts'ák̲'iẏek̲w ~ nts'ák̲'iẏek̲w [ts'a k̲'i ẏek̲w] bald. *adjective.*
ts'ak̲'k̲s [ts'ak̲' k̲s] hit on the nose, get. *verb(i).*
ts'ak̲'k̲w hit on the head, get. *verb(i).*
ts'ák̲'neẇasn [ts'ak̲' ne ẇa sn] hit (two things) together. *verb(t).*
ts'ák̲'nexw [ts'ak̲' nexw] have hit (someone); hit (someone) accidentally. *verb(t).*
ts'ak̲'sáẏ [tsak̲' saẏ] hit on the elbow, get. *verb(i).*
ts'ák̲'shenem [ts'ak̲' she nem] powwow dancing, do; dance powwow-style; stamp with foot [as done by **sxw7umten** when calling his power]. *verb(i).*
ts'ak̲'shn [tsa'k̲' shn] hit on the leg, get. *verb(i).*
ts'ak̲'ts hit on the mouth, get. *verb(i).*

ts'ak̲'tsk̲ [ts'ak̲' tsk̲] hit on the chin, get. *verb(i).*

ts'ak̲wáy̓new̓ásn [ts'a k̲way̓ ne w̓a sn] hit (someone) in the pit of the stomach. *verb(t).*

ts'áli7 [ts'a li7] heart [of body]. *noun.*

ts'alút [ts'a lut] grass mat used by sxw7umten as a head cover. *noun.*

ts'álhen [ts'a lhen] dampen (something). *verb(t).*

ts'alhshá7 ~ ts'echalhshá7 ~ ts'sáw̓ich [ts'alh sha7] ninety. *numeral.*

ts'álhtsam̓ [ts'alh tsam̓] put a little water in one's mouth. *verb(i).*

ts'ám̓chn ~ ts'á7mchn ~ ts'ám̓echn [ts'am̓ chn] bracelet. *noun.*

ts'ám̓echn ~ ts'am̓chn ~ ts'a7mchn [ts'a m̓e chn] bracelet. *noun.*

ts'am̓ín̓ [ts'a m̓in̓] lick (someone). *verb(t).*

ts'an ~ ts'aan hit (someone); punch (someone). *verb(t).*

ts'ántway̓ [ts'an tway̓] punch each another. *verb(i).*

ts'ántsut [ts'an tsut] thunder. *verb(i).*

ts'áp'an [ts'a p'an] delay (something); interrupt (someone); derange (someone); cause (someone) to slow down [in working]. *verb(t).*

ts'áp'antsut [ts'a p'an tsut] slow down; slow down [in working]. *verb(i).*

ts'áp'atsut [ts'a p'a tsut] slow down. *verb(i).*

ts'áp'nexw [ts'ap' nexw] distracted (someone), have. *verb(t).*

ts'áts'alh [ts'a ts'alh] come out of the house to look at something unusual or interesting; go to see [about everyone]; interested in someone coming, be. *verb(i).*

ts'áts'ayakw [ts'a ts'a yakw] worrying, be. *verb(i).*

ts'áts'ey̓x̲ [ts'a ts'ey̓x̲] busy, be; hurry. *verb(i).*

ts'áwam [ts'a wam] fresh [about water]. *adjective.*

ts'áwam stak̲w [ts'a wam stak̲w] fresh water. *noun.*

ts'awílhn [ts'a wi lhn] hit (someone) in the belly. *verb(t).*

ts'ax̲ sell cheaply. *verb(i).*

ts'ax̲áw̓txw [ts'a x̲aw̓ txw] second-hand store. *noun.*

ts'áx̲i [ts'a x̲i] bluejoint reedgrass [used for baskets]; white grass. *noun.*

ts'ax̲l̓ím̓n [ts'ax̲ l'i m̓n] go straight towards (something); take a straight course to (something); move in a perfectly straight course to (something). *verb(t).*

ts'áyakw [ts'a yakw] worry. *verb(i).*

ts'áyakwni [ts'a yakw ni] worry about (someone). *verb(t).*

ts'ay̓ántsut [ts'a yan tsut] get into the shade; shade, get into the. *verb(i).*

ts'ay̓éwilhtn [ts'a y̓e wilh tn] canoe shed. *noun.*

ts'áy̓tn [ts'ay̓ tn] umbrella. *noun.*

ts'áy̓tn tl'a stéwak̲in [ts'ay̓ tn tl'a ste wa k̲in] mushroom [literally, umbrella of the dead]. *noun.*

ts'áyts'ayk̲ay [ts'ay ts'ay k̲ay] white pine tree. *noun.*

ts'ayx̲shnám̓ [ts'ayx̲ shnam̓] make one's feet move fast. *verb(i).*

ts'ayx̲t rush (something). *verb(t).*

ts'áyx̲tas [ts'ayx̲ tas] rushwork. *verb(i).*

ts'áyx̲tsam̓ [ts'ayx̲ tsam̓] talk quickly. *verb(i).*

ts'áyx̲tsas [ts'ayx̲ tsas] hurry! *verb(i).*

ts'áyx̲tsut [ts'ayx̲ tsut] make oneself hurry; hurry. *verb(i).*

ts'a7á7mus [ts'a 7a7 mus] new dancer's headdress. *noun.*

ts'a7mchn ~ ts'ám̓echn ~ ts'ám̓chn [ts'a 7m chn] bracelet. *noun.*

ts'chel [ts' chel] kingfisher. *noun.*

ts'echalhshá7 ~ ts'sáw̓ich ~ ts'alhshá7 [ts'e chalh sha7] ninety. *numeral.*

ts'ékwa7 [tse' kwa7] fern plant root [steamed and eaten]. *noun.*

ts'ekwchalhshá7 ~ ts'ekwlhshá7 [tsekw chalh sha7] seventy. *numeral.*

ts'ekwlhshá7 ~ ts'ekwchalhshá7 [ts'e kwlh sha7] seventy. *numeral.*

ts'ékwts'ekw [ts'ekw ts'ekw] scabby. *adjective.*

ts'ekw'ntm [ts'e kw'n tm] wormed, be. *verb(p).*

ts'ekw'ts'ekw'álhx̲a [ts'ekw' ts'e kw'alh x̲a] sores on neck, have. *verb(i).*

ts'ek̲ leak. *verb(i).*

ts'ék̲e7em [ts'e k̲e 7em] hammer with hammer and chisel. *verb(i).*

ts'ek̲ní7kwup [ts'ek̲ ni7 kwup] split wood. *verb(i).*

ts'ek̲shenám [ts'ek̲ she nam] stamp foot [about **sxw7umten**]. *verb(i).*

ts'ek̲t woodpecker [smaller kind than **tmlhepsm**]. *noun.*

ts'ek̲'mín [ts'ek̲' min] dancer's rattle; deer-hoof rattle. *noun.*

ts'ek̲'míṅshn [ts'ek̲' miṅ shn] deer hooves used on new dancer's ankles. *noun.*

ts'ék̲'ts'ek̲' [ts'ek̲' ts'ek̲'] cracked hands, have. *verb(i).*

ts'ék̲wets' k̲wálhchem [ts'e k̲wets' k̲walh chem] marshy terrain. *phrase.*

ts'ek̲wlhalhshá7 [ts'ek̲w lhalh sha7] seventy [form used when counting money]. *numeral.*

ts'ek̲wts'k̲wálhch [ts'ek̲w'ts' k̲walhch] boggy. *adjective.*

ts'ék̲w'iya [ts'e k̲w'i ya] limpet. *noun.*

ts'ek̲w'uṁáẏ ~ ts'k̲w'u7emáẏ [ts'e k̲w'u ṁaẏ] blackcap berry bush [see **ts'k̲w'ú7em**]. *noun.*

ts'el lose all in a gamble; have nothing left; nothing left, have; left without sticks in **slhahál**, be. *verb(i).*

ts'el̓áls [ts'e l'als] unidentified stomach disorder, have an ["pain in stomach"]. *verb(i).*

ts'els shiny; cleaned [e.g., a pot cleaned with sand]. *adjective.*

ts'elsán [ts'el san] shine (something); polish (something). *verb(t).*

ts'elsemáẏus [ts'el se ma ẏus] dazed, be; semi-trance, be in a; go into a trance; trance, go into a; pass out; stunned, be [by a blow]. *verb(i).*

ts'elt act in vain. *verb(i).*

ts'elt' rough. *adjective.*

ts'elút [ts'e lut] head-covering used by **sxw7umten**, made from cattail. *noun.*

ts'elhalhshá7 [ts'e lhalh sha7] ninety [form used when counting money]. *numeral.*

ts'elhp' landed, be; come in for a landing; fall short [aiming for a point]; move off [being at a point]. *verb(i).*

ts'elhp'án [ts'elh p'an] throw (one's clothes) over a line; push (something) past an obstruction. *verb(t).*

ts'elhp'k̲w [ts'elhp' k̲w] disappear under [rising] water, have head or top. *verb(i).*

ts'élhts'elh [ts'elh ts'elh] cool place; cold, usually [about person]. *adjective.*

ts'elhts'úlh [ts'elh ts'ulh] cold [about a bunch of people]. *adjective.*

ts'eṁáal̓ [ts'eṁ máal̓] arrow. *noun.*

ts'eṁíl̓ [ts'e ṁil] thin; flat. *adjective.*

ts'emíl̓ayts'a [ts'e mi l'ay ts'a] thin cloth. *adjective.*

ts'eṁiln [ts'e ṁi ln] thin (something); make (something) thin. *verb(t).*

ts'emk̲'án [ts'em k̲'an] cut (something) with scissors. *verb(t).*

ts'émk̲'iẏek̲w [ts'em k̲'i ẏek̲w] cut hair on top of head. *verb(i).*

ts'emk̲'k̲án [ts'emk̲' k̲an] cut (someone's) rear end. *verb(t).*

ts'emk̲'shenán [ts'emk̲' she nan] cut (someone's) feet. *verb(t).*

ts'emk̲'tn [ts'emk̲' tn] scissors. *noun.*

ts'emts'umlháṁ ~ ts'umts'umlhám [ts'em ts'um lhaṁ] lately; newly arrived; just; little while ago. *verb(i).*

ts'ents'náẏach [ts'ents' na ẏach] swelling on one's hand, have a; lump on one's hand, have a. *adjective.*

ts'ep strong odour; body odour. *noun.* in rut, be [e.g., deer].

ts'epx̲wáyus [ts'ep x̲wa yus] sleep in one's eyes. *noun.*

ts'ép'iẏik̲w [ts'e p'i ẏik̲w] great-great-grandparent/aunt/uncle; great-great-grandchild. *noun.*

ts'ep'ts'áp' [ts'ep ts'ap'] neglect to do, just. *verb(i).*

ts'ep'ts'úp'neẇásen [ts'ep' ts'up' ne' ẇa sen] put (them) together end-to-end. *verb(t).*

ts'es nine. *numeral.*

ts'esk̲ nine o'clock. *noun.*

ts'ésts'es [ts'es ts'es] nine people. *numeral.*

ts'etkwán [ts'et kwan] take off a small piece from (something) [e.g., a piece of bread]. *verb(t).*

ts'etkwíṁ [ts'et kwiṁ] nibble at it. *verb(i).*

ts'étx̲em [ts'et x̲em] rattle [e.g., a window]; creak; make a noise like a grasshopper. *verb(i).*

ts'ét'ḵems [ts'et' ḵems] dripping, be. *verb(i).*
ts'et'ḵ'm [ts'et' ḵ'm] drip [about a drop of something]. *verb(i).*
ts'étsem [ts'e tsem] jingle [e.g., change in pocket]. *verb(i).*
ts'ets'eḵw'áls [ts'e ts'e ḵw'als] small black flies; flies [small black]. *noun.*
ts'ets'emíchen [ts'e ts'e mi chen] ant; gnat. *noun.*
ts'éts'etx̱m [ts'e ts'e tx̱m] jingling, be. *verb(i).*
ts'éts'et'ḵ'm [ts'e ts'et' ḵ'm] dripping, be. *verb(i).*
ts'éts'etsem [ts'e ts'e tsem] jingling, be. *verb(i).*
ts'éts'ichem [ts'e ts'i chem] drizzling, be. *verb(i).*
ts'ets'iḵáy̓ [ts'e ts'i ḵay̓] spring ritual of thanksgiving, do the. *verb(i).*
ts'ets'iḵw'á7els [ts'e ts'i ḵw'a 7els] blackfly. *noun.*
ts'éts'i7n [ts'e ts'i 7n] jingle; tinkle. *verb(i).*
ts'ets'p'át [ts'ets' p'at] distract (someone); interfere with (something); derange (something) all the time. *verb(t).*
ts'ets'xwítsut [ts'ets' xwi tsut] asking for something, be; plead, be; beg, be. *verb(i).*
ts'ets'x̱ [ts'e ts'x̱] away, be [about the moon]. *verb(i).*
ts'éts'x̱ntsut [ts'e ts'x̱n tsut] wane; decrease [about the moon; literally, consume itself]. *verb(i).*
ts'ewás [ts'e was] plead. *verb(i).*
ts'ew̓ts'íw̓eḵ [ts'ew̓ ts'i w̓eḵ] salmon that is covered in sores. *verb(i).*
ts'exw rotten, be; decay. *verb(i).*
ts'exwáyaḵap [ts'e xwa ya ḵap] fade away [e.g., noise or voice]. *verb(i).*
ts'éxwen [ts'e xwen] rot (something). *verb(t).*
ts'exwts'áxwi7 [ts'exw ts'a xwi7] rainbow. *noun.*
ts'ex̱ destroyed by fire, be; consumed, be; gone, be; burnt, be; burnt down, be; worn out, be. *verb(i).*
ts'éx̱min̓ [ts'ex̱ min̓] remains of a fire; something burnt out. *noun.*
ts'ex̱t gravel; gravel beach. *noun.*
ts'ex̱ten̓án̓ [ts'ex̱ te n̓an̓] poison (someone). *verb(t).*
ts'ex̱tn [ts'ex̱ tn] poison; rattlesnake. *noun.*
ts'ex̱ts'íx̱ [ts'ex̱ ts'ix̱] stinging nettle. *noun.*
ts'ex̱w waxberry. *noun.*
ts'éx̱wts'ex̱w [ts'ex̱w ts'ex̱w] waxberries [sg: **ts'ex̱w**]. *noun.*
ts'ex̱wts'x̱wáy̓ [ts'ex̱wts' x̱way̓] waxberry plant. *noun.*
ts'ex̱wts'x̱wélwetm [ts'ex̱wts' x̱wel we tm] wash [one's] clothes. *verb(i).*
ts'ex̱wts'x̱wénp [ts'ex̱wts' x̱wenp] wash the floor. *verb(i).*
ts'eyts'áyx̱tsut [ts'ey ts'ayx̱ tsut] overanxious, be. *verb(i).*
ts'icháy̓ay̓ ~ **ts'its'icháyay̓** [ts'i cha y̓ay̓] spruce tree. *noun.*
ts'ichn ~ **ḵ'p'ax̱w** [ts'i chn] hazelnut; nut [general term]. *noun.*
ts'íkts'ik [ts'ik ts'ik] buggie; car. *noun.*
ts'iḵ [ts'iḵ] leak [about boat or vessel]. *verb(i).*
ts'iḵt [ts'iḵt] common flicker. *noun.*
ts'íḵ'i [ts'i ḵ'i] soft and mushy, get; mushy, get soft and. *verb(i).*
ts'íḵ'i7 [ts'i ḵ'i7] muddy, be; get muddy [less muddy than **tekwt'kwi7**]. *verb(i).*
ts'ilsn [ts'il sn] sharpen (something). *verb(t).*
ts'im̓ [ts'im̓] dip food into grease; eat grease; take dried salmon and dip it in oil. *verb(i).*
ts'im̓ám [ts'i m̓am] lick plate. *verb(i).*
ts'im̓ín̓ [ts'i m̓in̓] lick (something). *verb(t).*
ts'imts'im̓áymixw [ts'im ts'i m̓ay mixw] caterpillar [literally, licking the ground]. *verb(i).*
ts'íp'ḵay̓usm [ts'ip' ḵa y̓u sm] wink; blink one's eyes. *verb(i).*
ts'ip'ḵáy̓usmin [ts'ip' ḵa y̓us min] wink at (someone). *verb(t).*
ts'íp'tsem̓ [ts'ip' tsem̓] close [e.g., clam]. *verb(i).*
ts'íp'usm [ts'i p'u sm] close one's eyes; shut one's eyes. *verb(i).*
ts'ísin̓ [ts'i sin̓] nail (something); nail up (something). *verb(t).*
ts'ísḵim̓ [ts'is ḵim̓] shoot burning arrows up in order to cause rain to stop [this would be done by children, while the grownups would shout "**kwúsen**" (star)]. *verb(i).*

ts'isk̲wáń [ts'is k̲wań] shoot (something) through the head. *verb(t).*
ts'isk̲wáy̓newásn [ts'is k̲way̓ ne ẁa sn] shoot (somethings/someone) in the stomach. *verb(t).*
ts'ísnexw [ts'is nexw] hit (something). *verb(t).*
ts'isshnáń [ts'is shnań] shoot (someone) through the foot. *verb(t).*
ts'istn [ts'is tn] antler; horn; nail. *noun.*
ts'ítiḿ [ts'i tiḿ] chew on a bone. *verb(i).*
ts'ítiń [ts'i tiń] chew on (a bone); nibble (something). *verb(t).*
ts'ít'ax̲w [ts'i t'ax̲w] grebe, horned or eared; horned grebe; eared grebe [type of bird]. *noun.*
ts'its'aháńtsut [ts'i ts'a hań tsut] "drumming" during mating season, be [about ruffed grouse]. *verb(i).*
ts'its'áp' [ts'i ts'ap'] work. *verb(i).*
ts'its'ap'áy̓m [ts'i ts'a p'a y̓m] want to work. *verb(i).*
ts'its'áp'en [ts'i ts'a p'en] work on (something). *verb(t).*
ts'its'áp'nexw [ts'i ts'ap' nexw] working on (something), have finished. *verb(t).*
ts'its'áp'ni [ts'i ts'ap' ni] work towards (something). *verb(t).*
ts'its'ap'númut [ts'i ts'ap' nu mut] work, manage to; work, able to; get a job; job, get a. *verb(i).*
ts'its'áp'shi [ts'i ts'ap' shi] work for (someone). *verb(t).*
ts'its'áp'wit [ts'i ts'ap' wit] they work. *verb(i).*
ts'íts'es [ts'i ts'es] nine animals. *numeral.*
ts'its'icháy̓ay̓ ~ ts'icháy̓ay̓ [ts'i ts'i cha yay̓] spruce tree. *noun.*
ts'íts'ik̲ [ts'i ts'ik̲] leaking, be [about boat or vessel]. *verb(i).*
ts'its'iḿáynexw [ts'i ts'i ḿay nexw] caterpillar [big haired]. *noun.*
ts'íts'inay̓ [ts'i ts'i nay̓] little bullhead. *noun.*
ts'íts'ixw [ts'i ts'ixw] helpful. *adjective.*
ts'its'ixwánan [ts'i ts'i xwa nan] kindness; pity. *noun.*
ts'its'íxwnewas [ts'i ts'ixw ne ẁas] kind to one another, be. *verb(i).*
ts'its'ixwnít [ts'i ts'ixw ni] take pity on (someone); pity on (someone), have; help (someone) out. *verb(t).*
ts'its'ixwnítway [ts'i ts'ixw ni way] nice to each other, be; take care of one another. *verb(i).*
ts'its'ixwnúḿut [ts'i ts'ixw nu ḿut] pitiful, be. *verb(i).*
ts'íts'usm [ts'i ts'u sm] [name of a river]. *place name.*
ts'its'xwsténaḿut [ts'its'xw ste na ḿut] asking for help, be [e.g., about a person who's been injured]; begging for mercy, be. *verb(i).*
ts'iẁ [ts'iẁ] close up solidly [e.g., a wound]. *verb(i).*
ts'íwam [ts'i wam] heal; heal over. *verb(i).*
ts'íwk̲'ay̓ ~ sts'íwk̲ay̓ [ts'iw k̲'ay̓] elderberry bush; red elderberry bush [see **sts'iwk̲'**]. *noun.*
ts'íxwen [ts'i xwen] pity (someone); help (someone) [out of trouble]. *verb(t).*
ts'íxwts'ixw [ts'ixw ts'ixw] osprey; fish-hawk. *noun.*
ts'ix̲ [ts'ix̲] singe. *verb(i).*
ts'íx̲iń [ts'i x̲iń] singe (something) by fire. *verb(t).*
ts'iyíkw'in [ts'i yi kw'in] pinch (someone); squeeze (someone) [with two fingers]. *verb(t).*
ts'iyíwen [ts'i yi wen] spiritual quest for power, go on a; go on a spiritual quest for power. *verb(i).*
ts'iy̓úḿnewas [ts'i y̓uḿ ne ẁas] stick together. *verb(i).*
ts'iy̓úḿnexw [ts'i y̓uḿ nexw] stuck (them) together, have. *verb(t).*
ts'i7 [ts'i7] loot from a raid. *noun.*
ts'i7ch [ts'i7ch] inner part of thick fir bark [powder-like]. *noun.*
ts'í7shten [ts'i7 shten] floor mat. *noun.*
ts'kw'átsut [ts' kw'a tsut] run. *verb(i).*
ts'kw'i7ns [ts' kwi 7ns] tuberculosis; TB [see also **ts'xwinas, hemlch,** and **sts'ekw'í7ens**]. *noun.*
ts'k̲'álhx̲a [ts' k̲'alh x̲a] kneel down. *verb(i).*
ts'k̲'álhx̲a7m [ts' k̲alh x̲a 7m] genuflect. *verb(i).*
ts'k̲walhch [ts' k̲walh ch] swamp; marshy terrain or land; bog. *noun.*
ts'k̲wiḿ [ts' k̲wiḿ] secretly take a share from someone; take from others. *verb(i).*

ts'k̲wúl̓ech [ts' k̲wu l'ech] mittens; gloves. *noun.*

ts'k̲wu7tstn ~ nts'k̲wu7tstn ~ snts'k̲wu7tstn [ts' k̲wu7ts tn] smoking pipe; pipe [for smoking]. *noun.*

ts'k̲w'i7k̲s [ts' k̲w'i7 k̲s] yellow-bellied sapsucker [tail feathers were used to adorn the **yasi7k̲w** of the **sxw7umten**]. *noun.*

ts'k̲w'ú7em [ts' k̲w'u 7em] blackcap berry [see **ts'ek̲w'uṁáẏ**]. *noun.*

ts'k̲w'u7emáẏ ~ ts'ek̲w'uṁáẏ [ts' k̲w'u 7e maẏ] blackcap berry bush. *noun.*

ts'lhulh [ts' lhulh] cold [to the touch]. *adjective.*

ts'lhúlhach [ts' lhu lhach] cold hands, have. *adjective.*

ts'lhúlhachen [ts' lhu lha chen] make (someone's) hands cold. *verb(t).*

ts'lhúlhen [ts' lhu lhen] make (something) cold. *verb(t).*

ts'lhúlhi7 [ts' lhu lhi7] cold, get really. *verb(i).*

ts'naẏ ~ sts'naẏ ~ sts'enáẏ [ts' naẏ] bullhead. *noun.*

ts'náẏach [ts' na ẏach] swelling on the hand. *noun.*

ts'salh [ts' salh] nine times. *verb(i).*

ts'sálhiyas [ts' sa lhi yas] nine days. *verb(i).*

ts'sámats' [ts' sa mats'] nine strands [of wool, rope, etc.]. *numeral.*

ts'sáẇich ~ ts'echalhshá7 ~ ts'alhshá7 [ts' sa ẇich] ninety. *numeral.*

ts'tsan [ts' tsan] rattle coin in pocket. *verb(i).*

ts'ukw [ts'ukw] not slippery. *adjective.*

ts'úkw'em [ts'u kw'em] fish scales; scale [of fish]. *noun.*

ts'úk̲wiṁ [ts'u k̲wiṁ] draw with mouth [about **sxw7umten**]; suck. *verb(i).*

ts'úk̲wuṅ [ts'u k̲wuṅ] suck (something). *verb(t).*

ts'úlayus [ts'u la yus] gunpowder [see also **k̲w'alh**]. *noun.*

ts'ulh [ts'ulh] cold. *adjective.*

ts'úlhi7 [ts'u lhi7] cold, get [only used to talk about the weather, not about a person]. *verb(i).*

ts'úlhuṁ [ts'u lhuṁ] cold, be; cold, become very [about human]. *verb(i).*

ts'umáyu [ts'u ma yu] barnacle. *noun.*

ts'úṁen [ts'u ṁen] hiss; whistle softly. *verb(i).*

ts'umlh [ts'umlh] newborn; recent; just; little while ago. *adjective.*

ts'umts'umlhám [ts'um ts'um lham] just; little while ago. *verb(i).*

ts'úp'els [ts'u p'els] newborn seal. *noun.*

ts'up'neẇásen [ts'up' ne ẇa sen] join (sticks) together; put (something) together. *verb(t).*

ts'úp'un [ts'u p'un] fill up (a hole) in the wall or ground; attach it to (something); connect it to (something) by inserting it. *verb(t).*

ts'ut'ayúsem [ts'u t'a yu sem] aim a gun with one eye shut. *verb(i).*

ts'úts'ulhuṁ [ts'u ts'u lhuṁ] cold, be feeling; cold, be/feel. *verb(i).*

ts'úts'uṁam ~ sets'úts'umam [ts'u ts'u ṁam] chickadee. *noun.*

ts'uẏk̲wáṅtem [ts'uẏ k̲waṅ tem] scalp (someone). *verb(p).*

ts'uys [ts'uys] crazy. *adjective.*

ts'uysánan [ts'uy sa nan] craziness. *noun.*

ts'úysi7 [ts'uy si7] crazy, get; become crazy. *verb(i).*

ts'úysus ~ nts'úysus [ts'uy sus] crazy face, have a; crazy-faced. *adjective.*

ts'úyuṅ [ts'u yuṅ] peel (fruit or vegetable). *verb(t).*

ts'u7 [ts'u7] disappear; melt; rotten, be. *verb(i).*

ts'u7 [ts'u7] come out [being pulled]. *verb(i).*

ts'u7k̲s [ts'u7 k̲s] come out [about small oblong object; e.g., nails]. *verb(i).*

ts'ú7mayshn [ts'u7 may shn] basket for carrying wood or sea urchins, made of heavy split root; basket [any basket with an open weave]; large basket carried on the back. *noun.*

ts'u7n [ts'u 7n] pull out (teeth, nail out of a wall). *verb(t).*

ts'u7tsáṅ [ts'u7 tsaṅ] uncork (a bottle). *verb(t).*

ts'xwáchxwiṁ [ts' xwach xwiṁ] start to go [about leaves]. *verb(i).*

ts'xwan [ts' xwan] overcook (something). *verb(t).*

ts'xwas [ts' xwas] steam-cook clams ["boil something for a long time and it gets really soft"]. *verb(i).*

ts'xwínas [ts' xwi nas] tuberculosis; TB [see also **ts'kw'i7ns, hemlch,** and **sts'ekw'í7ens**]. *noun.*

ts'x̱á7chep [ts' x̱a7 chep] burn things other than firewood [as an emergency measure]. *verb(i).*

ts'x̱wáy̓aps [ts' x̱wa y̓aps] button. *noun.*

ts'x̱wélut ~ ts'x̱wélwet ~ ts'x̱wélwetm [ts' x̱we lut] wash [one's] clothes. *verb(i).*

ts'x̱wélwet ~ ts'x̱wélwetm ~ ts'x̱wélut [ts' x̱wel wet] wash [one's] clothes. *verb(i).*

ts'x̱wélwetm ~ ts'x̱wélwet ~ ts'x̱wélut [ts' x̱wel we tm] wash [one's] clothes. *verb(i).*

ts'x̱wénp [ts' x̱wenp] wash the floor. *verb(i).*

U u

u [**7u**] if; when; [question particle that makes the sentence into a question]. *conjunction.*

úḵwum [**7u ḵwum**] carry water. *verb(i).*

uḵwuṁáẏem [**7u ḵwu ṁa ẏem**] want to go get water. *verb(i).*

-ul̓a [**-u l'a**] finger; little finger. *suffix.*

úlanch [**7u lanch**] orange. *adjective.*

-ullh [**-ullh**] young specimen (human or animal). *suffix.*

ulx̱t [**7ul x̱t**] put (something) away for eating. *verb(t).*

ulh [**7ulh**] teacher. *noun.*

-ulh [**-ulh**] belonging to; coming from [human or animal]. *suffix.*

-ulh ~ -wilh ~ -axwilh [**-ulh**] canoe {full word: **snexwílh**}; container; stomach; belly; bowels {full word: **s7étswilh**}. *suffix.*

ulhx̱t tkwa sts'úḵwi7 [**7ulh x̱t t kwa sts'u ḵwi7**] harvest any salmon. *verb(t).*

-um ~ -uṁ [**-um**] {intransitive suffix}. *suffix.*

-uṁ ~ -um [**-uṁ**] {intransitive suffix}. *suffix.*

úmat [**7u mat**] lazy; too lazy [to do something]. *adjective.*

-umi [**-u mi**] you. *suffix.*

-umiap ~ -umiyap [**-u mi ap**] you all. *suffix.*

úmich [**7u mich**] go upstream; upstream, go. *verb(i).*

-umiyap ~ -umiap [**-u mi yap**] you all. *suffix.*

úmsem [**7um sem**] wake up; awake, be [see also **s7úm'sem** and **es7úmsm**]. *verb(i).*

úmseman [**7um se men**] wake (someone) up. *verb(t).*

úmsemul̓a [**7um se mu l'a**] finger {full word: **nix̱ḵwúẏach**}. *suffix.*

-umulh [**-u mulh**] us. *suffix.*

-un ~ -uṅ [**-un**] {added onto some words so that you can use the object endings, see section on "object endings," p. 12; also called the directive}. *suffix.*

-uṅ ~ -un [**-uṅ**] {added onto some words so that you can use the object endings, see section on "object endings," p. 12; also called the directive}. *suffix.*

unálhen [**7u na lhen**] intercede. *verb(i).*

-unexw ~ -yunexw [**-u nexw**] wave, waves in the ocean {full word: **yúya7kw**}. *suffix.*

úni7 [**7u ni7**] lead singer in syewen. *noun.*

úpen [**7u pen**] ten. *numeral.*

úpen i kwi áṅus [**7u pen 7i kwi 7a ṅus**] twelve. *numeral.*

úpen i kwi nch'u7 [**7u pen 7i kwi n ch'u7**] eleven. *numeral.*

úpen kwis nách'aẇich [**7u pen kwis na ch'a ẇich**] one thousand. *numeral.*

upenálh [**7u pe nalh**] ten times. *verb(i).*

upenálhntsut [**7u pe na lhn tsut**] make a tenth attempt; attempt a tenth time; try for the tenth time. *verb(i).*

upenámats' [**7u pe na mats'**] ten strands [of wool, rope, etc.]. *numeral.*

úpenḵ [**7u penḵ**] ten o'clock. *noun.*

-us [**-us**] face {full word: **s7átsus** and **sme7ús**}. *suffix.*

-us ~ -was [**-us**] stick; wooden structure. *suffix.*

usáẏlh [**7u sa ẏlh**] teach. *verb(i).*

úsa7 [**7u sa7**] mountain blueberry. *noun.*

úsa7aẏ [**7u sa 7aẏ**] mountain blueberry bush. *noun.*

ústa [**7us ta**] noviciate. *noun.*

ústsaṅ [**7us tsaṅ**] teach (language); teach (something) verbally. *verb(t).*

úsuṅ [**7u suṅ**] teach (someone) how to do something; instruct (someone) how to do something; advise (someone) how to do something; show (someone) how to do something. *verb(t).*

ushenáẏlh [**7u she na ẏlh**] trainer. *noun.*

úshi [**7u shi**] request (something). *verb(t).*

-ut [**-ut**] {added onto some words so that you can use the object endings, see section on "object endings"}. *suffix.*

ut' [**7ut'**] stretch; stretched out, be [e.g., a sweater]. *verb(i).*

út'un [7u t'un] stretch (something) out [e.g., a rope]; extend (something); lengthen (something). *verb(t).*
út'us [7u t'us] long-faced; long face, have a. *adjective.*
utsám̓ [7u tsam̓] call witnesses. *verb(i).*
útsani [7u tsa ni] lynx; Canada lynx. *noun.*
útsax̱ánen [7u tsa x̱a nen] make an addition on the side of (something); build an annex on the side of (a house); lengthen (a house). *verb(t).*
útsiyan [7u tsi yan] dress with (something); put on (something). *verb(t).*
útsḵsan [7utsḵ san] splice (rope); splice (something) on; ply (rope) together. *verb(t).*
utsḵsn [7utsḵ sn] make an addition at the end of (something); splice on to (something). *verb(t).*
útsun [7u tsun] add on clothes to (someone); splice (rope). *verb(t).*
uts'ḵ [7uts'ḵ] go outside; outside, be. *verb(i).*
uts'ḵs [7uts'ḵs] take (someone) outside. *verb(t).*
uut [7uut] invite (someone) to a feast; call (someone) in; invite (someone). *verb(t).*
uxwenántem [7u xwn nan tem] frozen, be. *verb(p).*
úxwnan [7uxw nan] freeze (something). *verb(t).*
úxwumixw [7u xwu mixw] nation; village [houses and inhabitants]; villager. *noun.*
úx̱wim̓ [7u x̱wim̓] whittle; carve. *verb(i).*
úx̱wun̓ [7u x̱wun̓] whittle (something); cut (something); shave (something) down; shear (something). *verb(t).*
uys [7uys] go inside; come inside; enter [a house]. *verb(i).* take (someone) inside. *verb(t).*
-uy̓s [-uy̓s] large object; large piece; large chunk. *suffix.*
uysáy̓em [7uy sa y̓em] want to go inside. *verb(i).*
uysnúmut [7uys nu mut] inside, manage to get. *verb(i).*
úyt ka [7uyt kya] call (someone)! *verb(t).*
úyulh [7u yulh] board a canoe; go aboard; aboard, go; put cargo aboard. *verb(i).*
úyulh ta snéḵwem [7u yulh ta sne ḵwem] noon, be. *verb.*
úyulhs [7u yulhs] put (something) aboard a canoe. *verb(t).*
úyum [7u yum] slow, be. *verb(i).*
úyumen [7u yu men] slow (something) down. *verb(t).*
úyumentsut [7u yu men tsut] slow down. *verb(i).*
uyumíw̓as [7u yu mi w̓as] paddle slowly. *verb(i).*
úyumḵw [7u yumḵw] slow upstairs, be. *verb(i).*
uyumshenám̓ [7u yum she nam̓] walk slow; slow down when walking. *verb(i).*
u7 [7u7] first. *verb(i).*
u7elḵwús [7u 7el ḵwus] bent; domed. *adjective.*
ú7pen [7u7 pen] ten animals. *numeral.*
u7t ~ uut [7u7t] invite (someone). *verb(t).*
ú7ulh [7u 7ulh] teachers [sg: **ulh**]. *noun.*
ú7um̓at [7u 7u m̓at] feeling lazy, be; lazy, be feeling; be too lazy [to do something]. *verb(i).*
ú7um̓ich [7u 7u m̓ich] going upstream, be; upstream, be going. *verb(i).*
u7ús ~ ew̓ús [7u 7us] egg; eggs. *noun.*
ú7uts'ḵ [7u 7uts'ḵ] going out, be; out, be going. *verb(i).*
ú7uys [7u 7uys] coming inside, be; inside, be coming; entering, be. *verb(i).*
u7ú7 ~ a7ú7 [7u 7u7] first, be. *verb(i).*
ú7x̱ḵsáy̓ ~ ú7x̱wḵsáy̓ [7u7 x̱ḵ say̓] hardhack. *noun.*
u7x̱wim [7u7 x̱wim] whittling, be; carving, be. *verb(i).*
ú7x̱wḵsáy̓ ~ ú7x̱ḵsáy̓ [7u 7x̱wḵ say̓] hardhack. *noun.*

W w

wa [wa] imperfective; indicates continuation of action or process. *clitic.*

wa chexw wa slhálhk̲en [wa chexw wa slhalh k̲en] Behave youself. *sentence.*

wa chexw yuu [wa chexw yuu] Be careful!; Take care! *sentence.*

wa chexw yuusténam̓ut [wa chexw yuus tén nam̓ mut] Take care of yourself. *sentence.*

wa k̲'ay̓áchtn [wa k̲'a y̓ach tn] raise hands in thanks. *verb(i).*

wa lhna7s [walh na7s] place; where he/she/it is. *noun.*

wa lhsáy̓xwelh [walh say̓ xwelh] sibling or cousin of deceased parent; uncle [after death of parent or parent's sibling]; aunt [after death of parent or parent's sibling]. *noun.*

wa lhsíiy̓am̓ [walh síi y̓am̓] those honoured as chiefs. *noun.*

wa lhsiy̓ám̓ [walh si y̓am̓] someone honoured as a chief. *noun.*

wa lhsti7sh [walh sti7sh] size. *noun.*

wa lhtá7shn [walh ta7 shn] where one stands. *noun.*

wa lhtim̓á [walh ti m̓a] culture; ways [of doing something]; how [something is done]. *noun.*

wa lhtiná7 [walh ti na7] place of origin. *noun.*

wa lh7áy̓nexw [walh 7ay̓ nexw] life; spirit; soul; "what keeps a person alive" AP [see also **kw'elh7áynexw**]. *noun.*

wa lh7em̓út [walh 7e m̓ut] abode. *noun.*

wa lh7iy̓ím [walh 7i y̓im] strength. *noun.*

wa mílha7 [wa mi lha7] Indian dancer. *noun.*

wa s7utsáylh [was 7u tsaylh] teacher. *noun.*

wa u7lh [wa 7u7 lh] teacher. *noun.*

waa7 [waa7] bah [disparaging remark]. *interjection.*

wach hour; watch [timepiece]. *noun.*

wách'ustenumut [wa ch'us te nu mut] feel insulted; insulted, feel. *verb(i).*

wách'wach'tsam̓ [wach' wach' tsam̓] opening and closing mouth, be [about fish]. *verb(i).*

wak̲áy̓stn [wa k̲ay̓s tn] weapon. *noun.*

wák̲shenan̓ [wak̲ she nan̓] remove splinter from (someone's) feet. *verb(t).*

wak̲'ék̲ [wa k̲'ek̲] cricket. *noun.*

wálam [wa lam] echo. *verb(i).*

wals throw it away as a **swals**; give it away; make it a gift. *verb(i).*

wálwalem [wal wa lem] echoing, be. *verb(i).*

wál̓welk̲'als [wal' wel k̲'als] ask all over; ask everywhere. *verb(i).*

walh frightened away, get. *verb(i).*

wálhan̓ [wa lhan̓] chase away (an animal); shoo away (an animal); chase (someone) out. *verb(t).*

wálhk̲'an [walh k̲'an] chase (someone) away; order (someone) out. *verb(t).*

wanáxw [wa naxw] really; true. *verb(i).*

wanáxws [wa naxws] treat (someone) with respect; believe (someone); respect (someone); honour (someone). *verb(t).*

wánim [wa nim] orphan. *noun.*

wápatu [wa pa tu] Indian potato. *noun.*

-was ~ -us [-was] stick; wooden structure. *suffix.*

wáshan̓ [wa shan̓] move (something) away from the fire or heat; seat (a dancer); put (something) in the background; take (a pot) from the fire. *verb(t).*

wáshi7 [wa shi7] go into the background; background, go into the; away from the fire, be. *verb(i).*

wáts'an [wa ts'an] lever (something) up; pry (something) up; pry (something) loose. *verb(t).*

wáts'antsut [wa ts'an tsut] sit oneself down [about a dancer]. *verb(i).*

wáts'iyus [wa ts'i yus] basket made from interwoven pieces of red cedar inner cambium. *noun.*

wats'k̲'án̓ [wats' k̲'an̓] spread (something) apart. *verb(t).*

wats'tn [wats' tn] crowbar; anything used to pry. *noun.*

wáwalem [wa wa lem] echoing, be. *verb(i).*

wáwenti [wa wen ti] looking out, be; peeking, be. *verb(i).*

waw̓sh away from the fire, be; near the wall, be; keep away from the fire; sit in the back row [away from the fire]. *verb(i).*

waw̓shs seat (someone) away from the fire. *verb(t).*

way known, become. *verb(i).*

way I wonder whether; I wonder if. *clitic.*

-way ~ -ay one another; each other. *suffix.*

wáyat [wa yat] reveal (a secret); make (something) public; make an announcement about (something/someone). *verb(t).*

wáyatsut [wa ya tsut] show oneself as being a **sxw7umten**; reveal something about oneself [especially spiritual powers]. *verb(i).*

wáyti ~ iw̓áyti [way ti] maybe; I think; may. *adverb.*

wá7a [wa 7a] good heavens. *interjection.*

wa7éw̓elhch' [wa 7e w̓elhch'] wide open, be. *verb(i).*

wa7tk̲ [wa7 tk̲] man the stern of boat. *verb(i).*

wa7tshn [wa7t shn] foot end of bed platform. *noun.*

wá7us ~ wé7us [wa 7us] go after (someone); continue (something); carry on (something); keep after (something). *verb(t).*

wecháy̓nup [we chay̓ nup] wide piece of land. *adjective.*

wéchwechk̲s ~ nexwwéchwechk̲s [wech wechk̲s] wide nostril nose, have a; broad-nosed; flat-nosed. *adjective.*

wek̲'ék̲' [we k̲'ek̲'] snail; AP: "an animal that lives in a shell and makes a noise like a frog." *noun.*

wek̲w' arrived here from upriver, be/have. *verb(i).*

wel cattail; bullrush. *noun.*

welk̲w'áls [wel k̲w'als] ask a question. *verb(i).*

welk̲w'alsnúmut [wel k̲w'als nu mut] get to ask; ask finally. *verb(i).*

welh and; but; since; then; while; so that; for; until. *conjunction.*

welh disobedient; rough [physically]; wild. *adjective.*

welh na wa nkw'ekw'chúsem [welh na wan kw'ekw' chu sem] mirror, small hand; small hand mirror; hand mirror, small. *noun.*

welh nes tim̓á [welh nes ti m̓a] ways [of doing something]. *noun.*

welh wa yetl'k̲'ím̓ [welh wa yetl' k̲'im̓] paintbrush. *noun.*

welh wes x̲íp'im̓ [welh wes x̲i p'im̓] claws. *noun.*

welhchán [welh chan] spread out (blankets). *verb(t).*

welhchán̓ [welh chan̓] bring (something) into disarray; scatter (something). *verb(t).*

welhchántsut [welh chan tsut] open oneself up; open up. *verb(i).*

welhch'án̓ [welh ch'an̓] bring (something) into disarray; scatter (something). *verb(t).*

welhk̲wán [welh k̲wan] boil (something). *verb(t).*

welhk̲wm [welh k̲wm] boil water; boil. *verb(i).*

wélhwelh [welh welh] rough [about a group]. *adjective.*

wélhwelhk̲wm [welh welh k̲wm] boiling, be [a bunch at the same time]. *verb(i).*

welhx̲s [welh x̲s] time of the last snow, when the frogs come to life [AP: "probably March"]. *noun.*

wéskw'i7n [wes kw'i 7n] make a noise [about dry leaves]. *verb(i).*

weshk̲án̓ [wesh k̲an̓] search (something). *verb(t).*

wetk̲áy̓s [wet k̲ay̓s] back of house. *noun.*

wétwet [wet wet] completed; finished. *adjective.*

wetwetnúmut [wet wet nu mut] finish, manage to. *verb(i).*

wetl'ch' [wetl' ch'] twenty. *numeral.*

wetl'ch' i kwi áńus [wetl' ch' 7i kwi 7a ńus] twenty two. *numeral.*
wetl'ch' i kwi nch'u7 [wetl' ch' 7i kwi n ch'u7] twenty one. *numeral.*
wetl'ch'awánexw [wetl' ch'a wa nexw] twenty years. *verb(i).*
wetsách [we tsach] send with someone. *verb(i).*
wetswíts [wets wits] small snipe [type of bird]. *noun.*
wets'k̲'án [wets' k̲'an] spread (something) apart. *verb(t).*
wets'wáts'nexw [wets' wats' nexw] get (someone) all riled up; riled up, get (someone) all. *verb(t).*
wets'wáts'numut [wets' wats' numut] cranky, get really. *verb(i).*
wéw̓elhk̲wem [we welh k̲wem] boiling, be [about water]. *verb(i).*
wéwey̓xwem [we wey̓ xwem] falling, be. *verb(i).*
wéw̓shk̲em [wew̓sh k̲em] exploring, be; searching around, be [about kids]. *verb(i).*
wewts'át [wew ts'at] tease (someone). *verb(t).*
wew̓ts'átsut [wew̓ ts'a tsut] cranky, be; find ways to get cranky. *verb(i).*
wex̲és [we x̲es] frog. *noun.*
wex̲esúllh [we x̲e sullh] tadpole. *noun.*
wex̲nách [wex̲ nach] occasion of minimal difference between high and low tide; half tide. *noun.*
wé7u [we 7u] continue; carry on; keep doing something. *verb(i).*
wé7us ~ wá7us [we 7us] continue (something); keep after (something); carry on (something); go after (someone). *verb(t).*
wík̲it [wi k̲it] spread (a canoe). *verb(t).*
wik̲'tsáń ~ wik̲'tsń [wik̲' tsań] pull (something) open; force (something) open. *verb(t).*
wík̲'tsem̓ [wik̲' tsem̓] open one's mouth wide; pull open one's mouth [with one's hands]. *verb(i).*
wik̲'tsń ~ wik̲'tsáń [wik̲' tsń] pull (something) open; force (something) open. *verb(t).*
wilk̲w'nálhen [wilk̲w' na lhen] ask, finally get to. *verb(i).*
wilk̲w't [wil k̲w't] ask (someone). *verb(t).*
wílk̲w'tway [wilk̲w' tway] ask one another. *verb(i).*
-wilh ~ -ulh ~ axwilh [-wilh] canoe {full word: **snexwílh**}; container; stomach; belly; bowels {full word: **s7étswilh**}. *suffix.*
witáńen [wi ta ńen] trap (an animal). *verb(t).*
wít'ex̲ [wi t'ex̲] Northern-style canoe; canoe, Northern-style. *noun.*
wít'in [wi t'in] tease (something) [e.g., wool; pull the wool fibers apart]. *verb(t).*
wiwipáyk̲sen [wi wi payk̲ sen] icicles. *noun.*
wiwipáyk̲snem [wi wi payk̲s nem] hanging down, be [about small objects, such as icicles, leaves, etc.]. *verb(i).*
wiw̓k̲'tsám̓ [wiw̓k̲' tsam̓] open mouth, have an [about animals]. *verb(i).*
wiw̓lhch [wiw̓ lhch] open wide, be [e.g., a flower]. *verb(i).*
wiwtl'ch' [wiw tl'ch'] twenty animals. *numeral.*
wixwán [wi xwan] drop (something) intentionally. *verb(t).*
wixwím̓ [wi xwim̓] drop it intentionally. *verb(i).*
wí7elhch'an [wi 7elh ch'an] wide open, be. *verb(t).*
wí7k̲a [wi7 k̲a] baby boy at birth; newborn baby boy. *noun.*
wi7k̲a7án [wi7 k̲a 7an] type of dance [at the end of it, everyone shouts "**huy**"]. *verb(i).*
wí7ski ~ xwí7ski [wi7 ski] let's; let's do it. *interjection.*
wí7xwem [wi7 xwem] drop; fall; slide down. *verb(i).*
wi7xwí7k̲wm [wi7 xwi7 k̲wm] go down rapids. *verb(i).*
wí7xwnexw [wi7xw nexw] dropped (something), have. *verb(t).*
wuk̲w' ~ wúk̲w'i ~ txwwúk̲w'i ~ wúwk̲w'i [wuk̲w'] go downstream; downstream, go. *verb(i).*
wúk̲w'i ~ wuk̲w' ~ txwwúk̲w'i ~ wúwk̲w'i [wu k̲w'i] go downstream; downstream, go. *verb(i).*
wúk̲w'tsut [wuk̲w' tsut] pole upriver. *verb(i).*
wuun ~ wu7n [wuun] bark. *verb(i).*

wúwk̲w'i ~ wúk̲w'i ~ wuk̲w' ~ txwwúk̲w'i [wuw k̲w'i] going downstream, be. *verb(i).*

wuwk̲w'útsut [wuw k̲w'u tsut] go with the current; current, go with the. *verb(i).*

wúwu7n [wu wu 7n] barking, be. *verb(i).*

wu7n ~ wuun [wu 7n] bark. *verb(i).*

Xw xw

-xw still; yet. *suffix.*

xw- ~ n- ~ nexw- {location}. *prefix.*

xwa ~ xwaa starve; in a state of extreme starvation, be; starvation, be in a state of extreme; totally starved, be; have passed out from hunger; passed out from hunger, have; in the last stage of starvation, be; weak from hunger, be. *verb(i).*

xwaa ~ xwa [xwaa] starve; in a state of extreme starvation, be; starvation, be in a state of extreme; totally starved, be; have passed out from hunger; passed out from hunger, have; weak from hunger, be. *verb(i).*

xwáam̓am [xwáam̓ mam] on a road grown over from the sides, be. *verb(i).*

xwacháyusem [xwa cha yu sem] open one's eyes really big. *verb(i).*

xwach' stop raining. *verb(i).*

xwákw'i [xwa kw'i] drunk, get. *verb(i).*

xwákw'ishn [xwa kw'i shn] pins and needles in one's legs or feet, have. *verb(i).*

xwákw'iyantsut [xwa kw'i yan tsut] drunk, get; drink excessively. *verb(i).*

xwakw'iyáx̲a7n [xwa kw'i ya x̲a 7n] pins and needles in one's arm, have. *verb(i).*

xwám̓am [xwa m̓am] give encouragement; offer encouragement; keep someone company; make someone happy. *verb(i).*

xwam̓s child before twins. *noun.*

xwám̓us ~ xwhám̓us [xwa m̓us] have one's face covered; covered face, have a. *adjective.*

xwátan̓ [xwa tan̓] lighten (a load); take off (something) from someone; diminish (something); make (something) less [heavy]. *verb(t).*

xwátan̓tsut [xwa tan̓ tsut] relieve oneself. *verb(i).*

xwátshi [xwat shi] relieve for (someone); diminish something for (someone) [e.g., a load]. *verb(t).*

xway̓íl [xwa y̓il] hoot [about great horned owl]. *verb(i).*

xwáy̓k̲wem [xway̓ k̲wem] wash one's head. *verb(i).*

xwáyk̲wusentway [xway k̲wu sen tway] pass each other head on; pass head on. *verb(i).*

xwáyxwasustway̓ [xway xwa sus tway̓] facing each other, be [about buildings]. *verb(i).*

xwáy̓xwayéntsut [xway̓ xwa yen tsut] fan oneself. *verb(i).*

xwayxwáy̓k̲wem [xway xway̓ k̲wem] wash one's hair. *verb(i).*

xwáy̓xwaytn [xway̓ xway tn] fan. *noun.*

xwéch'li [xwech' li] individual. *adjective.*

xwech'shí7 [xwech' shi7] between, be; interspace, be the; space between, be. *verb(i).*

xwéch'shi7s [xwech' shi7s] put (something) in between. *verb(t).*

xwech'xwách' [xwech' xwach'] not raining, be. *verb(i).*

xwekw ~ xwukw [xwekw] used, be. *verb(i).*

xwekws ~ xwukws [xwekws] use (something); wear (something). *verb(t).*

xwekwxwíkwentway [xwekw xwi kwen tway] bathing each other in the river by brushing with sand, be. *verb(i).*

xwekw'xwíkw' [xwekw' xwikw'] grey. *adjective.*

xwek̲ strong smell, have a; smell, have a strong. *adjective.*

xwek̲wk̲ántway [xwek̲w k̲an tway] pass alongside. *verb(i).*

xwelítn [xwe li tn] white person. *noun.*

xwelitn̓áw̓txw [xwe lit n̓aw̓ txw] white man's house. *noun.*

xwelnílh [xwelh nilh] on account of. *verb(i).*

xwél̓shem [xwel' shem] leaking from container in large amounts, be [about water]. *verb(i).*

xwelxwalítn [xwel xwa li tn] white people [sg: xwelitn]. *noun.*

xwem̓élwit [xwe m̓el wit] "wife of wexes." *noun.*

xwémnech [xwem nech] dead, be all. *verb(i).*

xwená7k̲en [xwe na7 k̲en] change into another language; unintelligable, be. *verb(i).*

xweńíwch [xwe ńiwch] camp in a recess [for maximal protection against wild animals; literally, insert the back]. *verb(i).*

xwenkw' tired right out, be. *verb(i).*

xwes strong smell of a stable, have a; smell strongly like a stable. *verb(i).*

xwési7n [xwe si 7n] disappear suddenly. *verb(i).*

xweshét [xwe shet] spill (a pan full of water). *verb(t).*

xwet Swainson's thrush [type of bird]. *noun.*

xwétkwem [xwet kwem] flame up. *verb(i).*

xwetxwítim [xwet xwi tim] skipping, be. *verb(i).*

xwetl'xwútl'antwaý [xwetl' xwu tl'an twaý] fighting each other [about dogs; also about a couple]. *verb(i).*

xwets cut through, be [e.g., a block of wood or lumber]. *verb(i).*

xwets'k̲w' cut right off. *verb(i).*

xweẃáxw ~ xwu7áxw [xwe ẃaxw] not yet; be not yet the case. *verb(i).*

xwéwk̲en ~ sxwéwk̲en [xwew k̲en] swan. *noun.*

xwexwch'shí7ntsut [xwexwch' shi 7n tsut] come in between; move to the space between. *verb(i).*

xwéxwelsheḿk̲es [xwe xwel sheḿ k̲es] mucus dripping from nose, have. *verb(i).*

xwexweḿélwit [xwe xwe ḿel wit] big frog. *noun.*

xwéxwetkwem [xwe xwet kwem] flame up. *verb(i).*

xwéxwi7 [xwe xwi7] left behind, be [in a race]; losing, be [as in a race]. *verb(i).*

xwey ~ xwii ~ xwiy [xwey] appear; born, be; visible, become; show oneself. *verb(i).*

xwéyayus [xwe ya yus] shine for a while [about the sun or moon between clouds]. *verb(i).*

xweýk̲ have one's bottom exposed; exposed, have one's bottom. *verb(i).*

xweýk̲w uncovered, be; exposed, be. *verb(i).*

xweýk̲wán uncover (something); expose (something). *verb(t).*

xweym defecate [euphemism for **a7k̲**]. *verb(i).*

xwéyntsut [xweyn tsut] make an appearance; show oneself. *verb(i).*

xweýús ~ xwiyús [xwe ýus] hungry, be very; starving, be. *verb(i).*

xwéyusem [xwe yu sem] showing, be [about a face]; peaking out, be [about the sun]. *verb(i).*

xwéyusmiń [xwe yus miń] show one's face to (someone). *verb(t).*

xweýúsntsut [xwe ýu sn tsut] starve oneself. *verb(i).*

xwéyxwey ~ esxwéyxweý [xwey xwey] appearing, be; visible, be; sticking out, be. *verb(i).*

xwháḿus ~ xwáḿus [xw ha ḿus] have one's face covered; covered face, have a. *adjective.*

xwhiẃts ~ xwiẃts [xw hiẃts] shoved into one's throat, get. *verb(i).*

xwhíẃtsaḿ ~ xwíẃtsaḿ [xw hiẃ tsaḿ] stick feather or twig into one's throat [in order to cause vomiting]. *verb(i).*

xwii ~ xwey ~ xwiy [xwey] born, be; appear; visible, become; show oneself. *verb(i).*

xwikw [xwikw] rub against it. *verb(i).*

xwíkwin [xwi kwin] brush (something); wash (something) off at the river. *verb(t).*

xwíkwiń [xwi kwiń] brush (something/someone). *verb(t).*

xwíkwintsut [xwi kwin tsut] bathe using sand or branches; brush oneself [after swimming]. *verb(i).*

xwíkwińtsut [xwi kwiń tsut] rub against another person. *verb(i).*

xwíkwshnan [xwikw shnan] rub (someone's) feet. *verb(t).*

xwikwtn [xwikw tn] brush used for bathing. *noun.*

xwik' [xwik'] guessed wrong in **slhahál** game, be; get off without damage; have the pointer in **slhahál** guess wrong. *verb(i).*

xwíkw'i [xwi kw'i] grey, become. *verb(i).*

xwíkw'shenam̓ [xwikw' she nam̓] rub one's own feet. *verb(i).*

xwíkw'us [xwi kw'us] red-throated loon. *noun.*

xwík̲amamen [xwi k̲a ma men] strung onto (something), be. *verb(t).*

xwík̲emamim̓ [xwi k̲e ma mim̓] thread a needle. *verb(i).*

xwík̲itsut [xwi k̲i tsut] amuse oneself. *verb(i).*

xwík̲i7 [xwi k̲i7] happy, become. *verb(i).*

xwik̲wéllh [xwi k̲wellh] steamboat. *noun.*

xwim [xwim] discard; lose. *verb(i).*

xwínay̓lh [xwi na y̓lh] want something bad to happen to someone; malicious, be. *verb(i).*

xwiníl h [xwi nilh] instead. *verb(i).*

xwínin̓ [xwi nin̓] curse (someone); wish for (someone's) death. *verb(t).*

xwip'án [xwi p'an] brush (someone) off [using branches without touching the person with the branches]. *verb(t).*

xwip'ántsut [xwi p'an tsut] brush oneself off [as when praying]. *verb(i).*

xwíp'im [xwi p'im] scratch. *verb(i).*

xwíp'in [xwi p'in] brush (something). *verb(t).*

xwítim [xwi tim] jump. *verb(i).*

xwitimán̓ [xwi ti man̓] jump at (someone). *verb(t).*

xwitimchán̓ [xwi tim chan̓] jump over (something). *verb(t).*

xwitimíwsn [xwi ti miw sn] jump over (a body). *verb(t).*

xwiw̓ástn [xwi w̓as tn] fishing rod. *noun.*

xwiwk̲sán ~ xwíwk̲sen [xwiwk̲ san] put something in (someone's) nose; stick something in (someone's) nose. *verb(t).*

xwíwk̲sen ~ xwiwk̲sán [xwiwk̲ sen] stick something into (someone's) nose; put something into (someone's) nose. *verb(t).*

xwiw̓ts ~ xwhiw̓ts [xwiw̓ts] shoved into one's throat, get. *verb(i).*

xwíw̓tsam̓ ~ xwhíw̓tsam̓ [xwiw̓ tsam̓] stick feather or twig into one's throat [in order to cause vomiting]. *verb(i).*

xwíw̓tsem [xwiw̓ tsem] gag. *verb(i).*

xwíxwel̓ [xwi xwel'] branches, small [see xwíxwel'achxw]. *noun.*

xwíxwel̓achxw [xwi xwe l'a chxw] branch. *noun.*

xwíxwikw' [xwi xwikw'] domestic blueberry; oval-leafed blueberry. *noun.*

xwíxwikw'ay̓ [xwi xwi kw'ay̓] oval-leafed blueberry bush. *noun.*

xwíxwitim [xwi xwi tim] jumping, be. *verb(i).*

xwixwiyám [xwi xwi yam] beach flea; beach fleas. *noun.*

xwiy ~ xwey ~ xwii [xwiy] born, be; appear; visible, become; show oneself. *verb(i).*

xwiyaháya7n ~ yaháya7n [xwi ya ha ya 7n] right ear. *noun.*

xwiyahús [xwi ya hus] sunny side of the mountain. *noun.*

xwiyak̲sám [xwi yak̲ sam] sneeze through right nostril [a sign of good luck]. *verb(i).*

xwiyak̲w'án [xwi ya k̲w'an] shove through (something). *verb(t).*

xwiyáshn [xwi ya shn] right leg. *noun.*

xwiyáyus ~ nexwhiyáyus [xwi ya yus] big-eyed; big eyes, have [see also x̲wechx̲wáchayus]. *adjective.*

xwiyém̓tn ~ nexwyém̓tn [xwi yem̓ tn] belt. *noun.*

xwíy̓ep [xwi y̓ep] hollow socket at base of harpoon point or at base of gaffhook head. *noun.*

xwíy̓in̓ [xwi y̓in̓] bring (something) forward to be seen. *verb(t).*

xwiyintsút [xwi yin tsut] deny a lie; make an appearance; appearance, make an. *verb(i).*

xwiy̓ús [xwi y̓us] appear [about face]. *verb(i).*

xwiyús ~ xwey̓ús [xwi yus] starving, be; hungry, be very. *verb(i).*

xwiyuykwúla7em [xwi yuy kwu la 7em] trout. *noun.*

xwi7 [xwi7] lost, be; thrown away, be; loser, be a. *verb(i).*

xwí7lhayem [xwi7 lha yem] refuse to eat; eat, refuse to. *verb(i).*

xwí7nexw [xwi7 nexw] lose (something). *verb(t).*

xwi7s [xwi7s] discard (something); throw (something) away; chase (something) away; send (wife) home. *verb(t).*

xwí7ski ~ wí7ski [xwi7 ski] let's do it; let's. *interjection.*
xwí7stway [xwi7s tway] leave one another; separated, get; divorced, get; split up. *verb(i).*
xwk̲aẏáẏan [xwk̲a ẏa ẏan] left ear. *noun.*
xwléẏlim̓ay ~ nexwléẏlim̓ay [xwleẏ li m̓ay] little bottle [see **nexwlámay**]. *noun.*
xwmétl'metl'us [xwmetl' me tl'us] dirty face, have a; dirty-faced. *adjective.*
xwmets'ńálk̲p ~ nexwmets'ńálk̲p ~ nexwmets'tńálk̲p ~ xwméts'tńálk̲p [xwmets' ńalk̲p] lie; falsehood. *noun.* tell a lie. *verb(i).*
xwméts'tńálk̲p ~ nexwmets'tńálk̲p ~ xwméts'ńálk̲p ~ nexwmets'ńálk̲p [xwmets't ńalk̲p] lie; falsehood. *noun.* tell a lie. *verb(i).*
xwmikw'mámiń [xwmikw' ma miń] wash dishes. *verb(i).*
xwmíkw'usm [xwmi kw'u sm] wash one's own face. *verb(i).*
xwmiyíẃax̲an ~ nexwmiyíẃax̲an [xwmi yi ẃa x̲an] side. *noun.*
xwmiyíwa7n ~ nexwmiyíwa7n [xwmi yi wa 7n] cheek. *noun.*
xwmúkwutsim [xwmu kwu tsim] kiss. *verb(i).*
xwmu7ts ~ nexwmú7ts [xwmu7ts] drop something from one's mouth. *verb(i).*
xwp'a7áysus ~ ip'a7úysus [xwp'a 7ay sus] cave; hollow in rock. *noun.*
xwukw ~ xwekw [xwukw] used, be. *verb(i).*
xwukws ~ xwekws [xwukws] use (something); wear (something). *verb(t).*
xwúkw'aẏi [xwu kw'a ẏi] pull in one's net. *verb(i).*
xwúkw'en [xwu kw'en] drag (something); pull (something). *verb(t).*
xwúkw'k̲am̓ [xwukw' k̲am̓] drag one's rear end on the ground. *verb(i).*
xwukw'k̲áńtsut [xwukw' k̲ań tsut] drag one's rear end along the ground. *verb(i).*
xwúkw'shnem [xwukw' shnem] drag one's legs. *verb(i).*
xwúkw'uts [xwu kw'uts] barbecue small fish by skewering them on a stick. *verb(i).*
xwúkw'utstn [xwu kw'uts tn] stick for skewering small fish to barbecue. *noun.*
xwúkw'wilh [xwukw' wilh] haul canoe up the beach. *verb(i).*
xwútem [xwu tem] throb [as after being hit by nettle, or caused by being stung]. *verb(i).*
xwúyum [xwu yum] sell. *verb(i).*
xwu7áxw ~ xweẃáxw [xwu 7axw] not yet; be not yet the case. *verb(i).*
xwyaxwm [xwya xwm] hesitant, be; bashful about doing something, be. *verb(i).*
xw7ík̲w'usn [xw7i k̲w'u sn] make a gift to (a bereaved woman); give (a bereaved woman) a condolence gift. *verb(t).*

X̱ x̱

x̱aam ~ x̱am [x̱aam] cry. *verb(i).*
x̱aaṁáẏm [x̱aaṁ 7áẏ yem] feel like crying; want to cry; cry, want to. *verb(i).*
x̱áameṅtsut [x̱áa meṅ tsut] back up. *verb(i).*
x̱áamiṅ ~ x̱amíṅ [x̱aa miṅ] mourn for (someone); cry for (someone). *verb(t).*
x̱aamíntsut [x̱aa mín tsut] cry for oneself. *verb(i).*
x̱aamnít [x̱aam nít] make (someone) cry. *verb(t).*
x̱aan [x̱aan] look at (something) [e.g., a bottle] toward the light. *verb(t).*
x̱áa7útsen [x̱áa 7ú tsen] four days. *verb(i).*
x̱áchu7 [x̱a chu7] lake [x̱echx̱achu7]. *noun.*
x̱ach't fireweed. *noun.*
x̱ach'táẏ [x̱ach' taẏ] blanket of seeds of fireweed plant. *noun.*
x̱ahámaẏlh [x̱a ha ma ẏlh] have one's child crying; crying, have one's child; have a crying child. *verb(i).*
x̱ál̓u [x̱a l'u] wild sheep's horn spoon; spoon made from wild sheep's horn. *noun.*
x̱álhi7 [x̱a lhi7] hard in the cold, get [about grease]. *verb(i).*
x̱alhnách [x̱alh nach] red-necked grebe; grebe, red-necked. *noun.*
x̱am repair. *verb(i).*
x̱aṁ lose power. *verb(i).*
x̱am ~ x̱aam cry. *verb(i).*
x̱ámalhḵwu [x̱a malh ḵwu] snowy owl. *noun.*
x̱ámaṅ [x̱a maṅ] repair (something) [about canoes or shoes, not clothes]. *verb(t).*
x̱amáẏus [x̱a ma ẏus] something owned by a beloved one. *noun.*
x̱áṁentsut [x̱a ṁen tsut] reverse oneself; back up; withdraw. *verb(i).*
x̱améyulh [x̱a me yulh] go and sympathize with persons who sustained a loss; sympathize with persons who sustained a loss, go and. *verb(i).* mourner; wailer; mortuary office. *noun.*
x̱ámi [x̱á meẏ] grab and hold onto. *verb(i).*
x̱amíṅ ~ x̱áamiṅ [x̱a miṅ] cry for (someone); mourn for (someone). *verb(t).*
x̱ámwilh [x̱am wilh] repair a canoe. *verb(i).*
x̱anḵ lady fern. *noun.*
x̱ánx̱anítṁ [x̱an x̱a ni tm] perform a type of dance [during which one cuts oneself, drawing blood]. *verb(p).*
x̱ápaẏay [x̱a pa ẏay] red cedar tree; young cedar. *noun.*
x̱ápayaẏachxw [x̱a pa ya ẏa chxw] red cedar bough. *noun.*
x̱áp'en [x̱a p'en] crush (something small); split (something small). *verb(t).*
x̱átl'ustn [x̱a tl'us tn] ridgepole. *noun.*
x̱áts'ayan [x̱a ts'a yan] pawn (something). *verb(t).*
x̱aẇs fresh [about food]; new. *adjective.*
x̱aẇs lhḵaych' [x̱aẇs lh ḵaych'] new moon. *noun.*
x̱ax̱elḵwáṁ ~ x̱áx̱elḵwem [x̱a x̱el ḵwaṁ] cut one's hair. *verb(i).*
x̱áx̱elḵwem ~ x̱ax̱elḵwáṁ [x̱a x̱el ḵwem] cut one's hair. *verb(i).*
x̱áx̱elḵwen [x̱a x̱el ḵwen] cut (someone's) hair. *verb(t).*
x̱áx̱min [x̱ax̱ min] glacier. *noun.*
x̱ay rare; scarce; special; supernatural; in short supply. *adjective.*
x̱áẏanexw [x̱a ẏa nexw] admire (something); amazed by (something), be. *verb(t).*
x̱aym [x̱aym] laugh. *verb(i).*
x̱aymín [x̱ay min] laugh at (someone). *verb(t).*
x̱áymni [x̱aym ni] make (someone) laugh; laugh, make (someone). *verb(t).*
x̱aymnúmut [x̱aym nu mut] laugh, manage to. *verb(i).*
x̱ayms make (someone) laugh; laugh, make (someone); cause (someone) to laugh. *verb(t).*
x̱a7útsen [x̱a 7u tsen] four. *numeral.*
x̱a7útsenalh [x̱a 7u tse nalh] four times. *verb(i).*

x̱a7utsenámats' [x̱a 7u tse na mats'] four strands of wool. *numeral.*

x̱a7útsenaxwilh [x̱a 7ú tse na xwilh] four containers [pots, pans, canoes]. *numeral.*

x̱a7útsenayum̓ [x̱a 7u tse na yum̓] four berries. *numeral.*

x̱a7útseniwa [x̱a 7u tse ni wa] four trees. *numeral.*

x̱a7útsenk̲ [x̱a 7u tsenk̲] four o'clock. *noun.*

x̱a7utsenmút [x̱a 7u tsen mut] four pieces. *numeral.*

x̱chaw̓ch [x̱ chaw̓ch] outer river. *noun.*

x̱chusn [x̱ chu sn] remind (someone). *verb(t).*

x̱ch'ítax̱an [x̱ ch'i ta x̱an] near side. *noun.*

x̱ch'ítay̓ch ~ ch'ítay̓ch [x̱ ch'i tay̓ch] shortcut; nearest point at opposite side [as across water]; area close to where one is going; area close to one's destination; area close to one's own territory. *noun.*

x̱ch'itíwilh [x̱ ch'i ti wilh] near side of road or river, be. *verb(i).*

x̱ch'ít-tsa7 [x̱ ch'it tsa7] near side of road or river, be on the; on this side of the road or river, be. *verb(i).*

x̱echmíxws [x̱ech mixws] remind (someone) of something. *verb(t).*

x̱échnexw [x̱ech nexw] think of (something); remember (something); think back on (something). *verb(t).*

x̱echx̱áchu7 [x̱ech x̱a chu7] lakes [sg: x̱achu7]. *noun.*

x̱échx̱ech [x̱ech x̱ech] remember. *verb(i).*

x̱echx̱echm̓ám̓ [x̱ech x̱ech m̓am̓] think of the past; reminisce. *verb(i).*

x̱échx̱echs [x̱ech x̱echs] remember (something). *verb(t).*

x̱ék̲en [x̱e k̲en] straddle (something). *verb(t).*

x̱ek̲'x̱ík̲'in [x̱ek̲' x̱i k̲'in] scratch (an itchy spot). *verb(t).*

x̱el̓ write; etch; draw. *verb(i).*

x̱élem [x̱e lem] spinal cord of a sturgeon. *noun.*

x̱elk̲'án̓ [x̱el k̲'án̓] roll (something) down; knock (something) down; roll (something) off; knock (something) off. *verb(t).*

x̱élk̲'em [x̱el k̲'em] fall from a height; roll down; fall down from a raised position. *verb(i).*

x̱élk̲'nexw [x̱elk̲' nexw] drop (something). *verb(t).*

x̱el̓nálhn [x̱el' na lhn] write, able to; etch, able to; draw, able to; get to writing/etching/drawing. *verb(i).*

x̱él̓nexw [x̱el' nexw] write/etch/draw (something), manage to; write (something) finally; etch (something) finally; draw (something) finally. *verb(t).*

x̱el̓númut [x̱el' nu mut] write, able to; draw, able to; etch, able to; write/etch/draw finally; write/etch/draw, manage to. *verb(i).*

x̱el̓s architect. *noun.*

x̱él̓shi [x̱el' shi] write for (someone); draw for (someone); etch for (someone). *verb(t).*

x̱el̓t paint (something); write (something); etch (something); draw (something). *verb(t).*

x̱el̓tn [x̱el' tn] pencil. *noun.*

x̱el̓uséyalh [x̱e l'u se yalh] photographer. *noun.*

x̱elústntem [x̱e lus tn tem] checkered face, have a. *verb(p).*

x̱élx̱elk̲'em [x̱el x̱el k̲'em] fall from a height. *verb(i).*

x̱em heavy. *adjective.*

x̱émen [x̱e men] make (something) heavy. *verb(t).*

x̱emín̓ [x̱e min̓] heavier than . . . . *verb(i).*

x̱emí7 [x̱e mi7] heavy, get. *verb(i).*

x̱em̓ts heavy voice, have a [about a person]. *adjective.*

x̱émwilh [x̱em wilh] heavy [about a person]. *adjective.*

x̱emx̱ámi7 [x̱em x̱a mi7] hang on to it. *verb(i).*

x̱enáten [x̱e na ten] step on (something); walk on (something). *verb(t).*

x̱en̓hán [x̱en̓ han] walk in someone's place. *verb(i).*

x̱én̓x̱en [x̱en̓ x̱en] retrace family tree; recount one's descent; read one's family tree; tell one's family tree. *verb(i).*

x̱enx̱ín̓ [x̱en x̱in̓] feel a sudden chill. *verb(i).*

x̱epiyéwelh ~ x̱épiy̓ewelh ~ x̱epi7éwlh ~ x̱epi7úlh ~ x̱epiy̓éwelh [x̱e pi ye welh] shallow wooden bowl; cedar platter. *noun.*

x̱épiy̓ewelh ~ x̱epiyéwelh ~ x̱epi7éwlh ~ x̱epi7úlh ~ x̱epiy̓éwelh [x̱e pi y̓e welh] shallow wooden bowl; cedar platter. *noun.*

x̱epiy̓éwelh ~ x̱epi7éwlh ~ x̱epiyéwelh ~ x̱épiy̓ewelh ~ x̱epi7úlh [x̱e pi y̓e welh] shallow wooden bowl; cedar platter. *noun.*

x̱epi7éwlh ~ x̱epiyéwelh ~ x̱épiy̓ewelh ~ x̱epi7úlh ~ x̱epiy̓éwelh [x̱e pi 7ewlh] shallow wooden bowl; cedar platter. *noun.*

x̱epi7úlh ~ x̱épiy̓ewelh ~ x̱epi7éwlh ~ x̱epiyéwelh ~ x̱epiy̓éwelh [x̱e pi 7ulh] shallow wooden bowl; cedar platter. *noun.*

x̱ep' split; crack; break [e.g., plate, cup, etc.]. *verb(i).*

x̱ep'kw'áṅ [x̱ep' kw'aṅ] chew (something) up [so that the object cracks]. *verb(t).*

x̱ep'kw'ántem [x̱ep' kw'an tem] hurt, be; ache. *verb(p).*

x̱ép'kw'em [x̱ep' kw'em] make noise when eating; make popping sounds when chewing gum. *verb(i).*

x̱ep'kw'íwsentem [x̱ep' kw'iw sen tem] rheumatism, have; rheumatic, be. *verb(p).*

x̱ép'nexw [x̱ep' nexw] have broken (something); broken (something), have; break (something) accidentally. *verb(t).*

x̱ep'shínay̓ ~ x̱ex̱ep'shínay̓ [x̱ep' shi nay̓] Cascara tree; Casara bark. *noun.*

x̱ep'x̱áp'en [x̱ep' x̱a p'en] destroy (something) intentionally. *verb(t).*

x̱ep'x̱ep'íwsntm [x̱ep' x̱e p'iw sn tm] arthritic, be; arthritis, have. *verb(p).*

x̱esí7 [x̱e si7] try again. *verb(i).*

x̱ésshen [x̱es shen] deadfall trap; big trap with stone. *noun.*

x̱est'áṅ [x̱es t'aṅ] louse egg; louse eggs; nit; nits. *noun.*

x̱esheṅáṁ [x̱e she ṅaṁ] trap. *verb(i).*

x̱éta [x̱e ta] far. *adjective.*

x̱etáy̓wilh [x̱e tay̓ wilh] far side of road or river [see also x̱eta7tsá7]. *adjective.*

x̱eta7áx̱an [x̱e ta 7a x̱an] far side. *noun.*

x̱eta7áy̓ch [x̱e ta 7ay̓ch] far side of it. *adjective.*

x̱eta7áyikwup [x̱e ta 7a yi kwup] far side of the fire, other side of the fire. *adjective.*

x̱eta7tsá7 [x̱e ta7 tsa7] on the other side of road or river [see also **x̱etáy̓wilh**]. *adjective.*

x̱etx̱éta [x̱et x̱e ta] farther and farther each time, be. *verb(i).*

x̱etx̱ít7ayus ~ nx̱etx̱ít7ayus [x̱et x̱it 7a yus] far-sighted; able to see at great distance. *adjective.*

x̱et'ḵ'í7ḵin [x̱et' ḵ'i7 ḵin] dog [breed of short-haired]. *noun.*

x̱et'tánay [x̱et' ta nay] wild ginger; ginger, wild. *noun.*

x̱etl'x̱ítl'iṅ [x̱etl' x̱i tl'iṅ] chop (something) up into small pieces; chopping (them) continuously, be [e.g., pieces of wood]. *verb(t).*

x̱etsn [x̱et sn] put (something) on the fire. *verb(t).*

x̱étsx̱etsetsut [x̱ets x̱e tse tsut] overdo it. *verb(i).*

x̱ets'ḵ'ánsem [x̱ets' ḵ'an sem] gnash one's teeth. *verb(i).*

x̱ets'x̱íts'em [x̱ets' x̱i ts'em] itchy, become. *verb(i).*

x̱ets'x̱íts'i7 [x̱ets' x̱i ts'i7] embarrased, become. *verb(i).*

x̱eẇél̓ch [x̱e ẇel'ch] play cat's cradle; cat's cradle, play. *verb(i).*

x̱ewsálkwlh [x̱ew sal kwlh] new Indian dancer. *noun.*

x̱ewsálkwlhs [x̱ew sal kwlhs] initiate (someone) to be a new dancer. *verb(t).*

x̱éẇschem [x̱eẇs chem] half tide, be; coming in, be [about tide]. *verb(i).*

x̱ewtl' break. *verb(i).*

x̱éwtl'ach [x̱ew tl'ach] break one's hand or arm. *verb(i).*

x̱ewtl'áchnexw [x̱ew tl'ach nexw] break (someone's) hand accidentally. *verb(t).*

x̱ewtl'án [x̱ew tl'an] break (stick or bone). *verb(t).*

x̱ewtl'ápsem [x̱ew tl'ap sem] break one's neck. *verb(i).*

x̱ewtl'áyaṁit [x̱ew tl'a ya ṁit] break one's shoulder. *verb(i).*

x̱ewtl'á7i [x̱ew tl'a 7i] break one's rib. *verb(i).*

x̱ewtl'ch [x̱ew tl'ch] break one's back. *verb(i).*

x̱ewtl'chḵ [x̱ewtl' chḵ] break one's hip. *verb(i).*
x̱ewtl'íw̓as [x̱ew tl'i w̓as] break one's paddle [accidentally]. *verb(i).*
x̱éwtl'iwas [x̱ew tl'i was] paddle; oar. *noun.*
x̱ewtl'iyáx̱a7en [x̱ew tl'i ya x̱a 7en] break one's arm. *verb(i).*
x̱ewtl'ḵs [x̱ewtl' ḵs] break one's nose. *verb(i).*
x̱ewtl'ḵwúy̓ach [x̱ewtl' ḵwu y̓ach] break one's finger. *verb(i).*
x̱ewtl'ḵwúy̓shen [x̱ewtl' ḵwuy̓ shen] break one's toe. *verb(i).*
x̱éwtl'nexw [x̱ewtl' nexw] broken (something), have; break (something) accidentally. *verb(t).*
x̱éwtl'shen [x̱ewtl' shen] break one's leg. *verb(i).*
x̱ewtl'shnán [x̱ewtl' shnan] break (someone's) legs. *verb(t).*
x̱ewtl'úl̓a [x̱ew tl'u l'a] break one's finger. *verb(i).*
x̱ewx̱éwtl'an [x̱ew x̱ew tl'an] breaking (them), be [about a pile of things]. *verb(t).*
x̱ex̱ahám [x̱e x̱a ham] crying, be [about a group]. *verb(i).*
x̱ex̱amí7 [x̱e x̱a mi7] heavy, be getting. *verb(i).*
x̱éx̱apáy̓ay ~ x̱í7x̱ipáy̓áy [x̱e x̱a pa y̓ay] low red cedar growth. *noun.*
x̱ex̱a7útsn [x̱e x̱a 7u tsn] four people. *numeral.*
x̱ex̱ch'í7t [x̱ex̱ ch'i7t] insult (someone). *verb(t).*
x̱éx̱ech [x̱e x̱ech] remember. *verb(i).*
x̱éx̱echs [x̱e x̱echs] remember (something). *verb(t).*
x̱éx̱en̓ [x̱e x̱en̓] frost. *noun.*
x̱ex̱en̓ántem [x̱e x̱e n̓an tem] frozen, be [about the ground]. *verb(p).*
x̱ex̱epay̓áchxw [x̱e x̱e pa y̓a chxw] low cedar growth. *noun.*
x̱éx̱ep'kw'em [x̱e x̱ep' kw'em] making noise when eating, be; making popping sounds when chewing gum, be. *verb(i).*
x̱ex̱ep'shínay̓ ~ x̱ep'shínay̓ [x̱e x̱ep' shi nay̓] Cascara tree; Cascara bark. *noun.*
x̱ex̱ew̓ís [x̱e x̱e w̓is] newlyweds. *noun.* newly wed, be. *verb(i).*
x̱ex̱ey̓ám̓ ch'ew̓an̓ [x̱e x̱e y̓am̓ ch'e w̓an̓] tell a story about (someone). *verb(t).*
x̱éx̱eyts'em ~ x̱éyx̱eyts'em [x̱e x̱ey ts'em] itching, be. *verb(i).*
x̱ex̱í7 [x̱e x̱i7] lost, be; neutralized, be [about esch'awatm]. *verb(i).*
x̱ex̱tl'áḵ'tel [x̱ex̱ tl'aḵ' tel] argue. *verb(i).*
x̱ex̱ts'éy̓ten [x̱ex̱ ts'ey̓ ten] insult. *verb(i).*
x̱ey appear; visible, become. *verb(i).*
x̱ey̓ ~ x̱i7 [x̱ey̓] appear [out of nowhere]; created, be. *verb(i).*
x̱eyám [x̱e yam] stop one. *verb(i).*
x̱eyáy̓lhm [x̱e yay̓ lhm] cause one's child to stop being bad; discipline one's child. *verb(i).*
x̱ey̓tsán̓ [x̱ey̓ tsan̓] comfort (a crying baby); cause (someone) to stop crying or talking too much. *verb(t).*
x̱ey̓tsáy̓lh [x̱ey̓ tsa y̓lh] lullaby. *noun.* sing a lullaby; cause child to stop crying or talking too much. *verb(i).*
x̱éyts'em [x̱ey ts'em] itch. *verb(i).*
x̱éyts'em̓ach [x̱ey ts'e m̓ach] itchy hand, have an. *adjective.*
x̱eyts'em̓álhx̱a [x̱ey ts'e m̓alh x̱a] itchy throat, have an. *adjective.*
x̱éyts'emḵ [x̱ey ts'emḵ] itchy rear end, have an. *adjective.*
x̱éyts'emḵw [x̱ey ts'emḵw] itchy head, have an. *adjective.*
x̱éyts'em̓us [x̱ey ts'e m̓us] itchy face, have a. *adjective.*
x̱eyx̱ ~ x̱i7x̱ [x̱eyx̱] make war; war, be at. *verb(i).*
x̱ey̓x̱áy̓em ~ x̱éy̓x̱ey̓em [x̱ey̓ x̱a y̓em] laughing, be. *verb(i).*
x̱éyx̱entway [x̱ey x̱en tway] fight in battle. *verb(i).*
x̱eyx̱ewilh [x̱ey x̱e wilh] war canoe. *noun.*
x̱éy̓x̱ey̓em ~ x̱ey̓x̱áy̓em [x̱ey̓ x̱e y̓em] laughing, be. *verb(i).*
x̱eyx̱éyt ~ x̱ix̱ít [x̱ey x̱eyt] laugh at (someone). *verb(t).*
x̱éyx̱eyts'em ~ x̱éx̱eyts'em [x̱ey x̱ey ts'em] itching, be. *verb(i).*
x̱eyx̱ḵínm [x̱eyx̱ ḵi nm] war whoop. *noun.*
x̱ích'emḵw [x̱i ch'emḵw] bushy head, have a. *verb(i).*
x̱ích'intsut [x̱i ch'in tsut] raised hair on neck, have [e.g., a cat]; raise hackles. *verb(i).*

x̱ich'ní7kwup [x̱ich' ni7 kwup] cut wood. *verb(i).*

x̱íkw'in [x̱i kw'in] munch (something); chew (something) [about human, not at regular meal]. *verb(t).*

x̱íkw'usem [x̱i kw'u sem] make a face in disgust. *verb(i).*

x̱iḵ' [x̱iḵ'] scratched, be. *verb(i).*

x̱íḵ'in [x̱i ḵ'in] scratch (something). *verb(t).*

x̱íḵ'intsut [x̱i ḵ'in tsut] scratch oneself. *verb(i).*

x̱iḵ'ḵám̓ [x̱iḵ' ḵam̓] scratch one's behind. *verb(i).*

x̱íḵ'ḵwem̓ [x̱iḵ' ḵwem̓] scratch one's head. *verb(i).*

x̱íl̓ich [x̱i l'ich] spawned out and almost dead, be [about a salmon, a stage further than ma7at]. *verb(i).*

x̱íl̓x̱ilḵ'emáyu [x̱il' x̱il ḵ'e ma yu] roll down a slope intentionally. *verb(i).*

x̱im̓chúsen [x̱im̓ chu sen] grab the hair on (someone's) forehead. *verb(t).*

x̱ímin̓ [x̱i min̓] pull (someone's) hair; grab (someone) by the hair. *verb(t).*

x̱ímin̓sut [x̱i min̓ sut] grab one's own hair; pull one's own hair. *verb(i).*

x̱im̓x̱im̓náchtn [x̱im̓ x̱im̓ nach tn] kidney. *noun.*

x̱ip' [x̱ip'] knicked, be just; nipped, get; scratched, get; touched, get [by something flying by]. *verb(i).*

x̱íp'in [x̱i p'in] claw (something); scratch (something). *verb(t).*

x̱íp'inupten [x̱i p'i nup ten] rake [e.g., for collecting leaves]. *noun.*

x̱ísachí7ntem [x̱i sa chi 7n tem] cramped hands, have. *verb(p).*

x̱ísin̓tem [x̱i sin̓ tem] shrunk, be. *verb(p).*

x̱ísin̓tsut [x̱i sin̓ tsut] cramps, have; shrink. *verb(i).*

x̱isiwílhentem [x̱i si wi lhen tem] cramps, have stomach; stomach cramps, have. *verb(p).*

x̱isí7 [x̱i si7] fresh, be [about food]. *verb(i).*

x̱ísḵsem [x̱isḵ sem] move one's nose in disgust; turn up one's nose. *verb(i).*

x̱ishnán̓tem [x̱ish nan̓ tem] cramps in one's legs or feet, have. *verb(p).*

x̱ít'intsut [x̱i t'in tsut] stretch onself. *verb(i).*

x̱itl' [x̱itl'] chop; cut. *verb(i).*

x̱ítl'im̓ [x̱i tl'im̓] cut up; chop up. *verb(i).*

x̱ítl'in [x̱i tl'in] chop (something); cut (something) [especially wood]. *verb(t).*

x̱itl'iyúpsen [x̱i tl'i yup sen] cut off (animal's) tail. *verb(t).*

x̱ítl'min [x̱itl' min] wood chips from chopping with axe. *noun.*

x̱ítl'nexw [x̱itl' nexw] chop (something), manage to. *verb(t).*

x̱itl'ní7kwup [x̱itl' ni7 kwup] chop firewood. *verb(i).*

x̱its [x̱its] lie down. *verb(i).*

x̱itsḵ [x̱itsḵ] fell a tree. *verb(i).* tree that has fallen by chopping; fallen tree; timber. *noun.*

x̱itsḵán̓ ~ x̱ítsḵen [x̱its ḵan̓] fell (a tree). *verb(t).*

x̱ítsḵen ~ x̱itsḵán̓ [x̱its ḵen] fell (a tree). *verb(t).*

x̱íts'i [x̱i ts'i] embarrassed, be; bring shame upon onself [so that one has to blush]. *verb(i).*

x̱íxwa [x̱i xwa] giant red sea urchin; sea urchin, giant red. *noun.*

x̱ix̱a7útsen [x̱i x̱a 7u tsen] four animals. *numeral.*

x̱ix̱ít ~ x̱eyx̱éyt [x̱i x̱it] laugh at (someone). *verb(t).*

x̱íx̱itl'en [x̱i x̱i tl'en] chopping (something), be [e.g., wood]. *verb(t).*

x̱íx̱its'em [x̱i x̱i ts'em] itching, be. *verb(i).*

x̱íx̱its'i7 [x̱i x̱i ts'i7] feel cheap; cheap, feel. *verb(i).*

x̱ix̱p'ayáx̱a7n ~ x̱ix̱p'iy̓áx̱a7n [x̱ix̱ p'a ya x̱a 7n] carry an armful of something; carry a large bunch of something. *verb(i).*

x̱ix̱p'iy̓áx̱a7n ~ x̱ix̱p'ayáx̱a7n [x̱ix̱ p'i y̓a x̱a 7n] carry a large bunch in one's arms; carry an armful of something. *verb(i).*

x̱iyách [x̱i yach] separate from fighting. *verb(i).*

x̱íyan [x̱i yan] stop (them); quiet (someone); stop (them) from arguing, fighting, gambling. *verb(t).*

x̱iyúm [x̱i yum] food tube. *noun.*

x̱íyus [x̱i yus] menstruate [see also x̱7éyulh]. *verb(i).*

x̱i7 ~ x̱ey̓ [x̱i7] appear [out of nowhere]; created, be; appear suddenly. *verb(i).*

x̱í7kwen ~ sx̱í7kwen [x̱i7 kwen] kidney. *noun.*

x̱í7nim [x̱i7 nim] growl. *verb(i).*

x̱i7t [x̱i7t] transform (someone). *verb(t).*

x̱i7x̱ ~ x̱eyx̱ [x̱i7 x̱] make war; war, be at. *verb(i).*

x̱í7x̱ipáẏáy ~ x̱éx̱apáẏay [x̱i7 x̱i pa ẏay] low red cedar growth. *noun.*

x̱i7x̱ís [x̱i7 x̱is] feign at (something); make a feigning movement at (someone/ something); make believe (something). *verb(t).*

x̱í7x̱i7pay [x̱i7 x̱i7 pay] young red cedar. *noun.*

x̱i7x̱p' [x̱i7 x̱p'] smash the shell of a little-neck clam on a rock [in order to eat the inside raw]. *verb(i).*

x̱lhan [x̱ lhan] epidemic; sickness. *noun.*

x̱lhantm [x̱ lhan tm] visited by an epidemic, be; epidemic, be visited by an. *verb(p).*

x̱lhétsut [x̱ lhe tsut] drunk, get really. *verb(i).*

x̱paẏ [x̱ paẏ] red cedar. *noun.*

x̱paẏ yíẏulh [x̱ paẏ yi ẏulh] red cedar wood. *noun.*

x̱sháyup'em [x̱ sha yu p'em] breathe. *verb(i).*

x̱t'et [x̱ t'et] put a spell on (someone) [about **sxw7umten**]; put an evil spell on (someone). *verb(t).*

x̱t'etm [x̱ t'e tm] under a spell, be. *verb(p).*

x̱tsem [x̱ tsem] cedar bent box. *noun.*

x̱ts'aẏ [x̱ ts'aẏ] brand-new canoe; canoe that is just finished; unfinished canoe-hull. *noun.*

x̱7éyulh [x̱ 7e yulh] menstruate [see also **x̱íyus**]. *verb(i).*

X̱w x̱w

x̱wáḵamentsut [x̱wa ḵa men tsut] blow really hard and make noise [about wind]. *verb(i).*

x̱waḵ' anxious; eager. *adjective.*

x̱wáḵ'et [x̱wa ḵ'et] covet (something); desire (something); want (something). *verb(t).*

x̱waḵw'éń [x̱wa ḵw'eń] bar (something) shut. *verb(t).*

x̱wam ~ x̱wem run swiftly [about water]; swift water, be; swift, be [about water]. *verb(i).*

x̱wámi7 ~ x̱wemí7 [x̱wa mi7] running swiftly, be; swift, get [about water]. *verb(i).*

x̱wastn [x̱was tn] suet grease from bear, deer, etc.; hardened grease; fat. *noun.*

x̱way so hot it melts, be; hot, be so that it melts. *verb(i).*

x̱way ~ x̱wey die [plural]; wiped out by the enemy, be; go extinct; perish; become senseless; paralyzed, be; faint. *verb(i).*

x̱wáyach [x̱wa yach] paralyzed arm, have a. *adjective.*

x̱wáyat [x̱wa yat] slaughter (them); wipe (them) out. *verb(t).*

x̱wáẏay [x̱wa ẏay] Sitka willow tree. *noun.*

x̱wáẏelwas ~ x̱wá7ilwes [x̱wa ẏel was] excited, get. *verb(i).*

x̱waẏíl [x̱wa ẏil] neigh [about horse]; hoot [about owl]. *verb(i).*

x̱wáyiws [x̱wa yiws] paralyzed, be [throughout whole body]. *verb(i).*

x̱wayshn [x̱way shn] paralyzed leg, have a. *adjective.*

x̱wáẏten ~ x̱wa7ítn [x̱waẏ ten] bedpan; piss pot; potty. *noun.*

x̱wá7ilwes ~ x̱wiẏílus [x̱wa 7il wes] excited, be/become/get; disturbed, become. *verb(i).*

x̱wa7ítn ~ x̱wáẏten [x̱wa 7i tn] piss pot; potty; bedpan. *noun.*

x̱wechx̱wáchayus [x̱wech x̱wa cha yus] big-eyed; big eyes, have [see also **xwiyáyus** and **nexwhiyáyus**]. *adjective.*

x̱wech'x̱wích'em [x̱wech' x̱wi ch'em] make a lot of noise. *verb(i).*

x̱weḵ'iyúshntm ta ḵwlhi7shn [x̱we ḵ'i yu shn tm taḵw lhi7 shn] tie one's shoes. *verb(p).*

x̱weḵwíchen ~ sx̱weḵwíchen [x̱we ḵwi chen] net; spider; spider's net. *noun.*

x̱weḵw7áy [x̱weḵw 7ay] pocket. *noun.*

x̱weḵw' ~ x̱wiḵw' [x̱weḵw'] tied up, be; arrested, be. *verb(i).*

x̱weḵw'éwilh [x̱we ḵw'e wilh] lace up child in the xweqw'wilhtn. *verb(i).*

x̱weḵw'éwilhn [x̱we ḵw'e wi lhn] lace up (a child) in the **xweḵw'wilhtn**. *verb(t).*

x̱weḵw'éwilhtn [x̱we ḵw'e wilh tn] blanket cradle. *noun.*

x̱weḵw'iyúshentem [x̱we ḵw'i yu shen tem] tie (something) up. *verb(p).*

x̱wél̓shm [x̱wel' shm] flow. *verb(i).*

x̱welt make (a small channel) with a stick. *verb(t).*

x̱wéltem [x̱wel tem] make (a little ditch). *verb(p).*

x̱weltsút [x̱wel tsut] make a ditch by itself. *verb(i).*

x̱welúsen [x̱we lu sen] make (a ditch). *verb(t).*

x̱welwílem [x̱wel wi lem] camouflage a canoe. *verb(i).*

x̱welwíltn [x̱wel wil tn] boughs used for camouflaging a canoe. *noun.*

x̱welx̱wíl̓tsań [x̱wel x̱wil' tsań] open (them) up. *verb(t).*

x̱wem ~ x̱wam swift water, be; run swiftly [about water]; swift, be [about water]. *verb(i).*

x̱wemí7 ~ x̱wámi7 [x̱we mi7] swift, get; running swiftly, be [about water]. *verb(i).*

x̱wepḵwáńtsut [x̱wep ḵwań tsut] make a lot of noise. *verb(i).*

x̱wes fat; greasy. *adjective.*

x̱wesí7 [x̱we si7] get fat; fat, get. *verb(i).*

x̱wesmíń [x̱wes mińn] fatter than . . . , be. *verb(i).*

x̱wéshem [x̱we shem] splash; make a splashing noise. *verb(i).*
x̱wéshen [x̱we shen] rinse (something). *verb(t).*
x̱wéshi7n [x̱we shi 7n] splash. *verb(i).*
x̱wetspts [x̱wets pts] ripped mouth, have a [about fish; occurs when trolling and the mouth rips or when gaffhook rips through a fish]. *adjective.*
x̱wéts'ḵw'an [x̱wets' ḵw'an] cut (something) off. *verb(t).*
x̱wets'x̱wúts' [x̱wets' x̱wuts'] sit on a hard object; lie on a hard object. *verb(i).*
x̱wex̱wá7 [x̱we x̱wa7] imitate; copy. *verb(i).*
x̱wex̱wá7t [x̱we x̱wa7t] copy (someone); imitate (someone). *verb(t).*
x̱wex̱wá7usen [x̱we x̱wa 7u sen] make faces at (someone). *verb(t).*
x̱wex̱wekw'el̓s [x̱we x̱we kw'el's] potato, a kind of. *noun.*
x̱wex̱weẏáṁ [x̱we x̱we ẏaṁ] tell a story. *verb(i).*
x̱wex̱weytsús [x̱we x̱wey tsus] move perpendicular to something. *verb(i).*
x̱wex̱weẏúsen [x̱we x̱we ẏu sen] tell a legend to (someone). *verb(t).*
x̱wex̱wiẏáṁ [x̱we x̱wi ẏaṁ] tell a legend. *verb(i).*
x̱wex̱wiẏúsen [x̱we x̱wi ẏu sen] tell (someone) a story. *verb(t).*
x̱wex̱wsél̓ḵen ~ x̱wux̱wsél̓ḵen [x̱wex̱w sel' ḵen] mountain goat. *noun.*
x̱wex̱wsí7 [x̱wex̱w si7] getting fat, be; fat, be getting. *verb(i).*
x̱wéx̱wshem [x̱wex̱w shem] splashing continuously, be. *verb(i).*
x̱wey ~ x̱way wiped out by enemy, be; die [plural]; go extinct; perish; become senseless; paralyzed, be; faint. *verb(i).*
x̱weytsús [x̱wey tsus] move perpendicular to a force [current or gravity]. *verb(i).*
x̱we7ít [x̱we 7it] iron wedge; wedge. *noun.*
x̱we7ítaẏ [x̱we 7i taẏ] Western yew tree. *noun.*
x̱wích'em [x̱wi ch'em] humming noise, be a. *verb(i).*
x̱wích'intsut [x̱wi ch'in tsut] make a humming noise. *verb(i).*
x̱wiitl' [x̱wiitl'] span [unit of measurement the distance between stretched thumb and index finger]. *noun.*
x̱wiḵw' ~ x̱weḵw' [x̱wiḵw'] arrested, be; tied up, be. *verb(i).*
x̱wíḵw'aẏchaṅ [x̱wi ḵw'aẏ chaṅ] tie (something) up into a bundle. *verb(t).*
x̱wíḵw'iṅ [x̱wi ḵw'iṅ] put (someone) in jail; tie (something) up; arrest (someone); connect (something). *verb(t).*
x̱wiḵw'i7chán ~ x̱wíḵw'i7chen [x̱wi ḵw'i7 chan] bundle (something) up. *verb(t).*
x̱wíḵw'i7chen ~ x̱wiḵw'i7chán [x̱wi ḵw'i7 chen] bundle (something) up. *verb(t).*
x̱wíḵw'i7chtn [x̱wi ḵw'i7 ch tn] string or rope used for tying up bundles. *noun.*
x̱wíḵw'ḵsen [x̱wiḵw'ḵ sen] tie ribbon on (hairlock). *verb(t).*
x̱wíḵw'usm [x̱wi ḵw'u sm] hang oneself. *verb(i).*
x̱wíḵw'usn [x̱wi ḵw'u sn] hang (someone). *verb(t).*
x̱wil̓ [x̱wil'] come off [about lid]; come out [about nail or teeth]. *verb(i).*
x̱wíl̓am [x̱wi l'am] emptied, be [about container]. *verb(i).*
x̱wil̓ansántem [x̱wi l'an san tem] pull out (someone's) tooth. *verb(p).*
x̱wil̓áẏaḵínan [x̱wi l'a ẏa ḵi nan] remove guts from (something). *verb(t).*
x̱wil̓aẏáḵinem [x̱wi l'a ẏa ḵi nem] remove guts. *verb(i).*
x̱wil̓áẏaḵínexw [x̱wi l'a ẏa ḵi nexw] removed guts from (something), have. *verb(t).*
x̱wílaẏips [x̱wi la ẏips] come off [e.g., button]. *verb(i).*
x̱wíliḵw [x̱wi liḵw] duck. *noun.*
x̱wíl̓ḵsem [x̱wil'ḵ sem] blow one's nose. *verb(i).*
x̱wil̓ḵwáṅ ~ x̱wil̓ḵwn [x̱wil' ḵwaṅ] cut off the head of (something). *verb(t).*
x̱wil̓ḵwn ~ x̱wil̓ḵwáṅ [x̱wil' ḵwn] cut off the head of (something). *verb(t).*
x̱wíl̓mamin [x̱wil' ma min] empty it. *verb(i).*
x̱wílneẇas [x̱wil ne ẇas] fall apart. *verb(i).*
x̱wíl̓neẇás [x̱wil' ne ẇas] separated, be; divorced, get. *verb(i).*
x̱wílneẇásen [x̱wil ne ẇa sen] dismantle (something); take (something) apart. *verb(t).*

x̱wil̓new̓ásn [x̱wil’ ne w̓a sn] take (something) apart. *verb(t).*

x̱wil̓new̓áswit [x̱wil’ ne w̓as wit] separate [about spouses]. *verb(i).*

x̱wíl̓nexw [x̱wil’ nexw] open (something); open (something), manage to. *verb(t).*

x̱wíl̓numut [x̱wil’ nu mut] get away from, manage to. *verb(i).*

x̱wil̓s [x̱wil’s] take (something) off [about clothing]. *verb(t).*

x̱wil̓t [x̱wil’t] take (something) off. *verb(t).*

x̱wil̓ts ~ nx̱wil̓ts [x̱wil’ts] open, be. *verb(i).*

x̱wil̓tsáń ~ nx̱wil̓tsn ~ nx̱wil̓tsáń ~ x̱wil̓tsn ~ x̱wíl̓tseń [x̱wil’ tsań] open (something). *verb(t).*

x̱wil̓tsáyus [x̱wil’ tsa yus] open eyes, have. *verb(i).*

x̱wíl̓tseń ~ x̱wil̓tsáń ~ nx̱wil̓tsn ~ nx̱wil̓tsáń ~ x̱wil̓tsn [x̱wil’ tseń] open (something). *verb(t).*

x̱wíl̓tsim̓ [x̱wil’ tsim̓] open a door. *verb(i).*

x̱wil̓tsn ~ x̱wil̓tsáń ~ nx̱wil̓tsn ~ nx̱wil̓tsáń ~ x̱wíl̓tseń [x̱wil’ tsn] open (something). *verb(t).*

x̱wíl̓tsnexw ~ nx̱wíl̓tsnexw [x̱wil’ts nexw] open (something); open (something), manage to; opened (something), have. *verb(t).*

x̱wíl̓wilhtn [x̱wil’ wilh tn] laxative. *noun.*

x̱wíl̓x̱welmamin [x̱wil’ x̱wel ma min] empty inside, be; hollow, be. *verb(i).*

x̱wílx̱wil̓tsen [x̱wil x̱wil’ tsen] open (something). *verb(t).*

x̱wíni [x̱wi ni] curse (someone). *verb(t).*

x̱wítl’ulh ~ x̱wítl’wilh [x̱wi tl’ulh] quarter cup; 1/4 of a cup. *noun.* half-full, be. *verb(i).*

x̱wítl’wilh ~ x̱wítl’ulh [x̱witl’ wilh] half-full, be. *verb(i).* quarter cup; 1/4 of a cup. *noun.*

x̱wits’ [x̱wits’] lie on something hard; sit on something hard; step on something hard. *verb(i).*

x̱wíx̱wel̓em [x̱wi x̱we l’em] empty, be. *verb(i).*

x̱wíx̱wel̓ts [x̱wi x̱wel’ts] opened, be [about a box]. *verb(i).*

x̱wíx̱wich’am [x̱wi x̱wi ch’am] swish [about a stick]; howl [about the wind]; rattle [about a rattle]. *verb(i).*

x̱wíx̱wil̓tsań [x̱wi x̱wil’ tsań] opening (something), be. *verb(t).*

x̱wiyaḵw’án [x̱wi ya ḵw’an] shove through (dense mass of people or underbrush). *verb(t).*

x̱wiyaḵw’ántsut [x̱wi ya ḵw’an tsut] work one’s way through [dense mass of people or underbrush]. *verb(i).*

x̱wiyaḵw’éy [x̱wi ya ḵw’ey] get into [a dense mass; about people or underbrush]. *verb(i).*

x̱wiy̓ílus ~ x̱wá7ilwes [x̱wi y̓i lus] excited, be/become/get; disturbed, become. *verb(i).*

x̱wí7lem [x̱wi7 lem] rope; twine; string. *noun.*

x̱wi7lt [x̱wi7 lt] take (something) off. *verb(t).*

x̱wí7ltsayusem [x̱wi 7l tsa yu sem] open one’s eyes. *verb(i).*

x̱wí7stem [x̱wi7 stem] abandon (something). *verb(p).*

x̱wḵwíchen [x̱w ḵwi chen] make a net. *verb(i).*

x̱wúḵwem [x̱wu ḵwem] deep wooden bowl; bowl, deep wooden [used for eating soup]. *noun.*

x̱wúḵw’ayi [x̱wu ḵw’a yi] fish ready for cleaning, bunch of. *noun.*

x̱wúḵw’aytn [x̱wu ḵw’ay tn] rock corral [where fish are kept after being caught]. *noun.*

x̱wúḵw’en [x̱wu ḵw’en] snore. *verb(i).*

x̱wúḵw’tsut [x̱wuḵw’ tsut] pole up in a canoe. *verb(i).*

x̱wúmlhnalh [x̱wumlh nalh] throat; windpipe; gullet. *noun.*

x̱wuńúńtsut [x̱wu ńuń tsut] make bullroarer noise from cold weather. *verb(i).*

x̱wúńx̱wun [x̱wuń x̱wun] bullroarer. *noun.* make noise with bullroarer [in order to produce rain]; rattle for rain. *verb(i).*

x̱wúsim̓ [x̱wu sim̓] grab a handful. *verb(i).*

x̱wúsum [x̱wu sum] make Indian ice cream; prepare soapberries. *verb(i).*

x̱wúsumay̓ ~ sx̱wúsumay̓ [x̱wu su may̓] soapberry plant. *noun.*

x̱wúsuń [x̱wu suń] take a lot of (something) in one’s hand. *verb(t).*

x̱wútl’un [x̱wu tl’un] chew (something) up. *verb(t).*

x̲wútl'untway [x̲wu tl'un tway] fight each other [about dogs]. *verb(i).*

x̲wutsnálhntsut [x̲wuts na lhn tsut] make a fourth attempt; attempt a fourth time; try for the fourth time. *verb(i).*

x̲wutsnalhshá7 [x̲wuts nalh sha7] forty. *numeral.*

x̲wutsnalhshá7 i kwi an̓us [x̲wuts nalh sha7 7i kwi 7a n̓us] forty two. *numeral.*

x̲wutsnalhshá7 i kwi nch'u7 [x̲wuts nalh sha7 7i kwi n ch'u7] forty one. *numeral.*

x̲wuts' [x̲wuts'] stuck; bruised. *adjective.*

x̲wúts'ach [x̲wu ts'ach] hit one's hand on something hard. *verb(i).*

x̲wuts'shn [x̲wuts' shn] hurt one's foot; step on a rock. *verb(i).*

x̲wúts'un [x̲wu ts'un] block (something) up; squeeze (something) into something; lever (something) up. *verb(t).*

x̲wúts'untsut [x̲wu ts'un tsut] squeeze oneself in. *verb(i).*

x̲wuuk̲w' [x̲wuuk̲w'] sawbill duck; common merganser. *noun.*

x̲wúx̲wel̓k̲w [x̲wu x̲wel'k̲w] head covering. *noun.*

x̲wúx̲wk̲w'etsut [x̲wux̲w k̲w'e tsut] poling a canoe, be. *verb(i).*

x̲wux̲wsél̓k̲en ~ x̲wex̲wsél̓k̲en [x̲wux̲w sel' k̲en] mountain goat. *noun.*

x̲wúx̲wuts'un̓ [x̲wu x̲wu ts'un̓] blocking (something) up to make it higher, be; levering (something) up continuously, be. *verb(t).*

x̲wúx̲wuyumi7 [x̲wu x̲wu yu mi7] grey hair, be getting. *verb(i).*

x̲wúyumi7 [x̲wu yu mi7] grey hair, get; grey-haired, become. *verb(i).*

x̲wú7k̲in [x̲wu7 k̲in] marten [type of animal]. *noun.*

x̲wú7us [x̲wu 7us] unable to stop doing it. *verb(i).*

Y y

-y ~ -i ~ -i7 [-y] [inchoative suffix]; become; get. *suffix.*

ya [goes with haw; no translation]. *clitic.*

ya short for iya. *determiner.*

ya tl' sometimes. *adverb.*

yaa [yaa] I see [said when someone's telling a story]. *interjection.*

yaaṅ [yaaṅ] warn (someone). *verb(t).*

yaa7 ~ ya7 [yaa7] fixed, be [no longer loose]; stuck, be; tightened, be; tight, be; shut tightly, be; tied tightly, be. *verb(i).*

yach jarred, be. *verb(i).*

yaháya7n ~ xwiyaháya7n [ya ha ya 7n] right ear. *noun.*

yahíws ~ syahíws [ya hiws] right arm; right side. *noun.*

yahús [ya hus] face the sun; sunward. *adjective.* right eye [also syahus]. *noun.*

yáḵantem [ya ḵan tem] poke (someone) in rear. *verb(p).*

yaḵ' fall down; fallen, be [about tree]. *verb(i).*

yáḵ'an [ya ḵ'an] polish (something) by filing; sharpen (something) by filing. *verb(t).*

yáḵ'an [ya ḵ'an] cause (something) to fall down; fell (something) [as by the old method of using wedges and hot-rock burning]. *verb(t).*

yaḵw found, be. *verb(i).*

yaḵw extinguished, be; out, be [about a light or a fire]. *verb(i).*

yáḵwaṅ [ya ḵwaṅ] extinguish (a fire); put out (a fire); turn down (a light). *verb(t).*

yáḵwi [ya ḵwi] die down [about wind]. *verb(i).*

yáḵwi7 [ya ḵwi7] go out [about a fire]. *verb(i).*

yáḵwnexw [yaḵw nexw] discover (something); find (something); found (something), have. *verb(t).*

yaḵw' calm water, be; no wind, be. *verb(i).*

yáḵw'em [ya ḵw'em] sweat. *verb(i).* sweat. *noun.*

yáḵw'i [ya ḵw'i] stop; cease; abate [about wind]. *verb(i).*

yáḵw'i7 [ya ḵw'i7] calm, be [about water]. *verb(i).*

yalh just did something; finally; at last; after that; then. *verb(i).*

yalh ses therefore s/he; s/he just. *adverb.*

yáman ~ yámen [ya man] even if; even; although; yet. *conjunction.*

yámen ~ yáman [ya men] even; yet; even if; although. *conjunction.*

yanm [ya nm] take food to one's in-laws. *verb(i).*

yánmen [yan men] take food to (one's in-laws). *verb(t).*

yáṅten [yaṅ ten] pole for baby basket; swing for rocking children. *noun.*

-yap you, your (plural). *suffix.*

-yas ~ -yes days {full word: skwáyel}. *suffix.*

yásaẃay [ya sa ẃay] mountain alder tree. *noun.*

yaseĺáĺtxw [ya se l'al' txw] man who has more than one wife; bigamist. *noun.*

yasiḵwáṁ [ya si ḵwaṁ] put on one's hat. *verb(i).*

yási7ḵw [ya si7ḵw] hat; head-cover used by sxw7úmten. *noun.*

yasḵwáṅ [yas ḵwaṅ] put a hat on (someone). *verb(t).*

yátshen [yat shen] mainland. *noun.*

yátshen nékwem ta temíxw [yat shen ne kwem ta te mixw] earthquake. *phrase.*

yáwap [ya wap] sail. *verb(i).*

yáwap snexwílh [ya wap sne xwilh] sailboat. *noun.*

yáẃilh swáẏwi7ḵa [ya ẃilh swaẏ wi7 ḵa] bachelor. *noun.*

yaxwm [ya xwm] backwards, be [about doing or saying something]; hesitant, be; bashful about doing or saything something, be; have scruples. *verb(i).*

yax̱í7u [ya x̱i 7u] pit lamp for fish or ducks; go pit lamping for fish or ducks. *verb(i).*

yáx̱waṅ [ya x̱waṅ] thaw (something); melt (something). *verb(t).*

yáx̲wi7 [ya x̲wi7] melt. *verb(i).*
yáyak̲w'am [ya ya k̲w'am] sweat profusely; in a high fever, be; high fever, have a; fever, have a high. *verb(i).*
yáẏaxwm [ya ẏa xwm] have scruples. *verb(i).*
yaẏlh order (an object). *verb(i).*
yáyneẇas [yay ne ẇas] friends, become. *verb(i).*
yáẏwes [yaẏ wes] bed; bed platform. *noun.*
yá7a ~ yaa7 [ya 7a] stuck, get; tightened, be; fixed, be [no longer loose]; tight, be; shut tightly, be; tied tightly, be. *verb(i).*
ya7n [ya 7n] tighten (something); put (something) on; hold (something) tightly; tie (something) tightly. *verb(t).*
ya7t vomit. *verb(t).*
yá7tsaṅ [ya7 tsaṅ] lock (something); bar (something). *verb(t).*
yá7ya [ya7 ya] tightly; tight, be. *verb(i).*
yá7yamut [ya7 ya mut] shut tightly, be. *verb(i).*
yá7yamuts [ya7 ya muts] make (something) windproof; windproof, make (something). *verb(t).*
yá7yas [ya7 yas] put (something) on tightly; hold onto (something) tightly; tie (something) tightly. *verb(t).*
yá7yats [ya7 yats] stoppered tightly, be [about a bottle]. *verb(i).*
yech' full, be. *verb(i).*
yech'ét [ye ch'et] fill (something) up. *verb(t).*
yech'mámen [yech' ma men] fill (something) up. *verb(t).*
yech'númut [yech' nu mut] filled it up finally. *verb(i).*
yéch'wilh [yech' wilh] filled up, be [about stomach]; full stomach, have a. *verb(i).*
yech'yách'shen [yech' yach' shen] sore feet, be getting; bare feet on rocks, have. *verb(i).*
yeh I see; well, well; indeed! [used by listeners to a story]. *interjection.*
yekw'áyak̲'in [ye kw'a ya k̲'in] long upriver side of house built with its long sides perpendicular to the river; long landward side of house built with its long sides parallel to the river [same as **schishmax̲an**]. *noun.*
yekw'á7i [ye kw'a 7i] I think so; maybe; oh, yes. *interjection.*
yekw'tsá7min [yekw' tsa7 min] upstream, be. *verb(i).*
yek̲álesti [ye k̲a les ti] communion. *noun.*
yek̲í [ye k̲i] crawl; creep. *verb(i).*
yek̲ínem [ye k̲i nem] consumption, have; tuberculosis, have; TB, have. *verb(i).*
yek̲s nickname given to a baby girl because she would become a good berry-picker. *noun.*
yek̲' polished, be. *verb(i).*
yék̲'min [yek̲' min] dust from filing; filings. *noun.*
yek̲'yák̲'an [yek̲' ya k̲'an] fell (a lot of trees). *verb(t).*
yek̲w ~ yek̲wáẏ clothes. *noun.*
yek̲wáẏ ~ yek̲w [ye k̲waẏ] clothes. *noun.*
yék̲welchp [ye k̲wel chp] put wood on the fire. *verb(i).*
yek̲w' wood that is getting rotten [general term]; rotten wood or tree. *noun.*
yelak̲'í7chen [ye la k̲'i7 chen] fall on a house [about trees]. *verb(i).*
yel̓ánem ~ syel̓ánem [ye l'a nem] year. *noun.*
yéla7en [ye la 7en] wing. *noun.*
yelx̲ look for it. *verb(i).*
yelx̲íws [yel x̲iws] look for some missing body. *verb(i).*
yelx̲lhálem [yelx̲ lha lem] search for food; look for food. *verb(i).*
yelx̲t search for (something/someone); look for (something/someone). *verb(t).*
yélx̲tway [yelx̲ tway] look for one another. *verb(i).*
yelyá7els [yel ya 7els] sockeye salmon disease [from improperly cooked sockeye]. *noun.*
yelyélch' [yel yelch'] never know what kind of weather; mixed weather, be; unstable weather, be. *verb(i).*
yelyélk̲em [yel yel k̲em] stormy, be. *verb(i).*
yelhawá [ye lha wa] disappear. *verb(i).*
yelhyúlh [yelh yulh] get on fire; catch on fire; burn up completely. *verb(i).*
yelhyulhk̲wáẏneẇas ~ yulhk̲wáẏnewas [yelh yulh k̲waẏ ne ẇas] heartburn, have. *verb(i).*
yem cranky; ill-tempered; always mad. *adjective.*

yemts'k̲áṅ [yemts' k̲aṅ] barbecue (fish heads) by poking a single barbecuing stick through the back of the head. *verb(t).*

yemyémentsut [yem ye men tsut] hesitate. *verb(i).*

yemyémtsut [yem yem tsut] worry. *verb(i).*

yenís [ye nis] tooth; teeth. *noun.*

-yes ~ -yas days {full word: **skwayel**}. *suffix.*

yesyási7k̲w [yes ya si7k̲w] hats [sg: **yási7k̲w**]. *noun.*

yetwán [yet wan] red salmonberry; salmonberry [general term]. *noun.*

yetwánaẏ [yet wa naẏ] salmonberry bush; salmonberry shoots. *noun.*

yet'k̲w'ámten [yet' k̲w'am ten] tea towel; dishrag. *noun.*

yetl'k̲'ám [yetl' k̲'am] painted, be; wear paint. *verb(i).*

yetl'k̲'áṅ [yetl' k̲'aṅ] paint (something); rub (something). *verb(t).*

yetl'k̲'íṁ [yetl' k̲'iṁ] paint; rub. *verb(i).*

yetl'k̲'íwsm [yetl' k̲'iw sm] rub one's body. *verb(i).*

yétl'k̲'nexw [yetl'k̲' nexw] paint (something), manage to. *verb(t).*

yétl'k̲'ten [yetl'k̲' ten] paint [any colour; see also **syetl'k̲'**]. *noun.*

yetl'k̲w'úsm [yetl' k̲w'u sm] paint one's own face. *verb(i).*

yetl'k̲w'úsntsut [yetl' k̲w'u sn tsut] paint one's own face. *verb(i).*

yétsem [ye tsem] report; describe; tell. *verb(i).*

yetsyúts [yets yuts] hold it off with force. *verb(i).*

yéts'en [ye ts'en] step on (something). *verb(t).*

yéts'nexw [yets' nexw] stepped on (something), have. *verb(t).*

yéẇam [ye ẇam] make predictions. *verb(i).*

yeẇáṅ [ye ẇaṅ] first, be; before, be; ahead, be; former, be. *verb(i).*

yeẇáṅ chewáshs [ye ẇaṅ che washs] his first wife. *phrase.*

yeẇaṅálh [ye ẇa ṅalh] former time; previous time. *noun.*

yeẇánentsut [ye ẇa nen tsut] put oneself ahead of others. *verb(i).*

yeẇáṅiṁin [ye ẇa ṅi ṁin] before. *adjective.*

yeẇániwilh [ye ẇa ni wilh] before, be; in front of, be; front of, be in; ahead, be. *verb(i).*

yeẇás [ye ẇas] fish with hook and line; fish by means of a hook; fish with line ["mooching"]; fish with rod; fish with line in a river; angle [for fish]. *verb(i).*

yéẇat [ye ẇat] predict (something). *verb(t).*

yeẇíṅts [ye ẇiṅts] understand [speech]. *verb(i).*

yeẇíṅtsmiṅ [ye ẇiṅts miṅ] understand (someone). *verb(t).*

yeẇíṅtsni [ye ẇiṅts ni] understand (someone) [speaking]. *verb(t).*

yewt praise (someone); brag about (someone). *verb(t).*

yéwtsut [yew tsut] brag [literally, praise oneself]. *verb(i).*

yéẇyews [yeẇ yews] killer whale; orca; blackfish. *noun.*

yexwt before. *clitic.*

yex̲ far apart, be; have large openings [e.g., stakes of fence or mesh of net]. *verb(i).*

yéx̲entsut [ye x̲en tsut] spread apart, be. *verb(i).*

yex̲í7u [ye x̲i 7u] fish with a torch; use fire in hunting. *verb(i).*

yex̲w loose; untied; free. *adjective.*

yex̲wáẏchn [ye x̲waẏ chn] untie (bundle). *verb(t).*

yex̲wáyips [ye x̲wa yips] come undone [about a button]. *verb(i).*

yex̲wéla7 [ye x̲we la7] bald eagle [young]. *noun.*

yex̲wíṁ [ye x̲wiṁ] use dogs for hunting; release the hunting dogs. *verb(i).*

yex̲wn [ye x̲wn] turn (something) loose; set (something) free; untie (something). *verb(t).*

yex̲wúsn [ye x̲wu sn] unravel (something). *verb(t).*

yéya7t [ye ya7t] vomiting up (something) continuously, be. *verb(t).*

yéyel̓x̲t [ye yel' x̲t] searching for (something/someone), be; looking for (something/someone), be. *verb(t).*

yeẏk̲í [yeẏ k̲i] creeping, be; crawling, be. *verb(i).*

yích'it [yi ch'it] fill (something). *verb(t).*

yích'itsut [yi ch'i tsut] [expression when something serious happens]. *verb(i).*

yíkw'i [yi kw'i] come together. *verb(i).*

yiḵ [yiḵ] snow. *verb(i).*

yiḵyeḵí [yiḵ ye ḵi] crawl, be just beginning to; beginning to crawl, be just. *verb(i).*

yíḵ'itsut [yi ḵ'i tsut] plead with someone to give. *verb(i).*

yiḵw [yiḵw] you know. *clitic.*

yíḵwilhtax̱ [yi ḵwilh tax̱] Kwakiutl people. *noun.*

yíḵw'i [yi ḵw'i] bothered, get. *verb(i).*

yít'em [yi t'em] ooze out; run [about dye]. *verb(i).*

yits'its' [yi ts'its'] step on (something/someone). *verb(t).*

yiẇíṅem [yi ẇi ṅem] sing Indian songs; sing a song [a power song]; sing spiritual song. *verb(i).*

yix̱w [yix̱w] collapsed, be. *verb(i).*

yix̱wáchxw [yi x̱wa chxw] limbs far apart, have [about trees or bushes]. *verb(i).*

yíx̱wem [yi x̱wem] hesitate. *verb(i).*

yíx̱wementsut [yi x̱we men tsut] pouring rain, be; rain, be pouring. *verb(i).*

yíyeḵ'am [yi ye ḵ'am] filing, be [as in sharpening something]. *verb(i).*

yíyelḵem [yi yel ḵem] storm. *verb(i).*

yíyiḵ [yi yiḵ] snowing, be. *verb(i).*

yiyíl̓em [yi yi l'em] over, be [about storm]. *verb(i).*

yíẏulh [yi ẏulh] fire; firewood. *noun.* burn; have a fire burning. *verb(i).*

yíẏulhay [yi ẏu lhay] firepit. *noun.*

yí7yulhaẇtxw [yi7 yu lhaẇ txw] woodshed. *noun.*

yu [yu] soon; but then; but finally. *conjunction.*

yúkw'i [yu kw'i] shattered, be; smashed, be; busted, be; smashed up, be. *verb(i).*

yúkw'tsaṅ [yukw' tsaṅ] break into (a door). *verb(t).*

yúkw'un [yu kw'un] destroy (something); dismantle (something); take (something) apart; smash (something) up. *verb(t).*

yúla7 [yu la7] cow parsnip; Indian rhubarb. *noun.*

yuluṅ [yu luṅ] roll (something); sort (something) out; spin (something). *verb(t).*

yulh [yulh] 1. burn; burn up; 2. make a fire. *verb(i).*

yúlhcheẇan [yulh che ẇan] burn for (them). *verb(t).*

yúlhiṁ [yu lhiṁ] burning, perform a; perform a burning. *verb(i).*

yulhḵs [yulhḵs] 1. light a pipe; 2. burn one's nose. *verb(i).*

yulhḵsáṅ [yulhḵ saṅ] start (a fire); light (a pipe). *verb(t).*

yulhḵstn [yulhḵ stn] lighter. *noun.*

yulhḵwáẏnewas ~ yelhyulhḵwáẏneẇas [yulh ḵwaẏ ne was] heartburn, have. *verb(i).*

yúlhnalhn [yulh na lhn] get a fire going. *verb(i).*

yúlhnexw [yulh nexw] burn (something); burn (something) accidentally; burn (something), manage to. *verb(t).*

yúlhshi [yulh shi] burn food or clothing for (the dead). *verb(t).*

yúlhuṅ [yú lhuṅ] burn (something). *verb(t).*

yúlhut [yú lhut] burn (something). *verb(t).*

-yunexw ~ -unexw [–yu nexw] wave, waves in the ocean {full word: **yúya7kw**}. *suffix.*

yúp'its'tn [yú p'its' ten] diagonal sail-pole. *noun.*

yúp'un [yú p'un] shove (someone/something) with a pole. *verb(t).*

yútl'uṁ [yú tl'uṁ] knead bread. *verb(i).*

yútl'un [yú tl'un] knead (bread). *verb(t).*

yútsun [yú tsun] shove (someone) using one's hands; push (something) steadily. *verb(t).*

yúts'nexw [yúts' nexw] nudged (someone), have; nudge (someone) accidentally; shove (someone) with one's shoulder; push (someone) aside using one's shoulder; shove (someone) accidentally; push (someone) aside accidentally. *verb(t).*

yúts'un [yú ts'un] nudge (someone); shove (someone) [deliberately]; push (someone) aside [with elbow or shoulder]. *verb(t).*

yuu [yuu] bah! [term of digust]. *interjection.*

yuu [yuu] careful, be; take care. *verb(i).*

yuu chaxw [yuu chaxw] Take care! *sentence.*

yuult [yuult] choose (something); mix (something); sort (something) out. *verb(t).*

yuus [yuus] take care of (something). *verb(t).*

yuusténam̓ut [yuus tén na m̓ut] take care of oneself. *verb(i).*

yúustway [yúus tway] take care of one another. *verb(i).*

yúxway̓i [yú xwa y̓i] salmon roe ready for spawning. *noun.*

yúyak̲w [yú yak̲w] wave; current; rapids. *noun.*

yúya7kwm [yú ya7 kwem] undulate. *verb(i).*

yúya7kwms [yú ya7 kwems] make (waves). *verb(t).*

yú7yem [yú7 yem] alright, be; comfortable, be. *verb(i).*

The Dictionary / Ta Sḵexwts

English – Squamish

A a

a bit **tut**
a few **kw'in**
a little **tut**
a little, small **etsím**
a little, a little while **chiyáy ~ chá7i**
a little distance **tut**
a, any, some [feminine] **lha, álhi, kwlha, kwes**
a, the [generic] **ta, tay̓, kwa, kwi**
abandon (something) **x̱wí7stem**
abandon (something/ someone) **tuyn**
abate [about wind] **yáḵw'i**
able to do something, be **schew̓át ~ eschew̓át ~ eschechew̓át ~ chechew̓át**
able to open one's eyes, be **t'x̱áy̓usmnumut**
able to see at great distance **x̱etx̱ít7ayus ~ nx̱etx̱ít7ayus**
able, be **es7á7aw̓ts chechew̓át ~ eschechew̓át**
aboard, be **iy̓áy̓ulh nexw7iy̓áy̓ulh men iy̓áy̓ulh**
aboard, go **úyulh**
abode **wa lh7em̓út**
about what, be? [about speech] **txw7ín̓et**
above **chilh**
above, be **chílhiw̓ilh**
above, be [away from the beach] **chíshemiw̓ilh**
abscess **sḵw'chem**
absent, be **na7**
absent-minded **esmemey̓máy̓**
absent-minded person **nexwsmemey̓máy̓**
absent-minded, be **sháxwlhus**
absolved, be **esḵ'áw**
accept (someone) **lhím̓it lhím̓nexw**
accepted, be **lhim̓**
accident, have an **ha7mákwlh**
accompanied by a fast beat, to be **líx̱witem**
accompany (someone) **hewa7ní**
accompany someone **hewá7**
accompany when travelling, to **s-hew̓iwsem**
accomplish something **kwíyin̓tsut**
accordingly, be **tim̓á**
accounted for, be all **tl'aḵw'**
accuse (someone) **t'ḵet, tḵat, lhim̓íxwstem, héchaw̓ni**
accuse someone of taking something belonging to one **héchew̓**
accused of taking something, be **séchew̓**
accustomed to (someone), be **cháy̓exwni ~ chá7ixwni**
accustomed to, get **chá7ixw ~ cháy̓exw**
ache **x̱ep'kw'ántem, aa**
acne **slhém̓lhem̓kw'**
acquainted with (someone/ something), be **sḵ'i7s ~ eslhḵ'í7s ~ lhḵ'i7s ~ slhḵ'í7s**
acquired (something/ someone), have **lhím̓nexw**
across from, be **ínaḵa**
across, be **est'át'eḵ'**
across, be already **est'áḵ'**
act as go-between in a marriage proposal **chewáshem**
act completely **ts7it**
act in vain **ahúy̓numut ts'elt**
act like (someone/something) **tim̓ás**
act of murder, the **kwáyutsmixwn**
act suddenly **huyú**
act superior to someone **ch'úch'usum ~ ch'úsum**
act to a high degree **an**
act to a small degree **chá7i ~ chiyáy**
acting for **sxw-**
acting, be **kwekwiy̓ín̓tsut**
active, be **nexw7aw̓ítsay̓**
Adam's apple **lhits' melḵw**
add on clothes to (someone) **útsun**
add on to (something) **ch'xwit ~ ch'xwut**
add sugar to (something) **shúkwa7án**
add to (something) **híchit**
add water to (food in a cooking pot) **ch'xwálhḵwu7en**
add water to (something) **ch'xwálhḵwu7en**
address **ta7ts; tá7tsam̓**
adhere **mes**
administer medicine to (someone) **t'uy̓tn**
admire (something) **x̱áy̓anexw**
admire (something/ someone) **nexw7áx̱wn**
adopted child **shéwayim̓**

adult nekw tl'íyi7 stélmexw
advance txwhiẇ ~ txwiẇ
advertise work beforehand sheẇám
advice nexwníẇ; sneẇíyelh
advise nexwniẇéyalh ~ nexwneẇéyelh
advise (someone) nexwníẇit nexwneẇít
advise (someone) how to do something úsuṅ
adze kw'ets'alák̲s
adze (something) kw'ets'alák̲sen
afraid p'á7k̲w'alh ~ ip'áak̲w'ulh ~ p'áak̲w'alh
afraid of (someone), be i7ip'áak̲w'ulhni
afraid to snk̲w'úyiwan
afraid to, be nek̲w'úyiwan
afraid, be; be leary t'át'aṁátsut; t'ámatsut
afraid, become; have the chills sisilíws ~ silsilíws ~ sel̇selíws
after (someone), be aṅusmíṅ k̲ex̲míṅtem
after that yalh
after-birth á7aẇt
afterbirth s7aẇt
afternoon nekw k̲wetk̲ tex̲w; skwáyel
again k̲iẏát
against [something disliked] txwnaṁ
age stl'etl'elmú7tentsut
aged, be k̲'e7ílmi7
agitated, be p'ép'ikw'm
agitated, be [about water or object in it] p'eykw'm
agitated, be [about water, or object in it] p'ép'eykw'm
agree k̲'al̇ ánulh
agree with (someone) tiṁáshi
agreeable is
ahead, be yeẇániwilh; yeẇáṅ
ailing, be kw'áwi7
aim kw'enus
aim a gun with one eye shut ts'ut'ayúsem
aim at (someone/something) kw'eṅúsn
air bladder of fish [used as a container for oil] pláwa7
air-dried salmon ek̲wtús
Alaska blueberries iẏálk̲ep
Alaska blueberry iẏálk̲ep
Alaska blueberry bush iẏálk̲paẏ
Alaska blueberry bushes iẏálk̲paẏ
alcohol [general term] lam
alcoholic beverage lam
alder bark basket p'eyákw'as
alderbark basket sp'iyákw'us
alert, be on the t'ámatsut
alight t'ák̲'aṁ
alive, be áẏnexw á7aẏnexw ~ á7aynexw
all i7x̲w
all [that remains] txwuy ~ txwhuy
all accounted for, be tl'ak̲w'
all around, be sheych'
all bone, be txwshaẇ
all bone, become txwshaẇ
all day, be tl'émk̲en
all dressed up, be es-húyiws ~ es-huẏus
all gone, be i7x̲w
all in after a long run, be píkw'pikw'pikw'
all in, be finally [e.g., after a hunting expedition] k̲'ísnumut
all night, be tl'émk̲en
all of them í7x̲wax̲w; í7x̲wex̲wit
all one does men txwhuy
all the time ítl'i
allergic to (something), be k̲éyni
allergic, be nk̲élten
allow (someone) ánuṅ
almost chá7i ~ chiyáy; k̲ilh; chalh
alone, be men nch'ench'ú7
alone, be [about a person] ch'nch'u7 ~ nch'nch'u7 ~ ench'ench'u7
alone, left txwnch'nch'u7
along the waterfront, go peptúsm
alongside (a canoe), go tátaywilhs
alongside in a canoe, go p'ílhk̲'i
alongside, come right txwp'ilhk̲'
already nekw; kw
alright now, be txwstl'atl'm
alright, be hiyú7yem ~ yú7yem
also ímen
although yáman ~ yamn
always lhik̲'; men tl'ik̲'; men huy
always mad yem
amazed at such speed, be t'íẇtes
amazed by (something), be x̲áẏanexw
ambitious sxwéxwa7
amidst the trees, be eshíshch'
amidst vegetation, be eshíshch'
amiss, be kw'ay ~ skw'ay ~ eskw'áy
ammunition shat
amuse oneself xwík̲itsut
ancestors swa7áṁ
ancestral name kwshámin
anchor lhk̲éṅten

anchor (something) **lhk̲én̓at**
anchor line **lhek̲en̓éwilhtn**
anchored, be **eslhk̲én̓**
and **íkwi; ey ~ i ~ iy; welh**
and I **sen**
angel **lashás**
angle [for fish] **íw̓as ~ yew̓ás**
angle [not with a rod] **sts'em**
angry at (someone), be **t'áyak̲'ni**
angry face, have an **t'áyak̲w'us**
angry involuntarily, get [in spite of oneself] **t'ayak̲'númut**
angry, be **ch'ích'ikwem t'át'ayak̲'**
angry, be really **ch'í7ch'ik̲wem**
angry, get **t'áyak̲'**
animal cub **smím̓na7ullh ~ smín̓minullh ~ min̓min̓úllh**
animal hair **-i7k̲in; -ay̓us; t'ámin**
animal hide **kw'íx̲ta**
animal intestines [word only used in legends] **k̲w'etl'íwen ~ k̲w'utl'íwen**
animal skin **kw'í7k̲tn kw'el̓áw̓**
animal stomach **spexw**
animal tracks **nex̲én̓etn**
animals **k̲w'ín̓exw**
ankle **k̲wém̓x̲wshen sx̲wéts'k̲w'shen**
annoyed, be **ch'íwi**
another **k̲iy̓át**
another room, be in **nách'aw̓txw**
another's **snách'ulh**
answer **ntelk̲tn**
answer (someone) **ntelk̲t**
answer (someone) back **tá7tsan**
ant **ts'ets'emíchen**
antler **ts'istn**
anxious **x̲wak̲'**
anxious to do something, be **esx̲áx̲as**
anybody **men swátes**
anyone [from a group of people] **nech'nách'**
anything carved **sch'etxw**
anything fried **esch'éxwk̲**
anything one wears **s7íts'am ~ s7íts'am̓**
anything used to pry **wats'tn**
apparently **-ch'**
appear **x̲ey; xwey ~ xwii ~ xwiy**
appear [about big hole, as on road] **tk̲wám̓entsut**
appear [about face] **xwiy̓ús**
appear [out of nowhere] **x̲i7 ~ x̲ey̓**
appear before someone dies [about spirits] **shúyu**
appear suddenly **x̲i7 ~ x̲ey̓**
appearance, make an **xwiyintsút**
appearing, be **xwéyxwey ~ esxwéyxwey̓**
appetite, have no **itutálhx̲a**
apple(s) **ápels**
apple tree **apelsáy**
apply a big dab of (something) **t'elk̲án̓**
apply a splint to (someone) **ch'ást'a7en**
apply pitch to (something) **chemx̲án**
approach **ch'ími7; ch'ítentsut; lha7í7; tihem̓í; ch'ímin̓tsut**
approach (someone) sexually **tl'ik̲n**
approach (something) **lha7n**
approach someone **lhá7entsutiwes**
approaching **tihem̓í**
approaching, be **lhelha7í; lhalhéy̓**
approve (someone) [e.g., as a fiancé for one's daughter] **lhím̓it**
approved, be [e.g., as a fiancé] **lhim̓**
April [when salmonberry shoots are collected] **tem tsá7tsk̲ay**
Arbutus tree **lhúlhuk̲w'ay̓**
architect **x̲el̓s**
Are you leaving? **i chexw huyá7?**
Are you there? **nu chexw na7 tay̓?**
Are you well? **nu chexw men wa ha7lh?**
area **-i7ch ~ -ay̓ch**
area above, be **chíshem**
area below someone **áyalhk̲wmin̓**
area close to one's destination **ch'ítay̓ch ~ x̲ch'ítay̓ch**
area close to one's own territory **ch'ítay̓ch ~ x̲ch'ítay̓ch**
area close to where one is going **ch'ítay̓ch ~ x̲ch'ítay̓ch**
area higher up than where one is oneself **chíshem**
area of White Swan River **Xwlesh**
area where the ground levels off **slíx̲way̓shn ~ slix̲wáy̓shn**
argue **k̲'ek̲'x̲átay̓; x̲ex̲tl'ák̲'tel**
argue about (something) **k̲'ek̲'x̲átay̓ní**
arm **tax̲ntn**
arm {full word: **táxnten**} **-ach; -iy̓ax̲a7n ~ -ay̓ax̲a7n**
arm hair [including hair on the hands] **sk̲wínach**
armpit hair **sk̲winiyáx̲a7n**

armpits **nexw7átsiyax̱a7en**
around back of (something), go **ḵ'etchán̓**
around here, be **nexwtí7**
around the bend, go **ḵ'iwḵs**
around the feet of (someone lying down), go **ḵ'et-shnán̓**
around the head of (something), go **ḵ'etiy̓eḵwán̓**
around the point of (something), go **ḵ'etḵsán**
around there, be **nexwtá7**
arrest (someone) **nex̱wíḵw'in ~ x̱wíḵw'in̓**
arrest, be under **esx̱wíx̱wḵw'**
arrested, be **nex̱wíḵw' ~ x̱wiḵw' ~ x̱weḵw'**
arrive (here) **tl'iḵ**
arrive (there) **tsixw**
arrive at (something) **tsíxwni tsíxwen**
arrive on other shore **lheḵ**
arrived here from upriver, be/have **weḵw'**
arrived, have **estl'íḵnumut**
arriving there, be just **tsítsixw**
arriving, be **tl'ítl'iḵ**
arrow **ts'em̓áal̓**
arrow notch **sméḵ'nech nex̱wéts'ḵw'tn**
arrow used for practise **sméḵ'nech**
arrowhead [one which detaches] **sluxw**
arrowhead [type that breaks off the shaft when it hits something] **slhuxw**
arthritic, be **x̱ep'x̱ep'íwsntm**
arthritis, have **x̱ep'x̱ep'íwsntm**
as always **men t'ut**
as previously **men tl'ay**
as, be **tim̓á**
ascend **ket ~ kat kwum**
ascending, be **kwúkwum̓; ch'ech'a7chám̓**
Ash Slough **Yelhíxw**
ashamed, be **íx̱i ~ í7x̱i**
ashes [see also **ḵáyalhkwup**] **p'ich't**
ashes [see also **ḵwáyalhkwup** and **p'ich't**] **ḵáyalhkwup**
ask (someone) **wilḵw't**
ask (someone) if he/she really said something **tḵat**
ask (someone) what is going on **tḵat**
ask (someone) why he/she is saying something **tḵat**
ask a question **welḵw'áls**
ask all over **wál̓welḵ'als**
ask everywhere **wál̓welḵ'als**
ask finally **welḵw'alsnúmut**
ask for (something) **ḵ'ásat**
ask for a job **ḵwayax̱wsténam̓ut**
ask for assistance [in the form of supplies] **ch'awténm ~ tich'awténm**
ask one another **wílḵw'tway**
ask what price for (something)? **txwnch7am̓s?**
ask, finally get to **wilḵw'nálhen**
asking for help, be [e.g., about a person who's been injured] **ts'its'xwsténam̓ut**
asking for something, be **ts'ets'xwítsut**
asking suspiciously whether one has said bad things about him/her, be always **nexwsteḵtḵánaḵ**
asleep, be **í7tut**
assemble **ḵxwúsem**
assemble (them) **ḵ'éw̓new̓asn ~ ḵw'ú7new̓asn**
assembled, be **ḵxwus**
astray, go **sekw**
at [location or time], be **na7**
at last **yalh**
at the edge or end, be **ch'iyíp**
at which place? **éncha?**
at which time? **éncha?**
atone **ḵ'áwalhen**
attach it to (something) **ts'úp'un**
attach to (something) **esmém̓s**
attached, be **esmém̓s**
attempt **t'á7tsut**
attempt a fifth time **tsiyachisálhntsut**
attempt a fourth time **x̱wutsnálhntsut**
attempt a second time **tsam̓án̓tsut**
attempt a tenth time **upenálhntsut**
attempt for the third time **chanáxwntsut**
attentive, become **síwi**
attire **s7íts'am ~ s7íts'am̓**
audible, be **sáyi7n ~ sáy̓i7n**
August [when the salalberries are ripe] **tem t'áḵa7**
aunt **sáta7 ~ s-háta7**
aunt [after death of parent or parent's sibling] **wa lhsáy̓xwelh**
aunty (a term of address) **hatá7a**
autumn **tem eḵwáyanexw**
avenge oneself **mátl'tsut**
avoid something, manage to **p'étx̱numut**
awake, be [about a group] **em7úmsem**
awake, be [see also **s7úm̓sem** and **es7úmsm**] **úmsem**
awake, be [see also **úmsem**] **es7úmsm ~ s7úm̓sem**
awake, keep (someone) **es7úmsems**

aware of something that one can't see, be **síwi**
aware of the perimeter, be **eskw'úkw'ulh**
away from the edge [e.g., an object on a table] **lhup**
away from the fire, be **waw̓sh; wáshi7**
away, be [about the moon] **ts'ets'x̱**
awkward, be **sew̓íw̓**
awl **tl'échptn**
axe [see also **ḵw'aḵwemén** ~ **ḵw'ḵwémn**] **t'ḵwémen**
axe [see also **t'ḵwémen**] **ḵw'ḵwémn** ~ **ḵw'aḵwemén**

B b

baby sk̲ák̲el; s7íxwalh
baby boy at birth im̓; wí7k̲a
baby girl at birth ím̓shen
baby raccoon [see mélalus] melelus7úl-lh
baby rat [see hew̓ít] hew̓itúllh
babyish, be [e.g., when an older kid wants to get noticed] k̲ak̲el̓ántsut
baby's tent [a new dancer's tent] k̲'élch'tn
babysit ikw'álh ~ aykw'álh
babysit (someone) eykw'álhs; ns7éyx̲ni; eykw'álhen; aykw'álhs
babysitting, be ay̓txw
bachelor yáw̓ilh swáy̓wi7k̲a
back [of body or house] stay̓ch
back [of house] tay̓ch
back {full word: stay̓ch} -ch
back away tsekwk̲ám
back eddy sk̲'énts'x̲anem sk̲'ants'x̲ánm ~ esk̲'ants'x̲ánm
back hair sk̲win̓ch
back of head stay̓ápsem
back of house wetk̲áy̓s
back of the hand lha7lhchách ~ slhá7lhchach
back of the head sk̲wiy̓ápsem
back of the house táychiwilh tay̓cháyak̲'in
back of the neck stsek̲ápsem ~ sk̲apsm ~ stsk̲apsm
back of the neck {full word: sk̲apsm ~ stsk̲apsm ~ stsek̲ápsem} -apsám ~ -apsem ~ -psem
back of the room, be in the txwwash
back pain swáwts'aych
back side stay̓ch
back side [see also stay̓ch] tay̓ch
back up x̲áamen̓tsut; x̲ám̓entsut
backbone nexw7éx̲ts'ch ~ ex̲ts'ch ~ nx̲ats'ch
backbone [see also ex̲ch'ch] ex̲ts'ch ~ nexw7éx̲ts'ch ~ nx̲ats'ch
background, go into the wáshi7
backwards, be [about doing or saying something] yaxwm
backwards, be going k̲'ank̲'án̓atsut
backwards, go k̲'áx̲an̓tsut
bad k̲ey
bad dream k̲eyk̲eyáy̓ itut
bad to (someone), be k̲ey̓át
bad waves, be k̲eyúnexw
bad, be [about people] k̲éyk̲ey
bad, be [about terrain] esk̲éy̓
bad, be getting k̲ek̲ey̓í7
bad, become k̲éyi7
bag tl'pat; lesák̲
bag for belongings s7á7tem̓ay
bag of game or fish sk̲w'úynexw
baggage es7átetem s7á7tam̓
bah [disparaging remark] waa7
bah! [term of digust] yuu
bail (a canoe) ták̲wilhen
bail a canoe ták̲wilh
bail hay lhích'chk̲im̓
bailer ták̲wuy̓en ~ ták̲wilhtn ~ ták̲wi7n
bait mámi7
bait (something) mámi7n
balance oneself lying with the back across something nek̲'ík̲'ew̓ch
balanced, be nek̲'ík̲'ew̓ch
bald ts'ák̲'iy̓ek̲w ~ nts'ák̲'iy̓ek̲w
bald eagle sp'ák̲w'us
bald eagle [young] yex̲wéla7
bald forehead, have a ts'ák̲chus
bald head, have a nts'ák̲iyik̲w
bald, become ts'ak̲
ball ch'k̲wéla7
ball of the eye esntl'úm̓k̲ay̓us
balsam fir t'ú7xway̓
band [of cloth] k̲ít-shtn
bandage (someone's) foot k̲it-shnán̓
bandage (someone's) hand k̲itachí7n
bandage (something) k̲ítin̓
bandaged, be esk̲ík̲t
bang on (a canoe) kw'útswilhen
bannock sch'ex̲wk̲'
baptism [word used in the Catechism] lepáptism
baptized, be esmímkw'
bar (something) yá7tsan̓
bar (something) shut x̲wak̲w'én̓
bar in river eshashem̓ín̓was
bar passage nek̲'álh
barbecue (fish heads) k̲w'el̓k̲wán̓

barbecue (fish heads) by poking a single barbecuing stick through the back of the head yemts'ḵáń
barbecue meat or fish ḵw'élem
barbecue small fish by skewering them on a stick xwúkw'uts
barbecued fish head shíyukw'ḵw
barbecued salmon sḵw'élem
barbecued salmon head t'éweleḵw ~ t'éwliḵw
barbed spear point miyách
bare feet on rocks, have yech'yách'shen
barefoot, be esx̱wíx̱weláy̓ḵ
barely chiyáy ~ chá7i tut
bark [about dogs] wu7n ~ wuun
bark [thick] slaay̓
bark of tree -ay̓us
barking, be wúwu7n
barn [see steḵíw] staḵíw̓aw̓txw
barnacle ts'umáyu
barrel ḵ'eḵ'iy̓ás
bashful esyéxwyexw
bashful about doing or saything something, be yaxwm
bashful about doing something, be xwyaxwm
basic family tree eslhéḵ'
basket [any basket with an open weave] ts'ú7mayshn
basket [generic] sitn
basket [one pound berry basket for measuring] la7chs
basket for carrying wood or sea urchins, made of heavy split root ts'ú7mayshn
basket made from interwoven pieces of red cedar inner cambium wáts'iyus
basketful [type of measurement] t'anam̓áchtn
bat [type of animal] sḵáp'ḵap'tsaylh ~ ḵ'áp'ḵap'tsaylh
bath house shukw'umáw̓txw
bath, have had a eshúkw'
bathe shúkw'um; shukw'
bathe (someone) shúkw'ut
bathe one's child shukw'éyalh
bathe together [about a group] shekw'shúkw'em
bathe using sand or branches xwíkwintsut
bathed, be eshúkw'
bathing each other in the river by brushing with sand, be xwekwxwíkwentway
bathing, be shú7shukw'um
bathroom shukw'umáw̓txw
battleship ménya
bawl íxwitsut
bawl (someone) out kwíyentem; nechníchimiń
bawl out nechníchim
bay [see also átsnach ~ étsnach] s7átsnach
bay [see also s7átsnach] étsnach ~ átsnach
be a pity áyaxwnúmut
be able to walk ímeshnumut
be again in possession of (something) ḵ'énnexw ~ ḵ'énexw; ḵ'ánatsutnexw
be all stey̓sh
be all that is left txwuy ~ txwhuy
be at [a relative position in space or time] -iw̓ilh
be at home ay̓txw
be at lowest ebb ḵwey̓
be becoming weak keḵlími7
Be careful! wa chexw yuu
Be cautious going past! ḵw'aḵw'ay̓áx̱ ka
be cut lhich'
be getting dark lhálhachi7
be getting dimmer lhálhachi7
be getting fat ḵw'úḵw'uts'i7
be getting more ḵx̱i7
be laid down lixw
be no more háwḵi7
be noisy snélhem
be none hawḵ
be not the case haw
be not yet the case xwu7áxw ~ xwew̓áxw
be of the opinion tsut
be on the beach áyalhḵw
be outside something átsḵiw̓ilh
be prepared [to race] esḵw'úḵw'ulh
be ready es-hílkw
be ready [to race] esḵw'úḵw'ulh
be ready to go es-hílkw
be sorry lhikw'íwan
be still estétey̓sh
be swimming closely together near the shore while going to the spawning grounds [about group of fish] ḵwúlhuńtsut
be the same nílhnew̓as
be to a high degree an
be to a small degree chiyáy ~ chá7i
be too lazy [to do something] ú7um̓at
Be well prepared! tsewátsut chaxw!
be yet, to estétey̓sh
be your very best kwis tex̱wlám̓ es-húy
beach áyalhḵw

beach flea(s) xwixwiyám
beach side of áyalhk̲wmiń
beach side of, be on the áyalhk̲wiwi̓lh
beach, go up on the txwkwum
beach, have feet up on eskwúmshen
bead necklace sx̲wúp'a7en
beads [small] sk̲wínk̲wen
bear [black] míx̲alh
bear [brown] sméschem
bear [grizzly] stl'alhálem, sí7sintl'
bear a child smemn
bear cub mix̲alhúl-lh
beard sk̲wints
bears [black] mex̲míx̲alh
beat (someone) k̲w'úk̲wut
beat (someone) in a contest tl'xwet
beat (someone) up esk̲w'úk̲ws; kw'ál̓ak̲wust; k̲w'úyut
beat [e.g., as of a heart] snékwem; tétxwem
beat [of a song] sk̲'ewátem
beat a drum, to [see manáts'a] manáts'i7m
beat a drum rapidly, to stl'ets
beat a drum very rapidly, to stl'epx̲w
beat a slow rhythm, to [on drum or otherwise] stl'ets
beat the drum slowly, to ak̲'ík̲'exw
beat up, to k̲w'úyek̲'
beat wool into workable wool k̲w'ek̲ways
beautiful nach'íḿ
beautiful [about group of women] nech'nech'íḿ
beautiful [as in scenery] k̲ílus
beaver sk̲el̓áw̓
Beaver Lake [in Stanley Park] Ax̲áchu7

become -y ~ -i ~ -i7; mi ~ ḿi
become a ritualist kwtsí7tsi7
become a sxw7úmten sxw7úmteni7; esxw7umtnántsut
become all bone txwshaw̓
become bad k̲ek̲ey̓í7; k̲éyi7
become cloudy mi k̲atl'
become crazy ts'úysi7
become deaf tl'kwéni7i ~ tl'kwní7i
become hot kw'ákw'asi7
become many k̲x̲i7
become much k̲x̲i7
become really clear after a rain storm [about day or night] t'éch'i7n
become senseless x̲wey ~ x̲way
become shiny tl'uk̲'mí7
become soft k̲i7k̲i7í7
become stiff sespí7
become summer kw'ákw'asi7
become very thin txwshaw̓
become warm kw'ákw'asi7
become warm or hot kw'ási7
become weak k̲límí7
become wet k̲w'ts'i7
become wet [about snow] lhemxwnítem
bed yáy̓wes
bed {full word: yáy̓wes} -a7lh
bed platform yáy̓wes
bed with someone, be in eschéych
bedcover -a7lh
bedpan x̲wa7ítn ~ x̲wáy̓ten
bedstraw mamakw'útsinay̓
bee sesemáy̓
beer parlour [see lam] lamáw̓txw
before yexwt; yew̓áńiḿin

before, be yew̓áń yew̓ániwilh
beg ets'wás
beg ts'ets'xwítsut
begging for food, be [about a young dancer] imshlhálem
begging for mercy, be ts'its'xwsténaḿut
begin p'í7k̲siḿ
begin doing something kwen
begin singing one's power song kwen
beginning to crawl, be just yik̲yek̲í
begrudging nexw7étchus
begrudging of (someone), be nexw7étchusni
behave kwekwiy̓íńtsut
behave carefully ns7eyx̲sténaḿut
behave irregularly kwekwiy̓íńtsut
behave oneself ns7eyx̲sténaḿut
behave strangely kwekwiy̓íńtsut
Behave youself! wa chexw wa slhálhk̲en!
behind (something), go k̲'etcháń
behind {full word: s7atsk̲} -ay̓k̲
behind it, be áw̓tiwilh
behind of táychiwilh
behind something, be táychiwilh
behind, be aw̓t txwtay̓ch; tay̓ch
being as high as, be esch'ích'm
being in the shade ests'áts'i
being on, stíta7
belch k̲wach't
believe k̲'al̓
believe (someone) wanáxws k̲'álen

believe in (someone) **k̲'ál̓ni**
believe in what (someone) says **k̲'ál̓en**
belittle (someone) **lhilháts't t'k̲et**
bell **tíntin**
Bella Bella people **Pelpála**
Bella Coola people **Pélxwla**
bellow [about sealions, etc.] **k̲w'ák̲'am**
belly **-wilh ~ -ulh ~ axwilh**
bellybutton **méx̲weya**
belonging **swa7**
belonging to **-ulh**
belonging to a black bear **míx̲alhulh**
belonging to a black person **Sk̲'í7x̲iya7ulh**
belonging to a chief **siy̓ám̓ulh**
belonging to a Chinese person **Scháyminulh**
belonging to a seal **s7ásxwulh**
belonging to a white person **Sxwalítnulh**
belonging to an Indian **Stélmexwulh**
belonging to the Squamish **Sk̲wx̲wu7meshúlh**
belongings **es7átetem**
below, be [i.e., closer to the beach] **áyalhk̲wiw̓ilh**
below, be from **tilél̓s**
below, being **lil̓s ~ li7ls**
belt **xwiyém̓tn ~ nexwyém̓tn**
belt [woman's] **k̲itn**
bend, to **met'étsut;**
bend, a; elbow of a pipe **sk̲'enp'**
bend (something) **k̲wúmun**
bend (something) [in one direction] **pétsen**
bend (something) [in several directions] **kw'úts'un**
bend around (something) **k̲wúmun**
bend over **k̲wúsi**
bend over backwards **k̲'áx̲an̓tsut**
bends, be full of **sk̲'énk̲'enp'**
bent **u7elk̲wús**
bent, be **k̲w'elts'áchxwem pets**
bent, get **pétsem; k̲wúmutsut**
bequest to (someone) **áytxwmín̓en**
berries [sg: **skw'elám**] **sk̲w'elk̲w'elám̓**
berries that have already been picked **esyék̲**
berry [general term] **tewín̓xw**
berry [general term] **sk̲w'elám**
berry already picked [general term] **syek̲**
berry basket **k̲w'élemay sk̲w'elemáy**
berry bush **k̲w'elámay̓**
berry bush [general term] **sk̲w'elámay̓**
berry seeds **séts'ishen**
berry, fully ripe [general term] **sk̲w'k̲w'il̓**
besprinkle (something/someone) **lhitúsn**
bet **tsewásm; stsewásem**
bet (someone) **tsewasmín̓**
betray (someone) **tsúk̲wut**
better than someone/something, be **ha7lhmín̓**
better, be **hahelhí7 ~ háhalhi7 ~ hehelhí7**
better, be getting **háhalhi7 ~ hahelhí7 ~ hehelhí7**
better, get **halhí7 ~ helhí7**
betting, something used for **tsewasmín̓**
between, be **xwech'shí7**
bewitched **esx̲ét'x̲et'**
bewitched, be **esk̲'ewk̲'áw**
beyond, be **inayíwilh ~ ináy̓wilh**
big **hiyí**
big body, have [about person] **hiyíws**
big country **hiyí syátshen**
big deer with many "spikes" and a grey forehead **sx̲wel̓áx̲k̲in**
big eyes, have **nexwhiyáyus ~ xwiyáyus**
big eyes, have **xwiyáyus ~ nexwhiyáyus; x̲wechx̲wáchayus**
big fire **hiyíkwup**
big frog **xwexwem̓élwit**
big genitals, have **hiyáts'a**
big man's words [literally, a chief's thoughts] **siy̓ám̓ulh sk̲wálwen**
big mouth, have a **hiyí7ts**
big nose, have a **nexwhiyík̲s ~ nexwiyík̲s**
big part of **s-hiyí**
big raft [see also **t'álhi7k̲w**] **lháwlik̲w**
big toe **sintl'ak̲wúy̓shen**
big trap with stone **x̲ésshen**
big waves **hiyúnexw**
big, be getting **hehiyí**
bigamist **yasel̓ál̓txw**
big-bodied person, be **hiyíws**
big-eyed **xwiyáyus ~ nexwhiyáyus; x̲wechx̲wáchayus**
bigger than someone or something, be **hiyímin̓**
big-nosed **nexwiyík̲s ~ nexwhiyík̲s**
bile, be full of **nk̲w'elk̲s**
bird [general term] **sek̲w'ek̲w'í7nexw ~ s7ek̲w'7ek̲w'í7nexw ~ s7uk̲w'uk̲w'ín̓exw**
bird's nest **tsíptspi7lhten**
birthmark **smesch'ín̓**
biscuit **lépeskwi7**
bite **ch'em̓**
bite (someone) accidentally **txwch'em̓t**

bite (someone's) back
ch'em̓chán
bite (something or someone)
ch'em̓t
bite (something or someone) accidentally
ch'em̓nexw
bite (something's) rear
ch'em̓k̲án
bitten (something or someone), have
ch'em̓nexw
bitten, be ch'em̓tm
bitter sex̲;
t'ets';
sáyam;
lhes
bitter taste, have a lekw
black k̲'ex̲k̲'íx̲;
k̲'ix̲;
tl'ek̲'
black bear míx̲alh
black bear's míx̲alhulh
black bears [sg: míx̲alh]
mex̲míx̲alh
black brant [type of bird]
sx̲élx̲elch'
black codfish áyat
black duck t'élchepsem
black eye, have a
t'ák̲a7ayus
black katy chiton ekw's
black paint p'ich't
black person k̲'í7x̲iya
black turban [type of sea snail] k̲emáni
black twinberry bush
titin̓ústnay̓
black, be getting k̲'ík̲'ix̲i7
black, get k̲'íx̲i7
blackberry [wild]
sk̲w'elm̓xw
blackcap berry [see ts'ekw'um̓áy̓]
ts'k̲w'ú7em
blackcap berry bush
ts'k̲w'u7emáy̓ ~
ts'ek̲w'um̓áy̓
blackcap berry bush
[see ts'kw'ú7em]
ts'ek̲w'um̓áy̓ ~
ts'k̲w'u7emáy̓
black-chested wood-pecker k̲'ex̲k̲'íx̲ines
sts'ek̲w'í7k̲es
blacken (something) by holding it in smoke
p'ám̓an ~ p'am̓án̓
blacken (something) over a fire p'ám̓an ~ p'am̓án̓
black-eyed t'át'ak̲ayus
blackfish yéw̓yews
blackflies áx̲way̓
blackfly ts'ets'ik̲w'á7els;
áx̲way̓
blackjacket sesemáy̓
blanket hém̓ten;
mekwtn
blanket {full word: hém̓ten}
-lwit ~ -lwet ~ -elut ~
-elwit ~ -elwet
blanket cradle
x̲wek̲w'éwilhtn
blanket made of cedar bark
sléway̓uyt
blanket of fiber of cotton-wood stémx̲wulh
blanket of seeds of fireweed plant x̲ach'táy̓
blaze k̲wek̲í7
bleached, get p'ek̲'í7
bleed tsak̲w
bleeding ear, have a
tsak̲wáya7n
blend (something) tsitín̓en
blind k̲íx̲wus
blink lhílhipm;
lhiplh
blink one's eyes lhipay̓úsm;
ts'íp'k̲ay̓usm;
lhílhipmayus;
blinking, be lhílhipm
blister pem̓í7ach
block (something)
tk̲wú7tsen;
k̲átl'en
block (something) up
x̲wúts'un
blocked k̲'ets
blocked, be tk̲wu7ts
blocking (something) up to make it higher, be
x̲wúx̲wuts'un̓
blocking, be estk̲wú7ts
blond k̲wex̲wk̲wúx̲w
blond, become k̲wúx̲wi
blood stsátsi7n
bloom pák̲'em
bloom, be in pápk̲'am
blow (something) puut
blow (something) out
péx̲wen
blow (something) with mouth púxwun
blow [about the wind]
pahím̓
blow [as in an unfortunate event] tl'elakwan̓ánan
blow [e.g., sxw7umten]
px̲wim̓
blow a sore suun
blow at (something/someone) pahím̓ni
blow into fire paháyikwup
blow on (something) with mouth puut
blow one's nose x̲wíl̓k̲sem
blow really hard and make noise [about wind]
x̲wák̲amentsut
blow-hole [of a whale or dolphin] pxwaystn
blowing sound, make a [e.g., whale letting out water or air from its blow hole] pú7k̲w'em
blowing, be [about the wind]
pepahím̓
blown away by the wind, get
sik̲stm
blown off, be [by the wind]
puutm
blue skwáyel
blue camas spánanexw
blue eyes, have kwáylayus
blue grouse múm̓ten
blue jay kshaws ~
kwsháwes
blueback [type of fish]
pipixwáyus

bluejoint reedgrass [used for baskets] ts'áx̲i
bluff stáx̲aỷs
blunt k̲éyuts ~ k̲éyutsk̲s
blunt pointed stém̓k̲wek̲s
blunt-edged k̲éyuts ~ k̲éyutsk̲s
blush kwemi7
board a canoe úyulh
boast híchi7tsut
boastful, be es-héchhich
boat schá7twilh
bob and weave nák̲nak̲entsut
bob up and down on a board or branch míxwintsut
bobcat sp'elách'em
body sláláw̓
body {full word: sláláw̓} -iw̓s ~ -iws
body hair sk̲wíniws
body odour ts'ep
bog ts'k̲walhch
bog blueberry múl̓sem
bog blueberry bush múl̓sem̓aỷ
bog cranberry k̲wemchúl̓s
bog cranberry bush k̲wemchúl̓saỷ
boggy ts'ek̲wts'k̲wálhch
boil [abcess] sk̲w'chem
boil (food) k̲weỷsán
boil (something) k̲weỷsán; welhk̲wán
boil (something) by means of hot stones múyuỷsen
boil water welhk̲wm
boiling, be [a bunch at the same time] wélhwelhk̲wm
boiling, be [about water] wéw̓elhk̲wem
Bonaparte gull k̲w'ík̲w'ik̲w'
bone má7chen; shaw̓
bone game slhahál
bone in center of chest sx̲wáwinas
bone stuck in throat, have áak̲'alh
bone used in slhahál sk'ák'eltx̲
bones -ts'
bones [sg: shaw'] shusháw̓
bony face, have a shaw̓tsk̲
bony, be shusháw̓em; eskw'émkw'emts'
bony-faced shaw̓tsk̲
boogers ntl'iwk̲s
bore a hole in (something) shúyut
born, be xwii ~ xwey ~ xwiy; tsi7
borrow ix̲m
borrow (something) kwúlhens
borrow it kwúlhen
borrow it from (someone) kwúlheni
borrow it, manage to ix̲mnúmut
borrow something from (someone) ix̲mín̓
bosom st'elk̲wím̓ ~ stélk̲wim
both sides of something, be tiw̓ásiw̓ilh
bother (someone) lháts'i7n; téỷex̲wt; ch'íwi7min; táx̲wi7min
bothered by (someone), get ch'íwi7ni
bothered, be téỷex̲w
bothered, feel ch'íwi
bothered, get yík̲w'i
bothering, be téỷex̲wtsut
bothersome to (someone), be ch'íwi7min
bothersome, be kwílhimin̓; sch'íwi7min
bottle nexwlámay
bottom -aỷk̲; sles; les; s7atsk̲
bottom of foot nexw7átshen ~ nexw7átsshn
bottom, behind {full word: s7atsk̲} -k̲
boughs used for camouflaging a canoe x̲welwíltn
boulder syex̲ás ~ six̲ás
boulders syex̲yex̲ás ~ syex̲éyx̲as
bounce away t'úkwiỷen
bound t'úkwiỷen
bow [of boat] ílhchi
bow [type of weapon] téx̲wa7ch
bow of boat/canoe s7ílhchi
bow string ntsekwtn
bow tie k̲etlháytns
bowels s7étswilh
bowels {full word: s7étswilh} -wilh ~ -ulh ~ axwilh
Bowen Island Nex̲wlélex̲m
bowl, deep wooden [used for eating soup] x̲wúk̲wem
box kw'áxwa7; nexwnew̓íwstn
boxed lunch saw̓án
boxes [sg: kw'áxwa7] kw'exwkw'áxwa7
brace one's footing [e.g., when slipping down a hill] k̲átl'shnam̓ ~ k̲etl'shnám̓
bracelet ts'ám̓echn ~ ts'am̓chn ~ ts'a7mchn
bracken fern sx̲wútl'ekw
bracket fungus sk̲'étl'k̲'etl'
bracket fungus [term only used for syéwen] taw̓tewálak̲ep
brag [literally, praise oneself] yéwtsut
brag about (someone) yewt
brag about a killing hin̓ítsut
brag about one's success with a person of the opposite sex nin̓ítsut ~ nhin̓ítsut

brag about oneself híchi7tsut
brag of a murder hiṅítsut
braggart, be a es-héchhich
braid t'emshíṁ; st'emsh
braid (something) t'emshán
braid one's own hair t'emshk̲wáṁ
braid the edges of a cattail mat [literally, weave] lhéṅem
braided, be eslhéṅ
brain smets'álk̲en
brake (something) k̲ak̲'n
branch xwíxwelachxw; st'x̲achxw; stsek̲; st'ex̲
branch {full word: st'x̲achxw} -achxw
branch stripped from a tree tíx̲wachxw
branches [sg: st'xachxw] st'ex̲t'x̲áchxw
branches, small [see xwíxwel̓achxw] xwíxwel̓
branchy est'ex̲t'x̲áchxw
branchy, be t'ex̲t'x̲áchxwem
brand-new canoe k̲ék̲wilh x̲ts'aẏ
Brandt Canadian goose ex̲
brave sayamlíwen
brave [about a person] iẏím
bread seplín
bread [which one has baked] sp'áyak̲iṁ
bread, baked sp'áyak̲iṁ
bread, go get tiseplín
bread, homemade sp'áyak̲
bread, home-made sp'áyak̲iṁ
break x̲ewtl'
break (a rope) t'ák̲w'en
break (someone's) hand accidentally x̲ewtl'áchnexw
break (someone's) legs x̲ewtl'shnán
break (something) accidentally x̲ép'nexw; x̲éwtl'nexw
break (stick or bone) x̲ewtl'án
break [as of a rope] t'ek̲w'
break [e.g., plate, cup, etc.] x̲ep'
break in a song, type of st'ek̲w'
break into (a door) yúkw'tsaṅ
break loose t'k̲w'eṅ
break off lhemch'
break one's arm x̲ewtl'iyáx̲a7en
break one's back x̲ewtl'ch
break one's finger x̲ewtl'úl̓a x̲ewtl'k̲wúẏach
break one's hand or arm x̲éwtl'ach
break one's hip x̲ewtl'chk̲
break one's leg x̲éwtl'shen
break one's neck x̲ewtl'ápsem
break one's nose x̲ewtl'k̲s
break one's paddle [accidentally] x̲ewtl'íẇas
break one's rib x̲ewtl'á7i
break one's shoulder x̲ewtl'áyaṁit
break one's toe x̲ewtl'k̲wúẏshen
break out [about bunch of pimples or rashes] tl'ek̲
break trail for (someone) shewshewálhshi; shewálhshi
breaking (them), be [about a pile of things] x̲ewx̲éwtl'an
breast st'élk̲wiṁ ~ st'elk̲wíṁ
breast [children's term] skiṁ
breast {full word: st'elk̲wíṁ and st'élk̲wiṁ) -aẏamixw
breastfeed t'elk̲wíṁ
breastfeed [slang, children's language] kiṁ
breath slhákw'em
breathe x̲sháyup'em
breathe hard from being tired tsántem
breathe rapidly tsétsantem
breathing sx̲esháyup'em
breechcloth lhí7nek̲
bridge swetáwlh; seyk̲'ts
bridge of nose nshaẇk̲s
bridle lhíṅelstn
bright taw; tutáẇ
bright fire tutáẇikwup
bright on one, get taẇí7nitm
bright yellow lelch'
bright, become tetaẇí7
bright, get/become taẇí7
bright-coloured chíshkwaẏus
brighten taẇí7
brighten (something) taẇán
brightness stewtáẇ
bring (someone) along míẇnexw
bring (someone) back to life áynexwan ~ áẏnexwan
bring (someone) here míni
bring (something) tl'ik̲s ṁis ~ mis
bring (something) close ch'íten
bring (something) close to one's body to heat it k̲w'u7n
bring (something) down káwat
bring (something) down to the beach kaws
bring (something) forward to be seen xwíẏiṅ
bring (something) here tl'ik̲s; eṁís
bring (something) home hiẏáṁnexw; t'ukw's
bring (something) into disarray welhcháṅ

bring (something) out of the water **sháman̓**
bring (something) to shore **p'ésen**
bring (something) to the surface of the water **sháman̓**
bring (something) up **k̲íten̓**
bring (something) up to the surface **shát'an**
bring back a lost spirit **k̲'ániwan**
bring down (something) [e.g., a deceased person's name] **kaws**
bring down to the shore unfinished canoe-hull from the place where it was made [canoes are hollowed out wherever the tree is felled] **p'ékwilh**
bring food for lunch **esesaw̓án**
bring it to (someone) **tl'ík̲shi; míshi**
bring it up the hill for (someone) **kwúmshi**
bring oneself closer **ch'ítentsut**
bring oneself here, manage to **tl'ik̲nálhn**
bring shame upon onself [so that one has to blush] **x̲íts'i**
bring up a child **shewayáy̓lhem**
bringing (something) home, be **t'út'ukw's**
brittle, be **chéchepx̲wem; chépxwem**
broad, wide **lhk̲'at**
broad back, have a **lhek̲'ch**
broad face, have a **lhk̲'átus**
broad forehead, have a **lhk̲'átchus**
broad leaves, have **lhek̲'lhk̲'átachxw**
broad, be [about beach] **lhk̲'áy̓nup**
broad-leafed, be **lhek̲'lhk̲'átachxw**
broad-nosed **wéchwechk̲s ~ nexwwéchwechk̲s**
Brockton Point **Pápiyek̲**
broken **esx̲éx̲ewtl'**
broken (something), have **x̲ép'nexw; x̲éwtl'nexw**
broken hip, have a **esx̲éwtl'chk̲**
broken leg, have a **esx̲ex̲éwtl'shen**
broken off half **est'ék̲w'**
broken spine, have a **nex̲éwtl'ch**
broken-off half **t'ek̲w'mín̓**
brome grass **ták̲a7lh**
brooch **sk̲w'elhk̲ínes; sch'etxwínes**
brooch for the chest **lhák̲wanstn**
brood **tl'x̲wáy̓lhem**
brook trout **tl'ítl'ix̲way̓**
broom **ix̲wtn**
broth **k̲wa7álhk̲wu**
brought (something) close, have **ch'ítnexw**
brought (something) here, have **tl'ík̲nexw**
brought (something) home, have **hiy̓ám̓nexw**
brought in as a prisoner, be **p'ep'í7**
brown **p'ek̲w'p'ík̲w'**
brown bear **sméschem**
bruise **sts'ak̲'**
bruised **x̲wuts'**
bruised [so that the skin has the colour of a salal berry] **t'ák̲a7**
bruised all over, be **t'ek̲t'á7k̲a7**
bruised back, have a **nx̲wuts'ch**
bruised, be **p'its' t'ek̲t'á7k̲a7; t'ek̲w'**
brush **pixwayts'á7tn**
brush (someone) off [using branches without touching the person with the branches] **xwip'án**
brush (something) **xwíkwin; xwíp'in**
brush (something) using a brush **píxwin**
brush (something/someone) **xwíkwin̓**
brush for cleaning clothing **píxwayk̲in̓tn**
brush off (clothes) **píxwin**
brush oneself [after swimming] **xwíkwintsut**
brush oneself off [as when praying] **xwip'ántsut**
brush used for bathing **xwikwtn**
brush, be in the **eshíshch'**
brushed by **suts**
brushy place, be **nsk̲i7**
brushy terrain **nsk̲i7**
brushy, be very **nsk̲i7**
bubble **métk̲wem; péy̓tsem**
bubble up **métk̲wem**
bubbling, be **mém̓etk̲wm; pépey̓tsm**
buck **swéy̓wey̓k̲a sx̲wí7shen**
bucket **sntak̲wtn ~ ntak̲wtn ~ tak̲wtn**
bucket of water **sk̲wúk̲wel̓**
buckskin shirt **stsúyay̓wit**
budding a lot, be **pa7áchxw**
budding, be **pasm; pépa7achxw**
budding, start **mákwutsinem**
bug **sts'ekw'**
bug [general term **stl'itl'í7lk̲m**
buggie **ts'íkts'ik**
bugs **sts'ekw'**
bugs [literally, a bunch of little supernatural things] **stl'itl'á7alk̲em**
build **tahím̓ ~ ta7hím̓; ti-**

build (something) ta7s; tá7nexw
build a canoe chá7twilh
build a house tsíyeltxwem; tilám̓
build an annex on the side of (a house) útsax̱ánen
building -aw̓txw ~ -txw
building, be tethím̓
bull kelp k̲w'um̓
bullhead sts'nay̓ ~ ts'nay̓ ~ sts'enáy̓
bullroarer x̱wún̓x̱wun
bullrush wel; sts'á7k̲in
bully, be a eslhánch' ~ slhanch'
bum from (someone) tsewasmín̓
bumblebee [see also sekém'kem] sesemáy̓
bumblebee [see also sesemáy'] sekém̓kem
bump ts'a ~ ts'aa; tik̲w' ~ ntik̲w'
bump one's face ts'ahús
bump one's foot t'ém̓shn
bump one's head t'emk̲w ~ t'em̓k̲w; tík̲w'us ~ ntík̲w'us; ts'aak̲w
bump one's nose ts'ak̲s
bump the top of one's head ntík̲w'iy̓ek̲w
bump together tík̲w'new̓as
bumped head, have a ts'aak̲w
bumped, get tík̲w'nem
bumping noise, make a [e.g., a pot that falls, without breaking] lémxwi7n
bumpy [about surface] esxwetxwút
bumpy [surface] smékwmekw
bumpy, uneven surface, be esk̲ápk̲wep
bunch of native blankets slil
bunch of trees [sg: stsek] stsék̲tsek̲

bunched together, be [about trees] esk̲exwíwa7
bundle (something) up x̱wik̲w'i7chán ~ x̱wík̲w'i7chen
bundled up, be esx̱wíx̱wk̲w'i7ch
burden schem̓á7; s7ip'a7ím̓
burial blanket mekwtn
buried (something), have just k̲ém̓snexw
buried, be pen
buried, get pen
burl smekw
burn kw'askw'ás; kw'as; yíy̓ulh
burn (something) yúlhnexw; yúlhut; yúlhun̓
burn (something) accidentally yúlhnexw
burn (something), manage to yúlhnexw
burn food or clothing for (the dead) yúlhshi
burn for (them) yúlhchew̓an
burn off the hairs of a [seal] skin kw'íkw'sáyus
burn one's hands kw'ásach
burn one's mouth kw'asts
burn one's tongue kw'ásalxwtsalh
burn sliver off bottom of canoe k̲w'éywilh
burn things other than firewood [as an emergency measure] ts'x̱á7chep
burn up yulh
burn up completely yelhyúlh
burn without fire esyák̲wchew
burned accidentally, be txwyulh
burning nexwsyúlhim̓
burning one's mouth, be kw'askw'ásts

burning, do a kind of [e.g., of garbage] txwyulhim̓
burning, perform a yúlhim̓
burnt down, be ts'ex̱
burnt foot, have a kw'ásshen
burnt hands, have kw'ásach
burnt to nothing, be shew̓sh
burnt, be ts'ex̱
burnt, get esyúlh
burp k̲wach't
burr skwíts'ay̓
burr [small] memkw'útsin
Burrard Inlet Slíl̓utulh
Burrard Reserve étsnach ~ átsnach; Selíl̓witulh
burst (something) [by two-sided pressure k̲wem̓chán
burst (something) open tl'sháx̱en
burst [about flour] péych'em
burst [as of a balloon] k̲wem̓ch
burst [e.g., a boil] kw'a7ém̓ch
burst out péych'em
bury (something) pen̓k̲wán̓ pent
bush {full word: stsek̲} -ay̓
bushes, be in the eshíshch'
bushes, have feet in eshíshch'shen
bushy head, have a x̱ích'emk̲w; shípemk̲w
bushy terrain, be eshíshch'
busted, be yúkw'i
busy, be tétiy̓ex̱w; ts'áts'ey̓x̱
busy, get tí7ax̱w
but welh; huy
but finally yu
but then yu
butcher fish kw'ich'
butt (something) [about horned animals] lhíkw'in

butt cheek **lhélnach**
butt in **tátaỷs**
butt it **nek̲'álhentsut**
butt of tree **skwi7s**
butter clam **s7áx̲wa7 ~ s7áx̲wa**
butterfly **kílila**
button **ts'x̲wáỷaps; -ayips; k̲'ísayípstn**
button blanket **k̲'isayípstn hem̓tn**
buy (something) **sílh7an ~ silha7án ~ sílha7n**
buy a canoe **téxwilh**
buy clothing **sílha7cham̓**
buy it **sílha7**
buy it for (someone) **sílha7shi**
by **t-**
by the, by a **tl'a**

C c

cagey, be t'émt'em
calf of leg taẏémtn ~ tíminshen
calf of leg [literally, leg muscle] tíminshen ~ taẏémtn
call (someone) k̲'áyten nan
call (someone) down ex̲7í7x̲iṅ
call (someone) in uut
call (someone) names ex̲7í7x̲iṅ
call (someone)! úyt ka
call one's name nahím
call or give (someone) a name nan
call out (someone's) name nan
call out to (someone) núnstem
call to account (someone) suspected of spreading rumours about one tk̲at
call witnesses utsáṁ
called down, get kwíyentem
called that, be swé7ustem
called, be swé7u
callous k̲wuwí7ach; k̲'axw
callous, become k̲'áxwi7
callous, become very k̲'exwk̲'áxwi7
callous, gradually become k̲'ák̲'axwi7
calm water, be yak̲w'
calm, be [about water] yák̲w'i7
camouflage a canoe x̲welwílem
camp k̲'eym
camp in a recess [for maximal protection against wild animals xweṅíwch
camp over for a while estsítsixw
camp overnight esk̲'iẏíṁ
camping, be esk̲'ek̲'eẏíṁ esk̲'iẏíṁ
camping, be [about a group] esk̲'ík̲'iẏiṁ
campsite k̲'áẏmin
can es7á7aw̓ts
can work well eschechew̓át ~ chechew̓át ~ eschew̓át ~ schew̓át
Canada blueberry lhewk̲íṁ
Canada blueberry bush lhewk̲íṁay
Canada lynx útsani
candle heẏk̲wíṅ ~ heẏek̲wíṅ
candlefish sx̲wíw̓ach
cane t'chach
cannot kw'ay ~ skw'ay ~ eskw'áy
canoe snexwílh
canoe {full word: snexwílh} -axwilh ~ -wilh ~ -ulh
canoe pole sx̲wuk̲w'tn
canoe pulling, be ísun
canoe shed tsiyéwelhtn ts'aẏéwilhtn
canoe shelter tsiyéwelhtn
canoe that is just finished x̲ts'aẏ
canoe, "cut-off" st'k̲w'élhnalh snexwílh
canoe, Northern-style wít'ex̲
canoe, old sk̲eyúẏwilh
canoe, race or war táywilh ~ tayéwilh
canoe, small river snéch'elhp
canoe, small type p'elách'm snexwílh; p'elách'm
canoe-race tay
canoes [sg: snexwilh] snexwnexwílh
can't skw'ay ~ eskw'áy ~ kw'ay
can't reach it esk̲'tsáṁach
Capilano Xwmélts'stn ~ Xwmélch'tstn
capsize [about a canoe] kw'lhátsut
captain, beték̲w'em
captive, be esx̲wík̲w'
captive, be taken p'ep'í7
car ts'íkts'ik; tétxwem
card [wool] íkwusiṁ
carding implement [for wool] íkwustn
care about (something) na7s
careful to show respect, be asch'ew̓á
careful, be yuu kw'akw'chsténaṁut
careless [with things], be slhanch' ~ eslhánch'
carrot sháwik̲
carrot [originally referred to a type of wild carrot] sketk
carry (something) on one's back chemá7n
carry (something/someone) in one's arms íp'is
carry a large bunch in one's arms x̲ix̲p'iẏáx̲a7n ~ x̲ix̲p'ayáx̲a7n
carry a load cheṁá7
carry an armful of something x̲ix̲p'ayáx̲a7n ~ x̲ix̲p'iẏáx̲a7n
carry on wé7u

carry on (something) wé7us ~ wá7us
carry water úḵwum
carrying (something) on the back, be chemchem̓á7s
cartilage sx̱p'ekw'
carve úx̱wim̓; ch'etxw
carve (something) ch'etxwán
carver nexws7ú7x̱wim̓
carving sch'etxwim̓
carving, be ch'etxwím̓; u7x̱wim
Cascara bark x̱ex̱ep'shínay̓ ~ x̱ep'shínay̓
Cascara tree x̱ex̱ep'shínay̓ ~ x̱ep'shínay̓
cat push
cataract sḵwelx̱w
cataracts, have esḵwélx̱w
catch (a disease) ḵ'áp'nexw
catch (an animal) in a trap tl'éyḵ'nexw
catch (someone's) hand p'a7áchnexw
catch (something) txwp'i7t; sḵw'úynexw; p'í7nexw
catch (something) [that has been thrown] txwp'i7s
catch (something) with purse-seine or drag-seine ḵ'emts'án̓
catch a disease ḵ'ep' ~ ḵ'ap'
catch a glimpse of (something) p'élḵ'nexw
catch a glimpse of something sésiwi7
catch any salmon by any method sts'eḵwts'úḵwi7
catch breath when finishing crying sheḵlhálem
catch herring with herring rake lhét'em
catch of game or fish sḵw'úynexw
catch on fire yelhyúlh
catch sight of (someone/ something) kw'áchnexw
catch up with (somebody) cháynexw
catch upon a snag ḵwuy
catch with purse-seine or drag-seine ḵ'emts'ím̓
catch, manage to txwp'í7nalhn
Catechism Leketashísm
caterpillar sets'imts'imáymixw ~ ts'its'im̓áynexw
Catholic Kátulik
cat's cradle, play x̱ew̓él̓ch
cattail sts'á7ḵin; wel
caught (something) in a net, have lhín̓nexw
caught (something), have ḵw'úynexw
caught [in a net], get lhin
caught by cold weather, get t'íḵwi7nitm
caught by darkness, get tl'ḵw'í7nitem
caught by the hand, be ḵ'ap'achí7ntm
caught by the light, get taw̓í7nitm
caught by the wind, be pahím̓nitem
caught in (something), get [e.g., bad weather] ḵ'íw̓nem
caught in a net, be eslhílhn
caught out in the rain, be lhemxwnítem
caught sight of (someone), have tx̱wáy̓usnexw
caught, get ḵ'aa7 tl'eyḵ'
cause (someone) to elope lhew̓s ~ lhaw̓s
cause (someone) to laugh x̱ayms
cause (someone) to slow down [in working] ts'áp'an
cause (someone) to stop crying or talking too much x̱ey̓tsán̓
cause (someone) to take a steam bath ḵatán
cause (something) to fall down yáḵ'an
cause (something) to lean over cheyn
cause child to stop crying or talking too much x̱ey̓tsáy̓lh
cause many sparks t'ét'ey̓ḵwm
cause of sorrow selḵwmín̓
cause one's child to stop being bad x̱eyáy̓lhm
cause sparks péych'em
causing sparks, be pépeych'm
cave ip'a7áysus ~ xwp'a7áysus
cave in ḵikw
caw ḵáx̱chewan̓tem; ḵax̱
cease yáḵw'i
cedar bark súkw'em sléwi7 ~ sléway̓
cedar bark basket [inner] tl'pat
cedar bent box x̱tsem
cedar kettle or tub skwum sḵem
cedar leaves ch'am̓am
cedar platter x̱epiy̓éwelh ~ x̱epi7éwlh ~ x̱epiyéwelh ~ x̱épiy̓ewelh ~ x̱epi7úlh
cedar-bark cape nápus
centipede síw̓siw̓xwḵay̓mixw
centre, be in the énwilh; txw7énwilh
ceremonial mask sx̱wáyx̱wey
ceremony [involving donations] of "bringing out" a girl súyumay̓lh
chair ḵ'ay̓ḵ

challenge (someone) to a race heyk̲wt tkwi tl'etl'xwítay
change nách'i
change (someone's) appearance nach'aỷúsn
change (something) nexw7áỷn; nách'en; nexw7áỷs
change (something) around nexw7áỷn
change course [straight down káẁshenam
change course and come straight downward [about water] txwkáẁshenam
change expression mi nách'i
change expression in anger k̲wútusem
change into another language xwená7k̲en
change of clothes snexw7ayits'á7m ~ nexw7áỷits'm
change one's diet nách'ani7m
change the blanket of (the dead) nexw7áyits'á7n
change the colour of (something) nach'aỷúsn
change the subject txw7á7ik̲
change the topic [on purpose] txw7áỷak̲am̓
change to a friendly disposition [after being angry] k̲w'áỷatsut
changed, be nexw7áỷ
Changers X̲aays ~ Sx̲aays
changing one's appearance, be nách'nach'entsut
charcoal p'ich't
chase (someone) chayn
chase (someone) away wálhk̲'an
chase (someone) out wálhaṅ
chase (something) away xwi7s
chase away (an animal) wálhaṅ
chasing (something), be chicháỷs
chattering, be ch'eyx̲ántsut
chattering, be [about teeth] k̲'epkwtsám̓
Cheakmus Ch'iyák̲mesh
Cheakmus River Ch'iyák̲mesh Stak̲w
cheap lí7lk̲; nexwlí7lk̲
cheap, be tekw'
cheap, feel x̲íx̲its'i7
cheat k̲aṅ
check (something) tl'ápat
check up on someone, go tl'ítl'ish
checkered face, have a x̲elústntem
cheek xwmiyíwa7n ~ nexwmiyíwa7n
cheek {full word: nexwmiyíwa7n} -a7n ~ -a7án
cheek of rear end lhélnach
cheekbone sháẁus ~ nsháẁus
Cheekeye Reserve Nch'k̲aỷ ~ Ch'k̲aỷ
Cheekeye River Nch'k̲aỷ Stak̲w ~ Ch'k̲aỷ Stak̲w
cherries chílis
cherry chílis
cherry bark [wild] t'élem
cherry tree [wild] t'elem̓áỷ
chest s7ílinas
chest {full word: s7ílinas} -inas
chest hair sk̲wíninas
chest pain swáwts'inas
chew lhelh-
chew (something) [about human, not at regular meal] x̲íkw'in
chew (something) [about human] ísaẁen
chew (something) up x̲wútl'un
chew (something) up [so that the object cracks] x̲ep'kw'áṅ
chew [about human] ísaẁi
chew [especially grass] k̲'itl'áṅ
chew gum lhelhchéchmx̲
chew on (a bone) ts'ítiṅ
chew on a bone ts'ítim̓
chew resin lhelhchéchmx̲
chewing gum slhelhchéchmx̲
chickadee sets'úts'umam ~ ts'úts'um̓am
chickenhawk sx̲ip'im
chief siỷám̓
Chief Smallpox [term of fearful respect, used when smallpox was especially virulent] kwétsi siỷám̓ smex̲wíws
chiefs sííỷam̓
chief's siỷám̓ulh
chief's daughter chilhná7nch'
Chilcotin people Sx̲íx̲nam
child mím̓na; meṅ; s7íxwalh; stá7uxwlh
child {full word: meṅ} -aỷlh ~ -aylh ~ -íyalh
child after twins nk̲wúyum̓
child before twins xwam̓s
child from a senior line sintl'
child of a slave st'ashem
child of dead brother, sister, or cousin swenimáylh
child of living cousin stáyalh
child of living sibling stáyalh
child of parent's older sibling kwúpits
child of parent's younger sibling sk̲a7k̲

child, adopted shéwayim̓
child, have a esmémen̓
child-in-law's sibling skw'íwes
children smén̓hem; mén̓men; stá7uxwlh
children [sg: stá7uxwlh] stewtá7uxwlh
children from a senior line sensíntl'
children of parent's older sibling kwepkwúpits
Chilean person Chelína
chill creep up one's back [from cold or fright], have a sepspíwsntm
Chilliwack Sch'elxwik̲w
Chilliwack people Sch'elxwi7k̲w
chin slestsk̲
chin {full word: slestsk̲} -tsk̲
Chinese Scháyminulh
Chinese person Cháymin
Chinook Chíkmen
Chinook [see also chikmen] Chinúkw
Chinook canoe k̲'exwú7lh
Chinook language Chinúkwk̲in
Chinook money Chíkmen
chip slhemch'
chip (something) chepshán
chip (something) off lhemch'án
chip (something) off accidentally lhémch'nexw
chipmunk sx̲ex̲p'íchen
chipped (something) off, have lhémch'nexw
chipped off, be lhemch'
chipped-off piece slhemch'
chips of wood [for starting fire] se7sk̲'
chisel hálitn
chisel with an adze k̲íx̲wilh
Chocolate lily lhásem
choke ák̲'alh; t'kwínus ~ t'kwínas
choke (someone) p'eskw'elhnáyen; k̲w'uts'lhnáyn
choke on water slhem̓
choked [by food], get [cf. kw'én'ken] t'ekwínas
choked drinking water, get [cf. t'ekwínas] kw'én̓k̲en
choking, be p'es7álhx̲a
cholic, be nk̲w'elk̲s
choose (something) yuult
chop x̲itl'; t'k̲w'im̓
chop (someone's) hand t'em̓áchn
chop (someone's) head off t'emk̲wán̓
chop (something) t'ém̓en x̲ítl'in
chop (something) up t'émt'em̓n
chop (something) up into small pieces x̲etl'x̲ítl'in̓
chop (something), manage to x̲ítl'nexw
chop firewood sek̲'níkwup ~ sek̲'ní7kwup ~ sek̲'en̓í7kwup x̲itl'ní7kwup
chop one's hand accidentally t'em̓ách
chop up x̲ítl'im̓
chop up the ground k̲wéyk̲weytem
chopped foot, have a t'ém̓shen
chopped wood sek̲'mín
chopping (something), be t'ét'emen
chopping (something), be [e.g., wood] x̲íx̲itl'en
chopping (them) continuously, be [e.g., pieces of wood] x̲etl'x̲ítl'in̓
chum salmon k̲wáx̲nis
church kw'emaylháw̓txw ~ kw'enmaylháw̓txw
churn p'eykw'm
churning, be p'ép'eykw'm; p'ép'ikw'm
cinders p'ich't
circle (something) [inside of longhouse] sheych'án
circle around sheych'ántsut
circle when flying kw'ákw'em
clam sheykw
clam [littleneck] skem̓ts
clam shell k̲'ay̓ám̓in
clam shells k̲'ay̓ám̓in
clamp one's mouth shut [like a child who's pouting] chém̓chem̓ts
clamped shut, have one's mouth ch'ém̓ch'em̓ts
clams in one's nose ntl'iwk̲s
clams, go get tishéykw
clap lhak̲w'achí7m
clap hands lhak̲w'achí7m
claw (someone) t'elhk̲w'án
claw (something) x̲íp'in
claws welh wes x̲íp'im̓
clay seyk̲'; sts'ik̲'
clay used in making Indian blankets, kind of sp'etl'tn
clean mikw'; míkw'mikw'
clean (fish, fowl or game) kw'ích'in
clean (something) míkw'in
clean face, have a míkw'us
clean feet, be always having nexwmíkw'shn
clean feet, have [about a group of people] mikw'míkw'shn
clean fish, fowl or game kw'ich'
clean one's bed píxwa7lhm
clean one's feet míkw'shnam̓
clean one's hands míkw'achi7m
clean, become [can be used for ritual cleansing as well] míkw'i
cleaned [e.g., a pot cleaned with sand] ts'els

clear (a small area of land) tíyen
clear a large area of land tíyam
clear after a rain storm, become really t'éch'i7n
clear leaves and twigs from (blueberries or huckleberries) paháyumen
clear up tsápshen
clear up [about the weather] k̲wálhshen
clear, be estetích
clear, be [about water] nexw7íy̓em
clear-sighted nexwiyáy̓us ~ nexw7ey̓áy̓us
clench one's teeth ch'iyíkw'ní7n ~ ch'iyíkw'in
clever nek̲'ílus
clever, be eschechew̓át ~ chechew̓át ~ eschew̓át ~ schew̓át
cliff státax̲ay̓s; stáx̲ay̓s; stek̲shn
climb ket ~ kat
climb over a mountain seseyk̲'áy̓ch
climb up txwkat
climb up a hill or mountain ch'e7chám̓
climb up a tree or mountain kat ~ ket
climbed up already, have eskáket
climbing up, be kákat
close ch'it
close (a door or box) nek̲p'ét ~ nk̲p'et ~ k̲p'et
close (someone's) eyes up with pitch chemx̲áyusan
close (something) k̲p'et ~ nk̲p'et ~ nek̲p'ét
close [e.g., clam] ts'íp'tsem̓
close [on its own] nek̲ép' ~ nk̲ep' ~ k̲ep'
close by, be nexwch'ít
close family eslhék̲'
close one's eyes ts'íp'usm
close one's eyes tightly tl'éy̓ek̲wayusm ~ tl'iyik̲wayúsm
close one's mouth chem̓tsám
close relative swa7ám̓
close relatives, be eslhék̲'new̓as
close second in a race, be a ch'ích'it
close to edge, be ch'iyíp
close to giving birth, be ch'ími7
close to someone, be temstl'í7
close to something, be very eslhélha7 ~ slhélha7
close together tl'éts'em
close together, be ch'ítnew̓as tl'uts'
close together, be [with small openings tl'ech
close up solidly [e.g., a wound] ts'iw̓
close, be a little tutnexwch'ít
close, be getting [intentionally] ch'ímin̓tsut
close-limbed [about tree] tl'úts'achxw
closer to the front or fire, get híw̓i7
closer, be nexwch'ít
closer, be getting ch'ích'imi7 háxwatsut
closer, get ch'íti
closet k̲ep'tnáy
closing on, be ch'íkwi7tem
clot smém̓kw
cloth sil
cloth made of dog's hair with plumes of fireweed stém̓xwalh
clothes -ayts'a7 ~ -ayts'a ~ -its'a ~ -ts'a -elwet ~ -elut ~ elwit ~ -lwit ~ -lwet yek̲w ~ yek̲wáy̓ stsíyus
clothesline lhp'áyts'a7ten; ch'ixwáyts'a7ten
clothespin sáyips; tl'eyk̲'íts'tn
clothespin {full word: sáyips} -ayips
cloud sk̲atl'
clouds sk̲atl'
cloudy, be k̲atl' esk̲ák̲tl'
cloudy, be getting k̲ák̲atl'
cloudy, become mi k̲atl'
club kw'ála7k̲wus
club (someone) kw'ál̓ak̲wust
club for killing large fish slá7mats
clumsy k̲elk̲ímut
clumsy, be esk̲í7k̲elach
co- kw'elh
coal p'ich't
coarse mak̲'
coat kapú
coax (someone) chechshíw̓at
cockle stl'elú7em
cod áyat
cod lure k̲wak̲'p
codfish spawn kw'emkw'úm̓
co-elder kw'elhsyú7yuxwa
coffin néwakw'a
coho tsáw̓in
coho [small tsi7tsáw̓in
coho [small type tsítsaw̓in
coil (something) k̲'elk̲'án
coil (something) up k̲'elk̲w'úy̓sen; k̲'enp'án
cold ts'ulh st'ik̲w
cold [about a bunch of people] ts'elhts'úlh
cold [about air or weather] t'ik̲w

cold [to the touch] **ts'lhulh**
cold feet, have **tesí7shn**
cold hands, have **ts'lhúlhach** **tesí7ach**
cold inside a house **t'ik̲wmámin**
cold north wind **sútich**
cold weather, the **st'ik̲w**
cold, be feeling **ts'úlhum̓**
cold, be feeling **ts'úts'ulhum̓** **ests'elhts'úlh**
cold, be getting **t'ít'ik̲wi7**
cold, be getting [about air or weather] **t'ík̲wi7**
cold, be/feel **ts'úts'ulhum̓**
cold, become **tesí7**
cold, become very [about human] **ts'úlhum̓**
cold, feel **tet-si7**
cold, get [about air or weather] **t'ík̲wi7**
cold, get [about the weather, not about a person] **ts'úlhi7**
cold, get really **ts'lhúlhi7**
cold, has the quality of being [e.g., a house] **nt'ik̲wm**
cold, have chest stuck with **ch'útl'i7n**
cold, usually [about person] **ts'élhts'elh**
collapsed, be **yix̲w**
collarbone **ch'ch'ulh ~ ch'ich'úlh**
collect (something) **k̲éxwen**
collect them **k̲exwím̓**
collected, be [about a small quantity of water] **esk̲wúk̲wel̓**
colour **-ay̓us**
colour (something) with smoke from fire **p'am̓án̓ ~ p'ám̓an**
coloured [about material] **sx̲él̓x̲el**
coloured material **sx̲él̓x̲el**
colours **sx̲el̓**
colt **stek̲iw̓úllh ~ stak̲iwúllh**
comb **lhch'ímen; íkwustn**
comb (someone) **íkwusn**
comb of a bird **nek̲'íts'iy̓ik̲w**
comb one's hair **íkwusem**
comb, fine-toothed **méchenten**
combine (them) **lháts'new̓ásn**
come **em̓í; hem̓í; m̓i ~ mi; ham ~ ham̓**
come along **miw̓**
come alongside **p'ílhk̲'antsut**
come ashore **p'si ~ p'si7**
come at (someone) **txwhem̓íni**
come back **k̲'ánatsut**
come back to life **ay̓nexwí7**
come by way of some place **nexwtí7**
come close to **k̲ilh**
come downstream **mi wuk̲w'**
come face-to-face with a dead spirit **nchíshus**
come face-to-face with spirit **shú7nayus ~ shú7mayus**
come first **mi yew̓án̓**
come from behind **áw̓tiwilh titátay̓ch**
come here **miw̓**
come home **ham ~ ham̓; hiy̓ám̓; nahám̓**
come in **k̲w'ats'**
come in [about water] **k̲wul**
come in between **xwexwch'shí7ntsut**
come in for a landing **ts'elhp'**
come in stern of canoe [about water] **k̲wul̓k̲**
come inside **uys**
come into contact with dead spirit **shú7nayus ~ shú7mayus**
come loose **mek̲wem̓éy̓; kw'étxwem**
come off [about bark on tree] **lhek̲w'**
come off [about lid] **x̲wil̓**
come off [e.g., button] **x̲wílay̓ips**
come on **maalh**
come out **t'axw; t'áxwi; txwt'axw**
come out [about nail or teeth] **x̲wil̓**
come out [about small oblong object **ts'u7k̲s**
come out [being pulled] **ts'u7**
come out of a container **t'axw**
come out of the house to look at something unusual or interesting **ts'áts'alh; tsaay̓**
come right alongside **txwp'ilhk̲'**
come this way **txwm̓i ~ txwmi ~ txwem̓í; tihem̓í**
come through **kwénatsut**
come to (someone) **hem̓íni**
come to [after fainting] **p'lhiws; tel̓núm̓ut**
come to a dead end on account of high bluff **tséx̲wus**
come to an end [of a trail] **esáp'**
come to ask someone for assistance **ch'awténm ~ tich'awténm**
come to life **áynexwi7**
come to one [about wind] **pahím̓nitem**
come to shore [about a canoe] **p'ákwam̓**
come to surface of water **p'ákwan̓tsut; p'ákwam̓**
come to the space between **txwxwech'shí7**

come to the surface mi sham
come to the surface of the water shámaṅtsut
come together nchem̓ús ~ nchém̓us ~ chém̓us; yíkw'i
come towards this way txwm̓i ~ txwmi ~ txwem̓í ~ txwhem̓í
come undone [about button] yex̱wáyips
come up ch'iik̲
come/go towards lha7í7
comfort (a crying baby) x̱ey̓tsáṅ
comfortable, be yú7yem
coming after, be aw̓t; á7aw̓t
coming down, be t'ít'ixwi7
coming from [human or animal] -ulh
coming in, be [about tide] k̲w'ák̲w'ats'; x̱éw̓schem
coming inside, be ú7uys
coming into the harbour, bay, etc., be txwnénew̓ets
coming out, be [about plants] pasm
coming to an end, be tsetséy̓k̲s
coming to shore, be p'ep'sí
coming up [a hill], be kwúkwum̓
commiserate nexwnínlhewá7nem
commit suicide énmitsut ~ nmí7antsut
common flicker ts'ik̲t
common merganser x̱wuuk̲w'
communion yek̲álesti
Comox people Tsalhúlhtxw
companion sk̲'ew̓ ~ sk̲w'u7 ~ esk̲'ew̓ ~ esk̲w'ú7 ~ sk̲'ew̓
companions [sg: sk'ew' ~ skw'u7 ~ esk'ew' ~ eskw'u7] sk̲'ek̲w'ú7 ~ sk̲'ék̲'ew̓ ~ sk̲'ek̲'éw̓ ~ sk̲'ék̲w'u7
company sk̲w'ú7new̓as
compare (someone) nílhen
competing, be peptítsut
competion, have a peptítsut
complaining, be t'eyt'éykw'
complete (something) húynexw
completed wétwet
completed, be shek̲
completely tex̱wlám̓ ~ tex̱wlám̓ ~ tex̱wám̓
cone of evergreen tree sch'ích'inu
confess kw'sham
confront (someone) tk̲at
confuse (someone) shíshichnexw; milch't
confuse (them) [e.g., shoes or clothes] málk̲wnew̓ásn
confused, be shishích' ~ shíshich; melmílch'
congeal tl'x̱wi7
conger eel s7achcháwam ~ ns7achcháwam
connect (something) x̱wík̲w'iṅ
connect (them) méseṅ
connect it to (something) by inserting it ts'úp'un
connect oneself to something nelhnílhtsut
connected to it, be eslhílhkw'iws
connected, be slhílhkw'iws
connected, become tits'úp'
consent k̲'al; ánulh
consider nta7áw̓n ~ ta7áw̓n
consider (someone) to not be worthy k̲'iyát
consider (someone) too small or weak k̲'iyát
consider (something) a pity áyaxws
consisting of large pieces [referring to rocks, boulders, etc.] hiyúy̓s
constipation, have tl'ex̱wtl'ex̱wíw̓ilh
construct (something) ta7s
consume (something) húy̓nexw
consumed, be ts'ex̱
consumption sts'ekw'í7ens
consumption, have yek̲ínem
contagious disease, have an [one symptom of which is that one spits blood; "a kind of TB"] hemlch
contain a lot nk̲x̱am̓
container -ulh ~ -wilh ~ -axwilh; nexwnew̓íwstn
content tsá7tsaxw
content about (something), be tsá7tsaxwni
continue wé7u
continue (something) wé7us ~ wá7us
control weather suun
convulsions, have ch'ich'ich'ántem ~ ch'ech'ich'ántm
cook kwukw
cook (something) k̲w'élen k̲w'elt
cook by boiling k̲wey̓s
cook for (someone) k̲w'élshi
cooked (something), have esk̲w'élt
cooked, be k̲w'el
cooked, be [already] esk̲w'él
cooked, get it k̲w'elnálhen
cooked, manage to get it k̲w'elnálhen
cooking pot nk̲wi7stn
cool (something) off tesí7n
cool oneself off tesí7ntsut
cool place ts'élhts'elh
co-owned, be eṅáṅusmiṅ

co-parent-in-law skw'íwes
copper k̲wík̲wi; sk̲we7íls
copper ring k̲wík̲wi slemchís
copy x̲wex̲wá7
copy (someone) x̲wex̲wá7t
Coquitlam Kw'ikw'tl'ám
cork a boat tl'úk̲w'wilh
cormorant lhétsnech
corner, be in a estl'útl'k̲w
corpse shá7yu; stéwak̲in
correct tex̲w
correct (something) p'áyak̲en
correct, be estétx̲w
correcting (something), be p'áp'ay̓ak̲en
costume súyiws ~ s-húyiws; stsíyus
cottonwood tree k̲w'eník̲w'ay
cougar nswú7wu ~ swú7wu
cough éx̲wu7n
cough all the time ex̲w7éx̲wu7n
could es7á7aw̓ts
count (them) kw'shat
count (them) already kw'éshnexw
count them kw'shim̓
counted already, be eskw'ékw'sh
counted, be eskw'úkw'sh
counting (them), be kw'ekw'shát
country syátshen
cousin s7ek̲w'í7tel ~ sek̲w'í7tel ek̲w'í7tel
cousin [term of address] [see also sh7eylh ~ sh7ilh] eylh ~ ilh
cousin from a senior line sintl'
cousin of opposite sex áyish
cousin-in-law ch'emásh
cousins [sg: ekw'í7tel and sekw'í7tel ~ s7ekw'itel] sék̲w'ek̲w'i7tel ~ s7ék̲w'7ek̲w'i7tel ~ s7ék̲w'ek̲w'itel ~ sék̲w'7ek̲w'itel
cousins from a senior line sensíntl'
cousins of opposite sex [sg: áyish] i7áyish
cover nk̲ep'tn ~ nk̲ep'tán; k̲p'á7elch
cover (someone) all up with a blanket or towel esám̓k̲ws
cover (someone) with a blanket hám̓en es-hámk̲ws
cover (someone's) back táx̲chan̓
cover (someone's) head k̲ap'k̲wán̓
cover (someone's) mouth nk̲áp'tsan
cover (something) mékwu7n
cover (something) vertically táx̲wusen; táx̲tsan̓
cover (something) with ground pen̓k̲wán̓
cover (something/someone) with a blanket ham̓k̲wán̓
cover one's head hám̓k̲wam
cover one's mouth [with one's hand] táx̲tsam̓
cover oneself with a blanket hám̓entsut
covered face, have a xwhám̓us ~ xwám̓us
covered one's head, have esmém̓kw
covered up, be txwhám̓k̲wam̓
covered, be saam ham̓ ~ ham esám̓
covered, be [by blanket, by snow, etc.] ham̓k̲w ~ hamk̲w ~ es-hámk̲w
covering (something), be est'et'an̓íw̓s
covering, be stíta7
coversation sk̲wéy̓k̲wey
covet (something) x̲wák̲'et; shítimmin̓
cow músmes
cow parsnip yúla7
coward, be a nlhex̲wk̲
cowardly, be s7ip'ip'áak̲w'ulh
Cowichan language K̲aw̓íchn
Cowichan people K̲aw̓íchn
co-wife shá7yu
co-wives shishiyétel
crab ay̓x̲
crabapple k̲wu7úp ~ k̲we7úp
crabapple tree k̲wu7úpay̓ ~ k̲we7úpay̓
crab-infested, be áy̓x̲entem
crack x̲ep'; s7ay̓áx̲
crack (something) k̲wem̓chán
crack (something) with one's teeth [e.g., nits, gum, sunflower seeds] tl'emkw'án
crack finger joints kwet'k̲í7n
cracked foot from heat, have t'ech'shn
cracked hands, have ts'ék̲'ts'ek̲'
cracked, be sek̲'; esésk̲'; s7ay̓áx̲
cracking, have hand or foot t'ech'
cradle p'a7úts'us ~ p'úuts'us ~ p'e7úts'us
cradle basket p'e7úts'us ~ p'úuts'us ~ p'a7úts'us
cram (something) tl'ets'úyen

cramped hands, have x̲ísachí7ntem
cramps in one's legs or feet, have x̲ishnán̓tem
cramps, have x̲ísin̓tsut
cramps, have stomach x̲isiwílhentem
cranky k̲éywilh yem
cranky, be wew̓ts'átsut
cranky, get really wets'wáts'numut
crash and shake létx̲i7n
crawl yek̲í
crawl into something tl'uk̲wí7
crawl under hík̲i
crawl, be just beginning to yik̲yek̲í
crawling under, be híhik̲i
crawling, be yey̓k̲í
craziness ts'uysánan
crazy sts'its'úys; skáti; ts'uys
crazy face, have a ts'úysus ~ nts'úysus; skati7ús
crazy fellow, be a sts'its'úys
crazy, get ts'úysi7
crazy-faced nts'úysus ~ ts'úysus; skati7ús
creak t'éskw'em; ts'étx̲em; t'éskw'i7n
creak [e.g., door] k̲ítsem
creaking, be t'ét'eskw'i7n
creases stsém̓tsem̓k̲w ~ estsém̓tsem̓k̲w
created, be x̲ey̓ ~ x̲i7
Creator X̲ex̲e7ének̲
credulous nexwsk̲'ek̲'elk̲'ál̓
creek swá7elt
creeks [sg: swá7elt] swelwá7lt
creep yek̲í
creeping, be yey̓k̲í
creepy thing sisilíwsmen
crescent gunnel ns7achcháwam ~ s7achcháwam
cricket wak̲'ék̲
crippled leg, have eskw'áychk̲
crooked esk̲wék̲wey̓k̲w' k̲weyk̲w' ~ k̲wey̓k̲w
crooked jaw, have a esk̲wék̲wey̓k̲w'ts
crooked leg, have a sk̲w'ut'shen
crooked lip, have a esk̲wém̓ts
crooked, be esk̲wék̲wik̲w'
crooked, have gone kw'úts'untsut
crooked-legged sk̲w'ut'shen
cross st'át'k̲'new̓as; lekwá ~ lekwín; sk̲'ek̲w'ú7chk̲
cross (a mountain or hill) txwkawchs
cross (two things) t'ák̲'new̓asn
cross a river tuyts
cross a wide stretch of water shk̲wen̓
cross one's arms over one's chest k̲'ets'k̲'áts'chesténam̓
cross oneself p'tusm
cross over a gulf or ocean shk̲wen̓
cross over a road or bridge seyk̲'ts
cross over large body of water tuy
Cross, the lekwín ~ lekwá
crossbar in a canoe pkw'úyin
cross-eyed sk̲wúk̲wuts'ayus
cross-eyed, be est'át'k̲'ayus
crossing each other, be est'át'k̲'new̓as
crossing over a river, bridge, lake, etc., be séseyk̲'ts
crosspiece in a boat pkw'úyin
crosswise, be st'ák̲'its'
crosswise, become t'ak̲'
crouch esmí7mitl'
crow k̲'elák̲'ela ~ k̲'eláak̲'a
crowbar wats'tn
crowd kwchétem
crowd together k̲exwntsút
crown of head -ay̓ek̲w ~ -iy̓ek̲w
crown of the head nek̲'íts'iy̓ik̲w
crucifix lekwá ~ lekwín
crumble (something) up ch'etk̲w'án
crunchy, be chépxwem
crush (someone) [by one-sided pressure] mútl'un
crush (something small) x̲áp'en
crush (something) p'eltl'án̓ k̲wem̓chán
crushed, be p'eltl'í7
crusty p'ésxwem
cruxifix lekwín ~ lekwá
cry, a sx̲aam; sk̲'ewm
cry, to x̲aam ~ x̲am
cry for (someone) x̲amín̓ ~ x̲áamin̓
cry for oneself x̲aamín̓tsut; sx̲amín̓tsut
cry out really loud k̲w'ech'e7lák̲inem; kwekwáchem
cry unstoppably íxwitsut
cry, want to x̲aam̓áy̓m
crybaby sk̲íyalh
crybaby, be a stsa7x̲áy̓
crying all the time, be esx̲áx̲ay̓
crying, be [about a group] x̲ex̲ahám
crying, have one's child x̲ahámay̓lh
culture wa lhtim̓á
cup lepát
cupboard lhx̲áy̓tstnay̓
cups [sg: lepat] leplepát
cure lhaw̓ének̲

cure (hides) **kwik̲máman**
cure (someone) **lháw̓at ~ lháw̓et**
p'áyak̲en
cured (someone), have **lháw̓nexw**
cured hide **k̲wík̲x̲en**
súyuy̓
curing (someone), be **p'áp'ay̓ak̲en**
curious **tl'etl'atás**
curl **k̲'elp'ím̓**
curl (something) **k̲'elp'án**
curl up **tl'ípentsut**
curling one's own hair, be **k̲'elp'ántsut**
curling up, be **k̲'elp'ántsut**
curly hair, have **k̲'elk̲'elp'í7k̲in**
esk̲'elk̲'el̓p'í7k̲in
current **sx̲wem;**
yúyak̲w
current, go with the **wuwk̲w'útsut**
curse **k̲ey̓tsám̓**
curse (someone) **x̲wíni;**
xwínin̓;
k̲éy̓utsin
curse someone **kw'áwenek̲**
cursed, be **k̲éy̓utsinem**
cursing words **k̲éy̓utsin**
sníchim
curtain **ntáx̲wustn;**
táx̲wustn
cushion **sx̲wétl'k̲in**
cut **lhich';**
sx̲wets'k̲w';
x̲itl'
cut (a rope) **t'ák̲w'entem**
cut (a rope) in two **t'ák̲w'en**
cut (meat) **pákwan̓**
cut (someone's) feet **ts'emk̲'shenán**
cut (someone's) hair **x̲áx̲elk̲wen**
cut (someone's) neck **lhich'ilhx̲á7n**
cut (someone's) rear end **ts'emk̲'k̲án**
cut (something) **úx̲wun̓**
lhích'it
cut (something) [especially wood] **x̲ítl'in**
cut (something) a little at a time **tsépshan**
cut (something) accidentally **lhích'nexw**
cut (something) in half **nt'ek̲w'chán̓**
cut (something) off **x̲wéts'k̲w'an**
cut (something) with scissors **ts'emk̲'án**
cut (something), have **lhích'nexw**
cut (wound) **kwáshat**
kwáshan
cut across (water or mountains) **t'k̲w'ay̓ch**
cut hair on top of head **ts'émk̲'iy̓ek̲w**
cut hair, have **sx̲áx̲elk̲w**
cut off (animal's) tail **x̲itl'iyúpsen**
cut off one's hair **lhích'elk̲ínem**
cut off the end of (something) **t'ek̲w'k̲sán**
cut off the head of (something) **x̲wil̓k̲wn ~ x̲wil̓k̲wán̓**
cut one's hair **x̲ax̲elk̲wám̓ ~ x̲áx̲elk̲wem**
cut one's hair really short **esx̲ex̲ík̲'**
cut one's hand **lhích'ach**
cut one's neck deliberately **lhích'elhx̲a7m**
cut oneself **kwáshan̓tsut**
cut oneself off from someone **t'kw'ím̓**
cut oneself to let out bad blood **kwáshatsut**
cut open (game or fish) **kw'ék̲'en**
cut right off **xwets'k̲w'**
cut right off, be **esxwexwíts**
cut strips of (skin) **sex̲wn**
cut through, be [e.g., a block of wood or lumber] **xwets**
cut up **x̲ítl'im̓;**
t'k̲w'im̓
cut up (something) **kw'ích'in**
cut up fish **kw'ich'**
cut wood **lhich'ní7kwup;**
x̲ich'ní7kwup
cut, have one's hair **lhích'elk̲ín**
cutting (something) up continuously, be **lhech'lhích's**
cuttings **sek̲'mín**
Cut-up-in-chunks **St'ék̲w't'ek̲w's**

D d

dab (something) on t'elk̲áń
dab [dancer's paint] on quickly lhíwix̲wusentem
dad [see also man] máma
daddy mam
damp sa7sx̲w
damp, become sá7sx̲wi7
damp, get lhaḿí7
dampen (something) ts'álhen; lháḿan
dance {full word: kw'iyilsh) -alkwlh
dance [modern] k̲w'iyílsh
dance performed before a wedding mikw'tn
dance, a [done by a group of people going three times around a house, after which one dancer starts dancing a mílha7] tístsut
dance a bear dance mix̲alhálkwlh
dance a deer dance tl'ení sx̲wi7shenálkwlh
dance an Indian winter dance mílha7
dance hand movement with both hands at side at shoulder sk̲életsun
dance house tl'ashnáẃtxw; milha7áẃtxw
dance powwow-style ts'ák̲'shenem
dance suddenly txwk̲w'iyílsh
dance with a very rapid stamping of the feet [for which the stl'epxw serves as an accompaniment] tístsut
dance, do a war tsehénem
dance, make (someone) mílha7s
dancer, type of k̲w'éx̲wa7k̲s
dancer's rattle kwétsmin (Halkomelem); ts'ek̲'mín (Sk̲wx̲wú7mesh)
dancing a bunch, be melhmílha7
dancing gear mílha7uyts
dancing season tem mílha7
dangerous tl'i7
dangling, have one's legs séselk̲'mshn
dark tl'ek̲w'; lhach
dark inside a house tl'ek̲w'mámin
dark side of the mountain k̲i7k̲aẏús
dark spot on the road tl'k̲w'ík̲en
dark, be getting tl'etl'k̲w'í7; lhálhachi7; esk̲ák̲alhi7
dark, be just getting k̲ák̲alhi7
dark, get tl'k̲w'i7
darkness tl'k̲w'ánan
darling sheylh
daughter meń
dawn, be kwákwaẏel; mi ch'ik̲
dawning, be kwákwaẏel
day kwáyel; skwáyel
day after next tx̲íx̲ta
day after tomorrow tx̲íx̲ta
day before last tx̲íx̲ta
day before yesterday tx̲íx̲ta
daylight skwáyel
daylight, be k̲'eyt
day(s) {full word: skwayel} -yes ~ -yas
dazed, be ts'elsemáẏus
dead stéwak̲in; shá7yu
dead leaves and needles [of evergreen trees] k̲wiyám
dead man's cache smekw'a7ál
dead needle ch'ámem
dead needles ch'ámem
dead tired, be txwk̲w'uy; k̲w'úyayítut
dead tree sch'aẏ
dead, be esk̲w'úy
dead, be all xwémnech
deadfall t'kw'íḿek̲
deadfall trap x̲ésshen
deadfall tree kw'up'chk̲
deadpan face, have a sháxwlhus
deaf, be tl'kwéni7
deaf, become tl'kwéni7i ~ tl'kwní7i
dear ilh ~ eylh; tl'i7; stl'i7; sh7ilh ~ sh7eylh
dear [expression used by man and wife speaking to one another] naaẃ
dear [term of endearment for younger relative] k̲w'únek̲
debate k̲'ek̲'x̲átaẏ
decay ts'exw
deceased aunt sátat
deceased female cousin of parents sátat
deceased male cousin of parents sísi7t
deceased sibling's child sunimáylh ~ swanimáylh

deceased spouse's sibling or cousin **ch'áyaỷ**
deceased uncle **sísi7t**
deceive (someone) **nek̲'ík̲'els**
December **Etl'íḿ Lhk̲aych'**
decide **k̲welk̲wálwen**
deck of cards **slakáltem**
decline (one's daughter's suitor) **haws**
decorate (something/someone) **tsitíńen**
decorated with carving, be **ch'etxw**
decoration **tsítiń**
decoration carried on chest **sch'etxwínes**
decrease (fire) **lhaỷán**
decrease [about the moon] **ts'éts'x̲ntsut**
deep **les**
deep sea **ni7ch**
deep throat **les7álhx̲a**
deep water, be out in **ni7ch**
deep wooden bowl **x̲wúk̲wem**
deer **sx̲wí7shen**
deer [term used only in syewen] **tl'ení**
deer call, make a **t'i7n**
deer fern **pálapála**
deer hoof **k̲wúxwmin ~ kwúxwmin**
deer hooves **k̲wexwk̲wexwmín ~ kwexwkwúxwmin**
deer hooves [term used only in legends] **sk̲elúlax̲en**
deer hooves used on new dancer's ankles **ts'ek̲'míńshn**
deer-calling instrument **t'í7nten**
deer-hoof rattle **ts'ek̲'mín**
defeat (someone) **escheláẃs estl'éxws**
defeat (someone/something) **cheláẃnexw**
defeated, be **estl'éxw ~ stl'exw escheláẃ**
defecate **a7k̲ tl'etl'shí7k̲w**
defecate (something) **tl'etl'shí7k̲ws**
defecate [euphemism for a7k] **xweym**
defecate in pants **a7x̲mámin**
defective, be **eskw'áy ~ skw'áy ~ kw'ay**
defend (someone) **máwań**
defend (someone/something) **téỷwilhn ~ tíẃilhn**
definite, be **estétx̲w**
delay (something) **ts'áp'an**
delayed, be **estsítsixw**
deliver (something) **áḿek̲t**
deliver it for (someone) **áḿek̲shi**
deliver it to (someone) **áḿek̲shi**
delouse (someone) **chá7chen**
den of black bear **laḿ tl'a míx̲alh**
dented, be **tekw**
deny (someone) **háwshi**
deny a lie **xwiyintsút**
deny oneself **nemántsut**
depart **huyá7**
depart from one another **lhít'itsut**
depend on (someone) **ntahíńetni**
depend on someone **ntahíńet**
derange (someone) **ts'áp'an**
derange (something) all the time **ts'ets'p'át**
Derby hat **sp'á7wik̲w**
descend **t'íxwi**
descend [e.g., from a hill] **t'ixw**
descend [from a hill or tree] **kaw ~ kew**
descend on it [as a swarm of flies] **húmi7n**
descendants **sméńhem**
descending, be [e.g., from a hill] **t'ít'ixwi7**
descending, be [from a tree or hill] **kákaw**
describe **yétsem**
desire **stl'i7**
desire (someone) **tl'í7ni ~ tl'íni**
desire (something) **x̲wák̲'et**
destroy (something) **yúkw'un**
destroy (something) intentionally **x̲ep'x̲áp'en**
destroyed by fire, be **ts'ex̲**
deteriorate [about salmon after spawning] **ma7áti7**
determine which team gets the extra stick and begins holding the bones in **slhahál** **t'et'míteĺ**
devil **liyám**
devilfish **st'elx̲wts' ~ st'élx̲wets'; sk̲í7eḿk̲w**
devil's [see **liyám**] **liyámulh**
devil's club [type of plant **ch'ích'aya ~ ch'átyaỷ; pá7pawtn**
dew **slhéḿlhem**
dew on branches **slheḿxwmáchexw**
diagonal sail-pole **yúp'its'tn**
diapers **sk̲íyalh**
diaphragm **tek̲mín**
diarrhoea **eskw'élkw'el**
diarrhoea, have **eskw'élkw'elstm**
dice game **smet'áni**
die **hawk̲**
die [about a tree] **ch'áỷi**
die [plural] **x̲wey ~ x̲way**
die [singular] **k̲w'uy**
die away [about sound] **tsexwáyak̲ap**
die down [about wind] **yák̲wi**
die from hunger **tisxwám**

die in one's sleep tl'áyayax̲its'
diet ch'áytsut
diet, be on a ch'áytsut
differ from each other nech'nách'new̓as
different nach'
different colours, be of esx̲él̓x̲el
different, become nách'i
difficult tl'i7
dig t'ékw'enp; t'kw'ím̓
dig (something) t'ákw'en
dig (something) up t'ekw'tákw'en
dig a pit t'kw'ím̓
dig clams sheykw
dig into (something) lhúk̲wun
dig the ground t'ékw'enp
dig up potatoes tsik̲wálch
dig up the bones of the dead tsek̲wíyu7
digging around, be shéshey̓ik̲
digging stick sk̲aalx̲
diligent nexwskwéy; esxwexwá ~ esxwéxwa7; t'élhk̲'em
dim lhach
dim (light) lhay̓án
dime mit
diminish (something) xwátan̓ tl'ápat
diminish something for (someone) [e.g., a load] xwátshi
dimmer, be getting lhálhachi7
dip (something) repeatedly in the water máy̓muyun
dip (water) out k̲wult
dip food into grease ts'ím̓
dip head in water to get drink puy̓ch
dip net shéma7nten
dip oneself in water máy̓muyuntsut
dip water k̲wúl̓im̓
dip-net shéma7n
dipper [type of bird] smélmelx̲wits'a ~ mélmelx̲wíts'a ~ smalmelx̲wíts'a
dipper for water k̲wúk̲wul̓tstn
direct one's glance at something tx̲wáy̓usem
direct one's glance downward k̲ep'úsem
direction of, be in the ta7k̲s
dirt temíxw; sch'ek̲'
dirt, be in the txwpen
dirty matl'mín̓; esch'ék̲ch'ek̲ ~ sch'ék̲ch'ek̲
dirty (someone) mátl'nexw; matl'mín̓
dirty [about water] tik̲w
dirty face, have a memtl'ús; xwmétl'metl'us; esch'k̲wús
dirty feet, have [about a group of people] esch'ek̲ch'ék̲shn
dirty himself mátl'ntsut
dirty, be métl'metl'
dirty, get metl'
dirty, get one's hands metl'ách
dirty, get one's shoulder metl'áyam̓it
dirty, make (someone) mátl'en
dirty-faced xwmétl'metl'us
disabled, be kw'eykw'áy
disagree with (someone) haws
disagreeably surprised, be nexw7áwiwánm
disagreement resulting in a quarrel, have a kw'ikw'áynew̓as
disappear yelhawá; t'an̓íw̓; ts'u7; tsexw
disappear suddenly xwési7n
disappear under [rising] water, have head or top ts'elhp'k̲w
disappeared, be estsetsíxw
discard xwim
discard (something) xwi7s
discarded thing sxwiim̓
discipline one's child x̲eyáy̓lhm
discouraged, be nexw7áwiwánm
discover (something) tél̓nexw yák̲wnexw
discuss k̲wéy̓k̲way ~ k̲wéy̓k̲wey
discuss something/someone txwtéta7
discuss with (someone) k̲wéy̓k̲weys ~ k̲wéy̓k̲ways
discussion sk̲wéy̓k̲wey
disease sk̲w'uy
disguise oneself tl'ípentsut
dish shelf lhx̲áy̓tstnay̓
disheartened, be k̲eyí7inas
dishrag yet'k̲w'ámten
dislike ch'úch'usum ~ ch'úsum
dislike (something/someone) k̲eys
dislike one another k̲éystway
dismantle (something) x̲wílnew̓ásen; yúk̲w'un
disobedient welh
disrespected people [e.g., illegitimate children] st'ashem
distance, be in the chishkw
distant [about person] k̲w'ay̓

distract (someone) tsápnexw; ts'ets'p'át
distracted (someone), have ts'áp'nexw
distribute (something) lhít'it
distribute gifts at a potlatch lhit'
disturbed, become x̲wá7ilwes ~ x̲wiẏílus
dive shtam
dive continuously sheshtáṁ
dive head-first cheẏk̲wám
diver nexwshétshtam
divert water t'áṁshnaṁ
divide tsetsiẏák̲wustaẏ
divide (something) tsiyák̲en
divide (something) up tséyk̲neẇásn
divide and share sek̲'míntway
divide off (a part from a whole) tsiyák̲en
dividing and sharing, be sesk̲'míntway
divorced, be skwekwá7tl
divorced, get x̲wíl̓neẇás xwí7stway
dizzy from drinking, be shéych'em
dizzy from spiritual power, be siẏáẏus
dizzy, be getting shéych'em; siẏáẏus
do tí7shexw; ta7híṁ ~ tahíṁ
do (something) ti7cht
do (something) [about group] tl'amt
do (something) again txwiws
do (something) gently ayát ~ áyet
do (something) with care áyet ~ ayát
do (something) with kindness áyet ~ ayát
do (something), really kwens
do a war dance tsehénem
do again k̲iẏát
do as one is told [literally, do as (someone) tells one] tiṁás
do as the other did tal
do for (someone) tá7shi
do for a whole day or whole night tl'émk̲en
do good for (someone) ha7lhnítem
do it ti7sháṁ
do not haw
do penance k̲'áwalhen
do so tichám
do something kwíyiṅtsut
do something a little bit chiyáy ~ chá7i
do something else tk̲aẏ
do something else [on purpose] txw7áẏak̲aṁ
do something feet first nexwyaẇáṅshn
do something many times to (someone) k̲ex̲álhen
do to (someone) kwíyin
do what one does skwekwiẏíṅtsut
do what with (something)? cháshi?; chas?
do what? chánem?
Do your best! tsewátsut chaxw!
dodgeník̲iṁ
doe slhálheṅay sx̲wí7shen
dog sk̲wemáẏ; sk'énu; héwan
dog ["fluffy hide" type] pa7pa7í7k̲in
dog [breed of short-haired] x̲et'k̲'í7k̲in
dog [hunting] sk'énu
dog [old word for skwemaẏ] slhich'lk̲n
dog [short-haired type] tl'ími7k̲in
dog [type of long-haired dog with wool hanging over its eyes] k̲wepk̲wúpus
dog salmon k̲wáx̲nis
Dog Salmon River Kw'ál̓axwm
dog whelp stl'áx̲wtl'x̲waẏlh tsék̲w'ya
dog-faced sk̲wemaẏús
dogfish kw'aach'
dogfish skin sxwákw'ichn
doghouse sk̲wemaẏáẇtxw
dog-like sk̲wemaẏúmesh
dogs [sg: sk̲wemáẏ] sk̲wemk̲wemáẏ
doing (something), be ticht
doing something else, be titicháṁ
doing something, still be estéteẏsh
doing the same thing, just be estéteẏsh
doing what?, be chá7chanem? ~ chácha7nem?
doing wrong, be nánach'
doing, be kwekwiẏíṅtsut
doll míṁiṅ
Dolly Varden trout tl'ítl'elx̲iws
domed u7elk̲wús
domestic animal skw'íkw'iyuts
domestic blueberry xwíxwikw'
done, be esk̲w'ek̲w'íl; it; huynúmut; k̲w'el
don't go as far txwk̲'eẇ
don't know lhkwun
Don't overdo it! haw k̲'axw an x̲étsx̲etsetsut!
door k̲ep'tán; shewálh; nk̲ep'tán ~ nk̲ep'tn
dorsal fin sk̲'aẇíchshen ~ k̲'aẇíchshen
double blanket slhek̲tál̓
Double Mountain Goat Blanket Ntseẇásus

double up on (someone) an̓usmín̓
double, be nchem̓ús ~ nchém̓us ~ chém̓us
doubled up knee, have a métsḵw'i7n
doubled up over, be [about land] txwlhep'
doubled up, be espétspets
doubled up, be all [about person] sḵ'énḵ'enp'
doubt (someone) ḵwí7nexw
Douglas Fir [see also ch'shay̓] ch'sháya
Douglas fir [see also ch'sháya] ch'shay̓
Douglas fir bark slaay̓
down [as in the small feathers from a bird stl'eplḵn
down below, be áyalhḵw na7 ta les
down to, be txwti7
down towards the water, go txwkaw
down, be t'íxwi
downpour of rain, be a álhey̓shen
downstream area alhx̱án
downstream area, be elhx̱án
downstream of it, be alhx̱ániw̓ilh
downstream, go wuḵw' ~ wúḵw'i ~ txwwúḵw'i ~ wúwḵw'i
downtown iiḵ
downward to the ground, be txwt'ixw
dowry se7líl
drafty nt'iḵwm; sáy̓em̓s
drag (something) xwúkw'en
drag one's legs xwúkw'shnem
drag one's rear end along the ground xwukw'ḵán̓tsut
drag one's rear end on the ground xwúkw'ḵam̓
dragonfly lhelhenáya ~ lhelhenáy̓a ~ lhelhená7ya
draw x̱el̓
draw (something) x̱el̓t
draw (something) finally x̱él̓nexw
draw closer to (one) lhí7̓ni
draw for (someone) x̱él̓shi
draw water from (wood) suuḵsántem
draw with mouth [about sxw7umten] ts'úḵwim̓
draw, able to x̱el̓nálhn x̱el̓númut
drawn it onto (something), have esx̱éx̱el̓s
dream, to el̓éli
dream, a s7éli
dream about (something/someone) élini
dreaming about (something/someone), be el̓élini
dreams [sg: s7eli] s7el̓éli
dress tl'ítl'eptn
dress (someone) íts'ams
dress (someone) up huyiwsán
dress up húyiwsem
dress up warmly kw'asamút
dress warmly kw'ásmut
dress with (something) útsiyan
dressed up, be es-húyiws ~ es-huy̓us
dressed up, get all húyiwsem
dried (something), have ch'éy̓xwnexw
dried herring kw'elch'
dried salmon backbone sx̱ew̓
dried salmon put away for winter use nḵw'íḵw'lwas ~ nḵw'íḵw'lus ~ ḵw'íḵw'lus
dried salmon soaked in water st'éy̓ḵay
dried smoked salmon cut up thin sḵ'ey̓
dried whole salmon eḵwtús
drift seyx̱
drift ashore ḵwelh
drift back [as in a canoe] lhus
drift downstream seyx̱
drifting sesey̓x̱
drifting back in the river, be continually lhúlhusi7
driftnet seyx̱á7mten
driftwood t'kw'ím̓eḵ; ḵwlhay̓
drink taḵw; lhelh-
drink (something) táḵwan̓
drink directly from river [without scooping up water] puy̓ch
drink alcohol excessively xwákw'iyantsut
drink tea lhelhtí
drink, be getting a tiḵwúḵwel̓
drip [about a drop of something] ts'et'ḵ'm
dripping, be ts'éts'et'ḵ'm; ts'ét'ḵems
drive (a car) nékwen
driven back, be [e.g., a wick in a lamp or nail in the end of a stick] tl'up'
drizzling, be ts'éts'ichem
drooling. be lhílhix̱tem
drop wí7xwem
drop (small objects) [producing a rattling sound] tl'epx̱wán̓
drop (something) x̱élḵ'nexw
drop (something) accidentally mú7nexw
drop (something) intentionally mu7n; wixwán
drop (them) continuously mumú7nexw
drop [about dry salmon from being overheated] ch'elḵ

drop [about fish] ch'elk̲m
drop [as of barbecued fish] lhus
drop from being shaken [about leaves] píxwachxw
drop it intentionally wixwím̓
drop of water sts'ét'k̲'em
drop out of something tl'épx̲wem̓
drop something from one's mouth xwmu7ts ~ nexwmú7ts
dropoff sxwháy̓us ~ sxwaháy̓us
dropoff at bottom of beach shiyútsin
dropped (something), have wí7xwnexw
drought, be a t'ák̲wel̓
drown mut'; méymey
drum [specifically a skin drum] manáts'a ~ manáts'i
drum a fast rhythm líx̲witem
drum on boards with stick k̲'ewátem
drumstick [for a drum] schíchlhach; k̲'ewát
drunk, be esxwáxwkw'
drunk, be really esx̲ex̲ílh; sx̲ex̲lh
drunk, get xwákw'i; xwákw'iyantsut
drunk, get really x̲lhétsut
drunkard esxwékw'xwekw'
drunkard, be a sxwáxwkw'us
dry ch'eyxw ~ ch'ey̓xw
dry (someone's) tears ch'eyxwáy̓usn
dry (something) ch'eyxwán̓ ~ ch'ey̓xwán
dry (something), manage to ch'éy̓xwnexw
dry land, be on esháshm
dry one's own tears ch'eyxwáy̓usntsut
dry oneself off ch'eyxwán̓tsut
dry out [about living things] ch'áy̓i
dry something, just txwch'ey̓xwím̓
dry swamp mák̲wam
dry throat, have a ch'eyxwáy̓k̲in ~ ch'eyxwík̲in; ch'eyxwálhx̲a
dry, be t'ák̲wel̓; ch'eyxwí7; ch'i7xw
dry, be getting ch'ech'eyxwí7 ~ ch'eych'eyxwí7
dry, get ch'eyxwnúmut ch'eyxwán̓tm
drying pole for fish nek̲'áyiwstn
drying shed [see also ch'ixwimáw'txw] ch'ixwi7áw̓txw
drying things, be ch'ey̓xwím̓
duck (bird) x̲wílik̲w
duck, to mítl'intsut; ník̲im̓; tsípin̓tsut
duck down tl'íp'intsut
duck someone's head under water mík̲w'usem
dug (something) up, have t'ékw'nexw
dug already, be est'ét'kw'
dugout st'kw'im̓
dummy [literally, deer-face] sx̲wí7shnus
dung s7a7k̲
dung [euphemism for s7a7k̲] sxweym
dunk oneself in the water when bathing mík̲'intsut
during the day eskwáyel
dusk, be lháchi7
dust spúxwam; spekw'm
dust (something) up pák̲w'an
dust from filing yék̲'min
dusty, be very pépkw'am
Dwarf [specifically, little people who live in the forest; "if you see one don't tell anyone"] sk̲weyk̲wtáy̓mesh
dying, be k̲w'úk̲w'uy

E e

each other -way ~ -ay
each other -neẁas ~ -nẁas
each side inayíwilh ~ ináy̓wilh
eager x̱wak̲'
Eagle Harbour K̲'itl'álsem
ear k̲w'éla7en
ear {full word: k̲w'éla7n} -ayan ~ -ay̓a7n
earache, be having an lhek̲w-lhak̲wemáya7en
earache, have an lhák̲wemaya7n
eared grebe [type of bird] ts'ít'ax̱w
early daylight, be [later than natlh] k̲'it
early morning, be [earlier than k'it] natlh
earring s7útsiyim̓
earrings s7útsiyim̓
earrings, a pair of s7ets7útsiyim
ears full of wax, have t'sháyen
earth temíxw
earthquake yátshen néḵwem ta temíxw
ease off [about pain] tl'ékwentsut
eased up from pain, be mík̲wi7n
easing, be [about a poultice applied] tl'ék̲wentem
east telétsnech
east wind telétsnech
easy lí7lk̲
eat ílhen; lhelh-
eat (something) huy̓s
eat (something), manage to ilhnexw
eat [about a group] elh7ílhen
eat all of (something) i7x̱ws
eat bread lhelhseplín
eat fire lhelhyí7yulh
eat fish lhelhsts'úk̲wi7
eat grease ts'im̓
eat meat lhelhsméyts
eat much nk̲x̱am̓
eat potatoes lhelhsk̲áwts
eat secretly k̲anlhálem
eat soup lhum̓
eat suddenly txw7ilhn
eat, go out to ilhen̓íwlh
eat, manage to ilhennúmut
eat, refuse to xwí7lhayem
eater nexws7ílhen
eating (something), finish huy̓s
eating, be í7ilhen ~ i7ílhen
eating, finish huy̓ts
ebb chishkw
ebb, be at lowest [about tide] k̲wey̓
ebbing, be [about tide] shásham̓
echo swálam; iyálewen; wálam
echoing, be wáwalem; wálwalem
eddy sk̲'ants'x̱ánm ~ esk̲'ants'x̱ánm; k̲'iyáx̱atkwu7m
edge miyíw; -ts
edge [of anything] miyíẁax̱an ~ smiyíẁax̱an
edge of a cliff esk̲w'íwk̲ts
edge of anything esk̲w'íwk̲ts
edge of water p'en̓tskwú7
eelgrass chelm
egg(s) u7ús ~ eẁús
eight tk̲ach
eight animals a7tk̲ách
eight days ték̲k̲ách
eight o'clock tk̲achk̲
eight people tek̲tk̲ách
eight strands [of wool, rope, etc.] tk̲achámats'
eight times tk̲echálh
eight years tk̲áchawanexw
eighty tk̲echalhshá7
either side inayíwilh ~ ináy̓wilh
elbow s7áyk̲say
elbow {full word: s7áy̓k̲say̓} -k̲say̓
elbow of pipe sk̲'enp'
elder syú7yuxwa
elder child sintl'
elder children [sg: sintl'] sensíntl'
elder cousin kwúpits
elder cousins kwepkwúpits
elder sibling kwúpits
elder sibling [a term of address esh7íl ~ sh7il
elder siblings [sg: kwúpits] kwepkwúpits
elderberry bush ts'íwk̲'ay̓ ~ sts'íwk̲ay̓
elderberry tree sts'íwk̲'ay̓ ~ ts'íwk̲ay̓
elders sííy̓uxwa ~ siiyúxwa
eleven úpen i kwi nch'u7
eleven o'clock slhem̓k̲s ~ slhem̓k̲ ~ slem̓k̲s
eliminate (player of the opposite team in slhahál) by guessing in which hand s/he is holding the t'amten t'ámnexw
elk k̲'iyí7ch
elope lheẁím̓; lháẁstway
elope with (someone) lhaẁs ~ lheẁs
emaciated, become kwémts'i7

embarrassed, become x̱ets'x̱íts'i7
embarrassed, be x̱íts'i
embers [see also ḵáyalhkwup and ḵweḵwúlh] ḵwáyalhkwup
embers [see also ḵwáyalhkwup] ḵweḵwúlh
emerge with head above the water sháshamḵw
emit sparks p'eyts'em lhits'em
emitting sparks, be lhélheyts'em; pépeych'm
emphasizes sentence a
emptied bottle, be an nex̱wíl̓min̓
emptied, be [about container] x̱wíl̓am
empty berries into a different container kw'lham
empty inside, be x̱wíl̓x̱welmamin
empty it x̱wíl̓mamin
empty, be nex̱wíl̓em; x̱wíx̱wel̓em
encounter with a ghost, have an [see also shishá7yu7ntem] tewaḵinántem; shishá7yu7ntem
end stsey̓; tsey̓ḵs ~ tseyḵs
end (a story) tsey̓ḵsán
end [of something extended in length] stséy̓ḵs
end of a story, be the tsey̓ḵs ~ tseyḵs tseyḵs ~ tsey̓ḵs
end of a trip, get to the ḵ'iwḵs
endow (something) with life áy̓nexwan ~ áynexwan
endpoint stséy̓ḵs
enemies to one another, be shemánentway
enemies with one another, be sheshem̓án̓emnew̓as
enemy shemán
energetic nexwskwéy
energetic person, be an nexw7aw̓ítsay̓
energetic, be t'élhḵ'em
engaged to (someone), be es7áy̓as ~ s7áy̓as
engaged to each other, be esp'áp'iyiḵnew̓as
engaged to one another, be es7áy̓astway
engaged, be esp'áp'iyiḵnew̓as
enough, be tl'am; estl'átl'em; stey̓sh
enter new̓í
enter [a house] uys
entering, be ú7uys
entire, be ḵ'eḵ'sín̓
entrance s7uys
enveloped in (something), get ḵ'íw̓nem
envied, be nexw7étchusem
envious nexw7étchus
envious of (someone), be nexw7étchusni
envious, be ch'íḵam̓
epidemic x̱lhan
epidemic, be visited by an x̱lhantm
equal tsewás
equal, be [in strength, size, etc.] steta7átal̓
equilibrium, be in neḵ'íḵ'ew̓ch
erase (something) peylhán háwḵan
erased, be peylh
erect, be pex̱
erratically swimming back downstream after spawning, be [about salmon] tsutsuy̓úsem
errors st'emt'ám
escape ḵwanúmut; lhaw̓
escape [from something] tl'íw̓numut
escaped into the bush, be all skwemúm
Esquimault Sx̱imálhalh
etch x̱el̓
etch (something) x̱el̓t
etch (something) finally x̱él̓nexw
etch for (someone) x̱él̓shi
etch, able to x̱el̓númut x̱el̓nálhn
etched it onto (something), have esx̱éx̱el̓s
Eucharist lakalestí
eulachon from the Fraser River swí7u
eulachon from the Squamish River s7áynixw ~ áynexw ~ s7áynexw
eulachon grease/oil tl'ín̓a
euphoric, be esxwíxwiḵ
evaporated, be t'áḵwel̓
even, although yámen ~ yáman
even (opposite of uneven) tsewás
even beat on a drum, make an esḵéḵ
even if yámen ~ yáman
even, be steta7átal̓; estátel̓; statkw
even, be [in a match] esḵíḵtl'tel̓
evening, be ná7nat
evenly matched, be esḵ'íḵ'tel
eventful, be nexwlí7ls
ever ḵalh ~ ḵ'alh
every i7x̱w
everybody í7x̱wax̱w
everyone i7x̱w swat
everything i7x̱w stam
everywhere i7x̱w éncha
exactly tex̱wlám̓ ~ tex̱wl̓ám̓ ~ tex̱wám̓
exactly full, be ḵwíḵwitam
examine estx̱wáy̓usem
excess, be in esch'ech'íxw esch'ch'íxw

excessive tl'i7
excessively an
exchange (something) nexw7áy̓s
exchange with each other nexw7áy̓stway̓
excited, be/become/get x̱wá7ilwes ~ x̱wiy̓ílus
excited, get tí7ax̱w; x̱wáy̓elwas ~ x̱wá7ilwes
Excuse me! [said when trying to get past someone] k̲w'ak̲w'ay̓áx̱ ka!
exert oneself tímitsut
exhange nexw7áy̓
exhibit, an skw'áchmixway̓lh
exhibit, to kw'áchmixway̓lh
exhume body tsek̲wíyu7
exist tsi7
exist no longer txwawk̲ ~ txwhawk̲
expect nta7áw̓n ~ ta7áw̓n
expect (someone) kw'echkw'echní
expecting someone, be kw'échkw'ech
expensive tl'i7
expensive, become tl'a7í
expiate k̲'áwalhen
explode p'elhch; t'ekws
explode (something) t'ekwsán
explode [about dust or flowers] péych'em
exploring, be wéw̓shk̲em
expose (something) xwey̓k̲wán
exposed, be xwey̓k̲w
exposed, have one's bottom xwey̓k̲
extend (something) út'un
extent, be the stey̓sh estétey̓sh
extinguish (a fire) yák̲wan̓
extinguished, be yak̲w
extra sch'ech'íxw; slhems; hich
extra with regards to, be esí7chmin
eye k̲lum̓
eye {full word: k̲elúm̓} -ay̓us ~ -ayus
eyebrow tsúman
eyebrows [see also tsíplhten] tsúman
eyebrows [see also tsúman] tsíplhten
eyelash(es) lhiplhtn
eyelashes [see also tsiplháyus] tsíplhten
eyelashes [see also tsíplhten] tsiplháyus
eyes [sg: klum̓] k̲él̓k̲elum̓
eyes open, have one's t'ex̱t'x̱áy̓us

F f

face s7átsus; ta7ḵsám; sṁus
face [look] the other way tetúsayusem
face {full word: s7átsus and sm7us} -us
face a certain direction teta7ús
face like a dog, have a sḵwemaẏús
face powder páḵw'ustn
face the sun yahús
face this way tétus; tetúsem
face, be just a txw7utsus
face-peeling skin condition, have a p'elp'alaḵwúsi7
face-to-face with dead person's spirit, be chíshus
facing each other, be [about buildings] xwáyxwasustwaẏ
facing each other, be [about people] kw'awkw'chústway
fade pxwi7
fade away [e.g., noise or voice] ts'exwáyaḵap
faded pxwáẏus
faded, be getting pepxwí7
fading, be pepxwí7
faint ḵ'tsaṁ; x̱way ~ x̱wey; seṁ
fainter and fainter, be getting [about a sound off in the distance] nsesa7álhi
fall [the season] tem eḵwáyanexw
fall, to wí7xwem
fall [about a bunch of stuff] tl'épx̱weṁ
fall and get poked with a stick ch'út'a
fall apart x̱wílneẇas
fall asleep íttut
fall asleep [about leg] tl'úpshen
fall back [suddenly] txwtsḵálachen ~ txwḵálachen ~ txwtseḵálachen
fall backward tḵ'ax̱
fall backwards tsḵálachn t'ḵ'ax̱; txwtseḵálachen ~ txwḵálachen
fall down yaḵ'; lixw; lexwlíxw
fall down [e.g., an old tree on house] hep
fall down from a raised position x̱élḵ'em
fall down while walking lexwlíxw
fall from a height x̱élḵ'em x̱élx̱elḵ'em
fall from being shaken píxwachxw
fall head over heels kw'its'kw'its'léḵem
fall in hole txwchelhḵw
fall in the water [and sink] txwmuy
fall into txwneẇ
fall into an out-of-the-way-space txwtl'uḵw'
fall into the water peym; txwpeym
fall off cheyḵsám
fall on a house [about trees] yelaḵ'í7chen
fall on one's back txwtsḵálachen ~ txwḵálachen ~ txwtseḵálachen
fall on one's knees txwpelḵw
fall on the tops [about snow on the mountains] lixwḵwm
fall out shemáneẇas
fall out [about hair] eḵw
fall out of a container txwt'axw
fall over tsexwstm
fall overboard txwpeym peym
fall short elháp
fall short [about stone thrown] ḵ'tsaṁ
fall short [aiming for a point] ts'elhp'
fall silent ch'áxwi7
fall through ch'ixw ~ ch'exw
fall through a hole [about feet] chélhḵwshen
fall through a hole after trying to get through chelhḵwnúmut
fall through an opening [e.g., a hole in the floor] chelhḵw
fall under something txwhiḵ ~ txwiḵ
fallen needles on ground, an old word for "moss" ḵwiyám
fallen timber sx̱itsḵ
fallen tree x̱itsḵ
fallen, be [about tree] yaḵ'
fallen, be esx̱ítsḵ
falling out, have a kw'ikw'áyneẇas
falling, be wéweẏxwem
falling, be [about leaves] pixw
falls stséxwem
falsehood nexwmets'tṅálḵp ~ xwméts'tṅálḵp

family [the descendants of one head] nch'áy̓uw̓am
fan xwáy̓xwaytn
fan oneself xwáy̓xwayéntsut
far x̱éta
far apart, be yex̱
far end [of a lake] sx̱éta7ḵs
far side x̱eta7áx̱an
far side of it x̱eta7áy̓ch
far side of road or river [see also x̱eta7tsá7] x̱etáy̓wilh
far side of the fire, x̱eta7áyikwup
far-sighted nx̱etx̱ít7ayus ~ x̱etx̱ít7ayus
nexwiyáy̓us ~ nexw7ey̓áy̓us
fart steḵ'
fart teḵ'; pu7ḵ; má7kwelh
fart accidentally teḵ'númut
farther and farther each time, be x̱etx̱éta
farthest north tsipix̱áyx̱
fashion nexwníw̓
fast ch'áytsut; aw̓íts; ch'ey̓
fast drum beat tsix̱
fast noise, be a ḵ'etx̱ántsut
fast worker, be a nexw7aw̓ítsay̓
fat ḵw'uts; x̱wes; x̱wastn; sx̱wes
fat person [slang] t'elh
fat, be getting x̱wex̱wsí7; ḵw'úḵw'uts'i7
fat, get ḵw'útsi7; x̱wesí7
father man; mam; máma; chi7cht
fathom talh
fatten (someone) ḵw'útsun̓
fatter than, be x̱wesmín̓
favourite, be the temstl'í7
fawn [newborn] st'el̓úllh
fawn [yearling] sḵw'éḵw'ipa
feast tl'a7áshn ~ tl'ashn ~ tl'a7áshen
feast with extra food, have a ílhenay̓lh ~ ílhenaylh
feather stl'pál̓ḵen
feather [as part of Indian hairdo] sch'ḵw'ap
feather put in hair sch'ḵw'ap
feathers kw'íkw'lets'; stl'eplḵn; -ay̓us; stl'pál̓ḵen
February tem welhx̱s
feces s7a7ḵ
fed up with (someone), be ch'íwi7ni; lháts'ini
fed up, be lháts'i; aháy̓new̓as
fed up, get ch'íwi
feed (someone) ílhens
feed (someone) [about new dancers] p'í7tsan
feed (the dead) ílhenaylhs
feed the dead ílhenaylh ~ ílhenay̓lh
feel (someone) up tsestsástem
feel (something) táḵnexw; tsásnexw; tátaḵnexw
feel (something) with hands tsásan̓
feel a sudden chill x̱enx̱ín̓
feel a wish to be with someone níḵ'i
feel around for fish with butt end of harpoon tsatsḵs ~ tsa7tsḵs
feel cheap x̱íx̱its'i7
feel cold tesí7; tet-si7
feel good halhí7 ~ helhí7
feel insulted ch'usténamut
feel like crying x̱aam̓áy̓m
feel sad sélḵwtsut
feel some unseen thing kw'ulhnúmut
feel sorry for (someone) al̓s
feel sorry for oneself tesasténam̓ut; aalstén̓emut
feeling cold, be ests'elhts'úlh
feeling good, be [from drinking alcohol] shésheych'm
feeling lazy, be ú7um̓at
feeling sorry for oneself, be séselḵwtsut
feet [sg: sx̱en̓] sx̱énx̱en
feet in bushes, have eshíshch'shen
feet in the water, have one's esmúmey̓shen
feet on it, have [e.g., carving] esúts
feet stuck in mud, get t'ekwshn
feet up on beach, have eskwúmshen
feign at (something) x̱i7x̱ís
fell (a lot of trees) yeḵ'yáḵ'an
fell (a tree) x̱itsḵán̓ ~ x̱ítsḵen
fell (something) [as by the old method of using wedges and hot-rock burning] yáḵ'an
fell a tree x̱itsḵ
fellow kw'elh
felt (something), have táḵnexw
female [animal] slhálhen̓ay
female bear slhálhen̓ay míx̱alh
female cousin of parents sáta7 ~ s-háta7
female deer slhálhen̓ay sx̱wí7shen
female salmon after spawning kwémkwemts ~ skwém̓kwem̓ts

fence **k̲'iyáx̲en ~ k̲'iyáx̲an**
fence (something) in **k̲'iyáx̲enen**
fern plant root [steamed and eaten] **ts'ékwa7**
fern, type of **ptakwem**
fetch wood **chemáy̓kwup**
fever, have a **p'áp'ach'**
fever, have a high **yáyak̲w'am**
feverish **p'áp'ach'**
few **kw'in**
few animals **kw'íkw'in ~ kw'íkw'en**
few canoes **kw'ínaxwilh**
few left, be just a **txwkw'ínkw'in**
few people **kw'ínkw'en ~ kw'ínkw'in**
few strands of wool **kw'ínamats'**
few, be just a **txwkw'in**
few, become **kw'íni7**
few, become [about people] **txwkw'ínkw'in**
fidgety **eswéts'wets' ~ swéts'wets'**
field **estétey̓**
fifty **lhek̲'chalhshá7**
fifty one **lhek̲'chalhshá7 i kwi nch'u7**
fight **kwíntel ~ kwíltn kwílten**
fight back **ti7chám̓ tiyách**
fight each other [about dogs] **x̲wútl'untway**
fight for (someone) **kwíltenchew̓án̓**
fight in battle **x̲éyx̲entway**
fight one another **kwíltenstway**
fight over (something) **kwíltenchew̓án̓**
fighting each other [about dogs] **xwetl'xwútl'antway̓**
file **ch'k̲'en**
filed away, be **estl'útl'k̲w**
filing, be [as in sharpening something] **yíyek̲'am**
filings **yék̲'min**
fill (something) **yích'it**
fill (something) up **yech'ét yech'mámen**
fill (something) with a solid **nexwnew̓ám̓en**
fill (something) with liquid **kw'lhám̓en**
fill a can **nexwnew̓ámim̓ ~ new̓ámim̓**
fill out [as in body] **k̲'ech'**
fill up **mek̲'étsut**
fill up (a hole) in the wall or ground **ts'úp'un**
fill up [about mosquitoes] **k̲'chétem**
fill up hole in ground **penám̓en**
filled it up finally **yech'númut**
filled to the brim, be **k̲wík̲witam**
filled up, be [about stomach] **yéch'wilh**
filled, be **esyíy̓ch' ~ syíy̓ch'**
fillet **st'al**
fin **slhíplhipiyax̲a7ens**
final, be **huyálhtsut; tsey̓k̲s ~ tseyk̲s**
finally **yalh**
finally beat someone **kw'al̓ak̲wusnálhen**
finally get mad **t'ayak̲'númut**
finally get paid **k̲'awnúmut**
find **smékw'em**
find (something) **yák̲wnexw**
find (something) easy to do **li7lk̲s**
find (something/someone) strange **nach's**
find it **mékw'em**
find out about (something) **tél̓nexw**
find ways to get cranky **wew̓ts'átsut**
fine **is**
fine [about materials] **ník̲w'em**
fine-toothed comb **méchenten**
fine-work basket **kwél̓mexwus**
finger **-ul̓a nix̲k̲wúy̓ach**
finger {full word: **nix̲k̲wúy̓ach**} **úmsemul̓a; -k̲wuy̓ach**
fingernail(s) **k̲w'x̲wúy̓k̲wuy̓ach**
finish **it; huy**
finish (something) **i7x̲ws; tsey̓k̲sán; húynexw**
finish (something) [e.g., reading a book] **esáp'nexw**
finish [e.g., a story] **tsekw**
finish a course **esáp'**
finish eating **huy̓ts**
finish eating (something) **húy̓nexw; huy̓s**
finish for (someone) **esáp'shi**
finish it **shk̲étsut**
finish making (something) **tá7nexw**
finish, manage to **wetwetnúmut**
finished **wétwet**
finished giving a potlatch, get **shek̲**
finished packing (something), be **k̲ém̓snexw**
finished, be **huy; it; shek̲; tihúy; tsey**
finished, be [about season] **húyiyanexw**
finning, be [about porpoises or orcas/killer whales] **shamshám̓cham̓**

fir stick **ch'shaẏ**
fire, a; to burn **yíẏulh**
fire (a canoe) **k̲w'áyat**
fire (someone) **huys**
fire {full word: **yíẏulh**} **-chp ~ -chep; -ikwup ~ -ayikwup**
fire a gun **kwélash**
fire at (something) **kwélasht**
fire drill **shéychep**
fire hearth **nexwyíẏulhtn**
fire log **neshús**
fire log "aiming" direction of fire **sx̲étsni7kwup**
fire, be in the **txwyulh**
fired, be [about gun] **t'ekws**
firepit **yíẏulhay**
fireplace **nexwyíẏulhtn**
fireweed **x̲ach't**
firewood **yíẏulh**
firm, become [about glue, putty, etc.] **tichémx̲**
first **s7a7ú7 ~ u7**
first growth of young red cedar tree **t'áyamaẏ**
first man created at Gibson's **Tsk̲anchtn**
first white man **a7ú7 xwalítn swí7k̲a**
first, be **a7ú7 ~ u7ú7; yeẇáṅ**
fish [collective, all kinds] **scháyilhen**
fish [general term] **sts'úk̲wi7**
fish by means of a hook **íẇas ~ yeẇás**
fish cheek **slhík̲wus**
fish club **slá7mats**
fish club [more common term is **slá7mats**] **k̲w'úk̲wustn**
fish dam **tk̲ap**
fish fin **k̲'aẇítshen**
fish for salmon **tists'úk̲wi7**
fish head **sme7úsk̲w**
fish knife **kw'ich'tn**
fish nose **sx̲wumk̲s**
fish on their run to spawn up river **scháyilhen**
fish ready for cleaning, bunch of **x̲wúk̲w'ayi**
fish right up to the spawning grounds **schí7ulh**
fish scales **ts'úkw'em**
fish skin **kw'el̓áẇ**
fish slime **slish**
fish spreader [see also **ch'aẏústn**] **ch'aẏús**
fish spreader used in barbecuing [see also **ch'aẏús**] **ch'aẏústn**
fish stomach **k̲w'iẏúk̲w'**
fish tail [see also **swa7tshn**] **sx̲ép'shen**
fish trap **ch'iyák̲**
fish with a dip net **shéma7n**
fish with a harpoon **tsahímelh**
fish with a torch **yex̲í7u**
fish with hook and line **íẇas ~ yeẇás**
fish with line ["mooching"] **íẇas ~ yeẇás**
fish with line [not with a rod] **sts'em**
fish with line in a river **íẇas ~ yeẇás**
fish with net [in river] **mik̲'**
fish with rod **íẇas ~ yeẇás**
fish, a lot of **sts'ek̲wts'úk̲wi7**
fishhawk **ts'íxwts'ixw**
fishhook [general term] **kw'uykw**
fishing hook **k̲álhayu**
fishing line **kw'uykwél̓shen**
fishing line [modern] **sk̲w'úmk̲w'emaẏ**
fishing net **switn**
fishing rod **xwiẇástn**
fishing spot for a dip net **k̲tiṁ**
fist **sk̲ik̲p'ach**
fit [about clothes] **estl'átl'em**
fitting, be **estl'átl'em**
five **tsíyichis ~ tsíyachis**
five animals **tsitseẏáchis**
five berries **tsiyichisáyuṁ ~ tsiyachisáyuṁ**
five canoes **tsiyichisáxwilh**
five days **tsíyáchis**
five dollars **tsíyichisuẏs**
five houses **tsiyichisáẇtxw**
five o'clock **tsíyachisk̲**
five people **tsitsíyachis**
five rivers **tsiyichisálhk̲wu**
five rocks **tsíyichisuẏs**
five strands [of wool, rope, etc.] **tsiyachisámats'**
five teeth **tsiyichisáns**
five times **tsíyachisálh**
five trees **tsiyichisíwa7**
five years **tsiyichisáwanexw**
fix (something) **p'áyak̲en**
fix (something), manage to **p'áyak̲nexw**
fix it finally **p'ayak̲nálhen**
fix up (something) **p'áyak̲en**
fixed and leveled off, be **ha7lhínup**
fixed, be **p'áyak̲**
fixed, be [no longer loose] **yaa7 ~ ya7 ~ yá7a**
fixed, get **p'ayak̲nálhen**
fixing (something) up, be **p'áp'aẏak̲en**
flabby arms, have **lhélhp'i7**
flame **sxwétkwem; t'eẏk̲wm**
flame up **xwétkwem; xwéxwetkwem**
flapping foot, have a **lhelp'shn**
flash **kwék̲i7n; k̲wts'i7n; péych'em**
flash [about a light] **kwétsi7n pích'i7n**
flat **tsewás; ts'eṁíl**
flat [river, clothes, etc.] **lhk̲'at**
flat land **tsewásiṅup**
flat nose, have a **lhek̲'k̲s**
flat taste, have **pelh**
flatland **spálhx̲en**

flat-nosed wéchwechk̲s ~ nexwwéchwechk̲s
flats spálhx̲en
flea t'út'lhem
flea-ridden, be t'út'lhemántm
flee [about group of people] tl'utl'íw̓
flee into the bush [upward from village on the shore] skwemúm
fleeting glance esésixw
flesh slhik̲w
flies [small black] ts'ets'ek̲w'áls
flinch tsípin̓tsut
flint gun esk̲ílhpay
flip st'em̓
flirting, be mamts'á7nem sméts'mets'em
float p'áp'ekw
float (a canoe) p'ákwilhen
floating easily, be p'ékwp'ekw
floating high, be p'ékwp'ekw
flood over meymúy
flooded out, be mimúy
flooded, be mimúy
floor lhx̲énpten
floor {full word: lhx̲énpten} -nep ~ -np ~ -nup
floor mat ts'í7shten
floor on canoe to protect bottom nek̲wúyuy̓
flounder [black-dotted] p'ewáy̓
flow x̲wél̓shm
flower, a spák̲'em
flower, to pápk̲'am
flower child spák̲'em s7íxwalh
flower shop spak̲'em̓áw̓txw
fluid -alhk̲wu
fluid condition, be in esyáy̓x̲w
fluttering, be [about eyes] lhaplhipayúsm
fly, to sik̲
fly away [about bunch of birds] sek̲sík̲
flying dry snow, be púsham
flying dust, be pékw'em
flying squirrel sísik̲ smemel̓útsin
flying, be sísik̲ ~ sisík̲
foal stek̲iw̓úllh ~ stak̲iwúllh
foam, the sp'úk̲w'em
foam, to p'úk̲w'am
foamy, be púk̲w'emi7
fog sk̲wétshem ~ sk̲wétshen
fogged up kwalh
foggy, be k̲wetk̲wétshem
foggy, become kwálhi7
fold ptsim̓
fold (something) nchém̓usn ~ chém̓usn; pétspetsen; pétsen
fold itself over pétsentsut
folded, be pets
follow nep
follow (something) chayn
follow [a song or another speech] tay̓ts
follow [road, path] nsnen̓p
follow behind somebody txwtay̓ch
follow behind someone cháyak̲em
follow someone cháyak̲em
follow someone's speech with one's own speech tay̓tsám̓ ~ ti7tsám̓
following (something), be chicháy̓s
following after, be á7aw̓t
following behind someone, be chicháy̓ak̲em
following each other in single file, be chicháy̓stway
following, be chicháy̓ak̲em
food s7ílhen
food {full word: s7ílhen} -lhal
food donation [after a feast] smek̲w'ú7ts
food for a trip saw̓án
food or clothing burnt at funeral syúlhim̓
food sent home for women and children smek̲w'ú7ts
food taken on trip saw̓án
food tube x̲iyúm
fool (someone) nek̲'ík̲'els
foolish ways sts'úysánan
foot sch'iyípshen; sx̲en̓
foot {full word: sx̲en̓} -shen
foot end of bed platform wa7tshn
foot of mountain slix̲wáy̓shn ~ slíx̲way̓shn
footprint, have an impure eschíchen̓
footprints nex̲én̓etn
for -shi
for [something desired] txwnam̓
for a little while cha7lh ~ chá7lha
for the first time men yalh
forbid (someone) nemán
forbidden nemá
forbidden thing snemá
force (someone) out of his/her spot plhétem
force (something) full tl'ets'úyen
force (something) in tl'úk̲w'un
force (something) open wik̲'tsn̓ ~ wik̲'tsán̓
force one's way into a small spot pítsintsut
forecaster esyú7
forehead st'úk̲wchus ~ st'úkw'chus
forehead {full word: st'úkw'chus} -chus
forest stsék̲tsek̲
forfeit eschel̓áw̓

forget may
forget (something) máynexw
forgetful smeymáy̓ ~ meymáy̓ ~ smemey̓máy̓
forgetful person nexwsmemey̓máy̓
forgetful, very esmemey̓máy
fork sch'áḵw'els
fork in a stream, river or road st'x̱i
forked barbecuing knife or stick ḵw'élten
form clouds or puffs of dust pépkw'am
former men t'ut; t'ut
former state skwen
former time yew̓an̓álh
former, be yew̓án̓
fort ḵ'iyáx̱an
fortification ḵ'iyáx̱an
fortune-teller esyú7
forty x̱wutsnalhshá7
forty one x̱wutsnalhshá7 i kwi nch'u7
forty two x̱wutsnalhshá7 i kwi an̓us
forward, be txwhiw̓ ~ txwiw̓
found (something), have yáḵwnexw; p'í7nexw
found out (something), have tá7lnexw
found, be yaḵw
four x̱a7útsen
four animals x̱ix̱a7útsen
four berries x̱a7útsenayum̓
four containers [pots, pans, canoes] x̱a7útsenaxwilh
four days x̱áa7útsen
four o'clock x̱a7útsenḵ
four people x̱ex̱a7útsn
four pieces x̱a7utsenmút
four strands of wool x̱a7utsenámats'
four times x̱a7útsenalh
four trees x̱a7útseniwa
frame for tanning hides tpúlhtn
frame for weaving blankets tpúlhtn
Fraser River Sx̱wáymelh
free yex̱w
free (someone) tl'íw̓nexw
free, be esyéy̓x̱w
freeze (something) úxwnan
fresh [about food] x̱aw̓s
fresh [about water] ts'áwam
fresh water ts'áwam staḵw
fresh, be [about food] x̱isí7
Friday Stsiiyáchis
fried bread sch'ex̱wḵ'; esch'éxwḵ
friend siyáy̓; sh7eylh ~ sh7ilh
friendly ḵw'áḵw'ay̓
friendly terms with someone, be on siyáy̓ay̓
friendly with (someone), have become ḵw'áy̓nexw
friends [sg: siyay'] síiyay̓
friends to each other kw'elhtl'í7new̓ás
friends, become yáynew̓as tél̓new̓as
frighten (someone) tsetskw'ít ip'áaḵw'ulhs
frightened away, get walh
frightened of (someone/something), get ip'áaḵw'ulhni
frightened, be tsíkw'i7n
frightened, get sel̓selíws ~ silsilíws ~ sisilíws
frightened, have one's feet get sisilíwsshn
frightening, be ip'áaḵw'ulhimin
froe [type of tool] p'eḵwtn
frog wex̱és
frog leaves [literally, little bed of the frog] slhí7lhaw̓in̓ tl'a wex̱és
from ti-
from below, be til̓él̓s
from everywhere, be tiná7 i7x̱w
from here, be ti7í
from where?, be ti7éncha?
from, be tiná7
front leg síw̓ach ~ s-híw̓ách
front of house nicháyaḵ'in; néyney̓ch
front of something/someone, be txw7átsiḵn
front of the house átsus
front of the neck s7átsiḵen
front of, be in yew̓ániwilh
front room néyney̓ch; ninicháyaḵ'in
front side [see also átsus] s7átsus
front side [see also s7átsus] átsus
front side, be átsiḵen
front side, be at the txw7átsus
front, be in hiw̓ḵw
frost x̱éx̱en̓
froth métḵwem; péy̓tsem
frozen [about river] np'ats'
frozen, be uxwenántem
frozen, be [about the ground] x̱ex̱en̓ántem
fruit tree ḵw'elámay̓
fry (something) ch'ekwx̱án
frying pan ch'ékwx̱tn
frying, be ch'ekwx̱ím̓
full [e.g., a container] siy̓ích'
full, from eating [literally, have a sleepy throat] itutálhx̱a
full already [from eating], be esm̓íḵ'
full [from eating] for a while, have been sme7íḵ'
full grown, be ḵech
full moon sḵeḵích
full of bends, be sḵ'énḵ'enp'

full stomach, have a
yéch’wilh
full, be syíy̓ch’ ~ esyíy̓ch’;
yech’
full, be [about the moon]
esk̲ek̲ích;
k̲ech
full, be [from eating]
sme7ík̲’;
mek̲’
full, be finally mek̲’númut
full-blown, be k̲ech
full-grown [about berries, etc.] k̲cháyum̓
full-grown [about larger fruit] k̲chuy̓s
fully ripe, be [about berries]
skw’ek̲w’íl̓
fumble with a package
esk̲í7k̲elach
fun sk̲w’shétsut
funeral, a sk̲emsím̓;
funeral, to have a k̲em̓sám
funny, be eskwúy̓ts
fur kw’í7k̲tn
furious, be ch’íyakwem
ch’ích’ikwem
future generations kwi aw̓t stélmexw
future, be aw̓t;
á7aw̓t
fuzzy pá7pa

G g

gabled ends, have ntséwiyekw
gabled roof k̲'íts'iy̓ek̲w
gaff tsahímelh
gaff hook k̲álhayu
gag xwíw̓tsem
gall tl'ek̲'tn; mésen
gall bladder mésen
gamble k'ák'eltx̲; tl'etl'exwítay̓
gambling slhahál
game using two pieces of rubber tied on a stick nuk̲ws
gang up on (someone) k̲xwúsmin
gang up on (someone) [about two people] an̓usmín̓
garden npen̓em̓áy ~ pen̓em̓áy
gas boat hén̓xwilhem
gather k̲exw
gather (something) k̲éxwnexw
gather (them) together k̲w'ú7new̓asn ~ k̲'éw̓new̓asn; k̲éxwen
gather (them) up esk̲ék̲xws
gather (things) together k̲emsán
gather firewood k̲exwní7kwup
gather people together k̲xwúsem
gather together k̲exwk̲exwntsút
gathered already, be esk̲ék̲xw
gathered berries or roots syek̲
gathered together, be esk̲ék̲xw k̲exw
gathered together, be [about a body of water] esk̲éxwts'a
gathered together, be [about languages] esk̲éxwts
gathering sk̲ek̲xw
gathering (something), be k̲ék̲xwen
generations below smén̓hem
generous person nexwschechráchshay̓
generous, be s7íxwa7
genitals -ats' ~ -ats'a
gently áyetsut
genuflect ts'k̲'álhx̲a7m
geoduck swaam
get -y ~ -i ~ -i7
get (someone) all riled up wets'wáts'nexw
get (someone) hurt má7kwlhnexw ~ mákwlhnexw
get (someone) started singing kwenkwéns
get (someone) there tsixws
get (something) p'í7nexw
get (something) back k̲'énexw ~ k̲'énnexw
get (something) from where? ti7énchas?
get (something) home hiy̓ám̓nexw
get (something) into the water múynexw
get (something) open nx̲wíl̓tsnexw ~ x̲wíl̓tsnexw
get (something) together k̲w'ú7nexw
get (something), manage to [e.g., a deer] p'í7nalhen
get (them) together k̲exwnew̓ásn
get a chance to shoot kwelashnúmut
get a fire going yúlhnalhn
get a hold of (someone's) nose p'ík̲san ~ p'i7k̲sán̓
get a job ts'its'ap'númut
get a shot off, able to kwelashnúmut
get a taste t'á7nalhen
get a weapon p'ayk̲áy̓s
get a wife chewáshem
get a wife by blanket marriage tl'a7m
get after (someone) kwíyentem
get all poked up nek̲w'núk̲w'
get ashore [about group] kwemkwúm
get away t'am̓í ~ t'am̓éy lhaw̓
get away from rough weather tikw
get away from, manage to x̲wíl̓numut
get away, manage to lháw̓numut
get better kwan helhí7 ~ halhí7
get bread, go tiseplín
get busy tí7ax̲w
get caught tl'eyk̲'
get caught on a hook [about fish] lhikw'k̲w
get chipped off lhemch'
get clams, go tishéykw
get down tixw
get dressed íts'am
get dry ch'eyxwí7
get even mátl'tsut
get excited tí7ax̲w
get fat x̲wesí7
get here, manage to [similar to tl'iknumut] tl'ik̲sténam̓ut

get here, manage to [similar to tl’iksténam’ut] tl’ik̲númut
get hit tsexw
get hit in the face ts’ahús
get hit on one’s nose ts’ak̲s
get hit on top of the head tséxwiy̓ek̲w
get home hiy̓am̓númut; hihiy̓ám̓; nahám̓; hiy̓ám̓
get home finally hiy̓am̓númut
get home, manage to hiy̓am̓númut
get hooked lhikw’
get hot kw’ási7
get hung up k̲’á7a; lhep’
get hungry for (something) tem̓áy̓t
get hurt má7kwelh
get into [a dense mass x̲wiyak̲w’éy
get into a state of rapture kwen
get into action kwíyin̓tsut
get into the shade ts’ay̓ántsut
get it cooked k̲w’elnálhen
get its wool singed shew̓shík̲in
get left behind [in a race] chíchishkwstm
get less [about rain] tsápshen
get like tishám̓
get lost [old meaning] meymáy̓ ~ smeymáy̓ ~ smemey̓máy̓
get married melyí; p’ínew̓as
get married [about a woman] txwkwtams
get mixed up [about things or mentally] melmílch’
get more than one in one shot from gun k̲’ets’
get muddy [less muddy than tekwt’kwi7] ts’ík̲’i7
get near/close lha7í7
get off without damage xwik’
get old stl’etl’elmú7tentsut
get on fire yelhyúlh
get on to the road or trail nepí
get one’s foot caught tl’éyk̲’shen
get one’s foot caught [in something squeezing] p’its’shn
get one’s hand caught [in something squeezing] p’íts’ach
get one’s stuff ready k̲emsím̓
get one’s weapons in readiness húy̓k̲áy̓sm
get oneself out quickly shúshantsut
get oneself ready p’ayak̲éntsut
get oneself ready to go hilkwántsut
get out of someone’s way est’át’em
get out of the rain t’ápk̲am
get out of the way t’am̓í ~ t’am̓éy
t’am̓éy ~ t’am̓í
get paid k̲’aw; k̲’awnálhen
get poked/stabbed in the cheek tsík̲a7an
get poked/stabbed in the chest tsik̲ínas
get poked/stabbed in the chin tsik̲tsk̲
get poked/stabbed in the shoulder tsík̲ay̓ám̓it
get poked/stabbed on the top of the head tsík̲iy̓ek̲w
get ready shk̲étsut
get ready [to go] hilkw
get revenge múx̲wutsut
get scared p’áak̲w’alh ~ ip’áak̲w’ulh ~ p’á7k̲w’alh
get sliver in foot núk̲w’shen
get soft k̲i7k̲i7í7
get some money, go titála
get some water k̲wulím̓
get somewhere tsixw
get stuck in the mud t’ekw
get stuck on the bottom [of the water] shemshám
get tangled up around it k̲’élk̲’elk̲’
get the creeps silsilíws ~ sel̓selíws ~ sisilíws
get there tsixwnúmut
get tired feet k̲’ésshen
get tired waiting k̲’esíws
get to ask welk̲w’alsnúmut
get to go nam̓númut
get to shore p’es
get to the end of a trip k̲’iwk̲s
get to the other side [of a body of water] lhek̲
get to writing/etching/drawing x̲el̓nálhn
get together k̲w’u7new̓ásm
k̲w’ú7new̓as ~ k̲w’u7new̓ás ~ k̲’ew̓new̓ás; k̲exw; k̲xwúsem
get two or more with one shot lháts’new̓as
get up [a hill, a tree], finally katnúmut
get up [said to someone lying in bed] emút
get water for (someone) k̲wúlshi
get well eslhéw̓lhew; p’áyak̲; kwániws
getting (something) out of the way, be t’et’em̓án
getting (something), have been p’ep’í7nexw
getting a drink, be tik̲wúk̲wel̓
getting dark, be tl’etl’k̲w’í7
getting fat, be x̲wex̲wsí7
ghosted, be shishá7yu7ntem; tewak̲inántem

Giant Cannibal Woman k̲ál̓k̲alilh
giant red sea urchin x̲íxwa
giant salamander seỷíx̲yix̲es
giant wild person smáyl̓ilh
Gibson's Landing [see also Ch'k̲w'elhp] Scheńk̲
gift, a s7émnexw
gift, a [e.g., of seeing the future in dreams] esch'áwatm
gills of a fish sháỷay
ginger, wild x̲et'tánay
girl of upper class, girl raised strictly chilhná7nch' ~ schelhna7ench'
girl who picks berries sálu
give cháchshaỷ
give (a bereaved woman) a condolence gift xw7ík̲w'usn
give (daughter) in marriage líxwshi
give (one's daughter) as a wife émilhán
give (one's daughter) in marriage lixwt
give (someone) a disease k̲'áp'an
give (someone) a steam bath k̲atán
give (someone) a tough time [in a fight, game, etc.] kwíyin
give (someone) food for lunch saẁáńs; saẁáńen
give (someone) lots k̲ex̲s
give (someone) medicine t'uỷtenamen
give (someone) one nch'ú7muts
give (someone) permission ánuń
give (someone) something sátshi
give (something) táyak̲en; ixwn; sátań
give (something) a single poke in the fire tsík̲iń
give (something) around [especially gifts at a potlatch] lhít'it
give a big sigh [about a dancer] shék̲i7n
give a name to a child ninaháỷlhm
give a name to a person naháylhem
give a potlatch tl'e7énk̲ ~ tl'enk̲; tl'a7áshn ~ tl'ashn ~ tl'a7áshen
give advice nexwneẁéyelh ~ nexwniẁéyalh
give along écháỷ
give away presents cháchshaỷ
give birth tl'k̲ílh; smemn
give birth [LM: old word is ch'ach'lem] esméń
give birth [old word for esmen'] ch'ách'lem
give daughter in marriage líxwaỷlhem ~ lixwáỷlhem
give encouragement xwáḿam
give extra food away ílhenaylh ~ ílhenaỷlh ílhenaỷlh ~ ílhenaylh
give it sátiḿ
give it away wals
give it to (someone) éxwa7t
give medicine to (someone) t'uỷtn
give off a strong burning smell [e.g., burning rags or feathers] lhech
give off odour [about gall, when vomiting] lekw'
give one's daughter in marriage émilhaỷlh
give one's finger [in order to play klexw] sátk̲wuỷachí7m
give one's hand satachí7m
give out háwk̲i7
give out names to descendants naháylhem
give shape to (something) húyut
give something away at a feast lhit'
give the dead something to drink ták̲w7aylh
give way [e.g., about a plank under a weight] met'étsut
given to teasing people, be nexwswéts'wets'áỷlh ~ nexwswewts'áỷlh
glacier x̲áx̲min
glad tsá7tsaxw
glance k̲w'ux̲wáỷusem
glance at (something) p'elk̲'áń; k̲w'úx̲wuń; k̲w'ux̲wáỷusin
glare stewtáẁ
glasses [see tála] ntala7áyus
glasses on, have one's estetel̓áyus
glory [word used in the Catechism] Klúli
gloves ts'k̲wúl̓ech
glowing hot p'ach'
gnash one's teeth ch'iyíkw'ní7n ~ ch'iyíkw'in; x̲ets'k̲'ánsem
gnat ts'ets'emíchen
gnaw on (something) [e.g., about a rat gnawing a hole in the wall] ch'ítiń
gnawed, be ch'ítitem
go huỷ; naḿ
go aboard úyulh
go aboard a canoe with (someone) nak̲w'ú7wilhan
go across a body of water tuy
go across a river tuyts

go across a small body of water **txwtuy**
go across a stretch of water where the opposite shore is closest **t'k̲w'ay̓ch**
go after (someone) **wé7us ~ wá7us**
go against [wind or current] **k̲'ixwúsm**
go aground in canoe **txwtsekw**
go along **txwnam̓**
go along the road **nexwsnén̓p**
go alongside (a canoe) **tátaywilhs**
go alongside in a canoe **p'ílhk̲'i**
go and get (something or someone) **nám̓en**
go and stay with one's wife's people **kw'ílhiw̓**
go and sympathize with persons who sustained a loss **x̲améyulh**
go another way **txwáyak̲ep**
go around back of (something) **k̲'etchán̓**
go around something when travelling **seyk̲'áy̓ch**
go around the bend **k̲'iwk̲s**
go around the feet of (someone lying down) **k̲'et-shnán̓**
go around the front side of (something) **k̲'tusn; k̲'ek̲'túsn**
go around the head of (something) **k̲'etiy̓ek̲wán̓**
go around the point of (something) **k̲'etk̲sán**
go ashore **kwum**
go astray **t'emt'ám; sekw**
go away **huyá7; t'am̓éy ~ t'am̓í**
go back and forth from one end to the other **iséyk̲'k̲s**
go backwards **k̲'áx̲an̓tsut**
go behind **txwtay̓ch**
go behind (something) **k̲'etchán̓**
go berry picking **ilhen̓ám**
go by [referring to either a place or time] **k̲wetk̲**
go by inside route [e.g., between Bowen Island and the mainland] **nexw7áysay̓ch**
go by inside way **nexw7áysay̓ch**
go by way of some place **nexwtá7**
go by what means? [by canoe, by foot, etc.] **nexw7éncha?**
go by which route? **nexw7éncha?**
go by which way? **nexw7éncha?**
go check up on someone **tl'ítl'ish**
go deer pit lamping **hey̓k̲wínayus**
go down **t'íxwi; k̲enp**
go down [about health] **lhúsi**
go down [about swelling] **t'es**
go down [in the water] **míyatsut**
go down on one's knees **txwpelk̲w**
go down rapids **wi7xwí7k̲wm**
go down the wrong pipe **t'kwínus ~ t'kwínas**
go down towards the water **txwkaw**
go downstream **wuk̲w' ~ wúk̲w'i ~ txwwúk̲w'i ~ wúwk̲w'i**
go downwards **txwwí7xwéy**
go dry [e.g., a well] **t'ák̲wel̓**
go easy with (something) **túk̲wut**
go extinct **x̲way ~ x̲wey**
go far out into the sea **shk̲wen̓**
go fast while bouncing **kwemkwemshenám̓**
go for seals **ti7es7ásxw**
go get bread **tiseplín**
go head-first **chey̓k̲w**
go hide [as of a fish or rat, etc.] **tl'uk̲wí7**
go home **t'ukw'; txwt'ukw'**
go how? **nexw7éncha?**
go in the direction of the other side of a body of water **txwtuy**
go inside **uys**
go inside suddenly or unexpectedly **txw7uys**
go into a trance **máyk̲wsmut; ts'elsemáy̓us**
go into an inlet **txwnéwu7ts**
go into inlet **nexwnéwu7ts átl'k̲a7tsem**
go into the background **wáshi7**
go into the bush **shích'i**
go into the bush [about a group] **kwúm̓kwum**
go into the bushes [about a group] **shech'shích'i**
go into the water deliberately **múyuntsut**
go logging **tistsék̲**
go on a prolonged hunting trip [camping in the mountains] **t'elhnáym ~ tl'elhnáym**
go on a raid **snexwílh**
go on a short trip **men k̲á7is**
go on a spiritual quest for power **ts'iyíwen**
go on top of it **txwk̲'ay**
go out [about a fire] **yák̲wi7**
go out for the evening **tk̲ay̓**
go out quietly **sháshen̓tsut**
go out to eat **ilhen̓íwlh**

go outside **txw7ats'k̲;**
txw7utsk̲;
uts'k̲
go outside and sit down **átsk̲am**
go over a hill or mountain [rather than around it] **kwuṁch ~ kwumch**
go over a top or ridge **kwumch ~ kwuṁch**
go pick berries **ilheṅám**
go pit lamping for fish or ducks **yax̲í7u**
go right by **séseẇaẏ ~ séseẇyay**
go right through [e.g., arrow through object, person running in the front and out the back door] **séseẇaẏ ~ séseẇyay**
go short of **tl'emtl'íṁ**
go slowly **st'ek̲ís ~ estek̲ís**
go straight **ték̲w'em**
go straight ahead **ték̲w'em**
go straight towards **ta7k̲sám**
go straight towards (something) **ts'ax̲l̓íṁn**
go through a hole **chelhk̲wéy ~ chelhk̲wí ~ chélhk̲wi**
go through a hole or opening **chélhk̲wi ~ chelhk̲wí ~ chelhk̲wéy**
go through the same (thing) **nelhnílht**
go to **txwnánaṁ;**
txwnaṁ;
nánaṁ
go to another village to look for wife **tl'i7áẇ**
go to get clams **tishéykw**
go to get some money **titála**
go to school **skwul**
go to see [about a group] **ts'áts'alh;**
tsaaẏ
go to shore **p'si7 ~ p'si**
p'es
go to the area below **txw7alhx̲án**
go to the front side **txw7átsus**
go to the space between **txwxwech'shí7**
go to the space in front of something/someone **txw7átsik̲n**
go to waste **k̲elk̲el̓**
go under **hík̲i**
go up **ket ~ kat;**
txwkwum
go up (a hill, moutain) **ch'á7chaṁ**
go up [the coast, the river] **txw7úmich**
go up a little further [stream] **txwiẇ ~ txwhiẇ**
go up a mountain **txwch'a7ch**
go up on the beach **txwkwum**
go up rapids **ch'i7í7k̲wm**
go uphill **txwch'ech'a7úsm;**
ch'ech'e7úsem
go upstream **úmich**
txw7úmich
go upstream [only about salmon] **híẇiṅtsut**
go upward **txwkákat;**
kwum;
txwch'a7ch;
ch'ách'am
go very quietly **tl'ích'itsut**
go well for (someone who has died) **ha7lhnítem**
go where? **chánem?**
txwchánem?
go with someone **hewá7**
go with the current **wuwk̲w'útsut**
go with the wind **pepuk̲áṁ**
go with the wind [while canoeing] **puuk̲áṁ**
go wrong **kw'ikw'áy**
go, finally **naṁnúmut**
goatsbeard [type of plant] **pápu7ten**
God **Chilh Siẏáṁ**
going along, be **nánaṁ**
going backwards, be **k̲'ank̲'áṅatsut**
going by (something/someone), be **k̲wek̲wtk̲áṅ**
going by, be [in space or time] **k̲wek̲wtk̲**
going down, be [in the water] **mémeẏ**
going downstream, be **wúwk̲w'i ~ wúk̲w'i ~ wuk̲w' ~ txwwúk̲w'i**
txwwúwuk̲w'i
going home, be **t'út'ukw'**
going out, be **ú7uts'k̲;**
shráshaṁ
going out, be [about water] **sham**
going right behind, be **k̲'ák̲w'es**
going under, be **híhik̲i**
going up, be [a hill, mountain, etc.] **ch'ech'a7cháṁ**
going up, be [up the shore, from water] **kwúkwuṁ**
going uphill, be **kwúkwuṁ**
going upstream, be **ú7uṁich**
going where, be? **chácha7nem? ~ chá7chanem?**
going, be **nánaṁ**
gold **kwemkwím tála**
gold [money] **kwemkwím**
golden eagle **ch'ésk̲en**
goldeneye duck **shát-shtam**
gone by **k̲wetk̲pli**
gone dry, have **t'ák̲wel̓**
gone for a while, be **estsítsixw**
gone out, have [about tide] **sháshem**
gone short of one's intended spot, have **elháp**
gone, be **txwnánaṁ**
ts'ex̲
good **ha7lh**
good [about a group of people] **hahá7lh ~ há7ha7lh**

good [about berries] halháy̓um̓
good appetite, have a nexws7ilhením
good at doing something, be ta7ánu
good colour, have a halháyus ~ halháy̓us
Good day. [greeting used by person arriving] i chen tl'ik̲
Good day. [said to person arriving] chexw tl'ik̲
good fit, be a really tex̲wlám̓; men i7
good heavens wá7a
good mood, be in a ha7lhánan
good now, be tiha7lhí7
good order, be in hiyú7yem
good sense of smell, have a nexw7í7ik̲s
good time, have a is esxwíxwik̲; ayás
good wishes, have há7lhnew̓as
good worker sxwéxwa7
good, be feeling shésheych'm
good, become helhí7 ~ halhí7
goodbye huy melhálh
Goodbye. chexw huyá7; huy̓ melh halh
good-natured nexw7éy̓wilh
goodness ha7lhánan
good-smelling halháy̓ak̲ap
good-sounding [about drum] helháyak̲in
good-tasting halháy̓ak̲ap
goose tl'ákw'x̲en
gooseberry [wild] t'em̓xw
gooseberry bush, wild t'em̓xwáy̓
gorge hook ík̲'alhtn
got (someone) in a certain condition, have tí7shnexw
got (something) back again, have k̲'ánatsutnexw
got (something) to a certain point, have tí7shnexw
got home finally, have hiy̓am̓númut
got one t'ámnem
grab (someone) by the arm p'i7áx̲aní7n
grab (someone) by the ear p'a7áya7ní7n
grab (someone) by the hair x̲ímin̓
grab (someone) by the hand p'a7áchi7n
grab (someone's) ear p'i7áya7n
grab (someone's) foot or leg p'eshnán̓ ~ p'i7shnán̓
grab (someone's) hand k̲'áp'achi7n
grab (someone's) hand, manage to p'a7áchnexw
grab (someone's) hands ip'áchn
grab (someone's) head p'í7k̲wan̓
grab (someone's) leg or foot p'i7shnán̓ ~ p'eshnán̓
grab (someone's) mouth p'í7tsan
grab (someone's) nose p'i7k̲sán̓ ~ p'ík̲san
grab (something) p'i7t
grab (something/someone) íp'is
grab a handful x̲wúsim̓
grab all one can ch'ich'alíw̓en ~ nch'ích'elíw̓en
grab and hold onto x̲ámi
grab and sling (something) s7elk̲'ét
grab by the handfuls esx̲ix̲p'iy̓ách
grab by the nose p'í7k̲sim̓
grab one's own hair x̲ímin̓sut
grab the hair on (someone's) forehead x̲im̓chúsen
grab up (the swals) kwétxwet
grace laklás
graduate esáp'
grandaunt sí7la ~ si7l
grandchild ímats
grandchild of spouse's siblings or cousins sxw7ímats
grandchildren [sg: ímats] em̓ímats
grandfather páy̓iya
grandparent si7l ~ sí7la
grandparent/aunt/uncle of spouse sxwsi7l
grandparents [sg: si7l ~ si7la] selsí7l
granduncle sí7la ~ si7l
granny kíy̓a; kí7i; tesh; sí7la ~ si7l
grass sáx̲wi7
grass mat used by sxw7úmten as a head cover ts'alút
grass used for basket-making, type of tl'etl'
grasshopper sets'íts'itx̲em
grasslands sex̲wsáx̲wi7
grave smekw'a7ál; stéwak̲in
gravel ts'ex̲t
gravel beach ts'ex̲t
graveyard [see also smekw'a7ál] stéwak̲in
graveyard [see also stéwak̲in] smekw'a7ál
grazed, be just lhekw'
grease [liquid] sx̲wes
greased, be sax̲w ~ saxw; esásxw
greasy x̲wes
great blue heron nsmék̲w'á7 ~ smek̲w'á7
great fighter stamsh
great horned owl chíyetmixw
great talker nexwsníchim
great-grandchild métl'iy̓ek̲w sch'á7mik̲w

great-grandparent of spouse sxwch'á7mik̲w
great-grandparent/aunt/uncle sch'á7mik̲w
great-great-grandchild ts'ép'iy̓ik̲w
great-great-grandparent/aunt/uncle ts'ép'iy̓ik̲w
great-great-grandparent/aunt/uncle of spouse sxwts'ép'iy̓ik̲w
great-great-great-grandchild hékwiy̓ik̲w
great-great-great-grandparent, and all the same generation of relatives, of one's spouse sxwékwiy̓ik̲w
great-great-great-grandparent/aunt/uncle hékwiy̓ik̲w
great-great-great-great-grandchild temíxwiy̓ik̲w
great-great-great-great-grandparent/uncle/aunt temíxwiy̓ik̲w
grebe, horned or eared ts'ít'ax̲w
grebe, red-necked x̲alhnách
greedy, be esk̲énaxw; nch'ích'elíw̓en ~ ch'ich'alíw̓en
green tl'estl'ís; tl'is
green, becoming [about trees] pépa7achxw
green, get tl'ísi7; tl'ísusi7
greet shúyu
greet (someone) kw'enmán
grey xwekw'xwíkw'
grey hair sx̲wúyumk̲w
grey hair, be getting x̲wúx̲wuyumi7
grey hair, get x̲wúyumi7
grey hair, have sx̲wúyum
grey, become xwíkw'i
grey-haired, become x̲wúyumi7
grind (something) chík̲win̓
grind one's teeth setsk̲'etsántsut
grip (something) tl'eyk̲'án
grizzly [term of respect] sí7sintl'
grizzly bear skw'í7achn ~ skw'íy̓echen stl'alhálem
grizzly bear [term used only in syéwen] skw'íy̓echen ~ skw'í7achn
groan íyen̓tsut
ground {full word: tmixw} -np ~ -nup ~ -nep
group (them) together esk̲éxwnew̓ásen
group consisting of parents of surviving spouse and parents of deceased spouse kw'elh wa chet x̲aam
group of fish, be a esk̲ék̲xw
group of three consisting of parent(s) of surviving spouse and parent(s) of deceased spouse kw'enlh wa x̲aam
group of two composed of siblings and/or cousins, be a el̓áshtel
group of younger siblings s7áy̓ak̲w'a
grouped together, be sk̲áxwk̲axw
groups, be in esk̲áxwk̲exw
grouse [blue] múm̓ten
grouse [ruffed] sk̲wets'
grow shéway
grow all over shéshew̓ay
grow into a tree [about bark] new̓áy̓usm
growing in one's throat, have something shewaýálhx̲a
growing up, be shewaýántsut
growing, be shéshew̓ay
growl x̲í7nim
growl [as in stomach] k̲w'ixwántsut
grumble t'éykw'tsut
grumbling, be t'eyt'éykw'
guardian spirit s7éli
guardian spirit and song syéwen
guess (something) t'ámat
guess in slhahál t'am
guess wrong [in slhahál] txwt'am
guessed (someone), have t'ámnexw
guessed wrong in slhahál game, be xwik'
guest exw7úxwumixw
guest, be a stsá7yem
gull k̲w'iyítk̲
gullet x̲wúmlhnalh
gullible nexwsk̲'ek̲'elk̲'ál̓
gums smeytsáns
gun skwel̓ásh ~ s7ekwel̓ásh ~ sekwel̓ásh sekwelásh ~
gunpowder [see also k̲w'alh] ts'úlayus
gunpowder [see also ts'úlayus] k̲w'alh
guns [sg: s7ekwel'ásh ~ skwel'ásh ~ sekwel'ásh] s7ekw'á7kwlash
guts k̲'iyáx̲; s7étswilh
guts {full word: k̲'iyáx̲} -ay̓ak̲in ~ -ay̓

H h

habit of praying all the time, have the **nexwskw'enmáylh**
habit of rushing people, be in the **nexwsts'eyts'áyx̱aylh**
haft **p'a7áṁin ~ np'a7áṁin**
Haida people **Stek'ín**
hail [meterological] **kw'exwús**
hailing (the house), be **nuun**
hair **sḵw'úmaẏ**
hair {full word: **sḵw'úmaẏ**} **-ḵn ~ -ḵin**
hair hat **sḵwíḵwems**
hair hat [used by Cowichan dancers] **ḵwíḵwmes**
hair oil **snésḵen**
hair on **sḵwin-**
hair tied up in the Indian fashion, have [with a single feather] **esch'ḵw'áp**
hairy chest, have a **ḵwíninas**
hairy, become **ḵwíṅi7**
half **-min ~ -miṅ**
half [broken-off], be **est'éḵw'**
half [split off], be **lhseḵ' ~ eséḵ'**
half [split off], be [see also **nt'eḵw'ch**] **eséḵ' ~ lhseḵ'**
half a day, be **seḵ' skwáyel**
half a fathom, measured from breast bone to finger **snew̓ínas**
half dollar **sluḵ'**
half full, be [about bottle] **nt'eḵw'ch**
half moon, be **seḵ' lhḵaych'**
half tide **wex̱nách**
half tide, be **x̱éw̓schem**
half, be **seḵ';** **esésḵ'**
half, be [e.g., a fish, a meal, etc.] **est'éḵw'ch**
half, be [see also **eséḵ' ~ lhseḵ'**] **nt'eḵw'ch**
half-blind, be **esḵwélx̱w**
half-brother **ch'éwilh ~ snch'éwilh**
half-dried salmon **sxwa7ns**
half-full, be **x̱wítl'wilh ~ x̱wítl'ulh**
half-sibling **snch'éwilh**
half-sister **ch'éwilh ~ snch'éwilh**
halfway, be **é7enwilh**
halibut **scha7tx̱**
Halkomeylem language, the [see also **Ḵ'emíṅem**] **Sḵ'emíṅem**
Halkomeylem language, to speak the [see also **Sḵ'emíṅem**] **Ḵ'emíṅem**
halve (something) **lheḵ'cháṅ**
hammer **háma**
hammer with hammer and chisel **ts'éḵe7em**
hand **-chis;** **nax̱ch;** **ch'iyípach ~ sch'iyípach**
hand (something) over **sátaṅ**
hand {full word: **nax̱ch**} **-ach**
hand it down **lixw**
hand it to (someone) **éxwa7t**
hand mirror, small **welh na wa nkw'ekw'chúsem**
hand oneself over **sátaṅtsut**
hand or foot cracking, have **t'ech'**
hand to someone to deliver **échaẏ**
hand up **eslhílhkw'**
handcuffs **s7útsiyiṁ**
handful, be a **esx̱ix̱p'iẏách**
Hand-Gets-Stuck **Ts'iẏuṁách**
handkerchief **sx̱wéḵw'lhnalh ~ sx̱wéḵw'lhnilh**
handle [e.g., for a bucket] **np'a7áṁin ~ p'a7áṁin**
handsome **nach'íṁ**
handsome [about group of men] **nech'nech'íṁ**
hang **séselḵ'em**
hang (someone) **x̱wíḵw'usn**
hang (something) **lhíkw'in lháp'en**
hang (something) up **lhíkw'in**
hang (something) up [e.g., meat] **ḵ'áḵ'tsaṅ**
hang (something) up to dry **lháp'en**
hang broken on a tree [about branch] **kw'ḵach**
hang down **selḵ'm**
hang down [about head] **cheẏḵw**
hang it **lhep'**
hang on to **ḵ'áltxwiyu**
hang on to it **x̱emx̱ámi7**
hang oneself **x̱wíḵw'usm**
hang over **eslhélhp'**
hang up (a net) **hiw̓tsáṅ**
hang up [e.g., hooves on "stick" for protection] **ḵ'í7chintem**
hang up nets **híw̓tsiṁ**
hanging [on], be [about something hanging on

a nail, the wall, etc.] eslhíkw'k̲w
hanging down, be [about small objects, such as icicles, leaves, etc.] wiwipáyk̲snem
hanging face, have a seselk̲'em̓ús
hanging from one's nose, be having something séselk̲'mk̲s
hanging from one's rear end, be having something séselk̲'mk̲
hanging on [with one's hands], be ey̓áy̓ach
hanging up a net, be híw̓tsim̓
hanging up, be k̲'ak̲'ts
hanging, be séselk̲'em
happen scheli̓ls
happen to someone ta7ám
happen upon txwnep
happening to someone, be teta7ám̓
happy tsá7tsaxw; sxwéyxweyk̲
happy about (someone), be tsá7tsaxwni
happy for (someone), be tsá7tsaxwni
happy, be esxwíxwik̲
happy, become xwík̲i7
happy, get tsá7tsaxwi7
hard k̲'axw; tl'ex̲w
hard and stale, get k̲'exwk̲'áxwi7
hard in the cold, get [about grease] x̲álhi7
hard pulling, be [about canoe] k̲ék̲'em
hard to paddle [slow] k̲ék̲'em
hard wood sepíwa
hard, become [about bread or food] k̲'áxwi7
hard, get tl'x̲wi7
harden tl'x̲wi7
hardened k̲'axw
hardened grease x̲wastn
hardhack ú7x̲wk̲sáy̓ ~ ú7x̲k̲sáy̓; k̲álx̲ay̓
harpoon [for hunting seals, sea-lions, porpoises, etc.] shích'us
harpoon line of cedar bark sch'tíshm
harpoon with string miyách
harsh [about wind] sáyam
harvest any salmon ulhx̲t tkwa sts'úk̲wi7
hastiness sts'ayx̲tsutánan
hat yási7k̲w
hat {full word: yási7k̲w} -awek̲w ~ -aw̓ak̲w
hat made of straw tl'tl'áwik̲w
hatchet kw'íkw'k̲wémn
hate (something/someone) k̲eys
hate one another k̲éystway
hats [sg: yási7kw] yesyási7k̲w
haul canoe up the beach xwúkw'wilh
haul of game or fish sk̲w'úynexw
haunted, be getting shelshá7lutem ~ shelshal̓u7éntem
have tsi7
have (someone's) head resting on one's arm metmútk̲ws
have (something) p'í7nexw
have (something) here is
have (something) up high chilhs
have a "heavy," deep voice kwetxwmts
have a bite [as when fishing] ch'em̓tm
have a blunt edge k̲éyutsk̲s ~ k̲éyuts
have a branch hanging off kw'k̲ach
have a bruised back nx̲wuts'ch
have a child esmémen̓
have a cold [about human] tesí7
have a covered head es-hám̓k̲w ~ esám̓k̲w
have a crying child x̲ahámay̓lh
have a disagreement resulting in a quarrel kw'ikw'áynew̓as
have a dry throat ch'eyxwáy̓k̲in ~ ch'eyxwík̲in
have a faded colour pxwáy̓us
have a falling out kw'ikw'áynew̓as
have a feast with extra food ílhenaylh ~ ílhenay̓lh
have a fire burning yíy̓ulh
have a good time iyás
have a hold of (something) p'í7nexw
have a hole through it k̲waa
have a leak s7ay̓áx̲
have a liking for each other tl'í7new̓as
have a look at the content of one's net kw'ékw'chi7n
have a sad face nts'íts'xwus
have been included k̲'áp'nem
have been of assistance to (someone) ch'áwnexw
have broken (something) x̲ép'nexw
have canoe pointing this way mík̲sem
have caught (an animal) in a trap tl'éyk̲'nexw
have caught (something) k̲w'úynexw; p'í7nexw
have cut hair sx̲áx̲elk̲w
have dropped (something) mú7nexw
have escaped k̲wanúmut
have feet on it esúts
have forgotten (something) máynexw

have got (something) **p'í7nexw**
have got (something) back again **k̲'ánatsutnexw**
have hit (someone) **ts'ák̲'nexw**
have hoarse voice [about person] **k̲wéx̲k̲en**
have hold of (someone's) hand **p'a7áchnexw**
have hold of (someone's) leg **p'í7shnexw**
have hole in the bottom of a canoe or pot **k̲waak̲**
have hooked (something) up **lhíkw'nexw**
have hung (something) up **lhíkw'nexw**
have hurt (someone) **má7kwlhnexw ~ mákwlhnexw**
have its dampness removed [about firewood] **suk̲sántem**
have kicked (someone) **tsélk̲w'nexw**
have large openings [e.g., stakes of fence or mesh of net] **yex̲**
have liberated (someone) **tl'íw̓nexw**
have made a hole in (something) **k̲wánexw**
have many limbs [about a tree] **est'ex̲t'x̲áchxw**
have nothing left **ts'el**
have one child **nch'nch'áy̓lh**
have one of (something) **stí7tas**
have one's bottom exposed **xwey̓k̲**
have one's child crying **x̲ahámay̓lh**
have one's child nursing **t'elk̲wímay̓lh**
have one's eyes closed up with pitch **chemx̲áyus**
have one's eyes on it **k̲lumstm**
have one's face covered **xwám̓us ~ xwhám̓us**
have one's feet get frightened **sisilíwsshn**
have one's foot slip **k̲ix̲shnán̓tem**
have one's hair cut off **lhích'elk̲ín**
have one's hair shorn off **lhích'elk̲ín**
have one's head hanging down **chey̓k̲w**
have one's head lowered between shoulders **esk̲wúk̲wus ~ sk̲wúk̲wus**
have one's mouth clamped shut **ch'ém̓ch'em̓ts**
have one's mouth open **t'éx̲t'ex̲ts**
have one's shoes wear out **nts'ex̲shn**
have one's teeth chattering **k̲'epkwtsám̓**
have one's voice be changing [about a young man] **k̲w'ek̲w'ená7m**
have opened (something) **nx̲wíl̓tsnexw ~ x̲wíl̓tsnexw**
have paid for services [e.g., the **sxw7úmten** for a cure] **esk̲'áw**
have passed out from hunger **xwa ~ xwaa**
have power to cure **ay̓nexwének̲**
have saved onself **k̲wanúmut**
have scars on one's face **esk̲'ík̲'itl'us**
have scruples **yáy̓axwm yaxwm**
have scruples about (something) **áyaxws**
have sexual intercourse **hiw̓k̲m**
have smelly insides or intestines [about game] **sum̓ay̓ák̲in**
have something bad happen; to be unfortunate **tl'elekwán**
have something happen to itself **ta7-; tá7a**
have something in one's feces **tl'etl'shí7k̲wstem**
have something on one's breath [e.g., alcohol or food] **ch'emch'emím̓**
have spilled (something) **kw'élhkw'elhnexw**
have spilt (something) **kw'élhnexw**
have spilt (something) accidentally **kw'élhnexw**
have spoiled (something) **k̲elk̲él̓nexw**
have stopped leaking **t'ápi7**
have success [used only in the phrase: **haw kwelh na hiwhiw̓ám**, "they had no success"] **hiwhiw̓ám**
have ten children **ep7úpnay̓lh**
have a gift [e.g. of prophecy] **esch'áwatm**
have the habit of praying all the time **nexwskw'enmáylh**
have the head lowered between shoulders **sk̲wúk̲wus ~ esk̲wúk̲wus**
have the idea **tsut**
have the pointer in **slhahál** guess wrong **xwik'**
have three children **chenchánatay̓lh**
have to run away **txwtl'iw̓**
have to stop **txwtl'íya7**
have trimmed hair **sx̲áx̲elk̲w**
have two children **en̓7án̓usay̓lh**
have two legs together **k̲'éts'shen**
have worn-out shoes **nts'ex̲shn**

hawk nsx̲íp'im
hay sáx̲wi7
hazelnut k̲'p'ax̲w ~ ts'ichn
hazy, be [like fog] p'útl'am
he [absent] kwáwa
he [deceased male] kwétsit
he here ti tíwa
he himself menílh
he there tay̓
he, she, it, they -as, as
he, that [not present] kwétsi
head (one's canoes) for ta7k̲sán̓
head [in borrowings] -k̲in ~ -k̲n
head [of human, animal, fish] sme7ús
head {full word: sme7ús} -k̲w ~ -ek̲w
head cover used by a sxw7úmten hiyík̲w
head covered, get txwhám̓k̲w
head covering x̲wúx̲wel̓k̲w
head down, have sk̲wúk̲wus ~ esk̲wúk̲wus
head down, have ones esk̲wúk̲wus ~ sk̲wúk̲wus
head for ta7k̲sám; ta7k̲s
head hair sk̲w'úmay̓
head of bay slhe7án
head of river s-hiw̓ ~ siw̓
headache, have a aak̲w
head-cover used by sxw7úmten yási7k̲w
head-covering used by sxw7úmten, made from cattail ts'elút
headwaters, be up at hiw̓k̲wts'
heal lhaw̓ének̲; ts'íwam; k̲'eytl'
heal (a wound) [about medicine] k̲'eytl'án̓
heal (someone) lháw̓et ~ lháw̓at
heal over ts'íwam
healed (someone), have lháw̓nexw
healed up, be k̲'eytl'
hear tkwáya7n
hear (a message) íchnexw
hear (someone) tkwayá7nmin
hear finally tkwaya7nnúmut
hear, manage to tkwaya7nnúmut
heard, be sáyi7n ~ sáy̓i7n
hearing stkwáya7n
hearing a song from nature, be sá7say̓em
heart [as seat of affections or spiritual] sk̲wálwen
heart [of body] ts'áli7
heart [used for heart of new dancer] skweníwsem
heartbeat skweníwsem
heartburn, have yelhyulhk̲wáy̓new̓as ~ yulhk̲wáy̓newas
heat (something) in an oven setk̲wán
heat (something) up kw'ásan
heat [intense heat, as from a fire] sp'ach'
heat oneself nék̲wentsut; nek̲wchám̓
heat up p'ách'en̓tsut
heat up ["toast"] fish kw'ásem
heaven chilh temíxw
heavier than x̲emín̓
heavy x̲em
heavy [about a person] x̲émwilh
heavy feet, have [about person walking] kwékwem̓em ~ k̲wék̲wem̓em
heavy paste t'ep
heavy voice, have a [about a person] x̲em̓ts
heavy, be [about cord or yarn] mák̲'amats'
heavy, be getting x̲ex̲amí7
heavy, get x̲emí7
heavy-set, be [about person] kwésem
heel s7áy̓ek̲shen ~ s7áy̓k̲shen
hell [literally, low fire] les yíy̓ulh
hello nuuw
Hello. i chen tl'ik̲
Hello. [said to person arriving] tl'ik̲ chexw
help ch'áwalhen
help (someone) ch'ewch'áwni ch'áwat
help (someone) [out of trouble] ts'íxwen
help (someone) out ts'its'ixwní
help each other ch'áwatway
help one another ch'awch'áw̓stway ch'ewch'áwstway
help one another/each other ch'áw̓new̓as
help oneself ch'awnúmut ch'áwatsut
help oneself come up to the surface shát'antsut
help someone, manage to ch'awnálhen
help with feast tl'i7áw̓
help, just tl'i7áw̓
helped (someone), have ch'áwnexw
helper ch'awtn
helper [usually spiritual] sch'áwatn
helpful ts'íts'ixw; ests'exwts'íxw
helping one another/each other, be ch'ech'awátay̓
hemlock bough k̲wáy̓tsayachxw
hemlock boughs k̲wáy̓tsayachxw
hemlock tree k̲wáy̓tsay

hemmorage k̲wchim̓
hence, be txwnam̓
her -as
her [not present] kwlhawa
her own swa7s
here na
here, be i
i ti ~ i tti
herring slhawt’
herring rake lhét’emten
herring spawn ch’ém̓esh
herring time tem lhawt’
hers swa7s
herself menílh
hesitant, be xwyaxwm ~ yaxwm
hesitate yemyémentsut
yíx̲wem
hidden, be eskwákwi ~ eskwákway̓
hide tl’ípentsut;
kway
hide (something) tl’úk̲wun;
kwáyan;
estl’útl’k̲ws
hide [about a group] kwikwáy
hide from one another kwáy̓kway̓
hide oneself kwáyantsut
hideout ntl’í7tán ~ ntl’i7tn
hiding (something), be eskwákways
hiding, be eskwákwi ~ eskwákway̓
hiding, be in eskwákway̓ ~ eskwákwi
high chilh
high as, be being as esch’ích’m
high fever, have a yáyak̲w’am
high ground chílhihn̓up
high heel shoes chelhchílhshen
high mountain smánit
high seas ney̓ch
high tide, be esk̲wúk̲welayus;
k̲wúlay̓us;
k̲w’ats’
high up, be chílhiw̓ilh;
k̲’ay;
lha7lhch
high, be getting [while drinking] siy̓áy̓us
highbush cranberries kwú7kwuwel̓s
highbush cranberry kwú7kwuwel̓s
highbush cranberry bush kwu7kwuwél̓say̓
highbush cranberry bushes kwu7kwuwél̓say̓
high-class people [sg: sman̓álh] smenman̓álh
high-class person sman̓ánlh
highly honoured person siy̓ám̓
high-pitched voice, have a ek̲wísay̓k̲in
hike up ch’á7cham̓
hill schílhus
hillside sch’e7úsem
him over there [just out of sight] kwiyá
himself menílh
hind leg s7aw̓tk̲
hip [see also sk̲’ák̲’aw̓chk̲, sk̲’aw̓chk̲, smiyíwchk̲] sk̲íx̲wuts’ch
hip [see also sk̲íx̲uts’ch, smiyíwchk̲] sk̲’ák̲’aw̓chk̲ ~ sk̲’aw̓chk̲
hip [see also sk̲íx̲uts’ch, sk̲’ák̲’aw̓chk̲, sk̲’aw̓chk̲] smiyíwchk̲
hip {full word: sk̲’aw̓chk̲, smiyíwchk̲, sk̲’ák̲’aw̓chk̲, sk̲íx̲uts’ch} -chk̲
hippie spák̲’em s7íxwalh
hire (someone) k̲wáyexwn
hire someone k̲wáyexw
his -as;
swa7s
his first wife yew̓án̓
chewáshs
His heart is strong iy̓ím ta sk̲walwens
his own swa7s
his, hers, its -s
hiss ts’úm̓en
hit tsexwn
hit (someone) ts’aan ~ ts’an
hit (someone) accidentally ts’ák̲’nexw;
k̲w’úk̲wnexw
hit (someone) in the belly ts’awílhn
hit (someone) in the pit of the stomach ts’ak̲wáy̓new̓ásn
hit (someone) many times esk̲w’úk̲ws
hit (someone) on the head k̲w’uk̲wk̲wán ~ k̲w’úk̲wi7ek̲wn̓
hit (someone) on the top of the head nk̲w’úk̲wey̓ek̲wán
hit (someone) with a stick k̲w’úk̲wut
hit (someone) with burning cedar wood [was done to troublesome children] peych’án̓
hit (something) ts’ísnexw
nek̲’álhs
hit (something) [especially when one takes two things and bumps them together] ts’ák̲’an
hit (something) accidentally nek̲’álhnexw;
tséxwnexw
hit (something), have tséxwnexw
hit (target) nak̲’álhnexw
hit (them) together k̲w’uk̲wnew̓ásen
hit (two things) together ts’ák̲’new̓asn
hit accidentally, get k̲w’uk̲w
hit and crush (something) ts’ák̲’an
hit by something thrown, get tsexw
hit by sxw7úmten’s curse, be sx̲et’

hit chest so that blood comes shooting out of mouth [a type of syéwen] sk̲éyep ~ sk̲eyp
hit in the face, get tsxwus; ts'ahús
hit in the head, get ts'aak̲w
hit on one's nose, get ts'ak̲s
hit on the back of the head or neck, get ts'ák̲'apsm
hit on the back, get ts'ak̲'ch
hit on the bottom, get nts'ak̲'k̲
hit on the cheek, get ts'ák̲'a7en
hit on the chest, get ts'ák̲'inas
hit on the chin, get ts'ak̲'tsk̲
hit on the ear, get ts'ák̲'ay̓an
hit on the elbow, get ts'ak̲'sáy̓
hit on the eye, get ts'ák̲'ay̓us
hit on the forehead, get ts'ák̲'chus
hit on the hands, get ts'ák̲'ach
hit on the head new̓k̲w
hit on the head, get ts'ak̲'k̲w; nk̲w'úk̲wey̓ek̲w
hit on the hip, get ts'ak̲'chk̲
hit on the knee, get ts'ak̲'ayí7k̲wshen
hit on the leg, get ts'ak̲'shn
hit on the mouth, get ts'ak̲'ts
hit on the nose, get ts'ak̲'k̲s
hit on the shoulder, get ts'ak̲'ayámit
hit on the side, get ts'ák̲'ax̲n
hit on the stomach, get ts'ák̲'iwilh
hit on the tongue, get ts'ák̲'alxwtsalh
hit on the tooth, get ts'ák̲'ans
hit on top of the head, get tséxwiy̓ek̲w
hit one's hand on something hard x̲wúts'ach
hit oneself accidentally k̲w'uk̲wnúmut
hit oneself deliberately k̲w'úk̲wutsut
hit the ground with (something) ch'áxwk̲sen
hit upon txwnep
hit, be nek̲'álh
hit, get ts'a ~ ts'aa; ts'ak̲'
hitch up [horses] mesíwsem
Hit-low [name of a supernatural man who knocks down trees] K̲w'uk̲wchtk̲
hitting (someone), be always k̲w'uk̲w'úk̲ws
hitting (someone), keep kw'ál̓ak̲wust
hives sxwuxwupíws
hoarse from singing, be k̲wéx̲k̲eni7
hoarse, become sákwi7
hoist (something) up txwkats
hold (someone) on one's lap metmúts
hold (someone's) hand ip'áchs
hold (someone's) hand accidentally p'a7áchnexw
hold (something) p'í7nexw
hold (something) between one's teeth ch'émch'ems
hold (something) steady chen̓t
hold (something) tightly ya7n
hold (something/someone) íp'is
hold a baby in one's arms ip'áy̓lh
hold hands p'áchntway
hold it in one's hands ip'i7ím̓ ~ ip'a7ím̓ ~ p'a7ím̓
hold it off with force yetsyúts
hold much; hold a lot nk̲x̲am̓
hold new dancer during first dance kweníws
hold on to a canoe, dragging it along in the water ip'a7úy̓wilh
hold one's arms around (someone's) body k̲'áts'chan̓
hold one's arms around (someone's) head or neck k̲'áts'usen
hold one's arms on the back k̲'ats'íchn ~ nk̲'ats'íchn
hold oneself in check tl'ápatsut
hold onto (something) tightly yá7yas
holding (someone) around the waist, be k̲'ets'k̲'áts'chs
holding on to (something), be íp'ip'is
holding on with one's hands, be n7áy̓ach
hole esk̲wék̲wa7
hole in ear sk̲waháya7n
hole in it, have a [e.g., pail, canoe, ground, clothes] esk̲wék̲wa7
hole in nose sk̲wak̲s
hole in the bottom of a canoe or pot, have a k̲waak̲
hole in the ground est'ét'kw'
hole through it, have a k̲waa
holed, be k̲waak̲
holes in ears [as in pierced ears] sk̲waháya7n
holler k̲'ayt; kwáchem
hollering, be kwekwchám̓
hollow (something) out lhkwám̓en

hollow in rock ip'a7áysus ~ xwp'a7áysus
hollow socket at base of harpoon point or at base of gaffhook head xwíy̓ep
hollow, be x̱wíl̓x̱welmamin
Holy Spirit Súntuspri ~ Súntuspli ~ Sántuspli
Homalco X̱wamálhkwu
home alone, be ay̓txw
home settlement tl'eltl'élnup
home, be ay̓txw
home, be at em̓út
home, go txwt'ukw'
honey [literally, child of the bee] timéń ta sesemáy̓
honk (a horn) ḵ'ewms
honour (someone) wanáxws
honourable pride mets'entín
honoured ones [sg: siy̓ám̓] síiy̓am̓
honoured with donations, be súyum̓entem
hook (something) up lhíkw'in
hooked (something), have lhíkw'nexw
hooked [up], get lhikw'
hooked all over the body, be lhíkw'lhikw'iws
hooked in one's hand, get lhíkw'ach
hooked up, get ḵwuy
hooked, be lhikw' slhílhkw'iws
hoot [about owl] x̱way̓íl
horizontal pole of a loom t'át'alh
horn ts'istn
horned grebe ts'ít'ax̱w
horse steḵíw
horse clam swaam
horseback ride nsḵ'áḵ'i tkwi steḵíw
horses [sg: stekíw] steḵtaḵíw
Horseshoe Bay Ch'ax̱áy̓
horsetail [type of plant] sx̱ém̓x̱em
hospital ḵw'úy̓aw̓txw
hot kw'as; p'ach'; kw'askw'ás; p'áp'ach'
hot, be [about clothes] kw'ásmut
hot, be so that it melts x̱way
hot, become kw'ákw'asi7
hot, get kw'ási7; p'ách'i7
hound [normal word is skwemáy̓] héwan
hour wach
house lam̓
house {full word: lam̓} -txw ~ -aw̓txw
house location lam̓án
houseflies áx̱way̓
housefly áx̱way̓
housefly eggs íx̱wits'
housepost ḵaḵn
houses [sg: lam̓] lemlám̓
hover [about a bird] itl'iyáy
how [something is done] wa lhtim̓á
how are they related? txwnch7ám̓newas?
How are you? chexw wa texwnch7ám̓?
how many animals? kw'íkw'in? ~ kw'íkw'en?
how many canoes? kw'ínaxwilh?
how many people? kw'ínkw'in? ~ kw'ínkw'en?
how many pieces? kw'inmút?
how many times? kw'inálh?
how many years old? kw'ínawanexw?
how many? kw'in?
how much? kw'in? txwnch7am̓? ~ txwncha7ám̓? ~ nch'am̓?
how old? kw'ínawanexw?
how? txwnch7am̓? ~ txwncha7ám̓? ~ nch'am̓?
how? [literally, be doing what?] eschánem?
Howe Sound txwnéwu7ts Schel̓ḵ nexwnéwu7ts átl'ḵa7tsem
howl, a sḵ'ewm
howl, to ḵ'ewm
howl [about the wind] x̱wíx̱wich'am
huckleberry [red] sḵw'eḵwchs
huckleberry plant [red] sḵw'eḵwchsáy̓
hug (someone) ḵ'áts'usen ḵatúseń
hug oneself ḵ'ets'ḵ'áts'-chesténam̓ut
huge thing that could be sasquatch schíchlawem
hum chawn
human being stél̓mexw
human skin kw'el̓áw̓
humble (someone) lésen
humming noise, be a x̱wích'em
humming sound, make a [e.g., of people in another room] núńutam
hummingbird techtechnís
hump one's back ḵwúschem̓
humpback skwúm̓echn
humpback salmon lháwichen
humpback salmon [alternate name for lhaw'ichen] skwúm̓echn
hunchbacked sḵwéḵwem̓ch ~ sḵwu7mchen
hunched back, have a sḵwu7mchen ~ sḵwéḵwem̓ch

hung (something), have lhíkw'nexw
hung in the back-part of the house tax̱ch
hung up, get txwlhép'; lhep'; ḵ'á7a
hunger [see also ahánum] skw'ákw'aỷ
hunger [see also skw'ákw'ay'] ahánum
hungry for (something), get teṁáỷt
hungry, be kw'aỷ
hungry, be painfully ehánum
hungry, be very kw'ákw'aỷ; xweỷús ~ xwiyús
hungry, finally get kw'aỷnúmut
hungry, make (someone) kw'aỷs; kw'áỷnexw
hunt ch'áatl'am
hunt by canoe cháchu7
hunt deer ch'áatl'am
hunt in a canoe péyatulh
hunt mountain goat tl'elhnáyem
hunt small animals pepeỷátulh
hunter nexwspepiỷátulh
hunting dog sk'ínu7
hunting in a canoe, be pepeỷátulh
hunting trip in a canoe, go on a [literally, launch canoe] péyatulh
hunting trip on a canoe, be on a pepeỷátulh
hurry ts'áts'eỷx̱; ts'áyx̱tsut
hurry! ts'áyx̱tsas
hurry, be in a es7á7aẃts
hurt aa
hurt (someone) álheỷni; ha7mákwlhmiṅ
hurt (someone) accidentally má7kwlhnexw ~ mákwlhnexw
hurt (someone) unintentionally, have ha7mákwlhnexw
hurt (something) aas
hurt (something) [e.g., one's hands] álheỷnexw
hurt (something) unintentionally mákwlhnexw ~ má7kwlhnexw
hurt one's face t'éṁus
hurt one's foot t'éṁshen; x̱wuts'shn
hurt one's head t'emḵw ~ t'eṁḵw
hurt, be x̱ep'kw'ántem
hurt, get ts'a ~ ts'aa; má7kwelh; álheỷ
hurt, reason for someone getting ha7mákwlhmiṅ
husband kwtams
husband [term used by wife] kwáwa
husband of aunt sxwman
husband or wife [term of address used by spouse] néwa
husband, have a eskwtáms
husband's or wife's step-parent sxwse7x̱

I i

I -an;
an;
n-;
en-;
k̲en ~ k̲an ~ k̲'en;
chen;
k̲w'en ~ k̲w'an;
ents
I [emphatic] chan
I am doing okay i chen men wa ha7lh
I do chan
I don't know kw'aa
I have arrived. i chen tl'ik̲
I see yeh
I see [said when someone's telling a story] yaa
I still [from chen + xw] chenxw
I think wáyti ~ iw̓áyti
I think so yekw'á7i
I wonder if way
I wonder whether way
ice s7úxwen
ice skates kw'éch'tnshen
ice-skate k̲íx̲shenam̓
icicles wiwipáyk̲sen
idea, have the tsut
identify (someone/something) súxwten
identify oneself náatsut
if u
if I (future) k̲w'en ~ k̲w'an
if I [future tense] k̲w'an ~ k̲w'en
if s/he k̲'es ~ k̲es
if s/he [future tense] k̲w'as
if we [future tense] k̲w'at
if you k̲'axw
if you [future tense] k̲w'axw
if you all [future tense] k̲w'ap
ignoble descent, be of [e.g., sons of skasnekem] eskw'áyiws
ignorant, be sk̲í7k̲el ~ esk̲í7k̲el
ignore (someone) men huys
Ilahu River lyálahu
illegitimate child skásnekem
illegitimate children [sg: skásnekem] skeskásnekem
ill-tempered yem
illuminate (something) taw̓án
I'm sad. aa ensk̲wálwen
I'm sorry. aa ensk̲wálwen
imitate x̲wex̲wá7
imitate (someone) x̲wex̲wá7t
immediate family, be eslhék̲'new̓as
impatient waiting, get nexwwániw̓an
impatient, get k̲'esíws
imperfective wa
implement -tán ~ -tn ~ ten
implement for beating mountain goat wool kw'k̲waystn ~ k̲w'k̲waystn
implements for beating wool [sg: kw'kwaystn ~ kw'kwaystn] kw'ekw'k̲wáystn
important sxwexwkw tl'i7
important, be esxwéxwkw
impossible, be eskw'áy ~ skw'áy ~ kw'ay
impoverished, be estesás
impure footprint, have an eschíchen̓
in na7
in a high fever, be yáyak̲w'am
in a state of extreme starvation, be xwaa ~ xwa
in front of it, be nek̲'álh
in front of, be yew̓ániwilh
in great sorrow or trouble, be tl'elákwan
in labour, be smemn
in love with oneself, be tl'i7sténam̓ut
in order, be esp'áp'iy̓ek̲
in plain sight, be tech ítech
in rut, be [e.g., deer] ts'ep
in shallow water, be sham
in short supply x̲ay
in the bush, be txwshich'
in the daytime eskwáyel
in the direction of something, be txwnánam̓
in the direction of, be ta7k̲s
in the last stage of starvation, be xwa ~ xwaa
in the place of sxw-
in the way, be nek̲'álh
include (someone/something) k̲w'u7t
include (something/someone) accidentally k̲w'ú7nexw
included (something/someone), have k̲w'ú7nexw
included, be k̲w'ú7tsut;
k̲'ep' ~ k̲'ap'
included, have been k̲'áp'nem
increase ch'ixw ~ ch'exw;
k̲ek̲x̲í7
increase (something) híchit;
ch'xwut
increase [about the moon] k̲échk̲ech
increasing, be ch'ech'xw
increasing, be [about the moon] k̲ek̲ch ~ k̲ék̲ech

indeed! [used by listeners to a story] yeh
index finger t'ákw'ustn
Indian stélmexw
Indian (from India) Híntu
Indian consumption plant [seed used in fire to purify air] k̲'éx̲min
Indian currant sp'aats'
Indian dancer wa mílha7
Indian dancer's leggings kwéchak̲ens
Indian doctor sxw7úmten
Indian doctor, become an sxw7úmteni7
Indian doctors [sg: sxw7umten] sxwm̓úmten
Indian hellebore [type of plant] k̲wenálhp
Indian hockey game ch'k̲wéla7
Indian house s7iltxw
Indian paint fungus [a dark brown substance obtained from certain trees, which is boiled and used as a face lotion to prevent sunburn] tsek̲wlh
Indian plum smélhx̲wel
Indian plum bush smelhx̲weláy̓
Indian potato wápatu
Indian proposal, make an tl'a7m
Indian rhubarb yúla7
Indian rice lhásem
Indian tea mák̲wam
Indian winter dance smílha7 mílha7
Indian work Stélmexwulh sts'its'áp'
Indian's Stélmexwulh
indicate t'ákw'us
indicates continuation of action or process wa
indigestion, have ak̲wáy̓new̓as tl'ex̲wtl'ex̲wíw̓ilh
individual xwéch'li
individual specimen -mut
infant sk̲ák̲el
infect (someone) k̲'áp'an
infected with lice, be mechen̓ántem
infected, get k̲'ap' ~ k̲'ep'
infest (something) with housefly eggs, maggots or mites íx̲wits'n
infested with maggots, be ix̲wits'éntm ~ ix̲wits'ántm
inform (someone) hans
inform on (someone) tsúk̲wut
information syétsem
informed about (something), be íchnexw
ingest lhelh-
inhale (something) [as in smoking] sút'un
inhale [when smoking] lhelk̲'ém
initiate (someone) to be a new dancer x̲ewsálkwlhs
injure oneself ahíwsentsut
injured, be ha7mákwlh álhey̓
in-law, any close skw'íwes
in-laws [general term] slhá7elkw'
in-laws of the same generation ch'emásh
inlet txwnéwu7ts
inner cedar bark basket tl'pat
Inner Defence Island Chichm K̲w'émk̲w'em
inner part of thick fir bark [powder-like] ts'i7ch
inner red cedar bark sléwi7 ~ sléway̓
inner, be [in the sense of closer to shore] chichm
inquire tl'ísitsut
insect similar to a maggot [gets into dried salmon after it has been stored] ch'lhá7lew
inshore wind, be tichíchishem
inside {full word: s7étswilh} -iw̓s ~ -iws
inside back of house ets'ánax̲an
inside of it, be áysiw̓ilh
inside out, be turned k̲w'áyek̲'
inside, be ays; esn̓íw̓; áysiw̓ilh
inside, be coming ú7uys
inside, manage to get uysnúmut
inside, the s7étswilh
insides -ay̓ ~ -ay̓ak̲in
insist that (someone) refrain from doing something kw'íyat ~ kw'iyát
instances -alh
instantly sésiw̓yay
instead xwinílh
instruct nexwnew̓éyelh ~ nexwniw̓éyalh
instruct (someone) nexwníw̓it ~ nexwnew̓ít ~ nexwníw̓en
instruct (someone) how to do something úsun̓
instruct a child nexwniw̓éyalh ~ nexwnew̓éyelh
instructions nexwníw̓
instrument -tán ~ -tn ~ ten
instrument for beating inner red cedar bark ts'aháyexwtn
instrument for taking off cedar bark ts'aháyexwtn
insufficient, be esk̲'ék̲'its
insult x̲ex̲ts'éy̓ten
insult (someone) x̲ex̲ch'í7t t'k̲et íx̲iyen
insulted, feel ch'usténamut
intelligent nek̲'ílus

intercede **unálhen**
interested **shishík̲'**
interested in (something), be **tsékwem̓ni**
interested in someone coming, be **ts'áts'alh; tsaay̓**
interfere with (something) **ts'ets'p'át**
interrupt (someone) **ts'áp'an**
interspace, be the **xwech'shí7**
intestinal worm **k̲w'utl'íwen ~ k̲w'etl'íwen**
intestines **k̲'iyáx̲**
into, be **txwnew̓**
introduce oneself **náatsut**
introducing oneself, be **nántsut**
invite (people) **k̲éxwen**
invite (someone) **uut ~ u7t ~ uut**
invite (someone) on a hunting trip **hey̓k̲wt ~ heyk̲wt**
invite (someone) to a feast **uut**
invite to a feast **tl'ashn ~ tl'a7áshn ~ tl'a7áshen**
invite to a potlatch **tl'a7áshn ~ tl'ashn**
invited guest **stl'a7áshen**
involved in, be **ték̲tek̲**
iron **shupálitn**
iron wedge **x̲we7ít**
ironwood tree **k̲álx̲ay̓**
irritable **eswéts'wets' ~ swéts'wets'**
island **skwtsa7ts**
island on the northwest of Gambier Island **Wák̲w'wek̲w'**
it **-as**
it apparently turned out to be **i w̓ach' nilh**
it happened **tá7a**
it is **nilh**
it turned out to be something other than expected **iw̓ánilh**
itch **lhuts' x̲éyts'em**
itching, be **x̲íx̲its'em x̲éx̲eyts'em**
itchy face, have a **x̲éyts'em̓us**
itchy hand, have an **x̲éyts'em̓ach**
itchy head, have an **x̲éyts'emk̲w**
itchy rear end, have an **x̲éyts'emk̲**
itchy throat, have an **x̲eyts'em̓álhx̲a**
itchy, become **lhets'lhúts'; x̲ets'x̲íts'em**
it's **-as**
It's a pity! **áyaxwtas!**
It's getting to be a fine day. **helhí7 skwáyel**
It's going to spoil, too bad! **áyaxwnúmut ek̲'**

J j

jacket on, have a [see kapú] eskapú
jackscrew p'ak̲wtn
jail, be in esx̲wíx̲wk̲w'
jam (something) píts'in
jammed hands, have p'íts'ach
jammed, be p'its'
January mímn̓a lhk̲aych'
Japanese person chépani
jarred, be yach; tiw
jaundice tl'ítl'isi7
jaundiced tl'ítl'isi7
jaw kw'áwaschk̲
jealous nexw7étchus; pisténak̲; spipisténak̲
jealous of (someone), be nexw7étchusni
jealous, always be nexwspipisténak̲
jealous, be ch't'us
jellyfish kwá7kwelh
jerk (something) lhéshen̓
jingle ts'éts'i7n
jingle [e.g., change in pocket] ts'étsem
jingling, be ts'éts'etsem ts'éts'etx̲m
job sts'its'áp'
job, get a ts'its'ap'númut
join (someone) k̲w'u7t
join (sticks) together ts'up'new̓ásen
join (them) k̲'éw̓new̓asn ~ k̲w'ú7new̓asn
join (them) together mesnew̓ásen
join someone in fasting mákw'alhnayem
joint of body sx̲wets'k̲w'
joints of body [sg: sxwets'kw'] sx̲wets'k̲w'íws
joke eskwúy̓ts; kwikwitsám
jolly, be esxwíxwik̲
joyful tsá7tsaxw
juice nekwúy̓ik̲w; sx̲a7mts
July [when the blackberries are ripe] tem k̲w'élemexw
jump xwítim
jump [about fish] s7íxwiwat ~ es7íxwiwat
jump at (someone) xwitimán̓
jump from fright kwtl'étsut
jump over (a body) xwitimíwsn
jump over (something) xwitimchán̓
jump, use a pole to t'ech'k̲ám̓
jumping, be xwíxwitim
June [warm time] tem kw'eskw'ás
junior-line children sesáw̓t
junior-line children or cousins saw̓t
junior-line cousins [sg: saw̓t] sesáw̓t
just mn ~ men; ts'umts'umlhám; ts'umlh
just [recently] men yalh
just a few left, be txwkw'ínkw'in
just a few, be txwkw'in
just did something yalh
just right, be esp'áp'iy̓ek̲
just so much chiyáystexw
just whoever men swátes

K k

keen of scent, be nexw7í7ik̲s
keep (a name) in good repute ns7éyx̲ni
keep (name) in good repute ns7í7x̲ni
keep (someone) awake es7úmsems
keep (someone) company k̲ey̓múts
keep (someone) from going kw'íkw'iyas
keep (something) es-húys tl'alt
keep (something) close by ch'its
keep (something) here is
keep (something) on ets7útsis
keep (something) straightték̲w'ems
keep (them) together for safekeeping k̲ím̓k̲ims
keep after (something) wá7us ~ wé7us
keep away from the fire waw̓sh
keep doing something wé7u
keep it for (someone) sel̓í7shi
keep lifting (something) ch'ich'íin
keep one's head covered esám̓k̲w ~ es-hám̓k̲w
keep someone company xwám̓am
keep spilling (something) kw'élhnexw
keep still ítl'itl'i; ítl'i
keep straight ték̲w'em
keep time táteleltas
keep time with sticks k̲'ewátem
kelp greenling sts'émkwa
kelp leaves [literally, hair of the kelp] sk̲w'úmay̓ tl'a k̲w'um̓
kelp, lots of [sg: kw'um'] k̲w'emk̲w'úm
kept (something) away, have eslí7s
kerchief sx̲wék̲w'lhnilh ~ sx̲wék̲w'lhnalh
key leklí
kick tselk̲w'ím̓
kick (someone) tselk̲w'án
kick (someone) accidentally tsélk̲w'nexw
kick (someone) in the rear tselk̲w'k̲án
kicking (something) repeatedly, be tseltselk̲w'án
kidney x̲im̓x̲im̓náchtn; sx̲í7kwen ~ x̲í7kwen; sx̲ém̓x̲em
kill (game or fish) k̲w'úynexw
kill (someone) kwáyutsmixwn
kill (something) sk̲w'úynexw
kill it k̲w'uynálhen
kill oneself k̲w'uynúmut
kill someone kwáyutsmixw
killer whale yéw̓yews
kind, gentle nexw7éy̓wilh
kind of big hiyí7umesh
kind of red tutkwemkwím
kind of showing off, be sméts'mets'em
kind of sick, be [not sure what the illness is] sk̲w'uy̓úmish
kind to one another, be ts'its'íxwnew̓as
kindling sí7sek̲'
kindness ts'its'ixwánan ha7lhánan
kingfisher ts'chel
kinnikinnick berry tl'íkw'en
kinnikinnick berry plant tl'íkw'enay̓
kiss múkwuts ~ xwmúkwutsim
kiss (someone) múkwutsin mukwtst ~ nexwmúkwutsin
kitchen [see also chishemáyak̲'in] ílhenáw̓txw
kitchen [see also ílhenáw'txw] chishemáyak̲'in
kitten [see push] pushúllh
kittens [sg: pushullh] peshpúshullh
knead (bread) yútl'un
knead (dough) p'eltl'án̓
knead bread yútl'um̓
knee k̲wéni7k̲wshen
knee {full word: k̲wéni7k̲wshen} -ay̓k̲wshen
kneecap k̲p'alstn ~ k̲p'áy̓ek̲wshen ~ k̲p'áy̓ek̲wstn
kneel pelk̲wám; txwpelk̲w
kneel down ts'k̲'álhx̲a
kneeling, be pélpelk̲w
knicked, be just x̲ip'
knife [see also lhách'tn] sk̲'ápitixw ~ sk̲'ápitaxw
knife [see also sk̲'ápitaxw ~ sk̲'ápitixw] lhach'tn
knife used to clean/dress game kw'ich'tn
knitted tight, be tl'éts'em
knives [sg: lhách'tn] lhech'lhách'tn
knock k̲wélhk̲i7n; k̲welhk̲m

knock (something) down
hepét
x̲elk̲'áṅ
knock (something) off
x̲elk̲'áṅ
knock on (something)
kw'elk̲tsáṅ
knock on door kw'elk̲tsíṁ
knock on the door
k̲welhk̲tsíṁ
knocked off, be [about top of something] lhemch'
knocked out, be seṁ;
emtl'áy;
hik̲

knocking repeatedly, be
k̲wék̲welhk̲em
knot nk̲'ísin
knot (something) together
nk̲'ísin
knot [in a tree] st'x̲achxw
knotted, be k̲'is
know (someone/something)
lhk̲'i7s ~ sk̲'i7s ~
eslhk̲'í7s ~ slhk̲'i7s ~
lhsk̲'i7s
know (something)
tá7lnexw ~ téḷnexw

know (something) is around, seem to kw'úlhnexw
know how to do something
scheẇát ~ escheẇát
~ eschecheẇát ~
checheẇát
know one another
lhk̲'í7stway
known, become way
knuckle k̲weṁxw
Kuper Island Pená7lx̲ets'
Kwakiutl people Yík̲wilhtax̲

L l

lace up (a child) in the xwekw'wilhtn x̱weḵw'éwilhn
lace up child in the xwekw'-wilhtn x̱weḵw'éwilh
lacrosse match sk'éxwa7
lacrosse stick k'éxwa7ten
ladder kw'i7tn ~ nekw'í7tn
ladle (something) shát'an; kw'eńáń
ladle [deep serving spoon] kw'enáyachtn
ladle [type of serving spoon] shat'tn
ladle some out kw'eńíḿ
lady ḵ'á7maẏ
lady fern x̱anḵ
laid down, be lixw
laid down, have been [without permission, e.g., as of a marker] txwlixw
lair of black bear laḿ tl'a míx̱alh
lake [pl: xechxáchu7] x̱áchu7
lakes [sg: xáchu7] x̱echx̱áchu7
lame esx̱éwtl'chḵ
lament sx̱amíńtsut
lamp swách'it; heẏḵwíń ~ heẏeḵwíń
lance (boil) kwáshan ~ kwáshat
lance oneself kwáshatsut kwáshańtsut
land ashore p'si ~ p'si7; p'es
land, dirt temíxw syátshen
land [about a canoe] p'ákwaḿ
land [about bird] t'áḵ'aḿ ~ t'áḵ'eḿ
land a canoe tíwash
land ashore ḵwlhi7
land in the dirt txwpen
land in the fire txwyulh
land in the mud txwt'ekw
land into txwneẃ
land on it txwta7
land onto txwna7
land softly tsúpiẏen
landed, be ts'elhp'
landing ashore, be p'ésp'es
landing, be p'ep'sí
landslide s7axw
landward side, be on the chíshemiẃilh
language sníchim
language {full word: sníchim} -ḵn ~ -ḵin
large hiyí
large basket carried on the back ts'ú7mayshn
large butterfly [whose appearance is followed by the run of the kwu7s] sekwí7kwlus ~ s7ekwí7kwlus
large chunk -uẏs
large fishhook kw'uykw
large lizard siẏíx̱ix̱as
large mouth, have a hiyí7ts
large object -uẏs
large pebble mímikw'uẏs
large piece -uẏs
large rock six̱ás ~ syex̱ás
large rocks syex̱éyx̱as ~ syex̱yex̱ás
large rocks [sg: syexás] syex̱yex̱ás ~ syex̱éyx̱as
large shoot [general term] stsa7tsḵaẏíwa
large spark st'í7ḵwem
large swamp blueberry múl̓sem
larger amount, be a esch'xwúẏs
large-sized [about rope, or other thread-like things] hiyámats'
larynx melḵw
last stséẏḵs
last a long time hiń eḵ'
last month of the year tl'aḵt lhḵaych'
last night kwi txwná7nat
last one, be the huy aẃt
last year tpánu; kwi tpánu; tx̱íx̱ta7áwanexw; ḵwetḵ tpanu
last, be aẃt; tseyḵs ~ tseẏḵs
last, be very huy aẃt
late morning, be ḵ'i7t
late, be lhup
lately ts'emts'umlháḿ ~ ts'umts'umlhám
later tex̱w eḵ'
later on, be hiń
laugh x̱aym
laugh at (someone) x̱eyx̱éyt ~ x̱ix̱ít; x̱aymín
laugh hard tl'áx̱wetem
laugh, make (someone) x̱ayms; x̱áymni
laugh, manage to x̱aymnúmut
laughing all the time, be esx̱éẏx̱i
laughing, be x̱éẏx̱eẏem ~ x̱eẏx̱áẏem; esx̱eẏx̱áy; ch'ech'etx̱álhs
launch (canoe or boat) p'ákwań
launch canoe p'ákwilh
laundry smíḵw'ayts'a7m
laxative x̱wíl̓wilhtn
lay (something) down esx̱íts ~ ex̱íts

lazy semúmat;
    úmat;
    esemúmat
lazy, be kw'át'em
lazy, be feeling ú7umat
lazy, be getting semúmati7
lead shat
lead singer in syewen úni7
leaf [of any tree] sch'úlha7
leak ts'ek;
    s7aýáx
leak [about boat or vessel]
    ts'ik
leak [about roof or house]
    taam
leaking canoe s7aýáx
leaking from container in
    large amounts, be
    [about water]
    xwélshem
leaking, be [about boat or
    vessel] ts'íts'ik
leaking, be [about roof or
    house] tetam
lean, thin tetstíts
lean (something) over
    tuýún ~ túyun
lean against (something)
    tiyáyusen
lean against it schécheń
lean against it for support
    chéntsut
lean head through window
    or door [either to look
    inside or outside of the
    house] eschelhkwús
lean over tuýúntsut
    cheyntm
leaning on something, be
    esch'ch'íń
leaning over, be eschéchi7
leaning, be estútuy
    ests'úts'p'
learn (something) ta7lt
learnt (something), have
    tá7lnexw ~ télnexw
leather stsúyaý
leather buckskin stsúyaý
leave t'améy ~ t'amí;
    huyá7

leave (something) alone
    ítl'is
leave (something) inside [of
    a container] esńíws
leave (something) there
    na7s
    men na7s
leave (something/someone)
    tuyn
leave behind for (someone)
    nexwá7s
leave food behind k'í7xem
leave one another
    xwí7stway
leave one's net na7áýin
leave some for a future
    occasion k'í7xem
leave something with
    someone [for safe-
    keeping] kwewí7
leave space k'émasaynup
    nexwíxwelem
leave to (descendants)
    áytxwmíńen
leave, finally get to
    huyá7numut
leaves that have already
    fallen kwiyám
leery, be t'ámatsut;
    t'át'amátsut
left aboard, be men
    iýáýulh
left alone txwnch'nch'u7
left behind [in a canoe race],
    be chíchishkwstm
left behind, be [in a race]
    xwéxwi7
left ear xwkaýáýan
left eye káýus
left foot skáýka ~
    skáýshen
left hand skáýach;
    káýiws
left over in small numbers,
    be [about people]
    txwkw'ínkw'in
left over, be saats
left side skáýiws ~
    skáýiws
left without sticks in slhahál,
    be ts'el

left, be all that is txwuy ~
    txwhuy
left-handed káýiws
leftover [of food] simáń
leftover food saats
leftovers from a feast
    smekw'ú7ts
leg sxeń;
    -shen
leg hair skwínshen
legend sxwexwiýám
legend of how the Squamish
    eulachons appeared
    s7iyíxw
leggings used in dancing
    sxwíkw'iws
legs sxéńxen
legs in front, be with
    nexwyawáńshn
legs in front, have one's
    nexwyawáńshn
lend (something) kwúlhens
lend it to (someone)
    kwúlhens
length from arm to arm out-
    stretched talh
length in a canoe race
    k'iwks
length, be the estéýsh
lengthen (a house)
    útsaxánen
lengthen (something) út'un
lengthwise, be tá7lem
less than semyú7
less, get tsápshen
let (someone) be men huys
let (someone) have his/her
    way áńamit
let (something) down
    tl'ápat
let another go nach's
let go of (something) mu7n
let it be you news
let people mock one
    temslhilháts'-mixwaýlh
let people mock one's name
    temslhilháts'-mixwaýlh
let us do it húýska
let's wí7ski ~ xwí7ski
let's do it wí7ski ~ xwí7ski

level tsewás
level (something) off
tsewásn
level ground tsewásiṅup
lever (something) up
x̱wúts'un
wáts'an
levering (something) up continuously, be
x̱wúx̱wuts'uṅ
liberated (someone), have
tl'íẁnexw
lice méchen
lick (someone) ts'aṁíṅ
lick (someone) in a fight
ḵw'úyut
lick (something) ts'iṁíṅ
lick plate ts'iṁám
licorice root tl'asíp
licorice tea [type of fern found on maple tree]
tl'asíp
lid ḵp'á7elch
lie, to tell a
xwméts'tṅálḵp ~
nexwmets'tṅálḵp ~
lie [sleep] on the floor
esliilxwí7nup
lie dead shá7yu
lie down x̱its;
esx̱íts ~ ex̱íts;
líxwtsut;
cheṅáẁas ~
eschenáẁas
lie facing down ḵép'ḵp'us
lie on a hard object
x̱wets'x̱wúts'
lie on back with knees drawn up
tseḵtsḵáẏeḵwshn
lie on one's back tsḵálachn;
eschenáẁes
lie on something hard
x̱wits'
lie with head towards one
hemíḵw
life s7áynexw;
wa lh7áẏnexw
lift ch'iim;
ch'ahíṁ
lift (something) ch'ich'íin
lift (something) up ch'iin
lift it up for (someone)
ch'íshi
lift oneself up, manage to
ch'iinúmut
lift up one end of (something) ch'iḵsán
lift up one's arm
ch'ahácchi7m
lift up one's arms alternatingly ich'ahácchi7m
lift up one's child to offer for marriage
ch'aháẏlhm
lift up one's head
ch'ahúsem
lift up one's leg ch'ishnáṁ
lift up one's legs alternatingly ích'ishnam
light tutáẁ
light (a pipe) yulhḵsáṅ
light [such as an electrical light] heẏḵwíṅ ~
heẏeḵwíṅ
light eater, be a ch'eẏ
light in the water, be
p'ékwp'ekw
light in weight á7xwa
light of a star eskwúsen
light of a torch esxwách'it
light of the moon
eslhḵáych'
light of the stars [sg: eskwúsen] eskwúkwsen
light, become; become brighter tetaẁí7;
taẁí7
light-coloured hair, have
pépxweyeḵw ~
péxweyeḵw
lighten (a load) xwátaṅ
lighter, or match yulhḵstn
lightning st'x̱áyusem ~
st'x̱áyus;
t'x̱áẏus;
t'x̱áẏusm
like or want stl'i7
like (someone) tl'i7s
like (something) ha7lhs
like each other tl'í7neẁas;
tl'í7stway
like one another
há7lhstway
like, be tiṁá
Lillooet person Stl'áḷmexw
limb [of a tree] st'x̱achxw
limb of tree -achxw
limber met'
limbs close together, have
tl'úts'achxw
limbs far apart, have [about trees or bushes]
yix̱wáchxw
limp, be
ch'áxwch'axwḵsm
limpet lhmáḵ'a;
ts'éḵw'iya
line (them) up in a row
t'íṅiṅ
line connecting the harpoon heads to the pole or connecting gaffhook head to pole lhḵápten
line up canoes t'et'enínwilh
lining for a cradle sílawilh
lip -ts
lisp [literally, have the tongue between the teeth.]
esch'eṁálxwtsalh
listen tkwáya7n;
tkwaya7ní7m
listen to (someone)
tkwáya7nmixws;
tkwáya7nni;
tkwayá7nmin
listen to something or someone, have (someone)
tkwáya7nmixws
listless, be kw'át'em
litter of pups
stl'áx̱wtl'x̱waẏlh
little etsím;
etstsím;
kw'in;
s7etsím
little axe [see ḵw'akwemén ~ ḵw'ḵwémn]
kw'íkw'ḵwémn

little berry of the snake [another term for the black twinberry] sk̲w'ílk̲w'elem tl'a élhk̲aẏ
little bottle [see nexwlámay] xwléẏlim̓ay ~ nexwléẏlim̓ay
little box [see kw'áxwa7] kw'íkw'ixwa7 ~ kw'ákw'xwa7
little bullhead ts'íts'inaẏ
little bullrush sts'íts'ak̲in
little close, be a tutnexwch'ít
little cooking pot [see nk̲wi7stn] nk̲wí7k̲wistn
little crab [see aẏx̲] aẏíx̲elh
little face, have a etsím̓us
little finger -ul̓a
little finger saw̓tk̲wúl̓a ~ saw̓tk̲wúẏach saw̓túl̓a ~ esáw̓tul̓a etsím̓ul̓a
little house lí7lam̓ ~ lílam̓
little houses li7lemlám̓
little lake [see x̲áchu7] ax̲áchu7
little more than the other, be esch'ch'íxw
little nose [see mék̲sen] mí7mek̲sen
little ones etsímxw
little paddle sk̲'ík̲'imel
little shelter k̲'áyx̲ak̲'
little slave [see skw'iyúts] skw'íkw'iyuts
little stone [see smant] smí7mant
little table [see latám] lí7litam ~ lí7latam
little toe sáw̓tk̲wuẏshen
little toy [see sk̲w'shétsut] sk̲w'ík̲w'ishetsut ~ sk̲w'ík̲w'ishétsut
little while k̲á7is ~ k̲a7ís; cha7lh ~ chá7lha
little while ago ts'umts'umlhám; ts'umlh; ts'emts'umlhám̓
Little-Fence [village where Port Mellon is now located] K̲'ík̲'elx̲en
littleneck clam skem̓ts
live with wife's people kw'íkw'ilhiw̓
lively sxwéyxweyk̲
lively, be á7aẏnexw ~ á7aynexw
liver tl'ek̲'tn
living apart, be skwekwá7tl eskwkwá7tel
living somewhere, be em̓út
load s7ip'a7ím̓
load (a gun) nexwnew̓ám̓en
load a gun new̓ámim̓ ~ nexwnew̓ámim̓
load a rifle nexwnew̓ámim̓ ~ new̓ámim̓
loaded, be [about gun] nexwníw̓mamin
located, be tá7a; ta7-
lock (something) yá7tsan̓; kli7tsán ~ lekli7tsán
lock door nexwleklíts
lock one's mouth closed chém̓chem̓ts
lock something leklí
lodging made of cedar bark sukw'amáw̓txw
log stsek̲; k̲wlhaẏ
log around which fire is built, big sx̲étsni7kwup
log cabin t'ak̲'its'áw̓txw
log house st'ák̲'its'áw̓txw
log jam p'íp'a7em
logger stl'exwtl'éxw
logging, go tistsék̲
loincloth lhí7nek̲; tsiyách
lonely k̲w'ámi; séselk̲w
lonely for (someone), be k̲w'ámini
lonely, become séselk̲wi7
lonely, get sélk̲wtsut
lonesome séselk̲w
lonesome for (someone), be séselk̲wni
long [space or time] tl'ak̲t
long back, have a tl'ák̲taẏch
long cedar planks [used for walls or roofing] s7iltxw
long coat tl'ek̲túẏt
long downstream side of house built with its long side perpendicular to river alhx̲ánax̲an
long face, have a nexw7út'us; tl'ák̲tus; út'us
long for (someone) séselk̲wni
long hair, have tl'ák̲taẏch
long landward side of house built with its long sides parallel to the river yekw'áyak̲'in; schíshmax̲an
long legs, have tl'ek̲ttl'ák̲tshn
long shoreward side of house built with its long sides parallel to the river áyalhk̲wáx̲an
long since kwekwín̓ ~ kwukwín̓
long time ago kwekwín̓ ~ kwukwín̓
long time, be a eskwkwín̓ hin̓
long torso, have a tl'ák̲tamats'
long upriver side of house built with its long sides perpendicular to the river yekw'áyak̲'in
long-faced út'us
long-faced, be tl'ák̲tus

long-haired [about an animal] tl’ek̲ttl’ák̲ti7k̲in
longhouse tl’ák̲taw̓txw; tl’ák̲tax̲an
long-legged tl’ek̲ttl’ák̲tshn
long-sided house tl’ák̲tax̲an
look [away from speaker] ta7úsem
look [in the direction of the speaker] hen̓úsm; txwhen̓úsm
look after (someone) nś7éyx̲ni; kw’awchs
look after children íp’alh
look after someone ns7eyx̲
look alike nílhnew̓as
look around txwtim̓úsem; tim̓úsem; itim̓úsem
look around searching nexwyál̓yelx̲ay; nexwyelx̲áy̓
look at kw’ach
look at (something) kw’acht
look at (something) [e.g., a bottle] toward the light x̲aan
look at carefully estx̲wáy̓usem tx̲wáy̓usem
look at oneself kw’akw’chsténam̓ut
look at sideways tl’ích’k̲ay̓usem
look at that! kw’éna
look at the content of one’s net, have a kw’ékw’chi7n
look behind k̲’an̓átsutúsm tim̓úsem
look down on/into the water [for fish to spear] while shading the eyes kík̲p’usem
look down[ward] k̲ep’úsem
look for (a sick person’s lost spirit) k̲’ániwanen
look for (something/someone) yelx̲t
look for a sick person’s spirit [as done by sxw7úmten while performing a cure] k̲’ániwan
look for food yelx̲lhálem tis7ílhen
look for it yelx̲
look for one another yélx̲tway
look for some missing body yelx̲íws
look forward to (something) kw’echkw’echní
look in a certain direction ta7úsem
look in all directions itim̓úsem
look inside kw’achmámin
look over something kw’acháy̓s
look sideways k̲w’úx̲wim̓
look sideways at (something) k̲w’úx̲wun̓
look surprised eschechík̲’
look the other way txwtim̓úsem; tim̓úsem
look up tsek̲wúsem; ta7úsem; ch’in̓áyusem
look upwards tsek̲wúsem
look with surprise k̲wek̲’ ~ kwek̲’ ~ k̲w’ek̲’
look worried esámtm
looking [in the direction of the speaker], be txwhen̓ús ~ txwen̓ús ~ txwnu7s ~ hen̓ús
looking at (someone/something), be kw’akw’cht
looking down, be k̲ép’k̲p’us
looking for (something/someone), be yéyel̓x̲t
looking out, be wáwenti
looking the other way, be txwtéta7us
looking up, be tsek̲tsek̲wús ~ tsék̲tsek̲wus
looking upwards, be tsék̲tsek̲wus ~ tsek̲tsek̲wús
looking, be kw’akw’ch
looks up [about red-faced dancer] k̲w’éx̲wa7k̲s
loom [for weaving blankets] t’át’alh
loom, vertical pole of a tl’ík̲’eni7tn
loon skwákwel ~ swákwel
loose yex̲w
loose skin, have lhelp’úsi7
loose, be esyéy̓x̲w; mék̲wmek̲w; mék̲wem
loose, come mek̲weméy̓
loosen (something) mék̲wen
loot from a raid ts’i7
lose xwim̓; eschel̓áw̓
lose (something) xwí7nexw
lose [the game or the fight] tl’xwétem
lose a tooth tl’íxwans
lose all in a gamble ts’el
lose balance cheyk̲sám
lose one’s footing k̲étx̲em̓shen
lose one’s hair or fur ts’ak̲
lose one’s way [old meaning] meymáy̓ ~ smeymáy̓ ~ smemey̓máy̓
lose power x̲am̓
lose temper ch’ikwm
loser [in a game or fight] estl’éxw ~ stl’exw
loser, be a xwi7
losing, be [as in a race] xwéxwi7
lost, be x̲ex̲í7; xwi7
lots of driftwood k̲welhk̲wlháy̓
lots of money k̲ex̲álh tála
loud s7ey ~ ns7ey

loud person or skull
shaw̓k̲w
loud speaker, be a **ns7eyk̲w**
loud voice, have a **esx̲éts'k̲s**
louse **méchen**
louse egg(s) **x̲est'áń**
lousy, be **mecheńántem**
love (someone) **temstl'í7s**
tl'i7s
love one another **tl'í7new̓as**
tl'í7stway
love one's child **tl'ítl'i7ay̓lh**
love oneself **tl'i7sténam̓ut**
loved uncle or elder
en-sh7eylh
low **ns7alh;**
les
low cedar growth
x̲ex̲epay̓áchxw
low red cedar growth
x̲í7x̲ipáy̓áy ~
x̲éx̲apáy̓ay
low tide, be **sham**
low tide, be [furthest out]
k̲wey
low tide, be [way out]
chishkwts
low, be [about sound]
nsa7álh
low-class person **st'ashem**
lower (something) **tl'ápat**
lower (something) down
lhúsuń
lower (something) **lésen**
lower [as sail in a canoe]
lhúsum̓
lower arm **ch'iyípach ~**
sch'iyípach
lower leg **sch'iyípshen**
lower lip **slests**
lower part **les**
lower side of village or river,
be **elhx̲ániw̓ilh**
lowland **sliIxwí7nup**
lowlands **syátshen**
lucky **i7líwen**
lukewarm, be **sésetk̲wem**
lullaby, to **sx̲i7tsáy̓lh**
lullaby, to sing a **x̲i7tsáy̓lh;**
x̲ey̓tsáy̓lh
lumbago, have
lhek̲'lhék̲w'ilh
lumber **lepláśh**
lumber mill **múla**
Lumberman's Arch
X̲wáy̓x̲way
lump **skwém̓kwemts' ~**
skwúm̓kwum̓ts' ~
kwém̓kwemts';
smekw
lump [on skin, tree, etc.]
esmém̓kw
lump on a tree **smekw**
lump on one's hand, have a
ts'ents'náy̓ach
lumpy **esmém̓kw**
lumpy mouth, have a
esk̲wém̓ts
lumpy, be **esx̲wetx̲wút**
lunch bucket **saw̓ańáy**
lung(s) **sp'él̓xwem;**
tl'ek̲tín
lying aross, be **est'át'ek̲'**
lying down on back, be
schenáwes
lying down on one's back, be
tsek̲tsek̲wús ~
tsék̲tsek̲wus
lying down, be [about
people] **s7a7x̲íts**
lying down, be [about
things] **eslí7lxw**
lying down, be [about a
group] **eschí7ch**
lying on its side, be
esnéńsh
lying with hands raised
behind head
metmútk̲wem
lying, be **eslí7lxw**
lying, be [about a fallen tree]
esyáyk̲'
lynx **útsani**
lyrics **nch'élnech**

M m

mad **sts'its'úys**
mad at oneself, be getting **t'eyt'éykw'**
mad, be **t'át'aya<u>k</u>'**
mad, finally get **t'aya<u>k</u>'númut**
made (someone) pregnant, have **kw'áynexw**
made (something), have **es-húys; tá7nexw**
made a hole in (something), have **<u>k</u>wánexw**
maggot **ápeń**
maggot-infested, get **ápeńántm**
maggots [see also **ápeń**] **í<u>x</u>wits'**
maggots [see also **í<u>x</u>wits'**] **ápeń**
magic power **syeẃíń**
maiden **<u>k</u>'á7maẏ**
maiden daughter **<u>k</u>'á7maẏaẏlh**
maidens **<u>k</u>'ém<u>k</u>'emay**
mainland **yátshen; syátshen**
make **tahíḿ ~ ta7híḿ; ti-**
make (a ditch) **<u>x</u>welúsen**
make (a little ditch) **<u>x</u>wéltem**
make (a lot of smoke) from pipe or cigarette **pkw'et**
make (a small channel) with a stick **<u>x</u>welt**
make (money) **kwíyin**
make (someone) a chief **siẏáḿn**
make (someone) burp **<u>k</u>wach'ts**
make (someone) cry **<u>x</u>aamní**
make (someone) dance **mílha7s**
make (someone) dirty **mátl'en**
make (someone) fat **<u>k</u>w'útsuń**
make (someone) hungry **kw'aẏs; kw'áẏnexw**
make (someone) laugh **n<u>x</u>iya7mán; <u>x</u>áymni**
make (someone) out to be a priest [see **laplít**] **laplít7an**
make (someone) respectable **smeńálhen**
make (someone) rest **payms**
make (someone) sing **lúlums**
make (someone/something) out to be a man **swí7<u>k</u>as**
make (someone's) hands cold **ts'lhúlhachen**
make (something) **húyut; ta7s; cha7t**
make (something) cold **ts'lhúlhen**
make (something) crooked **kw'úts'un**
make (something) easy **li7l<u>k</u>s**
make (something) even **tsewásn**
make (something) heavy **<u>x</u>émen**
make (something) known **teĺmíxws**
make (something) less [heavy] **xwátań**
make (something) narrow **e<u>k</u>wísn**
make (something) one's business **na7s**
make (something) public **wáyat**
make (something) right **esp'áp'eẏe<u>k</u>s**
make (something) smaller or even by chopping **<u>k</u>í<u>x</u>iń**
make (something) smooth **ní<u>k</u>w'emen**
make (something) straight **tá<u>k</u>w'en**
make (something) tame **<u>k</u>w'á<u>k</u>w'iyán**
make (something) thin **ts'eḿiln**
make (something) tight **tl'áts'en**
make (something) watertight with pitch **chem<u>x</u>án**
make (something) wet **<u>k</u>w'éts'en**
make (something) windproof **yá7yamuts**
make (the sign of the cross) **lekwí7n**
make (waves) **yúya7kwms**
make a [verbal] will **titúyntsaḿ**
make a [verbal] will, manage to **titúyntsaḿnumut**
make a basket **k'xwum**
make a big sigh **she<u>k</u>lhálem**
make a big sigh [about a dancer] **she<u>k</u>lhálem**
make a clattering noise **<u>k</u>'et<u>x</u>án**
make a deer call **t'i7n**
make a dent in (something) **petsiẏúsn**
make a difference **nách'ani7m**
make a ditch by itself **<u>x</u>weltsút**
make a face in disgust **<u>x</u>íkw'usem**

make a fast drumbeat [almost a ruffle, with one drumstick] **stl'epx̲w**
make a feigning movement at (someone/something) **x̲i7x̲ís**
make a fifth attempt **tsiyachisálhntsut**
make a fold in (something) **petsiẏúsn**
make a fourth attempt **x̲wutsnálhntsut**
make a gift to (a bereaved woman) **xw7ík̲w'usn**
make a grab [about a group] **hámi7n**
make a hole in (something) **k̲wan ~ k̲waan**
make a hole in (something) accidentally **k̲wánexw**
make a hole in back of (something) **k̲wacháṅ**
make a humming noise **x̲wích'intsut**
make a lot of noise **k̲'áẏem; x̲wech'x̲wích'em; x̲wepk̲wáṅtsut**
make a lot of noise [about crows] **k̲áx̲chewaṅtem; k̲ax̲**
make a mat **timát**
make a nasal twang **nexwnútk̲s**
make a net **x̲wk̲wíchen**
make a noise **líx̲witsut; kwélhk̲i7n**
make a noise [about dry leaves] **wéskw'i7n**
make a noise [about screech owl] **kw'í7xwem**
make a noise from big wind [about house] **k̲ítl'em**
make a noise like a grasshopper **ts'étx̲em**
make a noise while moving in the bushes **shéshewch'm**
make a number of trips [to carry something] down **kéwkew**
make a plaything of it **temsk̲w'shétsut**
make a present of (something) **ixwn**
make a racket **snélhem**
make a raft from (something) **t'álhik̲wan**
make a rattling noise **k̲'etx̲án**
make a roaring noise in a stove [e.g., fire] **kwétxwem**
make a rumbling noise **kwétxwi7n; kwékwetxwm**
make a rustling noise while walking through the bush [about leaves] **shéshewch'm**
make a second attempt **tsaṁáṅtsut**
make a sharp noise **k̲wélhk̲i7n**
make a slow-paced beat **esk̲íyekw**
make a snorting sound **puk̲w'k̲sm**
make a soft plunking sound [e.g., cat jumping from table or distant cannon] **némi7n**
make a speech **nechníchim**
make a splashing noise **x̲wéshem**
make a tenth attempt **upenálhntsut**
make a third attempt **chanáxwntsut**
make a thumping noise **lémxwi7n; k̲welhk̲m**
make a thumping sound **kwémi7n**
make a U-turn [with car] **tiṁák̲sem**
make a U-turn with (a car) **tiṁak̲sáṅ**
make a whispering sound **nesk̲í7n**
make a whistling noise [as of a kettle] **séselts'em**
make an addition at the end of (something) **utsk̲sn**
make an addition on the side of (something) **útsax̲ánen**
make an announcement about (something/someone) **wáyat**
make an appearance **xwiyintsút; xwéyntsut**
make an end of (something) **tseẏk̲sán**
make an even beat on a drum **esk̲ék̲**
make an Indian proposal of marriage **tl'a7m**
make an indistinct hum [about people talking] **núṅutam**
make believe **tsut**
make believe (something) **x̲i7x̲ís**
make bread **p'áyak̲iṁ**
make bullroarer noise from cold weather **x̲wuṅúṅtsut**
make buttons **tik̲'esk̲'isayípstn**
make canoe watertight with pitch **chemx̲éwilh**
make cheaper **miyú7ts**
make chips of wood [for starting fire] **tisé7sk̲'**
make do with (something) **p'ákw'an**
make dust **pékw'entsút**
make expenditures in honour of (something/someone) **súyuṁen**
make faces at (someone) **x̲wex̲wá7usen**
make for (someone) **tá7shi**
make fun of **lhilháts'**
make fun of (someone) **lhilháts'n**
make himself out to be a priest [see **laplít**] **laplítntsut**
make holes in (something) with an awl **shúyuẏn**

make Indian ice cream **x̲wúsum**
make it a gift [the scramle] **wals**
make it for (someone) **húyshi**
make like (someone/something) **tiḿás**
make lunch for (someone) **saẃáńs; sesaẃáńen**
make lunch for oneself **sesaẃańí7m**
make many visits **txwnanch'áẃtxw**
make merry **is iyás**
make money **titála**
make motions with hands to (someone) **nax̲chachmín**
make movements **nékwentsut**
make noise **lepx̲wáńtsut**
make noise like a group of children **ch'eyx̲ántsut**
make noise when eating **x̲ép'kw'em**
make noise with bullroarer [in order to produce rain] **x̲wúńx̲wun**
make one's bed **p'ayak̲á7lhm**
make one's feet move fast **ts'ayx̲shnáḿ**
make one's way through (bushy spot) **p'ék̲en**
make oneself come up to the surface **shát'antsut**
make oneself fat **k̲w'útsuńtsut**
make oneself hard to see **tl'í7tsut**
make oneself hurry **ts'áyx̲tsut**
make oneself out to be a low-class person **st'ashemántsut**
make oneself weak **k̲líměńtsut**
make popping sounds when chewing gum **x̲ép'kw'em**
make predictions **yéẃam**
make present/gifts **cháchshaẏ**
make room **k̲'eḿásaẏnúpem**
make room for (something) **k̲'emásaynúpen**
make someone happy **xwáḿam**
make sounds like a sheep [see **lemetú**] **lemetu7íẏk̲in**
make spread motion in **slhahál** game [pick the two outside] **pik̲w'**
make strokes in canoeing **ísun**
make sure **tetx̲wáya7ní7m ~ tx̲wáya7ní7m**
make sure of (something) **estétx̲ws**
make the fast beat of stick Indian dance or Indian war dance **líx̲witem**
make the sign of the cross **p'tusm**
make toys **tisk̲w'shétsut**
make up one's mind **k̲welk̲wálwen**
make use of (something) **áyaxwat**
make use of (something) almost useless **p'ákw'an**
make war **x̲i7x̲ ~ x̲eyx̲**
make waves [about the bow of a fast moving boat] **puum**
make waves by dragging something in water **péẃem**
make yeast bread **puḿíḿ**
makes a stronger command **ka**
making a lot of thumping noises, be **kwenkwenshenáḿ**
making a noise, be [about a group] **laplepx̲wáńtsut**
making a sharp noise continually, be **k̲wék̲welhk̲em**
making a thumping noise, be **k̲wék̲weḿem ~ kwékweḿem**
making dust or smoke, be **pépkw'am**
making inquiries, be **lhák̲'lhek̲'elelmen**
making lots of noise, be **léplepx̲wem**
making lots of steps, be **teytayak̲shnáḿ**
making noise when eating, be **x̲éx̲ep'kw'em**
making popping sounds when chewing gum, be **x̲éx̲ep'kw'em**
making strokes, be **í7sun**
making sure of the news, be **táx̲wtex̲wayani7m**
Malahat **Málax̲alh**
male [animal] **swéẏweẏk̲a**
male cousins of parents **sísi7**
malicious, be **xwínaẏlh**
mallard duck **ténk̲sen**
mamma **kíẏa; tá7a**
man **swí7k̲a**
man and wife, be **tetélnewas**
man the bow of a boat/canoe **ílhchi**
man the centre of the boat **énwilh**
man the stern of boat **wa7tk̲**
man who has more than one wife **yaseláltxw**
man, become a **swi7k̲a7í7**
manage to escape **tl'íẃnumut**
manage to get full **mek̲'númut**
manage to get it cooked **k̲w'elnálhen**
manage to get there **tsixwnúmut**

manage to kick (someone) tsélk̲w'nexw
manage to move (something) nékwnexw
manage to open (something) nx̲wíl̓tsnexw ~ x̲wíl̓tsnexw
manage to recognize suxwtnálhen
manage to taste t'á7nalhen
manage to walk ímeshnumut
manhood, going into swi7k̲a7án̓tsut
manners nexwníw̓
man's private parts s7átsiy̓ek̲w
man's private parts [literally, body of the man] slálaw̓s ta swí7k̲a
many animals k̲ik̲x̲
many canoes k̲ex̲áxwilh
many of them, be ch'éch'ewtl'em
many people k̲éx̲k̲ex̲
many times k̲ex̲álh
many, be k̲ex̲
many, become k̲x̲i7
many-limbed tree est'ex̲t'x̲áchxw
maple sugar tl'asíp
maple syrup tl'asíp
maple tree k̲'emeláy̓
March tem lhawt'
mark, a t'ánem̓tn
mark (something) tl'ákwan t'ánam̓en
marked, be est'ánem̓
marks on the back, be having nx̲éx̲el̓ch
marmot sk̲wik̲w
married to each other, be tetél̓new̓as
married, be tetelástelwit
married, be [about a man] eschewásh
married, be [about a woman] eskwtáms
married, get [about a woman] txwkwtams
marrow nx̲wesshn nex̲wésshn
marry melyí
marry deceased spouse's sibling or cousin ch'áyay̓m ~ tich'áyay̓m
marry each other p'ínew̓as
marshy terrain ts'ék̲wets' k̲wálhchem
marshy terrain or land ts'k̲walhch
marshy water sk̲w'ax̲
marten [type of animal] x̲wú7k̲in
mask nexw7áy̓amustn; áy̓emustn
mass of driftwood [sg: kwlhay̓] k̲welhk̲wlháy̓
mast nexwyawapáy
master (something) [e.g., a language] tl'xwet
mat mat; slhen̓
match [for camping] pená7k̲
match, have a peptítsut
mat-creaser [implement used in making mats] k̲elhw̓álstn ~ k̲elhew̓álstn
mate, a sk̲'ík̲w'u7
mate, to p'í7tway
mat-making needle for bullrush mat sch'ámts'a7ten
mattress [originally referred to a large cattail mat] slhaw̓ín̓
may, might wáyti ~ iw̓áyti
May [when the salmonberries ripen] tem yetwán
may be occurring right now i
maybe lhkwun; na7lhkwun; iw̓áyti lhkwun; iw̓áyti ~ wáyti; yekw'á7i
McNab Creek Kw'ech'ténem
me n-; -ts
me [used only with -nexw verbs] -msh
meadow spálhx̲en
mean, be sk̲ey̓únek̲
mean to one another, be eslhánch'tway
mean, be slhanch' ~ eslhánch'
measure t'ánamtn; -anm ~ -anam
measure (something) t'ánam̓en
measure something stey̓sh
measurement t'ánem̓tn
meat smeyts
meat-head smeytsk̲w
medicinal plant [general term] k̲'éytl'tanay̓ ~ k̲'eytl'tánay̓
medicine t'uy̓t
medicine to restore appetite [e.g., tl'asíp, the licorice fern root] ilhténten
meet chém̓us ~ nchem̓ús ~ nchém̓us
meet (someone) chém̓usn ~ nchém̓usn nchechem̓úsen
meet [a spirit] nchíshus
meet accidentally k̲w'u7new̓ás ~ k̲'ew̓new̓ás ~ k̲w'ú7new̓as
meet each other chém̓usnew̓as
meeting (someone), be chechem̓úsn
melt yáx̲wi7; ts'u7
melt (something) yáx̲wan̓
melted, be míxwi7
men [sg: swí7ka] siw̓í7k̲a
menstrual pad tsiyách
menstruate [see also x̲7eyulh] x̲íyus
menstruate [see also x̲íyus] x̲7éyulh

messenger schéshen
midday, be nuk̲w
middle child, be the énun̓tach
middle finger s7enwilhk̲wúy̓ach ~ s7enwilhúl̓a
middle, be the énwilh sek̲’
middle-aged person tl’étl’iyi7 stélmexw
middle-aged, be [literally, stop one’s development] tl’étl’iyi7
midnight sek̲’ snat
might lhk̲wun
milt sp’él̓xwem
milt of fish kwíyukw
mind, thoughts, feelings -iwan sk̲wálwen
mine nswa7
minister laplít
mink chechík̲’en
Mink [name only used in legends] K̲ayx̲
mink pelts used by sxw7úmten skwúlsem
minnow skikimelú7; slhímel
mirror kw’échmen; kw’achémen̓; nkw’ekw’chústn; kw’chustn ~ kw’ek̲wchústn nkw’ekw’chústn
mirror, small hand welh na wa nkw’ekw’chúsem
mischievious ak̲áy
misfire k̲’etl’kw
misfortune tl’elakwan̓ánan
miss txwt’át’em; txwt’am; lhílhay
miss (someone) k̲wélulusni séselk̲wni
miss (something) [opposite of hit a shot] k̲esnán̓en
miss a shot nexwt’át’em
miss a shot at something k̲esnán̓
miss someone lhélhenay
miss something hiyáy
missing something, be héchew̓
missing, be estsetsíxw
Mission Indian Reserve #1 Eslha7án̓ ~ Slha7án̓
mite ch’lhá7lew
mites íx̲wits’
mittens ts’k̲wúl̓ech
mix (something) yuult malk̲wt
mix (them) up málk̲wnew̓ásn
mixed together, be málk̲wnew̓as
mixed up, be or confused shíshich ~ shishích’; melmílch’
mixed weather, be yelyélch’
mixed, be malk̲w
moccasin stl’ék̲’shen
moccasins [see also mek̲wú7shtn] stl’ék̲’shen
moccasins [see also stl’ék̲’shen] mek̲wú7shtn
model canoe [see snexwílh] sní7nixwilh
modern haircut [to shoulder-level] slhích’apsm
modern race canoe táywilh ~ tayéwilh
modest person slhálhk̲’an
moisture dripping from trees; dew slhem̓xwmáchxw
molasses meláshis
mole [type of animal] k̲w’elk̲’chís
mom, mum, elder lady tá7a
Monday sk̲wetk̲álhyes
money tála
money bag tála7ay ~ ntala7áy
mongrel skepalú7
monster stl’álk̲em
moon lhk̲aych’
moonlight eslhk̲áych’
mooring line k̲’íswilhtn
moose or elk k̲’iyí7ch
mop si7inúptn
more than, be es-héch
more, be getting k̲x̲i7
morning, be k̲’it
mortuary office of professional mourner x̲améyulh
mosquito k̲wen̓ímach
mosquitoes k̲wen̓ímach
moss mák̲wam
mother chésha7; kíy̓a; tá7a
mother (someone) cheshá7min
Mother Mary Ha7lh Máli
mother to (them) all cheshchésha7ni
mother to many [see chésha7] cheshchésha7
mother to many, be cheshchésha7min
motherly towards (someone), be cheshá7min
mould (something) húyut
mouldy pek̲wpúk̲w
mouldy, be getting melmílkw k̲ek̲ey̓í7
mouldy, get púk̲wi7
moult ék̲wentsut
mound eskwékwep
mount ch’á7cham̓
mount an animal k̲’áyan̓tsut
Mount Currie people Lúx̲wels
Mount Garibaldi Ch’k̲ay ~ Nch’k̲ay̓
mountain smánit
mountain alder tree yásaw̓ay
mountain blueberry úsa7
mountain blueberry bush úsa7ay̓

mountain goat **x̲wex̲wsél̓k̲en ~ x̲wux̲wsél̓k̲en**

mountain goat blanket **swek̲w'elhúyt ~ swék̲w'elh ~ swéwk̲w'elh**

mountain goat wool **p'eskw'úy̓ ~ sp'eskw'úy̓**

mountain pass **sch'ikw**

mountains [sg: **smánit**] **smenmánit**

mourn **téwak̲in ~ tíwik̲en**

mourn for (someone) **x̲amín̓ ~ x̲áamin̓**

mourner [professional] **x̲améyulh**

mourning for (someone), be in **nemán**

mourning, be in **estéwak̲in ~ téwak̲in**

mouse **kw'át'an**

mouth **tsútsin**

mouth {full word: **tsútsin**} **-ts**

mouth closed tightly, have the **ch'ém̓ch'em̓ts**

mouth of a river **éy̓uts ~ s7éy̓uts**

mouth of river **íy̓uts**

mouth of the river **s7éy̓uts ~ éy̓uts**

move **nekwm ~ nékwem̓**

move (someone) up **híw̓k̲an**

move (something) **táyak̲en**

move (something) accidentally **nékwnexw**

move (something) away from the fire or heat **wáshan̓**

move (something) closer **ch'íten**

move (something) from one container to another **kw'én̓nexw**

move (something) from one place to another **sínit ~ sínin**

move (something) over **sínit ~ sínin; t'am̓án**

move (something) over accidentally **sínnexw**

move (something) to less heat **t'íw̓in**

move (something) up higher **kats**

move (something), manage to **nékwnexw**

move [from one house to another] **táyak̲i**

move [residence] all the time **taytáy̓ak̲i**

move ahead **híw̓k̲wam̓**

move along **txwnam̓**

move around **nékwentsut**

move around something **shich'átsut ~ sheych'ántsut**

move away **lhúpuntsut**

move back and forth **i-**

move closer to the edge **k̲w'ítin̓tsut**

move down **lhúsi**

move down to **txwti7**

move forward **txwhiw̓ ~ txwiw̓**

move from one canoe to another **kw'an̓í**

move from one village to another **eslúl̓elh**

move in a perfectly straight course to (something) **ts'ax̲l̓ím̓n**

move in front of something/someone **txw7átsik̲n**

move inland **txwnéwu7ts**

move off [being at a point] **ts'elhp'**

move on **txwiw̓ ~ txwhiw̓**

move one's feet [e.g., to the music] **nínkwk̲wuy̓shnem**

move one's foot [over] **sínshnam**

move one's nose in disgust **x̲ísk̲sem**

move one's residence **nékwentsut**

move one's toes **nínkwk̲wuy̓shnem**

move oneself up **híw̓k̲wk̲antsut**

move onto **txwti7**

move out of a container **txwt'axw**

move over **t'am̓éy ~ t'am̓í; sin; sínitsut**

move perpendicular to a force [current or gravity] **x̲weytsús**

move perpendicular to something **x̲wex̲weytsús**

move slowly [about water] **méchmechem**

move through it **txwchelhk̲w**

move to live at wife's village **kw'ílhiw̓**

move to the back of the room [the space farthest away from the fire] **txwwash**

move to the centre **txw7énwilh**

move to the outdoors **txw7utsk̲**

move to the side of something **txwmiyíw̓ax̲an**

move to the space between **txwxwech'shí7; xwexwch'shí7ntsut**

move to the space under something **txwik̲ ~ txhik̲**

move under something **txwik̲ ~ txhik̲**

move up to **txwti7**

move upstream **txwhiw̓ ~ txwiw̓; txw7úmich**

moved (something) accidentally, have **sínnexw**

movements [to something, e.g., the beats of a song] **snékwen**

movie k̲ék̲ey̓x̲em
moving one's feet, be níńkwemshen
moving, be néńkwem; nánam̓
much, be k̲ex̲
much, become k̲x̲i7
mucus smét'k̲sen
mucus dripping from nose, have xwéxwelshem̓k̲es
mud st'ík̲el; sts'ik̲'
mud, a kind of st'éwak̲w'
muddy st'ek̲t'ík̲l ~ est'ek̲t'ík̲l; tik̲w
muddy [about water] tik̲wáyatk̲wu
muddy [muddier than ts'ík̲'i7] tek̲wtík̲w
muddy, be ts'ík̲'i7
muddy, be [saltwater condition that occurs every April] k̲elem̓í7
muddy, be very t'ekwt'kwí7
muddy, get very t'ekwt'kwí7
muddy, very t'ékwt'ekw
multiple of ten -lhsha7 ~ -alhsha7
multiply k̲ek̲x̲í7
munch (something) x̲íkw'in
murder (someone) kwáyutsmin
murder (someone) [see also kwáyutsmin] kwáyutsmixwn
murder someone kwáyutsmixw
murdered (someone), have skwáyutsmin
murre [type of bird] sx̲ayts'
murrelet [type of bird] piyís
muscle tímin
muscles [of body] t'álaw
mushroom [literally, umbrella of the dead] ts'áy̓tn tl'a stéwak̲in
mushy, become t'ík̲'i
mushy, get soft and ts'ík̲'i
music kwek̲eléylstn
muskrat sk̲'éx̲k̲'ex̲
Musqueam Métskwiyam ~ Xwmétskwiyam
Musqueam people Métskwiyam ~ Xwmétskwiyam
Musqueam Reserve (place name), territory where situated Mám̓li
mussel lháw̓k̲em
must be lhkwun
my en- ~ n-
my [close by: from sa + n] san, sen
my [ta + n] tan
my late father [literally, the late one who I came from] kwa wenlh tinená7t
my late mother kwes wenlh tinená7t
myth, story, legend sx̲wex̲wiy̓ám̓

N n

nail ts'istn
nail (something) ts'ísiṅ
nail up (something) ts'ísiṅ
naked, be lhílheẇits'
name, to naa ~ na7
name, a sna7 ~ sna
name (someone) nan
name of a place in Squamish P'eẇyáṁ
name of a small rock west of Slhxi7lsh, just off the beach S7ents
name of a tribe up north Tíwet
name of mountain near Squamish Nexwyúxwem
named that, be swé7ustem
named, be swé7u
naming, a snahíṁ
Nanaimo Snenáymexw ~ Snanáymexw
Nanaimo people Snanáymexw ~ Snenáymexw
Nanoose Snéwnews
napkin si7áchtn
narrow ek̲wís
narrow face, have a ek̲wísus
narrow nose, have a ek̲wísk̲s
narrow passage schelhk̲wí sch'ikw
narrow-faced ek̲wísus
nation úxwumixw
navel méx̲weya
near ch'it
near side x̲ch'ítax̲an
near side of road or river, be x̲ch'itíwilh
near side of road or river, be on the x̲ch'ít-tsa7
near the wall, be waẇsh
near, get ch'ími7
nearest at opposite side [as across water] ch'ítaẏch ~ x̲ch'ítaẏch
nearest point at opposite side [as across water] x̲ch'ítaẏch ~ ch'ítaẏch
nearly chiyáy ~ chá7i
neck -alhx̲a
neck [front part of] k̲énaxw
neck {full word: sk̲apsm ~ stsk̲apsm ~ stsek̲ápsem} -psem ~ -apsám ~ -apsem
neck pain swáwts'apsem
necklace sx̲wúp'a7en
needle p'ats'tn; ch'áman
needle [weaving] sch'ámts'a7ten
needles ch'áman
neglect to do, just ts'ep'ts'áp'
neigh [about horse] x̲waẏíl
neighbour s7úxwumixw
nephew stáyalh
nephew, niece [when your sibling is deceased] swenimáylh
nervous k̲w'áyk̲w'aẏax̲
nervous, be sisilíws ~ silsilíws ~ sel̇selíws
net -aẏi ~ -aẏin ~ i7aṅ; x̲wek̲wíchen ~ sx̲wek̲wíchen
net float p'ekwtín
net floater line hiẇtstn
net line sinker shátax̲en
net-hanging twine t'ach'apáx̲tn
net-making twine p'áts'iyeṅten
net-marking buoy t'áneṁtn
neutralized, be [about esch'áwatm] x̲ex̲í7
never [only used in certain sentences with "haw" and "txwhaw"] k̲alh ~ k̲'alh
never come to hik̲
never know what kind of weather yelyélch'
never mind (someone) men huys
never parted, be ch'ítneẇas
new x̲aẇs
new Indian dancer's headband [made of cedar bark] k̲itk̲w
new Indian dancer's wool headdress ts'a7á7mus
new Indian dancer's staff [with deerhooves on top] sk̲w'k̲wem
new Indian dancer x̲ewsálkwlh
new Indian dancer's belt sp'eskw'úy nexwyéṁtn
new moon x̲aẇs lhk̲aych'
newborn ts'umlh
newborn baby boy iṁ; wí7k̲a
newborn baby girl íṁshen
newborn seal ts'úp'els
newly arrived ts'emts'umlháṁ ~ ts'umts'umlhám
newly wed, be x̲ex̲eẇís
newlyweds x̲ex̲eẇís
news syétsem
next day, be the kwáyel
next month kwi heṁí lhk̲aych'; kwi x̲aẇs lhk̲aych'; kwi xwey lhk̲aych'; kwi nch'u7 lhk̲aych'
next room, be in nách'aẇtxw

next to someone, be ch'ích'it
next year tpánu; tpánu es ek̲'; kwi nch'u7 syel̓ánem; kwi hem̓í syel̓ánem
nibble (something) ts'ítin̓
nibble at it ts'etkwím̓
nice is
nice person slhálhk̲'an
nice to each other, be ts'its'ixwnítway
nice weather, be es7ay̓ílem
nick (something), just lhemts'án
nickle [literally, half a dime] lhsík̲'mit
nickname niná7min
nickname given to a baby girl because she would become a good berry-picker yek̲s
niece stáyalh
night snat; txwná7nat
night time, be esnát
night, be nat
night, be at esnát
nighthawk p'ik̲w'
nightmare k̲eyk̲eyáy̓ itut
nine ts'es
nine animals ts'íts'es
nine days ts'álhiyas
nine o'clock ts'esk̲
nine people ts'ésts'es
nine strands [of wool, rope, etc.] ts'sámats'
nine times ts'salh
ninety ts'sáw̓ich ~ ts'echalhshá7 ~ ts'alhshá7
ninety [form used when counting money] ts'elhalhshá7
nipped, get x̲ip'
nit x̲est'án̓
nits x̲est'án̓
no haw
no longer be háwk̲i7
no longer be there txwhawk̲ ~ txwawk̲
no longer the case, be txwhaw ~ txwaw
no moon, be estse7át
no more, be txwhaw ~ txwaw
no one hawk̲ swat
no taste, have pelh
no tide, be ítl'i7atk̲wum
no wind, be méchmechem yak̲w'
nocturnal, be esnát
nod one's head ník̲wusm
nodding onion k̲weláwa
noisy, be lél̓epx̲wm
none hawk̲
none of them hawk̲ swat
noon tex̲w skwáyel
noon, be nuk̲w; úyulh ta snék̲wem
Nootsack Xwsa7k̲
Nootsack people Xwsa7k̲
north sútich
north wind sútich
northern lights sexwsáxwi7
Northern-style canoe wít'ex̲
nose mék̲sen
nose {full word: mék̲sen} -k̲s
nose hair sk̲wink̲s
nose ornament nlhink̲stn ~ lhink̲stn
nose, bridge of nshaw̓k̲s
nose-dive [e.g., bird] chey̓k̲wám
no-see-um(s) ch'ech'ús ~ ch'ch'us
nosy shíshik̲
not allow (something) to go to waste áyaxwat
not be haw
not be raining so hard chay̓
not dare nek̲w'úyiwan
not dare to snk̲w'úyiwan
not eat much ch'ey̓
not enough, be esk̲'ék̲'its
not genuine s7á7ik̲
not good at doing something, be esk̲í7k̲el ~ sk̲í7k̲el
not horizontal, be eschéchi7
not know how to do something sk̲í7k̲el ~ esk̲í7k̲el
not leaking anymore, be t'ápi7
not like (something) ch'úsumin̓
not look for fear kw'ewxwayúsem
not moving, be ítl'i
not much room, be skwekwích
not quite reaching around something, be espx̲átm
not quite reaching, be esk̲'tsám̓ ~ sk̲'tsam̓
not raining, be xwech'xwách'
not real [used in sentences with haw and sentences where the outcome is not certain] k̲
not slippery ts'ukw
not willing to discuss a dead person, be múlutsinem
not yet xwew̓áxw ~ xwu7áxw
not yet know how to do something sk̲í7k̲elxw ~ esk̲í7k̲elxw
not yet ripe tewín̓xw
nothing hawk̲ stam
Nothing happened. Hhawk̲ k̲ stam na shán̓as
nothing left, have ts'el
nothing wrong, have esp'áp'iy̓ek̲
November tem ek̲wáyanexw
noviciate ústa
now kw tíwa ts'umlh
nudge (someone) yúts'un
nudge (someone) accidentally yúts'nexw
nudged (someone), have yúts'nexw

nuisance to (someone), be a táx̱wi7min
nuisance, be a sch'íwi7min
numb tl'eptl'áp
tnulh
numb [from sitting in one position] tl'up
numb bum, have a ntl'up
numb feet, have tl'úpshen
number them kw'shim̓
numerous, be ḵeḵx̱í7
nurse kim̓
nurse (a baby) t'elḵwím̓s
t'elḵwán̓
nurse [about a baby] t'elḵwím̓
nurse one's child t'elḵwímay̓lh
nut [general term] ts'ichn ~ ḵ'p'ax̱w

O o

oar **x̲éwtl'iwas; putíw̓as**
oars [sg: **putíw̓as**] **putputíw̓as**
oars used to row a boat **k̲'án̓atsutíwes**
obedient **nexwsk̲'elk̲'al̓**
obey **k̲'al̓; ánulh**
obey (someone) **k̲'ál̓en tim̓ás**
object possessed by someone **swa7**
obstructed, be **esk̲ék̲tl'**
obstruction **-i7k̲w**
occasion of minimal difference between high and low tide **wex̲nách**
ocean **shk̲wen̓**
o'clock **-k̲**
October **tem p'í7tway**
octopus **st'élx̲wets' ~ st'elx̲wts'**
octopus [the more common word is st'elxwts'] **sk̲í7em̓k̲w**
odds and ends **aháw̓amut**
of him/ of that [see **tay̓**] **ttay̓**
of that/of him [see **kwétsi**] **tkwétsi**
of the/of a **tl'a**
of the/of a [see **kwi**] **tkwi**
of this [see **ti**] **tti**
offended, be **estélanumut ~ aalstén̓emut; lhilháy̓l**
offer daughter in marriage **líxway̓lhem ~ lixwáy̓lhem**
offer encouragement **xwám̓am**
offer it **sátim̓**
offer one's condolence to (someone) **kw'enmán**
offer one's finger [to play klexw] **sátk̲wuy̓achí7m**
offshore wind, be an **tinéney̓ch**
offspring [of person] **men̓**
offspring [sg: **men̓**] **mén̓men**
often **k̲ex̲álh; lhik̲'**
oh, yes **yekw'á7i**
oil **sx̲wes**
oil for eating **sts'ím̓**
oil one's hair **nsk̲ínem ~ nesk̲ínem**
oil one's own hair **sáx̲wk̲wam̓**
oil something on the inside **sax̲wmámin**
old [something] **men t'ut**
old canoe **sk̲eyúy̓wilh**
old man **swi7k̲a7áws**
old man's beard [type of lichen] **mimts'**
old mountain goat **sína7kw**
old people [sg: **stl'elmút ~ st'elmut**] **stl'eltl'elmút**
old people [sg: **syú7yuxwa**] **siiyúxwa ~ síiy̓uxwa**
old person **stl'elmú7t ~ st'elmú7t; syú7yuxwa**
old warpy hat [used jokingly] **slép'lep'áw̓ak̲w**
old word for tem cháyilhen **tem kwáx̲nis**
old phrase for **tem p'i7tway tem p'í7tway ta sx̲wí7shen**
old, be [about things] **eskwkwín̓**
old, be very **k̲'e7ílmi7**
old, get **stl'etl'elmú7tentsut k̲'e7ílmi7**
old, getting [about people or things] **syu7yuxwa7í7**
older person **syu7yuxwa7áws**
older sibling **kwúpits**
older siblings **kwepkwúpits**
older step-brother **sxwkwúpits**
oldest child **sintl'**
oldest of **síntl'aywilh**
oldsquaw [type of duck] **a7a7ní7**
on **na7**
on a road grown over from the sides, be **xwáam̓am**
on account of **xwelnílh**
on back with feet put up in the air, be **tsek̲tsek̲shenám̓**
on behalf of **-shi**
on behalf of, for **-chew̓an**
on guard, be [aware] **sisiwiyínek̲**
on it, be **txwta7**
on one's guard, be **t'ámatsut; t'át'am̓átsut**
on something, be **txwhiw̓ ~ txwiw̓**
on the alert, be **t'ámatsut**
on the evening of the day after tomorrow **tx̲íx̲ta txwná7nat**
on the evening of the day before yesterday **kwi tx̲íx̲ta txwná7nat**
on the other side of road or river [see also **x̲etáy̓wilh**] **x̲eta7tsá7**
on this side of the road or river, be **x̲ch'ít-tsa7**

on top of it, be txwk̲'ay
on, be esk̲'ák̲'ey
on, be [a road] nsnen̓p
on, be [about a spot] st'ét'elk̲w ~ est'ét'elk̲w
once nach'áxw
one snch'u7 ~ nch'u7 ~ ch'u7
one (thing) for each, be nch'nch'u7ni
one animal nínch'u7
one another -ay ~ -way
one berry nch'áyum̓
one berry at a time, be en̓ench'áyum̓
one chunk nch'ú7uy̓s
one container [pots, pans, canoes] nách'axwilh
one house nách'aw̓txw
one human nch'nch'u7 ~ ench'ench'ú7 ~ ch'nch'u7
one hundred nách'aw̓ich
one large piece nch'ú7uy̓s
one large rock nch'ú7uy̓s
one left, just txwnch'nch'u7
one o'clock nch'u7k̲
one of (something), have stí7tas
one of a pair s7ínak̲a
one of them men nch'ench'ú7
one person ench'ench'ú7 ~ nch'nch'u7 ~ ch'nch'u7
one piece nch'ú7mut
one roll of 50 blankets nch'áw̓an
one small oblong object nch'u7k̲s
one thousand úpen kwis nách'aw̓ich
one time nach'áxw
one tree nch'íwa
one unit, be nch'ú7mut
one who was given in marriage s7émilh
one who works in place of someone else sxwsts'its'áp'
one whole [large] piece shiy̓úkw'uy̓s
one whole [small] piece shiy̓úkw'ayum̓
one whole rock shiy̓úkw'uy̓s smant
one, be at nch'ú7mut
one, the ína ta ína
One-Legged Monster Nínch'u7shen
one's breath slhákw'em
one's business swa7 sk̲wálwen
one-year-old shoots stsa7tsk̲ay̓íwa
onion [wild] sx̲wíl̓nach
only mn ~ men; huy; men huy
only three people left txwchenchánat
onto, be txwti7
ooze out yít'em; t'íts'em
opaque kwalh
opaque, become kwálhi7
open (a box) nex̲wíl̓tsen̓ ~ nex̲wil̓tsán̓
open (something) x̲wíl̓tsnexw ~ nx̲wíl̓tsnexw x̲wil̓tsán̓ ~ nx̲wil̓tsn ~ nx̲wil̓tsán̓ ~ x̲wil̓tsn
open (something), manage to x̲wíl̓tsnexw ~ nx̲wíl̓tsnexw x̲wíl̓nexw
open (them) up x̲welx̲wíl̓tsan̓
open a door x̲wíl̓tsim̓
open area estétey̓
open eyes, have x̲wil̓tsáyus
open for (someone) nex̲wíl̓shi
open it nx̲wil̓ts ~ x̲wil̓ts
open mouth, be with an t'éx̲t'ex̲ts
open mouth, have an [about animals] wiw̓k̲'tsám̓
open one's eyes t'x̲áy̓usm; x̲wí7ltsayusem; t'x̲áy̓usmnumut
open one's eyes really big xwacháyusem
open one's mouth t'ex̲tsám̓
open one's mouth wide wík̲'tsem̓
open oneself up welhchántsut
open space in woods t'échu
open up welhchántsut
open wide, be [e.g., a flower] wiw̓lhch
open, be x̲wil̓ts ~ nx̲wil̓ts
opened (something), have nx̲wíl̓tsnexw ~ x̲wíl̓tsnexw
opened, be [about a box] x̲wíx̲wel̓ts
opened, be [about a door, window, etc.] nex̲wíx̲wel̓ts
opening -ts
opening (something), be x̲wíx̲wil̓tsan̓
opening and closing mouth, be [about fish] wách'wach'tsam̓
operate on (someone) kw'ích'in
opinion sk̲wálwen
opinion, be of the tsut
oppose (someone) k̲'ítl'usen
opposite, be turned k̲w'ák̲w'iy̓ek̲'
or iy ~ i ~ ey; eyk̲
orange úlanch
Orange honeysuckle kítu7 tl'a stéwak̲in
orca yéw̓yews
order (an object) yay̓lh
order (someone) tsun
order (someone) out wálhk̲'an

Oregon grape bush **séliy̓ay̓**
originate from **tiná7**
originating from, be [with reference to the locality where one's ancestors were created] **sx̱í7x̱a7us**
ornament **stíy̓iws ~ stíyiyews**
orphan **wánim**
osprey **ts'íxwts'ixw**
other hand **s7ín̓ach**
other head **s7ínaḵwa**
other side **inayíwilh ~ ináy̓wilh; ílheḵa**
other side [of a body of water] **ílheḵa7min**
other side of river **ínaḵskwu**
other side of something **íniw̓ilh**
other side of the fire **x̱eta7áyikwup**
other side, be on the **ílheḵa**
other side, the **ta ína**
other, the **ína**
other's, the **snách'ulh**
otter **sḵ'aatl'**
our **-chet**
ours **s7ulh**
out in deep water, be **ni7ch**
out of [a container], get **t'exwt'áxwi7**
out of a container, be **txwt'axw**
out of breath, be **sheḵlhálem**
out of control because of rage, be **t'á7x̱wetem**
out of order, be **eskw'áy ~ skw'áy ~ kw'ay**
out of order, be [i.e., not work] **skw'eykw'áyach**
out of reach, be **lhup esḵ'tsám̓ach**
out of shape, be **láp'entsut**
out of sight, be/get **t'an̓íw̓**
out of the rain, get **t'ápḵam**
out of the way, be **lhukw**
out when it starts raining, be **lhemxwnítem**
out, be [about a light or a fire] **yaḵw**
out, be going **ú7uts'ḵ**
outdoors **atsḵ**
outdoors, be **txw7utsḵ**
Outer Defence Island **Níni7ch Ḵw'émḵw'em**
outer red cedar bark **súkw'em**
outer river **x̱chaw̓ch**
outer, be [in the sense of "farther offshore"] **níni7ch**
outguessed, be **t'ámnem**
outside [of an object] **slha7lhch**
outside the perimeter [see also **atsḵ**] **átsḵiw̓ilh**
outside, be [see also **átsḵiw̓ilh**] **atsḵ**
outside measurement, be **átsḵiw̓ilh**
outside of the outside, be on the **átsḵiw̓ilh**
outside, be **atsḵ; nexw7áts'ḵ; uts'ḵ**
oval-leafed blueberry **xwíxwikw'**
oval-leafed blueberry bush **xwíxwikw'ay̓**
over the side, be **nexwchílhiwilh**
over/above, be **chílhiw̓ilh**
over/done/completed, be **sheḵ**
over, be [about a storm] **yiyíl̓em**
overanxious, be **ts'eyts'áyx̱tsut**
overcoat **tl'eḵtúy̓t**
overcook (something) **ts'xwan**
overdo it **nemnáam; x̱étsx̱etsetsut**
overdo something **tl'xwétem**
overeat **tismeḵ'méḵ'm; meḵ'étsut**
overeaten, have **esḵénaxw**
overflow **kw'lhay̓ch; p'ip'íy̓em**
overflowing, be **ḵwíḵwitem**
overpowered, be **tl'xwétem**
over-smoked fish [from too much heat, causing the skin to separate from the flesh, so that the oil goes rancid] **ḵw'elús**
own the same thing [about two people] **en̓án̓usmin̓**
owner **temswá7**
oyster **tl'éx̱wtl'éx̱w**

P p

Pacific dogwood tree lháw̓k̲amay̓
Pacific tomcod [also called whitefish] k̲wíniyatsen
pacify (someone's) child hay̓án̓
pack (something) on one's back chemá7n
pack (them) close together lhelwá7stays; tl'úts'un̓
pack (things) together k̲emsán
pack a child on one's back chem̓chem̓áylh
pack one's belongings k̲emsántsut
pack them tightly together tl'ets'wíyen
pack things on one's back chem̓á7
packed lunch saw̓án
packed tight, be tl'ets'
packed together, be k̲ems
packstrap chém̓etn
pad (something) tsúpen
paddle, to ísun
paddle, a sk̲'émel; x̲éwtl'iwas
paddle (someone/something) ísunt
paddle [little] [see sk̲'émel] sk̲'ík̲'imel
paddle for (someone) í7sunk̲an
paddle quietly sux̲wsux̲wmíw̓as
paddle rapidly tsíx̲iw̓as
paddle slowly uyumíw̓as
paddling, be í7sun
padlock má7k̲wel
paid for services rendered, be esk̲'áw
paid, be esk̲'áw; k̲'áwalhen
paid, finally get k̲'awnúmut
paid, get k̲'aw; k̲'awnálhen
pain in the leg, have a ashn
painfully hungry, be ehánum
pains in body s7ahíws
paint yetl'k̲'ím̓
paint (someone) with red paint temlhán
paint (someone's) face tsit
paint (something) x̲el̓t yetl'k̲'án̓
paint (something), manage to yétl'k̲'nexw
paint [any colour yétl'k̲'ten
paint [see also yétl'k̲'ten] syetl'k̲'
paint one's body temlhíwsem
paint one's face temlhúsem
paint one's face black p'ích'tusem
paint one's hair témlhk̲wám̓
paint one's own face yetl'k̲w'úsntsut; yetl'k̲w'úsm
paint oneself tsítsut
paintbrush welh wa yetl'k̲'ím̓
painted, be esyéy̓etl'k̲'; yetl'k̲'ám
pair consisting of brother and sister, be a el̓áshtel
pair of brothers or sisters, be ek̲w'í7tel
Pakistani person híntu
pale spexw
pale [colour of grass] tl'estl'ís
pale face, have a p'ek̲w'ús
pale, be getting pepxwí7
pale, become tl'is7ántsut
pale, get tl'ísi7; tl'pi7
pale, get/become pxwi7
pallial muscle of clam chém̓etn
palm of hand np'ahách; nexw7átsach
pant tsántem
pants síwayk̲
paper pípa
paper money [bills] pípa tála
parallel, be tá7lem
paralyzed arm, have a x̲wáyach
paralyzed leg, have a x̲wayshn
paralyzed, be k̲w'uy; x̲wey ~ x̲way
paralyzed, be [throughout whole body] x̲wáyiws
paranoid, be nexwstek̲tk̲ának̲
parent chi7cht; elhtách
parent- or child-in-law se7x̲
parent-in-law after death of spouse; child-in-law after death of child slhik̲wáylh
parent or sibling of parent chi7cht
parent, become a elhtáchntsut
parents elhtách
parents of child-in-law [sg: skw'íwes] skw'ikw'íwes
part, be est'ánem̓
parted from one another, be shíimnew̓as
parted, be shiim
partial measure [less than a cup] nx̲wítl'ulh
partner nk̲w'ú7nexw sk̲w'u7 ~ sk̲'ew̓ ~ esk̲'éw̓ ~ esk̲w'ú7

partner in a canoe nḵw'ú7wilh
partners kw'elhtl'í7neẁás
party tl'a7áshen ~ tl'ashn ~ tl'a7áshn
party house tl'ashnáẁtxw
pass (something) sátań
pass alongside xweḵwḵántway
pass by ḵ'eḵ'tús; ḵwetḵ
pass by (something) ḵwetḵán
pass each other head on xwáyḵwusentway
pass head on xwáyḵwusentway
pass in front of it ḵ'eḵ'tús
pass out máyḵwsmut; ts'elsemáy̓us
pass out (food) at a potlatch lixwiḵán
pass over a flat surface seyḵ'ḵs
pass over a mountain ridge seyḵ'áy̓ch
pass over a ridge seseyḵ'áy̓ch
pass over top of something, just esḵ'áy
pass over water seyḵ'ḵs
pass right out seḿ
pass through a hole hither or this way mi chelhḵwi
pass through a hole or opening chelhḵw
pass through opening chelhḵwéy ~ chelhḵwí ~ chélhḵwi
passed out from hunger, have xwaa ~ xwa
passing away, be hahávḵ
passing by (something/someone), be ḵweḵwtḵáń
passing by, be ḵweḵwtḵ
passing something over, be sásatiḿ
past ḵwetḵpli
pat (something) tátsań
patch (something) up t'émuy̓n; t'émuy̓en
patch of wood without underbrush skwéxwnach
patch up t'émuy̓íḿ
patch up all the time t'emt'emuyíḿ
patella lhmáḵ'a
path shewálh
pattern for making clothes t'anemnách
paw for food [about animal] tsu7p
pawn (something) x̱áts'ayan
pay ḵ'aw
pay (someone) ḵ'áwat néẁnacht
pay (someone) for a cure ḵ'áwat
pay attention to (someone) nexwníẁeni; síshulhni7en; sheshúlhni
pay attention to (someone's) instruction nexwníẁen
payment sḵ'aw
peace, be at ha7lhánan ayás
peace, be at [i.e., not at war] a7áyas
peaceful atmosphere ha7lhánan
peaking out, be [about the sun] xwéyusem
pebbles smí7mant
peck lhékwem
peck (someone's) eye out lhekwáyusen
peck at (something) lhékwen
pee one's pants ḵw'ets'mámiḿ
peek tl'ich'ayúsm
peeking, be wáwenti
peel (fruit or vegetable) ts'úyuń
peel (something) [e.g., bark] tsúyun
peel (thin bark) lhúḵw'un
peel off a layer from (something) [especially thick bark] kwu7n
peeled off, be [as heavy bark of tree] lhuḵw'
peep tl'ích'ḵay̓usem
peer tl'ích'ḵay̓usem
peg (a canoe) nuḵw'tsḵwú7n
penance snemá
penance, do ḵ'áwalhen
pencil x̱el̓tn
penis shel̓
penpoint gunnel s7achcháwam ~ ns7achcháwam
people -aylh ~ -ay̓lh ~ -íyalh
people [sg: stélmexw] steltélmexw
people {full word: stélmexw} -mesh
people of times to come kwi aẁt stelmexw
people of White Swan River Xwlesh
perceive (something) by touch tsásań
perch [pile or striped] swacháy̓
perforate (someone's) nose ḵwáḵsán
perforate (something) ḵwan ~ ḵwaan
perforate (something) accidentally ḵwánexw
perforated (something), have ḵwánexw
perforated, be ḵwaa
perforation in nose, have a esḵwéḵwa7ḵs ~ esneḵwéḵwa7ḵs ~ sḵwéḵweḵs
perform (something) with all one's might tímit
perform a bear dance mix̱alhálkwlh

perform a burning yúlhim̓
perform a cure lhaw̓ének̲
perform a dance characterized by the shaking of the head k̲w'éx̲wa7k̲s
perform a dance characterized by the use of a rattle sk̲éyep ~ sk̲eyp
perform a deer dance sx̲wi7shenálkwlh
perform a spirit quest k̲'áníwan
perform a spirit quest for (a sick person's lost spirit) k̲'áníwanen
perform a type of dance [during which one cuts oneself, drawing blood] x̲ánx̲anítm
perish x̲way ~ x̲wey
permament encampment lam̓án
person -íyalh ~ -aylh ~ -ay̓lh; stélmexw
person [only used in the Catechism] pix̲súun
person from India, Pakistan, etc. Híntu
person of high class [also used to address a woman, as a counterpart to siy̓ám̓] sman̓ánlh
person who drinks a lot of water k̲wuch's
person who has been cursed by sxw7umten sk̲'ewk̲'áw
person who is always absent-minded nexwsmemey̓máy̓
person who is always forgetting nexwsmey̓máy̓
person who is always getting lost nexwsmey̓máy̓
person with magic power kwtsi7ts
persons steltélmexw
pet skw'íkw'iyuts
pet (something) tátsan̓
petticoat slil̓sáy̓ek̲s
phone call, make a new̓tsám̓
photographer x̲el̓uséyalh
pick (berries) k̲éxwen
pick (berries) individually [e.g., salmonberries, raspberries] lhémen
pick (blueberries or huckleberries with leaves) tl'éxwen
pick (someone) up nám̓en
pick (something) in handfuls [for berries, such as huckleberries] lhemch'án
pick berries for (someone) [berries which are picked individually, such as salmonberries] lhémshi
pick berries in handfuls [e.g., huckleberries] lhemch'ím̓
pick berries individually lhemím̓
pick berries, go ilhen̓ám
pick it up mékw'em
pick on (someone) [about a group] k̲ex̲mín̓tem
pick one's teeth shishew̓ánsem
picked (berries) in handfuls, have [e.g., huckleberries] lhémch'nexw
picked berries esyék̲
picked clean, be [about berries] lhilhemáyum̓
picked, be already [about berries] esyák̲
picking things up, be mémkw'em
piece -min̓ ~ -min -mut
pieces of bone sháw̓min
pierce (someone's) ear k̲waháya7ni7n
pierce (someone's) nose k̲wák̲sán
pierce (something) k̲wan ~ k̲waan
pierce (something) with a stick, or sharp object ch'út'a7n
pierced ears, have esk̲wek̲weháya7n
pierced nose, have a esk̲wék̲wa7k̲s ~ esnek̲wék̲wa7k̲s ~ sk̲wék̲wek̲s
pierced with sharp object, get ch'út'a
pierced, be esk̲wék̲wa7
piercer tl'échptn
pig kweshú
pigeon [wild] nsex̲á7x̲em ~ sex̲á7x̲em
piggyback chem̓á7
piggyback each other chemá7ntway
pigmy owl sxwaxw
pile (something) up k̲'aynew̓ásen
pile (things) up lhánew̓ásen
pile upon (one another) tsek̲w'new̓ásen
pileated woodpecker témlhepsem
pilot bread lépeskwi7
pimply, be lhém̓lhem̓ts'
pin sáyips
pin feather kw'íkw'lets'
pinch (someone) ch'iyíkw'in ts'iyíkw'in
pinch (something) tl'eyk̲'án
pink tut-kwemkwím
pink salmon lháwichen
pinned down, be tek̲
pins and needles in one's arm, have xwakw'iyáx̲a7n
pins and needles in one's legs or feet, have xwákw'ishn
pinto abalone s7áay̓u
pipe [for smoking] nts'k̲wu7tstn ~ ts'k̲wu7tstn ~ snts'k̲wu7tstn
piss pot x̲wáy̓ten ~ x̲wa7ítn

pit st'kw'iṁ
pit [hole dug in the ground] est'ét'kw'
pit lamp for deer [on land] heẏk̲wínayus
pit lamp for fish or ducks yax̲í7u
pitch chemx̲
pitch (someone's) eyes chemx̲áyusan
pitch (something) chemx̲án
pitiful tesás
pitiful [about person] ests'exwts'íxw
pitiful looking nts'íts'xwus
pitiful person, be a sort of seláwa7
pitiful, be ts'its'ixwnúṁut; seláwa7
pity ts'its'ixwánan
pity (someone) ts'íxwen aỉs
pity on (someone), have ts'its'ixwní
pity, be a áyaxwnúmut
place lhna7; wa lhna7s
place [near to where one is] lh7i
place above chíshem
place below someone áyalhk̲wmiṅ
place hands behind neck esk̲'ets'íchen
place hands on hip ip'a7ámats'em
place in the Squamish Valley Sátiẏilh
place of division sx̲wets'k̲w'
place of origin wa lhtiná7; tl'eltl'élnup
place on (something) [as a blanket over a mat] lhashán
place on Bowen Island Xwlíỉx̲wem
place on the Squamish River where a number of canoes were changed into stone by the Xaaẏs K̲'ák̲'apnach
place to keep clothes nexwneẃíwstn
place where water runs over anything [falls, rapids, stones in mountain stream, etc.] skw'lháẏak̲alh
plain view, be in estetích
plainfin midshipman [type of fish] sx̲wíẃach
Plains-style Indians lhek'éta
plan k̲welk̲wálwen
plant spéṅem
plant that relieves muscle soreness pá7pawtn
plant things péṅem
plate lhx̲áẏtstn
platter [white] lhx̲áẏtstn
play k̲w'shétsut; heẃélem; k̲w'ík̲w'ishétsut
play a game k̲w'shétsut
play cards lakáltem
play catch tsexwshítway
play cat's cradle x̲eẃélch
play hide and seek kwáẏkwaẏ
play 'hit the bones' game mítl'ela
play lacrosse [modern] k'éxwa7
play pulling "lazy stick" contest lhesh
play 'pulling fingers' game klexw
play slhahál k'ák'eltx̲
play string game [e.g., cat's cradle] heẃélch
play the shuttlecock and battledore game ekwiyí
play tug-of-war [using a stick] lhesh
play with (something/someone) k̲w'shet
play with toy canoe p'íp'ikwilh ~ p'áp'akwilh
plead ts'ewás
plead with someone to give yík̲'itsut
plead, be ts'ets'xwítsut
pleat (something) [as in a dress] k̲w'úp'un
plenty, be k̲ex̲
pliable met'
pluck (something) kw'étsen
pluck feathers kw'ekw'tsáyus ~ kw'ikw'tsáyus
plug (something) in tl'úk̲w'un
plug tobacco esch'éch'ich' sp'útl'am
ply (rope) together útsk̲san
pocket x̲wek̲w7áy ~ nex̲wék̲wal ~ nexwlek̲we7áy
pocket knife heỉkw
pockmarked face, have a lhéṁlheṁts'us
pockmarked face, with lhéṁlheṁts'us
pock-marked, be lhéṁlheṁts'
point, to t'akw'usíṁ; t'ákw'us
point, a -k̲s
point (them) both ways [spreading both thumb and index-finger in slhahál] p'ik̲w's
point (them) down [in slhahál] txwmik̲'s
point at (something) t'ákw'usen
Point Atkinson [in West Vancouver] Sk̲'íẃitsut
point canoe in this direction mík̲sem
Point Grey Élk̲sn
Point Hood, Gambier Island Kwéṁshem
point of any sharp object s7ayk̲s ~ s7aẏk̲s
point of land s7ayk̲s ~ s7aẏk̲s

point to the left side
txwk̲áẏiwsm
point to the right side
txwyahíwsem
point, be to the esnéṅp
pointed, be ests'éẇk̲s
pointer [in slhahál]
st'amáẏs
pointer in slhahál, be the
t'amáẏs
points of land s7i7áẏk̲s
points, of any sharp object
s7i7áẏk̲s
poison ts'ex̲tn
poison (someone)
ts'ex̲teṅáṅ
poke (someone) in rear
yák̲antem
poke (something) tsík̲iṅ
núk̲w'un
poke it accidentally
nuk̲w'nálhen
poke it finally nuk̲w'nálhen
poke it, manage to
nuk̲w'nálhen
poked in the cheek, get
tsík̲a7an
poked in the chest, get
tsik̲ínas
poked in the chin, get
tsik̲tsk̲
poked in the shoulder, get
tsík̲aẏáṁit
poked on the top of the
head, get tsík̲iẏek̲w
poked up, get all
nek̲w'núk̲w'
poked, be/get tsik̲
poked, get nuk̲w'
poker (for a fire) hí7chistn
pole [e.g., for a clothesline]
sxwk̲w'áyek̲w
pole for baby basket yáṅten
pole of a loom, vertical
tl'ík̲'eni7tn
pole of gaffhook s7enám
pole of harpoon s7enám
pole up in a canoe
x̲wúk̲w'tsut
pole upriver wúk̲w'tsut
police officer
nexwsx̲wik̲w'em
poling a canoe, be
x̲wúx̲wk̲w'etsut
polish (something) ts'elsán
polish (something) by filing
yák̲'an
polished, be yek̲'
pond sk̲wúk̲wel̓
pond in Ambleside Park
[this pond used to be a
lagoon] Swáẏwey
pool esk̲wuk̲wláẏak̲alh
pool in river [where the fish
swim around] k̲tiṅ
poop [see also sxweym]
sx̲wits'
poor [about people]
testesás
poor, be estestesás
estesás
Pope, the Lipáp
porcupine k̲wúk̲wusem
porpoise kw'únut'
Porteau Cove
Swechwáchayem
possession of (something),
be again in k̲'énnexw
~ k̲'énexw;
k̲'ánatsutnexw
possession of (something/
someone), be
lhíṁnexw
possibly lhkwun
posterity sméṅhem
pot hanger tsk̲aṅtn
potato sk̲awts
potato, a kind of
x̲wex̲wekw'el̓s
potlatch tl'e7énk̲ ~ tl'enk̲
Potlatch Creek Tsítsusm
potlatch house
tl'e7enk̲áẇtxw ~
tl'enk̲áẇtxw
potty x̲wa7ítn ~ x̲wáẏten
pour (something)
kw'lhálhk̲wu7n
pour (something) out
kw'lhat
pour water on (someone/
something) kw'lhúsen
pour water over (someone)
who is lying in bed
kw'lhá7lhen
pouring (something), be
[about a group]
kw'elhkw'lhát
pouring rain, be
yíx̲wementsut
pout nexw7út'us;
k̲weṁch
powder (someone)
p'ák̲w'usen
powder one's face
pák̲w'usem
powerless, be eskw'áy ~
skw'áy ~ kw'ay ~
eskw'áy
powwow dancing, do
ts'ák̲'shenem
prairie spálhx̲en;
sex̲wsáx̲wi7
praise (someone) yewt
pray kw'enmáylh
pray for (someone)
kw'enmaylhcheẇán
prayer skw'enmáylh
praying all the time, be
nexwskw'enmáylh
predict (something) yéẇat
predictor syeẇ
pregnant, be es7á7tsiẇen
eskw'áy ~ skw'áy ~
kw'ay
prepare (something) húyut
prepare soapberries
x̲wúsum
prepare someone to do
something p'áyak̲alhen
prepare to start k̲w'úlhutsut
prepared to start, be
esk̲w'úk̲w'ulh
prepared, be [about ground,
e.g., in preparation for a
house] ha7lhínup
presents sx̲weṁ
preserve it k̲'í7x̲em
press (something) down
mík̲'in

press (them) together mik̲'neẃásen
press down mek̲'mík̲'
pressed down already, be esmímk̲'
pretty nach'íḿ
prevent one from using (something) k̲'ets'iwá7sentem
previous time yeẃańálh
previously men t'ut; t'ut
price, a skweshnách
price, to kwéshnach
price (something) kwéshnacht
prick one's ears síwi
priest laplít
priests [sg: laplit] lepleplit
prisoner, be taken p'ep'í7
probably lhkwun
produce an interrupted beat [every second or fourth beat silent] esk̲'ík̲'xw
produce nasal sounds nexwnútk̲s
produce offspring [used only in the phrase timéń ta sesemáy̓] timéń
promontory -k̲s s7ayk̲s ~ s7ay̓k̲s
prong of antler st'ex̲
proper, be esp'áp'iy̓ek̲
proposal, make an Indian tl'a7m
propose marriage chewáshem
propose to (someone) to do something together hey̓k̲wt ~ heyk̲wt
prostrate, be eslí7lxw
protect (someone/something) tíẃilhn ~ téy̓wilhn
protected téy̓wilh; estéteyw̓ilh
protuberance smekw
proud smáts'en
proud of oneself, be sméts'mets'em
provide lunch for (someone) saẃáńen; saẃáńs
provided with food on trip, be esesaẃán
pry (something) loose wáts'an
pry (something) up wáts'an
puberty, reach tsetsíx̲w; k̲w'ek̲w'ená7m
pubic hair sk̲wínats'
pucker one's lips kwút-tseḿ
puffball [literally, dust on nose] spáxwpxwél̓k̲sen
pull (a canoe) ashore tsékwilhen ~ tsékwilh
pull (someone's) hair x̲ímiń
pull (something) tsékwen; xwúkw'en; lhésheń
pull (something) apart lhík̲w'in
pull (something) off kwu7n
pull (something) open wik̲'tsń ~ wik̲'tsáń wik̲'tsáń ~ wik̲'tsń
pull (something) tight tákw'en
pull (something) towards oneself lhíḿit
pull (them) on tsékwtsekwen
pull a canoe ashore tsékwilh ~ tsékwilhen
pull a long face in anger kwútusem
pull a muscle t'u7
pull a muscle in (someone's) hand t'ú7achen
pull a muscle in one's head t'u7k̲w
pull face back k̲'eẃúsem
pull in one's hand k̲'eẃáchi7m
pull in one's head k̲'eẃúsem
pull in one's leg k̲'eẃshnám
pull in one's net xwúkw'ay̓i
pull long face in anger k̲wútusem
pull one's jaw sideways k̲wey̓k̲w'tsáḿ
pull one's own hair x̲ímińsut
pull oneself back tsekwk̲ám
pull open one's mouth [with one's hands] wík̲'tseḿ
pull out (feathers) kw'étsen
pull out (plants) kw'úp'chk̲ań
pull out (someone's) tooth x̲wil̓ansántem
pull out (teeth, nail out of a wall) ts'u7n
pull the wool fibers apart] wít'in
pulled apart, be kwu7
pulled apart, be [e.g., by a grizzly] t'elht'ílhikw'entem
pulled off, be [about bark] kwu7
pulled, be tsekw
pulling canoe, be í7sun
pulse beat slhákw'emachs
punch ts'ahíḿ
punch (someone) ts'an ~ ts'aan
punch (someone) in the eye ts'aháyusn
punch (someone) in the nose ts'ak̲sán ~ ts'ák̲san
punch (someone) on the back ts'ácháń
punch each another ts'ántway̓
punched in the head, get ts'aak̲w
punish (someone) k̲'áwalhens
punish oneself for the sake of another mákw'atsut
punished, be k̲'áwalhen
punishment sk̲'áwalhen
pupil of the eye k̲'elx̲áyus
puppy sk̲wemay̓úllh

purchase it sílha7
pure ch'eych'
purified esch'éy̓ch'
purify (someone) kw'áyat
purify onself kw'áyatsut
purify ritually kw'ayáylhm
purple ests'áts'i
purse ntala7áy ~ tála7ay
pursuade (someone) chechshíw̓at
pursue (someone) an̓usmín̓; chayn
pursue someone cháyak̲em
pursued by angry person, be kwíyentem
pus máts'ulh
push (someone) tsx̲et
push (someone) accidentally tséx̲nexw
push (someone) aside [with elbow or shoulder] yúts'un
push (someone) aside accidentally yúts'nexw
push (someone) aside using one's shoulder yúts'nexw
push (something) híw̓k̲an
push (something) around the fire tsík̲'in
push (something) away in all directions lhekwlhúkwun̓
push (something) out of the way lhúkwun̓
push (something) past an obstruction ts'elhp'án
push (something) steadily yútsun
push by oneself tsex̲nálhen
pushed (someone), have tséx̲nexw
pushed, be tséx̲ném
put (a baby) in its cradle p'e7úts'usn
put (a bullet) in a gun new̓k̲sán
put (a plug) in a socket new̓k̲sán; new̓mámin
put (an object) down lixwt
put (fish) on stick [through gills] shiw̓etsán
put (kettle) on stove páak̲wen
put (pot) over heat pakw'k̲án̓
put (someone) in jail nex̲wík̲w'in ~ x̲wík̲w'in̓
put (someone) in seclusion k̲'elch'án
put (someone) to sleep ítuts
put (someone's) coat on for him/her kapú7n
put (something) aboard a canoe úyulhs
put (something) across t'ák̲'an
put (something) around something k̲'íw̓it
put (something) as a dot on t'elk̲wán̓
put (something) aside t'am̓án
put (something) at an incline tuy̓ún ~ túy̓un
put (something) away lhúpun
put (something) away [for safekeeping] li7t
put (something) away for eating ulx̲t
put (something) close ch'íten
put (something) close to the edge k̲w'ítin̓
put (something) down gently ayát ~ áyet
put (something) in between xwéch'shi7s
put (something) in pleats [as in a dress] k̲w'úp'un
put (something) in the background wáshan̓
put (something) in the centre ´énwilhs
put (something) in the shade t'an̓íw̓n
put (something) in the water máy̓muyun; p'ákwan̓; múyun̓
put (something) in the way nek̲'álhn
put (something) inside ays néw̓en
put (something) into a collection k̲w'u7t
put (something) into it néw̓en
put (something) lengthwise tá7lems
put (something) on ya7n
put (something) on its side néshen
put (something) on the fire x̲etsn
put (something) on the surface of it lhá7lhchan
put (something) on tightly yá7yas
put (something) on top k̲'áyan̓
put (something) out of reach lhúpun; k̲'tsám̓achi7n
put (something) out of the way t'an̓íws
put (something) over smoke of fire pákw'en
put (something) over smoke to colour p'em̓án̓
put (something) over the top k̲'íw̓it
put (something) through a hole chelhk̲wán̓
put (something) together ts'up'new̓ásen
put (something) under water shtams
put (something) underneath hík̲it
put (something) up high chilhs
put (something) where? énchas?

put (them) close together tl'úts'un̓

put (them) down parallel to each other tá7lems

put (them) side by side lhelwá7stays; p'ílhk̲'new̓ásn

put (them) together kw'ú7new̓asn ~ k'éw̓new̓asn; mésen̓

put (them) together [can also be used for killing two ducks with one shot] lháts'new̓ásn

put (them) together end-to-end ts'ep'ts'úp'new̓ásen

put a belt on (someone) nexwyem̓tnán ~ nexwyém̓tenan

put a hat on (someone) yaskw̲án̓

put a hole in the bottom of (something) k̲wak̲án̓

put a little bit of pressure on (something) k̲án̓an

put a little water in one's mouth ts'álhtsam

put a spell on (someone) [about sxw7umten] xt'et

put a spell on someone [about ritualist] k̲éy̓utsinem

put an evil spell on (someone) xt'et

put arms around (someone) k̲'áts'chan̓

put arms around (someone's) head or neck k̲'áts'usen

put away a corpse, just k̲ém̓snexw

put away in a box and fall out, be t'exwt'áxw

put away in a small space, be estl'útl'k̲w

put away, be [about a dead body] esk̲ék̲ms

put behind áw̓tiwilh

put cargo aboard úyulh

put charcoal on one's face [as done by dancers] p'ích'tusem

put fish on split barbecuing stick tl'eyk̲'áls

put food in (someone's) mouth náp'tsan̓

put hair oil on sáxwkwam̓

put hand over (someone) mútl'un

put hand over mouth k̲'áp'tsam̓

put it away for (someone) lí7shi

put it down lixw

put it up high for (someone) chílhshi

put lid on (box) k̲p'a7elchán

put more on to (something) ch'xwut

put on (something) útsiyan

put on hair oil nsk̲ínem

put on one's hat yasik̲wám̓

put on two of the same thing án̓usmut

put one's head down k̲ep'úsem

put one's jacket on kapú7m

put one's shoes on k̲wlhi7shnám̓

put oneself ahead of others yew̓ánentsut

put oneself forward híw̓intsut

put oneself in someone's place nexwnínlhewá7nem

put oneself way back lhúpuntsut

put out (a fire) yák̲wan̓

put pitch in someone's eyes chemx̲áyus

put something in (someone's) nose xwiwk̲sán ~ xwíwk̲sen

put something into (someone's) nose xwíwk̲sen ~ xwiwk̲sán

put splints on (someone) ch'ást'a7en

put together, get mesnew̓ás

put up hand to protect oneself t'íx̲iyachi7m

put up its hair [about animals] shípintsut

put wood on the fire yék̲welchp

putting (things) away, be k̲ék̲xwen

Q q

quarrel shemánew̓as;
huhuystwáy̓
quarter cup x̱wítl'ulh ~
x̱wítl'wilh
question (someone)
nin̓chím̓s
question particle nu
quick, quicker, quickly
siwáy̓ ~ siw̓ay ~
s-hiw̓ay;
aw̓íts
quickness aw̓ítsanum
quiet (someone) x̱íyan
quiet, be eslhálhḵen;
es7álh;
esch'áxw
quiet, be [about person]
p'áxwem
quit tl'íyi7 ~ tl'íya7
quit (something) tl'íyen

R r

rabbit **nsúhupit ~ súhupit ~ ns-húhupit**
raccoon **mélalus**
race [in canoes] **tay**
race canoe **táywilh ~ tayéwilh**
rack for drying nets **ch’ixwi7án̓ten**
raft **t’álhi7k̲w, lháwlik̲w**
rags around legs **k̲ít-shen**
raid some place **snexwílh**
railroad **lílat**
rain, to **lhem̓xw**
rain, the **slhem̓xw**
rain flower **k̲wílayus**
rain flower bush **k̲wílayusay̓**
rain hard **tímitsut**
rain, be pouring **yíx̲wementsut**
rainbow **ts’exwts’áxwi7**
rainbow trout **syuyk̲w’úlu7 ~ syúyk̲w’ula**
rained out, be **lhemxwnítem**
raining continuously, be **lhélhemxw**
raining hard, be **estítim̓ lhélhemxw**
raining so hard, not be **chay̓**
raining, be **lhélhemxw**
rainproof coat **kw’exweláwet**
raise **ch’iim**
raise (something) **ch’iin chilhs**
raise (something) up a little bit in order to get a look at it **kw’úwen**
raise a child **shewayáy̓lhem**
raise hackles **x̲ích’intsut**
raise hands in thanks **wa k̲’ay̓áchtn**
raise it for (someone) **chílhshi**
raise one’s child **ch’aháy̓lhm**
raise oneself slightly from a sitting position **ch’ík̲am̓**
raised hair on neck, have [e.g., a cat] **x̲ích’intsut**
raised, be **ch’iim**
rake (berries) off a berry bush [e.g., huckleberries] **lhemch’án**
rake [e.g., for collecting leaves] **x̲íp’inupten**
rancid odour, have a **kw’ech’**
ransom **se7líl**
rap **k̲welhk̲m; k̲’etx̲án**
rap (a dish) **k̲’etx̲iy̓úlhn**
rap on something **k̲wélhk̲i7n**
rapids **yúyak̲w; swi7xwí7k̲wm; sx̲wem; sch’i7í7k̲w**
rapids {full word: **sch’i7í7k̲w**} **-i7k̲w**
rapping on something repeatedly, be **k̲wék̲welhk̲em**
rapture, be in a state of **eskwekwín**
rapture, get into a state of **kwen**
rare **x̲ay; stl’álk̲em**
rash, have a **tl’k̲íws**
raspberries **al̓íl̓a7**
raspberry **al̓íl̓a7**
raspberry bush **al̓íl̓a7ay̓**
raspberry bushes **al̓íl̓a7ay̓**
rat **hew̓ít**
ratfish **skwúma**
rationed, be **rationstm**
rattle **ch’í7ten ~ nch’í7ten**
rattle [about a rattle] **x̲wíx̲wich’am**
rattle [e.g., a window] **ts’étx̲em**
rattle coin in pocket **ts’tsan**
rattle for rain **x̲wún̓x̲wun**
rattlesnake **ts’ex̲tn**
rattling, be **k̲’etx̲ántsut**
raven **sk̲ewk̲’**
ravine **est’ét’ch’; estl’étl’esh**
raw **tew̓ín̓**
reach (something) **tsíxwen**
reach destination **tsixw**
reach out **tsáx̲wam**
reach puberty [about a female] **tsetsíx̲w**
reach puberty [about a male] **k̲w’ek̲w’ená7m**
reach the flatlands or valley floor **líxway̓shen**
reach there **txwta7**
reached, be just about **tsíxwach**
reaching up to, be **esch’ích’m**
read one’s family tree **x̲én̓x̲en**
ready for, be **esk̲w’ek̲w’íl**
ready one’s weapons **húy̓k̲áy̓sm**
ready to go, be **esx̲áx̲as**
ready to help **ests’exwts’íxw**
ready to leave, be **es-hílkw**
ready to start, be **esk̲w’úk̲w’ulh**
ready, be **es-húy tsey**
ready, be already **es-húy**
real home **tl’eltl’élnup**
realize **tel̓núm̓ut**
realize (something) **tél̓nexw**

really ts7it; tex̱wlám̓ ~ tex̱wl̓ám̓ ~ tex̱wám̓; wanáxw; an
really do (something) kwens
really hot p'áp'ach'
rear end s7atsḵ
rear end showing, have one's esxwéyxweyḵ
reason for someone getting dirty matl'mín̓
recede chishkw
receive (a message) íchnexw
receive a blow [figuratively] tl'elekwán
receive help tl'el̓ím̓
receive it at a potlatch liḵ
receive more esí7ch
receive much help from someone tl'el̓ím̓
receive one's syewen lhakw'ámentm
receive syewen [about new dancer] ímshalkwlh
received (something), have p'í7nexw
received a bath, have eshúkw'
recent ts'umlh
recently men yalh
recline ex̱íts ~ esx̱íts; chen̓áw̓as ~ eschenáw̓as
recognize (someone) esḵ'eyḵ'eyx̱ní; súxwtnexw
recognize, manage to suxwtnálhen
recount one's descent x̱én̓x̱en
recount one's family tree or descent ch'ách'ew̓am
recover lhaw̓; kwan; kwániws; eslhéw̓lhew; p'áyaḵ
recovering, be lhálhaw̓
red kwemkwím; eskwímkwim
red alder tree kwelúl̓ay
red cedar x̱pay̓
red cedar bough x̱ápayay̓achxw
red cedar root basket [with watertight weave] kwélmexwus
red cedar tree x̱ápay̓ay
red cedar wood x̱pay̓ yíy̓ulh
red elderberry [see ts'íwḵ'ay̓] sts'iwḵ'
red elderberry bush [see sts'iwḵ'] ts'íwḵ'ay̓ ~ sts'íwḵay̓
red flowering currant ḵwílayus
red flowering currant bush ḵwílayusay̓
red hot [about fire or person in fever, not water or weather] p'ach'
red huckleberry sḵw'eḵwchs
red laver seaweed lhéḵ'es
red ochre temlh
red paint temlh
red salmonberry yetwán
red snapper teḵwtúḵw
red, get kwemi7
redback salamander ép'enshen
red-hot, be nax̱wáxway̓
red-necked grebe x̱alhnách
red-throated loon xwíkw'us
reduced to bone, be txwshaw̓
reed shách'els
reef tl'ítl'ep
reef in river [see also eshashemáy̓ch] eshashem̓ín̓was
refrain from action ítl'i
refuse kw'iyátsut
refuse (someone) kw'iyáshi; kw'íyat ~ kw'iyát; haws
refuse (someone) permission kw'ayshí
refuse to eat xwí7lhayem
refuse to give to (someone) kw'íyat ~ kw'iyát
regret náyatsut
reinjure a wound ḵelh
related to someone, be siyáy̓ay̓ eslhílhkw'iws
related, be eḵw'í7tel; lha7lhahíws; lhíkw'lhikw'iws
relative skwtsi7ts; s7eḵw'í7tel ~ seḵw'í7tel
relative [general term] stl'ḵilh
relative of the same generation áyish
relatives swa7ám̓
relatives [sg: swa7ám̓] swewa7ám̓
release (something) mu7n
release one's grip ma7ayachí7m
release the hunting dogs yex̱wím̓
released because hooked-up part rips, be [e.g., fish] tl'esh
relieve (someone) kwaan
relieve for (someone) xwátshi
relieve oneself xwátan̓tsut
relieved, be [about headache] kwanḵw
rely on someone tl'el̓ím̓ntsut
remain as the only person txwnch'nch'u7
remain sitting men em̓út
remain stuck [about something thrown, etc.] ḵ'aa7
remaining txwuy ~ txwhuy
remains of a fire ts'éx̱min̓

remember (something) x̱échnexw; x̱éx̱echs; x̱échx̱echs
remind (someone) x̱chusn
remind (someone) of something x̱echmíxws
reminisce x̱echx̱echm̓ám̓
remove (something) t'am̓án
remove (something) [e.g., bark] tsúyun
remove (something) from the fire t'íw̓in
remove (something) out of sight t'an̓íw̓n
remove from (someone) t'ám̓shi
remove guts x̱wil̓ay̓ák̲inem
remove guts from (something) x̱wil̓áy̓ak̲ínan
remove hair from (a hide) ék̲wen
remove splinter from (someone's) feet wák̲shenan̓
removed guts from (something), have x̱wil̓áy̓akínexw
removed, be t'aam̓
removed, be [about berries from a bush, dust from clothing, etc.] pixw
repair t'émuy̓ím̓; x̱am
repair (something) p'áyak̲en; t'émuy̓n ~ t'émuy̓en
repair (something) [about canoes or shoes, not clothes] x̱áman̓
repair (them) all the time t'émt'emuy̓n
repair a canoe x̱ámwilh
repair net p'áts'iyen
repay (someone) k̲ik̲'t; nú7nacht; mátl'nexw
repaying, be new̓néw̓nech
replace (a person's) lost spirit líxwayíwa7ntem
replace (something) nexw7áy̓n
report, a syétsem
report, to yétsem
report on (someone) tsúk̲wut
represent (something) nexw7áy̓n
request (something) úshi
rescue (someone) k̲wat
resemble nexwnílhus
resemble one another nexwnílhusnew̓as
reserved k̲w'ay̓
resin chemx̱
resin for chewing slhelhchéchmx̱
respect (someone) smen̓álhs wanáxws
respect (someone) like a chief siy̓ám̓s
respectable person slhálhk̲'an
respected feeling man̓alhánan
respectful form esh7íl ~ sh7il
rest páyem
rest finally paymnúmut
rest, get to paymnúmut
restaurant ílhenáw̓txw
resting after a pain, be tl'ú7u
resting now, be pápey̓m
resting on, be estsútsp
resting, be espápey̓m
restless lhats'
restless, be getting [about spirits] shíshipem
resume txwiw̓ ~ txwhiw̓
resume, manage to txwiwnúmut
retrace family tree x̱én̓x̱en
retrace one's family tree k̲enshewáy̓em
retrace one's steps k̲'enshewáy̓em
retraced, be k̲enshewáy̓em
retracted, be tl'up'
return k̲'ánatsut
return (someone/something) ám̓ek̲t
return (someone/something) home ám̓ek̲t
return (something) k̲'énexw ~ k̲'énnexw
return [move back in the same direction] tk̲'ánatsut
return home hiy̓ám̓
return it for (someone) ám̓ek̲shi
return it to (someone) k̲'ánatsutshi; ám̓ek̲shi
return to it k̲'ánatsut
return to where one was nek̲'ánatsut
returning the way one has come, be txwk̲'ak̲'an̓átsut; tk̲'ák̲'an̓átsut
reveal (a secret) wáyat
reveal (something) tel̓míxws
reveal something about oneself [especially spiritual powers] wáyatsut
revenge on (someone), get mátl'nexw
revenge, get matl'númut
reverse oneself x̱ám̓entsut
revive áynexwi7; p'lhiws
rheumatic, be x̱ep'kw'íwsentem
rheumatism, have x̱ep'kw'íwsentem
rib(s) lewx̱
rich person siy̓ám̓
ride (a horse, etc.) k̲'áyan̓tsut
ridgepole x̱átl'ustn
ridicule (someone) lhilháts't
rifle skwel̓ásh ~ s7ekwel̓ásh ~ sekwel̓ásh ~ sekwelásh
rifles s7ekw'á7kwlash

right arm **syahíws ~ yahíws**
right away **siw̓ay ~ siwáy̓ ~ s-hiw̓ay**
right behind (someone) **men ch'ích'its**
right behind something **men slhélha7 ~ men eslhélha7**
right by, be **nexwch'ít**
right ear **yaháya7n ~ xwiyaháya7n**
right eye [also **syahús**] **yahús**
right eye [see also **yahús**] **syahús**
right foot **syáshen ~ syáka̱**
right hand **syahách**
right leg **xwiyáshn**
right now **tits'áts'ey̓x̱; tisew̓áy̓**
right side **yahíws ~ syahíws**
right size, be the **stl'átl'am**
right, be **estétx̱w**
right, be just **esp'áp'iy̓ek̲**
rile (someone) **lhilháts't**
riled up, get (someone) all **wets'wáts'nexw**
riling people, be always **eslhéts'lhets'**
rill **sx̱weláyshn**
ring **slemchis**
ring [for the finger] **syelemchís**
ring a bell **tíntin**
ring around the moon **esnuwákw'a snewákw'a**
ring-necked pheasant **tl'ák̲tiyups**
rinse (something) **x̱wéshen**
rinse laundry **k̲w'útsem**
rip **tl'eńsh; sak̲'**
rip (fish or animal) open **k̲w'ík̲'in**
rip (something) **síkw'nexw; sák̲'an ~ sák̲'en**
rip (something) off accidentally [as of branches on a tree] **tíx̱wiń**
rip (something) up **sík̲wintem**
rip off **tl'esh**
rip off [about a fish on a hook] **tl'eshts**
ripe, be **k̲w'el; esk̲w'ek̲w'íl**
ripped mouth, have a [about fish] **x̱wetspts**
ripped up [about body] **sék̲'wilh**
ripped, be **sek̲'**
ripped, be [e.g., fish] **tl'éshtl'ensh**
ripped, get **sikw'**
ripple **méymey̓em**
rise **ch'ách'am**
rise (up a hill, mountain) **ch'á7chaḿ**
rise [about sun/moon] **ch'ik̲**
rise [about sun/moon] **ch'iik̲**
rise [about the tide] **k̲w'ats'**
rise from one's seat **ch'ík̲aḿ**
rise to surface **p'ákwańtsut**
rise to the surface **shámańtsut**
rise to the surface [in water] **ch'íintsut**
rise to the surface of the water **p'akwḿ**
rise up **txwkat**
rising, be **k̲w'ák̲w'ats'**
ritual words, use **tisyew̓íń**
ritualist **kwtsi7ts**
ritualist, become a **kwtsí7tsi7**
ritualist's incantation **syew̓íń**
ritualist's rattle **nch'í7ten ~ ch'í7ten**
ritualist's spell on someone **k̲iy̓utsinem syewen**
river **stak̲w**
river otter **sk̲'aatl'**
river bottom **slesk̲**
riverbank **miyíw̓ts**
rivers [sg: **stak̲w**] **stek̲wták̲w**
river's mouth **íy̓uts**
road **shewálh**
roar [as a waterfall does] **kwékwetxwm**
roar [i.e., roar of the north wind] **sxwák̲amentsut**
roast (something) **átsak̲wan**
roasted potatoes **s7átsak̲w**
roasting rack **nek̲'áyiwstn**
rob **k̲ań**
rob (someone) **k̲áńen**
robin **skw'ek̲ák̲**
rock **smant**
rock (a boat) **kw'i7k̲'áń**
rock [large] **syex̱ás ~ six̱ás**
rock a canoe **kw'ilhkw'ilhátsut**
rock back and forth **k̲'ex̱k̲'áx̱entsut**
rock cod **sts'ák̲shelik̲w ~ ts'ák̲shelik̲w**
rock corral [where fish are kept after being caught] **x̱wúk̲w'aytn**
rock mallet used for splitting or making a canoe **telhchís**
rock one's baby **nikw'íyalh ~ nekwíyalh**
rock that sticks out **sxweyxwey̓úy̓s**
rockbar **eshashemáy̓ch**
rocks [large] **syex̱éyx̱as ~ syex̱yex̱ás**
rockslide **s7axw**
rocky shore, be a **smenmántm**
roll **hílitsut**
roll (something) **yuluń**
roll (something) [e.g., under a tree] **hílit**
roll (something) down **x̱elk̲'áń**
roll (something) off **x̱elk̲'áń**
roll down **x̱élk̲'em**
roll down a slope intentionally **x̱íl̓x̱ilk̲'emáyu**
roll of 50–60 blankets **-awań**

roll oneself **txwhílitsut**
rolling (something), be **híhili̓t**
rolling around, be **hal-hílitsut**
rolling, be **híhili̓tsut**
roof **schlhútsin; s7ik̲ch; slha7lhútxw**
roof of cedar shakes **s7iltxw**
room **-txw ~ -aw̓txw**
rooster **lekwák̲w**
root [general term] **t'kw'ámyexw**
root already picked [general term] **syek̲**
root digger **sk̲aalx̲**
roots {full word: **t'kw'ámyexw**} **-amyexw**
rope **x̲wí7lem**
rope made of twisted cedar bark **sch'tish**
rope made of twisted cedar withes **slishm**
rope, yarn, etc. **-amats'**
rosary **sk̲wínk̲wen**
rot (something) **ts'éxwen**
rotten tree [dead] **kw'up'chk̲**
rotten wood **p'eyk̲w'**
rotten wood or tree **yek̲w'**
rotten, be **ts'exw; ts'u7**
rough **ts'elt'**
rough [physically] [about a group] **wélhwelh**
rough [about surface] **esxwetxwút**
rough [physically] **welh**
rough land **státax̲ay̓s**
rough, be **slhanch' ~ eslhánch'; esx̲wetx̲wút**
rough, be [about water] **k̲eyúnexw**
round **shíshi7ch**
round ["washed"] stone **mímikw'uy̓s**
rub **yetl'k̲'ím̓**
rub (someone) with oil **sáx̲wan̓ ~ sáxwan̓**
rub (someone's) feet **xwíkwshnan**
rub (something) **yetl'k̲'án̓**
rub (something) off **ík̲w'in**
rub against another person **xwíkwin̓tsut**
rub against it **xwikw**
rub oil in one's hair **nsk̲ínem sáx̲wk̲wam̓**
rub one's body **yetl'k̲'íwsm**
rub one's own feet **xwíkw'shenam̓**
rub oneself off **ík̲w'intsut**
rubbed, be **ik̲w'**
rudder **ték̲w'emtn**
rude **ak̲áy**
rude, be **eslhánch' ~ slhanch'**
ruffed grouse **sk̲wets'**
rumble **nelhm**
run **ts'kw'átsut**
run (something) out [e.g., a rope] **túxwun**
run [about dye] **yít'em**
run aground **txwtsekw**
run aground [about boat] **tik̲w' ~ ntik̲w'**
run aground [in a boat] **shemshám**
run away [about a captive] **tl'iw̓; lhaw̓**
run away from (someone) **lháw̓en**
run away, have to **txwtl'iw̓**
run into (something) by chance **nek̲'álhnexw**
run into, be **nek̲'álh**
run short [e.g., when sewing something] **esk̲'tsám̓ ~ sk̲'tsam̓**
run swiftly [about water] **x̲wam ~ x̲wem**
running away, be **lhálhaw̓**
running swiftly, be **x̲wámi7 ~ x̲wemí7**
running swiftly, be [about water] **x̲wemí7 ~ x̲wámi7**
running that way, be [about river] **tá7shen**
running, be **tsetskw'átsut**
rush (something) **ts'ayx̲t**
rushing current **sx̲wem**
rushwork **ts'áyx̲tas**
rust **skwetl'**
rusty, get **kwetl'i7**
rutting season of the deer [literally, when the deer mate] **tem p'í7tway ta sx̲wí7shen**

S s

s/he, if k̲w'as
s/he just yalh ses
sack lesák̲
Sacrament [word used in the Catechism] sáklament
sad séselk̲w
sad about (someone), be séselk̲wni
sad face, have a seselk̲w7ús nexwts'its'usnítus
sad look, have a nexw7í7xwen̓us
sad, become selk̲w
sad, feel sélk̲wtsut
sad-faced nts'íts'xwus seselk̲w7ús
sad-looking nexw7í7xwen̓us
safe estítkw ~ títkw; estéteyw̓ilh
saggy arms, have lhelp'í7
said, be tsuntm
sail yáwap
sail into [harbour, bay, etc.] néneẁets
sail out of [harbour, bay, etc.] átl'k̲a7tsem
sailboat yáwap snexwílh
salal berry t'ák̲a7
salal berry bush t'ák̲a7ay̓
saliva sxwelhch; lhix̲t
salmon sts'úk̲wi7
salmon after spawning ma7át
salmon backbone sx̲eẁ
salmon eggs t'amkw'
salmon eggs preserved for winter use stl'amkw'
salmon harpoon miyách
salmon head sme7úsk̲w
salmon knife kw'ich'tn
salmon milt tl'k̲w'ay̓
salmon roe ready for spawning yúxway̓i
salmon that is covered in sores ts'eẁts'íẁek̲
salmon weir ch'iyák̲
salmon, air-dried ek̲wtús
salmon, pink or humpback lháwichen
salmonberry [general term] yetwán
salmonberry bush yetwánay̓
salmonberry shoots yetwánay̓ stsá7tsk̲ay
salt tl'álhem
salt water kw'utl'kw; tl'álhem
Salvation Army Salawéshn
same menílh
same length, be exactly the estéy̓sh
same size, be the stey̓sh
same, be the nílhneẁas
sample (something) t'a7t
sand k̲wpíchen
sandbar [see also eshashem'ín'was] eshashemáy̓ch
sandflies ch'ch'us ~ ch'ech'ús
sandhill crane sliim, slim
sandpaper sxwákw'ichn
sap sx̲a7mts
sapling s7íxwalhiwa
Saskatoon berry [see nástem̓ay] snástem
Saskatoon berry plant [see snástem] nástem̓ay
satisfied with self, be tsetsiẁántsut
satisfy (someone) chíwi7min; stsítsiyiẁan; tsétsaẁan
Saturday t'ák̲w'entem
saucer stl'epnách
save (someone) áy̓nexwnexw; k̲waat; k̲wat
save (something) túk̲wut
save (something) for later tútuk̲wut
save oneself k̲wanúmut
saw [a tool] lhích'tn
sawbill duck x̲wuuk̲w'
saw-whet owl sxwaxw
say tí7shexw; tsut
say so tichám
say to someone txwtsut
say what? ínet?
saying one's own name, be nántsut
saying what, be? txw7ín̓et?
saying, be txwtsútsut
scabby ts'ékwts'ekw
scabby, be lhuts'
scabby, become lhets'lhúts'
scabies slhuts'
scald kw'askw'ás; kw'as
scale [of fish] ts'úkw'em
scallop shell(s) kwenám̓in
scalp kwá7sek̲w
scalp (someone) ts'uy̓k̲wán̓tem
scalped, be st'em̓k̲w
scar sk̲'itl'
scarce x̲ay
scare (someone) ip'áak̲w'ulhs; ip'áak̲w'ulhmin
scared p'á7k̲w'alh ~ ip'áak̲w'ulh ~ p'áak̲w'alh
scared of (someone/something), be ip'áak̲w'ulhni
scared, get sisilíws ~ silsilíws ~ sel̓selíws

scaredy cat, be a s7ip'ip'áak̲w'ulh
scar-faced esk̲'ík̲'itl'us
scarred face, have a esk̲'ík̲'itl'us
scars [sg: sk̲'itl'] sk̲'ík̲'itl'
scatter (feathers, seeds, etc.) pák̲w'an
scatter (ordered things) peylhán
scatter (something) welhchán̓; lhít'in; peylhán; lhít'it; pekw'n; welhch'án̓; lhekwlhúkwun̓
scatter (something) around lhúkwun̓
scatter (something) in clouds pékw'en
scatter in all directions tl'shátsut
scattered all over, be pek̲w'pák̲w'
scattered all over, be [as of ducks or dead birds] pek̲pák̲
scattered around, be malk̲w
school skwul
school of fish sts'ek̲wts'úk̲wi7
school of fish, be a esk̲ék̲xw
scissors ts'emk̲'tn
scold (someone) náyat k̲éy̓nexw
scoop up water with one's hands k̲wulachí7m
scorch (something) shewshán̓
Scotch thistle i7íyu7ts lhek̲'lhk̲'átachxw
scramble for (the swals) kwétxwet
scramble gift swals
scrape (hides) ík̲'in
scrape (something) sáx̲an̓
scraped, be ix̲
scratch xwíp'im; ix̲
scratch (an itchy spot) x̲ek̲'x̲ík̲'in
scratch (something) x̲ík̲'in; x̲íp'in
scratch one's behind x̲ik̲'k̲ám̓
scratch one's head x̲ík̲'k̲wem̓
scratch oneself íx̲itsut; x̲ík̲'intsut
scratched, be x̲ik̲'
scratched, get x̲ip'
scream kwáchem
screech kw'í7xwem
screech owl shá7yu; kw'í7xwem
sea cucumber el̓és ~ el̓ás
sea eggs skw'íts'ay
sea lion k̲wex̲nís
sea otter témus
sea urchin shells íkw'imin
sea urchin, giant red x̲íxwa
sea wrack [type of seaweed] k̲w'úk̲wik̲w
seagrass lham̓áy̓
seagull k̲w'iyítk̲
seagull [when it is mature and has a large and yellowish-orange coloured beak] k̲wayk̲s
seagull, small black-headed k̲w'ík̲w'ik̲w'
seal asxw
seal fat s7ásxwulh sxwes
seal hunting, be ti7es7ásxw
seal's s7ásxwulh
search (one's) clothing tsayiyíts'entem
search (something) weshk̲án̓
search for (something/someone) yelx̲t
search for food yelx̲lhálem
search for syewen in the ocean imshálkwu ~ imshálkwu7ts
searching around, be [about kids] wéw̓shk̲em
searching for (something/someone), be yéyelx̲t
season tem; tpánu
seat (a dancer) wáshan̓
seat (someone) away from the fire waw̓shs
Sechelt Shishá7lh
Sechelt people Shishá7lh
second tsam̓á
second [thing] stsem̓á
second attempt stsemántsut
second man created at Gibson's X̲eláltn
second piece s7án̓usmut
second-hand store ts'ax̲áw̓txw
secretary sxwsx̲ex̲i̓
secretly take a share from someone ts'k̲wim̓
see (someone [about a group] kw'echkw'áchnexw
see (someone) off ám̓ek̲t
see (someone), be able to kw'awchs
see (someone/something) kw'áchnexw
see (someone's) face kw'áchusnexw
see (something) in a dream s7élis
see for oneself kw'áchnamen
see one another kw'echkw'áchn̓was
see, be able to kw'áchnalhn
see, finally kw'áchnalhn
seed spén̓em
seed [of salmonberry, apple, orange, etc.] nts'á7lhten
seem tim̓á
seem to know (something) is around kw'úlhnexw
seen walking around, be [about dead person] tut ch'itentsut
seer esyú7

seize (someone's) hand [especially with mouth or beak] k̲'áp'achi7n
seize (something) p'i7t
seized, be k̲'ep' ~ k̲'ap'
sell xwúyum
sell "Indian blanket" se7líl
sell cheaply ts'ax̲
semi-trance, be in a ts'elsemáẏus
send (someone) cheshn
send (someone) away huyá7s
send (wife) home xwi7s
send someone to do something cheshnám
send with someone wetsách
send word this way mítsaṁ
senior-line child or cousin sintl'
senior-line children or cousins sensíntl'
sense (something) tátak̲nexw
ták̲nexw
sensible nek̲'ílus
sensitive ch'i7x̲
separate (something) sek̲'wílhn
separate (them) tsiyek̲neẇásn
separate [about spouses] tuyntwáẏwit; x̲wil̇neẇáswit
separate bed nách'aẇalh
separate from fighting x̲iyách
separate house, be in nách'aẇtxw
separated, be skwekwá7tl; x̲wíl̇neẇás; eskwkwá7telneẇas
separated, get xwí7stway
September tem cháyilhen
September [when the dog-salmon run] tem kwáx̲nis
set (something) free yex̲wn
set (something) near the fire to heat kw'ách'sen
set [about sun or moon] k̲enp
set net ma7áyk̲'
set out from shore [of river, strait, etc.] txwtuy
set out one's net muẏaẏi; na7áẏin
settle down líxwelh
settled tex̲w
settled down, be lexwlíxwalh
seven t'akw'usách
seven animals t'at'kw'usách
seven days t'ékw'kw'usách
seven o'clock t'akw'usáchk̲
seven people t'ekw't'ákw'usách
seven strands [of wool, rope, etc.] t'akw'usachámats'
seven times t'akw'usachálh
seventh time st'akw'usachálh
seventy ts'ekwchalhshá7 ~ ts'ekwlhshá7
seventy [form used when counting money] ts'ek̲wlhalhshá7
several nach'
sew p'áts'iṁ
sew (something) p'áts'an
sewing box p'ats'tenáẏ
sewn (something), have p'áts'nexw
sex with (someone), have kw'átl'an; nexwníẇiwsentem
sex, be someone who is always having kw'étl'kw'etl'
sex, have kw'atl'; ti7sháṁ
sexual intercourse, have hiẇk̲m
sexually forward, be lha7í7
sexually harrass (someone) eslhánch'stem
shade sts'áts'ey ~ ests'áts'i
shade, get into the ts'aẏántsut
shaded, get ts'aaẏ
shadow k̲íṅk̲iṅx̲ni
shady side of mountain k̲eẏús
shake nék̲weṁ ~ nekwm
shake (someone's) hand p'a7áchi7n
shake (something) nék̲wen
shake [as at explosion or heavy fall] letx̲
shake hands p'a7áchiyelh
shake hands with (someone) p'áchi7n
shake one's head nekwnekwúsem; nekwúsem
shaking from rage, be lhálhetx̲em
shaking, be [about a person] lhet'k̲em
shaking, have one's head lhetx̲úsem
shaking, have whole body lhét'k̲emiws
shallow t'alh
shallow wooden bowl x̲epi7úlh ~ x̲épiẏewelh ~ x̲epi7éwlh
shallow, get t'át'alhi; t'álhi
shame s7íx̲i
shame, have íx̲i ~ í7x̲i
share tsetsiẏák̲wustaẏ
share in (someone's) sorrow or discomfort esmáṁakw'as
share someone's fate voluntarily mákw'atsut
shark kw'aach'
shark, type of kw'ach'áẏinkwu
kw'ach'ák̲alh
sharp i7íyu7ts; íyu7ts

sharp [about small oblong objects] íyu7tsḵs
sharp edge [of something] s7íyu7tsáx̱an
sharp edge, have a éyu7ts
sharp grass shách'els
sharp noise, make a ḵwelhḵm
sharp of hearing, be estx̱wáy̓a7n
sharp point of spear or hunting knife kwéts'i7n
sharp point, have a íyu7tsḵs
sharp-edged éyu7ts
sharpen (a knife) nexwiḵw'úsn ~ nexwyeḵw'úsn
sharpen (a point) tsíyel̓sen
sharpen (something) iyu7tsán; ts'ilsn
sharpen (something) by filing yáḵ'an
sharpener íyu7tstn
sharp-pointed íyu7tsḵs
shattered, be yúkw'i
shattering, be ch'éch'epxwm
shave sáx̱tsam̓
shave (something) down úx̱wun̓
shawl s7ats'ám̓es; se7á7ems
she -as
she [can't be seen and unknown to speaker] kwsáwa
she [not present] kwélhi
she [over there] álhi
she [here] tsíwa
she herself menílh
shear (something) úx̱wun̓; lhích'it
shed where salmon is dried sḵ'ey̓áw̓txw
shed where things are dried [see also ch'ixwi7áw̓txw] ch'eyxwimáw̓txw

shedding bark, be [about tree] lheḵw'
sheep lemetú
sheep's wool [see lemetú] lemetu7í7ḵin
sheer bluff, cliff státax̱ay̓s
shell clams, to lhewíl̓ew
shelter téy̓wilhtn
shelter from the rain, take t'ápḵam
sheltered titkw ~ estítkw
sheltered, be [from wind, sun, rain, etc.] ts'aay̓
shimmering, be p'ép'elḵ'em
shin bone sch'iyípshen
shine (something) ts'elsán
shine for a while [about the sun or moon between clouds] xwéyayus
shingles [roof] siḵch
shining, be tl'etl'ewḵ'ém̓
shiny ts'els
shiny, be tl'etl'ewḵ'ém̓
shiny, be [e.g. wood] tl'étx̱em
shiny, become tl'uḵ'mí7
shirt stl'píw̓en
shiver lhétx̱em
shoe ḵwlhi7shn
shoes ḵwlhi7shn
shoes, have worn-out nts'ex̱shn
shoo away (an animal) wálhan̓
shoot kwélash
shoot (someone) through the foot ts'isshnán̓
shoot (something) kwélasht
shoot (something) accidentally kwélashnexw
shoot (something) continuously kwelkwélasht
shoot (something) through the head ts'isḵwán̓
shoot (something), manage to kwélashnexw
shoot (somethings/someone) in the stomach ts'isḵwáy̓new̓ásn

shoot at (something) kwélasht
shoot burning arrows up in order to cause rain to stop [this would be done by children, while the grownups would shout "kwusen" (star)] ts'ísḵim̓
shoot for planting spén̓em
shoot oneself accidentally kwelashnúmut
shoot oneself intentionally kwelashtsút
shoot string kwélash
shoot, manage to kwelashnálhn
shooting, be kwelkwélash
shoots of any tree s7íxwalhiwa
shop sxwimála
shop for food táw̓tsam̓
shopping, be silha7áys
shore eskwúkwem
shore, be at the eskwúkwem
shore, get to p'es
shoreward side, be on the áyalhḵwiw̓ilh
shorn, have one's hair lhích'elḵín
short [about person] etl'ímay̓ḵwem
short [in length] etl'ím
short and stubby, be kwésem
short ass, have a ítl'em̓ḵ
short cedar planks for roofing ch'a7lhx̱w
short day, be a etl'ím skwáyel
short downstream side of house built with its long sides parallel to river alhx̱ánḵs
short end of [rectangular] house s7ay̓ḵs ~ s7ayḵs
short ends of [rectangular] house [sg: s7ay̓ḵs ~ s7ayḵs] s7i7áy̓ḵs

short landward side of house built with its long sides perpendicular to the river **schishmḵs**
short shoreward side of house built with its long sides perpendicular to the river **áyalhḵwḵs**
short trip, go on a **men ḵá7is**
short upriver side of house built with its long sides parallel to the river **syekw'ḵs**
short wide canoe **péx̱wilh**
short, be [when ends don't meet] **esḵ'tsám̓ḵs**
short, be too **esḵ'tsám̓ ~ sḵ'tsam̓**
shortcut **ch'ítay̓ch ~ x̱ch'ítay̓ch; st'eḵw'áy̓ch**
shorten (something) **etl'ím̓en**
short-tailed animal **ntemxw**
shot **shat**
shot through the back, be **ḵwaach**
shoulder **ḵwéḵ'tan**
shoulder {full word: **kweḵ'tán**} **-ay̓am̓it**
shoulder blade **múl̓ḵstn**
shoulder joint **tax̱ntn**
shoulder strap of basket **chém̓etn**
shout **ḵ'ayt**
shove **tsx̱im̓**
shove (someone) **tsx̱et**
shove (someone) [deliberately] **yúts'un**
shove (someone) accidentally **yúts'nexw**
shove (someone) using one's hands **yútsun**
shove (someone) with one's shoulder **yúts'nexw**
shove (someone/something) with a pole **yúp'un**
shove (something) **híw̓ḵan**
shove (something) through a hole **chelhḵwáń**
shove a little canoe in the water **p'íp'ikwilh ~ p'áp'akwilh**
shove through (dense mass of people or underbrush) **x̱wiyaḵw'án**
shove through (something) **xwiyaḵw'án**
shoved into one's throat, get **xwiw̓ts ~ xwhiw̓ts**
shoveller [type of bird] **shapl̓ts**
show (someone) how to do something **úsuń**
show dimples in one's cheeks [e.g., when experiencing a sour taste] **shishuyaní7ntm**
show it to (someone) **kw'áchmixws**
show one's face to (someone) **xwéyusmiń**
show oneself **xwii ~ xwey ~ xwiy; xwéyntsut**
show oneself as being a **sxw7umten wáyatsut**
show pictures in the longhouse **kw'achmixwaylh**
shower, have a **lhet'kw'íwsntsut**
showing (something), be **sxwéyxweys**
showing of pictures **skw'áchmixway̓lh**
showing off, be **mamts'á7n**
showing, be [about a face] **xwéyusem**
showing, have one's rear end **esxwéyxweyḵ**
shriek **ḵ'ewm**
shrink **x̱ísińtsut**
shrunk, be **x̱ísińtem**
shun (someone) **esch'úsumni**
shunned, be **est'ánem̓ esch'úsum**
shut (a door or box) **neḵp'ét ~ nḵp'et ~ ḵp'et**
shut [on its own] **neḵép' ~ nḵep' ~ ḵep'**
shut one's eyes **ts'íp'usm**
shut one's eyes [in disgust] **t'áp'elh**
shut tightly, be **yá7yamut yá7a ~ yaa7**
shuttlecock and battledore game **s7ekwiyí**
shy, be **ḵw'áyḵw'ay̓ax̱**
shy, be [see also **es7í7x̱i** and **es7éx̱7ex̱i**] **esx̱ets'x̱íts'**
shy, be [see also **esx̱etsx̱its'**] **es7í7x̱i ~ es7éx̱7ex̱i**
sibling **seḵw'í7tel ~ s7eḵw'í7tel ~ eḵw'í7tel**
sibling of opposite sex **áyish**
sibling or cousin of deceased parent **walh sáy̓xwelh**
sibling-in-law **ch'emásh**
siblings and cousins **séḵw'7eḵw'itel ~ séḵweḵw'itel ~ s7éḵw'7eḵw'itel ~ s7éḵw'eḵw'itel**
siblings [see also **eḵw'í7tel**] **seḵw'í7tel ~ s7eḵw'í7tel**
siblings and cousins [see also **seḵw'í7tel ~ sḵw'í7tel**] **eḵw'í7tel**
sibling's child **stáyalh**
siblings of opposite sex **i7áyish**
sibling's parent-in-law **skw'íwes**
sick and tired, be **aháy̓new̓as**
sick, be **esḵw'úy**
sickly, be **esḵíyalh; sḵw'uy̓úmish**
sickness **sḵw'uy; x̱lhan**
side **-chḵ; nexwmiyíw̓ax̱an ~ xwmiyíw̓ax̱an ~ miyíw̓ax̱an ~ miyíw ~**

smiyíw̓ax̱an;
-min̓ ~ -min;
-ḵa;
t'et'i7náy̓en̓
side {full word: nexwmiyíw̓ax̱an} -ax̱an
side by side, be sp'íp'lhḵ'new̓as
side by side, come sp'íp'lhḵ'new̓as
side of body sḵ'aw̓chḵ ~ sḵ'áḵ'aw̓chḵ; smiyíw̓ax̱an ~ miyíw̓ax̱an; nset'ḵ'íws ~ set'ḵíws
side of dried deer suḵw'
side of house [see also say̓án̓] s7ay̓án̓ ~ s7ey̓án̓
side of something, be to the txwmiyíw̓ax̱an
side with (someone) in an argument máwan̓
sidehill sch'e7úsem
sigh shéḵi7n
sighing, be kw'áwi7
sign t'ánem̓tn
signal to (someone) with the hand or hands nax̱chachmín
signal with the hand or hands nax̱cháchi7m
silent, be esch'áxw
silent, be or become ch'áxwi7
silver dollar chíkmen tála
silver-scaled serpent that is said to live underground or in trees and is said to be the food of Thunderbird Ch'ínkw'u
similar menílh
since welh
sinew tl'a7ímen ~ tl'a7ímin
sinew lhits'; lhiils
sinew from the back of the deer ḵw'ich'tn
sing lúlum
sing a lullaby x̱ey̓tsáy̓lh
sing a song [a power song] yiw̓ín̓em
sing about (someone) lúlumchew̓an
sing for (someone) lúlumchew̓an
sing Indian songs yiw̓ín̓em
sing one's syewen tisyéwan
sing out lyrics nch'élnechim̓
sing song of a dead person [literally, bring down] kewkáwim̓
sing spiritual song yiw̓ín̓em
sing sxw7umten's song lhaw̓ének̲
sing the song of a dead person kewkéwim̓
sing the words to a song nch'élnechim̓
sing to (someone) lúlumin
singe ts'ix̱; kw'askw'ás; kw'as
singe (something) shewshán̓
singe (something) by fire ts'íx̱in̓
singe (something) over a fire chíx̱in̓
singe feathers on a bird kw'ekw'sáyus
singe hair on (a seal) kw'asayúsen
singe the outer skin of (a red cod) kw'asayúsen
singed, be shew̓sh
singed, get its wool shew̓shíḵin
singing one's power song, begin kwen
singing war dance, be strongly [about a man] eslhelhích
single blade, have a síst'ḵ'els
single stick onto which fish are threaded shíw̓etstn ~ shiy̓útstn
single-bladed síst'ḵ'els
single-bladed axe síst'ḵ'els ḵw'ḵwémen
sink mey
sinker-line on net shátax̱en
sinking, be mémey̓
sip (tea or water) lhút'un
sit (someone) down emúts
sit [about a group] em̓emút
sit [on a chair] ḵ'ay̓ḵám̓
sit down [on any raised surface] ḵ'ay̓ḵám̓
sit down [said to someone standing up] emút
sit down on someone's lap mútaw̓i
sit in the back row [away from the fire] waw̓sh
sit on a hard object x̱wets'x̱wúts'
sit on eggs tl'x̱wáy̓lhem
sit on ground síts'ḵam̓
sit on someone's lap metmútaw̓i
sit on something neḵ'áḵ'ey̓ḵ
sit on something hard x̱wits'
sit on the ground mútḵem
sit oneself down [about a dancer] wáts'antsut
sit side by side lhelwá7stay
sit with someone ay̓txw
Sitka willow tree x̱wáy̓ay
sitting down, be em̓út
sitting on a chair, be neḵ'á7ḵ'ay̓ḵ
sitting on something, be ḵ'áḵ'ey̓ḵ; em̓út
sitting on the ground, be nsists'ḵ
sitting with legs open, be nḵwíḵwix̱
sitting, remain men em̓út
six t'áḵ'ach
six [containers] t'aḵ'acháxwilh

six animals t’át’k̲’ach
six days t’ák̲’ách
six o’clock t’ák̲’achk̲
six people t’ek̲’t’ák̲’ach
six strands [of wool, rope, etc.] t’ak̲’achámats’
six times t’ak̲’achálh
sixty t’éx̲malhsha7
size wa lhsti7sh
size something stey̓sh
skate [type of fish] k̲’ák̲’aw
skating along, be k̲ik̲ix̲ítsut
skewed, be láp’entsut
skewered, be ch’út’a
skids for launching a canoe k̲wík̲witsawilhtn
skim (something) off paalt
skimmed off, be paaltm
skin kw’el̓áw̓iws
skin (something) kw’ích’in
skin [animal] kw’í7k̲tn
skin {full word: kw’el̓áw̓} -ay̓us
skin and bones, be p’éli7
skin any animal kw’ich’
skin disorder [general term] slhém̓lhem̓kw’
skin on face nkw’el̓áw̓us
skin on foot kw’el̓áw̓shen
skin on hands kw’el̓áw̓ach
skin, fish, animal or human kw’el̓áw̓
skin, with attached flesh, that is peeled off whole barbecued salmon heads t’éwlik̲w ~ t’ewelek̲w
skinless part of salmon cut in half lhík̲wachn
skinned up, be all [about hands] eslhúk̲’ach
skinny sháw̓us ~ nsháw̓us; kwémkwemts ~ skwém̓kwem̓ts
skinny [about a person] tetstíts
skinny, be eskw’émkw’emts’
skinny, become tetstítsi7
skinny, become very txwshaw̓
skinny, get tetstítsntsut
skinny, make oneself tetstítsntsut
skipping, be xwetxwítim
skull shaw̓k̲w
skunk smets’ín̓
skunk cabbage ch’úukw’a
skunks [sg: smets’ín̓] smemets’ín̓
sky kwáyel; skwáyel
slab esp’ék̲w
slack tide, be méchmechem
slanted roof, have a [as opposed to gabled] lhílhk̲w’us
slanted, be eschéchi7
slap (someone) lhák̲w’an
slap (someone) many times lhek̲w’lhák̲w’an
slap (someone) on the head lhak̲w’ey̓ek̲wán
slap (someone’s) face lhák̲w’usn
slap (someone’s) hand lhak̲w’achí7n
slap on the face nlhák̲w’us
slapping with one’s feet, be lhák̲w’lhak̲w’shenam
slaughter (them) x̲wáyat
slave skw’iyúts
slaves [sg: skw’iyúts] skw’ikw’iyúts ~ skw’eykw’iyúts
slay someone shen̓ch
sledgehammer mul
sleep s7ítut; ítut
sleep during the day kwáylayl ítut
sleep in one’s eyes ts’epx̲wáyus
sleep, manage to get to itutnúmut
sleeping together, be eschí7ch
sleeping, be í7tut
sleepy, be í7tutem
sleet á7lhk̲en
slept, have finally íttut
Sliammon Slhay̓ámin
slide k̲étx̲em̓; k̲íx̲itsut; k̲íx̲item
slide down lhus; lhúsum̓; k̲wuxwk̲wu-xwyá7k̲em ~ k̲wuxwk̲wuxw-yé7k̲em; wí7xwem
slide on one’s behind k̲ix̲k̲ántem
slide one’s feet k̲íx̲shenam̓
sliding, be k̲ik̲ix̲ítsut
slim ek̲wís
slimy face, have a eslhíshus
slimy, get lhemx̲wí7
slingshot sch’élk̲’es
slip k̲étx̲em̓shen; k̲ix̲shnán̓tem; k̲íx̲item; k̲íx̲itsut; k̲étx̲em̓
slip [about foot] k̲étx̲em̓shen
slip [on purpose] k̲ix̲k̲ántsut
slip and fall k̲íx̲item
slip down k̲étx̲em̓
slippery [e.g., sports or ice] t’élhk̲em̓
slippery, be tl’étx̲em
slipping, be k̲i7k̲étx̲em; tlhu7lhúsi
slither k̲íx̲itsut
sliver [in finger] sch’ach
sliver in foot, get a núk̲w’shen
sliver in one’s foot, have a shech’shn
slobber lhíx̲tem
slobbering, be lhílhix̲tem
slope sch’e7úsem
sloping ground eschécheynup
slough sk̲w’ax̲
slow (something) down tl’ápat; úyumen; k̲ak̲’n

slow down ts'áp'atsut; úyumentsut; k̲ák̲'ntsut; ts'áp'antsut
slow down [about water] mechemí7
slow down [in working] ts'áp'antsut
slow down when walking uyumshenám̓
slow upstairs, be úyumk̲w
slow working, be es7úyumi7
slow, be st'ek̲ís ~ estek̲ís; úyum
slow-paced beat, make a esk̲íyekw
slug lhíx̲wem
slurp (something) lhút'un
small s7etsím
small [about animals] etstsím
small [about object] etsím
small [about person] ixwn
small actions skwikwekwiy̓ín̓tsut
small all-cedar bark basket ap'á7en
small black flies ts'ets'ek̲w'áls
small black-headed seagull k̲w'ík̲w'ik̲w'
small bullrush mat k̲'ey̓shn
small canoe kwí7kwelh
small eulachon s7áynexw ~ áynexw ~ s7áynixw
small fish, similar to a small cod [never known to be eaten] k̲w'pel
small fishhook kw'ekw'iyúkw
small game arrow smék̲'nech
small green cod k̲w'elíx̲iya
small green sea urchin skw'íts'ay
small hand mirror welh na wa nkw'ekw'chúsem
small house lílam̓ ~ lí7lam̓
small house [see lam̓] lí7lam̓ ~ lílam̓
small houses [see lam̓] li7lemlám̓
small knife [see lhách'tn] lhí7lhach'tn
small mouth, have a etsím̓ts
small object -ayum̓
small oblong object -k̲s
small quantity of collected water sk̲wúk̲wel̓
small river canoe snéch'elhp
small shelter [made, e.g., of branches] k̲ík̲p'iy̓ek̲w
small snipe [type of bird] wetswíts
small span [unit of measurement from thumb and knuckle of bent index finger] spelk̲wach
small type of canoe made of cedar in such a way that the heart of the tree is at the bottom of the boat p'elách'm snexwílh p'elách'm
smaller etsími7
smallpox smex̲wíws
smart nek̲'ílus
smart, be chechew̓át ~ eschechew̓át ~ eschew̓át ~ schew̓át
smash (something) chík̲win̓
smash (something) up ch'etk̲w'án; yúkw'un; chík̲wnexw
smash the shell of a littleneck clam on a rock [in order to eat the inside raw] x̲i7x̲p'
smashed up, be yúkw'i
smashed, be yúkw'i
smear (someone) mátl'en
smear (someone) with dirt mátl'en
smear one's face kw'lhúsem
smear over one's face kw'lhíyak̲wam̓
smell sum̓; -ay̓ak̲ap; súsum̓
smell (something) hák̲wnexw; súm̓nexw; sum̓ún̓
smell [give off an odour] sum̓
smell from burning lhech
smell it sum̓nálhen
smell rancid kw'ech'
smell strongly like a stable xwes
smell the stink súsum̓
smell, have a strong xwek̲
smelling (something), be súsum̓nexw
smelt schá7k̲wem
smile nx̲iyá7ms
smile, manage to nx̲eya7mnúmut
smoke stl'ík̲w'am; sp'útl'am; spúxwam; lhelh-; pépkw'am
smoke (fish/meat) a little bit pikw'án̓
smoke (something) pikw'án̓
smoke [about a fire] p'útl'am
smoke [e.g., about a stove] tl'ik̲w'm
smoke [tobacco] lhelhsp'útl'am
smoke a pipe lhelhnts'k̲wú7tstn
smoke cigarettes lhelhsp'útl'am
smoke fish a lot pikw'álxwim
smoke from house fire stl'ík̲w'am
smoke salmon pikw'álxwim
smoked salmon sk̲'ey̓
smokehouse stl'ik̲w'em̓áw̓txw; k̲'ey̓áw̓txw

smoking pipe ts'k̲wu7tstn ~ nts'k̲wu7tstn ~ snts'k̲wu7tstn
smoking, be [cigarettes] p'úp'utl'am
smoking, be [e.g. about a stove] tl'ítl'ik̲w'm
smoky, be p'útl'am
smooth ník̲w'em; tsewás
smothered, get mutl'ts
smudged, be peylh
snag sch'aẏ; t'kw'íṁek̲
snagged, be k̲wuy
snail k̲'iyátl'an; wek̲'ék̲'
snake élhk̲aẏ
snakeberry bush titiṅústnaẏ
snap up st'eṁ
snare tl'éyk̲'shen
sneak esk̲wúk̲wus ~ sk̲wúk̲wus
sneak along tl'itl'ich'ítsut
sneak up tl'itl'ch'ál̇k̲m
sneak up to (something) tl'ích'it
sneaking, be[about an animal] esk̲w'úk̲w'ulh
sneeze éshe ẇen
sneeze through right nostril [a sign of good luck] xwiyak̲sám
sneeze through the left nostril [a sign of bad luck] k̲áẏk̲sém
sniff at (something) suṁúṅ
snipe [type of bird] sp'ep'elách'
snore x̲wúk̲w'en sx̲wúk̲w'en
snort puk̲w'k̲sm
snort [about deer] k̲éx̲en ~ k̲éx̲em
snort [about sea-lions, etc.] pxwaẏs
snot smetk̲sn
snow [fallen] syik̲; mák̲a7
snow, to yik̲
snow eagle ch'ésk̲en
snow heavy flakes tl'ák̲wentsut
snow really hard lhák̲w'antsut
snowbird seṁá7mak̲a t'émt'em
snowing, be yíyik̲
snowshoe(s) stl'ál̇x̲en ~ tl'ál̇x̲en
snowslide s7axw
snowy owl x̲ámalhk̲wu
snub t'áp'elh
snub (someone) t'áplhni
so melh
so hot it melts, be x̲way
so that welh
so, be tiṁá
soak (something) t'éẏk̲aẏen ~ t'eẏk̲án; múyuṅ
soak himself k̲w'éts'entsut
soaked fish st'éẏk̲ay
soaked, be t'í7tk̲em; lheṁí; muy; lhel̇k̲
soaked, be [about dried salmon in water] t'éẏk̲i
soaking, be [about dried salmon in water] t'ét'eẏk̲i
soapberries sx̲wúsum
soapberry plant x̲wúsumaẏ ~ sx̲wúsumaẏ
sob shék̲w'u7m; shék̲w'i7n; shék̲wu
sober (someone) up p'lhet
sober up p'lhi7; p'lhiws; p'elh
sober up finally p'elhnúmut
sober, be esp'ep'ílh; p'elh
sockeye salmon stsék̲i7
sockeye salmon disease [from improperly cooked sockeye] yelyá7els
socks mekwshn
soft ník̲w'em
soft [about voice] ns7alh
soft [as cloth] ník̲w'em
soft [e.g., butter] k̲í7k̲i
soft and mushy, get ts'ík̲'i
soft cloth, be a ník̲w'mayits'
soft hair, have ník̲w'umaẏ
soft salmon roe tl'k̲w'aẏ
soft spot on baby's head k̲wek̲wtúniẏik̲w
soft, be [about grease or butter] míx̲wmex̲w
soft, become [about fish] t'ík̲w'i
soft, get k̲i7k̲i7í7
soft, get [about meat or fish, e.g., when leaving fish in] ník̲'i
soft, getting [about down feathers] nik̲w'eṁí7
soggy, be t'ekw
soggy, become t'pi
soldier súlchis
soldiers [sg: súlchis] sulsúlchis
sole [type of fish] lhémk̲w'a
sole of foot np'a7shn; nexw7átshen ~ nexw7átsshn
solid round objects shishiẏúkw'aẏuṁ
some kw'in; nach'
some, be tsi7
someone honoured as a chief wa lhsiẏáṁ
someone that crowds or shoves nexwyútsiṁ
someone who prays all the time, be nexwskw'enmáylh
someone who talks a lot nexwsníchim
something burnt out ts'éx̲miṅ
something discarded sxwiiṁ

something gotten rid of or thrown away **sxwiim̓**
something in one's eye **penáyus**
something owned by a beloved one **x̲amáy̓us**
something stolen **sk̲an̓**
something that is frightening **sisilíwsmen**
something to be exhibited **skw'áchmixway̓lh**
something used for betting **tsewasmín̓**
something wrong **st'emt'ám**
sometimes **ya tl'**
son **men̓**
song **slúlum; syéwen**
song sung by **sxw7úmten** while healing **slhaw̓ének̲**
soon, sooner **chaylh ~ chiyálh ~ chalh; siwáy̓ ~ siw̓ay ~ s-hiw̓ay; k̲á7is ~ k̲a7ís; yu**
soot **k̲w'áy̓chep**
soothe **tinán**
sore **aa; ch'i7x̲; sk̲elh**
sore feet from exertion, get **pawshn**
sore feet, be getting **yech'yách'shen**
sore muscles, get **pewpáw**
sore throat, have a **shuwayálhx̲a**
sores on neck, have **ts'ekw'ts'ekw'álhx̲a**
sorrow, be in great **tl'elákwan**
sorrow, cause of **selk̲wmín̓**
sorry **séselk̲w**
sorry about (someone/something), be **séselk̲wni**
sorry for oneself, feel **aalsténemut**
sort (something) out **yuult**
sort (something) out **yulun̓**
sort of **tut**
soul **kw'elh7áynexw; wa lh7áy̓nexw**
sound **kwémi7**
sound like a group of children **ch'eyx̲án̓tsut**
sound right **estátel̓**
soup **slhum̓**
sour **sáyam; sex̲; lhes**
south **temchál̓ek̲w**
south wind **temchál̓ek̲w telyésh**
south, be from the [literally, be from the high seas] **tinéney̓ch**
space behind something **stay̓ch; tay̓ch**
space between, be **xwech'shí7**
space between, be in the **txwxwech'shí7**
span [unit of measurement the distance between stretched thumb and index finger] **x̲wiitl'**
spank (someone) **lhák̲w'k̲an̓**
spare (something) **áyaxws**
spark **t'ey̓k̲wm; t'éyt'ey̓k̲wm; péych'em; slhíts'em**
spark from a fire **st'í7k̲wem**
sparking, be **pépeych'm**
sparks **sp'ach'**
sparrow **sx̲wix̲w**
spawn, to **achcháwam ~ echcháwm**
spawned out and almost dead, be [about a salmon, a stage further than **ma7at**] **x̲íl̓ich**
spawned out, be [about salmon] **ma7át**
spawning place **achcháwten**
spawning season [salmon] **tem achcháwem ~ tem eshcháwm**
speak **níchim**
speak about it **txwta7**
speak about some very strong person **k̲'itl'**
speak Chinook [see also **Chinúk̲win**] **Chenékwk̲en Chinúkwk̲in**
speak quickly **tsix̲ts**
speak the Halkomeylem language **K̲'emín̓em**
speak the **Sto:lo** language **Títk̲in; Téytk̲in**
spear **s7enám**
spear (something) **tsík̲in̓**
spear for catching salmon **miyách**
speared, be/get **tsik̲**
spearhead **miyách**
spearshaft **s7enám**
special **x̲ay; stl'álk̲em**
special [magical] words **syew̓ín̓**
special, be very **nexwlí7ls**
speckled trout **tl'ítl'elx̲iws**
speech **sníchim**
spell put on, have a **esx̲ét'x̲et'**
spend goods or money in honour of (something/someone) **súyum̓en**
spend money or blankets on (someone) **tsúyum̓en**
spend time with (someone) **esmám̓akw'as**
spherical **shíshi7ch**
spider **sx̲wex̲wek̲wíchen x̲wek̲wíchen ~ sx̲wek̲wíchen**
spider web **switn**
spider's net, web **x̲wek̲wíchen ~ sx̲wek̲wíchen**
spiked hair, have ["how they wear their hair today"] **shepshípmk̲w**

spill (a pan full of water) xweshét
spill (something) kw'elhs kw'lhat
spill (something) accidentally kw'élhnexw; kw'élhkw'elhnexw
spill (something) already kw'élhnexw
spill a lot of (something) kw'élhnexw
spill accidentally kw'elh
spill it, finally kw'elhnálhen
spill it, manage to kw'elhnálhen
spill repeatedly kw'élhkw'elh
spill water on middle of one's head kw'élheỷek̲wem
spill water on one's head kw'élheỷk̲wem
spilling, be kw'lhim̓; kw'élhkw'elh
spilt (something) accidentally, have kw'élhnexw
spilt (something), have kw'élhnexw
spilt (something), have already kw'én̓nexw; kw'án̓nexw
spin (something) selúsen
spin (something) yulun̓
spin (something) [e.g., wool] seltém
spin thread or wool nsélus ~ sélus
spinal cord of a sturgeon x̲élem
spindle whorl sél̓seltn
spine -ts'
spinning around, be shishich'án̓tsut
spinning wool sélus ~ nsélus
spirit -iwan; wa lh7áỷnexw; kw'elh7áynexw; s7áynexw
spirit of the water kwelh7áỷnexw
spirit touches one and one goes numb tení7i7
spirit who cuts people's throats nexwslhich'álhx̲a
spiritual helper ch'awtn
spiritual power [of kwtsi7ts, exercised through words] siw̓ín̓
spiritual power of a sxw7umten [exercised through dancing and singing] sna7m
spiritual quest for power, go on a ts'iyíwen
spit lhx̲wélhch; eslhélhch
spit (blood) k̲wchet
spit (something) out lhex̲wút
spit at (someone) péx̲wen
spit at (something/someone) lhéx̲wen
spit blood k̲wchim̓
spit for drying fish [e.g., herring] shiỷútstn ~ shíw̓etstn
spit into (something) lhex̲wám̓en
spit medicine on (someone) péx̲wen
spit on (something/someone) lhéx̲wen
spit on one's hands lhex̲wáchi7m
spit run from mouth, have lhíx̲tem
splash x̲wéshi7n; pékw'i7n; x̲wéshem
splash (liquid) lhitán̓
splash [about fish] chex̲wentsút
splash one's eyes kw'lháyusem
splash one's eyes with water lhet'kw'áyusm
splash water [about skipper of canoe] lhúk̲wk̲am̓
splash water on (something/someone) lhitúsn
splashed with mud or dirt, be métl'metl'
splashed, be pékw'i7n
splashing continuously, be x̲wéx̲wshem
splice (rope) útsk̲san; útsun
splice (something) on útsk̲san
splice on to (something) utsk̲sn
splint ch'ást'a
splinter sch'ach
splinter in one's hand, have a shech'ách
splinter in the rear end, have a nshech'k̲
split x̲ep'; t'éch't'ech'
split (a canoe) in half sák̲w'ilhen
split (a head) in two [can refer particularly to skewering a fish head for barbecuing] sek̲'k̲wán̓
split (red cedar) into shakes ch'um̓ún̓
split (shakes) p'ékwa7en
split (something small) x̲áp'en
split (something) sek̲'chán̓; kwelhn; sák̲'an ~ sák̲'en
split (something) [e.g., cedar shakes] p'ék̲wu7n
split (something) in half sek̲'chán̓
split (something) in half [about something large, like a log] kwelhchán̓
split and share sek̲'míntway
split apart with one trunk to top end, be [about tree] k̲w'ek̲
split firewood sek̲'níkwup ~ sek̲'ní7kwup ~ sek̲'en̓í7kwup

split hands, have t'ech't'ách'ach
split in half, be kwelhch
split it sek̲'íḿ
split open, be kwelhch
split shakes ch'uḿ
split something sp'ek̲wa7íḿ
split up xwí7stway
split wood sek̲'íḿ; ts'ek̲ní7kwup
split, be sek̲'; p'ek̲w; esésk̲'
split, be [about tree] k̲w'ek̲
split, be [e.g., a log] kwelh
split-off material sp'ek̲wa7íḿ
spoil k̲éyi7; k̲ek̲eỷí7; k̲elk̲eĺ
spoil (something) k̲elk̲éĺnexw
spoil (something) [intentionally] k̲elk̲eĺílt
spoil a child k̲alílk̲em
spoiled k̲elk̲él
spoiled, be k̲éyi7
spoiled, get ník̲'i
spoon [modern] ch'aẃáỷ
spoon made from wild sheep's horn x̲áĺu
spoonbill duck shapĺts
spot estl'ék̲
spot [on an animal] st'elkw'
spot on something, be a st'ét'elk̲w ~ est'ét'elk̲w
spot-eyed st'elkw'áyus
spots, have estl'éptl'epx̲ ~ stl'éptl'epx̲
spotted [like a chicken] eschék̲chek̲; estl'éptl'epx̲ ~ stl'éptl'epx̲
spotted [like a dog] st'élt'elkw'
spouse sk̲w'u7 ~ sk̲'eẃ ~ esk̲'éẃ ~ esk̲w'ú7
spouse of spouse's sibling snch'ínak̲
spouse's in-laws of the same generation snch'ínek̲
sprain (someone's) hand p'álk̲w'achnexw
sprain (something) p'álk̲'nexw
sprain a wrist p'elk̲w'ách
sprain one's ankle p'álk̲w'shen
sprain one's toe tsuḿk̲wúỷshen
sprained ankle or any part of leg, have a p'élhk̲w'shen
sprained ankle, have a p'álk̲w'ach
sprained hand, have a t'ú7ach
sprained wrist or any part of arm, have a p'elhk̲w'ách
sprained, be p'alk̲'
spray spúshem
spread (a canoe) wík̲it
spread (something) páchan
spread (something) apart wets'k̲'án ~ wats'k̲'áń
spread (something) behind [vertically] táx̲chań
spread (something) in the back táx̲chań
spread (something) out vertically táx̲ań
spread [e.g., people from an ancestor or shoots from a weed] páchańtsut
spread apart, be yéx̲entsut
spread one's fingers tix̲k̲wuỷachí7m
spread out (blankets) welhchán
spread out (something) páchan
spread out, be míchem páchańtsut
spring ritual of thanksgiving, do the ts'ets'ik̲áỷ
spring salmon kwu7s
spring salmon [very first run during high water] schí7ulh
spring tide, be huhú7chem
spring water tiléĺs stak̲w
spring-raining, be pa7áchxwiḿ
spring-tied tree [type of weapon] kw'k̲winstn
springtime, be k̲w'eỷús
sprinkle lhet'kw'íḿ
sprinkle (liquid) lhitáń
sprinkle (something) with water lhet'kw'úsn
sprinkle (something/someone) with water lhitúsn
sprinkled, get lhét'kw'em
sprouting a lot, be pa7áchxw
sprouting, be pasm pépa7achxw
spruce tree ts'icháỷaỷ ~ ts'its'icháyaỷ
spun, be [about wool] eseseĺús
spy tl'ich'ayúsm
Squamish [language, people, village] Sk̲wx̲wú7mesh
Squamish canoe snexwílh
Squamish River, the Sk̲wx̲wú7mesh Stak̲w
Squamish's own Sk̲wx̲wu7meshúlh
square est'ék̲w't'ek̲w'k̲s ~ t'ék̲w't'ek̲w'k̲s
squash (something) p'eltl'áń
squat mítsińtsut
squeak [e.g., buggy, door, mouse] k̲ítsem
squeal on (someone) tsúk̲wut
squeeze (someone) [with two fingers] ts'iyíkw'in
squeeze (someone's) eyes píts'ayusn
squeeze (someone's) mouth p'í7tsan

squeeze (someone’s) neck **p’eskw’elhnáyen**
squeeze (something) **tl’iyík̲win̓** **p’íts’in**
squeeze (something) accidentally **p’íts’nexw**
squeeze (something) in one’s hands **p’eltl’án̓**
squeeze (something) into something **x̲wúts’un**
squeeze (something) together **p’íts’in**
squeeze (something) with tongs **tl’eyk̲’án; p’eskw’án**
squeeze (something), manage to **p’íts’nexw**
squeeze oneself in **x̲wúts’untsut**
squeezed between two things, get [about head] **p’its’k̲w**
squeezed, get **p’its’**
squirrel **smemel̓útsin**
squirt (something) **t’elts’án̓**
squirted by a skunk, get **smemets’ín̓entem ~ memets’ín̓tm**
squished up, be [about berries, such as thimbleberries] **esmelmélch’**
Stawamus **St’á7mes**
stab (someone) in the back of the head **tsik̲apsámen**
stab (someone) in the behind **tsik̲k̲án**
stab (someone) in the cheek **tsík̲a7áni7n**
stab (someone) in the chest **tsik̲inásn**
stab (someone) in the ear **tsik̲áya7ní7n**
stab (someone) in the mouth **tsik̲tsán**
stab (someone) in the shoulder **tsík̲ay̓ám̓itn**
stab (someone) in the teeth **tsík̲ansn**
stab (someone) in the throat **tsik̲alhx̲á7n**
stab (someone) on the top of the head **tsik̲iy̓ek̲wán**
stab (something) **tsík̲’in** **tsík̲in̓**
stab (something/someone) all over **estsík̲s**
stab (something/someone) many times **estsík̲s**
stab at (someone’s) tongue **tsik̲alxwtsálhen**
stabbed in the cheek, get **tsík̲a7an**
stabbed in the chest, get **tsik̲ínas**
stabbed in the chin, get **tsik̲tsk̲**
stabbed in the shoulder, get **tsík̲ay̓ám̓it**
stabbed in the thigh, get **tsík̲alap**
stabbed on the top of the head, get **tsík̲iy̓ek̲w**
stabbed, be/get **tsik̲**
stagger **sukw’**
stagger along **súsukw’**
staggering, be **sakw’súkw’**
stained, get **metl’**
stalk (something) **tl’ích’it**
stalk an animal **tl’etl’ch’ál̓k̲m**
stall (someone) **kw’íkw’iyas**
stamp (something) **tl’ákwan** **tl’ák̲wan̓**
stamp foot [about **sxw7úmten**] **ts’ek̲shenám; ts’ák̲’shenem**
stamping, be **kwemkwemshenám̓**
stand **lhx̲ilsh**
stand (something) up **chén̓chens**
stand (something) up [e.g., pole or mast] **tsék̲en**
stand in the shade **t’an̓íw̓ntsut** **t’an̓íw̓**
stand up **lhx̲ilsh**
stand up finally **lhx̲ilshnúmut**
stand up, manage to **lhx̲ilshnúmut**
stand with one’s foot on it **esk̲’ák̲’eyshn**
Standing-up [Squamish name for Siwash Rock in Stanley Park] **Slhx̲i7lsh**
standing up, be **lhílhx̲i7lsh**
standing up, be [already] **eslhx̲ílsh**
standing water, be **ítl’i7atk̲wum**
standing, be **lhílhx̲i7lsh**
Stanley Park, Lumberman’s Arch **X̲wáy̓x̲way̓**
star **kwúsen**
stare at (someone) **kw’ákw’chust**
stare, just **sháxwlhus**
starfish **túmlk̲elh**
staring at (someone), be **kw’áwchust**
staring, be **kw’áwchus**
start **mi ~ m̓i; kwen**
start (a fire) **yulhk̲sán̓**
start (a song) **sít’it**
start an engine **nekwm ~ nékwem̓**
start being possessed (about a dancer) **kwen**
start budding **mákwutsinem**
start to go [about leaves] **ts’xwáchxwim̓**
start to ripen [about berries] **k̲w’elk̲wám̓**
start to smell it **sum̓nálhen**
start to take on trees [about leaves in the spring] **p’a7áchxwim**
startle (someone) **tsetskw’ít**
startled, be **tsítskw’i7n**
startled, be/get **tsíkw’i7n**
starvation, be in a state of extreme **xwa ~ xwaa**

starve xwaa ~ xwa; tísxweỷúsm; kweỷús
starve oneself xweỷúsntsut
starve to death tisxwám
starving, be xweỷús ~ xwiyús
state of rapture, be in a eskwekwín
stay men i
stay close to (someone) [literally, cause someone to be near] ch'ích'its
stay here men i
stay overnight k̲'eym
stay there for a while estsetsíxw
steady (something) chen̓t; chén̓chens
steady flow, be a tsíx̲wem
steal k̲én̓k̲en̓ ~ k̲én̓k̲en; k̲an̓
steal (someone) lhew̓s ~ lhaw̓s
steal food k̲anlhálem
steal from (someone) k̲án̓shi
steal something to eat k̲en̓lhálem
steam, the spúxwam
steam, to púxwam
steambath k̲'élya
steamboat xwik̲wéllh
steam-cook clams ["boil something for a long time and it gets really soft"] ts'xwas
steelhead sk̲iw̓x̲
steep tsitsk̲ ~ tsi7tsk̲ ~ tsi7ts
steer [boat, car] ték̲w'em
steer (something) ték̲w'ems
steer one's boat to shore p'esentsút
step on (something) yéts'en x̲enáten
step on (something/ someone) yits'its'
step on a rock x̲wuts'shn
step on something hard x̲wits'
step over (something) kw'én̓wilhn
step-(relative) sxw-
step-brother ch'ú7wilh
stepchild sxwmen̓
step-child's husband or wife sxwse7x̲
stepfather sxwman
step-grandchild sxw7ímats
step-grandparent/aunt/uncle sxwsi7l
stepmother sxwchésha7
step-mother cheshá7min
stepped on (something), have yéts'nexw
steps stáyak̲shnam̓
step-sister ch'ú7wilh
stern man swa7tk̲
stern of a boat swa7tk̲
stick -was ~ -us; stsek̲
stick (a fish) through the gills shíw̓elhx̲a7n
stick (something) into tl'úk̲w'un
stick (something) on it mésen̓
stick (something) out of the water shámam̓
stick feather or twig into one's throat [in order to cause vomiting] xwíw̓tsam̓ ~ xwhíw̓tsam̓
stick for arranging things in a fire tl'eyk̲'áỷstn
stick for digging clams sk̲aalx̲
stick for hanging meat on to smoke k̲'ew̓át-shen
stick for holding salmon above fire nk̲w'ík̲w'lus ~ k̲w'ík̲w'lus ~ nk̲w'ík̲w'lwas
stick for keeping time k̲'ewát
stick for skewering small fish to barbecue xwúkw'utstn
stick it into (someone's) nose nexwhiw̓k̲sán ~ nexwhíwk̲sán ~ nexwíwk̲sán
stick out esxwíxwi7 ~ esxwéyxweỷ ~ xwéyxwey
stick out of the water sham
stick out one's hand tsáx̲wam
stick something in (some-one's) nose xwiwk̲sán ~ xwíwk̲sen
stick something into (some-one's) nose xwíwk̲sen ~ xwiwk̲sán
stick to something mes
stick together ts'iỷúm̓new̓as
stick tongue out lháx̲walu lhexwlháxwala
stick used to raise fish up to the drying racks k̲'ayén̓ten
sticking in the ground, be estútx̲w
sticking out [of a container, etc.], be est'át'xw
sticking out, be xwéyxwey ~ esxwéyxweỷ esxwíxwi7
sticks on which the wool is strung up k̲'íw̓its'a
sticky burrs of bedstraw mamakw'útsin
stiff sep
stiff arm, have a sepiyáx̲a7en
stiff body sepíws
stiff body, get a sepíwsi7
stiff cloth sepíts'
stiff, become sespí7
stiff, get sepí7
still men tl'ay; ítl'i; -xw; tl'ay
still [from na7 + xw] na7xw
still, be ítl'i

still, be [about water] **ítl'i7atk̲wum**
stillfishing **sts'em**
sting [about a bee] **kwélash**
stinging feeling, have a **ch'ách'em**
stinging nettle **ts'ex̲ts'íx̲**
stingy **esyú7kw;** **ntl'i7**
stingy with food, be **kw'iyamlhnáym**
stink **k̲eyáẏak̲ap;** **súsuṁ;** **suṁ**
stink currant [see **p'áats'ay'**] **sp'aats'**
stink currant bush [**sp'aats'**] **p'áats'aẏ**
stinky, be getting [about salmon that is being smoked] **chíx̲emi7**
stir **nekwm ~ nékweṁ**
stir (a liquid) [e.g., soup] **nekwálhk̲wu7n**
stir (something) **nek̲wálhk̲wu7n**
stir up (fire) **tsík̲'in**
stitch (things) together **p'ats'neẇásn**
stockade **k̲'iyáx̲an**
stolen goods **sk̲aṅ**
stomach **kw'el̓;** **-wilh ~ -ulh ~ axwilh;** **s7étswilh**
stomach {full word: **kw'el̓**} **-k̲wáẏneẇas**
stomach ache, have a **eskw'élkw'el**
stomach cramps, have **x̲isiwílhentem**
stomach part [the stomach part left after a hunter finishes cleaning a deer] **puxwmíṅ**
stomach where tripe comes from **spexw**
stomping, be **k̲wék̲weṁem ~ kwékweṁem**
stone **smant**
stone hammer **ntélhchis**
stoop **tsípiṅtsut;** **mítl'intsut**
stoop over **k̲wúsi**
stooped over from age, be [about a person] **k̲wúsuṅtem**
stop **tl'íya7 ~ tl'í7i7;** **huy;** **yák̲w'i**
stop (someone who is moving) **k̲'atl'n**
stop (something) **tl'íyen;** **k̲átl'en**
stop (something) from leaking **k̲áts'en**
stop (something) leaking **tl'áts'en**
stop (them) **x̲íyan**
stop (them) from arguing, fighting, gambling **x̲íyan**
stop an argument **p'ayk̲áẏs**
stop leaking **t'ápi7**
stop one **x̲eyám**
stop raining **k̲wálhshen;** **tsápshen;** **xwach'**
stop suddenly **k̲etl'shnáṁ ~ k̲átl'shnaṁ**
stop talking **ch'áxwi7**
stop walking **k̲átl'shnaṁ ~ k̲etl'shnáṁ**
stop, have to **txwtl'íya7**
stopped, be **k̲etl'**
stoppered tightly, be [about a bottle] **yá7yats**
store **sxwimála**
store (something) away **li7t**
storm **yíyelk̲em**
stormy, be **yelyélk̲em**
story [realistic] **syets**
storyteller **nexwsx̲wex̲wiẏáṁ**
stout **nexwiyíwilh**
stove **nexwyiẏulháy;** **stup**
straddle (something) **x̲ék̲en**
straight, be **ték̲w'em;** **tek̲w'**
straighten (something) **ták̲w'en**
straighten oneself up **p'lhétsut**
straightened out **tex̲w**
strain **t'u7**
strain off water from (something) [while cooking] **kw'lhálhk̲wu7n**
strained, be **t'u7**
strait **sch'ikw**
strands **-amats'**
stranger **nch'élmexw**
strangle (someone) **p'its'lhnáẏn;** **ch'ich'úsn;** **ch'ich'k̲wán**
strap (something) on one's back **lhíṅcháṅ**
strap of basket over chest **s7áti7nes**
strap of basket over head **chemcheṁáẏek̲w**
strap used with Indian baby basket **ch'áptstn**
strapped up, be **lhin**
straw **sáx̲wi7**
straw hat **tl'tl'áwik̲w**
strawberry **schí7i**
strawberry plant **schi7i7áẏ;** **chí7i7aẏ**
strawberry plants **chí7i7aẏ**
stray from **txwt'am**
strength **tímin;** **wa lh7iẏím**
strengthen (something) **iẏíms;** **iẏímen**
stretch **ut'**
stretch (a hide) on board frame **tpulhn**
stretch (something) out [e.g., a rope] **út'un**
stretch animal skin on stretching board **tpúlhiṁ**
stretch legs **tsákw'shenam**
stretch one's neck **shít'im**
stretch onself **x̲ít'intsut**
stretch out (a hide) **tpulhn**

stretch out one's arms tsáx̱wam
stretch skins all the time nexwsteptpúlhim̓
stretched out, be [e.g., a sweater] ut'
stretching-board tpúlhtn
strike (an obstacle) accidentally nek̲'álhnexw
strike (someone) k̲w'úk̲wut
strike (someone) accidenally k̲w'úk̲wnexw
string x̱wí7lem
string or rope used for tying up bundles x̱wík̲w'i7chtn
string out túx̱wuntsut
string up wool on the loom k̲'íw̓its'a
strip (limbs off tree) tíx̱win̓ tíx̱wachxwn
strip (something) lhew̓íts'n
stripped off, be [about branches] tix̱w
strips slhich'm
stroke (something) tátsan̓
stroke, have a [literally, get thrown] tsexwstm
strokes, be making í7sun
strokes, make ísun
strong iy̓ím
strong [about materials] tl'ex̱w
strong [about taste] sex̱
strong dancer, be a estsetsík̲w
strong odour ts'ep
strong odour, be a k̲'lháy̓ak̲ap
strong smell of a stable, have a xwes
strong smell, have kw'ech'
strong smell, have a chíx̱em xwek̲
strong wind making the snow fly on mountain peaks, be puuk̲w
strong, get iy̓ími7
strongest of s7iy̓imtán
strongly singing war dance, be eslhelhích
strong-smelling, be kw'ech'
struggle t'elhk̲'ántsut
struggle [before dying] mélch'tsut
struggle before dying k̲w'á7axwt; k̲wéx̱tsut
strung onto (something), be xwík̲amamen
strutting, be kwúkwtsem
stubborn eshéshiy̓us ~ shéshiy̓us
stubborn and wanting to be begged, be k̲ek̲'k̲'ítsut
stuck x̱wuts'
stuck (them) together, have ts'iy̓úm̓nexw
stuck in the mud, get txwt'ekw; t'ekw
stuck in throat, be t'kwínus ~ t'kwínas
stuck to something, get mes
stuck together, get mesnew̓ás
stuck, be yaa7 ~ ya7; ests'iy̓úm̓
stuck, get k̲ts'am̓; yá7a ~ yaa7
stuck-up, be sméts'mets'em
study (something) ta7lt
studying who one is, be tel̓tel̓númut
stuff es7átetem; s7á7tam̓
stuff (something) tl'ets'úyen
stuff oneself [full of food] tismek̲'mék̲'m
stumble lhíkw'shen
stumble along lhekw'lhíkw'shn
stumble upon txwnep
stumbling, be lhekw'lhíkw'shn
stump of tree skwíkwi7
stunned, be [by a blow] ts'elsemáy̓us
stunted, be [about a tree] k̲w'elts'áchxwem
sturgeon k̲wtáytsn; skwá7wach
stutter es7éch7ech
stuttering, be es7éch7ech
stye shelshelk̲áy̓us
submerge múyuntsut muy
submerge oneself míyatsut
suck ts'úk̲wim̓
suck (something) ts'úk̲wun̓
suck blood k̲'chétem
suck blood [about mosquitoes] lhk̲wíw̓ilh
sucker [someone who is easily fooled] nexwsk̲'ek̲'elk̲'ál̓
sudden, be k̲'ák̲w'es
suddenly txwhiyú7; k̲'ák̲w'es
suet grease from bear, deer, etc. x̱wastn
suffer ahíws
suffer under a sxw7umten esx̱ét'
sufficient, be estl'átl'em
suffocate (someone) mútl'un
sugar shúkwa
sugar container shukwa7áy
suggest to (someone) to do something together heyk̲wt ~ hey̓k̲wt
suggest to (someone) to something together hey̓k̲wt ~ heyk̲wt
suicidal, be nmi7antsutáy̓m
summer tem kw'eskw'ás
summer [old word for tem kw'eskw'ás] tem yeys
summer, become kw'ákw'asi7
sun snék̲wem
Sunday Sx̱elhnát ~ Sx̱ex̱elhnát
sunk in the mud, be shek̲w
sunken, be esmúmi7

sunny side of the mountain
xwiyahús
sunny, be aỷílem;
esnéńk̲wm
sunrise sch'ik̲ ~ sch'eyk̲
sunstroke, have kw'ásalk̲en
sunward yahús
supernatural x̲ay;
stl'álk̲em
supernatural creature elk̲áỷ
supple met'
support (someone) in an argument máwań
support (someone's) head metmútk̲ws
support (something)
ch'ích'is
cheńt
support one another
chéńchenstway
surf scoter [type of duck with white spot on back of neck] t'élchepsem
surface slha7lhch
-i7ch ~ -aỷch
surface after being under water for some time
shat'
surface of it, be on the
lha7lhch
surface, help oneself come up to the shát'antsut
surface, make oneself come up to shát'antsut
surf-grass lhaḿáỷ
surplus of anything siḿáń
surprise oneself
ch'ek̲'númut
surprised by (something), be
ch'ék̲'ni
surprised, be esch'ich'ík̲'
sch'ich'ík̲;
k̲wek̲' ~ kwek̲' ~
k̲w'ek̲'
ch'eyk̲' ~ ch'ek̲';
ch'aa;
k̲wék̲chek̲
surprised, be very
nexw7áwiwánm
surprised, look eschechík̲'
surrounded by, be [bushes]
eshíshch'
surveying, be titiẃéńek̲
suspect (someone)
tátak̲nexw;
kw'ákw'ayakw'ni
suspenders k̲w'uwínstn
suspicious, be
nexwstek̲tk̲ának̲
Swainson's thrush [type of bird] xwet
swallow (something)
k̲'émnexw;
k̲'émen
swallow [type of bird]
k̲w'ek̲w'ík̲w'ehatl' ~
sek̲w'ík̲w'ehats
swallow the wrong way
slheḿ
swamp mák̲wam;
ts'k̲walhch
swamp gooseberry [older growth stage bush with more distinctive and numerous spines]
ilhteńáỷ
swamp gooseberry [younger growth-stage bush]
k̲elíplhk̲aỷ
swan sxwéwk̲en ~
xwéwk̲en
sway back and forth
k̲'áx̲ańtsut
swaying, be séselk̲'em
swear words sk̲eỷtsáḿ
swearing sk̲eỷtsáḿ
swearing, be k̲éỷk̲eyts
sweat yák̲w'em
sweat profusely
yáyak̲w'am
sweathouse k̲'élya
sweep (something) íx̲wiń
sweet k̲'át'am
sweet cicely ták̲a7lh
sweetheart siỷá7
swell chx̲etm;
puḿ
swell up [about bread]
puuḿ;
puḿch
swelling on body, have
chexwétem;
kwépentsut
swelling on one's hand, have a ts'ents'náỷach
swelling on the back, have a
puḿch
swelling on the hand
ts'náỷach
swelling, be eschechíxw
swelling, be [e.g., bread]
púpuḿ ~ pépuḿ
swift á7xwa
swift tide sx̲wem
swift water, be x̲wem ~
x̲wam
swift, get x̲wemí7 ~
x̲wámi7
swiftness aẃítsanum
swim t'íchim
swim so that the backfin repeatedly emerges from the water
shamsháḿchaḿ
swim under water
sheshtáḿ
swimming, be t'ít'ichim
swing kítu7
swing (someone) níkwit
swing for rocking children
yáńten
swing oneself níkwitsut
swinging, be níkwitsut
swish [about a stick]
x̲wíx̲wich'am
switch i-
switch feet sík̲'shen
switch hands [e.g., when paddling with a one-bladed paddle or in slhahál] sík̲'ach ~
séyk̲'ach
switch hands [e.g., when paddling with the one-bladed paddle or in slhahál] séyk̲'ach ~
sík̲'ach
swollen back, have a
puḿch

swollen up, be **espépum̓**
sword fern **pálapála; tsx̱álem**
sxw7úmten's hat **sxw7umtnáwek̲w**
sxw7úmten's knife **kwashtn**
sympathize with (someone) **esmám̓akw'as**
sympathize with persons who sustained a loss, to go and **x̱améyulh**

T t

table latám
table cover tsíyaỷtstn; tsiyíchsten
tablecloth tsiyíchsten
taboo nemá
taboo name for grizzly bear sí7sintl'
taboo thing snemá
tadpole wexesúllh
tail skw'ukw'ts
tail {full word: skw'ukw'ts} -i7ups
tail end nsháwiỷups
tailbone nsháwiỷups
tail-part of fish [see also sx̱ép'shen] swa7tshn
tainted salmon eggs stl'amkw'
take (a pot) from the fire wáshaṅ
take (someone) along nánaṁs
take (someone) away huyá7s
take (someone) inside uys
take (someone) outside uts'ḵs
take (someone) prisoner p'í7nexw
take (someone) somewhere naṁs
take (someone/something) ashore kwuṁs ~ kwums
take (someone/something) home áṁeḵt
take (someone's) part máwaṅ
take (something) p'i7t
take (something) across the gulf lheḵs
take (something) apart yúkw'un; x̱wílnewásen; x̱wiḷnewásn
take (something) away finally huyá7nexw
take (something) down kaws; t'íxwiṅ
take (something) home t'ukw's
take (something) off x̱wiḷt ~ x̱wi7lt
take (something) off [about clothing] x̱wiḷs
take (something) out of a container t'áxwaṅ
take (something) up [from the ground] kwums ~ kwuṁs
take (something) upward kwuṁs ~ kwums
take (things) out one by one t'exwt'áxwaṅ
take a child by the hand p'a7áchiyelh
take a long time hiṅ
take a look ta7úsem
take a look at (something) kw'acht
take a lot of (something) in one's hand x̱wúsuṅ
take a picture pekcha7áṁ
take a picture of oneself pekcha7ántsut
take a quick look at (something) and then look away p'elḵ'áṅ
take a short cut seyḵ'áỷch; t'ḵw'aỷch
take a shot, manage to kwelashnúmut
take a small piece off of (something) [e.g., of wood] chepshán
take a steam bath ḵatántsut
take a steambath ḵ'élya
take a step táyaḵshneṁ
take a straight course to (something) ts'ax̱ḷíṁn
take a sweatbath ḵatántsut
take a trek into the woods on spirit song search [about novice dancer] iṁshálkwlh
take a wee bit off of (something) at a time chépsan
take advantage of (someone) lánexw
take alternate route txwáyaḵep
take away sch'iyámut
take away from (someone) ch'íỷit
take care yuu
take care of (something) yuus
take care of (statement) ns7í7x̱ni
take care of one another ts'its'ixwnítway; yúustway
take care of oneself yuusténaṁut; ns7eyx̱sténaṁut
Take care of yourself. wa chexw yuusténaṁut
Take care! wa chexw yuu yuu chaxw
take dried salmon and dip it in oil ts'iṁ
take fast steps tsix̱shn
take food along on a trip sesaẃán
take food out of one's mouth [about shá7yu] ch'ich'itsántem
take food to (one's in-laws) yánmen
take food to one's in-laws yanm
take from others ts'ḵwiṁ

take in lhelh-
take it ashore for (someone) kwúmshi
take it away from (someone) ch'éy̓shi
take it easy estek̲ís ~ stek̲ís; kwánatsut; st'ek̲ís ~ estek̲ís
take it from (someone) ch'éy̓shi; p'í7shi
take it over (someone) ch'éy̓shi
take it up the hill for (someone) kwúmshi
take medicine t'úy̓tentsut
take off (something) from someone xwátan̓
take off [about a bird] ch'íintsut
take off a small piece from (something) [e.g., a piece of bread] ts'etkwán
take off blanket lhewíts'a7m
take offence lhilháy̓l
take out (a dead body) through the door shéw̓alhms
take part in táy̓ach
take pity on (someone) ts'its'ixwní
take pity on others ests'exwts'íxw
take revenge for (someone) mátl'nexw
take revenge on (someone) mátl'et
take shelter from the rain t'ápk̲am
take some of (something) out of a container t'exwt'áxwan̓
take the breast kim̓
take to (someone) nám̓shi
taken out of a container, be t'axw
taken, have p'í7nalhen
taking (something) home, be t'út'ukw's
taking medicine, be t'uy̓tenam
taking, be [about leaves on a tree] pa7áchxwim̓
talk sk̲wéy̓k̲wey k̲wéy̓k̲way ~ k̲wéy̓k̲wey; níchim
talk [about group] nechníchim
talk a little louder tut ns7ey
talk a lot nechníchim
talk about (someone) txwteta7ní
talk about something/someone txwtéta7
talk excessively k̲wélk̲wel
talk funny eskwúy̓ts
talk nasally nexwnútk̲s
talk quickly ts'áyx̲tsam̓; tsix̲ts
talk rough esx̲éts
talk to (someone) k̲wéy̓k̲ways ~ k̲wéy̓k̲weys
talk to each other k̲wéy̓k̲waystway
talk to one another níchimstway
talk to oneself k̲wey̓k̲weysténam̓ut
talk too much kw'áwi7 k̲wélk̲wel
talk, manage to nichimnúmut
talkative nexwsk̲wéy̓k̲wi
talkative, be k̲wélk̲wel
talking through one's nose, be nexwnútk̲s
tall [about a person] tl'ák̲tay̓k̲wem
tall [about a tree] tl'ák̲tiw̓a
tame k̲w'ay̓
tame (something) k̲w'áy̓at
tame [about animal] k̲w'ák̲w'i
tame, very k̲w'ák̲w'ay̓
tangled ch'ích'ich'
tangled [about string, hair, etc.] k̲'élk̲'elp'
tangled up around it, get k̲'élk̲'elk̲'
tap one's feet nínkwk̲wuy̓shnem
target shooting, be tit'álak̲
target-shooting arrow k̲w'ík̲w'tl'us
taste -ay̓ak̲ap
taste (something) t'a7t húy̓nexw
taste bad k̲eyáy̓ak̲ap
taste, manage to t'á7nalhen
tasted (something), have t'á7nexw
tattletale nexwsyétsyets
TB sts'ekw'í7ens; ts'xwínas; ts'kw'i7ns; yek̲ínem
tea towel yet'k̲w'ámten
teach nexwniw̓éyalh ~ nexwnew̓éyelh; usáy̓lh
teach (language) ústsan̓
teach (someone) nexwnew̓ít ~ nexwníw̓it
teach (someone) how to do something úsun̓
teach (something) verbally ústsan̓
teacher nexws7usáyelh; wa s7utsáylh; wa u7lh; ulh
teachers [sg: ulh] ú7ulh
teaching nexwníw̓
teapot ti7áy
tear k̲wú7us ~ snk̲wú7us ~ nk̲wú7us; sak̲'
tear (something) sák̲'an ~ sák̲'en; síkw'it; síkw'in
tear (something) continuously sek̲'sák̲'an

tears ḵwú7us ~ snḵwú7us ~ nḵwú7us
tease (someone) wewts'át
tease (something) [e.g., wool wít'in
teased sexually, be eslhánch'stem
teat s7ayḵs ~ s7aỷḵs
teats s7i7áỷḵs
teeming, be ch'éch'ewtl'em
teenage boy, become a swiẁlus7áṅtsut
teeth yenís
teeth {full word: yenís} -ans
telephone nexwnéẁtstn ~ neẁtstn
tell yétsem
tell (someone) nechníchimiṅ; níchimin; tsun; hans
tell (someone) a story x̱wex̱wiỷúsen
tell a legend x̱wex̱wiỷáṁ
tell a legend to (someone) x̱wex̱weỷúsen
tell a lie xwméts'ṅálḵp ~ nexwmets'ṅálḵp ~ xwméts'ṅálḵp
tell a story x̱wex̱weỷáṁ
tell a story about (someone) x̱ex̱eỷáṁch'eẁaṅ
tell news tisyétsem
tell on (someone) tsúḵwut
tell one's family tree x̱éṅx̱en
tell oneself something tsúntsut
temples [anatomical] nts'ahémin
temporary shelter ḵ'íḵ'p'ikw
ten úpen
ten animals ú7pen
ten o'clock úpenḵ
ten people ep7úpen
ten strands [of wool, rope, etc.] upenámats'
ten times upenálh
Ten Trees (place name) Upaníwa
tender ch'i7x̱
tender part of nose of fish sp'éxwi7ḵs
tent siḷáẁtxw
territory áysaỷch
territory where Musqueam Reserve is situated Máṁli
test (something) t'a7t
testicle máchen
than txwnaṁ
thank (someone) kw'enmán
Thank you. huy chexw a
that guy over there [can't see him and don't know who he is] kwiyáwa
that I kwins na
that I [future] kwins
that is nilh
that one there [visible to speaker, but not within touching distance] taỷ
that s/he kwi ses
that you kwis na
that you [future] kwis
that-a-way, be txwnaṁ txwnánaṁ
that's the one nilh
thaw (something) yáx̱waṅ
the late -t
the Lord Chilh Siỷáṁ
The moon rises ch'iḵ ta lhḵaych'
The moon set na ḵeṅp ta lhḵaych'
the other ta ína
the other's snách'ulh
The sun rises na ch'iḵ ta snéḵwem
The sun set na ḵeṅp ta snéḵwem
the year after next tx̱íx̱ta7áwanas
the, a [masculine, not present] kwa
the, a [close to speaker] ti
the, a [feminine, not present] kwlha
the, a [feminine] lha
theatre ḵéḵeỷx̱em
their -as
their own swá7swit
theirs swá7swit
them [right here] iyáwa
themselves manaṅílh
then mn ~ men; melh; ikw; kw; halh; welh; yalh
then I sen
then s/he ses
there! [said when handing something to someone] na!
there is na7
there is [available] tsi7
there is no hawḵ
There is no wind na téxwlam
there is not hawḵ
There was a falling star na wí7xwem ta kwúsen
There was a forest fire na yulh ta stséḵtseḵ
there, be na7
therefore halh
therefore s/he yalh ses
these iyá
these [people right here] iyáẁit
these people [not sure of who they are] kwiyáẁit
they -aswit
they [not here] kwétsiẁit
they [not present] kwaẁit
they [right here] iyáwa
they say eḵa
they work ts'its'áp'wit
thick hiyámats'; plhulh
thick [about rope, yarn, wool, etc.] maḵ'
thick [about tree] hiyíẁa
thick bark slaaỷ
thick cloth plhúlhayts'a; plhits

thick lips, have **pelhts**
thick, be [about rope] **mák'amats'**
thicked-lipped, be **pelhts**
thicker, be getting **peplhúlhi7**
thief **kénken ~ kénken**
thigh **smekw'álap**
thigh {full word: smekw'álap} **-alap**
thimbleberry [see **t'ákw'emaẏ** and **t'kw't'akw'emáẏ**] **st'ákw'em**
thimbleberry bush [see **st'ákw'em** and **t'kw't'akw'emáẏ**] **t'ákw'emaẏ**
thimbleberry shoots **stsá7tskay**
thimbleberry tree [see **st'ákw'em** and **t'ákw'emaẏ**] **t'ekw't'akw'emáẏ**
thin **ts'emíl**
thin (something) **ts'emiln**
thin [about rope] **ekwísamats'**
thin [about tree] **ekwísiwa**
thin [e.g., rope] **ekwís**
thin bark, have **p'éli7**
thin cloth **ts'emílayts'a**
thin, become very **txwshaw**
thin, get very **kwémts'i7**
thing(s) **s7á7tam**
thing [to be] given away **scháchshaẏ**
thing desired or wanted **stl'i7**
things given away [e.g., at a potlatch] **sxwem**
think **ta7áwn ~ nta7áwn; tsut; kwelkwálwen**
think about (something/ someone) **nta7áweni**
think back on (something) **xéchnexw**
think of (something) **xéchnexw**

think of the past **xechxechmám**
think things over **telwánim**
third **chanáxw**
thirsty **ch'eyxwíkin ~ ch'eyxwáẏkin**
thirsty, be **tiskwú7kwu; eskwúkwel; ch'eyxwántm**
thirty **lhéxwlhsha7 ~ lhexwlhshá7**
thirty one **lhéxwlhsha7 i kwi nch'u7**
thirty two **lhéxwlhsha7 i kwi ánus**
this one **ti**
this one here **tíwa**
this one here [female] **tsíwa**
this, the, a [female, within reach] **tsi**
Thompson Indian(s) **Lhekápmexw**
those **ítsi ~ íytsi**
those [people] **ítsiwit ~ íytsiwit**
those honoured as chiefs **wa lhsíiẏam**
those ladies [not here yet] **kwlhawit**
those sitting farthest away from the fire **nexwwáwsh**
those sitting in front [closest to the fire] **hiwíkn**
those sitting in the back row **nexwwáwsh**
thread a needle **xwíkemamim**
thread fish onto a single stick through the mouth and the gills **shíwets**
threaten (someone who is present) **k'emk'ámt**
threaten [someone who is present] **k'emk'ámay**
three **chánat**
three animals **cháchenat**
three berries **chanatáyum**
three containers [pots, pans, canoes] **chánaxwilh**

three days **chánxwyes**
three hundred **lhíxwelech**
three o'clock **chánatk**
three people **chenchánat**
three people left, only **txwchenchánat**
three rocks **chánatuys**
three rolls of 50 blankets **chanatáwan**
three strands [of wool, rope, etc.] **chanatámats'**
three times **chanatálh; chanáxw**
three trees **chanatíwa**
three years **chanatawánexw**
three-year old deer [with two-pronged antlers] **t'xatsn**
thrice **chanáxw**
throat **kénaxw; xwúmlhnalh**
throat {full word: **kénaxw**} **-alhxa**
throat {full word: **xwúmlhnalh**} **-kn ~ -kin**
throat, inside of {full word: **xwúmlhnalh**} **-lhnay**
throb **ets'k'ántsut**
throb [about a sore] **tl'ixántsut**
throb [as after being hit by nettle, or caused by being stung] **xwútem**
throb really bad **tsík'intsut**
through it, be **txwchelhkw**
throw **tsexwím**
throw (one's clothes) over a line **ts'elhp'án**
throw (something) **tsexws**
throw (something) away **xwi7s tsexws**
throw (something) down **tsexws**
throw (something) overboard **peymán**
throw (something) through a hole **chelhkwán**

throw (things) **tl'epx̲wán̓**
throw it away as a **swals wals**
throw off large chips of glowing [cedar] wood **t'ey̓k̲wm**
throw off large sparks **t'ey̓k̲wm**
throw off sparks **t'ét'ey̓k̲wm t'éyt'ey̓k̲wm**
throw on a big dab of (something) **ch'elk̲án̓**
throw one's voice **k̲wex̲tsám̓**
throw oneself overboard **peymántsut**
throw overboard **peym**
throw punches **ts'ahím̓**
throw something at (someone/something) **tsexwn**
throw to (someone) **tsexwshí**
throwing oneself around, be **tsáxwtsexwsténam̓ut**
thrown away, be **xwi7**
thrown into convulsions, be **ch'ich'ich'ántem ~ ch'ech'ich'ántm**
thrown, be **tsétsxwes**
thrush, have [a fungal infection of the mouth, usually found in children] **ch'ík̲'aluts**
thumb **sintl'ak̲wúy̓ach**
thump [i.e., the sound of something dropping] **kwémi7n**
thump continuously **kwékwem̓em ~ k̲wék̲wem̓em**
thumping noise, make a **lémxwi7n; k̲welhk̲m; lítem̓**
thumping, be always **k̲wék̲wem̓em ~ kwékwem̓em**
thunder **in̓inyáx̲a7n; ts'ántsut**
Thunderbird **in̓inyáx̲a7n**
Thursday **Sx̲aa7útsens**
tickle (someone) **chichipán**
tickle (someone's) feet **chichipshnán̓**
tickle (someone's) hands **chichipáchen**
tickling, be **chíchip**
ticklish **nexwschíchip**
ticklish face, have a **chichipús**
ticklish feeling in throat, have a **chíchipem**
ticklish hands, have **chíchipach**
tide **sx̲wem**
tide pool **sk̲wúk̲wel̓**
tidied (something) up, have **k̲ém̓snexw**
tidy up **k̲emsím̓**
tie (someone) up **nex̲wík̲w'in**
tie (something) around the middle **k̲'iswílhn**
tie (something) tightly **yá7yas; ya7n**
tie (something) up **k̲'ísin̓ ~ nk'ísin; x̲wík̲w'in̓; x̲wek̲w'iyúshentem**
tie (something) up into a bundle **x̲wík̲w'ay̓chan̓**
tie (them) together [e.g., the ends of two ropes] **k̲'áp'new̓ásn**
tie one's shoes **x̲wek̲'iyúshntm ta k̲wlhi7shn**
tie ribbon on (hairlock) **x̲wík̲w'k̲sen**
tie up **k̲'ísin̓tsut**
tie up hair in back **k̲'ts'ap**
tie up hair with one feather in it [in the Indian fashion] **ch'k̲w'ap**
tied tightly, be **yaa7 ~ ya7**
tied up in a bundle, be **esx̲wíx̲wk̲w'i7ch**
tied up, be **esk̲'ík̲'s; x̲wek̲w' ~ x̲wik̲w'**
tied, be **k̲'is**
tied, be [in a canoe race] **steta7átal̓**
tight squeeze, be **skwekwích**
tight squeeze, be a **lhiy̓áts'**
tight wad, be a **tekw'**
tight, be **yaa7 ~ ya7; yá7ya**
tight, be [e.g., about clothes] **tekw'**
tight, be very **espx̲átm**
tight, become **tekw'em̓í7**
tighten (something) **tákw'en; ya7n**
tighten up, as in a cramp [about muscle] **k̲íp'intsut**
tightened up and tired, get [about body] **pewpáw**
tightened, be **yá7a ~ yaa7**
tight-lipped, be **ch'ém̓ch'em̓ts**
tightly **yá7ya**
till the ground **k̲wéyk̲weytem**
tilt (something) **tew̓á7n**
tilted, be **eschéchi7**
timber **x̲itsk̲**
time **-anam ~ -anm; tem-; t'ánamtn; -anm ~ -anam**
time between autumn and early winter, be the **t'ít'ik̲wi7**
time for salmon to spawn [approximately mid-August to mid-November] **tem eshcháwm ~ tem achcháwem**
time of spring salmon [approximately July] **tem kwu7s**
time of the eulachon [approximately April] **tem s7áynixw**

time of the last snow, when the frogs come to life welhx̱s
times -alh
tin can ḵ'éḵ'x̱el
tinkle ts'éts'i7n
tippy, be kw'ílhkw'ilh
tips of fish ḵaẏt
tire (someone) out lhchiwsn
tired feet, have ḵ'ésshen
tired muscles from over-exertion, get paw
tired neck, get a ḵ'esápsem
tired neck, have a ḵ'esápsem
tired of (someone), be lhchíwsni
tired of waiting, be ḵ'esíws
tired right out, be xwenkw'
tired, be lhelhchíws
tired, get lhchiws
tired, get [short form] chiws ~ lhchiws
tired, get/become txwlhchiws
tissue si7ḵstn
title sna ~ sna7
to t-; txwnaṁ
to no purpose txwuy ~ txwhuy
to the, a tl'a
toasting the xwastn, be [literally, warming it for the mouth] kw'ákw'stsam
tobacco sp'útl'am
today ti stsi7s
today [only in the phrase ti stsi7s] stsi7s
toddler s7íxwalh
toe nix̱ḵwúẏshen
toe {full word: nix̱ḵwúẏshen} -ḵwuẏshen
toe jam st'ech'shn
toenail(s) ḵw'x̱wúẏḵwuẏshen
toes sch'iyípḵwuẏshen
together with [only with lh] kw'a-lh
together with, be esḵ'éḵ'eẇ ~ esḵ'eḵw'ú7 ~ esḵ'éḵw'u7 ~ esḵ'eḵ'éẇ
together, be sḵ'eḵw'ú7ṅwas ḵw'ú7neẇas ~ ḵw'u7neẇás ~ ḵ'eẇneẇás esḵ'eḵw'ú7neẇas esḵw'ú7neẇas
together, be [about people] ḵxwus
together, come nchéṁus ~ ncheṁús ~ chéṁus
together, get ḵw'u7neẇásm
togetherness esḵw'ú7neẇas
toilet paper si7ḵtn
told, be tsuntm
tomboy heṁsh
tommycod sts'émkwa
tomorrow kwáyel; tsixw kwáyles
tomorrow night kwáyles txwná7nat
tomorrow, be kwáyles
tongs tl'eyḵ'áẏstn
tongue meḵálxwtselh
tongue {full word: meḵálxwtsalh} -alxwtsalh
tonight ti txwná7nat
too an; ímen
too lazy [to do something] úmat
toot a horn púḵw'tsaṁ
tooth -ans; yenís
toothache, have a seḵ'sáḵ'ans
top -iẏeḵw ~ -aẏeḵw; chilh; -ḵw ~ -eḵw; s7elḵn
top [in borrowings] -ḵin ~ -ḵn
top [spinning toy] syilíḵ'
top of foot slha7lhchshn
top of hand lha7lhchách ~ slhá7lhchach
top of head {full word: nḵ'áytsiẏ'eḵw} -aẏeḵw ~ - iẏeḵw
top of it, be on esḵ'áḵ'ey
top of something, be on tḵ'ay
top of the hand slhá7lhchach ~ lha7lhchách
top of the head neḵ'íts'iẏiḵw
top part of it chílhix̱en
top, be at the élḵen
top, be on lha7lhch; lhá7lhchiẇilh; ḵ'ay
torch swách'it; heẏḵwíṅ ~ heẏeḵwíṅ
torchlight esxwách'it
torn (something), have sáḵ'nexw
torn body, have a séḵ'wilh
torn, be esésḵ'
torso slhéḵ'wilh
tossing, be [when sleeping] tsáxwtsexwsténaṁut
totally starved, be xwa ~ xwaa
totem of a man holding a fish Wáx̱ayus
totem pole sch'etxw
touch (something) [with hands] lha7n
touched by rising water, be muy
touched, be lhá7a
touched, be just lhuts
touched, get [by something flying by] x̱ip'
touchy swéts'wets' ~ eswéts'wets'
tow ḵ'éḵ'p'nach
toward, be txwnánaṁ
towards txwnaṁ
towards [this way], be txwmi ~ txwṁi ~ txweṁí ~ txwheṁí
towards the beach, be áyalhḵwiẇilh

towel **nsa7ústn**

town **táw̓n**

toy **sew̓úl̓em ~ s-hew̓úl̓em**; **sk̲w'shétsut**

toy canoe **sk̲w'shétsut**; **snexwílh**; **sní7nixwilh**

trade **nexw7áy̓stway̓**

trade (something) **nexw7áy̓s**

trade (something) in **nexw7áy̓s**

trail **shewálh**

train (someone) to be a **sxw7umten kw'áyat**

train in or follow (a tradition) **nexw7áy̓n**

train oneself for sports **p'ayak̲éntsut**

train to become a **sxw7umten kw'áyatsut**

trainer **ushenáy̓lh**

training **skw'áyatsut**

trance **smáyk̲wsmut**

trance, go into a **máyk̲wsmut**; **ts'elsemáy̓us**

transfer from one container to another **kw'an̓ím̓**

transfer weight repeatedly from one foot to the other **iséyk̲'shn ~ isík̲'shn**

transform (someone) **x̲i7t**

transform (something) **nách'en**

transform oneself **nexw7áy̓entsut**

Transformers **X̲aays ~ Sx̲aays**

trap **x̲eshen̓ám̓**

trap (an animal) **witán̓en**

trap [leg-hold] **tl'éyk̲'shen**

trapped, get **p'its'**; **tl'eyk̲'**

travel by any conveyance (e.g., a car) **nexw7iy̓áy̓ulh**

travel by canoe **nexw7iy̓áy̓ulh**

travel by horse **nsk̲'ák̲'i tkwi stek̲íw**

travel on foot **men í7im̓esh**

treat (someone) kindly **ayát ~ áyet**

treat (someone) like a chief **siy̓ám̓s**

treat (someone) like a high-class person **smen̓álhs**

treat (someone) like a low-class person **st'áshemni**

treat (someone) with respect **wanáxws**

treat it irreverently **temsk̲w'shétsut**

tree **stsek̲**; **-ay̓**

tree {full word: **stsek̲**} **-iwa ~ -iwa7**

tree that has fallen by chopping **x̲itsk̲**

trees **stsék̲tsek̲**

tremble [from fear or cold] **lhétx̲em**

trembling aspen **p'ep'elk̲'emáchxw**

tried (something), have **t'á7nexw**

trimmed hair, have **sx̲áx̲elk̲w**

trip **lhíxwshenantem**

trip (someone) **lhíkw'shnan**

trip when one's foot gets caught **lhekw'lhíkw'shn**

tripe **spexw**

troll **kw'úykwem**

trolling line **kw'uykwél̓shen**

trouble, be in great **tl'elákwan**

trout **syuyk̲w'úlu7 ~ syúyk̲w'ula**; **xwiyuykwúla7em**

trout-like fish, any **syuyk̲w'úlu7 ~ syúyk̲w'ula**

true **wanáxw**; **ts7it**

true story **syets**

truly **tex̲wlám̓ ~ tex̲wl̓ám̓ ~ tex̲wám̓**

trunk **nexwnew̓íwstn**; **-k̲**

trunk of tree **slhék̲'wilh**

try **tsut**; **tl'átl'i**; **t'á7tsut**

try (something) **t'a7t**

try a second time **tsam̓án̓tsut**

try again **x̲esí7**

try for the fifth time **tsiyachisálhntsut**

try for the fourth time **x̲wutsnálhntsut**

try for the tenth time **upenálhntsut**

try for the third time **chanáxwntsut**

try to best one another **memtl'ítsut**

try to find out **tl'ísitsut**

try to get (someone's) attention [by signs, sounds] **sesew̓ít**

try to out do one another **men tl'ítsus**

try to recognize **k̲wáts'ayúsem**

try to recognize someone **súxwtim̓**

trying hard, be **estítim̓**

Tsawwassen **Schu7útsn**

Tsimshian people **Ts'amshiyán**

tuberculosis **ts'xwínas**; **ts'kw'i7ns ~ sts'ekw'í7ens**

tuberculosis, have **yek̲ínem**

tuck (something) in **k̲w'útl'un**; **pétsen**

tucked in already, be **esk̲w'úk̲w'utl'**

Tuesday [literally, second day] **Stsámyes**

tug (something) tsékwen
tumpline chéṁetn
turn (someone) into a salmon sts'ukw'i7án
turn (someone) into a whale kwenísen
turn (someone) upside down chéẏkwsan
turn (something) around sheych'án; tiṁaksáṅ
turn (something) around lengthwise sik'ksán ~ seyk'ksán
turn (something) inside out nkw'áyk'an
turn (something) into stone smántn
turn (something) loose yexwn
turn (something) over kw'áyak'n ~ kwáyk'an
turn (something) upside down cheẏkwáṅ
turn around ch'ich'
turn around a bend k'íẇitsut
turn around a canoe, car, etc. tiṁáksem
turn canoe/can/box over kp'i7kwm
turn down (a light) yákwaṅ tl'úp'un
turn inside out nkw'áyak'
turn into stone smánitm
turn oneself around sheych'ántsut; shich'átsut; ch'ich'ántsut
turn oneself right over kw'áyak'ántsut ~ kw'áyk'antsut
turn oneself upside down chéẏkwentsut
turn out to be of assistance to (someone) ch'áwnexw
turn so that one faces the other way txwtiṁúsem tiṁúsem
turn to the right txwyahíwsem
turn up one's nose xísksem
turned inside out, be kw'áyek'
turned opposite, be kw'ákw'iẏek'
turning itself into a steelhead at the head of the Squamish River, be [about salmon] kiwkiẇxántsut
turning, be [when sleeping] kw'áykw'ayk'
turnip sxwelawú7
twelve úpen i kwi áṅus
twenty wetl'ch'
twenty animals wiwtl'ch'
twenty cents aṅus7áyum mit
twenty one wetl'ch' i kwi nch'u7
twenty two wetl'ch' i kwi áṅus
twenty years wetl'ch'awánexw
twice áṅusalh; tsaṁá
twig shí7sheway
twilight, be lháchi7
twine xwí7lem
twins sch'iyúy ~ ch'iyúy ~ ch'ich'iyúy ~ sch'eych'eyúy
twist ch'ich'
twist (a cedar bough) to make a rope pútsuṅ
twist (something) ch'ich'án
twist one's mouth kweẏkw'tsáṁ
twisted ch'ích'ich'
twisted, be esch'éch'ich'; ch'ich'
two áṅus
two animals áaṅus
two berries aṅusáyuṁ
two canoes travelling together stsátsaṁáxwilh
two containers [pots, pans, canoes] tsámaxwilh
two days tsámyas
two hundred tsáṁich
two legs together, have k'éts'shen
two o'clock áṅusk
two people en7áṅus
two pieces áṅusmut
two strands [of wool, rope, etc.] aṅusámats'
two times tsaṁá
two trees áṅuswa ~ áṅusiwa
two years aṅusawánexw
Two-Headed Serpent Sínulhkaẏ
two-headed snake pá7chalem
two-year old deer [with one-pronged antlers] kálaxwus
type of dance [at the end of it, everyone shouts "huy"] wi7ka7án
type of plant, a kíkwes

U u

ugly k̲eỷím̓ut;
k̲eyús
ugly face, have an
ch'esp'i7ús
ugly looking k̲eỷím̓ut
ugly, be ch'ésp'i
ugly-faced ch'esp'i7ús
ultimate huy
umbrella ts'áỷtn
unable to stop doing it
x̲wú7us
unable, be sew̓íw̓
kw'ay ~ skw'ay ~
eskw'áy
unaware of surroundings, be
sháxwlhus
uncle sísi7
uncle [after death of parent or parent's sibling] wa lhsáỷxwelh
unconscious, be hik̲;
esesím̓
uncork (a bottle) ts'u7tsán̓
uncover (something)
xweỷk̲wán
uncovered, be xweỷk̲w
under a spell, be x̲t'etm
under ground, be espépen̓
under house, be esíik̲
under something, be txwhik̲
~ txwik̲
under, be lésiw̓ilh
under, being li7ls ~ lil̓s
underarm hair
sk̲winiyáx̲a7n
underarms sikw'íwen
underbrush nsk̲i7
undergo ta7-;
tá7a
underground house
espen̓úỷtxw;
sk̲amún
underground tunnel
sk̲wacháỷs
underneath, be lésiw̓ilh
underpants or shirt
tl'itl'eptnáỷk̲
undershirt tl'itl'eptnáỷts'a
understand (someone)
yew̓ín̓tsmin̓
understand (someone) [speaking] yew̓ín̓tsni
understand [speech]
yew̓ín̓ts
understood (something), have tá7lnexw
undress (someone)
lhew̓íts'n
undress oneself
lhewíts'a7m
undulate yúya7kwm
unfinished canoe-hull
x̲ts'aỷ
unhappy séselk̲w
unidentified stomach disorder, have an ["pain in stomach"]
ts'el̓áls
unintelligable, be
xwená7k̲en
unit of measurement from elbow of right arm to tip of finger sptach
unit of measurement from shoulder to top of finger of right hand sák̲wula
unity, be in nch'ú7mut
unravel (something)
yex̲wúsn
unripe tew̓ín̓
unripe [about a berry]
sayamáyum̓
unschooled, be sk̲í7k̲el ~
esk̲í7k̲el
unschooled, be still
esk̲í7k̲elxw ~
sk̲í7k̲elxw
unsettled, be nach'í7mixw
unsettled, be very k̲eyk̲iyí7
unskilled, be esk̲í7k̲el ~
sk̲í7k̲el
unskilled, be still sk̲í7k̲elxw
~ esk̲í7k̲elxw
unstable weather, be
yelyélch'
untie (bundle) yex̲wáỷchn
untie (something) yex̲wn
untied yex̲w
until ikw;
welh
up around head, be hiw̓k̲w
up away from the beach, be
chíshem
up front, be hiw̓k̲w
up on the beach, go
txwkwum
up to, be txwti7
up, be hiyíwilh
upbringing nexwníw̓
upbringing, have the
nexwnínew̓
uphill, go
txwch'ech'a7úsm
uphold one another
chén̓chenstway
upper arm tax̲ntn
upper end of a village
schishmk̲s
upper leg smekw'álap
upper lip schilhts
upper part chilh
upper part of some place, be in the chíchshem
uprooted, be [about tree]
kw'up'k̲
upset canoe/can/box
k̲p'i7k̲wm
upside down, be cheỷk̲w
upstream area hiw̓ ~ hiw
upstream region siw̓ ~
s-hiw̓ ~
hiw ~ hiw̓

upstream, be **txwiw̓ ~ txwhiw̓; yekw'tsá7min; txw7úmich; hiw̓ ~ hiw**
upstream, be going **ú7um̓ich**
upstream, go **úmich**
uptown **iiḵ**
urchin net **ikw'íyentn**
urge (someone) **chechshíw̓at**
urinate **séx̱wa7**
urinate on (something) **séx̱wa7n**
urinating, be **sésx̱wa7**
urine **séx̱wa7**
us **nímalh; -umulh**
use (a ladle) **kw'en̓án̓**
use (something) **xwukws ~ xwekws**
use (something) almost useless **p'ákw'an**
use (something) as a last resort **p'ákw'an**
use (something) for the lack of anything better **p'ákw'an**
use (something) up **i7x̱ws**
use a driftnet **seyx̱á7m**
use a pole to jump **t'ech'ḵám̓**
use dogs for hunting **yex̱wím̓**
use fire in hunting **yex̱í7u**
use magic power **tisyew̓ín̓**
use ritual words **tisyew̓ín̓**
use, be in **esxwéxwkw**
used to (someone), be **cháy̓exwni ~ chá7ixwni**
used to, get **chá7ixw ~ cháy̓exw**
used up, be **i7x̱w**
used with making mud pies **t'elḵán̓**
used, be **esxwéxwkw xwekw ~ xwukw**
useful **sxwexwkw**
useful, be **esxwéxwkw**
using (something), be **esxwéxwkws**

V v

valley sk̲wexwnách; sx̲wéx̲wel; slix̲wáy̓shn ~ slíx̲way̓shn
valuable tl'i7
Vancouver Lighthouse Pápiyek̲
vanished, be estsetsíxw
vanquish (someone) k̲w'úyut; tl'xwet
varied thrush [type of bird] sx̲wish
variegated, be esx̲él̓x̲el
vegetables speńeḿáy
vein tl'a7ímin ~ tl'a7ímen
velvet témus
venereal disease háts'ek̲
venereal disease, have a háts'ek̲
venture tl'átl'i
vertabra [see also ex̲ts'ch ~ nexw7éx̲ts'ch ~ nx̲atsch] ex̲ch'ch
very an ha7lh; an
very edge of a cliff esk̲w'ík̲w't
very hungry, be kw'ákw'ay̓
very ill, be skw'ay ~ eskw'áy ~ kw'ay
very low tide, be chishkwts
very near k̲ilh
vibrate letx̲
Victoria Sts'ams; Metúliya
view ínexw
view (something) ínexwan
village [houses and inhabitants] úxwumixw
villager úxwumixw
villagers exw7úxwumixw
vine maple tree t'ek̲t'k̲áy̓
virgin ch'eych'
visible as far as one's face is concerned, be esxwéyxwiy̓us
visible as far as one's hands are concerned, be esxwéyxwiy̓ach
visible, be xwéyxwey ~ esxwéyxwey̓ ~ esxwíxwi7; estetích
visible, become xwii ~ xwey ~ xwiy; x̲ey
vision s7éli; kw'áchmin
vision about (something/someone), be having a el̓élini
vision about (something/someone), have a élini
visit txwnách'awtxw
visit (someone) txwnách'aẃtxwni
visited by an epidemic, be x̲lhantm
visiting, be always txwnanch'áẃtxw
visitor txwnách'aẃtxwtn; exw7úxwumixw
visor smek̲sáń
voice nek̲wéltn
vomit ya7t; k̲wchiḿ
vomit (something) up k̲wchet
vomiting up (something) continuously, be yéya7t
vulva sts'uunts'

W w

wade síx̱wim
wading, be sísix̱wim
wailer x̱améyulh
wait iỷáỷshim
wait for (someone/something) iỷáỷs
wake (someone) up úmseman
wake up úmsem
wake up unexpectedly txw7umsm
walk, a s7ímesh
walk, to ímesh
walk [about a group] em̓ím̓ash
walk alongside of it t'in̓ín̓tsut
walk at edge of water memelshenám
walk back and forth ḵ'anḵ'án̓atsut
walk in a dazed condition sax̱waỷúsem
walk in one's sleep se7píḵwem
walk in someone's place x̱en̓hán
walk into the water síx̱wim
walk on (something) x̱enáten
walk quickly tsix̱shn
walk right on a trail [of an animal] nexwsnén̓p
walk slow uyumshenám̓
walk with hands behind back ḵ'ts'íchen
walk, be able to ímeshnumut
walk, be just starting to im̓ímesh
walk, manage to ímeshnumut
walking around, be em̓ím̓ash
walking heavily, be kwékwem̓em ~ ḵwéḵwem̓em
walking staff t'chach
walking stick t'chach
walking strongly and smartly, be kwúkwtsem
walking, be í7imesh ~ í7im̓esh ~ í7mash
walking, shaking one's rear end, be nexwnákwnakwḵam
wall s7aỷán̓ ~ s7eỷán̓
wall mat [small mat made from cattail] tax̱ch
wall mats [sg: súyi7ch] súyaỷch;
súyi7ch
wander around men wa í7im̓esh
wandering around, be titiw̓én̓eḵ
wane ts'éts'x̱ntsut
want stl'i7
want (something) tl'i7s
x̱wáḵ'et
want something bad to happen to someone xwínaỷlh
want to {full word: stl'i7} -aỷem
want to arrive there tsíxwaỷm
want to be breastfed t'elḵwím̓aỷm
want to borrow íx̱maỷm
want to cry x̱aam̓áỷm
want to dance ḵw'iyílsh7aỷem
want to drink ch'eyxwáỷḵin ~ ch'eyxwíḵin;
táḵwaỷm
want to eat ilhen̓áỷem
want to eat bear meat lhelhmíx̱alhaỷm
want to fart pú7ḵaỷm
want to go huyá7aỷm
want to go along hew̓álus ~ hewa7áỷm ~ hew̓áỷm
want to go and see someone níḵ'i
want to go get water uḵwum̓áỷem
want to go home t'ukw'áỷm
want to go inside uysáỷem
want to go someone with hew̓áỷm ~ hewa7áỷm ~ hew̓álus
want to leave but something holds one back tsékwem̓
want to paddle isun̓áỷm
want to play ḵw'shetsutáỷm
want to propose chewashem̓áỷm
want to rest paym̓áỷm
pápeỷm
want to swim shúshukw'aỷm
want to whistle shupen̓áỷm
want to work ts'its'ap'áỷm
war kwílten
war canoe tayéwilh ~ táywilh
x̱eyx̱ewilh
war club ḵw'úḵwustn
war dance, do a tsehénem
t'ashénem
war whoop x̱eyx̱ḵínm
war, be at x̱eyx̱ ~ x̱i7x̱
ward shéwayim̓
warm kw'as;
kw'askw'ás
warm (something) near the fire néḵwen

warm food near fire kw'ásaỷus
warm one's feet nek̲wshnáḿ
warm one's hands nek̲wáchi7m
warm oneself nék̲wentsut
warm oneself by the sun neńk̲wíchen
warm weather kw'as skwáyel
warm, become kw'ákw'asi7 kw'ási7
warmer, be getting [about weather] kw'eskw'ás
warming hands, be sítk̲wachi7m
warn (someone) yaań
warped, be láp'entsut
warped, be all eslép'lep'
warrior nexwsx̲éỷx̲ ~ nexwsx̲éyx̲; stamsh
warrior's spear sxwmats'tn
wart sch'épxweḷ
wart on face near eye, have a st'elkáyus
wart on one's face, have a t'elkáyus
wash (someone's) face míkw'usn
wash (someone's) feet míkw'shnan
wash (someone's) hands mikw'achí7n
wash (something) míkw'in
wash (something) off at the river xwíkwin
wash [one's] clothes ts'x̲wélwetm ~ ts'x̲wélwet ~ ts'x̲wélut; ts'ex̲wts'x̲wélwetm
wash away (ground) [as done by a swollen river] k̲'atl'n
wash dishes xwmikw'máminˊ
wash face with water p'lhúsem
wash one's face míkw'usm
wash one's feet míkw'shnaḿ
wash one's hair xwayxwáỷk̲wem
wash one's hands míkw'achi7m
wash one's head xwáỷk̲wem
wash one's own face xwmíkw'usm
wash one's own mouth mikw'tsm
wash oneself míkw'intsut
wash the dishes mikw'mámin
wash the floor ts'ex̲wts'x̲wénp; ts'x̲wénp
wash the insides of (an animal) míkw'aỷák̲inan
washed mikw'; smimkw'
washed, be esmímkw'
washed, be already esmíkw'
washing smíkw'ayts'a7m
waste (something) k̲eḷk̲eḷílt
waste time in a vain effort ahúỷnumut
waste wood after splitting sek̲'mín
waste, go to k̲elk̲eḷ
wasted [anything] áyexw
wasted food áyexw
wasteful, be k̲ax̲k̲ex̲ás
watch (statement) ns7í7x̲ni
watch [timepiece] wach
watch oneself kw'akw'chsténaḿut
watchful, be t'át'aḿátsut
watching (someone), be kw'awcht
watching (someone/something), be kw'akw'cht
watching, be kw'awch
water stak̲w
water (plant) kw'lhúsen
water (plants) around the roots kw'elhchk̲áń
water [used in cooking] {full word: stak̲w} -alhk̲wu
water for (someone), get k̲wúlshi
water, get some k̲wulíḿ
water, have one's feet in the water esmúmeỷshen
waterfall stséxwem
waterfront, go along the peptúsm
waterproof garment k̲w'xwélwet
water's edge miyíẃts
watertight, be tl'éts'em
Watt's Point Xwelxwalítn
wave yúyak̲w
wave (stick, weapon, etc.) at someone k̲ix̲wúsn
wave hitting beach sk̲wlha7lk̲
wave, waves in the ocean {full word: yúya7k̲w} -unexw ~ -yunexw
wax, have one's ears be full of wax t'sháyen
waxberries [sg: ts'ex̲w] ts'éx̲wts'ex̲w
waxberry ts'ex̲w
waxberry plant ts'ex̲wts'x̲wáỷ
way of tying a dog k̲ilxwtn
way off, be lhup
way out, be [about sea] k̲weỷ
way out, be [about the tide] est'át'elh
ways nexwníẃ
ways [of doing something] welh nes tiḿá; wa lhtiḿá
we at; chat; chet; nímalh; k̲w'at
we ourselves men nímalh
we, our -at
weak [about a person] k̲lim

weak but willing to try, be kw'úmutsut
weak from hunger, be xwaa ~ xwa
weak, be chépxwem
weak, be becoming k̲ek̲límí7
weak, get k̲límí7
weapon -k̲aýs; wak̲áýstn
wear (clothes) ets'7íts'am̓s
wear (something) ets7útsis; xwekws ~ xwukws
wear a blanket ets'7íts'am
wear glasses estela7áyus
wear out, have one's shoes nts'ex̲shn
wear paint yetl'k̲'ám
wearing glasses, be esteteláyus
wearing, be ets'7íts'am
weasel ch'éshnech
weave tahím̓ ~ ta7hím̓; ti-
weave (blankets) lhen̓t
weaving (something) all the time, be lhenlhén̓t
weaving needle sch'ámts'a7ten
wedge k̲wílhus; x̲we7ít
Wednesday Schánxwyes
weed shéwaýnup ~ shewaýnúp ~ shewáýnup
weigh (something) t'ánam̓en
well [with drinking water] est'ét'kw'
well brought up, be nexwnínew̓
well water est'ét'kw' stak̲w; tiléls stak̲w
well, well yeh
well-behaved person slhálhk̲'an
well-developed, be k̲ech
well-grained for splitting, be [about a log] sek̲'máýus

west teltíwet
West Coast-style canoe k̲'exwú7lh
West Sister Mountain [one-half of what is now commonly referred to as the Lions] Elhx̲wín̓
west wind teltíwet
western birch tree k̲wélhi7n
Western Grebe [type of bird] skwelkwélts
Western yew tree tl'emk̲'áý; x̲we7ítaý
wet k̲w'ets'
wet (something) k̲w'éts'en
wet oneself accidentally. k̲w'ets'númut
wet snow, be á7lhk̲en
wet, get k̲w'ts'i7
whale k̲wenís
what age? kw'ínawanexw?
what are you doing? chexw wa chánem?
what befalls one skwekwi7ín̓tem
what day? kw'ínlhyes?
what did .... say? ínet?
what happened? shan̓? ~ eshán̓?
what happens to one skwekwi7ín̓tem
what is told stsúntem
what kind of canoe is it? tamévilh? ~ stamévilh?
what kind of house is it? tamáw̓txw? ~ stamáw̓txw?
what kind of smell is it? stam̓áýak̲ap?
what kind of tree is it? stamáý? ~ tamáý?
what kind of wool is it? stam̓í7k̲in?
what kind? txwncha7ám̓? ~ txwnch7am̓? ~ nch'am̓? txwnch7am̓? ~
what one's ch'emash is called after the death of one's spouse ch'áyaý

what to do with (something)? txwchas?
what what one is doing skwekwiýín̓tsut
what? stam?
what's the matter with? shan̓? ~ eshán̓?
wheezing, be séselts'emk̲s
when u; ikw
when he/she/they k̲neskw
when I lhan ~ lhen; tl'an; kwins na
when I [from s + 7an] sen
when I [future] kwins
when it tl'as
when s/he k̲'es ~ k̲es tl'as kwi ses
when s/he, when they lhas ~ lhes
when the eagle comes to take a dead person away nkw'amtn
when they tl'as
when we lhet ~ lhat tl'at
when you lhexw ~ lhaxw; kwis na; k̲'axw; tl'axw
when you [future] kwis
when you all lhap ~ lhep; tl'ap
when? temtám?
where he/she/it is wa lhna7s
where is ..... going? txwchacha7ném?
where one stands wa lhtá7shn
where, be? éncha?
where?, from ti7éncha?
whetstone tsíyelstn; íyu7tstn
which? éncha?
while welh
whip with boughs [while training] k̲w'uk̲wéyelh

whirl [about water in a whirlpood] k̲'iyáx̲atkwu7m
whirlpool sk̲'iyáx̲atk̲wu7em
whiskey lam
whisper lhák̲em; eslhák̲
whisper to (someone) lhák̲at
whispering to oneself, be lhálhak̲m
whispering, be es7álhk̲en
whistle sxwúxwlem shúpen
whistle [about animal, steamboat, etc.] k̲'ewm
whistle at (someone) shupns
whistle softly ts'úm̓en
whistling at (someone), be shushúpns
whistling noise, make a séselts'em
whistling prolongedly [e.g., a melody, or the whistling of a bird], be shúshpen
whistling repeatedly, be shúshpen
whistling, be shúshpen
white p'ek̲'
white [about animals] p'ip'k̲'
white blanket p'ek̲'élwet
white bone in slhahál t'ámten
white fir t'ú7xway̓
white fir [silver] kwéxwemay̓
white grass ts'áx̲i
white man's house xwelitn̓áw̓txw
white man's language sxwalítnulh sníchim
white paint [used in making blankets] sp'etl'tn
white people [sg: xwelitn] xwelxwalítn
white person xwelítn
white pine tree ts'áyts'ayk̲ay
white, become p'ek̲'í7
whiteman's blanket p'ek̲'élwet
whittle úx̲wim̓
whittle (something) úx̲wun̓
whittling, be u7x̲wim
who? swat?
whole day or night, be a tl'émk̲en
whole dried deer suk̲w
whole dried salmon nxwúkw'us ~ nexwúk̲w'uts
whole piece of shí7mu7t
why, then? men shan̓ melh?
why? men shan?; men eshán̓ melh?; eshán̓ ~ shan̓?
wide lhk̲'at
wide forehead, have a lhk̲'átchus
wide nostril nose, have a wéchwechk̲s ~ nexwwéchwechk̲s
wide open kw'ék̲em̓ts
wide open, be wí7elhch'an wa7éw̓elhch'
wide piece of land wecháy̓nup
widgeon [type of duck] ch'áw̓ax̲an
widow syá7ten
widower syá7ten
widowers [sg: syá7ten] siy̓á7ten
widows siy̓á7ten
wife chewásh
wife by blanket marriage, get a tl'a7m
wife of uncle sxwchésha7
wife, have a eschewásh
wild welh
wild blackberry [see k̲w'elm̓xwáy̓] sk̲w'elm̓xw
wild blackberry bush [see sk̲w'elm̓xw] k̲w'elm̓xwáy̓
wild cherry t'élem
wild cherry tree t'elem̓áy̓
wild crabapple k̲we7úp ~ k̲wu7úp
wild crabapple tree k̲we7úpay̓ ~ k̲wu7úpay̓
wild game in late winter, any t'elh
wild ginger x̲et'tánay
wild goose ex̲
wild gooseberry bush t'em̓xwáy̓
wild lily of the valley [plant leaves used for eyewash] pepsen̓á7
wild lily of the valley plant pepsen̓á7ay
wild onion sx̲wíl̓nach
wild rosebud k̲al̓k̲
wild rosebush k̲ál̓k̲ay
wild sheep's horn spoon x̲ál̓u
wild, be [about animal] k̲w'áyk̲w'ay̓ax̲
will [future tense ek̲'
win tl'xwenk̲
win (something) tl'xwet
win a contest tl'xwenk̲
wind spahím̓
wind (something) around k̲'elk̲'án
wind (string) into a ball k̲'elk̲w'úy̓sen
wind, go with the pepuk̲ám̓
wind-dried salmon from the Fraser River lhích'us
window nkw'ekw'chústn ~ kw'chustn ~ kw'ek̲wchústn ~ nkw'chustn
window of house kw'ekw'chustnáw̓txw
windpipe x̲wúmlhnalh slhákw'amay nlhakw'máy
windproof, make (something) yá7yamuts
windy, be pepahím̓
wing yéla7en

wink ts'íp'k̲aỷusm
wink at (someone)
ts'ip'k̲áỷusmin
winning all the time, be
tl'exwtl'exwénk̲
winter tem t'ik̲w
wipe (someone's) face
si7úsn
wipe (something) íp'in;
ík̲w'in;
si7n
wipe (them) out x̲wáyat
wipe one's face si7úsm
se7úsm
wipe one's hands
se7áchi7m
wipe one's mouth sí7tsam̓
wipe one's nose sí7k̲sam̓
wipe one's rear end sí7k̲am̓
wiped out by enemy, be tek̲;
x̲wey ~ x̲way
wise nek̲'ílus
wish for (a certain kind of food) tem̓áỷt
wish for (someone's) death
xwínin̓
wish for (something) tl'íni
~ tl'í7ni
wish to -aỷem
wish to accompany someone
hewa7áỷm ~
hew̓áỷm ~ hew̓álus
wish to go nam̓áỷm
wish to go home
t'ukw'áỷm
wish to sing lulum̓áỷm
wish to swim
shúshukw'aỷm
wishing for someone else's food, be shítim
witchcraft siw̓ín̓
with a view to, be txwnam̓
with an open mouth, be [as from surprise]
t'éx̲t'ex̲ts
with, be [more than one person] esk̲'ék̲w'u7
~ esk̲'ek̲w'ú7 ~
esk̲'ék̲'ew̓ ~ esk̲'ek̲'éw̓
with, be [one person]
esk̲w'ú7
withdraw tsekwk̲ám;
x̲ám̓entsut
withering leaves, have [in the fall]
nek̲w'úyachxw
within, be esn̓íw̓
witness to (a statement), be a
ns7éyx̲ni
witness to (statement), be
ns7í7x̲ni
wives [sg: chewash]
chewchewásh
wolf tk̲áya
wolf [term used in long-house] stk̲áya
wolf-like tk̲aya7úmesh
wolverine k'élk'ech
woman slhánaỷ
woman, become a
slhánaỷi7
woman's firstborn schilh
woman's last child
s-huyáỷlh
woman's paddle
lheni7él̓wes
woman's private parts
ests'únts'
women [sg: slhánaỷ]
slhenlhánaỷ
won't eat because one's friend won't
mákw'alhnayem
won't flow [about water]
k̲ts'am̓
wood stsek̲
wood chips from chopping with axe x̲ítl'min
wood duck míten
wood that is getting rotten [general term] yek̲w'
wooden spoon ch'aw̓áỷ
wooden structure -us ~
-was
woodland stsék̲tsek̲
woodpecker [pileated]
témlhepsem
woodpecker [smaller kind than tmlhepsm] ts'ek̲t
woodshed yí7yulhaw̓txw
wool lemetu7í7k̲in
wool {full word:
lemetu7í7k̲in} -i7k̲in
wool blanket [made of mixed dog and mountain goat hair]
sk̲wemáỷak̲in
wool braided for protection at wrist, below knees, and at ankles k̲'i7chtn
wooly pá7pa
word sníchim
words of a kwtsi7ts syew̓ín̓
words to a song nch'élnech
work or a job sts'its'áp'
work, to ts'its'áp'
work (something) around in the fire tsík̲'in
work for (someone)
ts'its'áp'shi
work on (something)
ts'its'áp'en
work one's way through [dense mass of people or underbrush]
x̲wiyak̲w'ántsut
work towards (something)
ts'its'áp'ni
work unexpectedly
txwts'its'áp'
work, able to
ts'its'ap'númut
work, manage to
ts'its'ap'númut
worked up, get really [about Indian dancer] tsek̲w'
working hard, be stítim̓
working on (something), have finished
ts'its'áp'nexw
world k̲'ek̲'sín̓ ti siyát-shen
worm sts'ekw'
worm ed, be ts'ekw'ntm
worms sts'ekw'
wormy, be sts'ékw'ts'ekw'
wormy, get sts'ekw'nítem
worn out, be ts'ex̲
esk̲wáak̲wa
worried, look esámtm

worry **yemyémtsut; ts'áyakw**
worry about (someone) **ts'áyakwni**
worrying, be **ts'áts'ayakw**
worse, be getting [about sick person] **kw'ay̓**
wound **snek̲'álhs**
wound (someone) **s7á7kwlashs**
wound around, be **k̲'elk̲'**
wound it **s7ekw'á7kwelash**
wounded, be **es7á7kwlesh s7á7kwlash s7ekw'á7kwelash**
woven mat **slhen̓**
woven material [general term] **slhen̓**
wrap (something) **tsúpen mékwu7n**
wrap one's own leg up in something **mekwshnám̓**
wrapped around a body, be **esk̲wek̲wúk̲wuwilh**
wrapped around someone's waist, be **esx̲wix̲wik̲w'úwilh**
wrapped in a blanket, be **esém̓k̲wu**
wrapped, be **mékwu7**
wrecked **k̲elk̲él**
wren **t'émt'em**
wrestle **kwekwntál̓**
wretched, be [about person] **estesás**
wring (something) **k̲w'úts'un̓**
wrinkled, be **eslép'lep'**
wrinkled, become **kw'úp'untsut ~ kw'úpuntsut; láp'entsut**
wrinkles **lhelp'ús stsém̓tsem̓k̲w ~ estsém̓tsem̓k̲w**
wrinkles on hand, have **lhelp'ách**
wrinkles on legs, have **lhelp'shn**
wrinkles, have **lhelp'í7 lhelp'úsi7**
wrinkly hands, have **lhelp'ách**
wrist **sx̲wets'k̲w'ách nexw7átsach**
write **x̲el̓**
write (something) **x̲el̓t**
write (something) finally **x̲él̓nexw**
write for (someone) **x̲él̓shi**
write, able to **x̲el̓númut x̲el̓nálhn**
write/etch/draw (something), manage to **x̲él̓nexw**
write/etch/draw finally **x̲el̓númut**
write/etch/draw, manage to **x̲el̓númut**
written it onto (something), have **esx̲éx̲el̓s**
wrong **nach'**
wrong, be **kw'ay ~ skw'ay ~ eskw'áy; nánach'**
wrong, be doing **nánach'**

Y y

yarrow [type of plant]
si7semáchxw
yawn ewáyani7m ~
ewáy̓a7m
year yel̓ánem ~ syel̓ánem;
-awanexw
year after next year
tx̲íx̲ta7áwanexw
year before last year
tx̲íx̲ta7áwanexw
years {full word: syel̓ánem}
-awanexw
yeast bread spúmim̓
yell kwáchem
yellow p'ek̲w'p'ík̲w';
lelch'
yellow cedar tree k̲'elhmáy̓
yellow leaves, get [about trees in autumn]
pí7pek̲'láchxwm
yellow paint [kind that is found in the mountains]
p'ek̲w'p'ík̲w'
yellow salmonberry sepík̲
yellow shiner perch slhímel
yellow slime mould
ch'elík̲'ay̓us
yellow, become p'ík̲w'i7
yellow-bellied sapsucker [tail feathers were used to adorn the yasi7k̲w of the sxw7úmten]
ts'k̲w'i7k̲s
yellowjacket sesemáy̓
yes i7
yesterday kwi chel̓ák̲lh

yet tl'ay;
men tl'ay;
-xw;
yámen ~ yáman
yet, be ítl'i
yew wooden wedge k̲wílhus
you a-;
axw;
-umi;
ta new;
néwi ~ new;
chexw;
k̲w'axw;
k̲'axw;
-axw
you all -ap ~ -ayap;
ap;
k̲w'ap;
cháyap;
-umiyap;
ta néwyap;
chap
you guys néwyap
You have arrived chexw
tl'ik̲
tl'ik̲ chexw
you know yik̲w
you! ta new
you, your (plural) -yap
young boy swí7k̲a7ullh
young cedar x̲áp̓ay̓ay
young fir tree íl̓ilay
young fir trees íl̓ilay
young girl [see slhanay̓]
slhen̓yúllh
young horse stek̲iw̓úllh ~
stak̲iwúllh
young horse [see stek̲íw]
stak̲iwúllh ~
stek̲iw̓úllh

young ladies [sg: k̲'á7may̓]
k̲'émk̲'emay
young man swíw̓lus
young men [sg: swíw̓lus]
sew̓íw̓lus ~ swáw̓lus
young mountain goat
í7mk̲iya
young of any animal
min̓min̓úllh ~
smín̓minullh ~
smím̓na7ullh
stl'áx̲wtl'x̲way̓lh
young red cedar x̲í7x̲i7pay
young second-growth Douglas fir tree
k̲wek̲wel-háy̓
young specimen (human or animal) -ullh
young woman k̲'á7may̓
young women k̲'émk̲'emay
younger children sesáw̓t
younger children of parents' younger siblings
[sg: sk̲a7k̲] s7áy̓ak̲w'a
younger sibling s7ék̲ek̲;
sk̲a7k̲
younger siblings s7áy̓ak̲w'a
youngest child saw̓t
youngest of family [term of pity not as strong as
sk̲w'únek̲] s7ék̲ék̲
youngest, dearest child
sk̲w'únek̲
your a-
your [pl] a- . . . -yap
your all a- . . . -yap

Z z

zigzag [e.g., in a canoe]
kw'ets'kw'úts'untsut